MW00630268

LEARN OF ME

LEARN OF ME

History and Teachings of the New Testament

BYU RELIGIOUS STUDIES CENTER

EDITED BY JOHN HILTON III
AND NICHOLAS J. FREDERICK

Published by the Religious Studies Center, Brigham Young University, Provo, Utah, in cooperation with Deseret Book Company, Salt Lake City, Utah.
Visit us at rsc.byu.edu.

Printed in the United States of America by Sheridan Books, Inc.

Cover design by Emily V. Rogers, interior design by Carmen Durland Cole

ISBN: 978-1-9503-0433-2

Library of Congress Cataloging-in-Publication Data

Names: Hilton, John, III, editor. | Frederick, Nicholas J., editor.
Title: Learn of me : history and teachings of the New Testament / edited by John L. Hilton III and Nicholas J. Frederick.
Description: Provo, Utah: Religious Studies Center, Brigham Young University, [2022] | Includes index. | Summary: "This volume of collected essays is intended to assist disciples of Jesus Christ in coming to a deeper understanding of the Savior and his ministry through their personal study of the New Testament. Because the period and culture of the New Testament can be daunting to modern readers, the editors gathered the work of Latter-day Saint scholars who have devoted time and research to gaining a greater understanding of the New Testament. The editors included essays written from a variety of perspectives to highlight the different lenses that can productively be brought to bear on the New Testament. Some of these essays are overtly devotional, while others are more explicitly academic, but all are written with the intent to help each of us accomplish one goal: to learn of him"—Provided by publisher.
Identifiers: LCCN 2022010434 | ISBN 9781950304332 (hardback)
Subjects: LCSH: Bible. New Testament—Criticism, interpretation, etc. | Church of Jesus Christ of Latter-day Saints—Doctrines. | Mormon Church—Doctrines.
Classification: LCC BS2361.3 .L43 2022 | DDC 225.6—dc23/eng/20220615
LC record available at https://lccn.loc.gov/2022010434

Contents

Part 3: Acts to Revelation

Introduction

In a 2017 address, President Russell M. Nelson promised, "If you proceed to learn all you can about Jesus Christ, I promise you that your love for Him, and for God's laws, will grow beyond what you currently imagine."[1] Truly the more we learn about Jesus Christ, the more we love him. The more we love him, the more we will desire to follow him.

This volume of collected essays is intended to assist disciples of Jesus Christ in coming to a deeper understanding of the Savior and his ministry through their personal study of the New Testament. Because the period and culture of the New Testament can be daunting to modern readers, we've gathered the work of Latter-day Saint scholars who have devoted time and research to gaining a greater understanding of the New Testament. We have included essays written from a variety of perspectives to highlight the different lenses that can productively be brought to bear on the New Testament. Some of these essays are overtly devotional, while others are more explicitly academic, but all are written with the intent to help each of us accomplish one goal: to *learn of him*.

In the first section, we've selected three essays that give important background information. Why is it so important to specifically focus on Jesus

Christ in our study of the New Testament (and other scripture)? What were some of the political and religious sentiments held by different groups of Jews? How did the process of canonization of the New Testament come about? These and other questions are answered in this section.

The essays in the second section focus on the four Gospel accounts of Jesus's mortal ministry. Readers will come to more fully understand how to approach each of the four Gospel accounts and learn additional insights about Jesus Christ. They will come to know the Savior better by broadening their perspectives on his miracles, teachings, and interactions with people from all walks of life. We particularly highlight the climax of the Savior's ministry—his passion—with essays on events that took place in Gethsemane, Golgotha, and the garden tomb.

In the third section, we explore the second half of the New Testament, typically the part of the New Testament that can be less familiar to readers. Essays in this section include discussions of Paul and his letters, Peter's pivotal role in the expanding church, the forthcoming apostasy, the role of women in the New Testament, and how Jesus can be found in texts such as the letter to the Hebrews, the General Epistles, and the book of Revelation. For those who interested in additional scholarly resources, we've included a lengthy appendix that surveys New Testament scholarship and provides a list of some of the most important work being done on this remarkable text.

In the April 2020 general conference, President Russell M. Nelson taught, "As we seek to be disciples of Jesus Christ, our efforts to *hear Him* need to be ever more intentional. It takes conscious and consistent effort to fill our daily lives with His words, His teachings, His truths."[2] Our hope is that the essays gathered in this volume can assist you in your intentional efforts to learn all you can about Jesus Christ.

NOTES

1. Russell M. Nelson, "Prophets, Leadership, and Divine Law" (worldwide devotional, January 8, 2017), https://www.ChurchofJesusChrist.org/broadcasts/article/worldwide-devotionals/2017/01/prophets-leadership-and-divine-law?lang=eng.
2. Russell M. Nelson, "Hear Him," *Ensign*, May 2020, 89.

Part One

BACKGROUND

Chapter One

"We Talk of Christ, We Rejoice in Christ"

CHAD H WEBB

With many of you, I think often of our opportunity to teach and how we might teach others with more power in helping them to build deep and abiding faith in the Lord Jesus Christ. As I've considered this important question, I've reflected on an idea shared by Elder Kim B. Clark when he said that the Savior's invitation to learn of Him first means that we must learn to know Him. And second, that we must learn from Him. He quoted Elder Neal A. Maxwell, who referred to the Savior's invitation to "learn of me" and added, "There is no other way to learn deeply."[1]

I have come to understand and believe that the single most important way in which we can help increase faith is to more fully place Jesus Christ at the center of our teaching and learning by helping our students and children come to know Him, to learn from Him, and to consciously strive to become like Him. Every day, we must "talk of Christ, . . . rejoice in Christ, . . . [and] preach of Christ."[2]

Many of you have already begun to respond to this invitation, intentionally preparing lessons and discussions with these ideas in mind and looking for opportunities to testify of Jesus Christ and of His divine attributes, His boundless power, and His unfailing love. In your gospel discussions, there has been an increased influence of the Holy Ghost, more expression of gratitude for the Savior, more meaningful and relevant personal application, and more people acting in faith.

Of course, the most important way we can help our students and loved ones come to know the Savior is to help them prepare for sacred priesthood ordinances and to keep their covenants.[3] To help them qualify for the blessings of the temple is to help them know and follow Jesus Christ. But there are other things we can do, while they are with us, that will help them to rely on Him and on His teachings and Atonement.

To this end, may I suggest four ways that we can place Jesus Christ more in the center of our learning and teaching every day?

Focus on the Titles, Roles, Character, and Attributes of Jesus Christ

First, focus on the titles, roles, character, and attributes of Jesus Christ. President Russell M. Nelson gave us an invitation to "let the scriptural citations about Jesus Christ in the Topical Guide become [our] personal core curriculum."[4] This invitation is intended to help us go beyond knowing about the things Jesus did and help us to come to know Him—His attributes and character.

For example, one of the titles of Jesus Christ is Creator. Under the direction of His Father, Jesus created the heavens and the earth. Creator is also one of His divine roles and speaks to His nature. As we study how and why Jesus created the earth, we might ask, "What does this teach us about who He is? What does it teach us about His motives, His love, and His power? What divine attributes of the Savior are revealed in His role as the Creator?"

You may remember that President Boyd K. Packer was an accomplished artist who enjoyed carving wooden birds. One day he was a passenger in a car driven by Elder A. Theodore Tuttle, and one of his carvings rested on the backseat of the car. At an intersection Elder Tuttle slammed on the brakes, and the carving tipped upside down on the floor and broke into pieces. Elder Tuttle was devastated, but President Packer was not. He simply said, "Forget it. I made it. I can fix it." And he did. He made it stronger than it was and even improved it a bit. President Packer explained, "Who made you? Who is your Creator? There is not anything about your life that gets bent or broken that He cannot fix and will fix."[5]

When those we teach understand Jesus's role as the Creator, and as they ponder the scripture accounts that witness of His incredible power to fix and heal His creations, their hearts will long to experience that power and promise in their own lives. They will then act in faith to experience His incredible power to fix what is broken in them.

Another of Jesus's sacred titles is Redeemer. The scriptures refer to Him in this role 930 times. What does this title teach us about His character and attributes? What did His redeeming power mean for Alma, Saul, and the woman taken in adultery? What did it mean to Matthew, the publican and Gospel writer?

I find it interesting that we learn of Matthew's call to the Twelve in the same chapter as the accounts of Jesus performing miracles and "healing every sickness and every disease among the people."[6] The motive for these miracles was that Jesus was "moved with compassion."[7] But why does Matthew alone, of all the Gospel writers, include his call in the midst of these miracles? It may have been a chronological account, but I think there is something else we can learn. Is it possible that Matthew recognized that the greatest miracle that Jesus did was redeem us by forgiving and loving and lifting and showing a person his or her true identity and potential, just as He had done for Matthew?

Another way to help our students and others recognize Jesus's attributes is to focus not just on scripture events but on what those events teach us about the Savior. For instance, why do we teach the story of Ammon cutting off the arms of men who scattered King Lamoni's sheep? Is it to talk about the greatness of Ammon? Or is this story actually about the greatness of God? What does this story teach us about the Lord and the way He blesses those who put their trust in Him? Ammon's own account concludes with this enthusiastic testimony: "I do not boast in my own strength. . . . I know that I am nothing; . . . therefore . . . I will boast of my God, for in his strength I can do all things."[8]

A few months ago, I was with a group of wonderful teachers and asked them to choose any scripture story or event in Church history and to think about what it reveals about the nature of God. The first teacher responded with, "Polygamy." My first thought was, "Thanks a lot! You couldn't have chosen a more difficult topic." But as we started to talk, a wonderful thing happened. People began to bear testimony to the fact that Heavenly Father loves all His children and wants them to be cared for. Another talked about the Lord's willingness to ask hard things of us but that He always sustains us and rewards our obedience. Another spoke of God as someone who loves families and wants children to be taught by loving parents. As the conversation went on, I realized that the Spirit was witnessing of the nature and character of God, that we felt closer to our Father in Heaven and His Son Jesus Christ, and that we had come to know and love Them a little more.

Jesus Christ is our Creator. He is our loving and forgiving, compassionate Redeemer and Deliverer. He is also Immanuel, the Lamb of God, the Messiah, the Holy One of Israel, and the Author and Finisher of Our Faith. As we focus on His titles, roles, character, and attributes, the Spirit will testify of Him, bringing greater understanding and love for who He truly is and a greater desire to become like Him.

Emphasize the Example of Jesus Christ

A second way to place Jesus at the center of our teaching is to recognize and emphasize that He is the perfect example, the embodiment and expression of all gospel principles.[9] One of our teachers recently shared with me that for their family scripture study, they've decided to read the New Testament again. But this time, rather than focusing on what Jesus said, they're focusing primarily on what Jesus did. Focusing on His perfect example also invites the Holy Ghost to testify of Him.

Even when Jesus is not directly referred to in a story we're teaching, we can still point to Him as the example of the principle that the story illustrates. For example, after identifying and analyzing a principle, we might ask, "Can you think of a time in the scriptures when Jesus exemplified this principle?" Or, "When have you seen Jesus exemplify this principle in your life or on your behalf?" One student was recently asked that question with regard to the Savior's example of gentleness. Her thoughts and feelings raced to the gentle way in which the Savior has always treated her. This experience, right in a classroom, created in her a deep desire to be more Christlike and gentler with the people who depend on her, as she depends on the Lord.

You could scour all the books ever written and not find a better illustration of each gospel principle than is found in the scripture accounts of Jesus and His eternal ministry. Pondering examples of the Lord in His roles as Jehovah, the mortal Christ, and the resurrected Savior will increase the power and capacity of our students and loved ones to take effective, righteous action. It will take our lessons beyond discussions about ethics and self-mastery and connect those we teach to the power of the Savior and the eternal plan of happiness.

By way of illustration, how might we teach the principle of honesty? Simply as the "best policy," because people will trust us more if we are honest? Or is integrity central to the character of Christ? If we're to be like Him, must we learn to follow His perfect example in being totally honest? The same types of questions could be asked for every principle of the gospel.

Arthur Henry King taught this idea beautifully when he said, "We symbolize [good] in a real individual—Jesus Christ, the Son of God. He is a man, not a principle, a man who includes all principles. . . . And following a man is very different from following a principle. . . . We do not have to work out philosophical complexities of ethics. It has nothing to do with that. We have to study the Gospels, see what Christ did, and try to identify ourselves with what he did. It is because we catch the spirit of the Master, the Master's love, and because we have soaked ourselves in the gospel, that we know what it is that we must do. The gospel which we have stored within us enables us at any moment to feel what we should do in a certain situation."[10]

There is power that comes when we connect our efforts to live the gospel to Jesus Christ. If we ever feel we are just going through the motions or that living the gospel has become a list of tasks to perform, we may have disconnected from the source of the grace and joy we seek. We might even be doing all the right things but find that we are missing the mark. The gospel is not a list of demands; it is the good news that Jesus Christ overcame sin and death. Jesus Christ is the central figure in our Father in Heaven's plan to help us to become like Him. He is the perfect example of how we are to live and the source of the divine enabling power we need. As we learn to follow His example and connect our efforts to live the gospel to Him, we will find joy in being His disciples.

Look for Types and Shadows of Jesus Christ

Third, we should look for types and shadows[11] of the Savior in the lives of prophets and other faithful men and women as they are recorded in the scriptures. As the prophet Jacob taught, "All things which have been given of God from the beginning of the world, unto man, are the typifying of him."[12]

Because of this idea, when I taught the Old Testament in seminary, I placed large pieces of paper on the back wall of the classroom. On the top of each paper I wrote the name of an Old Testament prophet. When we had finished studying a section of the Old Testament, I asked the students to think of the things they had learned about the prophet we had been studying and how his experiences foreshadowed or reminded them of the Savior. After learning about Adam, students wrote things like "Adam was a son of God." "He was immortal." "He went into a garden." "He voluntarily took upon himself death that we might live." It would not take long before someone would ask, "Are we still talking about Adam, or are we talking about Jesus?"

During that time, a student came early to class to share with me her experience studying the scriptures. The night before she had been reading about the consequences of the Fall of Adam in Moses 4, which says, "Thorns also, and thistles shall it bring forth to thee."[13] Since she had learned to ask the question, "How does this account testify of Christ?," she was led to ask, "Did Jesus know when He was speaking to Adam that someday He would literally wear the consequences of the Fall as a crown of thorns?"

Our students found another example in the life of Joseph of Egypt, identifying over sixty ways in which he is a type of the Savior. Students pointed out that both of them were beloved by their Father, despised by their brothers, and sold for the price of a slave. They noticed the similarities in their temptations and in the fact that God was always with them. These connections are so much more than merely something interesting to note. The lives of the Lord's chosen prophets are types of Him and teach us of His divine attributes. When used effectively, this set of lenses can help us come to know Jesus better and to be more like Him.

My wife, Kristi, was recently teaching this same scripture account of Joseph in Egypt and asked the class, "What Christlike characteristics do you see in the example of Joseph?" We talked of his ability to turn every trial into a blessing.[14] We talked of his obedience, his patience, his willingness to remember those in need, and his willingness to forgive. The question caused me to remember a previous time studying this story and imagining what it was like when Joseph revealed himself to his brothers. The scriptures say they were "troubled at his presence."[15] Can you envision what that moment must have been like and how they must have felt, knowing what they had done? But Joseph responded to them, "Come near to me. . . . I am Joseph your brother. . . . Be not grieved, . . . for God did send me before you to preserve life."[16] As I picture that event in my mind, I better understand what it will be like when we stand before the Lord at Judgment Day. Certainly I can imagine that we will remember our sins and may feel "troubled" being in His presence. But I can also imagine Him saying as He lifts us from our knees, "Come to me, come near to me, I am your brother. God did send me to preserve life."

When we focus on types and shadows of Jesus Christ, we can then help those we teach recognize His attributes and characteristics by asking questions such as

- "What Christlike characteristics do you see in the life of this prophet?"
- "When have you been blessed because Jesus possesses this attribute?" Or, "How has the Savior demonstrated this characteristic on your behalf?"
- "What could you do to become more like Jesus Christ and acquire this divine attribute?" Or, "What have you learned about your Father in Heaven and Jesus Christ that inspires you to act in faith to follow Them?"

And when those we teach give answers like "pray" or "read the scriptures," we would do well to help them connect those actions to Heavenly Father and Jesus Christ by asking them questions like

- "How will your prayers be different knowing whom you are talking to?"

- "How will you study the scriptures in a way that will help you know the Savior better and be more like Him?"

These types of questions will help those we teach develop greater power and capacity to know the Savior and to learn from Him.

Bear Pure Testimony of Jesus Christ

The fourth thing that we can do is to bear pure testimony of Jesus Christ.

We need to speak of Him more often and more powerfully and with more reverence, adoration, and gratitude. We need to share our own testimonies, and we must find effective ways to invite those we teach to share their testimonies with each other. In a recent class discussion on the principle of prayer, a teacher invited students to consider what the Lord's invitation to pray and His promise to teach us about the nature of our Father in Heaven. They were then invited to consider the attributes of the Savior that allow us to pray in His name. With these simple questions, a lesson on prayer turned into the opportunity for students to bear testimony of the power and love of our Father in Heaven and His Son, Jesus Christ. Students left with increased appreciation for their relationship with Deity and for the incredible blessing we have been given to pray in the name of Jesus Christ, who is our Advocate with the Father.

Another essential way to testify of Jesus Christ is to allow the testimony of prophets, both ancient and modern, to be heard in our discussions. The apostle Peter said we are "witnesses chosen before of God. . . . He commanded us to . . . testify that it is he which was ordained of God. . . . To him give all the prophets witness."[17]

More recently, Elder Robert D. Hales made a statement that has caused me much reflection. He said, "We watch, hear, read, study, and share the words of prophets to be forewarned and protected. For example, 'The Family: A Proclamation to the World' was given long before we experienced the challenges now facing the family." And then he added this thought: "'The Living Christ: The Testimony of the Apostles' was prepared in advance of when we will need it most."[18]

I am not one who is given to gloom and doom, but it has become evident why the proclamation was given in advance of the strong winds that have been blowing against traditional families. And to hear a prophet say that the "Living Christ" document was given "in advance of when we will need it most" makes me think that additional winds will be blowing, battering the faith of our students and our children.

"The Living Christ: The Testimony of the Apostles" declares:

> We offer our testimony of the reality of His matchless life and the infinite virtue of His great atoning sacrifice. . . . He was the Great Jehovah of the Old Testament, the Messiah of the New. . . . He walked the roads of Palestine, healing the sick, causing the blind to see, and raising the dead. He taught the truths of eternity. . . . He gave His life to atone for the sins of all mankind. . . . He rose from the grave to "become the firstfruits of them that slept." . . . He and His Father appeared to the boy Joseph Smith, ushering in the long-promised "dispensation of the fulness of times." . . . We testify that He will someday return to earth . . . [and] rule as King of Kings and reign as Lord of Lords. . . . Jesus is the living Christ, the immortal Son of God. He is the great King Immanuel, who stands today on the right hand of His Father. He is the light, the life, and the hope of the world. . . . God be thanked for the matchless gift of His divine Son.[19]

This witness of God's prophets was given before the time our students and our children will need it most. We must help them plant this testimony deeply in their minds and hearts. There is nothing we can do that will bless our students and children more than to help them to come to know Jesus Christ. We must help them to love Him, follow Him, and intentionally strive to become like Him. To the witness of God's prophets I add my humble testimony that Jesus is the Christ, the Son of God and Savior of the world.

In the sacred name of Jesus Christ, amen.

Chad H Webb is administrator of Seminaries and Institutes of Religion.

Modified from a Seminaries and Institutes of Religion annual training broadcast, June 12, 2018, and printed in the *Religious Educator* 20, no. 3 (2019): 17–25.

NOTES

1. Kim B. Clark, "Learn of Me" (evening with a General Authority, January 26, 2018).
2. 2 Nephi 25:26.
3. Doctrine and Covenants 84:19–22.
4. Russell M. Nelson, "Drawing the Power of Jesus Christ into Our Lives," *Ensign*, May 2017, 39.
5. Boyd K. Packer, "The Instrument of Your Mind and the Foundation of Your Character" (Church Educational System devotional for young adults, February 2, 2003), 9, speeches .byu.edu.
6. Matthew 9:35.
7. Matthew 9:36.
8. Alma 26:11–12.
9. See Charles W. Penrose, "Discourse Delivered by Elder Chas. W. Penrose," *Deseret Evening News*, November 29, 1884, 1; *Lectures on Faith* (Salt Lake City: Deseret Book, 1985), 79.
10. Arthur Henry King, *The Abundance of the Heart* (Salt Lake City: Bookcraft, 1986), 123.
11. *Teachings of Presidents of the Church: Joseph Smith* (Salt Lake City: The Church of Jesus Christ of Latter-day Saints, 2007), 49.
12. 2 Nephi 11:4.
13. Moses 4:24.
14. When we look to the Lord, we can see how He is there even when we're facing trials: "I have been reminded by the Lord's prophet, President Russell M. Nelson, that 'counting our blessings is far better than recounting our problems' ["The Story behind My Global Prayer of Gratitude," ChurchofJesusChrist.org]. I've learned from him of the blessings available to covenant Israel and that when we let God prevail, we experience healing, find answers, receive courage to face temptation and strength to fight our battles. . . .

    "I recently participated in a virtual class. In preparation for the class, students read Ether 2:25: 'And behold, *I prepare you* against these things; for ye cannot cross this great deep *save I prepare you* against the waves of the sea' [emphasis added]. Members of the class discussed this verse and how the Lord prepared the Jaredites for their journey. One student shared that she was in the middle of a trial, which she described as the most devastating thing she had ever experienced.

    "Then a question was asked that I believe was inspired by the Holy Ghost. What has the Lord already done to prepare you for this trial—even before it happened? What experiences has He already given you, and what lessons has He already taught you that you can draw on now? What a great question to cause us to think about how the Savior reaches out to us in love, even when that means anticipating our needs. The person who was going through the trial spoke of many ways in which the Lord had prepared her. She realized she'd had experiences she could draw on and a deep understanding and testimony of the principles she needed to know to react to this trial in great faith. A number of other members of the class shared how they had been supported by the Lord in their trials and how they have come to know that He loves them and wants to bless them.

    "As you and [those you teach] see the Lord's hand in blessing the people we come to know in the scriptures, you will be able to help them also recognize the role He is currently playing in their lives. As the Book of Mormon urges, we can help them 'remember how merciful the Lord hath been unto the children of men' [Moroni 10:3]." Chad H

Webb, "Empathy" (Seminaries and Institutes annual training broadcast, January 26, 2021), ChurchofJesusChrist.org.

15. Genesis 45:3.
16. Genesis 45:3–5.
17. Acts 10:41–43.
18. Robert D. Hales, "General Conference: Strengthening Faith and Testimony," *Ensign*, November 2013, 7.
19. "The Living Christ," *Ensign*, May 2017, inside front cover.

Chapter Two

Bridging the Biblical Gap

The History of Judea between the Testaments of the Bible

JOSHUA M. MATSON

The four centuries that precede the Common Era are known by a variety of names. The Jews refer to this time as the Second Temple period, emphasizing the return of the faith's central sacred space. Protestant Christians often refer to this time as the intertestamental period, acknowledging the interlude between the faith's two primary collections of sacred text. Orthodox Christians and Catholics prefer the deuterocanonical period, highlighting the production and acceptance of additional religious texts such as the Apocrypha. In recent years, some Christians have also named it the Four Hundred Silent Years, suggesting a lack of prophetic activity between the prophet Malachi and the New Testament apostles. The varied names of this period serve as a fitting introduction to a time that is omitted from the texts of the Bible but was fraught with division according to the historical record.

The biblical record reveals little concerning the events of these four centuries. Only the books of Ezra, Nehemiah, Haggai, Zechariah, and Malachi are contemporaneous with events following the Babylonian exile (after 539 BC). Malachi, composed around 420 BC, completes the record of the Old Testament, leaving a considerable gap of commentary on the political, social, and religious developments in the time between the conclusion of the Old

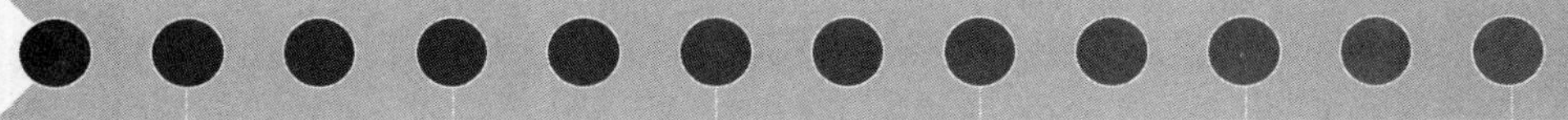

Time line between the Old and New Testaments.

Testament and the beginning of the New Testament. While various historical sources shed additional light on the history of this period in Judea, recent discoveries such as the Dead Sea Scrolls and a renewed appreciation and acceptance for noncanonical Jewish literature have added a considerable amount of information pertaining to the Jewish history that preceded the events of the New Testament. From these historical sources, a picture of division can be painted that bridges the gap between the testaments of the Bible.

The Period of Destruction and Exile (721–538 BC)

Prior to the destruction of the northern Israelites in 722 BC and the exile of Jews from Judah in 587 BC, divisions existed among the Israelite people. The books of 1–2 Kings and 2 Chronicles preserve the history of this division between the northern kingdom of Israel and the southern kingdom of Judah. These kingdoms divided themselves along lines of political, social, economic, and religious ideologies. Beginning in the late tenth century BC, tension abounded as these separate kingdoms attempted to navigate the shifting geopolitical landscape of Israel. While the southern kingdom of Judah outlasted the northern kingdom by a century and a half, ultimately both fell to domineering world powers that imposed on them their forms of conquest. These conquests began the diaspora, or the displacement of Jewish people from the land of Judea.

The Assyrian conquest of the northern kingdom of Israel is well documented in the histories of the Old Testament (see 2 Kings 15:29 and 17:3–6) and in Assyrian inscriptions. Conquering Israel in 722 BC, the Assyrians destroyed Samaria, the capital of the northern kingdom, and imposed their method of exile upon the Israelites by scattering nearly all the inhabitants of the ten northern tribes throughout the vast Assyrian Empire.[1] A mass return of these Israelite exiles to Judea following the fall of the Assyrian Empire is not found among the biblical or historical record, and these tribes are often designated as the lost ten tribes of Israel in later religious texts (see Mishnah, Sanhedrin 10:3; Babylonian Talmud, Shabbat 147b; and Numbers Rabba 9:7). These lost tribes dispersed themselves throughout the world in many ways in the following centuries and legends concerning their scattering are found in the writings of Josephus,[2] Pliny the Elder,[3] and rabbinic texts (Genesis Rabba 73:6 and Sanhedrin 10:6/29b). The Assyrian conquest of the kingdom of Israel foreshadowed the events of the Babylonian conquest of the kingdom of Judah a century later.

The Babylonian conquest of the southern kingdom of Judah is similarly documented in the histories and prophetic literature of the Old Testament (see 2 Kings 25:8–12 and 2 Chronicles 36:17–21) and the Babylonian Chronicles.[4] Jeremiah and Ezekiel are the primary prophetic commentators of the events that are described in the histories of 2 Kings and 2 Chronicles. The Babylonian model of conquest differed from that of the Assyrians, but not radically. Instead of scattering the inhabitants of Judah throughout the empire, the Babylonians focused on exiling waves of Judahite elites over a twenty-year period. First in 606 BC and again in 587 BC, Babylonians carried members of the priestly and royal families of Judah away into captivity. The captivity of 587 BC differed from its predecessor as the Babylonians employed a greater level of destruction by razing the walls of Jerusalem, burning the city, and destroying the temple. In response to the destruction of the city and their central place of worship, the people of Judah in exile remained largely intact and were left to reflect on unfulfilled promises, mourn the loss of their promised land, and devise new ways in which to continue to practice their religion.[5]

While the biblical record focuses primarily on the captivity of the inhabitants of the northern and southern kingdoms, the non-elites who remained in the land of Judea after 587 BC are almost completely lost in the narrative of exile (see 2 Kings 25:12). The peasantry and those situated in villages and towns throughout the countryside of Judea faced many of the same challenges as the exiles. Left to themselves for a half century, these inhabitants devised their own mechanisms to cope with unfulfilled promises and developed new practices for their religion, though in many ways they still maintained a similarity to those of the returning exiles.[6] These decisions would become a focal point in divisions in the period following the exile and in the New Testament (see Ezra 4:4 and 9:1).

The experiences of the elites taken into Babylon dominate the narrative of exile found in both biblical and historical records. Babylonian traditions heavily influenced exiled elites' responses to the loss of their cultural, religious, and political identity. Because exiles could meet in congregations in Babylon, local synagogues appear to have replaced the temple as the central place of worship. Aramaic replaced Hebrew as the primary language spoken by the people (Ezra 4:7). The Jewish calendar was replaced by the Babylonian. New narratives, including some found in the additional Old Testament writings named the Apocrypha, focus on individuals faithfully living the Mosaic law in exile rather than dwelling in a land of promise (see especially Daniel and Esther). These changes occurred in almost every Jewish community throughout the Babylonian Empire.

Jewish communities also held vehemently to the traditions that made them a peculiar people. These communities attributed their failure to remain faithful to God as the primary factor in their captivity. The communities of exiles instituted a religious reform to combat a similar captive fate in the future. These reforms are made manifest in the records produced by the returned exiles. Everyday life appears to have been viewed through the lens of exile, and the religious perspective of the southern kingdom of Judah focused on returning to the genesis of Jewish culture, religion, and politics. Exclusive monotheism (Nehemiah 9:6), a renewed adherence to the Mosaic law (Nehemiah 8:2–18), an abhorrence for intercultural marriage (i.e., exogamy, Ezra 9), and a greater commitment to the institutions of the Aaronite Priesthood and the Davidic monarchy became trademarks of Jewish identity shortly after the exiles' return from Babylon. These ideologies likely developed during the period of exile but flourished once the Jewish communities returned to Judea.

Returning from Exile and Judea under Persian Rule (538–331 BC)

The Persian Empire approached conquered peoples differently than the Assyrian and Babylonian Empires. When the Persians defeated the Babylonians in the mid-sixth century BC, they allowed those exiled under Babylonian rule to return to their original lands and maintain an amount of political, cultural, and religious autonomy. In 538 BC, the Persian king Cyrus the Great authorized the rebuilding of the Jerusalem temple and allowed the sacred vessels for the temple to be returned to the city. Coupled with the autonomy that they were granted by the Babylonians, some Jewish communities of the Babylonian exile began to return to Jerusalem, although many remained in Babylon despite Cyrus's edict (Ezra 1:4–6). These communities intended to carry out their reforms in the promised land free from the divisions and strife that had plagued them prior to the exile. Unsuspectingly, however, they found the land they were returning to inhabited by peoples who had different religious, cultural, and political expectations than their own (Ezra 9:1). The reestablishment of these reformed Jewish communities would take over a hundred years to be realized.

The return of the Jewish communities from exile proved divisive almost immediately. The *'am haggôlâ* (people of the deportation/exile) desired to distinguish themselves from the people they found in the land. The *'am ha'aretz* (people of the land) inhabited the countryside and villages in Judea and were the descendants of the peasantry that remained in the land during the Babylonian exile (2 Kings 25:12). The "adversaries of Judah and Benjamin" (Ezra 4:1–3) settled in the parts of the old northern kingdom of Israel following the Assyrian exile and may have had a connection with the Samaritans. The Edomites were the descendants of Esau who moved into Judea following the Babylonian exile due to political pressure from neighboring kingdoms. The people of the exile, being the descendants of those who originally comprised the noble and priestly classes, felt entitled to the

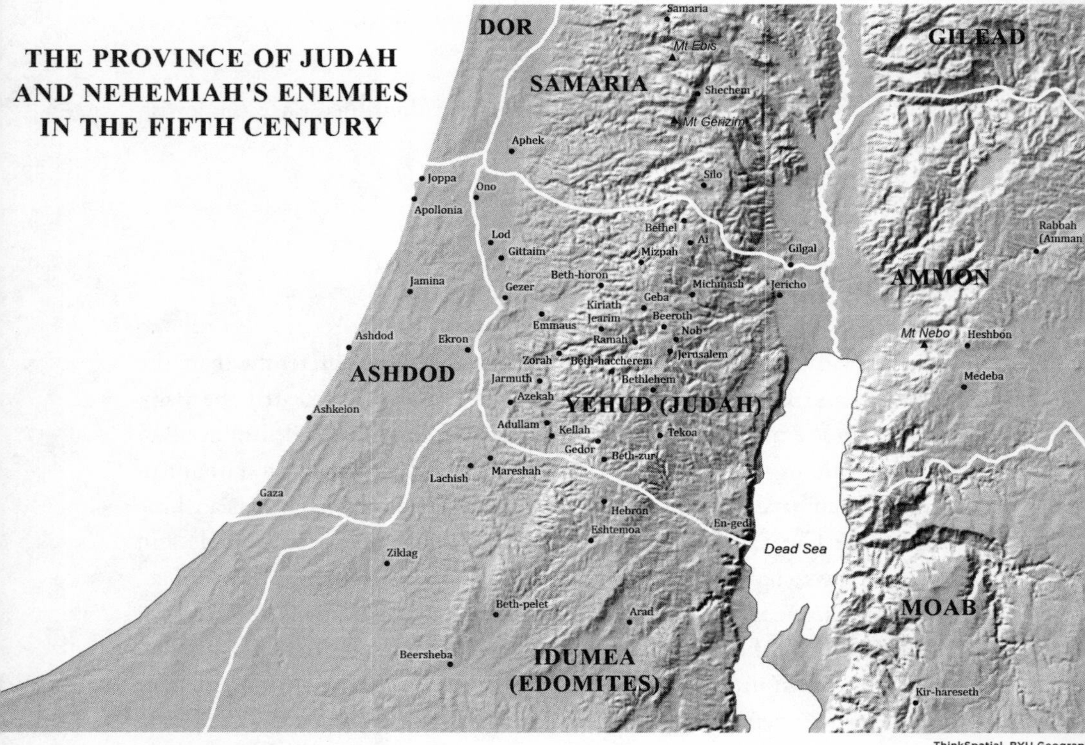

Map of postexile Judea.

land and positions of leadership in the newly autonomous region. These elites progressively imposed themselves as the new aristocracy.

The exiles who returned to their promised land moved quickly to regain control of Judea from the people of the land, the adversaries of Judah and Benjamin, and the Edomites. The introduction of new religious and political practices developed in Babylon by the people of the exile and the syncretism of religion and culture by the people already in Judea resulted in contention. Different cultural histories also contributed to this outcome. Haggai, Zechariah, Ezra, and Nehemiah preserve partial histories of this period from the perspective of the returnees from the exile. These records recount the disputes that led to the eventual dividing of Judea into three distinctive regions during the fifth century BC. The people of the land remained in the villages and countryside of Judea as subjects to the people of the exile and vocally opposed the political and religious reforms instituted by the returned exiles, including the building of the Jerusalem temple

(Ezra 4:4–5). The adversaries of Judah and Benjamin inhabited the vacated northern territories of Ephraim and Manasseh. Later generations renamed this land Samaria, after the central city of the northern kingdom, and named the people Samaritans. Like the reference to "Samaritans" in 2 Kings 17:29, it is uncertain if this is a reference to the same group discussed in the New Testament, as the term is employed to describe both the inhabitants of Samaria and members of the religious group. While the origination and connection of the Samaritans that appear in the New Testament with these settlers in Samaria is unclear, the tensions exhibited at this early period, as well as confrontations discussed below, illustrate why there would be great animosity between Jews and Samaritans in Jesus's day. Making the cultural landscape even more diverse were the Edomites who inhabited the southern region of Judea, which was later named Idumea (Ezekiel 36:5). Ultimately, the people of the exile regained control of the land of Judah and the city of Jerusalem, but only after a lengthy period of reconstruction and consolidation.

After gaining control of the region, the people of the exile focused on rebuilding the temple in Jerusalem. The books of Haggai and Zechariah were written during this period, while Ezra recounts these events from a later perspective. These accounts are fragmentary and unclear on the chronology of rebuilding the temple. The Jerusalem community, under the political direction of the governor Zerubbabel (a descendant of the old royal house of David) and the religious direction of the high priest Jeshua, rebuilt the altars and structure of the temple, establishing Jerusalem as the center of the religious hierarchy. This temple was only a shell of the former one built by Solomon, but its establishment centered the religious activities of Judea in Jerusalem for the returned exiles. The dedication of the temple in 515 BC brought religious centrality back to Jerusalem (Nehemiah 12:27–13:3). After the mysterious disappearance of Zerubbabel, Jeshua reappropriated the office of high priest into a central political figure appointed by the ruling nation, creating a small priestly temple-state that received autonomy from the Persian Empire. These events created religious centrality in Jerusalem, but the city remained a place of insecurity with voids in religious and political law.

After nearly a century of reinstatement in Judea, the people of the exile continued to wrestle with the other inhabitants of Judea to restore Jerusalem to its former glory. Aware of the instability in the city and region, Persian kings appointed Nehemiah and Ezra to return to Jerusalem to usher in the restoration of the social, political, cultural, and religious community that had once thrived within its walls. While the sequence of events in the fifth century BC is still unclear, Ezra and Nehemiah sought to reestablish political and religious stability. Strict adherence to the law of Moses, the paying of tithes, Sabbath day observance, and laws against intermarriage with those outside of the community were among the laws instituted during this time, and they played a prominent role in the history of the Jewish people throughout the period. Additionally, Ezra, acting as a scribe and priest within the Jerusalem community, initiated the study of Torah, or the Law contained in the first five books of the Old Testament, ushering in a distinct period of studying religious texts among the Jewish people.

Jewish communities took various approaches to authoritative religious texts following the exile. Although all Jewish communities at the time accepted the Torah, they disputed the authoritative nature of other Jewish texts. Throughout the Second Temple period, authoritative religious texts (primarily the Torah) played an important role in shaping Jewish communities and their interpretation of the Law with each Jewish community maintaining a different opinion of what constituted authoritative scripture. However, groups like the Samaritans interpreted these authoritative texts very differently than the Jews in Jerusalem. Unlike other Jewish communities of the Second Temple period, the Samaritans only adhered to their own version of the Torah (known as the Samaritan Pentateuch) with divergent traditions. One such tradition is the belief that the properly designated location for a central place of worship was Mount Gerizim, not Mount Ebal or, as later dictated, Jerusalem (see Samaritan Pentateuch, Deuteronomy 27:4). This belief was further manifested at this time by the building of a temple. While concerns about the proper interpretation of authoritative texts elevated tensions in Judea during the time of Malachi (420 BC), it served as a primary indicator of each Jewish community's identity during the Hellenistic period. Judea maintained near complete autonomy throughout the remainder of the dominance of the Persian Empire in the eastern Mediterranean area. Religious communities took advantage of this autonomy.

The biblical and historical records are silent regarding Judea and the events of the next century and a half. Although the Persians engaged in a variety of political and cultural entanglements, the inhabitants of Judea were primarily unaffected by them. This autonomy would be maintained throughout the Persian period but diminished with the overthrowing of the Persian Empire by Alexander the Great and the introduction of Hellenism to Judea.

THE HELLENIZATION OF JUDEA (331–164 BC)

As mentioned above, the biblical record is silent about events that occur after the fifth century BC, requiring scholars to look to other sources to create a history of the period. The writings of Flavius Josephus are one prominent source scholars refer to when discussing the history of the Second Temple period. Josephus was a Roman Jew who lived during the first century AD. A political diplomat, military general, and historian, Josephus wrote extensively about the history of the Jewish people. While Josephus wrote other works, *Jewish Antiquities* and *The Jewish War* are valuable histories that preserve information about the time between the Old and New Testaments. *Jewish Antiquities* preserves a history of the Jewish people from the creation of the world to the days of Gessius Florus, the Roman procurator of Judea from AD 64–66. Most of the early chapters of this work are drawn from the history presented in the Old Testament. *The Jewish War* overlaps with *Jewish Antiquities* and preserves a war history of the Jewish people from the rule of the Seleucid king Antiochus IV Epiphanes (175–164 BC) to the aftermath of the destruction of the Jewish temple (AD 70). Many of the things that are known to scholars today about the intertestamental period are based on the histories of Josephus and the Maccabean histories included in the Apocrypha.

Alexander the Great rapidly conquered the Persian Empire through military campaigns between 334 and 324 BC. Alexander gained control of the region of Judea between 333 and 331 BC with a series of campaigns in the western border of the Persian Empire.[7] Alexander is credited with attempting to unify his conquered empire with the spread of Hellenism (Greek culture and language). The spread of Hellenism through the region of Judea, and to Jews throughout the diaspora, marked a period of shifting ideals and manifestations within Judaism.

Hellenism spread throughout Jewish communities in various ways. Greek became the preferred language of the elite throughout the empire, although Hebrew and Aramaic remained in general use among the inhabitants of Judea. The Hebrew scriptures were translated into Greek in Egypt and utilized throughout the empire. Hellenistic structures like the gymnasium and the stadium became the social centers of communities, even in Jerusalem. Some Jewish inhabitants removed the distinguishing mark of circumcision through a variety of methods, including an operation known as *epispasm*. Others, including some high priests, took Greek names.[8] Education of elite citizens emphasized Hellenistic culture over traditional Jewish history. Jewish communities adopted and fought against Hellenism to varying degrees. While some communities believed that the adoption of some elements of Hellenistic culture did not weaken Jewish identification, others became outraged and rose in rebellion against it.

The inhabitants of Judea found themselves in a precarious political situation following the death of Alexander the Great in 323 BC. Immediately following his death, Alexander's generals divided the conquered lands among themselves. These generals began dynasties that determined the destinies of various lands throughout the empire. The Ptolemies in Egypt and the Seleucids in Syria-Mesopotamia governed the people living in Judea for almost two hundred years. Originally, the Ptolemies ruled Judea. Under Ptolemaic control, the inhabitants of Judea experienced a change in imperial protocol. While the Persians had allowed a great degree of autonomy to the people of Judea, the Ptolemies constructed a large bureaucracy that wielded considerable political power. On the whole, Jews in Judea and Egypt flourished under Ptolemaic control and had a certain degree of autonomy.

Located on the border between these two dynasties, Judea observed battles between the Ptolemies and the Seleucids that penetrated community dynamics. These battles forced individuals and communities to take sides, hoping that their side would prevail and reward them for their loyalty. High priests, now the preeminent position of authority and power among the Jewish people in Judea, aligned themselves with outside forces for political gain, appointment, and advancement. In 198 BC, the Seleucids wrestled control of Judea away from the Ptolemies.

Under Seleucid rule, the Jewish communities in Judea experienced a lessening of religious and political autonomy. While the Seleucids approached ruling their territories through cooperation with established elites, these elites often failed to cooperate with those who had opinions differing from those within the Seleucid hierarchy. In Judea, the Seleucids provided financial and political incentives to the elites of high priestly families in exchange for loyalty to Syrian rulers and the implementation of hellenization. As individuals obtained the position of high priest by bribery, rather than lineage, and Jewish communities disputed the appropriate degree of hellenization allowed by the Jewish law, considerable divisions arose among the Judean people. The Maccabean histories, found in the Apocrypha as 1 and 2 Maccabees, preserve an account of the events surrounding this period.

According to the Maccabean narrative, the ascension of Antiochus IV Epiphanes to the throne of Seleucid Syria marked the decisive moment in the divisive atmosphere in Judea between Jews and Hellenistic rulers. Around 175 BC Antiochus raised taxes on the inhabitants of Judea to fund his failed military campaigns into Egypt. Additionally, Jason, a highly hellenized Jew, successfully bribed Antiochus to appoint him to the position of high priest. Three years later, Menelaus, a highly hellenized Jew devoid of priestly lineage, acquired the position from Jason. In 167 BC, Antiochus collaborated with the hellenized Jewish elite in Jerusalem to convert the Jerusalem temple into a pagan shrine. Some sources, including 1 and 2 Maccabees, suggest that Antiochus instituted these changes to force Greek culture, religion, and language upon the inhabitants of Judea (see 1 Maccabees 1:10–15). Scholars of the Second Temple period debate Antiochus's motives and the extent of his forced reform. However, the results of Antiochus's decisions are undisputed as they led to a revolution in Judea against Hellenistic rule.

A Period of Revolt and Restitution (165–160 BC)

Mattathias, a priest from outside of Jerusalem, together with his five sons, led the revolt against Hellenistic rule. Employing guerrilla-style tactics, the rebels attempted to drive the Seleucids out of Judea and reinstate political, cultural, and religious autonomy to the region (see 1 Maccabees 2:1–14). Mattathias and his supporters initiated their assaults on the villages and towns of Judea in 167/166 BC. This tactic isolated Jerusalem from the rest of Judea. Mattathias left control of the revolt in the hands of his sons when he died in 166/165 BC.

Judas, one of Mattathias's sons who was given the new name of Maccabeus or Maccabee (fighter or hammer), became the primary leader of the rebellion (see 1 Maccabees 3:1–9). Under Judas's leadership, the revolutionaries defeated the Seleucid forces near the city of Jerusalem in 164 BC.[9] Following their victory, they easily regained control of the city. Almost immediately, Judas's followers focused on purifying and rededicating the temple in Jerusalem. Future generations commemorated the events of this rededication with the festival of Hanukkah. Around the same time the revolutionaries gained control of Jerusalem, Antiochus died, igniting a succession crisis in the Seleucid Empire. The Jews took advantage of the political instability, and what began as a fight for religious freedom became an all-out war for Jewish independence.[10]

After restoring the temple in Jerusalem and appointing a high priest whom they believed to be the rightful successor to the position (a decision that would further divide other Jewish communities who did not agree), Judas and his followers focused on forcing the Seleucids out of Judea. Judas marshaled a series of successful military campaigns throughout Judea in the following years. In 160 BC, however, Judas was killed by Seleucid forces, creating a leadership crisis among the rebelling Jews. Disoriented by their defeat, Judas's forces retreated to the countryside of Judea. The Seleucids quickly regained control of Jerusalem and appointed Alcimus, a highly hellenized Jew outside of the lineage of the high priestly families, to the position of high priest. The revolutionaries regrouped and appointed Jonathan, one of Judas's brothers, as their new leader. In 159 BC Alcimus died, and Jonathan led a successful campaign to regain Jerusalem.[11]

While Jonathan ruled as a general for the ensuing years, in 152 BC he tactfully negotiated with the Seleucid rulers and obtained an appointment to be high priest in Jerusalem. The official recognition of Jonathan by the Seleucids began a period of autonomous rule like that enjoyed under the Persians. Descendants of the family of Mattathias officiated in the role of both political leader and high priest for over a century, creating the Hasmonean dynasty.[12] Although Jonathan was not from a high priestly family line, he convinced the Jewish people that he and his posterity would maintain the position of high priest only until the advent of another prophet who could

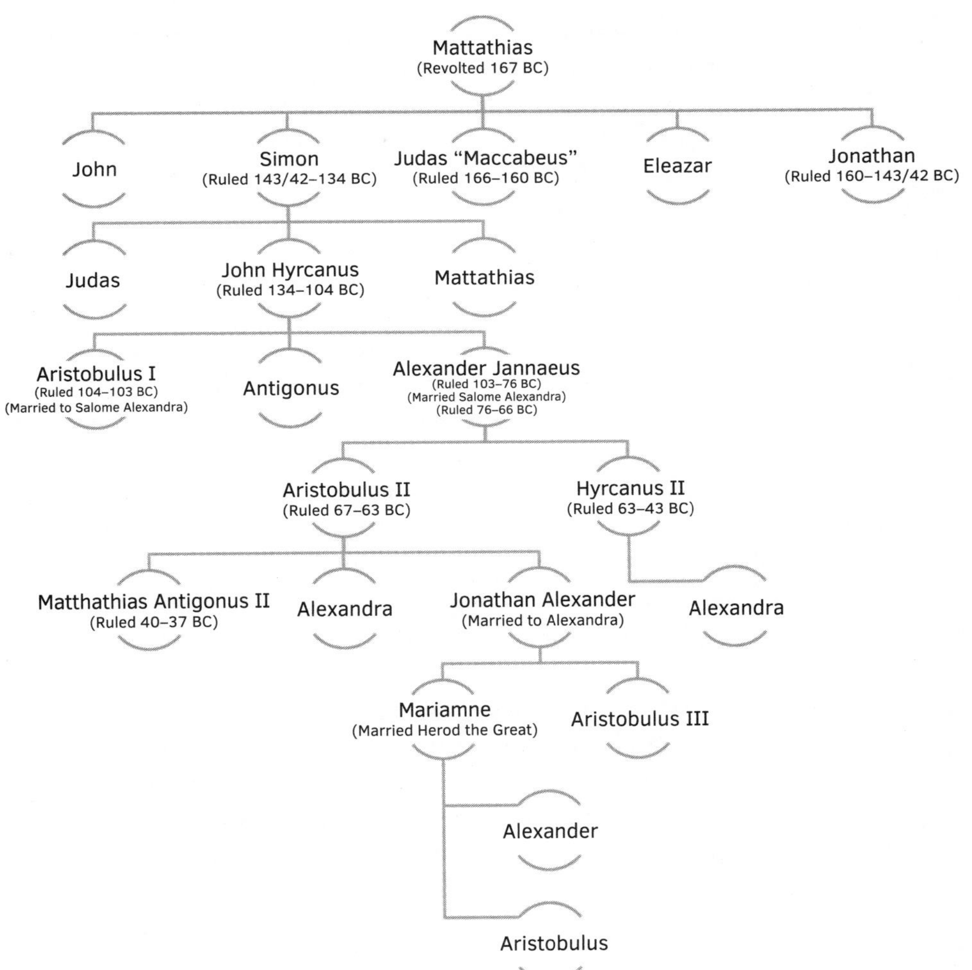

Hasmonean family tree.

successfully identify a rightful successor (see 1 Maccabees 14:41). This change in religious practice, coupled with the divisions throughout Judaism over Hellenism and the revolt against it, led to the creation of various Jewish factions, including the Pharisees, Sadducees, and Essenes.[13] These groups constantly contended with one another over religious and political matters. Some of these religious factions, including the community that authored some of the Dead Sea Scrolls, moved away from Jerusalem to establish their own religious communities, free from the rule of the Hasmoneans.

The Hasmonean Dynasty (160–63 BC)

Political instability in the Seleucid Empire ensured that the beginnings of the Hasmonean dynasty were anything but ideal and smooth. The Seleucids engaged in various internal battles between claimants to the throne. Although Jonathan and his family had been granted autonomous authority in Judea, the Seleucid claimants persuaded him to participate in numerous military campaigns to maintain that autonomy.[14] During one of these campaigns, those antagonistic to the Hasmoneans and the claimant they supported killed Jonathan, leaving the Jewish state without a leader. The Jerusalem assembly appointed Simon, the last remaining brother of Judas, as ethnarch (ruler of the people) and high priest.[15]

Simon continued the campaign for Judean independence. One of the claimants to the Seleucid throne, Demetrius II, made concessions with Simon and the Jewish people in 142 BC in exchange for their support in obtaining control of the empire. Complete Jewish independence was among these concessions. In 141 BC, Simon led a successful campaign against one of the final remaining Greek and highly hellenized Jewish communities at the Acra fortress, marking the beginning of Jewish independence (1 Maccabees 13:52–14:15).

Jewish independence preceded the restitution of the Jewish state to lands that were part of Davidic and Solomonic kingdoms in earlier times. Simon's son-in-law orchestrated Simon's assassination in 135 BC, leaving the throne of Judea and the position of high priest in the control of Simon's son John Hyrcanus. Although Antiochus VII, the ruler of the Seleucids, attempted to regain some of the lands the Hasmoneans had captured during

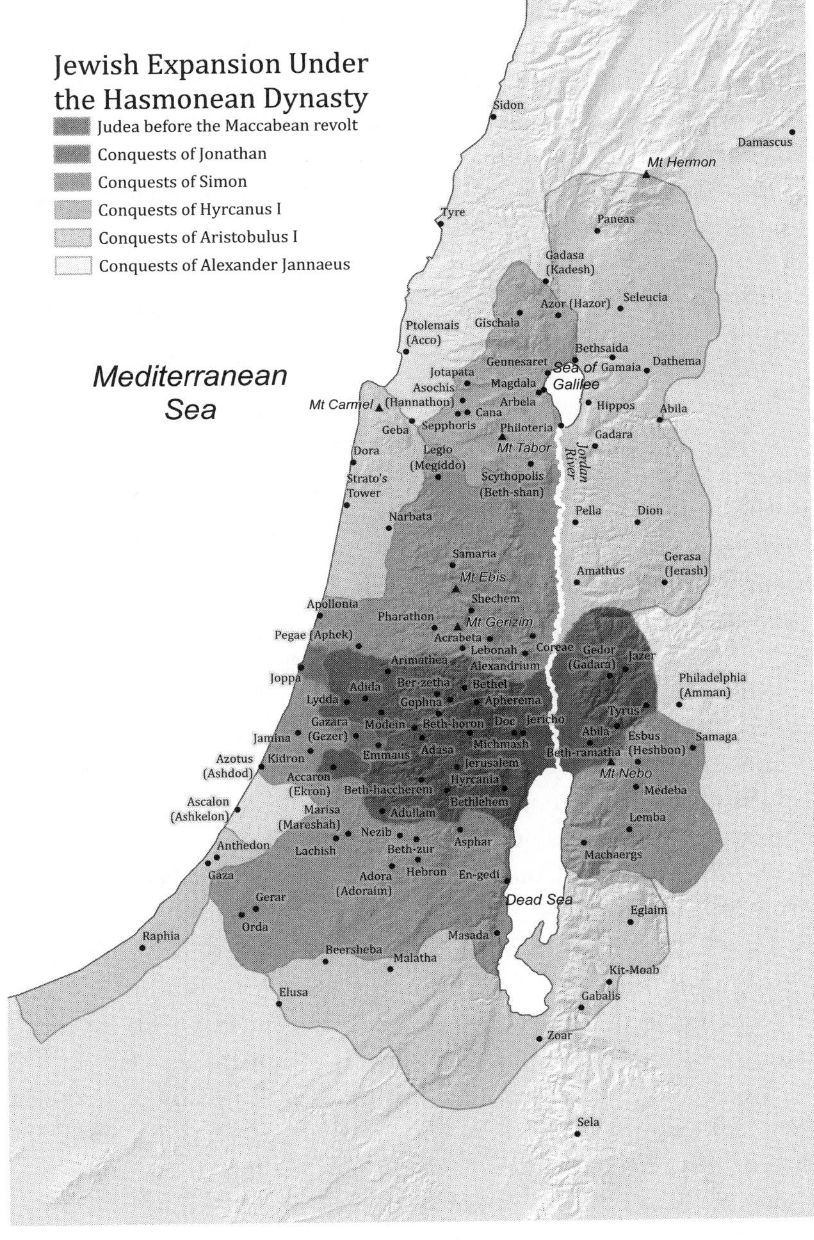

Expansion of the Hasmonean Empire.

the revolts, Hyrcanus negotiated a deal with the Seleucids to maintain autonomy in Judea in exchange for tribute payments for the cities in their control. This agreement ensured that Hyrcanus reigned for over twenty years and allowed him to lead military campaigns to restore the borders of the old kingdom.[16] Among these campaigns, Hyrcanus annexed Idumea in the south and persuaded the inhabitants to convert to Judaism. He also moved to the north and acquired Galilee and Samaria. In Samaria, he destroyed the temple on Mount Gerizim, causing a final divisive blow between the Samaritans and the Jews. Hyrcanus died in 104 BC, leaving the throne to his son Aristobulus I.[17]

Aristobulus I ruled over Judea for only a year but changed the Hasmonean state for the remainder of the dynasty. After gaining control of Judea, Aristobulus continued to push the boundaries of the Hasmonean state toward those that existed during the kingdoms of David and Solomon. Further, Aristobulus took upon himself the title of king.[18] Previous rulers in the dynasty had avoided the title for a variety of reasons, but now the rulers would be known as both priests and kings. This development reflected and molded Jewish expectations of the coming messianic age and proved divisive among the various Jewish factions throughout Judea.

Aristobulus's heir to the throne, his brother Alexander Jannaeus, furthered the divide in Judea during his twenty-seven-year reign. Jannaeus continued to expand the borders of the Hasmonean state, attaining the borders of the earlier kingdom of Solomon, and took upon himself the title of king. Jannaeus faced a rebellion from the Pharisees and other Jewish factions because of his support for the Sadducees and his adoption of many Hellenistic practices. These internal conflicts soon spilled over into civil war.[19] The opponents of Jannaeus solicited the help of Demetrius III, a rival to the Seleucid throne, and engaged in a lengthy series of battles. Jannaeus ultimately prevailed and executed eight hundred of his opponents during a victory feast in Jerusalem. Following Jannaeus's death in 76 BC, his wife Alexandra Jannaea Salome became queen. This form of succession, from husband to wife, resembled that of other Hellenistic kingdoms.[20] The dynasty that started as a defense of religious freedom and independence against Hellenistic rule now resembled Hellenism itself.

Salome reigned masterfully from 76 to 67 BC and facilitated further divisions among the Judeans. She shifted the religious alliances of the crown and aligned herself with the Pharisees, a move that angered the Sadducees, who had been supported by her husband. Salome's support for the Pharisees included placing them among the ruling class of the society. Further, Salome installed her son Hyrcanus II to the position of high priest and expanded the power of the Sanhedrin, a ruling body of religious leaders. This move granted the Sanhedrin power to pronounce judgment in religious matters that had previously been reserved for the high priest. Salome's death signaled the beginning of a civil war between Hyrcanus II and his brother Aristobulus II and began the decline of the Hasmonean dynasty.[21]

The civil war between Hyrcanus and Aristobulus introduced the Romans into political matters in Judea. Aristobulus almost immediately seized the throne from Hyrcanus. After the bitter takeover, Hyrcanus fled to Petra and allied himself with Rome's eastern opponents, the Nabateans. Convinced that his brother would continue to pursue him until his death, Hyrcanus led a joint assault on Jerusalem with his newfound allies. During the fierce battle, both Hyrcanus and Aristobulus appealed to Rome for intervention.[22] The Romans conquered the remnants of the Seleucid Empire in the seventies BC and began to expand throughout the Eastern Mediterranean. Rome intervened and expelled the Nabateans, opening the way for Aristobulus to again prevail over his brother. Eventually, the Roman general Pompey interrogated both brothers to decide who should reign. Aristobulus and his supporters made numerous fateful mistakes, so the Romans sided with Hyrcanus and assigned him to the positions of high priest and ethnarch, revoking the title of king and taking control of the Hasmonean kingdom.[23] Again, the inhabitants of Judea found themselves under the control of a foreign power.

Roman Rule through the Herodian Dynasty (63 BC–AD 70)

Roman rule over Judea began in a way that divided the Jewish people from their new overseers religiously and geographically. Following the intervention of the Romans in the civil war between Hyrcanus and Aristobulus, Pompey explored the Temple Mount in Jerusalem. Curiously, Pompey visited the Holy of Holies, which he had heard was void of any cultic objects.[24] Jewish communities joined together to express their anger over the insensitivity of this Roman ruler. Additionally, although Hyrcanus II ruled over Jerusalem and the temple-state, the Romans divided the remaining lands that had been part of the Hasmonean kingdom and restored independence to each region. In this realignment, the Samaritans, Idumeans, and other Jewish and non-Jewish regions of the Eastern Mediterranean were placed under the control of the Roman proconsul of Syria.

The realignment of the region lasted through the life of Pompey. Following Pompey's death in 48 BC, Hyrcanus II obtained the support of Julius Caesar. Caesar appointed Antipater, the trusted advisor of Hyrcanus, to the position of governor of Judea and reconfirmed the position of high priest upon Hyrcanus with added political powers. Furthermore, Caesar returned lands that had been realigned by Pompey to the jurisdiction of Judea. For the remainder of Caesar's reign, the remnants of the Hasmoneans controlled Judea with little intervention from the Romans.[25]

Caesar's death in 44 BC triggered another period of instability throughout the Mediterranean. In Judea, Aristobulus II's son Antigonus seized the opportunity to take back control of the region and establish an independent kingdom. Antigonus allied with Rome's primary opponent in the East, the Parthians, and attacked Hyrcanus in Judea. After capturing Jerusalem, the forces of Antigonus killed Antipater and imprisoned Hyrcanus. Antigonus proclaimed himself king of Judea and attempted to reestablish the autonomy of the Hasmonean dynasty. However, the Romans appointed Herod, one of Antipater's sons, to establish their own dynasty over Judea.[26]

Herod stands as an example of the complex worlds of Judea in the final century before Christ. Herod's family is situated at the crossroads of the old and the new in many ways, bridging divides and creating new ones. Herod presented his ancestry as deriving from the tribe of Judah and the Babylonian exile. His grandfather and father were Idumeans and converts to Judaism. Both acquired social status and position in the Hasmonean state under Salome and Hyrcanus II. Herod's mother came from a Nabatean family that likely aligned themselves with Hyrcanus in his campaign to regain the throne from his brother. Herod married Mariamne I, the granddaughter of both Aristobulus II and Hyrcanus II. Herod's marriage tied him directly to the Hasmonean royal line. Ultimately, Herod's father, Antipater, appointed Herod governor of Jerusalem in 47 BC. The assault by Antigonus in 44 BC limited Herod's original appointment, but political allegiances reinstated him.

The Romans grew tired of the Hasmonean struggles to regain autonomous power in Judea and looked for a suitable replacement. Herod's knowledge of the political system of the Romans and the Jews, as well as his ability to maintain both systems, made him an ideal candidate for appointment. Herod's lineage, however, prevented him from being accepted by the Jews as a legitimate heir to the position of high priest. Instead, Rome proclaimed Herod king of Judea, Galilee, and Perea in 40 BC, and together they recaptured Jerusalem from Antigonus and the Parthians in 37 BC. Herod's appointment was not an autonomous kingship, but the role of a client king. Herod and his descendants occupied such positions in Judea until almost AD 100.

Herod's rule over Judea mirrored that of the Hasmoneans and those that ruled an independent Judea before them. The support Herod received from the overseeing Romans distinguished him from the earlier kingdoms. Herod expanded the borders of Judea to the size that had been obtained by the Hasmoneans. Herod fortified these borders by erecting fortresses throughout the region. Additionally, he initiated an extensive building project to rebuild the Tomb of the Patriarchs and the capital of Samaria and to construct new cities. Herod's renovations to the Jerusalem temple returned the sacred edifice to the glory and prestige that it had enjoyed in the days of Solomon. Herod also engaged in construction projects that were clearly Hellenistic. In Jerusalem, Herod constructed a theater, an amphitheater, a hippodrome, temples to foreign deities, and a golden eagle above the gate to the temple. The Jews in Judea oscillated in their support for their complicated client-king.

Herod executed laws and judgment in erratic ways to preserve his position of power. He ordered that Aristobulus III, a high priest of Jerusalem and the brother of his wife Mariamne, be drowned so that he could appoint a less established family to the high priesthood. This appointment, and the consistent appointing and disposing of high priests, ensured loyalty to Herod and prevented the possibility of revolt by the temple-state. Similarly, he executed his wife Mariamne and two of her sons to prevent familial conflict between the children he fathered from his ten wives that could jeopardize his authority in the eyes of the Romans. Ultimately, following

Herod's death in 4 BC, the Romans left the region of Judea in control of his descendants.

Herod's posterity who ruled over Judea play a central role in the narrative of the New Testament. Rome appointed Herod's son Archelaus ethnarch of Judea. Archelaus's brother, Antipas, became the tetrarch (ruler of a quarter) of Galilee. Philip, the half brother of Archelaus and Antipas, became the tetrarch of the gentile region of Iturea on the eastern side of the Jordan River. The history of New Testament Judea predominantly occurs in the areas ruled by these three sons of Herod. Archelaus's inability to control the region of Judea in a similar manner to his father led to his removal in AD 6. Instead of appointing another ethnarch, Rome installed a prefect of equestrian rank over Judea. Pontius Pilate served as the fifth prefect over Judea. Shortly after his rule, the title of governor was changed to that of procurator and the Jews were again limited to controlling the temple-state while others controlled the political landscape of Judea.

Two of Herod's grandsons appear prominently in Judea throughout the New Testament narrative. Rome exiled Antipas in AD 37 and appointed Agrippa I, Herod's grandson by Mariamne, first as heir to Philip's tetrarch and then in AD 39 expanded his rule over Antipas's tetrarchy. Additionally, Rome allotted the expanse of Judea to mirror the borders of previous kingdoms. Following Agrippa I's death in AD 44, Rome reinstated their own rulers over Judea because Agrippa II was too young to rule in his father's stead. In AD 50, the Romans appointed Agrippa II as overseer of the kingdom of Chalcis in the north. Additionally, the Romans appointed Agrippa II as high priest, where he deposed the Sadducee high priest Ananus, adding to the tumultuous tension between Jews and Romans that would eventually erupt in rebellion. These revolts ultimately led to the temple's destruction in AD 70 and the removal of the Jews from Judea.

Conclusion

A brief overview of the history of the Second Temple period highlights that this was a time of divisiveness within Judaism. Jewish communities of this period were at odds with those who ruled over them. These tensions, especially against the Hellenistic rulers that followed an age of autonomy under

Persian rule, grew as Jewish communities experienced constant fluctuation between autonomy and oppression. Additionally, Jews frequently found themselves at odds with one another. From the earliest days of their return from exile, the Jews of this period struggled to create a cohesive identity, holding to traditions and adaptations that were at the core of their uniqueness, no group wanting to sacrifice their identity at the cost of another. This history emphasizes the consistent attempts made by Jewish communities and outside leaders to bridge the divides that existed in the social, cultural, political, and religious aspects of their time. It also emphasizes that while attempts were made to bridge these divides, those bridges frequently were adorned with the peculiarities of those in power at the cost of those who were not. Although the biblical sources for this period are scarce, the historical record reveals seeds that were planted within the Old Testament history that grew in adversity and sprouted roots of discord and contention among the Jews that span throughout the text of the New Testament.

Joshua M. Matson is a religious educator with Seminaries and Institutes of Religion.

Joshua M. Matson, "Between the Testaments: The History of Judea Between the Testaments of the Bible," in *New Testament History, Culture, and Society: A Background to the Texts of the New Testament*, ed. Lincoln H. Blumell (Religious Studies Center, Brigham Young University; Salt Lake City: Deseret Book, 2019), 3–18.

Further Reading

Brown, S. Kent, and Richard Neitzel Holzapfel. *Between the Testaments: From Malachi to Matthew*. Salt Lake City: Deseret Book, 2002.

Goodman, Martin. "Jewish History, 331 BCE–135 BCE." In *The Jewish Annotated New Testament*, edited by Amy-Jill Levine and Marc Zvi Brettler, 507–13. New York: Oxford, 2011.

Grabbe, Lester L. *A History of the Jews and Judaism in the Second Temple Period*, vol. 4. New York: Bloomsbury Academic, 2006.

Holzapfel, Richard Neitzel, Eric D. Huntsman, and Thomas A. Wayment. *Jesus Christ and the World of the New Testament*. Salt Lake City: Deseret Book, 2006.

NOTES

1. Avraham Faust, "Settlement, Economy, and Demography under Assyrian Rule in the West: The Territories of the Former Kingdom of Israel as a Test Case," *JAOS* 135 (October–December 2015): 765–89.
2. Josephus, *Jewish War* 7.96–97.
3. Pliny the Elder, *Historia Naturalis* 31:24.
4. See Babylonian Chronicle for the year 605–594 BCE, British Museum BM 21946.
5. Joel Weinberg, "The Babylonian Conquest of Judah: Some Additional Remarks to a Scientific Consensus" *ZAW* 118 (2006): 597–610.
6. Gary N. Knoppers, *Jews and Samaritans: The Origins and History of Their Early Relations* (Oxford: Oxford, 2013), 131–32.
7. Josephus, *Jewish Antiquities* 11.8.
8. Josephus, *Jewish Antiquities* 12.5.
9. Josephus, *Jewish War* 1.1.
10. Josephus, *Jewish Antiquities* 13.7.
11. Josephus, *Jewish War* 1.2.
12. The origin of the name *Hasmonean* is a point of uncertainty among scholars. The term originates in the histories of Josephus and may not have been used prior to his written histories. For Josephus, the name pays homage to an ancestor of Mattathias named *Hašmônay*, who was a descendant of Joiarib (See *The Jewish War* 1.36 and *Jewish Antiquities* 11.111 and 20.190, 238). This name would be significant as it would tie Mattathias and his children into a priestly line of the Aaronite Priesthood. An alternative scholarly opinion is that the name Hasmonean is linked to the village of Hesbon (see Joshua 15:27), making the reference perhaps a link to Mattathias' ancestral home. A final opinion among scholars is that the name Hasmonean is taken from the Hebrew "Ha Simeon," a reference to the tribe of Simeon, one of the twelve tribes of Israel.
13. Josephus, *Jewish Antiquities* 18.1.
14. Josephus, *Jewish Antiquities* 13.5.
15. Josephus, *Jewish Antiquities* 13.6.
16. Josephus, *Jewish Antiquities* 13.8.
17. Josephus, *Jewish Antiquities* 13.10.
18. Josephus, *Jewish Antiquities* 13.11.
19. Josephus, *Jewish Antiquities* 13.13.
20. Josephus, *Jewish Antiquities* 13.16.
21. Josephus, *Jewish Antiquities* 14.1.
22. Josephus, *Jewish Antiquities* 14.3.
23. Josephus, *Jewish War* 1.6.
24. Josephus, *Jewish War* 1.7.
25. Josephus, *Jewish Antiquities* 14.8.
26. Josephus, *Jewish Antiquities* 14.9.

Chapter Three

The Canonization of the New Testament

DANIEL BECERRA

By the end of the first century AD, all of the twenty-seven documents that now constitute the New Testament were written and had begun to circulate among early Christians. However, it was not until centuries later that these texts were collectively named as part of the authoritative body of Christian scripture. The process by which this occurred is called "canonization." The term *canon* comes from the Greek word *kanōn*, meaning "measuring rod" or "measuring stick," and was frequently applied in the ancient church to the collection of texts that informed the beliefs and practices of the Christians who read them.[1] While the terms *scripture* and *canon* are often used interchangeably, there is a subtle yet important distinction between the two: *scripture*, as the term is commonly used by scholars, denotes the inspired and authoritative status of a written document, whereas *canon* typically refers to a defined list of such documents.[2] This distinction is significant because Christians did not begin to create, much less agree upon, such lists until long after the death of Jesus Christ (ca. AD 30). Thus, for several centuries, the earliest Christians considered many texts to be scriptural but had no commonly accepted canon.

To reconstruct the process by which twenty-seven early Christian documents became the official scripture of the church, modern scholars rely on different sources of evidence.[3] These include, first of all, the actual use of these writings by early Christian authors. By noting the frequency and manner of their citations by ecclesiastical leaders, for example, scholars infer the value that the earliest Christians attached to them. Second, scholars also rely on explicit statements and decisions made by both individual Christian authors and ecclesiastical councils relating to the authority of various writings. And finally, the contents and arrangements of ancient manuscript collections also tend to reflect which texts were most important to early Christians.[4]

Broadly speaking, the process of canonization occurred in three overlapping stages:

1. In the first and second centuries, there was no formally closed group of authoritative Christian literature. The four Gospels, several Pauline letters, 1 Peter, and 1 John were widely used and highly regarded by many early Christians. Hebrews, 2 Peter, 2–3 John, James, Jude, and Revelation, on the other hand, held less prominence and authority in Christian communities throughout the Roman Empire.

2. In the second through early fourth centuries, additional Christian writings were composed and read alongside the aforementioned documents. Debates regarding the authoritative status of newly composed texts, such as the Shepherd of Hermas, as well as the literature that would eventually comprise the New Testament, continued well into the fourth century. While there still did not exist any formally closed canon during this period, the scope of the church's authoritative writings was beginning to solidify as individual texts began to be consciously grouped into collections. One reason for this growing canon-consciousness was encounters with teachings and texts deemed heretical by early church leaders.

3. In the fourth and fifth centuries, early Christians struggled earnestly to define and distinguish between authoritative and nonauthoritative texts. During this period many lists of canonical books were drafted by church leaders. The first such list to advocate the exclusive use of the twenty-seven books that now comprise the New Testament was written in the year AD 367. This list was later ratified by several church councils in subsequent years, effectively closing the New Testament canon for many Christians.

The purpose of this chapter is to trace the contours of this centuries-long canonization process in more detail by discussing four related topics: (1) the authoritative texts and teachings of the earliest Christians, (2) factors leading to the selection and closure of the canon, (3) the criteria by which canonicity was determined, and (4) important canon lists.

The Authoritative Texts and Teachings of the Earliest Christians

The Scriptures of Israel and Teachings of Jesus

At its inception, Christianity was a largely Jewish movement, meaning that Jesus and the majority of his earliest followers were Jews. The New Testament records that Jesus and the apostles quoted extensively from Old Testament[5] books like Deuteronomy, the Psalms, Isaiah, and others, thus demonstrating that the early church considered the scriptures of Israel—albeit in their Greek translation—to be one authoritative source for moral instruction as well as determining matters of doctrine and practice.[6] In contrast to their Jewish neighbors, however, the followers of Jesus understood the Jewish scriptures to be fulfilled primarily in the life and mission of Jesus of Nazareth. Although no known Christian writings were produced until the decades following Jesus's death, the earliest Christians preserved the teachings and acts of Jesus in memory and passed them on orally.[7] These teachings were understood to have the highest authority in Christian communities and constituted the basis for Christian discipleship.

Beginning in the middle of the first century, about twenty years after Jesus's death, Christians began to produce their own writings, which gradually increased in variety and number to include Gospels, letters, narratives of apostolic "acts," and other genres of literature. Throughout the second and third centuries, Christians across the Roman Empire treasured such texts—not all of which would be included in the New Testament—even though no church council had formally legitimized or mandated their exclusive use. These documents informed the worship, preaching, and teaching of many Christian communities.

The canonization of the New Testament texts may be profitably understood not so much as a process of collecting these documents individually, but as assembling smaller collections of texts. The four major components of the New Testament include three such "minicollections": a collection of letters attributed to Paul, a collection of four Gospels, and a collection of what are commonly referred to as "universal" (or "catholic") epistles, so named on account of their general rather than specific intended audience. Only the books of Acts and Revelation stand apart from these three collections. It will be helpful at this point to provide a brief overview of when these four different components of the New Testament began to take shape.[8]

The Letters of Paul

Paul's letters are almost certainly the earliest surviving Christian documents—although not all were written at the same time—and were tailored to the particular circumstances of the persons and communities to whom they were individually addressed.[9] Paul, therefore, did not likely anticipate that his letter to the Thessalonians, for example, would be read by those in Corinth, or his letter to Philemon read by Timothy and Titus.[10] Furthermore, the thirteen letters traditionally attributed to Paul and currently in the New Testament were certainly not the only ones he wrote to Christian communities. In 1 Corinthians 5:9 for example, Paul mentions a letter he had sent previously to the saints at Corinth. Ephesians 3:3 alludes to an earlier, but lost, letter to the Ephesians. Elsewhere, Paul similarly mentions a letter he sent to saints at Laodicea (Colossians 4:12). None of these documents, however, survive today.

The earliest evidence that Paul's letters were being compiled and read together as a single collection comes from the beginning of the second century, making Paul's writings not only the first to be composed but the first to be gathered into a collection.[11] While the earliest such collection included only ten of Paul's letters (excluding 1 and 2 Timothy and Titus), by the end of the second century, collections containing all thirteen letters of Paul were common in Christian communities.[12] The book of Hebrews, however, was viewed with suspicion even into later centuries on the grounds that many Christians doubted that Paul wrote it, not least because the letter itself does not claim to have been written by the apostle.[13]

The Four Gospels

The four Gospels were likely written in the second half of the first century in order to (1) preserve and testify of the teachings and acts of Jesus, which up to this point were primarily, if not exclusively, transmitted through word of mouth, and (2) adapt and apply these traditions to the particular circumstances in which Christian communities found themselves (hence the distinctive character of each Gospel).[14] Two of the Gospels are attributed to apostles of Jesus (Matthew and John), while the other two (Mark and Luke) are attributed to men who were followers of Jesus and companions of apostles, but not apostles themselves (see Acts 12:25; 2 Timothy 4:11).[15]

The current scholarly consensus is that the Gospel of Mark was written first, being composed in the midsixties to early seventies AD, some three to four decades after the death of Jesus, and fifteen to twenty years after the earliest surviving letter of Paul was written. The Gospels of Matthew and Luke followed shortly after, being written in the seventies and eighties respectively, and reflect significant reliance on Mark's Gospel as a source. The Gospel of John was likely composed sometime between AD 80 and AD 100.

As with the letters of Paul, the four Gospels were originally addressed to individual Christian communities and thus were not at first read as a collection. It is not until the end of the second century that evidence emerges of Christians reading them together and arguing for their exclusive use. The earliest such evidence is a statement from a bishop and theologian named Irenaeus (ca. AD 180), who argues that the Gospels can be neither "more or less in number" than four.[16] Before the second century, the Gospel of John seems to have been the least widely used in some regions, perhaps, as some scholars have argued, because of its differences in substance, style, and outline from other, more popular Gospels.[17]

The collection of four Gospels gained wide acceptance by the mid-third century, although the order in which the books were placed differed in some regions. Christian communities in the Western Roman Empire, for example, preferred the order Matthew, John, Luke, Mark, apparently privileging those Gospels written by apostles. Because of the vast distances that separated Christian inhabitants of the Roman Empire, as well as their general cultural diversity, it was not uncommon for Christian communities in different geographical regions—some of which might be thousands of miles apart—to favor some texts above others, or even to highly value texts rejected in, or unknown to, other congregations.[18]

The Universal Epistles

The third minicollection included in the New Testament comprises the letters 1 and 2 Peter, 1–3 John, James, and Jude. Because these letters are not addressed to particular communities or individuals, they are commonly referred to by scholars as the "universal" or "catholic" epistles. The term *catholic* derives from the Greek word *katholikos*, which means "universal," referring to the general rather than specific intended audience of these epistles. All seven letters were likely written in the latter half of the first century. Early on, however, only 1 John and 1 Peter were widely read by Christians; the other five letters were still used but only regionally. One of the reasons for this was that some early Christians questioned the apostolic authorship of these letters. The Universal Epistles were not likely being read together as a collection until the third century.[19]

Acts of the Apostles and Revelation

The Acts of the Apostles and the book of Revelation are the only two documents to stand outside the three minicollections that compose the New Testament and have their own history of acceptance. The book of Acts and the Gospel of Luke are two volumes of the same work and were both written by Luke in the late first century. Whereas the Gospel records the ministry of Jesus, Acts records the first missionary efforts of Jesus's apostles. In contrast to Luke's Gospel, however, the book of Acts did not gain wide popularity until the end of the second century.

The book of Revelation is what is known as an "apocalypse," from the Greek word *apocalypsis*, meaning "uncovering," and is a genre of literature that claims to disclose something hidden, often being revealed by heavenly beings in symbolic language and frequently pertaining to the end of the world. By the end of the first century, Revelation was widely read, although more so in Christian communities in the Western Roman Empire than in the East. Reasons for its slower acceptance as scripture in the East, which didn't occur until the late fourth century, include disputes over the apostolic origins of the book and disagreements regarding whether the events described therein should be understood literally or symbolically.[20]

Other Authoritative Texts

While all of the above-mentioned texts would eventually become part of the New Testament canon, they were not the only writings valued by Christians in the early centuries of the church. Numerous other letters, gospels, acts, and apocalypses were read and considered authoritative in Christian communities across the Roman Empire. Many letters, for example, were sent from early church leaders to diverse Christian individuals and communities. These were intended to provide their addressees with instruction regarding Christian living, and like Paul's letters, were tailored to the individual circumstances of those to whom they were written. Some of these documents, however, were also disseminated widely and read beyond their original intended audience. First Clement and the Epistle of Barnabas are two examples of letters that were considered broadly authoritative but that ultimately were not included in the New Testament. First Clement was written in the late first century and is attributed to Clement, the third bishop of Rome. Addressed to the saints in Corinth, the letter attempts to resolve disputes among the clergy and congregation in that community.[21] The Epistle of Barnabas was likely written sometime between AD 70 and 135 and is attributed to Paul's missionary companion, Barnabas. It addresses Christianity's relationship with Judaism and argues that Christians are the true inheritors of God's covenant with Israel.[22]

In addition to letters, there were also numerous gospels composed. Gospels attributed to Peter, Thomas, Judas, Mary, and Phillip, for example, were circulated and read in some, although not all, Christian communities. While these gospels purport to have been written by followers of Jesus, modern scholars and many early Christians generally agree that such was not the case. It was not uncommon in the ancient world for such "pseudonymous" (i.e., falsely named) texts to be written by one person and attributed to another on the grounds that the author understood his work to be inspired by, in honor of, or true to the mind and teachings of the person for whom he named it.[23] Whether and to what degree such authors were trying to intentionally deceive their readers is a matter of debate.[24] Additionally, another text popular in the Eastern Roman Empire until the fourth century was the Diatesseron, which harmonized the four Gospels into a single coherent narrative. The Diatesseron was written sometime in the second century and attributed to an author and theologian named Tatian.

Numerous accounts of the missionary endeavors, or "acts," of the apostles were also written in the second century, including the Acts of John, Acts of Peter, Acts of Andrew, Acts of Paul, and Acts of Thomas. These works were composed anonymously, circulated independently of one another, and claim to record the deeds of Jesus's apostles as they spread his message throughout the known world. Many of the stories contain accounts of miracles such as healings, exorcisms, and raising the dead. While these stories were certainly popular in some Christian communities, many ancient Christians also viewed them with suspicion, not least on account of some of their "unorthodox"[25] theological content, which is one of the primary reasons they were never included in the canon. Modern scholars generally do not view these texts as historically reliable accounts of what Jesus's apostles actually did.

Texts of the same genre as the book of Revelation were also widely read by Christians in the second century. The Apocalypse of Peter, for example, purports to have been written by the Apostle Peter—a claim ultimately rejected by both many ancient Christians and modern scholars—and records a conversation between the resurrected Christ and Peter in which Jesus describes the destruction of the world, final judgment, and destinies of the righteous and wicked. The Shepherd of Hermas, another apocalyptic text, was written in the early second century by a man named Hermas and contains a series of visions and parables delivered by an angel. These texts teach principles relating to ethical life and the final judgment. Although viewed as scripture by many early Christians, the Shepherd of Hermas was ultimately excluded from the canon because its author was not an apostle.

Factors Leading to the Selection and Closure of the Canon

As a large number of Christian texts were being composed in the first and second centuries, Christians became increasingly aware of the need to delimit the number and scope of their authoritative literature. This was a complex process that not only spanned centuries but varied in pace among the different regions of the Roman Empire. Scholars have argued that a number of social, technological, and theological factors contributed to the selection and closure of New Testament canon.[26] The most prominent of these include the following.

Creation of the Codex

Prior to the end of the first century, Christians likely copied their sacred texts on scrolls made of papyrus (2 John 12; compare 2 Timothy 4:13), a paper-like material made from the papyrus plant, which was indigenous to Egypt. The maximum length of a single scroll was about thirty feet, which was roughly enough space to fit the Gospel of Luke and the book of Acts.[27] Parchment, a writing material made from animal skin (typically sheep, goats, and calves), was also sometimes used by Christians, although less frequently given that it was more expensive to produce.[28] One technological development that facilitated the eventual gathering of authoritative books together in a single volume was the invention of the codex, or leaf-book, which closely resembles a modern book. When Christians adopted the codex form of book for their scriptural writings, this allowed them to gather many more documents into a single volume. This format would also eventually help standardize the order of the New Testament books.

Marcion

Another likely influence on the formation of the canon was a man named Marcion. Marcion was a wealthy Christian shipowner living in Rome in the mid-second century. He believed that the God of the Old Testament could not possibly be the same loving and merciful God described by the Gospels. Consequently, he sought to establish a collection of authoritative writings that removed any mention of what he understood to be a cruel and vengeful deity. His efforts led to what some scholars have called the first verifiable—although eventually rejected—canon of the New Testament. Marcion's canon included only the Gospel of Luke and ten letters of Paul, which were all edited to exclude any mention of the Jewish scriptures and the God described therein. Marcion gained a substantial following in the second and third centuries, but he was ultimately excommunicated for his views. In responding to the teachings of Marcion, early church leaders were impelled to become more reflective about the scope of the church's scriptures and the degree to which they might be subject to alteration.

Gnosticism

Gnosticism, derived from the Greek word *gnosis* and meaning "knowledge," is a broad term used by scholars to designate groups of Christians who claimed to possess special knowledge that would enable them to gain a higher degree of salvation than anyone else.[29] While gnostic Christians valued most of the same literature as other Christians, they also produced their own texts that they claimed contained secret teachings of Jesus and the apostles. Some of these include the Gospel of Philip, Gospel of Mary, and Gospel of Thomas, the last of which claims to record secret sayings delivered by Jesus to the apostle Thomas. Many early Christian authorities criticized gnostic Christians not only for their use of these books but for the way they interpreted more widely accepted writings like the Gospel of John. One bishop's response to such interpretative practices was to establish what he referred to as a "rule of faith," which was founded on the teachings of the more traditional texts, like the four Gospels and writings of Paul, and intended to be a standard by which proper Christian teaching could be determined. Numerous other early authorities would follow suit, condemning the esoteric writings of the gnostics as heretical; in the process they advocated for the exclusive use of many of the texts that would eventually compose the New Testament.

Montanism

Another second-century influence on the closure of the canon was a movement led by a man named Montanus (ca. AD 170). This movement emerged in Asia Minor and spread throughout the Roman Empire. Montanus and his associates, two women named Prisca and Maximilla, believed themselves to be inspired instruments of the Holy Spirit and adhered to what they understood to be the true form of Christianity. They taught that other Christians lacked spiritual gifts and that the Heavenly Jerusalem would soon descend and be located in the small town of Pepuza, the same place where the three resided, spoke in tongues, and uttered prophecies that were recorded for their followers. The larger church strongly opposed the prophetic messages of the Montanists and was faced with the question of how new revelations should be treated in light of existing information revealed in scriptural texts. As a step toward the adoption of a more fixed canon, many Christian authorities at this time emphasized the absolute authority of apostolic writings for determining matters of faith and adjudicating the continuing activity of the Holy Spirit in the church.

Persecution

The persecution of Christians by the Roman government was another factor that likely contributed to the finalization of the canon. Christians in the Roman Empire experienced sporadic persecution from the mid-first century to early fourth century. In AD 303, during what is commonly known as "the Great Persecution," the emperor Diocletian (AD 284–305) issued an order that all Christian scriptures were to be confiscated and burned. Accordingly, when imperial authorities demanded the surrender of these documents, Christian believers (primarily the clergy) were forced to decide which books to hand over and which to try to save. Many faithful individuals hid copies of those most valued texts and handed over writings considered less authoritative in order to placate the Romans and avoid punishment. Persecution, therefore, offered early Christians another occasion to make deliberate judgments regarding which texts they held in highest regard.

Emperor Constantine

Finally, several decades following the Great Persecution, when Christians were free to worship relatively unmolested in the Roman Empire, the emperor Constantine (AD 306–37) ordered fifty deluxe copies of the scriptures to be made in an effort to organize and promote Christian worship in his new capital, Constantinople. These copies were intended to furnish Christian churches in the region and encourage uniformity in belief and practice. The production of these codices suggests that the matter of which books were most valued was close to settled by the fourth century. Although it is a minority opinion, some scholars argue that at least two surviving New Testament manuscripts—Codex Vaticanus and Codex Sinaiticus—may have been among Constantine's original fifty copies, or were perhaps influenced by them.[30] The survival of Constantine's codices notwithstanding, scholars posit that if these deluxe copies included the current twenty-seven books of the New Testament, then this likely would have had a profound impact on the eventual finalization and acceptance of the canon as it exists today.[31]

Criteria for Canonicity

During the second through the fourth centuries, as early Christians sought to define and distinguish between authoritative and nonauthoritative texts, there were primarily three criteria by which the canonicity was determined: apostolicity, orthodoxy, and widespread use.

Apostolicity

Arguably the most important criterion for church leaders was a text's apostolicity, meaning its authorship by or close connection with an apostle. The Shepherd of Hermas, for example, was a popular book but was ultimately denied entry to the canon in part because it was not written by an apostle. The Gospels of Mark and Luke, on the other hand, while not written by apostles, were nevertheless validated because of the authors' close associations with Peter and Paul.[32] In accordance with this criterion, texts accepted into the canon were typically composed at an earlier date than those that were excluded, reflecting a preference for books written by eyewitnesses to Jesus Christ's ministry. The books of Hebrews, Revelation, 2–3 John, James, and Jude were slow to be formally accepted on a large scale due to some doubts regarding their apostolic origins.

Orthodoxy

Another criterion was a text's conformity with a tradition of fundamental Christian beliefs. This tradition of orthodoxy, although it developed over time, was understood to have been received from the apostles and passed down from generation to generation. It was also sometimes referred to by early Christian authors as the "rule of faith," "canon of truth," and "ecclesiastical canon."[33] These phrases encompassed widely held beliefs relating to things like the nature of the Godhead; the reality of the incarnation, suffering, and resurrection of Jesus; the creation and redemption of humankind; proper scriptural interpretation; and the rituals of the church. The texts known as the Gospel of Peter and Gospel of Thomas, to name two examples, were rejected on the grounds that their portrayal of Christ was incongruent with this inveterate tradition of orthodoxy.

Widespread Use

Another criterion for canonicity was a text's widespread and continuous usage, especially by respected Christian authorities and in the large metropolitan centers of the Roman Empire, such as Rome, Ephesus, Antioch, Alexandria, and Constantinople. The broad use of a text implied its value for determining matters of faith and practice on a large scale and thus its relevance to the church beyond specific regional locales. For example, the Eastern Church's high valuation of the book of Hebrews influenced the West to adopt it, while the Western church's usage of Revelation led to its acceptance in the East. Because the popularity and liturgical use of a book frequently led to its formal acceptance, canonization should be understood not only as a process by which authority is conferred but as a means of recognizing already-authoritative literary works.

Canon Lists

It wasn't until the fourth and fifth centuries that the majority of lists of authoritative books were drafted. During this time, early Christian leaders arguably did not impose anything new on the church, but rather formally ratified what was already widely accepted. Three of the most important lists that attest to the establishment of the New Testament canon as it exists today are the Muratorian canon, the canon of Eusebius, and Athanasius's thirty-ninth Festal Letter.[34]

Muratorian Canon

The Muratorian Canon is a fragmentary document named after Ludovico Muratori, the man who discovered it in the eighteenth century. Scholars disagree on when it was written, estimating its date of composition to be sometime between the second and fourth centuries. The document contains a list of twenty-four books accepted for reading in the church. These include the four Gospels, Acts, thirteen letters of Paul, Jude, and 1–2 John. It likewise includes two books that would never become canonical (Wisdom of Solomon and Apocalypse of Peter) and excludes five that would (Hebrews, 1 and 2 Peter, James, and 3 John). Finally, the document also explicitly rejects several other books: Shepherd of Hermas, two letters falsely attributed to Paul (one to the Laodiceans and another to the Alexandrians), and other unnamed writings of heterodox groups.

Canon of Eusebius

Another canon list comes from an ancient church historian named Eusebius (ca. AD 260–339) and was written in the early fourth century. Eusebius divides his list of books into four categories. The first category enumerates twenty-one books accepted without qualification in the church: the four Gospels, Acts, fourteen letters of Paul, 1 John, and 1 Peter. He adds, however, that the book of Revelation may also be used if desired. The second category lists books that were commonly used but whose authority was still under dispute at the time: James, Jude, 2 Peter, and 2–3 John. Eusebius notes that some Christians would place the books of Revelation and Hebrews in this category as well. The third category contains books Eusebius considers illegitimate: Acts of Paul, the Shepherd of Hermas, the Apocalypse of Peter, the Epistle of Barnabas, and the Didache (also known as "Teaching of the Twelve Apostles"). The final category lists those books deemed heretical and thus to be completely rejected. These include gospels attributed to Peter, Thomas, and Matthias, to name a few, as well as books claiming to record the acts of Andrew, John, and other apostles.

Athanasius's Thirty-Ninth Festal Letter

The first canon list to name all twenty-seven books of the New Testament as exclusively authoritative was written by Athanasius, who was the bishop of Alexandria, Egypt, and a prominent theologian. His *Thirty-Ninth Festal Letter* was sent out on Easter of the year AD 367 and recommended a list of canonical books to church members in North Africa. This list was later ratified by the Council of Carthage in AD 397 and subsequent councils as well.[35] Athanasius concludes his letter with a statement regarding the value of these books for Christians: "These [books] are fountains of salvation, so that they who thirst may be satisfied with the living words they contain. In these alone is proclaimed the doctrine of godliness."[36]

New Testament Canons Today

The acceptance of Athanasius's Festal Letter by most Christians should not overshadow the fact that there still does not exist a single universally agreed-upon New Testament canon. In fact, given the diversity of Christianity in both ancient and modern times, no canon list ever produced has been binding on all those who claim to be Christian. The modern Syrian Orthodox and Chaldean Syrian churches for example, reject 2 Peter, 2–3 John, Jude, and Revelation. The Greek Orthodox Church likewise rejects the book of Revelation. On the other hand, the Ethiopian Church, in addition to the commonly accepted twenty-seven books of the New Testament, also includes the Shepherd of Hermas, two letters of Clement, and a collection of church law called the *Apostolic Constitutions* in their canon.[37]

Conclusion

The canonization of the New Testament was a long and complicated process, and numerous factors led to the formation of what is now arguably the most beloved volume of Christian scripture. By understanding the history of the canon, Latter-day Saints should not only gain a greater appreciation for this remarkable book of scripture but find themselves deeply indebted to those ancient Christians who faithfully recorded, preserved, defended, and transmitted the teachings of Jesus and his earliest followers.

Daniel Becerra is an assistant professor of ancient scripture at Brigham Young University.

Daniel Becerra, "The Canonization of the New Testament," in *New Testament History, Culture, and Society: A Background to the Texts of the New Testament*, ed. Lincoln H. Blumell (Provo, UT: Religious Studies Center, Brigham Young University; Salt Lake City: Deseret Book, 2019), 772–86.

Notes

1. The word wasn't applied to Christian writings in the sense of an authoritative collection of texts until the fourth century. Before that point, it referred more to a set of governing Christian beliefs, something akin to the Articles of Faith in the modern Church of Jesus Christ of Latter-day Saints.
2. Some scholars, however, understand the word *canon* in a much more capacious sense, as referring to normative texts, beliefs, and traditions, even before such things become formally ratified through conscious deliberation and ecclesiastical mandates.

3. For a brief introduction to prominent issues relating to the formation of the biblical canon more broadly, see Lee Martin McDonald and James A. Sanders, "Introduction," in *The Canon Debate*, ed. Lee McDonald and James A. Sanders (Peabody: Hendrickson, 2002), 3–17. For issues relating specifically to the New Testament, see Harry Gamble, "The New Testament Canon: Recent Research and the Status Quaestionis," in *Canon Debate*, 267–94. For a more in-depth discussion of the formation of the biblical canon from a Latter-day Saint perspective, see Daniel Becerra, "The Biblical Canon," in *Biblical Studies and the Latter-day Saint Tradition*, ed. Taylor Petrey, Cory Crawford, and Eric Eliason (Salt Lake City: University of Utah Press, forthcoming 2023).
4. Those manuscripts and collections that survive to the present tend to be those whose contents were circulated most widely. The earliest of such collections date to about the fourth century. See Harry Gamble, "Canon, New Testament," in *The Anchor Bible Dictionary*, ed. David Noel Freedman (New York: Doubleday, 1992), 1:853.
5. Some scholars believe, however, that Christianity did not inherit a fixed canon from Judaism, for Judaism had not yet fully set limits on its scripture in the first century. See Gamble, "Canon," 853.
6. See for example, Jared W. Ludlow, "Paul's Use of Old Testament Scripture," in *How the New Testament Came to Be: The Thirty-Fifth Annual Sidney B. Sperry Symposium*, ed. Kent P. Jackson and Frank F. Judd Jr. (Provo, UT: Religious Studies Center, Brigham Young University; Salt Lake City: Deseret Book, 2006), 227–42.
7. One early Christian author named Papias (ca. AD 60–130) alludes to this process of oral transmission, saying, "But if anyone ever came who had been a follower of the elders, I inquired into the words of the elders—what Andrew, Peter, Phillip, Thomas, James, Matthew, or any other of the Lord's disciples had said, and what Ariston and the elder John, the Lord's disciples, said. For I did not think that information from books would profit me as much as the word of a living and surviving voice." See Eusebius, *Ecclesiastical History* 3.39.4. It is also possible that a collection of Jesus's sayings and other teachings was composed and circulated at a very early date. Scholars refer to this hypothetical written source for some of the Gospels as "Q," a shorthand for the German word *Quelle*, meaning "source."
8. For the format and content of following summary, I am indebted to Gamble's helpful article in the *Anchor Bible Dictionary*: "Canon," 852–61.
9. For a brief introduction to Paul's letters and the reasons they were written, see Eric D. Huntsman, "The Occasional Nature, Composition, and Structure of Paul's Letters," in Jackson and Judd, *How the New Testament Came to Be*, 190–207.
10. One exception to this is the letter to the Colossians in which the author explicitly states that it should be read by the saints in Laodicea (Colossians 4:16).
11. Second Peter, which may have been written toward the end of the first century, refers to a collection of Pauline letters; see 2 Peter 3:15–16.
12. Gamble, "Canon," 853–54.
13. For a brief introduction to issues relating to authorship of Hebrews, see Terrence Szink, "Authorship of the Epistle to the Hebrews," in Jackson and Judd, *How the New Testament Came to Be*, 243–59.
14. Gamble, "Canon," 854; Thomas A. Wayment, "First-Century Sources on the Life of Jesus," in Jackson and Judd, *How the New Testament Came to Be*, 109–22.
15. Authorship is a complex phenomenon and involves not only the telling a story but conscious choices regarding what to include in one's account as well as how to present that information to the reader. Accordingly, some scholars have highlighted the role of the

Gospel authors as editors. For one example, see Gaye Strathearn, "Matthew as an Editor of the Life and Teachings of Jesus," in Jackson and Judd, *How the New Testament Came to Be*, 141–56.

16. Irenaeus, *Against Heresies* 3.11.8.
17. Gamble, "Canon," 855.
18. Unlike today, in which the ease of travel and communication across large distances, as well as a centralized ecclesiastical authority, promote uniformity in worship, doctrine, and practice, in the ancient church there existed more regional variety with respect to such things.
19. Evidence for this comes from a fourth-century Christian author and historian, Eusebius, who says that these seven letters were being read publicly in many churches. See Eusebius, *Ecclesiastical History* 2.23.25.
20. Gamble, "Canon," 855.
21. Michael Holmes, ed., *The Apostolic Fathers: Greek Texts and English Translations*, 3rd ed. (Grand Rapids, MI: Baker Academic Press, 2007), 33–43.
22. Holmes, *Apostolic Fathers*, 370–75.
23. K. Aland, "The Problem of Anonymity and Pseudonymity in Christian Literature of the First Two Centuries," *Journal of Theological Studies* 12 (1961): 39–49. For the implications of pseudonymity for understanding the formation of the New Testament, see Kent D. Clarke, "The Problem of Pseudonymity in Biblical Literature and Its Implications for Canon Formation," in McDonald and Sanders, *Canon Debate*, 440–68. For one Latter-day Saint perspective on this issue, see also Stephen E. Robinson, "Lying for God: The Uses of the Apocrypha," in *Apocryphal Writings and the Latter-day Saints*, ed. C. Wilfred Griggs (Provo, UT: Religious Studies Center, Brigham Young University, 1986), 133–54.
24. Thomas A. Wayment, "False Gospels: An Approach to Studying the New Testament Apocrypha," in *How the New Testament Came to Be*, 292–303.
25. At this point in time the boundaries of orthodoxy were still being established and were thus somewhat more fluid than in later centuries.
26. For a more detailed discussion of these factors, see Everett Ferguson, "Factors Leading to the Selection and Closure of the New Testament Canon: A Survey of Some Recent Studies," in McDonald and Sanders, *Canon Debate*, 295–320.
27. Bruce Metzger, *The Canon of the New Testament: Its Origin, Development, and Significance* (New York: Oxford University Press, 1997), 108–9. However, this is a debated point. David Brack argues, "Considering the size of Luke and Acts, it would be too unwieldy to glue both papyri into one papyrus roll, and Luke's preface makes clear that there were two rolls. See *Luke's* Legato *Historiography: Remembering the Continuity of Salvation through Rhetorical Transitions* (Eugene OR: Pickwick, 2017), 26.
28. For more on the early Christian production of texts, see Lincoln H. Blumell, "Scripture as Artefact," in *The Oxford Handbook of the Early Christian Interpretation of Scripture*, ed. Paul M. Blowers and Peter W. Martens (Oxford, UK: Oxford University Press, 2019), 7–32.
29. For a more detailed treatment of the relationship of Gnosticism and the canon, see Pheme Perkins, "Gnosticism and the Christian Bible," in McDonald and Sanders, *Canon Debate*, 355–71.
30. Kirsopp Lake, "The Sinaitic and Vatican Manuscripts and the Copies sent by Eusebius to Constantinople," *Harvard Theological Review* 11 (1918): 32–35; T. C. Skeat, "The

Use of Dictation in Ancient Book-Production," *Proceedings of the British Academy* 42 (1956): 195–97.

31. Lee McDonald, *The Formation of the Christian Biblical Canon* (Peabody: Hendrickson, 1995), 188; Metzger, *Canon of the New Testament*, 205.
32. According to Eusebius, Papias identifies Mark as Peter's interpreter. See Eusebius, *Ecclesiastical History* 3.39.15–16. See also Acts 12:25 and 2 Timothy 4:11.
33. Metzger, *Canon of the New Testament*, 252.
34. For additional lists see "Appendix D: Lists and Catalogues of New Testament Collections," in McDonald and Sanders, *Canon Debate*, 591–97.
35. Though there had been general agreement for centuries, the Roman Catholic Church did not formally establish its canon of scripture until the sixteenth century at the Council of Trent.
36. Athanasius, *Festal Letter* 39.6.
37. Alexander B. Morrison, "Plain and Precious Things: The Writing of the New Testament," in Jackson and Judd, *How the New Testament Came to Be*, 25.

Part Two

THE GOSPEL ACCOUNTS

Chapter Four

Teaching the Four Gospels

Five Considerations

GAYE STRATHEARN

Speaking of the Bible, the Prophet Joseph Smith declared, "He who reads it oftenest will like it best."[1] One of the challenges any teacher of the New Testament faces is being able to engender in his or her students a desire to read the Bible *often enough* that they will come to appreciate its rich doctrinal teachings and its powerful testimony of Jesus Christ. The four New Testament Gospels are, in particular, a treasure trove of information about his life, ministry, teachings, Atonement, and Resurrection, much of which is not available anywhere else in scripture.

The purpose of this paper is to discuss some issues that may be of worth for those teaching the New Testament. The five issues that we will address are the genre and purposes of the individual Gospels, the challenges of teaching the four Gospels as a whole, *exegesis* and *eisegesis* (i.e., approaches to interpreting the scriptural texts), specific passages that can be difficult to teach, and the value of Restoration scripture in teaching the New Testament Gospels. The discussion in each of these sections is limited. We will only have space to discuss a couple of examples. Nevertheless, the hope is that this discussion will introduce teachers to some of the depth, richness, and complexity of the four Gospels.

Genre and Purposes of the Four Gospels

Genre

The genre of a "gospel" seems to have been invented by Mark. He is the only New Testament Gospel author who identifies his work as such: "The beginning of the gospel of Jesus Christ, the Son of God" (Mark 1:1). The Greek word for gospel, *euangelion*, literally means "the good message," and for Mark the good message begins at the baptism where "a voice from heaven [declares], Thou art my beloved Son, in whom I am well pleased" (Mark 1:11). Mark's concept of a gospel seems to have been generally informed by the Greco-Roman biography, or *bios*, which was "less concerned with relating historical events than with showing the character of the main figure through his or her words, deeds, and interactions."[2] What distinguishes it from the *bios* is its reliance on the Old Testament, its emphasis on Jesus's divine purpose rather than on extolling his virtues, and its usefulness in the preaching of the Church. One scholar has noted, "The close association of the Gospels with early Christian worship and proclamation suggests that we should see them as church documents with a certain biographical character rather than as biographies with a religious tone."[3]

The Gospels of Matthew, Mark, and Luke are remarkably similar to each other, yet very different from the Gospel of John. They are often referred to as the "synoptic Gospels," which means that they present the life of the Savior in similar ways, including frequent verbal parallels. The similarities are so significant that many scholars have proposed a literary relationship between the first three Gospels. The most common explanation of this literary relationship, known as Markan Priority, posits that Mark's Gospel was written first and then Matthew and Luke each used the Gospel of Mark as a source for their own accounts, to which they added sayings of Jesus and some of their own unique material.[4]

Although not all scholars accept the argument of Markan priority, three points in particular make this conclusion probable. First, Matthew and Luke generally follow the Markan sequence of events, even though Papias (an early second-century bishop of Hierapolis) says that Mark was not interested in writing the events in order.[5] When Matthew and Luke disagree with Mark's chronology, the differences can usually be explained as the result of Matthean and Lukan editorial tendencies. Significantly, Matthew and

Luke never agree on the sequence of events when they differ from Mark. Second, there is evidence that Matthew and Luke have "corrected" the Markan account. For example, when Mark uses a rare or difficult word, Matthew and Luke render the passage using more common terminology, and they often improve his grammar.[6] Sometimes they will modify passages that provide theological difficulties for them. For example, Mark 6:5 says that Jesus "could there do no mighty work, save that he laid his hands upon a few sick folk, and healed them." Matthew's account avoids the implication that Jesus's power was in any way limited: "And he did not many mighty works there because of their unbelief" (Matthew 13:58). Third, a primary reason for concluding that the Gospel of Mark is the earliest Gospel is the fact that it is the shortest. It is more likely that Matthew and Luke would later add additional material about the life of Christ than that Mark would purposefully omit so many good stories about the Savior. Mark does not have a tendency to shorten stories, because when Matthew, Mark, and Luke contain the same story, Mark often preserves the longer version.[7]

John's Gospel is very different from the Synoptic Gospels. In fact, the majority of its teachings, stories and miracles are *not* found in the Synoptic Gospels. It uses a high Christology to describe Jesus, meaning that, to a greater extent than the Synoptic Gospels, from its opening chapter John's Gospel emphasizes Jesus's divinity.[8] Thus, Clement of Alexandria described it as "a spiritual gospel."[9]

Purposes

As we would expect, all four Gospels testify that Jesus is the Messiah or Son of God, although each does it in different ways, with different emphases, because the authors are all writing to different audiences.

Mark does not appear to be an eyewitness of Jesus's ministry. Instead, Papias, the second-century bishop of Hierapolis, records that "Mark, having become Peter's interpreter, wrote down accurately everything he remembered, *though not in order*, of the things either said or done by Christ. For he neither heard the Lord nor followed him, but afterward, as I said, followed Peter, who adapted his teachings as needed but had no intention of giving an ordered account of the Lord's sayings. Consequently, Mark did nothing wrong in writing down some things as he remembered them, for he made it his one concern not to omit anything which he heard or to make any false statement in them."[10] Thus, although Mark was apparently a second-generation Christian,[11] he wrote down the memories of Peter.

Mark appears to be writing to a gentile audience who live outside of Palestine because he explains geography (Mark 13:3), translates Aramaic phrases (5:41; 15:34), uses Latin terms such as *legion* (5:9, 15) and *centurion* (15:39), interprets Jewish customs (7:3–4), and mentions Roman, rather than Jewish, divorce laws (10:11–12).

After the baptism, Mark's account moves quickly. It focuses on showing that Jesus's teachings and deeds were astonishing to his audiences (1:22; 5:42; 6:2; 7:37; 10:24, 26; 11:18). It shows that there is a cost in choosing to be one of Jesus's disciples. The result of John the Baptist's preaching was that he was "put in prison [*paradidomi*]" (Mark 1:14). The result of Jesus's preaching was that he was "betrayed [*paradidomi*] into the hands of sinners" (Mark 14:41). Likewise, for the disciples, who are also expected to preach, there is an expectation that they will also be delivered up (*paradidomi*; see Mark 13:9–10). Lastly, it emphasizes the suffering and eventual vindication of the Savior. Sometimes Mark's Gospel is described as "a Passion narrative with an extended introduction."[12] In other words, the account frequently points the reader to, and focuses on, the events on the cross (3:6; 8:31; 9:31; 10:33–34, 45; 15:15–41). The Resurrection is God's vindication of Jesus after the horrible events of the passion.[13] Mark's Gospel is written to show that despite opposition, misunderstanding, suffering for sins, and an ignominious death, Christ was able to triumph over all things.[14]

Matthew was a member of the Twelve writing to a Jewish audience for two main purposes. He wrote to convince his audience that Jesus was the fulfillment of messianic prophecy. Matthew goes to great lengths to attach Old Testament prophetic statements to Jesus's deeds. He frequently uses the phrase "as it is written" (Matthew 2:5; 4:4, 6–7, 10; 11:10; 21:13; 26:24, 31), although on one occasion he attributes the passage to Jeremiah when it is actually from Zechariah (see Matthew 27:9; see by comparison Zechariah 11:13). Additionally, Matthew seeks to show that Jesus is the "new Moses." He is the only Gospel author to link Jesus's story to that of Moses by including the stories of the holy family's trip to Egypt and the slaughter of the innocents (see Matthew 2:14, 16). Just as Moses received the law on a mountain, Jesus goes up into a mountain to give the new law (Matthew 5:1; in contrast with the Lukan version, Luke 6:17, where it is given on a plain).

Given his Jewish audience, it is not surprising that he includes in Jesus's apostolic commission the directive to "go not into the way of the Gentiles and into any city of the Samaritans enter ye not: but go rather to the lost sheep of the house of Israel" (Matthew 10:5–6).

But Matthew's Gospel seems also to have been written to convince his audience to accept the gentile mission.[15] In a number of places he includes gentiles, showing that they were an important part of the kingdom: he includes four gentile women in Jesus's genealogy (Matthew 1:1–6); he includes the story of the Wise Men, whom Matthew sees as gentiles, who recognize the child Jesus when the people of the covenant, who had access to the prophecies, do not (Matthew 2:1–11); and he includes stories which show times when Gentiles' faith is so remarkable that it overshadows that of the covenant people (see Matthew 8:5–13; 15:21–29). All these aspects of Matthew's Gospel prepare the reader for Jesus's final words on the Mount of Olives, "Go ye therefore, and teach all nations, baptizing them in the name of the Father, and of the Son, and of the Holy Ghost" (Matthew 28:19).

Like Mark, Luke also appears to be a second-generation Christian writing to a gentile audience. He opens his Gospel with his own "statement of intent" to Theophilus: "Forasmuch as many have taken in hand to set forth in order a declaration of those things which are most surely believed among us, even as they delivered them unto us, which from the beginning were eyewitnesses, and ministers of the word; it seemed good to me also, having had perfect understanding of all things from the very first, to write unto thee in order, most excellent Theophilus, that thou mightiest know the certainty of those things, wherein thou hast been instructed" (Luke 1:1–4).

The major purpose of Luke's writings (including the book of Acts) is to show that the gospel of Jesus Christ is available to all. Luke, unlike Matthew, extends Jesus's genealogy back to Adam, the father of all humans, rather than just to Abraham (see Luke 3:38; see by comparison Matthew 1:1). His is the only Gospel to include the calling of the Seventy (Luke 10) in addition to the Twelve (Luke 6:13–16; 9:1–6). The number seventy may have reference to the seventy nations mentioned in Genesis 10 and may, therefore, prefigure the expanded mission in Acts that includes the Gentiles.[16] Luke includes Jesus's sermon given on a plain to "the company of his disciples, and a great multitude of people out of all Judaea and Jerusalem, and from the sea coast of Tyre and Sidon [i.e., Gentiles]" (6:17). He shows

Jesus's concern for those who were deemed "marginal" in Jewish society: the poor (6:20), the Samaritans (10:29–37; 17:11–19), and women, often using couplets of men and women such as Simeon and Anna testifying of Jesus at the temple (2:25–38) and the disciples and the women accompanying Jesus on his journey to Jerusalem (8:1–3).

John also includes a specific "statement of intent," although unlike in Luke, it is at the conclusion of his Gospel. He indicates that he chose what to include in his Gospel (and what to leave out) for a specific reason: "But these things are written, that ye might believe that Jesus is the Christ, the Son of God; and that believing ye might have life through his name" (John 20:31). Unlike the Synoptic Gospels, which concentrate on Jesus's Galilean ministry, John's Gospel concentrates on his Judean ministry. In addition, John includes frequent passages that contribute to this Gospel's high Christology. John opens his Gospel with a statement of Jesus's divinity in the premortal realm. "In the beginning was the Word and the Word was with God and the Word was God" (John 1:1). This theme is then expanded throughout the text. He frequently records Jesus using the divine name to identify himself ("before Abraham was, I am [*egō eimi*]" in John 8:58 but also in John 4:25–26; 6:20). He also records numerous dialogues where he, as the "one from above," converses with those that are "of the earth" (John 3:31; see also 3:12–13; 8:23). The purpose of these dialogues is for Jesus to help his listeners throw off the earthly blinders that limit their perspective so that they can begin to see as he sees and gain an eternal perspective (e.g., 3:1–21; 4:5–42; 9:1–41; 11:1–16).[17]

Thus, each of the four Gospels adds a distinctive witness to his life and ministry, which if recognized, can add an important and enriching element to teaching the life and ministry of the Savior.

Challenges of Teaching the Four Gospels

Teaching the four Gospels is a rewarding opportunity, but there are also some challenges that teachers must face. Here I will briefly describe just two.

The first challenge New Testament teachers may have is to convince their students of the value of studying the Bible. As is often noted, the Prophet Joseph taught, "I believe the Bible as it read when it came from the pen of the original writers. Ignorant translators, careless transcribers, or designing and corrupt priests have committed many errors."[18] This teaching may, at first glance, suggest that the Prophet had serious reservations about the accuracy of the Bible. Yet it must also be remembered that the Prophet loved the Bible and frequently taught from it in his sermons.[19] So what should Latter-day Saints think about the accuracy of the biblical text?

The translation of the New Testament is a complex issue. We have no autographs, or original manuscripts, of any New Testament text. Our earliest text is the Rylands papyrus (P^{52}), a fragment from John 18, which dates from the first quarter of the second century. This means that all the approximately 5,700 extant manuscripts of the New Testament are at best copies of copies and at worst manuscripts that are over a thousand years removed from their autographs. Within these manuscripts scholars estimate that there are between 200,000 and 400,000 textual variants.[20] These numbers, at first glance, seem daunting and may reinforce some skepticism of the accuracy of the New Testament. But a careful study of the variants shows that many of them are not malicious scribal attempts to alter the text but are the result of innocent copying errors. In other words, very few of these variants are theologically significant.[21] One example of a passage from the Gospels that is important for Latter-day Saints is Matthew 5:22. The KJV reads, "But I say unto you, That whosoever is angry with his brother *without a cause* shall be in danger of the judgment" (emphasis added). The phrase "without a cause" is found in some late New Testament manuscripts but is not attested in earlier ones.[22] The phrase seems to be a later scribal addition to "allow room for righteous indignation,"[23] maybe even to allow for Jesus's actions when he cleansed the temple (see Matthew 21:12–14). Most modern translations do not include the phrase.[24] For Latter-day Saints in particular, this point is significant because the phrase is not found in either the corresponding passage in the 3 Nephi account (3 Nephi 12:22) or the Joseph Smith Translation (JST).

In addition to the Prophet's statement, the Bible may be underappreciated because the Book of Mormon teaches that, as a result of the great and abominable church, "there are many plain and precious things taken away from the [Bible], which is the book of the Lamb of God" (1 Nephi 13:28). While it is possible that the loss of plain and precious things may be the result of the removal of key passages and teachings, the manuscript tradition shows that the text of the New Testament is remarkably stable. It is therefore possible that the loss is the result of the *reinterpretation* of doctrine rather than from large-scale removal of passages. For example, early Christians debated at some length about the doctrine of the virgin birth and how that impacted the nature of the mortal Christ, and they also debated about the nature of the Resurrection. The existence of these debates did not result in the removal of the birth and the Resurrection narratives from the text, but the early Christians interpreted the accounts in sometimes drastically different ways, which eventually influenced the Christian Creeds.[25]

Therefore, I would suggest that we be cautious in our interpretation of 1 Nephi 13:28. If we are not careful, our interpretation may overshadow our confidence in the truth and power of the Bible and might even influence where we put our emphasis when we recite the eighth Article of Faith. If we put our emphasis on the first part of the sentence, "We believe the Bible to be the word of God," we can have a very different understanding of the Bible than if we put our emphasis on the second part, "as far as it is translated correctly." The first, while acknowledging some textual and translational issues, reaffirms our commitment to the Bible and its teachings as the "word of God." The second, if we are not careful, may justify a neglect of or marginalization of the Bible. Elder Neal A. Maxwell has taught, "Occasionally, a few in the Church let the justified caveat about the Bible—'as far as it is translated correctly' (A of F 1:8)—diminish their exultation over the New Testament," but then he goes on to remind us, "Inaccuracy of some translating must not, however, diminish our appreciation for the powerful *testimony* and ample *historicity* of the New Testament. . . . These pages are a treasure trove testifying of Jesus."[26] Additionally, it is important to remember that in other places the Book of Mormon is quite complementary of the importance of the Bible. For example, both Lehi and Mormon teach the importance of combining the truths taught in both the Bible and the Book of Mormon. Lehi teaches his son Joseph that the Bible and the Book of Mormon "shall grow together, unto the confounding of false doctrines and laying down of contentions, and establishing peace among the fruit of thy loins, and bringing them to the knowledge of their fathers in the latter days, and also to the knowledge of my covenants, saith the Lord" (2 Nephi 3:12). Likewise, Mormon implores latter-day readers of the Book of Mormon to "lay hold upon the gospel of Christ which shall be set before you, not only in this record but also in the record which shall come unto the Gentiles from the Jews, which record shall come from the Gentiles unto you" (Mormon 7:8).

A second challenge that teachers of New Testament Gospels face is how they are going to organize their class. Having four Gospels poses a challenge not found when teaching other scriptural texts. Should we use a harmony approach, similar to those used by Elder James E. Talmage and Elder Bruce R. McConkie and, for a long time, followed by the Sunday School and institute New Testament manuals?[27] The major advantage of this approach is that it gives students a sense of the life and ministry of Jesus in some sort of chronological order. The Gospels, and any subsequent harmony of them, do not narrate the entire life of the Savior but rather present highlights of the ministry and unique portraits of his life. It is significant that the Joseph Smith Translation designates the Gospel of Matthew and the Gospel of John "testimonies" rather than "gospels."[28] A limitation of the harmony approach is illustrated in a statement by Papias, who taught that Mark "wrote down accurately everything he remembered, *though not in order*, of the things either said or done by Christ."[29] To further complicate the matter, the Synoptic Gospels of Matthew and Luke, who generally follow Mark's order, sometimes record a different sequence of events. If Mark was not concerned with preserving all the events of the life of the Savior in their precise chronological order, and since the other Gospels occasionally differ in their order of events, it then becomes very difficult to establish a precise chronology for a harmony.[30]

An alternate approach is to teach each of the Gospels individually. The advantage of this approach is that it allows the students to appreciate the unique emphases, teachings, and interpretations of each of the Gospels that are often lost in a harmony approach.[31] Certainly, each evangelist wrote his Gospel thinking that it would read as an autonomous whole rather than as part of a harmony.[32] The challenge with this approach is that there will be a lot of overlap, especially in teaching the Synoptic Gospels, which cover much of the same material. Personally, I use a mixed approach. I spend three class periods at the beginning of the course going over background material: the world of the New Testament; the formation of the Bible; and the unique characteristics of each of the four Gospels. During this time I have the students read the Gospel of Mark so that they become familiar with the basic story of Jesus's ministry. Then I work through a harmony of Matthew and

Luke (with, because of personal interest, an emphasis on Matthew), adding in the material of the Gospel of John where appropriate.

Exegesis and Eisegesis: Approaches to Interpreting the New Testament Gospels

Exegesis is a hermeneutical, or interpretive, approach to scriptural texts that attempts to understand a passage within the context of the text itself. This approach to scripture is different from *eisegesis*, which seeks to interpret the text from the perspective of the reader and often interprets the text divorced from its original context.[33] It is the latter approach to scriptures with which many Latter-day Saints are most familiar, particularly when they desire to identify a principle that can be applied for modern readers. While there is value to this approach, there are times when exegesis will help teachers and students to identify important principles that are difficult to ascertain simply from eisegesis.

Exegesis can be as simple as realizing that the context for the parable of the talents in Matthew 25:14–30 has nothing to do with the modern understanding of talents as an ability to sing or to dance or to be a good public speaker and so forth. Rather, the word *talents* is a transliteration of the Greek word *talanton*, which refers to a weight or measure—to money. Thus, the parable is about slaves who have been entrusted with their master's business affairs.[34] As one scholar has noted, "The 'talents' . . . represent not the natural gifts and aptitudes which everyone has, but the specific privileges and opportunities of the kingdom of heaven and the responsibilities they entail."[35] This particular parable is one of a series of parables used in the Olivet Discourse. In the first part of the discourse, Jesus, in part, describes the conditions preparatory to his Second Coming. The parables that follow teach principles of how to prepare for that event. Therefore, the parable of the talents must be understood in this context. The talents therefore represent any stewardship with which we are entrusted and must magnify to help build the kingdom in preparation for the Second Coming.

Exegesis can also be achieved recognizing the editorial hand of the author.[36] Latter-day Saints are familiar with this process in the Book of Mormon where Mormon and Moroni frequently act as editors, both by choosing which texts to include and by inserting their voice into the text. The four Gospels are uniquely situated to help us recognize editorial emphases because we often have three, or sometimes four, accounts of a particular story. In these instances, it is just as important to recognize the differences in the accounts as it is to emphasize the similarities. A question that is helpful for readers to ask is not just what does the story say, but why did the author choose to record it *this* way?

One example where we see Matthew's editorial hand is in his recounting of the miracle of the stilling of the storm (see Matthew 8:23–27). This story is found in all three of the Synoptic Gospels. Mark and Luke use the story to show that Jesus has power over the physical elements (see Mark 4:35–41; Luke 8:22–25), but, while Matthew's account acknowledges this power, he uses the story differently.[37] In chapters 8 and 9 Matthew has collected a series of miracles, one of which is the stilling of the storm.

What is interesting in this collection is the passage that immediately precedes the stilling of the storm:

> Now when Jesus saw great multitudes about him, he gave commandment to depart unto the other side.
>
> And a certain scribe came, and said unto him, Master, I will follow thee whithersoever thou goest.
>
> And Jesus saith unto him, The foxes have holes, and the birds of the air have nests; but the Son of man hath not where to lay his head.
>
> And another of his disciples said unto him, Lord, suffer me first to go and bury my father.
>
> But Jesus said unto him, "Follow me; and let the dead bury their dead. (Matthew 8:18–22)

These verses stand out in a chapter that deals with miracles because they focus on discipleship and the cost of choosing to follow Jesus. In contrast to Matthew, Luke uses them to introduce the calling of the Seventy (see Luke 9:57–10:16).

Besides changing the context for the story, Matthew's editorial hand is evident in four other ways that indicate he has a different emphasis in recounting this miracle. First, in describing the storm, Matthew uses the Greek word *seismos*, translated in the KJV as "tempest," whereas both Mark and Luke use *lailaps*, translated as "storm" (see Figure 1). At first glance this change may seem insignificant, but in the New Testament *seismos* is almost universally associated with the destructions and tribulations that take place at the end of the world (see Matthew 24:7; Mark 13:8; Luke 21:11; Revelation 6:12; 8:5; 11:13, 19; 16:18; the exception is Acts 16:26). The tempest in Matthew thus becomes a symbol for the difficulties disciples face as they choose to enter the ship or, in other words, the Church.

Second, in Matthew's account, the cry of the disciples is different. In both Mark and Luke, the disciples address Jesus with "Master," which is "a human title of respect"[38] (Mark uses the Greek word *didaskalos*; Luke uses *epistata*). However, in Matthew's account they cry out, "Lord, save us." Here the disciples use the term "Lord" (the Greek word *kyrios*), which can be translated as "a lord" or "a master," but it also can be understood as a term for deity. It is a term which in the Septuagint (the Greek Old Testament) is "used as an expository equivalent for the divine name" YHWH.[39] The New Testament frequently uses *kyrios* as a title for God, either in the quotations of passages from the Old Testament (see Matthew 27:10; Mark 1:3; 12:36) or independently (see Matthew 1:20, 24; Mark 5:19; 13:20). Thus, Matthew emphasizes that it is a divine being, not just a great human who is in the ship.

Third, in Mark and Luke the disciples cry to Jesus because they are going to perish, but in Matthew's account the disciples add a plea for Jesus to "save [*sozō*] us," a plea that can have both a physical and a spiritual dimension.[40] Thus, Matthew's story emphasizes Jesus acting in his divine capacity, not just as someone who has power over the physical elements but also as someone who has the power to save his disciples from physical and spiritual buffetings they experience when they choose to follow Jesus and enter into the ship.

Fourth, in contrast to Mark and Luke, Matthew changes the position of Jesus's question about the disciples' faith. In Mark and Luke, Jesus awakes, rebukes the wind and the sea, and then asks about their faith. In Matthew, however, Jesus awakes, asks about the disciples' faith first, and then rebukes the wind and the sea. Thus, the emphasis in Matthew is on the disciples' faith, or lack thereof, rather than the power to rebuke the wind and the sea. As one scholar has noted, "The expression ὀλιγοπιστία (or ὀλιγόπιστος) [i.e., "little faith"] is a favourite word of Matthew's; apart from Luke 12.28 he is the only evangelist to use it (6.30; 8.26; 14.31; 16.8; 17.20) and it always denotes a faith that is too weak, that is paralysed in the storm (8.26; 14.31) and in anxiety (6.30; 16.8), and thus is exposed as an appearance of faith (17.20) which is not sufficiently mature to withstand the pressure of demonic powers."[41]

Matthew 8:23–26	Mark 4:35–40	Luke 8:22–25
23. And when he was entered into a ship, his disciples followed him.	35. And the same day, when the even was come, he saith unto them,	22. Now it came to pass on a certain day, that he went into a ship with his disciples: and he said unto them,
	Let us pass over unto the other side. 36. And when they had sent away the multitude, they took him even as he was in the ship. And there were also with him other little ships.	Let us go over unto the other side of the lake. And they launched forth. 23. But as they sailed he fell asleep:
24. And, behold, there arose a great **tempest** [*seismos*] in the sea, insomuch that the ship was covered with the waves:	37. And there arose a great **storm** [*lailaps*] of wind, and the waves beat into the ship, so that it was now full.	and there came down a **storm** [*lailaps*] of wind on the lake; and they were filled with water, and were in jeopardy.
but he was asleep. 25. And his disciples came to him, and awoke him, saying,	38. And he was in the hinder part of the ship, asleep on a pillow: and they awake him, and say unto him,	24. And they came to him, and awoke him, saying,
Lord, save us: we perish. 26. And he saith unto them, **Why are ye fearful, O ye of little faith?**	**Master** [*didaskalos*], carest thou not that we perish?	**Master, master,** [*epistata*] we perish.
Then he arose, and rebuked the winds and the sea; and there was a great calm.	39. And he arose, and rebuked the wind, and said unto the sea, Peace, be still. And the wind ceased, and there was a great calm. 40. And he said unto them, **Why are ye so fearful? how is it that ye have no faith?**	Then he arose and rebuked the wind and the raging of the water: and they ceased, and there was a calm. 25. And he said unto them, **Where is your faith?**

Table 1. The Gospel writers' editorial hand.

So what does all of Matthew's editorial activity mean? By introducing the miracle stories with verses about discipleship, Matthew indicates to his readers that the miracle of the stilling of the storm should be interpreted through the lens of discipleship. The costs of following Jesus mentioned in verses 18–22 are the costs a disciple must be willing to pay to follow Jesus into the ship. The ship then is a metaphor for the Church. Perhaps disciples might think that following Jesus into the ship/church would mean that their struggles in life would be over; that they would have a pleasant, calm voyage across the sea. But the storm comes quickly. Tribulations are a part of discipleship. In such a situation, abandoning the ship, or walking away from the Church, is not the best option. Rather there is safety in the ship because that is where the Son of God is. Even though he is asleep, he has the power to protect the ship and all who are in it, even though they might not have sufficient faith initially when the winds arise. Here is the important miracle that Matthew has for his readers: the miracle that Christ can save in spite of the very real and powerful physical and spiritual buffetings that a disciple experiences.

The stilling of the storm is just one example of the importance of understanding not just what the passage says but understanding why the author said it *this way.* Thus, exegesis can be a powerful tool to enhance eisegesis, or, in other words, understanding the intent of the original author provides opportunities to identify and teach principles that will help modern readers live the gospel.

Considerations When Teaching Some Difficult Passages

As with teaching any text, there are always some passages that present either historical or doctrinal difficulties for modern readers. Readers of ancient texts, even the scriptures, must be able to deal with a certain amount of ambiguity. An important role for teachers is to help their students learn to deal with this ambiguity. Latter-day Saints do not believe in scriptural inerrancy, so we are in some ways theologically better equipped to deal with it in the Gospels. Ambiguity can come from a number of sources. For example, we have access to limited information about the ancient world. Although we try to recreate the world of the New Testament Gospels, this limitation means that, at best, we create an approximation—an educated approximation but an approximation, nevertheless. Of course, as we have noted above, this does not mean that we shouldn't try to examine and understand the historical context, but it does mean that sometimes we cannot answer all the questions. At times those limitations can be clarified by the prophetic word and Restoration scripture (as we shall see below), but generally prophetic sources weigh in on theological rather than historical issues.

Another difficulty arises because, although the ancient authors were inspired, they often relied on other sources and other people's memories of events. They did not have access to video recordings of events or eyewitness testimonies where they could check the events and eyewitness quotes. Even if they did, eyewitness testimonies, in ancient and modern times, seldom align perfectly with each other. Each eyewitness focuses on and remembers different things and remembers in different ways. This fact will have an effect on the text, especially when there are three or four texts telling the story. For example, when Jesus was arrested and Peter three times denied that he was one of Jesus's disciples, the four accounts are unified in stating that initially it was a maid who confronted Peter (see Matthew 26:69; Mark 14:66; Luke 22:56; John 18:17). However, there is some discrepancy in each of the accounts about who evokes Peter's second denial. In Mark it is the same maid (Mark 14:69); in Matthew it is another maid (Matthew 26:71); in Luke it is someone else—a man (Luke 22:58); and in John it is not an individual but a group (John 18:25). Given the limited information that we currently have, it is difficult to reconcile these passages.

Sometimes the intent of the Gospel author and his audience will influence what they include in their accounts and how they include it. For example, if a person was reading the New Testament accounts of Jesus's birth for the first time, it is understandable that they might not think that the accounts in Matthew and Luke were telling the same story. Matthew and Luke include very different genealogies (see Matthew 1:1–17; Luke 3:23–38) and different stories. Matthew recounts the birth from Joseph's perspective and includes the story of the Wise Men's visit to the young Jesus and the holy family's subsequent trip to Egypt (see Matthew 1:18–2:15). Luke recounts the birth from Mary's perspective and includes her visit to Elizabeth, the Roman census, and Joseph and Mary's subsequent trip from

Nazareth to Bethlehem where it is the shepherds, rather than the Wise Men, who worship the young baby (see Luke 2). If a reader is looking for differences in the two accounts, then there are plenty to be found. These differences have led some scholars to question the historicity of the two birth narratives.[42] However, it is important to note that although the accounts are very different as to the historical events, Joseph A. Fitzmyer reminds us that there is an important nucleus of material where the two accounts are in agreement:

> 1. Jesus's birth is related to the reign of Herod (Luke 1:5; Matt 2:1)
> 2. Mary, his mother to be, is a virgin engaged to Joseph, but they have not yet come to live together (Luke 1:27,34; 2:5; Matt 1:18)
> 3. Joseph is of the house of David (Luke 1:27; 2:4; Matt 1:16, 20).
> 4. An angel from heaven announces the coming birth of Jesus (Luke 1:28–30; Matt 1:20–21)
> 5. Jesus is recognized himself to be a son of David (Luke 1:32; Matt 1:1)
> 6. His conception is to take place through the Holy Spirit (Luke 1:35; Matt 1:18,20)
> 7. Joseph is not involved in the conception (Luke 1:34; Matt 1:18–25)
> 8. The name "Jesus" is imposed by heaven prior to his birth (Luke 1:31; Matt 1:21)
> 9. The angel identifies Jesus as "Savior" (Luke 2:11; Matt 1:21)
> 10. Jesus is born after Mary and Joseph come to live together (Luke 2:4–7; Matt 1:24–25)
> 11. Jesus is born at Bethlehem (Luke 2:4–7; Matt 2:1)
> 12. Jesus settles, with Mary and Joseph, in Nazareth in Galilee (Luke 2:39,51; Matt 2:22–23).[43]

Theologically, the accounts of Matthew and Luke are in agreement on the most important questions about Jesus's birth.

Another significant historical difficulty is the discrepancy in the timing of the Passover meal during the passion week. In the Synoptic Gospels, Jesus met with his disciples on "the first day of the feast of unleavened bread" (Matthew 26:17; see also Mark 14:12; Luke 22:7). More specifically, Mark adds, "when they killed the Passover" (Mark 14:12; see also Luke 22:7). In all these accounts, Jesus's meal with his disciples is understood to be the Passover *seder*. In John's Gospel, however, Jesus's meal with his disciples took place the evening before the Passover (see John 13:1), with his crucifixion occurring the afternoon before the Passover meal (when lambs were being killed for that evening's festivities). The Jews wanted to expedite the crucifixion by breaking Jesus's legs "because it was the preparation [day]" (John 19:31).

In the nineteenth and early twentieth centuries, this discrepancy was a virtual nonissue because many assumed that the synoptic accounts were historically more accurate than that found in John. Primarily, this position reflected the dominant scholarly view that John's Gospel was a late document and was therefore historically unreliable. In recent years, however, the scholarly pendulum has swung in favor of the historical reliability of the fourth Gospel. Archaeologists have found and excavated the pool of Bethesda with its five porches (John 5:1–2).[44] The Dead Sea Scrolls show that John's use of dualism between light and darkness (John 1:5; 3:19; 12:35–36), which for a long time scholars attributed to second-century philosophy, is at home in the Jewish Palestinian milieu of the first century.[45] In addition, John's knowledge of Samaritian beliefs, worship on Mount Gerizim, and the site of Jacob's well are all accurate.[46] Thus, the scholarly surge in favor of John's historicity has highlighted the chronological differences between the accounts of the Last Supper in the synoptic Gospels and John. While many theories have been proposed to explain the differences,[47] the reality is that, until more information is discovered, modern readers again face the dilemma of dealing with some ambiguity in the four Gospels of the New Testament.

In teaching both the birth narratives and the Last Supper, teachers should not be afraid of the ambiguity. Rather, they should help their students recognize it when it appears and help them understand that in ancient texts, even scriptural texts, there will be times when the appropriate answer to the question "why?" is "here are some possibilities, but at present we don't have enough information to give a definitive answer."

Historical ambiguities, however, are not the only type of difficult passages to teach. Sometimes there are also passages that are theologically difficult. For example, Jesus teaches, "And I say unto you, Whosoever shall put away his wife, except it be for fornication [*porneia*], and shall marry another, committeth adultery [*porneia*]: and whoso marrieth her which is put away doth commit adultery [moichaō]" (Matthew 19:9; see also Mark 10:11; Luke 16:18). In both Matthew and Mark this teaching is part of a longer discussion where the Pharisees tried to discredit Jesus by asking the question, "Is it lawful for a man to put away his wife?" (Mark 10:2). In Mark the issue is whether Jesus allows divorce. In Matthew's version the Pharisees assume that Jesus allows divorce and they instead question: "Is it lawful for a man to put away his wife *for every cause*?" (Matthew 19:3; emphasis added). In this instance the issue seems to be tied to one of debates in the first century between the schools of Hillel and Shammai, who interpret the Mosaic injunction in radically different ways. Deuteronomy 24:1 reads, "When a man hath taken a wife, and married her, and it come to pass that she find no favour in his eyes, because he hath found some uncleanness in her: then let him write her a bill of divorcement, and give it in her hand, and send her out of his house." The followers of Shammai's interpretation focused on the phrase "because he hath found some uncleanness in her" and taught that infidelity was the only justification for divorce. The followers of Hillel, however, focused on the phrase "she find no favour in his eyes" and interpreted it much more loosely.[48]

In Matthew's account, Jesus's response about marrying someone who is divorced seems to be given to the Pharisees who were part of a larger crowd. In Mark, however, the response is given at a later time only to the disciples: "And in the house his disciples asked him again of the same matter. And he saith unto them, Whosoever shall put away his wife, and marry another, committeth adultery against her" (Mark 10:10–11). Elder Bruce R. McConkie thus taught, "This strict law governing divorce was not given to the Pharisees, nor to the world in general, but to the disciples only, 'in the house,' at a later time as Mark explains. Further, Jesus expressly limited its application. All men could not live such a high standard; it applied only to those 'to whom it is given' [Matthew 19:11]."[49] President Joseph Fielding Smith interpreted this law in terms of a temple sealing.[50] Elder Dallin H. Oaks teaches, "The kind of marriage required for exaltation—eternal in duration and godlike in quality—does not contemplate divorce. In the temples of the Lord, couples are married for all eternity. But some marriages do not progress toward that ideal. Because 'of the hardness of [our] hearts,' the Lord does not currently enforce the consequences of the celestial standard. He permits divorced persons to marry again without the stain of immorality specified in the higher law. Unless a divorced member has committed serious transgressions, he or she can become eligible for a temple recommend under the same worthiness standards that apply to other members."[51]

Another example of a difficult doctrinal passage is the discussion between Jesus and the Sadducees about marriage in the Resurrection (see Matthew 22:29–30; Mark 12:24–25; Luke 20:34–35). The Sadducees came to Jesus, "Saying, Master, Moses said, If a man die, having no children, his brother shall marry his wife, and raise up seed unto his brother." They then go on to apply the Mosaic teaching to a hypothetical situation where seven brothers each in turn married a woman until eventually all the brothers and the woman had passed away. The Sadducees then asked, "Therefore in the resurrection whose wife shall she be of the seven? For they all had her" (Matthew 22:23–28). Jesus's response is sometimes brought up by those who try to discredit the Latter-day Saint teaching on eternal marriage.[52]

What this debate seems to lose sight of, however, is that this passage is only secondarily about marriage. The real issue that the Sadducees are pushing with Jesus is about the Resurrection because, as all three Synoptic authors emphasize, the Sadducees did not believe in it (Matthew 22:23; Mark 12:18; Luke 20:27). "Jesus answered and said unto them, Ye do err, not knowing the scriptures, nor the power of God. For in the resurrection they neither marry, nor are given in marriage, but are as the angels of God in heaven. But as touching the resurrection of the dead, have ye not read that which was spoken unto you by God, saying, I am the God of Abraham, and the God of Isaac, and the God of Jacob? God is not the God of the dead, but of the living. And when the multitude heard this, they were astonished at his doctrine" (Matthew 22:29–33). As one scholar has noted, the Sadducees' question "does not pose a serious question; it is simply designed to show how absurd is the belief in a future resurrection."[53] It is possible, therefore, that Jesus's response about marriage in the Resurrection was a form of parody. Jesus tells the Sadducees that they don't understand either the scriptures about Levirate marriage nor the power of God to bring about the Resurrection. In effect, he may be saying to them, "If, as you believe, there is no resurrection, then obviously the wife will not belong to any of the brothers because *you don't even believe that there will be a resurrection*."

The Four Gospels and Restoration Scripture

Unlike other Christians, Latter-day Saints have additional tools to enrich their study of the New Testament. Here I will briefly discuss three major ways that Restoration scripture can aid the student of the New Testament Gospels.

First, Restoration scripture confirms to truthfulness of the New Testament teachings in a time when their historicity is sometimes under attack. Two examples will suffice. The Sermon on the Mount in Matthew (Matthew 5–7) is very different from the sermon in Luke (Luke 6:17–49). Some scholars argue that the Lukan sermon is the historical sermon that Jesus gave and that the Matthean sermon was a later compilation of Jesus's sayings to supplement the Lukan material.[54] One of the difficulties scholars see in the Matthean account of the sermon is the disjointed nature of the text; there does not appear to be any coherence to the sermon. For Latter-day Saints however, who have in 3 Nephi a text remarkably similar to the Matthean sermon,[55] there is no doubt that Jesus taught this as a unified sermon. John W. Welch has argued that the unifying theme of the sermon, which has eluded scholars, is the temple.[56] In short, the 3 Nephi account confirms the historicity of the Matthean Sermon on the Mount.

Another example of how Restoration scripture confirms the teachings of the New Testament Gospels is found in Luke's account of the Garden of Gethsemane. Luke records that Jesus's "sweat was as it were great drops of blood falling down to the ground" (Luke 22:44). Modern scholarship has questioned the historicity of this event. The textual history for this verse is difficult. Some scholars argue that this verse was not original to Luke's Gospel but had been added at a later date because the verse is omitted in some important early manuscripts. As a result, some modern English translations of Luke 22:43–44 either put a footnote after verse 44 saying that many manuscripts do not have verses 43 and 44 (e.g., see New International Version; English Standard Version) or omit the verses in the text, with a footnote saying that other ancients texts add verses 43 and 44 (Revised Standard Version). It is, however, possible that the verses were removed by some scribes for theological reasons because they seemingly showed a weak Jesus who was not prepared for his upcoming death.[57]

But Restoration scripture, in both the Book of Mormon and the Doctrine and Covenants, confirms the reality that Jesus sweat blood while in the Garden of Gethsemane. In the Book of Mormon, King Benjamin teaches that the bloody sweat was a real part of the Atonement: "And lo, he shall suffer temptations, and pain of body, hunger, thirst, and fatigue, even more than man can suffer, except it be unto death; for behold, blood cometh from every pore, so great shall be his anguish for the wickedness and the abominations of his people" (Mosiah 3:7). Likewise, the Savior himself declares to the Prophet Joseph in a revelation, "Which suffering caused myself, even God, the greatest of all, to tremble because of pain, and to bleed at every pore, and to suffer both body and spirit—and would that I might not drink the bitter cup, and shrink" (Doctrine and Covenants 19:18).

Second, at times Restoration scripture expands and enumerates the doctrine of the Gospels. One example in this category is the use of the New Testament word "gospel" (*euangelion*), which is found twelve times in Matthew and Mark, although it is not used in Luke or John. The Greek word means "good news," but nowhere in the Gospels is it specifically defined. In the Book of Mormon, however, the Savior himself gives a definition in 3 Nephi 27:13–21. The good news is that Jesus "came into the world to do the will of [his] Father," that he was "lifted up upon the cross" so that he could "draw all men unto [him], that . . . men be lifted up by the Father, to stand before [Christ], to be judged of their works, whether they be good or whether they be evil" (verses 13–14). In addition, the good news is that through faith, repentance, coming unto Christ, being baptized and sanctified by the Holy Ghost, and enduring to the end we can be judged "guiltless before [the] Father" and "stand spotless before [Christ] at the last day" (verses 16, 20).[58] While all of these aspects are taught and expounded in the New Testament, nowhere are they brought together in such a succinct and complete definition of the gospel.

Elder Neal A. Maxwell gives another example: "'Except ye be converted, and become as little children, ye shall not enter into the kingdom of heaven.' (Matthew 18:3.) What is the full significance of becoming childlike? The Book of Mormon delineates with specificity: 'And becometh as a child, submissive, meek, humble, patient, full of love, willing to submit to all things which the Lord seeth fit to inflict upon him, even as a child doth submit to his father' (Mosiah 3:19)."[59]

Third, the JST is a valuable tool for the study of the New Testament Gospels. It is important however to understand what the JST is and is *not* doing. The editors of the critical edition of the JST have identified five types of changes that the JST makes to the biblical text, all of which can be specifically identified in the Gospels:[60]

"1. Restoration of original text." It is difficult to determine whether a JST change fits into this category. As we will see with some of the other categories of changes, just because the JST includes material that is not in our current text does not mean that it is automatically the restoration of original text. Thomas A. Wayment has identified one example where that may be the case. He has examined places where the JST agrees with the Latin version of the New Testament and argues that in some of these places the JST may be restoring lost or altered text.[61] One example that he gives is Luke 9:44. Both the Latin version and the JST replace "ears" (as found in the Greek manuscripts) with "hearts" and thus read, "Let these sayings sink down into your *hearts*: for the Son of man shall be delivered into the hands of *man*" (italics indicate JST changes).[62]

"2. Restoration of what was once said or done but which was never in the Bible." This type of change is also difficult to confirm, but it may include passages that are expanded in the JST but for which there is no evidence in the textual tradition that they were ever part of the written Gospels. For example, in the KJV account of John the Baptist, Matthew writes that John the Baptist declares to the Pharisees and Sadducees, "Bring forth therefore fruits meet for repentance" (Matthew 3:8). The JST, however, includes a lengthy introduction to this statement. "*Why is it, that ye receive not the preaching of him whom God hath sent? If ye receive not this in your hearts, ye receive not me; and if ye receive not me, ye receive not him of whom I am sent to bear record; and for your sins ye have no cloak. Repent therefore, and* bring forth fruits meet for repentance" (JST, Matthew 3:8; italics indicate JST changes).

"3. Editing to make the Bible more understandable for modern readers." Sometimes this form of editing is simply to help modern readers understand archaic King James language. For example, Matthew 13:20 reads, "But he that received the seed into stony places, the same is he that heareth the word, and anon with joy receiveth it." According to Laurence M. Vance, "Anon is a compound of the Old English *on an*, 'in one,' that signified 'in one moment.'"[63] It translates the Greek word *euthus*, which is often translated as "immediately."[64] Given that *anon* is rarely used in modern English, the JST changes it to read, "But he that received the seed into stony places, the same is he that heareth the word, and *readily* with joy receiveth it" (JST, Matthew 13:20). But sometimes the editing is more substantial, as is the case with the JST of Matthew 24. Here the JST changes were so substantial that they are included, along with the Book of Moses, as a separate part of the Pearl of Great Price: Joseph Smith—Matthew. One of the significant changes of the JST version was the reordering of the material. The discourse consists of Jesus's answers to two of his disciples' questions, "When shall these things [i.e., the destruction of the temple] be? and what shall be the sign of thy coming, and of the end of the world?" (Matthew 24:3). In Matthew 24 there is no distinction between these questions in Jesus's answer. In the JST, however, the answers to the two questions are delineated. Verses 5–21 answer the first question and verses 21–37 answer the second question. Verse 21 is the turning point between the two answers and the addition of the word "again" in verses 21, 30, 31, and 32 shows that the signs for the coming destruction of the temple in the first century would be repeated when the Savior returned. As one scholar has noted,

> When the Prophet made his revision of the Olivet discourse he moved three verses (7, 8, and 9) from their position in the King James text and placed them at various points later in the narrative. This change gave the prophecy a new chronological sequence, or more accurately, it gave it a more definite chronological sequence. This was enhanced by the repetition of three verses [verses 6, 9 to verses 21–22; verse 10 to verse 30; verse 12 to verse 32] which showed that there was to be a recurrence of ancient events in the latter days. It is this reordering and repetition of passages which brings understanding to that area in which there has been the greatest confusion among Bible scholars.[65]

"4. Editing to bring biblical wording into harmony with truth found in other revelations or elsewhere in the Bible." John 1:18 provides an example of this kind of change. The KJV reads, "No man hath seen God at any time." The JST reads, "No man hath seen God at any time, *except he hath borne record of the Son*" (JST, John 1:19; italics indicate JST changes). It is clear from other biblical passages and from events of the Restoration that people have in fact seen God. In other places in John's writings the statement is clarified. For example, John 6:46 reads, "Not that any man hath seen the Father, save he which is of God, he hath seen the Father." Another example may be the JST of John 20:1 which adds that there were two angels sitting at the sepulchre, which brings the story into harmony with the account in Luke 24:1–4.

"5. Changes to provide modern readers teachings that were not written by original authors." Two brief examples of this type of change may be Matthew 4:1 and 7:1. In the KJV, Matthew 4:1 reads, "Then was Jesus led up of the Spirit into the wilderness to be tempted of the devil." The JST reads, "Then was Jesus led up of the Spirit into the wilderness to be *with God*." The JST change here makes sense. Jesus's time in the wilderness was a preparatory experience for him before he began his mortal ministry. But the JST change here should not negate the fact that Jesus also went into the wilderness to be tempted by the devil. Elder Jeffrey R. Holland quotes Malcolm Muggeridge: "Christ withdrew alone to the desert to fast and pray in preparation for a dialogue with the Devil. Such a dialogue was inescapable; every virtue has to be cleared with the Devil, as every vice is torn with anguish out of God's heart." Then Elder Holland goes on to teach that he believes "such dialogues are entertained day after day, hour after hour—even among the Latter-day Saints."[66]

The KJV of Matthew 7:1 reads, "Judge not, that ye be not judged." The JST reads, "Now these are the words which Jesus taught his disciples that they should say unto the people. Judge not unrighteously, that ye be not judged: but judge righteous judgment." In this case, the JST does not seem to be restoring lost text because the corresponding teaching in 3 Nephi reads, "Judge not, that ye be not judged" (3 Nephi 14:1). In this case, the JST seems to be adding an additional level of teaching that, given the corresponding 3 Nephi account, was probably not originally spoken by Jesus as he taught the Sermon on the Mount.[67]

Conclusion

President Gordon B. Hinckley taught, "We are sometimes told that we are not a biblical church. We are a biblical church. This wonderful testament of the Old World, this great and good Holy Bible is one of our standard works.

We teach from it. We bear testimony of it. We read from it. It strengthens our testimony."[68] Teaching the New Testament Gospels is an opportunity to expand the minds of our students so that they will have the desire to embark on an ongoing study of the life, ministry, and teachings of Jesus Christ so that *they* will recognize that we are a biblical church. If we are to take President Hinckley's teaching seriously, then it is our charge to prepare our students so that they are prepared to "teach from it," to "bear testimony of it," and to use it to strengthen their testimonies. Again, as the Prophet Joseph stated, "He who reads it oftenest will like it best."

Gaye Strathearn is a professor of ancient scripture at Brigham Young University.

Gaye Strathearn, "Teaching the Four Gospels: Five Considerations," *Religious Educator* 13, no. 3 (2012): 79–107.

NOTES

1. "Letter to the Church, circa March 1834," p. 142, The Joseph Smith Papers.
2. Bart D. Ehrman, *The New Testament: A Historical Introduction to the Early Christian Writings*, 3rd ed. (Oxford: Oxford University Press, 2004), 65.
3. Larry W. Hurtado, "Gospel (Genre)," in *Dictionary of Jesus and the Gospels*, ed. Joel B. Green, Scot McKnight, and I. Howard Marshall (Downers Grove, IL: 1992), 279.
4. Robert H. Stein, *Studying the Synoptic Gospels: Origin and Interpretation*, 2nd ed. (Grand Rapids, MI: Baker Academic, 2001), 49–96; see also Elder Bruce R. McConkie, *Doctrinal New Testament Commentary*, 3 vols. (Salt Lake City: Bookcraft, 1965–73), 1:69.
5. English translation from Michael W. Holmes, ed., *The Apostolic Fathers: Greek Texts and English Translations* (Grand Rapids, MI: Baker Books, 1992), 569.
6. For more detailed discussions, see W. D. Davies and Dale C. Allison Jr., *A Critical and Exegetical Commentary on the Gospel According to Saint Matthew* (Edinburgh: T&T Clark, 1988), 1:105–6; and Stein, *Studying the Synoptic Gospels*, 56–59.
7. For examples, see Stein, *Studying the Synoptic Gospels*, 50–56.
8. For a Latter-day Saint discussion on the sources for the four Gospels, see Thomas A. Wayment, "First-Century Sources on the Life of Jesus" in *How the New Testament Came to Be*, ed. Kent P. Jackson and Frank F. Judd Jr. (Provo, UT: Religious Studies Center, Brigham Young University; Salt Lake City: Deseret Book, 2006), 112–22. For a non-LDS discussion, see James D. G. Dunn, *Jesus Remembered*, vol. 1 of Christianity in the Making (Grand Rapids, MI: William B. Eerdmans, 2003), 1:139–72.
9. Eusebius, *The History of the Church from Christ to Constantine*, trans. G. A. Williamson (New York: Penguin, 1965), 192.
10. English translation from Michael W. Holmes, ed., *The Apostolic Fathers: Greek Texts and English Translations* (Grand Rapids, MI: Baker Books, 1992), 569; emphasis added. Another

fragment from Papias outlines his intent in recording remembrances of the teachings of the early Church leaders, "I will not hesitate to set down for you, along with my interpretations, everything I carefully learned then from the elders and carefully remembered, guaranteeing their truth. For unlike most people I did not enjoy those who have a great deal to say, but those who teach the truth. Nor did I enjoy those who recall someone else's commandments, but those who remember the commandments given by the Lord to the faith and proceeding from truth itself. And if by chance someone who had been a follower of the elders should come my way, I inquired about the words of the elders—what Andrew or Peter said, or Philip, or Thomas or James, or John or Matthew or any other of the Lord's disciples, and whatever Aristion and the elder John, the Lord's disciples, were saying. For I did not think that information from books would profit me as much as information from a living and abiding voice." English translation from Holmes, *Apostolic Fathers*, 565.

11. Some have speculated that the unnamed young man in Mark 14:51 was a reference to Mark, although there is no scriptural basis for it. For a brief discussion, see R. T. France, *The Gospel of Mark: A Commentary on the Greek Text* (Grand Rapids, MI: Eerdmans; Carlisle, England: Paternoster Press, 2002), 595–96.
12. Dennis C. Duling, *The New Testament: History, Literature, and Social Context*, 4th ed. (Belmont, CA: Thomson Wadsworth, 2003), 324.
13. The issue of where Mark's Gospel ends is complex. For two recent LDS discussions on the issues, see Thomas A. Wayment, "The Endings of Mark and Revelation," in *The King James Bible and the Restoration*, ed. Kent P. Jackson (Provo, UT: Religious Studies Center, Brigham Young University; Salt Lake City: Deseret Book, 2011), 75–81; and Lincoln H. Blumell, "A Text-Critical Comparison of the King James New Testament with Certain Modern Translations," *Studies in the Bible and Antiquity* 3 (2011): 89–96. For a non-LDS discussion, see France, *The Gospel of Mark*, 695–98.
14. Gaye Strathearn and Frank F. Judd Jr., "The Distinctive Testimonies of the Four Gospels," *Religious Educator* 8, no. 2 (2007): 60–64.
15. For an expanded discussion, see Strathearn and Judd, "Distinctive Testimonies," 64–69.
16. Richard D. Draper, "Counting the Cost: The Apostolic Mission of the Twelve and Seventy," in *The Life and Teachings of Jesus Christ*, vol. 2, *From the Transfiguration through the Triumphal Entry*, ed. Richard Neitzel Holzapfel and Thomas A. Wayment (Salt Lake City: Deseret Book, 2006), 35–40. Some important manuscripts indicate that the number was seventy-two. See for example, Codices Sinaiticus, Alexandrinus, Ephraemi, Regius. Nevertheless, scholars still see this passage as indicative of an expanded mission. See, for example, I. Howard Marshall, *The Gospel of Luke: A Commentary of the Greek Text* (Grand Rapids, MI: Eerdmans, 1978), 415.
17. Gaye Strathearn, "Johannine Christology through the Lens of Three of Its Dialogues," in *Thou Art the Christ, the Son of the Living God: The Person and Work of Jesus in the New Testament*, ed. Eric D. Huntsman, Lincoln H. Blumell, and Tyler J. Griffin (Provo, UT: Religious Studies Center, Brigham Young University; Salt Lake City: Deseret Book, 2018), 153–74.
18. History, 1838–1856, volume E-1 [1 July 1843–30 April 1844], p. 1755, The Joseph Smith Papers. It should be noted that the second half of this statement ("Ignorant translators, careless transcribers, or designing and corrupt priests have committed many errors.") was an editorial addition to the Prophet's statement after his death. See *The Words of Joseph Smith*, comp. and ed. Andrew F. Ehat and Lyndon W. Cook (Provo, UT: Religious Studies Center, Brigham Young University, 1980), 256. For a discussion of how the writings of the Prophet Joseph in *History of the Church* were compiled and

edited, see Kent P. Jackson, *The Restored Gospel and the Book of Genesis* (Salt Lake City: Deseret Book, 2001), 59–61.

19. He made reference to passages from the New Testament Gospels 1,148 times in the material collected in *Teachings of the Prophet Joseph Smith*, according to a count of the scriptural references in Richard C. Galbraith, *Scriptural Teachings of the Prophet Joseph Smith*, comp. Joseph Fielding Smith (Salt Lake City: Deseret Book, 1993), 462–67.
20. Bruce M. Metzger and Bart D. Ehrman, *The Text of the New Testament: Its Transmission, Corruption, and Restoration*, 4th ed. (New York and Oxford: Oxford University Press, 2005), 52; Bart D. Ehrman, *Misquoting Jesus: The Story Behind Who Changed the Bible and Why* (New York: HarperSanFrancisco, 2005), 14–15.
21. For discussions of some of the issues surrounding the King James Version of the Bible and modern translations, see Blumell, "Text-Critical Comparison," 67–126; and Gaye Strathearn, "Modern English Bible Translations," in *The King James Bible and the Restoration*, ed. Kent P. Jackson (Provo, UT: Religious Studies Center, Brigham Young University; Salt Lake City: Deseret Book, 2011), 234–59.
22. The phrase is found in a seventh-century correction made in Codex Sinaiticus, and in Codicies Bezae (fifth century), Regius (eighth century), Freer (fourth–fifth century), and Koridethi (ninth century). But the Madalen papyrus (c. AD 200), the original hand of Codex Sinaiticus, and Codex Vaticanus (fourth century) all omit the phrase.
23. Davies and Allison, *Gospel According to Saint Matthew*, 1:512n4.
24. Although, the English Standard Version does include a footnote saying, "Some manuscripts insert *without a cause*."
25. Gaye Strathearn, "*Sōma sēma*: The Influence of 'The Body Is a Tomb' in Early Christian Debates and the New Testament," in *The Life and Teachings of the New Testament Apostles: From the Day of Pentecost Through the Apocalypse*, ed. Richard Neitzel Holzapfel and Thomas A. Wayment (Salt Lake City: Deseret Book, 2010), 276–98.
26. Neal A. Maxwell, "The New Testament—A Matchless Portrait of the Savior," *Ensign*, December 1986, 20; emphasis in original.
27. This approach to the New Testament has ancient roots. Tatian, an early Christian apologist, used the four Gospels to create one single harmony, the *Diatessaron* (c. AD 175). This text was very influential in Syria during the third and fourth centuries. An English translation of the Arabic version is found in Allan Menzies, ed., *The Ante-Nicene Fathers*, 5th ed. (Grand Rapids, MI: Eerdmans, 1980), 10:43–129. In antiquity, Ephrem the Syrian wrote a commentary on the *Diatessaron*. See Carmel McCarthy, *Saint Ephrem's Commentary on Tatian's Diatessaron: An English Translation of Chester Beatty Syriac MS 709 with Introduction and Notes* (Oxford: Oxford University Press, 1993).
28. Although the current LDS version of the King James Bible says that the JST identifies all four New Testament Gospels as "testimonies," Joseph Smith only made that addition for the Gospels of Matthew and John, not Mark and Luke. See Scott H. Faulring, Kent P. Jackson, and Robert J. Matthews, eds., *Joseph Smith's New Translation of the Bible: Original Manuscripts* (Provo, UT: Religious Studies Center, Brigham Young University, 2004), 235 and 442. For a convenient collection of the JST changes in the New Testament, see Thomas A. Wayment, ed., *The Complete Joseph Smith Translation of the New Testament* (Salt Lake City: Deseret Book, 2005).
29. Papias, quoted in Holmes, *Apostolic Fathers*, 569.
30. For example, in Luke's Gospel the account of John the Baptist's imprisonment is in Luke 3:19–20, *before* he baptized Jesus in Luke 3:21–22. In Mark and Matthew, the imprisonment takes place some time after the baptism (Mark 6:17–29; Matthew 14:3–12). In this instance, logic favors the chronology presented in Mark and Matthew over that of

Luke. In other instances, however, the decision is not so straightforward. For example, in Matthew's Gospel, Jesus raised Jairus's daughter immediately after John's disciples ask about fasting (Matthew 9:14–26). In Mark's and Luke's Gospels, however, the two events are separated by three chapters (Mark 2:18–22; 5:21–43; Luke 5:33–39; 8:41–56). Determining the chronology in this instance is much more difficult.

31. For a more expanded discussion of the individual emphases of the Gospel writers, see Strathearn and Judd, "Distinctive Testimonies," 59–85.
32. For a discussion on the importance of reading Matthew as a whole, see Ulrich Luz, *The Theology of the Gospel of Matthew*, trans. J. Bradford Robinson (Cambridge: Cambridge University Press, 1995), 1–21.
33. For discussion of *exegesis* and *eisegesis* in interpreting scriptural texts, see Eric D. Huntsman, "Teaching through Exegesis: Helping Students Ask Questions of the Text," *Religious Educator* 6, no. 1 (2005): 107–26.
34. For a discussion, see John Nolland, *The Gospel of Matthew: A Commentary on the Greek Text* (Grand Rapids, MI: Eerdmans, 2005), 1010–21.
35. R. T. France, *The Gospel of Matthew* (Grand Rapids, MI: Eerdmans, 2007), 951.
36. For a more detailed discussion of Matthew's editorial hand, see Gaye Strathearn, "Matthew as an Editor of the Life and Teachings of Jesus," in *How the New Testament Came to Be*, ed. Kent P. Jackson and Frank F. Judd Jr. (Provo, UT: Religious Studies Center, Brigham Young University; Salt Lake City: Deseret Book, 2006), 141–56; Graham Stanton, "Matthew as a Creative Interpreter of the Sayings of Jesus," in *The Gospel and the Gospels*, ed. Peter Stuhlmacher (Grand Rapids, MI: Eerdmans, 1991), 257–72.
37. This editorial process was first noticed by Günther Bornkamm, in "The Stilling of the Storm in Matthew," in *Tradition and Interpretation in Matthew*, ed. Günther Bornkamm, Gerhard Barth, and Heinz Joachim Held, trans. Percy Scott (Philadelphia: Westminster Press, 1963), 52–57.
38. Bornkamm, "Stilling of the Storm," 55.
39. Gerhard Kittel, ed., *Theological Dictionary of the New Testament*, trans. and ed. Geoffrey W. Bromiley, 10 vols. (Grand Rapids, MI: Eerdmans, 1965), 3:1058.
40. For examples where *sozō* is used in a physical sense, see Matthew 14:30; 27:40, 42, 49; Mark 15:30; and Acts 27:20, 31. For examples where *sozō* is used in a spiritual sense, see Luke 19:10; John 12:47; 1 Timothy 1:15; and 2 Timothy 4:18 (where the KJV translates it as "preserve").
41. Bornkamm, "Stilling of the Storm," 56.
42. For example, see E. P. Sanders, *The Historical Figure of Jesus* (London: Penguin, 1993), 85–88. An important question about the birth narratives is, where did Matthew and Luke get their information? For a discussion of the difficulties, see Raymond E. Brown, *The Birth of the Messiah: A Commentary on the Infancy Narratives in the Gospels of Matthew and Luke*, updated ed. (New York: Doubleday, 1993), 32–37. For many scholars today the historicity of the birth narratives has receded in the scholarly debate. Interest is now often focused more on what the birth narratives tell us about what later Christians thought about Jesus than on their historical reliability. For example, Henry Wansbrough writes, "The importance of the infancy narratives lies not in the precise historicity of the events but in what these narratives show about Jesus, or rather, about Christian belief in Jesus." Henry Wansbrough, "The Infancy Stories of the Gospels since Raymond E. Brown," in *New Perspectives on the Nativity*, ed. Jeremy Corley (London: T&T Clark International, 2009), 5.

43. Joseph A. Fitzmyer, *The Gospel According to Luke (I–IX)*, The Anchor Bible (New York: Doubleday, 1981), 307.
44. John J. Rousseau and Rami Arav, *Jesus and His World: An Archaeological and Cultural Dictionary* (Minneapolis: Fortress Press, 1995), 155–57. James H. Charlesworth notes the significance of this find: "No other ancient writer—no author or editor of the Old Testament, the Pseudepigrapha, not even Josephus—mentions such a significant pool in Jerusalem. Moreover, no known ancient building was a pentagon, which was apparently what John was describing with the five porticoes." James H. Charlesworth, "Reinterpreting John: How the Dead Sea Scrolls Have Revolutionized Our Understanding of the Gospel of John," *Bible Review* 9 (1993): 20.
45. James H. Charlesworth, "The Dead Sea Scrolls and the Gospel according to John" in *Exploring the Gospel of John: In Honor of D. Moody Smith*, ed. R. Alan Culpepper and C. Clifton Black (Louisville, KY: Westminster John Knox Press, 1996), 65–97. Charlesworth argues for a direct link between John and Qumran. In this he has probably exceeded the evidence. See David E. Aune, "Dualism in the Fourth Gospel and the Dead Sea Scrolls: A Reassessment of the Problem" in *Neotestamentica et Philonica: Studies in Honor of Peder Borgen*, ed. David E. Aune, Torrey Seland, and Jarl Henning Ulrichsen (Boston: Brill, 2003), 281–303. Aune shows that there is a greater affinity with other Jewish sources than the Dead Sea Scrolls. For a more recent discussion on the relationship between John and Qumran, see Mary L. Coloe and Tom Thatcher, eds., *John, Qumran, and the Dead Sea Scrolls: Sixty Years of Discovery and Debate* (Atlanta: Society of Biblical Literature, 2011).
46. For some discussions of historically accurate information about Samaritan belief, practices and places, see Robert J. Bull, "An Archaeological Footnote to 'Our Fathers Worshipped on this Mountain,' John 4:20," *New Testament Studies* 23 (1977): 460–62; Rousseau and Arav, *Jesus and His World*, 131.
47. For a discussion on possible ways of resolving these differences, see David Rolph Seely, "The Last Supper According to Matthew, Mark, and Luke" in *From the Last Supper through the Resurrection: The Savior's Final Hours*, ed. Richard Neitzel Holzapfel and Thomas A. Wayment (Salt Lake City: Deseret Book, 2003), 64–74.
48. Mishnah *Gittin* 9:10:

    A. The House of Shammai say, "A man should divorce his wife only because he has found grounds for it in unchastity,

    B. "Since it is said, *Because he has found in her indecency in anything* (Dt. 24:1)."

    C. And the House of Hillel say, "Even if she spoiled his dish,

    D. "Since it is said, *Because he has found in her indecency in anything*."

    E. R. Aqiba says, "Even if he found someone else prettier than she,

    F. "Since it is said, *And it shall be if she find no favor in his eyes* (Dt. 24:1)."

    English translation from *The Mishnah: A New Translation*, ed. Jacob Neusner (New Haven: Yale University Press, 1988), 487. Josephus says that he divorced his first wife because he was "not pleased with her behaviour." "Life of Flavius Josephus," in *Josephus: Complete Works*, trans. William Whiston (Grand Rapids, MI: Kregel, 1981), 21.
49. Bruce R. McConkie, *Doctrinal New Testament Commentary*, 3 vols. (Salt Lake City: Bookcraft, 1979), 1:548.
50. See Joseph Fielding Smith, in Conference Report, April 1961, 48–50.
51. Dallin H. Oaks, "Divorce," *Ensign*, May 2007, 71.

52. Many scholars interpret Jesus's answer as teaching that resurrected life transcends the mortal life and that marriage will no longer be part on an angelic existence. For examples, see Ulrich Luz, *Matthew 21–28: A Commentary*, trans. James E. Crouch (Minneapolis: Fortress Press, 2005), 70; W. D. Davies and Dale C. Allison Jr., *A Critical and Exegetical Commentary on the Gospel according to Saint Matthew* (Edinburgh: T&T Clark, 1988), 3:227–30. At least one, however, argues that Jesus's statement that "no new marriages will be initiated in the eschatological [resurrection] state" is "surely not the same as claiming that all existing marriages will disappear in the eschatological state." Ben Witherington, *The Gospel of Mark: A Socio-Rhetorical Commentary* (Grand Rapids, MI: Eerdmans, 2001), 328. Tertullian argues that in the Resurrection marriages will continue to be recognized. See Tertullian, *On Monogamy*, in *The Ante-Nicene Fathers*, 5th ed. (Grand Rapids, MI: Eerdmans, 1980), 4:66–67.
53. Ulrich Luz, *Matthew 21–28*, 70.
54. John S. Kloppenborg, *The Formation of Q: Trajectories in Ancient Wisdom Collections*, Studies in Antiquity & Christianity (Philadelphia: Fortress Press, 1987), 171–72. For an LDS reading that sees the two sermons as different accounts of the same sermon, see Thomas A. Wayment, "The Sermon on the Plain," in *The Life and Teachings of Jesus Christ*, vol. 1, *From Bethlehem through the Sermon on the Mount*, ed. Richard Neitzel Holzapfel and Thomas A. Wayment (Salt Lake City: Deseret Book, 2005), 355–78.
55. Although the texts are remarkably similar, they are not the same. See Krister Stendahl, "The Sermon on the Mount and Third Nephi," in *Reflections on Mormonism: Judaeo-Christian Parallels* (Provo, UT: Religious Studies Center, Brigham Young University, 1978), 139–54. Stendahl emphasizes that Jesus's frequent use of the phrase "come unto me" is the key textual element that distinguishes the Matthean and 3 Nephi accounts.
56. John W. Welch, *Illuminating the Sermon at the Temple and Sermon on the Mount* (Provo, UT: Foundation for Ancient Research and Mormon Studies, 1999). For an academic treatment, see John W. Welch, *The Sermon on the Mount in the Light of the Temple* (Burlington, VT: Ashgate, 2009).
57. Blumell, "Text-Critical Comparison," 96–103; see also I. Howard Marshall, *The Gospel of Luke: A Commentary of the Greek Text* (Grand Rapids, MI: Eerdmans, 1978), 831–33. For a more in-depth examination of why these verses may have been removed from the original Lukan text, see Lincoln H. Blumell, "Luke 22:43–44: An Anti-Docetic Interpolation or an Apologetic Omission?," *TC: A Journal of Biblical Textual Criticism* 19 (2014): 1–35.
58. See also 2 Nephi 31:2, 9–21 and 3 Nephi 11:31–39. Another term for the gospel is the "doctrine of Christ" (Jacob 7:6).
59. Neal A. Maxwell, "The New Testament—A Matchless Portrait of the Savior," *Ensign*, December 1986, 25.
60. Scott H. Faulring, Kent P. Jackson and Robert J. Matthews, eds., *Joseph Smith's New Translation of the Bible: Original Manuscripts* (Provo, UT: Religious Studies Center, Brigham Young University, 2004), 8–11.
61. Thomas A. Wayment, "Quest for Origins: The Joseph Smith Translation and Latin Version of the New Testament" in *A Witness for the Restoration: Essays in Honor of Robert J. Matthews*, ed. Kent P. Jackson and Andrew C. Skinner (Provo, UT: Religious Studies Center, Brigham Young University, 2007), 61–91.
62. Wayment, "Quest for Origins," 80–81.
63. Laurence M. Vance, *Archaic Words and the Authorized Version*, rev. ed. (Pensacola, FL: Vance Publications, 1999), 16.

64. For examples in the KJV, see Matthew 4:22; Mark 1:12, 42. The King James translators used a number of words to translate *euthus*, including "straightway" (e.g. Matthew 4:20; 14:27; Mark 1:10, 18, 20), "by and by" (Matthew 13:21), and "forthwith" (Mark 1:29, 43).
65. Richard D. Draper, "Joseph Smith—Matthew and the Signs of the Times," *Studies in Scripture*, vol. 2: *The Pearl of Great Price*, ed. Robert L. Millet and Kent P. Jackson (Salt Lake City: Randall Book, 1985), 290. These are not the only JST changes to the Olivet Discourse. For discussion of all the changes, see the entirety of Draper's article and Kent P. Jackson, "The Olivet Discourse," in *The Life and Teachings of Jesus Christ*, 2:318–43.
66. Jeffrey R. Holland, "The Inconvenient Messiah," *Ensign*, February 1984, 68.
67. For a discussion of both elements of judging, see Dallin H. Oaks, "'Judge Not' and Judging," *Ensign*, August 1999, 7–13.
68. "Selections from Addresses of President Gordon B. Hinckley," *Ensign*, March 2001, 64.

Chapter Five

Marcan Christology

Narrating the Christ

AMY EASTON-FLAKE

Halfway through the Gospel of Mark, Jesus asks his disciples, "Whom do men say that I am?" (Mark 8:27), and then more piercingly, "But whom say ye that I am?" (8:29). Perhaps the earliest of the Gospels to have been written and likely a major source for both Matthew and Luke, the narrative of Mark presents a powerful Christological understanding of Jesus's identity and salvific work. It loosely fits the genre of a first-century Roman biography, which has been defined as a "prose narration about a person's life, presenting supposedly historical facts which are selected to reveal the character or essence of the individual, often with the purpose of affecting the behavior of the reader."[1] Its fast-moving, vivid, action-packed story invites the reader into the narrative world to experience Jesus's mortal ministry and crucifixion through the perspective of his disciples. Mark's presentation of Jesus is also generally considered to be the most human and relatable portrait of Jesus because of the range of strong emotions Jesus displays.[2] At the same time, however, Mark's portrait of Jesus invites awe and wonder at Jesus's divinity, thus making Jesus's dualism as both human and divine a central aspect of the Marcan Jesus.[3]

While there are many ways to explore Mark's presentation of Jesus, the compelling story aspect of Mark's Gospel makes the use of a narrative lens particularly apt. By considering the work of scholars who take seriously Mark's narrative Christology—what Jesus says and does in the context of the narrative and actions of others—Latter-day Saints can gain new insights into Mark's presentation of Jesus. Through a focused, close reading of the scriptures, we can come to see a Savior who is fully human and fully divine; who experiences and portrays strong human emotions as he teaches, provides miracles, and challenges perceptions; and who acts as the model disciple, showing us all the necessity of service, suffering, and sacrifice.

Background of the Gospel of Mark

Though formally anonymous, early Christian tradition attributed this Gospel to John Mark and suggested that it was written in Rome (AD 60–75) as a record of Peter's teachings.[4] In the early centuries of Christianity, the Gospel of Mark was often overshadowed by the other Gospels because it was seen as an abbreviated version of Matthew. Its increase in popularity and scholarly attention in the nineteenth and twentieth centuries is largely due to the reversal of the traditional view that Matthew was the earliest Gospel.[5] Most New Testament scholars today favor Marcan priority because of the way the Gospels of Matthew and Luke follow the Marcan wording and ordering of events.[6] In recent years, scholars have also come to appreciate the Gospel of Mark as a carefully crafted story—most likely shared orally—that presents its own theological themes and understanding of Jesus.[7] Close analysis of the text reveals that Mark's Gospel is a highly structured literary work with a three-stage geographical progression, topical ordering of events, intercalation or sandwiching (placing one story within another), triads or sets of three, repetition, parallel scenes, foreshadows and echoes, and vivid details.[8] Each of these elements makes the text more memorable and performable, and collectively they indicate that Mark's Gospel was likely constructed as an oral text and performed multiple times before being written down.[9]

The Gospel of Mark had its beginning in an oral culture.[10] In first-century Mesopotamia, storytelling was ubiquitous, writing was largely seen as a representation of speech, oral communication was considered true communication, and people wrote to transfer oral stories rather than to replace oral performances.[11] Scholars estimate that in the ancient Roman Empire only between 5 and 10 percent of the people—mostly wealthy elites—were able to read or write in the first century; consequently, the vast majority of people experienced everything they learned aurally.[12] As Whitney Shriner reports, "Good speakers were admired and attracted the sorts of large crowds that we would associate with rock stars. Crowds would fill up theaters to hear a famous rhetorician from out of town."[13] Performance of sacred stories was also an important part of worship services, and letters such as those written by Paul would have been performed for their intended recipients.[14] Most people would have experienced the Gospel of Mark as an engaging two-hour performance because they had neither access to the text nor the ability to read it.[15]

From Titles to Narrative Christology

Recognizing that the Gospel of Mark most likely originally functioned as an oral story has important implications for our understanding and study of Mark's Gospel and its portrait of Jesus. First, this recognition invites a perceptual shift to consider the many aspects that make up a performative event: the storyteller, audience, location, sociohistorical circumstances, and rhetorical impact. The interpretive process largely shifts from the reader to the performer as the presentation of Jesus depends a great deal on who is telling the story. How does Jesus sound? What is his tone? What clues or suggestions does the text offer as a script for storytelling performances?[16] Second, it reinforces the importance of studying Mark's portrayal of Jesus from a narrative vantage point since the Gospel of Mark was intended to be experienced as a single story in a single sitting.

Earlier discussions on New Testament Christology focused almost exclusively on the titles for Christ found within the Gospels—namely, Son of God, Son of Man, Christ, and Lord—and what these titles revealed when placed within a historical or theological context.[17] While there is still value to such Christological approaches, innovative approaches to the Gospels help us to see and understand the person and work of Jesus in new ways. Since Robert Tannehill introduced the term *narrative Christology* in 1979,[18] many scholars have begun looking at Mark's narrative holistically, arguing that Jesus can be grasped only within the narrative.[19] As M. Eugene Boring states simply, "Mark's narrative is already a Christology."[20] In essence, advocates of narrative Christology believe that "we learn who Jesus is through what he says and does in the context of the actions of others."[21] In other words, the narrator of Mark's Gospel does not offer many evaluative words or judgments of Jesus, preferring instead to show who Jesus is through Jesus's actions and dialogue and others' actions and dialogue in relation to him. Other aspects to consider when analyzing Mark's portrayal of Jesus are what drives and motivates Jesus, what his traits are, how they are illuminated by comparison or contrast with other characters, and what Jesus seeks and works for.[22] Narrative structure and plot must also be given due consideration as they too may reveal character.

A strength of narrative Christology, as pointed out by Boring, is its ability to hold ideas in tension and "allow paradox without synthesis."[23] Mark, for instance, composes a narrative in which Jesus is presented as both divine and human without qualification or dilution.[24] As Jacob Naluparayil writes, "The use of the narrative method produces an overall tendency to incorporate the different aspects of the Marcan presentation of Jesus instead of stressing one aspect at the expense of others."[25] This in turn allows us to see Jesus in his full complexity. Another strength of the narrative approach is the recognition that this is someone's depiction of Christ. Even though Jesus was a real, historical figure, any story that one hears of him is necessarily mediated through the teller.[26] This recognition encourages us to seek out and learn from the different portraits of Jesus offered by a myriad of individuals in the Bible, the Book of Mormon, and other Restoration scripture. Each of us—including the Gospel writers—has experienced Christ differently in our lives, and the narrative approach allows us to celebrate and learn from these differences rather than dismiss them. I begin with an analysis of Mark's narrative Christology in Mark 1 to illustrate how a close, careful reading of the text illuminates Mark's portrait of Jesus.

God's Beloved, Obedient Son

The prologue to Mark's Gospel (Mark 1:1–15) establishes Jesus's significance and prepares the audience to trust Jesus through statements made by the narrator, by John the Baptist, and by God. With the opening line, "The beginning of the gospel of Jesus Christ, the Son of God" (1:1), the narrator establishes Jesus as the central figure of his story. The opening line acts as a title for the work[27] and is highly distinctive as the only place where the narrator pronounces a direct, generalized assessment of Jesus—elsewhere, the narrator prefers to show who Jesus is through actions and dialogues and to place assessments of Jesus in the mouths of the characters.[28] At the outset of the story, however, the narrator wants to make it known that Jesus is "Christ or the anointed one"[29] and "the Son of God," but what these titles mean in the first century is highly debatable and becomes clear only as we explore the narrative as a whole.[30] The next assessment of Jesus is uttered by John the Baptist: "There cometh one mightier than I after me, the latchet of whose shoes I am not worthy to stoop down and unloose. I indeed have baptized you with water: but he shall baptize you with the Holy Ghost" (1:7–8). John's statement establishes Jesus's importance and authority as greater than that of a prophet and prepares us for what God will say about Jesus after his baptism: "Thou art my beloved Son, in whom I am well pleased" (1:11). God's proclamation of Jesus as his Son confirms the narrator's assessment of Jesus and is crucial to establishing Jesus's authority and the narrator's credibility.[31] Both can now be trusted because God, the highest authority in Mark's narrative world, has ratified Jesus's status as his Son. Thus, by the time Jesus speaks his first words, "The time is fulfilled, and the kingdom of God is at hand: repent ye, and believe the gospel" (1:15), the audience is prepared to listen to him and trust whatever he may say or do.

Looking closely at what Jesus says and does in chapter 1 of Mark's Gospel reveals Jesus's basic character. First, Jesus is obedient to God. His first act, baptism (see Mark 1:9), signals his submission to God; and his second act, being "driven" by the Spirit into the wilderness (1:12), confirms his willingness to be obedient to God even when it is difficult. Significantly, God's pronouncement of Jesus as the one he loves and with whom he is "well pleased" (1:11) comes after Jesus has displayed his obedience by being baptized. Mark's concise version of Jesus's forty days in the wilderness—mentioning only that "angels ministered unto him" and Satan "tempted" him (1:13)—helps the audience see Jesus on a cosmic scale as he associates with immortal beings. It also announces a major theme of Mark's Gospel: Jesus is at battle with Satan and Satan's dominion.[32] After the trial in the wilderness, we have Jesus's first spoken utterance: "The time is fulfilled, and the kingdom of God is at hand: repent ye, and believe the gospel" (1:15). This is a significant line because it encapsulates what Jesus cares about: teaching the gospel and preparing people for "the kingdom of God." As David Rhoads, Joanna Dewey, and Donald Michie write, it also "discloses his understanding of himself as an agent of God and his purposes."[33] His next spoken line, uttered as he calls his first disciples, Simon and Andrew, propels this motif of repentance and preparation for God's kingdom forward as it indicates Jesus's role in the process. It is by following Jesus as the enabler—"Come ye after me, and I will make you to become fishers of men" (1:17)—that we may become something more than we are, that we may become whom he sees us as. Simon, Andrew, James, and John were fishermen until Jesus gave them a vision of what more they could be and suggested a path forward. Other foundational aspects of Jesus's character as a teacher, healer, and exorcist are set forth in rapid succession, as Mark moves quickly from one act of Jesus's to the next. Jesus teaches (see 1:21–22), casts out an unclean spirit (see 1:23–27), heals Simon's mother-in-law (see 1:30–31), heals the sick and casts out devils (see 1:32–34), departs to a solitary place to pray (see 1:35), preaches (see 1:39), casts out devils again (see 1:39), and heals a leper (see 1:40–45). Throughout all these actions, Mark emphasizes Jesus's authority and the crowd's astonishment.

By the end of chapter 1, Mark has established the image of Jesus's identity and salvific work that informs the first half of the story. Jesus is God's beloved, obedient Son, who acts to further God's kingdom through preaching and healing. Significantly, this image of Jesus will likely resonate with most believers' understanding of Christ because the similarities among the Gospel writers' Christologies are greater than their dissimilarities.

Mark's More Human Jesus

However, as we continue to pay close attention to what Jesus says and does and what others say about him, we will find in Mark a more human Jesus—a more emotional and harder to define Jesus—than that found in the other canonical Gospels, which will enrich our understanding of the Savior of the world. Mark's understanding of Jesus as one who felt and portrayed strong emotions may come as a surprise to the many individuals who picture an always composed and never ruffled Jesus—such as that presented in *The Life of Jesus Christ Bible Videos* made by The Church of Jesus Christ of Latter-day Saints. Notably, these moments of human realism in Mark are often omitted or toned down in the Gospels of Matthew and Luke.[34] For instance, Matthew and Luke omit the compassion that Jesus feels toward a leper that he heals—"And Jesus, moved with *compassion* [or *pity* in the New International Version],[35] put forth his hand, and touched him" (Mark 1:40–41, emphasis added; compare Matthew 8:1–2; Luke 5:12–13)—as well as the love that Jesus feels for the rich young man—"Then Jesus beholding him *loved* him" (Mark 10:21, emphasis added; compare Matthew 19:16–22; Luke 18:18–22). Matthew and Luke also omit mentions of Jesus's anger, such as the anger he feels toward the Pharisees for questioning the lawfulness of healing a man with a withered hand on the Sabbath—"And when he had looked round about on them with *anger*, being *grieved* [or *deeply distressed* in the NIV] for the hardness of their hearts" (Mark 3:5, emphasis added; compare Matthew 12:9–14; Luke 6:6–11)—and the displeasure Jesus feels when the disciples forbid the little children to come unto him—"But when Jesus saw it, he was much *displeased* [*indignant* in the NIV and the New Revised Standard Version or *angry* in the Common English Bible and the Good News Translation]" (Mark 10:14, emphasis added; compare Matthew 19:13–15; Luke 18:15–17). The moment when Jesus expresses surprise at the Nazarenes' unbelief is also omitted in the Gospels of Matthew and Luke—"And he *marveled* [*was appalled* in the CEB, *greatly surprised* in the GNT, *was amazed* in the NIV] because of their unbelief" (Mark 6:6, emphasis added; compare Matthew 13:53–58; Luke 4:16–30). Jesus's desire for solitude and need to commune with God for strength and direction is also more apparent in Mark's narrative (see Mark 1:35; 6:45–46).

As illustrated above, reading other translations may help us gain a better sense of the strong emotions that Jesus displays because the early modern English of the King James Version may in some instances mask Jesus's emotions to readers' contemporary ears. One example of this is when Jesus expresses his frustration at his apostles' inability to cast a spirit out of a young boy or, more likely, his frustration at the general lack of faith he perceives in all of Israel—"O faithless generation, how long shall I be with you? How long shall I suffer you?" (Mark 9:19). The much more prevalent translation of this statement—"You faithless generation, how much longer must I be among you? How much longer must I put up with you?" (Mark 9:19 NRSV)—changes the tone of Jesus's statement and makes his frustration much more palpable, as it seems he is being compelled to be with them—"how much longer must I"—rather than choosing to be with them. These differences in tone may be simply the result of our disconnect from early modern English or they may reflect a desire on the part of the King James translators, similar to that of the authors of Matthew and Luke, to soften Mark's portrayal of Jesus. Mark's portrayal of a more expressive Jesus, however, should be appreciated and studied because it provides a more relatable Jesus who has felt the emotions that we all commonly experience.

Both Human and Divine

One of the most notable aspects of Mark's Christology, however, is how he depicts a Christ that is both divine and human without qualification or dilution. In a narrative these oppositional aspects may exist together uncontested in a way that they could not in a theological treatise because the story may simply highlight different aspects at different moments.

Jesus's divinity may be seen most clearly in his actions and others' reactions to him. Jesus's power to heal and cast out spirits is a tangible manifestation of his divinity and authority from God. The other miracles he performs, such as calming the seas (see Mark 4:38–41), walking on water (see 6:47–51), feeding the five thousand and four thousand (see 6:34–44; 8:1–9), raising Jarius's daughter from the dead (see 5:35–43), and—perhaps most significant—forgiving sins (see 2:5), are also manifestations of his divinity and authority. The most common reaction to Jesus, his teachings, and his works is astonishment and, for many, a desire to follow him.[36] Repeatedly throughout the Gospel, the narrator reports that all were astonished (see 1:22; 7:37; 10:24, 26; 11:18) or amazed (see 1:27; 2:12; 6:51; 9:15; 10:32) or that they marveled (see 5:20; 12:17; 15:5) because his teachings and works set him apart from any mortal being. Jesus also commonly evokes fear in his apostles as he shatters their understanding of what is possible when he calms the sea (see 4:41), walks on water (see 6:50), transfigures before them (see 9:2–6), and tells them of his life path to be killed and then rise the third day (see 9:31–32). In Mark's Christology, Jesus shares the human situation as a fellow human being even as he is the Son of God exercising divine power, evoking awe in all, and challenging mortal understanding. Such a display of seemingly contradictory elements shows how narrative Christology may incorporate the different aspects of the Marcan Jesus rather than flatten the multidimensional Jesus apparent within the text. For us readers, such a portrait is beneficial because it not only brings us much closer to the reality of Christ, which is of course complex, but it also helps us accept the complexity and paradoxes that invariably arise when we seek to more fully understand almost any aspect of theology.

Jesus's Understanding of Himself

Another important layer of Mark's Christology is ascertaining how Jesus sees himself. That Jesus sees himself as the agent through whom the kingdom of God is proclaimed and effected is clearly evident from the first line Jesus speaks—"The time is fulfilled, and the kingdom of God is at hand: repent ye, and believe the gospel" (Mark 1:15)—until his crucifixion on the cross.

While the Marcan Jesus is a Jesus of deeds, with Mark reporting the miracles of Jesus in the most fulsome and descriptive way of any of the Gospels and sharing Jesus's teaching in parables and short, pithy statements rather the longer sermons and discourses reported in the other Gospels, Jesus emphasizes that he came primarily to teach. At the beginning of his ministry, Jesus tells Simon explicitly, "Let us go into the next towns, that I may preach there also: *for therefore came I forth*" (Mark 1:38; emphasis added); Mark portrays Jesus teaching or preaching more than any other act; and Jesus prioritizes his teaching over his healing. For instance, Jesus's desire for individuals not to share the miracles he performs seems to be motivated out of his desire to preach (see 1:43–45; 7:36–8:1). While news of his healings and miracles draws many people to him, it also seems to make it difficult at times for him to preach (1:45). On occasion, Mark depicts Jesus leaving the miracle-seeking crowds so that he may find other communities and individuals to share his message with (see 3:7–10; 6:31–34). Jesus also turns every situation into a teaching moment. For example, when his mother and brethren come seeking him, he uses it as a moment to explain a new conception of family—that all who do the will of God are Christ's family (see 3:31–35); when his disciples are disputing over who will be the greatest, he uses their concern to teach them what it actually means to be the greatest (see 9:33–35; 10:35–45); and when he sees the poor widow casting in her two mites, he uses her example to explain how God judges our actions and sacrifices (see 12:41–44).

Jesus Challenging Perceptions

Teaching is central to Jesus's mission because preparing people for the kingdom of God entails teaching them to see and judge as God does rather than as man does; consequently, the Jesus of Mark constantly challenges one perception after the other. One of the first religious practices that Jesus challenges is appropriate Sabbath-day observance. He does this first through his actions, as he performs his first two miracles (casting out a spirit and healing a disease) on the Sabbath (see Mark 1:21–31). He later challenges the Pharisees' views of the Sabbath explicitly through dialogue after they condemn his disciples' plucking ears of corn on the Sabbath and his healing a withered man's hand on the Sabbath because they viewed both as a form of work (see 2:23–3:5). Jesus uses these moments to teach the Pharisees that they have failed to understand what the Sabbath is for: "The sabbath was made for man, and not man for the sabbath" (2:27). Or in other words, the Sabbath is to give individuals rest from their troubles and worries; consequently, there could not be a more fitting time to heal someone.

Jesus also challenges Jewish purity laws (what makes a person clean or unclean). The catalyst for this discussion is when the Pharisees find fault with the disciples eating with unwashed hands (see Mark 7:1–5). Jesus uses their critique to first point out that they place the traditions of men above the commandments of God because the requirement to wash pots and cups before eating came from man, not God (see 7:6–9). He then goes on to redefine their understanding of what makes one clean or unclean when he proclaims, "There is nothing from without a man, that entering into him can defile him: but the things which come out of him, those are they that defile the man" (7:15). This statement shows Jesus to be revolutionary because if taken literally it essentially means that Jesus was nullifying a significant portion of the Levitical law code.[37] Cleanliness and purity were now to be determined by one's moral actions and attitude, not by one's eating or washing practices or those people one comes into contact with. Jesus taught this principle through his actions as well, as he regularly interacted with those who were considered unclean, such as sinners and those with various diseases (see 2:15–17). In this way, he also challenged the treatment of the marginalized and outcast. All were to be treated with kindness and invited to be part of the kingdom of God (2:17).

The most important perception Jesus alters is what it means for him to be the Christ and, by extension, what it means to be his disciple. Peter is correct when he answers Jesus's question "But whom say ye that I am?" with "Thou art the Christ" (Mark 8:29). But it is also clear from the text that Peter does not understand what it means for Jesus to be the Christ. This verse has often been seen as the turning point in Mark's Gospel because the rest of the Gospel may be seen as Mark's attempt to help his audience understand what it means for Jesus to be the Christ.[38] In many ways, being the Christ is not the glorious calling one would expect; instead, it is about suffering, sacrifice, and resurrection. Or, as Jesus explains to his disciples, "the Son of man must suffer many things, and be rejected of the elders, and of the chief priests, and scribes, and be killed, and after three days rise again" (8:31). Here, Jesus radically redefines the role of the Messiah and then proceeds to radically redefine what it means to be his follower: "Whosoever will come after me, let him deny himself, and take up his cross, and follow me" (8:34). Clearly, this description of discipleship does not suggest ease and worldly accolades; instead, it asks disciples to forgo this world for the next and to follow his example of servant leadership. As Jesus will later explain to his disciples, "And whosoever of you will be the chiefest, shall be servant of all.

For even the Son of man came not to be ministered unto, but to minister, and to give his life a ransom for many" (10:44–45).

Mark makes it clear that Jesus's disciples do not understand this message by juxtaposing Jesus's statements about his suffering and sacrifice with his disciples' continual desire for honor and prestige. The irony is palpable when Jesus's statement "The Son of man is delivered into the hands of men, and they shall kill him; and after that he is killed, he shall rise the third day" (Mark 9:31) is immediately followed by the disciples disputing among themselves who is the greatest (see 9:33–34). And then again a chapter later, when Jesus's statement "Behold, we go up to Jerusalem; and the Son of man shall be delivered unto the chief priests, and unto the scribes; and they shall condemn him to death, and shall deliver him to the Gentiles: And they shall mock him, and shall scourge him, and shall spit upon him, and shall kill him: and the third day he shall rise again" (10:33–34) is immediately followed by James and John asking to sit on his right hand and on his left hand in the next life (see 10:35–37). In both instances, Jesus uses their inappropriate question to reorient their understanding of what it means to be the greatest and what it means to have authority: "But whosoever will be great among you, shall be your minister: And whoever of you will be the chiefest, shall be servant of all" (10:43–44). Observant readers may note that these juxtaposed events are actually separate events that may not necessarily have taken place one after another. This observation should in turn highlight for readers that Mark has deliberately constructed his narrative to emphasize the disciples' inability to comprehend what Jesus was teaching them about his role as well as theirs. A possible reason for this is that Mark's Jesus teaches both in words and in actions that suffering, service, and sacrifice are essential aspects of being part of God's kingdom—"If any man desire to be first, the same shall be last of all, and servant of all" (9:35)—and his disciples' inability to comprehend Jesus's message about himself and his followers indicates just how radical, unexpected, and difficult his teachings were.

Jesus's Suffering

At the center of Mark's Christology is Jesus as the suffering servant who faithfully follows God's will and gives his life before rising three days later.

He is the model disciple who shows us that service, suffering, and sacrifice are necessary qualifications for being part of God's kingdom. While this may be ascertained by looking at Jesus's words and actions, as we have discussed thus far, perhaps it is best emphasized by looking at Mark's basic narrative structure and plot. Mark's Gospel is generally divided into a prologue (Mark 1:1–1:13 [15]) followed by three major divisions: Jesus's authoritative ministry in and around Galilee (1:14 [16]–8:22 [26]), Jesus's journey to Jerusalem (8:27–10:52), and Jesus in Jerusalem (11:1–16:8).[39] Dividing Mark's Gospel in half is Jesus's crucial question to Peter: "But whom say ye that I am?" (8:29). In the first half of the narrative, Mark presents Jesus as the Messiah and Son of God, who teaches and acts with authority and power and grows in popularity. Miracle working, teaching, and challenging norms and perceptions are central to Mark's depiction of Jesus in the first half of the narrative and affirm that Jesus is indeed the Messiah. The second half of the narrative then shifts the focus to Jesus's suffering, death, and resurrection to reorient the meaning of being the Messiah.

That Mark wants the passion narrative—the account of Jesus's suffering, death, and resurrection—to be the center of his story is indicated by the fact that the narrative slows down significantly once Jesus enters Jerusalem. This fact has not been lost on readers, as Mark's Gospel has famously and repeatedly been described as "a passion narrative with an extended introduction" because Mark proportionally spends more time expounding on Jesus's suffering, death, and resurrection than any other Gospel writer.[40] As Donald H. Juel further explains, "One-third of Mark's Gospel is devoted to an account of Jesus's last few days [other scholars will more accurately list this as 40 percent].[41] One-sixth to his last twenty-four hours."[42] Up until this point, Mark's narrative has offered a fast-moving overview of the highlights of Jesus's ministry, but now the narrative moves slowly, offering a detailed look at the events leading to Jesus's death and resurrection. We see Jesus's escalating confrontations with the scribes and Pharisees as he continues to perform miracles, teach, and challenge accepted norms. Most moving is Mark's depiction of Jesus in Gethsemane, where we see a very human Jesus cry out to God his Father, "Abba, Father, all things are possible unto thee; take away this cup from me: nevertheless not what I will, but what thou wilt" (Mark 14:36).

Though Mark does not share the significance of what occurs in the Garden of Gethsemane (that is disclosed only in Restoration scripture), he does share an image of Jesus that encapsulates much of what Mark wants his audience to understand about Jesus: his faith, humility, and absolute obedience to God (Mark 14:36); his common humanity that allows him to feel that his "soul is exceeding sorrowful unto death" and causes him to shrink from the suffering and death that awaits him (14:33–35); his compassion towards and understanding of his disciples' human frailties (see 14:38–41); and his divinity that enables him to see the future and to meet it resolutely (see 14:41–49). This portrait is reinforced through Jesus's trials and time on the cross. With his death as the critical act, his last words—"My God, my God, why hast thou forsaken me?"—indicate the depth to which Jesus has had to suffer in order to be God's saving agent (15:34). Mark's very brief depiction of events after the resurrection—ending, as most scholars agree, with the women finding his empty tomb and being told by a messenger that Jesus is risen and to go and "tell his disciples and Peter that he goeth before you into Galilee: there shall ye see him, as he said unto you" (16:7) and their subsequent fear, amazement, and silence (see 16:8)[43]—keeps the narrative focused on the crucial acts of Jesus's death and resurrection. And the open, rather than closed, nature of the ending invites Mark's audience into the narrative to take the place of the women at the empty sepulchre and to share the message of Christ's crucifixion and resurrection.[44] Through the precision with which he constructs his narrative, and, in particular, that final week of Jesus's life, Mark has created his Christology.

Coming to Know Jesus through Mark

Jesus's question to Mark, "But whom say ye that I am?" (Mark 8:29), is the crucial question for each of us. There are many ways that we may come to know that Jesus is the Christ: prayer, scripture study, experience, following the counsel of the Spirit, and modeling our life after Jesus all help us answer that piercing question. For many, a critical aspect of knowing that Jesus is the Christ is seeking to learn about and understand the mortal Messiah who lived two thousand years ago. Because each of the Gospels provides unique insights into Jesus's life, ministry, and death, a close, careful narrative reading of the texts helps reveal aspects of the text and Jesus's life that may otherwise remain unnoticed. In Mark's Gospel, we find a Savior who is fully human and fully divine. The Son of Man experiences and portrays strong emotions as he teaches, heals, and acts with divine authority and power. He is God's Beloved Son and the agent through whom the kingdom of God is proclaimed and effected. He is the suffering servant who faithfully follows God's will and gives his life before rising three days later. He is the model disciple who shows us all that service, suffering, and sacrifice are necessary qualifications for being part of God's kingdom. He is as declared in the opening line of the Gospel of Mark, "Jesus Christ, the Son of God" (1:1), and it is by coming to know him and following his example that we may become his disciples.

Amy Easton-Flake is an associate professor of ancient scripture at Brigham Young University.

Amy Easton-Flake, "Marcan Christology: Narrating the Christ," in *Thou Art the Christ, the Son of the Living God: The Person and Work of Jesus in the New Testament*, ed. Eric D. Huntsman, Lincoln H. Blumell, and Tyler J. Griffin (Provo, UT: Religious Studies Center; Salt Lake City: Deseret Book, 2018), 92–111.

NOTES

1. Charles H. Talbert, *What Is a Gospel? The Genre of the Canonical Gospels* (Philadelphia: Fortress, 1977), 17. For more information on how Mark fits within the genre of first-century Roman biographies, see Ben Witherington III, *The Gospel of Mark: A Socio-Rhetorical Commentary* (Grand Rapids, MI: Eerdmans, 2001), 5–7; R. T. France, *The Gospel of Mark*, The New International Greek Testament Commentary (Grand Rapids, MI: Eerdmans, 2002), 5–6, 10; John R. Donahue and Daniel J. Harrington, *The Gospel of Mark*, Sacra Pagina, vol. 2 (Collegeville, MN: Liturgical Press, 2002), 14–15. Written in the vernacular of popular spoken Greek, the Gospel of Mark belongs more in the category of popular literature than the elite literary works scholars typically analyze. For more information, see Mary Ann Tolbert, *Sowing the Gospel: Mark's World in Literary-Historical Perspective* (Minneapolis: Augsburg Fortress, 1996), 70–78.
2. Scholars who discuss this include Mark L. Strauss, *Four Portraits, One Jesus: A Survey of Jesus and the Gospels* (Grand Rapids, MI: Zondervan, 2007), 294; John R. Donahue, "Jesus as the Parable of God in the Gospel of Mark," in *Interpreting the Gospels*, ed. James Luther Mays (Philadelphia: Fortress Press, 1981), 159–60; Stephen H. Smith, *A Lion*

with Wings: A Narrative-Critical Approach to Mark's Gospel (Sheffield: Sheffield Academic Press, 1996), 58.

3. M. Eugene Boring, "The Christology of Mark: Hermeneutical Issues for Systematic Theology," *Semeia* 30 (1984): 138–39.
4. For a brief discussion of this, see Strauss, *Four Portraits*, 201; Witherington, *Gospel of Mark*, 24–26; France, *Gospel of Mark*, 7–8, 38–40
5. For more information, see Strauss, *Four Portraits*, 173; Donahue and Harrington, *Gospel of Mark*, 3–4; France, *Gospel of Mark*, 15–16.
6. For more information, see Donahue and Harrington, *Gospel of Mark*, 4–5; Witherington, *Gospel of Mark*, 18–19.
7. For an extended discussion, see David Rhoads, Joanna Dewey, and Donald Michie, *Mark as Story: An Introduction to the Narrative of a Gospel*, 3rd ed. (Minneapolis: Fortress Press, 2012). For a brief overview, see France, *Gospel of Mark*, 16–20.
8. For more information, see Strauss, *Four Portraits*, 174–77; Donahue and Harrington, *Gospel of Mark*, 16–19; France, *Gospel of Mark*, 11–14.
9. Scholars who discuss this include Philip Ruge-Jones, "The Word Heard: How Hearing a Text Differs from Reading One," in *The Bible in Ancient and Modern Media: Story and Performance*, ed. Holly E. Hearon and Philip Ruge-Jones (Eugene, OR: Cascade, 2009), 102; Richard A. Horsley, "Oral and Written Aspects of the Emergence of the Gospel of Mark as Scripture," *Oral Tradition* 25, no. 1 (2010): 95; Joanna Dewey, *The Oral Ethos of the Early Church: Speaking, Writing, and the Gospel of Mark* (Eugene, OR: Cascade, 2013), 158–60; France, *Gospel of Mark*, 9–10.
10. Some of the best works on this issue include Whitney Shriner, *Proclaiming the Gospel: First-Century Performance of Mark* (Harrisburg, PA: Trinity Press, 2003); Dewey, *Oral Ethos*; Hearon and Ruge-Jones, *Bible in Ancient and Modern Media*.
11. For more information, see Dewey, *Oral Ethos*, 160; David Rhoads, "What Is Performance Criticism," in *Bible in Ancient and Modern Media*, 85–86; Whitney Shriner, "Oral Performance in the New Testament World," in *Bible in Ancient and Modern Media*, 49–51; Ruge-Jones, "Word Heard," 102.
12. Rhoads, "What Is Performance Criticism," 85; Shriner, "Oral Performance," 49; Horsley, "Oral and Written Aspects," 95, 104–8.
13. Shriner, "Oral Performance," 51.
14. Dewey, *Oral Ethos*, 160; Rhoads, "What Is Performance Criticism," 86.
15. Shriner, "Oral Performance," 49; Christopher W. Skinner, "The Study of Character(s) in the Gospel of Mark: A Survey of Research from Wrede to the Performance Critics (1901 to 2014)," in *Character Studies and the Gospel of Mark*, ed. Christopher W. Skinner and Matthew Ryan Hauge (London: Bloomsbury, 2014), 32.
16. Holly E. Hearon, "The Storytelling World of the First Century and the Gospels," in *Bible in Ancient and Modern Media*, 22; For a fuller discussion of the implication of biblical performance, see Rhoads, "What Is Performance Criticism," 88–99.
17. See France, *Gospel of Mark*, 23; Jacob Chacko Naluparayil, "Jesus of the Gospel of Mark: Present State of Research," *Currents in Research: Biblical Studies* 8 (2000): 192–93.
18. Robert C. Tannehill, "The Gospel of Mark as Narrative Christology," *Semeia* 16 (1979): 57–95.
19. Leading scholarship on narrative Christology includes Elizabeth Struthers Malbon, *Mark's Jesus: Characterization as Narrative Christology* (Waco, TX: Baylor University Press, 2009); Rhoads, Dewey, and Michie, *Mark as Story*; Ole Davidson, *The Narrative Jesus: A Semiotic Reading of Mark's Gospel* (Aarhus, DK: Aarhus University Press, 1993); Jacob

Chacko Naluparayil, *The Identity of Jesus in Mark: An Essay on Narrative Christology*, Studium Biblicum Franciscanum Analecta, no. 49 (Jerusalem: Franciscan Printing Press, 2000); Paul L. Danove, *The Rhetoric of the Characterization of God, Jesus, and Jesus' Disciples in the Gospel of Mark* (New York: T&T Clark, 2005).

20. Boring, "Christology of Mark," 136–37.
21. Tannehill, "Narrative Christology," 58.
22. Rhoads, Dewey, and Michie, *Mark as Story*, 100.
23. Boring, "Christology of Mark," 138.
24. Boring, "Christology of Mark," 138–39.
25. Naluparayil, "Jesus of the Gospel of Mark," 217.
26. For more on this idea, see Smith, *Lion with Wings*, 16; James L. Resseguie, *Narrative Criticism of the New Testament: An Introduction* (Grand Rapids, MI: Baker Academic, 2005), 121; Scott S. Elliott, *Reconfiguring Mark's Jesus: Narrative Criticism after Poststructuralism* (Sheffield: Sheffield Phoenix Press, 2011), 8–9.
27. Donahue and Harrington, *Gospel of Mark*, 60; Malbon, *Mark's Jesus*, 59.
28. Malbon, *Mark's Jesus*, 60–61, 66.
29. The Greek word *christos* means anointed; the Hebrew word *māšîaḥ* means anointed one. Donahue and Harrington, *Gospel of Mark*, 25.
30. For an overview of some of the meaning of these terms in the first century, see Malbon, *Mark's Jesus*, 62–66. For instance, "son of God" in the Bible refers to "a person or people with a special relationship to God, often with a special role in salvation history" (65).
31. Rhoads, Dewey, and Michie, *Mark as Story*, 104; Malbon, *Mark's Jesus*, 77.
32. Witherington, *Gospel of Mark*, 59.
33. Rhoads, Dewey, and Michie, *Mark as Story*, 105.
34. Donahue and Harrington, *Gospel of Mark*, 17; Witherington, *Gospel of Mark*, 18–19.
35. There are, however, some textual problems with this passage, with some early manuscripts reading "stirred with anger" rather than compassion. See Bruce M. Metzger, *A Textual Commentary on the Greek New Testament*, 2nd ed. (Stuttgart: Deutsche Bibelgesellschaft, 1994), 65; Huntsman, *Miracles of Jesus*, 45, 148n9.
36. Expressions of astonishment and a desire to follow Jesus are repeated fifteen times in the Gospel of Mark.
37. For more information and the debate surrounding Jesus's statement, see Witherington, *Gospel of Mark*, 227–29.
38. Among the many scholars who have made this observation are Strauss, *Four Portraits*, 183–85; Witherington, *Gospel of Mark*, 239; Donahue and Harrington, *Gospel of Mark*, 264–65; France, *Gospel of Mark*, 11.
39. France, *Gospel of Mark*, 11–14; Donahue and Harrington, *Gospel of Mark*, 46–50.
40. Martin Kahler, *The So-Called Historical Jesus and the Historic Biblical Christ* (Philadelphia: Fortress Press, 1964), 80.
41. Witherington, *Gospel of Mark*, 301.
42. Donald H. Juel, *The Gospel of Mark* (Nashville: Abingdon, 1999), 139.
43. Strauss, *Four Portraits*, 194; Rhoads, Dewey, and Michie, *Mark as Story*, 9; Donahue and Harrington, *Gospel of Mark*, 460; Witherington, *Gospel of Mark*, 412–13.
44. For a discussion of an open versus a closed story, see Wolfgang Iser, *The Implied Reader* (Baltimore: John Hopkins Press, 1974), especially chapter 11. For a look at how New Testament scholars have used the idea of an open ending to explain the unsettling conclusion of Mark's Gospel, see Thomas E. Boomershine and Gilbert L. Bartholomew, "The Narrative Technique of Mark 16:8," *Journal of Biblical Literature* 100 (1981):

213–23; David J. Hester, "Dramatic Inconclusion: Irony and the Narrative Rhetoric of the Ending of Mark," *Journal for the Study of the New Testament* 17, no. 57 (1995): 61–86; Norman R. Petersen, "When Is the End Not the End? Literary Reflections on the Ending of Mark's Narrative," *Interpretation* 34, no. 2 (1980): 151–66.

Chapter Six

In Times of Discouragement, Remember the Widow of Nain

KEITH J. WILSON

Sometimes in the ups and downs of life, we can feel like God is not very active in our day-to-day lives. Our patterns seem rather tedious and monotonous. Not much changes, and it is hard to point to one area where God has directly intervened in our circumstances. Whenever I am hit with these pedestrian feelings in my own life, I often think of a woman in the New Testament who may have felt this way. She is not named in the scriptures but is simply known by the name of her village and by her marital status.

The woman is the widow of Nain, and only the evangelist Luke records her amazing story. For me she represents the essence of the Savior's personalized ministry and how He reached out to the overlooked and forgotten of his society. This account soundly settles the issue about whether God knows us and cares about us.

A brief synopsis of the miracle from Luke chapter 7 depicts Jesus intercepting a burial procession and miraculously bringing a dead young man back to life. But there is much more to understand about the setting. As with all miracles, but especially so with this one, the context is vital to understanding this incident. Having taught at the Brigham Young University

Jerusalem Center, let me share with you some personal insights about this miracle.

Nain was a small farming village at Jesus's time, nestled up against Mount Moreh, which defined the east side of the Jezreel Valley. The town itself was off the beaten path. Access to it was limited to a single road. During Jesus's time, this hamlet would have been small and relatively poor, and it has remained that way ever since. At times in its history, this town has encircled as few as thirty-five homes and just 157 people. Today it is home to about 1,500 inhabitants.[1]

Luke begins his vignette by noting that Jesus was in Capernaum the day before and had healed the Centurion's servant (see Luke 7:11). Then we learn that "*the day after*" (verse 11; emphasis added), the Savior went into a city called Nain, accompanied by a large group of disciples. This sequence is very important. Capernaum is situated on the northern shore of the Sea of Galilee, at an elevation of 600 feet (183 m) below sea level. Nain is about thirty miles (forty-eight km) away from Capernaum at 700 feet (213 m) above sea level, thus requiring an arduous, uphill climb to Nain. In order to walk from Capernaum to Nain, it would have taken at least one or two days. Recently it took a group of youthful BYU Jerusalem Center students ten hours to walk this route on paved roads. This means that Jesus probably had to arise very early or possibly even walk during the night in order to intercept the burial procession "the day after."[2]

As Christ approached the city after a very taxing journey, a young man in his twenties was being carried out on a burial slab. Luke tells us that this young man was a widow's only son, and some scholars interpret the Greek text to imply that she has no other offspring.[3] A large group of villagers accompanied her in this most unfortunate family tragedy.

Obviously, having a son die would be a tragedy for anyone, but consider the implications for this widow. Just what would it have meant socially, spiritually, and financially to be a widow without an inheritor in ancient Israel? In Jewish culture, it was believed that when a husband died before old age, it was a sign of God's judgment for sin. Thus, through the law of retribution, God was meting out punishment upon this surviving widow. In the Old Testament, when Naomi was widowed at an early age, she bemoaned, "After all, the Lord is against me, and the Almighty has broken me" (Ruth 1:21, International Standard Version).[4]

Not only was there spiritual and emotional pain, but this widow of Nain was also facing financial ruin—even staring starvation in the face. Upon marriage, a woman was assigned to her husband's family for financial protection. If he died, then her care was delegated to her birthright son. Now that this widow's birthright and only son was dead, she was at the end of her rope financially. She probably was a middle-aged woman, living in a small, secluded farm town, and now found herself spiritually, socially, and financially destitute.

Precisely at the narrow window of time when the villagers were carrying this woman's son out to be buried, Jesus happened upon the procession and has "compassion on her" (Luke 7:13). Actually, this might be Luke's greatest understatement. Jesus somehow sensed the utterly desperate situation of this widow. Perhaps she had spent the night sprawled on her dirt floor, begging Heavenly Father to know why. Perhaps she had even openly questioned why he was requiring her to live any longer on this earth. Or perhaps she was terrified of the pending loneliness that she was facing. We do not know. But we do know that the Savior chose to leave Capernaum immediately, which likely required him to walk through the night in order to intercept the burial procession right before they put the body in the ground.

Yes, when he saw her tear-stained face walking behind that slab, Jesus felt great compassion for this woman—but it came from feelings that he experienced long before he just "happened" to intercept that burial entourage. He had clearly planned to be there in her moment of need.

Jesus then told the widow to "weep not" (verse 13). Unafraid of ritual uncleanness, he touched the palette, and the procession "stood still." He then forcefully commanded, "Young man, I say unto thee, Arise.

"And he that was dead sat up, and began to speak. And [Jesus] delivered him to his mother" (verses 14–15). Naturally, the crowd of villagers and Jesus's followers were awestruck as their shared grief turned to pure joy. But this miracle was not just about impressing a small farming community. It was all about rescuing one desperate soul. Jesus was aware that something was very wrong for this woman—someone who was a true "nobody" in their culture. Her situation cried out for his immediate attention, even if he had to skip a night's rest. He knew her desperate situation, and he came running. President Thomas S. Monson spoke undeniable truth when he said, "One day, when we look back at the seeming coincidences of our lives, we will realize that perhaps they weren't so coincidental after all."[5]

Now, as uplifting as this incident is, it must become much more than a cool Bible story to us. It verifies unmistakably that Jesus knew about this poor, forgotten, and destitute widow. Especially when we feel forgotten or overlooked or insignificant, we must remember: Jesus hurried to the widow, and he will hurry to us as well. Additionally, a second reason we all must remember this account is that the Lord intends for you to bless others around you. Many within your circle will be discouraged from time to time. If you can tell them about "Sister Nain" and how the Lord knew precisely her discouragement and great personal crisis, it will change night to day. Remember President Spencer W. Kimball's great observation: "God does notice us, and he watches over us. But it is usually through another person that he meets our needs."[6]

Of all Jesus's miracles during his time on earth, few are as tender and compassionate as his ministering to the widow of Nain. It reminds us that we matter to him, that he will never forget us. We cannot forget that.

Keith J. Wilson is an associate teaching professor of ancient scripture at Brigham Young University.

Keith J. Wilson, "In Times of Discouragement, Remember the Widow of Nain," *Ensign,* April 2019, 12–17.

NOTES

1. See E. Mills, *Census of Palestine 1931: Population of Villages, Towns and Administrative Areas* (Jerusalem: Palestine Government, 1932), 75.
2. See S. Kent Brown, *The Testimony of Luke: Brigham Young University New Testament Commentary* (Provo, UT: BYU Studies, 2015), 364; also see D. Kelly Ogden, *Verse by Verse: The Four Gospels* (Salt Lake City: Deseret Book, 2006), 229.
3. See Brown, *The Testimony of Luke,* 365.
4. In Isaiah 54:4, the Lord tells the widow Israel that she will "no longer remember the disgrace of [her] abandonment" (New English Translation).
5. Thomas S. Monson, in Joseph B. Wirthlin, "Lessons Learned in the Journey of Life," *Ensign,* December 2000, 7; *Liahona,* May 2001, 38.
6. *Teachings of Presidents of the Church: Spencer W. Kimball* (Salt Lake City: The Church of Jesus Christ of Latter-day Saints, 2006), 82.

Chapter Seven

They Ministered unto Him of Their Substance

Women and the Savior

CAMILLE FRONK OLSON

Various images symbolize and typify Jesus Christ in scripture. He is Alpha and Omega (see Revelation 1:8; Doctrine and Covenants 19:1; 35:1) and the author and finisher of our faith (see Hebrews 12:2). He personifies the love of God in the tree of life (see 1 Nephi 11:7; 15:36) and the Bread of Life in the manna in the wilderness (see John 6:31–35). Often, the typology of Christ conveys male imagery; for example, the Savior is the male lamb without blemish that is sacrificed for sin (see Exodus 12:5), the mighty man of war who conquers every enemy (see Isaiah 42:13), and the Good Shepherd who gives his life for his sheep (see Isaiah 40:11; Hebrews 13:20; Helaman 7:18).

Other scriptural metaphors of Christ express female imagery. He is as the pained woman in childbirth, crying in anguish as she brings forth life (see Isaiah 42:14); the mother who caresses and comforts her troubled child (see Isaiah 66:13; Psalm 131:2); and the mother hen who gathers her chicks under her wings (see 3 Nephi 10:4–6; Doctrine and Covenants 10:65; Luke 13:34). The Savior's merciful mission of salvation is further linked to the pains and unselfishness of motherhood by the same Hebrew root (*rhm*) that produces the word for Christ's compassion and a mother's womb.

In spite of such ways that the Messiah was likened to women, Jewish society at the time of Christ did not typically acknowledge the value of women or consider ways that women could contribute to their religious worship. On the contrary, men in first-century Palestine frequently marginalized women and distrusted their witness. For example, on that first Easter morning, the disciples questioned the women's report of the empty tomb, concluding that their words were merely "idle tales" (Luke 24:11). Even today these New Testament women and their testimonies are easily overlooked, which obscures their potential to inspire us. This chapter will consider the Savior's sacrifice and victory over death from the perspective of these women with the hope that they may lead us to a renewed appreciation for his enabling power and promises.

A couple of general observations will be helpful in establishing the larger context for this paper.

First, a comparison of the testimonies of Matthew, Mark, Luke, and John reflects conflicting details surrounding the witnesses of Christ's resurrection. Attempts to perfectly harmonize the various accounts have proved disappointing except to conclude that an unspecified number of men and women in Palestine had a personal encounter with the resurrected Lord. Exactly who saw him where and when must remain somewhat nebulous.

The Nephites' witness of the resurrected Christ provides a parallel scenario in that the specific order in which a multitude approached their Savior seems irrelevant. From the Book of Mormon we simply know that 2,500 men, women, and children came forward "one by one" to see with their eyes and feel with their hands the prints of the nails in their Redeemer's resurrected body. Each of them could thereafter bear record that he was unquestionably Jesus Christ, whom the prophets had testified would be slain for the sins of the world (3 Nephi 11:10–15).

My second general observation: the purpose of scripture is to testify of the Savior's victory over sin and the grave. Holy writ proclaims that none is like Jesus Christ; he alone is Redeemer and Savior. Therefore, the focus of the Gospel narratives is not to communicate that any of the disciples was more deserving, more loved, or more righteous than the other followers of Jesus. They were not written to indicate that God views an apostle's witness with greater merit than one professed by other disciples or that a man's testimony is more valuable than a woman's. Furthermore, the scriptures do not teach that women are innately more spiritual or receptive to revelation than men, or that either men or women have less need of Christ's enabling power than the other. Rather, the scriptures jointly testify that each of us is lost and in desperate need of a Redeemer. In this way, every man, woman, and child who encountered the resurrected Lord in the meridian of time is a type of each of us. Through their individual and combined experiences, we are led to discover and proclaim our own personal witness of Jesus Christ.

The Women's Identity

Who were the women near the cross and at the empty tomb? Collectively, Matthew, Mark, Luke, and John name several women in the passion narratives, noting that they all came from Galilee.

1. Mary, the mother of Jesus (see John 19:25)

2. Mary Magdalene, the only woman named in all four Gospels (see Matthew 27:56; 28:1; Mark 15:40; 16:1, 9; Luke 24:10; John 19:25; 20:1, 11–18)

3. Mary, the mother of James and Joses (see Matthew 27:56; 28:1; Mark 15:40; 16:1; Luke 24:10; perhaps the same as number 1 because she also had sons named James and Joses; see Matthew 13:55; Mark 6:3)

4. The mother of Zebedee's children (perhaps the same as number 5; see Matthew 27:56)

5. Salome (perhaps the same person as "the mother of Zebedee's children" because they appear in nearly identical lists of women in two of the Gospels) (see Mark 15:40; 16:1)

6. Joanna (see Luke 24:10)

7. The sister of Jesus's mother (see John 19:25)

8. Mary, the wife of Cleophas (see John 19:25)

9. "And many other women which came up with him [from Galilee] unto Jerusalem" (Mark 15:41; see also Luke 23:49, 55–56)

Of all the Gospel writers, only Luke introduces us to these "Galilean women" *before* the death and resurrection of Christ. Because Luke records few of their names in his earlier narrative, we cannot definitively conclude that all of these women were also those at the cross. We can, however, glean general insights into those women who attended the Savior at his death and burial from a study of these women who became disciples earlier in Galilee.

In Luke 8:1–3, in addition to Mary Magdalene and Joanna, (here identified as "the wife of Chuza, Herod's steward"), we learn that a woman named Susanna and "many others [women]"[1] in Galilee, received the Savior's healing from "evil spirits and infirmities." With their lives transformed, these women formed an important core to the Savior's unofficial entourage as he and the Twelve traveled "throughout every city and village" (verse 1). They were not, however, merely tagging along. Jesus and his itinerant company depended on the goodness of others to provide daily nourishment and a place to sleep. Apparently these good women assisted in the Lord's sustenance because they "ministered unto him of their substance" (verse 3), meaning they supported him from their own resources.

The implication here is that these women had access to ample means and the freedom to divest of it in the way they deemed pertinent. Additionally, they appear to have had the support and blessing of husbands or families to be relieved of traditional domestic duties in order to serve the Savior in this way. At least one of the women, Joanna, was married. Others may have been widowed or single. One wonders at the social ramifications for a group of women who traveled around the country with Jesus and his Apostles. Did they attend the entourage during the day and return to their own homes at night? Were any of them related to one of the male disciples? Did their children ever accompany them, or had they already reared their children? Whatever the circumstance, their commitment to the Savior was not episodic; these women continued to follow him to Jerusalem—to his crucifixion, his burial, and his resurrection.

In Luke 7–8, in verses surrounding Luke's brief description of these generous women from Galilee, he recounts the stories of specific women whose lives were forever changed through encounters with the Savior. Notably, we read of the widow of Nain (see Luke 7:11–15), the woman who loved the Savior so much that she washed his feet with her tears (see Luke 7:36–50), the mother of Jesus (see Luke 8:19–21), the daughter of Jairus (Luke 8:41–42, 49–56); and the woman who was healed of a serious illness by touching the hem of the Savior's clothing (see Luke 8:43–48).

Were at least some of these women among the Galilean ensemble that shared their resources to support Jesus along with Mary Magdalene, Joanna, and Susanna? Were any of these specific women of Galilee among those who stood by Jesus as he hung on the cross and was buried in the tomb? Although no conclusive answer to these questions is possible, except in the case of the mother of Jesus and Mary Magdalene, we can at least think of these women as representative of the faithful Galilean women who attended the Savior in the passion narratives. More importantly, they can teach us about coming to Christ and laying hold on his Atonement.

Widow of Nain

Upon his arrival in Nain, Jesus encountered a funeral procession just exiting the village. Jesus immediately identified the mother of the dead man, knowing that she was a widow and that the dead was her only son. The small village of Nain is located about seven miles southeast of Nazareth, the village where the Savior grew to manhood. One wonders, was Jesus previously acquainted with the widow's family? Recognizing that he was in Capernaum the day before, a distance of some thirty miles,[2] Jesus would have had a rigorous and speedy walk to arrive in Nain at precisely the moment between the young man's death and burial. The details of the story suggest he came knowingly and specifically to help this widow.

We better appreciate the Lord's instinctive compassion for the widow when we realize that at her husband's death, his estate would have first gone to their son, then after the son's death, to the closest male relative.[3] Without her son, the widow had no means of support and would be left a vulnerable target for exploitation in her society.

Into this poignant funeral scene walked Jesus. He approached the mourning mother and uttered a seemingly impossible command, "Weep not" (Luke 7:13). As the only One with power to give hope and joy in the face of loss, the Savior brings life even when we have not asked. With a touch of his hand and the power of his word, the young man arose, and Christ "delivered him to his mother" (verses 14–15). Through his atoning sacrifice, the Savior heals broken hearts, restores families, and gives life, even eternal life. No distance is too great to separate us from his mercy and grace.

The Woman Who Loved Much

While a Pharisee named Simon hosted Jesus for dinner, a Galilean woman entered his house carrying an alabaster vial filled with expensive ointment. The scriptures introduce her as simply "a woman in the city, which was a sinner" (Luke 7:37). The Greek verb here is a past tense, suggesting that she was known in the town and *had been* a sinner but was a sinner no longer.[4] She had changed.

We do not know what her specific sins were, only that they were "many" (verse 47). The most common assumption is that she was a prostitute—because she was a woman of means, indicated by her possession of an expensive vial of ointment, and had committed publicly known sins. Many other possibilities could qualify for public "sins" committed by women at the time. For example, the woman may have openly interacted with gentiles or others considered "unclean" for her livelihood. Simon knew her sin because he belonged to the town but expected Jesus to know it by inspiration, if he really was the Prophet,[5] leading us to surmise that one could not deduce her sinful life by her outward appearance.

By teasing out the scriptural text, we may conclude that the woman must have already repented of her sins after a previous encounter with the message of salvation. When she knew that Jesus was at Simon's house, she made preparations to demonstrate her gratitude to him by anointing his feet with the ointment.

Actually being in the presence of Jesus after her repentance, however, caused deeper emotions in the woman than she may have anticipated. She began to weep when she saw him, and her tears flowed with the ointment. Wiping his feet with her hair rather than a cloth suggests that her tears were spontaneous and she had no other means to wipe them.[6] Repentant and profoundly humble, she fell at her Savior's feet and kissed them with overwhelming reverence.

By contrast, Simon's self-righteousness bore unspoken witness that he felt that he needed no Redeemer. While the woman wept in humble adoration, Simon silently rebuffed Jesus for allowing a sinner to touch him thus, concluding that this was evidence that Jesus was no prophet. Knowing Simon's thoughts, Jesus told him the parable of two debtors, each of whom were subsequently forgiven of their debts: "There was a certain creditor which had two debtors: the one owed five hundred pence, and the other fifty. And when they had nothing to pay, he frankly forgave them both. Tell me therefore, which of them will love him most?" (Luke 7:41–42).

In a question pointed to Simon but also meant to be heard by the woman, Jesus asked, "Tell me therefore, which of them will love [the creditor] most?" Simon logically and accurately answered, "I suppose he, to whom he forgave most" (Luke 7:42–43). Only those who have truly repented of sins and willingly turned their lives over to Jesus Christ see themselves as owing more than they can ever repay.

Who loves the Savior most? All those who recognize they have sinned, fallen short, and are forever lost without the atoning blood of Jesus Christ. Bankrupt in spirit and burdened by sin, we come to Christ as unprofitable servants. In such a helpless plight, none of us claims that our sin is merely a fifty-pence problem. Our debt is greater than we can ever repay, time immemorial.

Although the story of her repentance is not explicitly detailed in scripture, it is clearly implied. Christ acknowledged the woman's soul-felt repentance by telling Simon, "Her sins, which are many, are forgiven; for she loved much: but to whom little is forgiven, the same loveth little." Then turning directly to the woman, Jesus proclaimed, "Thy sins are forgiven. . . . Thy faith hath saved thee; go in peace" (7:47–50). The Savior's forgiveness of the woman was not a consequence of her love for him at that moment, or of her tears and expensive ointment. Her love for the Savior was a product of his cleansing gift of repentance. Through her sincere acceptance of the Lord's Atonement, the Galilean woman who loved much teaches us to reverence our Redeemer because of his gifts of repentance and complete forgiveness. How can we not, therefore, fall at his feet and manifest our profound love and gratitude to him?

The Mother of Jesus

Luke next identifies the mother of Jesus among the Galilean women. Presumably still a resident of Nazareth, Mary the mother of Jesus and her other sons went to hear Jesus when he came to town. How rarely did she get to talk with him alone or care for him as his mother? Did her other sons, whom we know did not believe in Jesus's mission at the time (John 7:3–5), keep her from following him when he was away? On this particular day, because of the "press" of the crowd, she was again too far away to see him (Luke 8:19). Some of those in the crowd recognized her and her other sons as the family of Jesus and sent word to Jesus that they were there: "Thy mother and thy brethren stand without, desiring to see thee" (verse 20). One expects Jesus to part the crowd to allow his family to be in front near him, but that is not what happens. Instead Jesus answered, "My mother and my brethren are these [did he motion toward the entire crowd of people?] which hear the word of God, and do it" (verse 21). With his mother near the back of the crowd, Jesus explained that rather than biological kinship, his family consisted of all those who receive and follow his teachings. Being numbered within the household of God is not, therefore, based on lineal descent but rather on a willing acceptance of his commandments to live by them.

Mary exemplified what the Lord meant by hearing the word of God and doing it from the time the angel appeared to her to announce that she would bear the Son of God. She responded with faith, "Be it unto me according to thy word" (Luke 1:38), not knowing what hardships her discipleship would require of her. Her conviction to do whatever God required echoed the greater words of passion and assurance that her Son cried in the Garden of Gethsemane, "Father, if thou be willing, remove this cup from me: nevertheless not my will, but thine, be done" (Luke 22:42).

When Mary and Joseph took the infant Jesus to the temple to offer a sacrifice according to the law (see Leviticus 12:6–8; Numbers 18:15), the Holy Spirit taught an elderly man named Simeon that this baby was the long-awaited Messiah. When Simeon spoke, however, he did not say that he saw the Messiah but that his eyes were looking upon God's salvation. By revelation, he knew that embodied in this tiny babe were all our hopes and promises for eternity.

Speaking prophetically, Simeon then soberly declared, "This child is set for the fall and rising again of many in Israel; and for a sign which shall be spoken against" (Luke 2:34). Turning to Mary, he continued, "A sword shall pierce through thy own soul also that the thoughts of many hearts may be revealed" (verse 35). In other words, because of this child's future mission, many in Israel would be faced with a decision that would lead them either to destruction or to the highest heights. That option for Israel, however, would come at a tremendous cost to Jesus through their rejection of his teachings and Atonement and through his humiliating death on the cross.

Furthermore, this clash of reactions to the Savior would not leave his mother unscathed. Mary's soul would also be wounded during her Son's ministry through divisions within her own family.[7] Discipleship with Jesus Christ transcends family ties. When we are born again, when we "hear the word of God, and do it" (Luke 8:21), Jesus Christ becomes our Father, and we become his daughters and his sons. As Mary waited to see Jesus from the back of the Galilean crowd, was her heart pierced when she realized that her Son was not hers alone, but only hers to give to the world? And when Jesus hung on the cross, his mother "stood" right there by him (John 19:25). Rather than hiding away, she assumed the shame and pain of crucifixion by her very presence at the cross. Her witness required no words; she stood for truth and righteousness.

As a model of discipleship, Mary demonstrates another important principle for us. Mary is part of the Savior's family not because she gave birth to him but because she received God's word and followed it. The fact that she was his mother did not reduce her need to "hear the word of God, and do it" any less than us. Mary reminds us that blood lineage is no substitute for the enabling blood of the Atonement of Jesus Christ. Every one of us, whatever our particular circumstance or family background, is invited to accept Christ's gift of salvation and join his holy family.

The Daughter of Jairus and the Woman Who Touched the Hem of His Garment

The stories of Jesus raising the daughter of Jairus from the dead and healing the woman with the issue of blood are intertwined in the Luke 8 account. They are therefore most meaningful when viewed together.

Jairus's only daughter, probably his only descendant (see verse 42),[8] was dying at the age of twelve, just as she was coming of age as an adult in her society. Jairus, a ruler of the local synagogue, was forthright and confident yet humbly knelt at Jesus's feet to petition for his help. The Lord had more to teach Jairus, however, before answering his request. The girl was dead when they finally arrived at Jairus's home, but that was part of Jesus's lesson for her father. In the interim, Jairus witnessed someone with greater faith in the Savior's power than he possessed at his first petition to Christ. Walking toward his home with Jesus, Jairus saw such faith exemplified in the form of a woman who had been ill for as long as his daughter had lived.

The woman, known not by her name but by her disease, was not dead but was just as good as dead, considering her hopeless circumstance that isolated her from society. The scriptures do not specify the cause of her bleeding, but it is generally considered to have been gynecological in nature. According to the law of Moses, such an illness rendered the woman ritually unclean and anything or anyone that she touched was subsequently rendered unclean (see Leviticus 15:25–31). Her bed, eating utensils, and food she prepared were tainted. Most likely, her family members no longer touched her, and her friends abandoned her long ago.

Luke reports that the woman "spent all her living upon physicians" without a positive resolution (Luke 8:43). This description suggests that she was a wealthy woman at one time—but no more. The woman therefore represents depletion in nearly every way—physically, socially, financially, and emotionally—but not spiritually.[9] In the midst of all her distress, buried in the impossibility of her circumstance, she had one shining hope. With a boldness and determination that must have stretched her weakened body to its limits, the woman crafted a plan to access her Savior without anyone's notice. Accustomed to being invisible to society and likely physically weakened by her disease to preclude her from standing much, the woman reached out from her reduced position on the ground to touch the border of the Savior's robe as he passed by.

Luke tells us that "immediately" the woman knew she was healed physically (verse 44). The Savior's Atonement, however, extends beyond mending physical pain. He heals broken hearts and sick souls. He makes us whole, spirit and body. At that very moment she knew her body was healed, Jesus turned to ask, "Who touched me?" (verse 45). The surrounding crowd was oblivious to what was happening. This was between the woman and her Savior. Jesus had a further gift to offer to this woman—but it would require even greater faith on her part. By touching merely the hem of his garment, the woman may have believed that she could be healed without rendering the Savior unclean and without calling down further denunciation and disgust from her neighbors. Now she must stretch her faith to publicly acknowledge what she had done.

After confessing before the townspeople, including a leader of the synagogue, that she was the one who touched him, the Savior called her "daughter" (verse 48). This marginalized woman exemplified the faith needed to "hear the word of God and do it." Because of her exceeding faith in him, Jesus openly numbered her among his family and pronounced her whole. She was healed both inwardly and outwardly.

As one of the awestruck bystanders who witnessed this miracle, Jairus suddenly received word, "Thy daughter is dead; trouble not the Master" (verse 49). To him, Jesus said, "Fear not: believe only, and she shall be made whole" (verse 50). How different did these words of assurance sound to Jairus after witnessing this woman's great faith? Was anything too hard for the Lord? When we wholeheartedly come to Christ in our distress, knowing that he is our only hope, he renews, enlarges, and enhances the quality of our lives through his atoning blood.

MARY MAGDALENE

In all but one of the twelve times that Mary Magdalene is mentioned in the four Gospels, she is alone or named first in a list of women. The sole exception is in John's account of the women at the Crucifixion, when the mother of Jesus is listed before her (see John 19:25). The primacy of her name in these lists and the frequency of her mention suggest that Mary Magdalene was a leader among the women and the Christian movement. Perhaps that is one reason that Luke specifically named her as one of the Galilean women who ministered to Jesus in his travels and the one out of whom Jesus cast "seven devils" (Luke 8:2).

Mary's ailment involving seven devils may say more about the magnitude of Christ's power to heal than her previous spiritual, emotional, or moral health. The number seven in scripture often connotes completeness and wholeness. In announcing Mary's cure, Luke may simply be confirming that through the power of Christ, Mary was completely healed, she was made whole, or that she was completely liberated from her illness, whatever its nature.[10]

In all four Gospels, among the Galilean women who followed Jesus to Jerusalem, Mary Magdalene is specifically mentioned. She was clearly one of the women who was an active witnesses of his Crucifixion.[11] As sheep without their shepherd, these women joined the burial procession to observe where the body was buried and perhaps to observe which burial procedures were completed. Scripture implies that time did not allow for the customary sprinkling of spices and perfumed ointment on the strips of cloth used to wrap around the body prior to burial.[12] Because women were typically the ones who prepared and applied the fragrances, the women of Galilee may have concluded the need to return after the Sabbath for this purpose.

The Gospel narratives as well as traditions that preceded their writing imply that Mary Magdalene and other women from Galilee were the first to discover the empty tomb early on that first Easter morning.[13] Shortly afterward, other disciples witnessed the empty tomb and departed again, filled with their own questions and desires to understand what had occurred, leaving Mary Magdalene alone at the scene. The Gospel of John directs us to follow her quest and subsequent revelation, but no doubt other disciples could testify of their own parallel experience. Mary remained stationed at the empty tomb, seemingly determined not to depart until she learned what had happened to the body of Jesus.

Mary Magdalene did not recognize the Savior when he first appeared and spoke to her, calling her by a nonspecific term, "Woman" (John 20:13). She assumed that he was the gardener. Was her eyesight sufficiently blurred because of her tears, or had Jesus' physical appearance changed to obstruct recognition? Importantly, Mary did not comprehend the Savior's resurrection when she discovered the empty tomb or even when she saw the resurrected Christ with her natural eyes. Perhaps the risen Lord wanted Mary Magdalene to recognize and know him through her spiritual eyes and ears. In a similar way, the two disciples on the road to Emmaus could not initially recognize the resurrected Christ because their "eyes were holden" (Luke 24:16). Only after he departed did they decipher what had just happened. "Did not our heart burn within us, while he talked with us by the way, and while he opened to us the scriptures?" (Luke 24:32). The resurrected Lord wanted them to know him by the spirit and not through their physical sight. Furthermore, the Savior's use of the generic term "woman" in addressing Mary Magdalene may invite each of us, whether man or woman, to put ourselves in Mary's place to likewise use our spiritual sight to discern divine truth.

When the Lord said her name, "Mary," something clicked in her, and her spiritual eyes were opened (John 20:16). Suddenly her encounter with the resurrected Lord had become very personal. In an example of what Jesus taught by way of metaphor in John 10, Mary heard the voice of the Good Shepherd when "he calleth his own sheep by name, and leadeth them out" (John 10:3).

Addressing him as her Master, Mary must have instinctively reached out to him and touched him in some way because the Lord's response, "Touch me not," directed her to discontinue whatever it was that she was doing (John 20:17).[14] Other translations of the Savior's directive are, "Don't cling to me" or "Don't hold me back," which is reflected in the Joseph Smith Translation, "Hold me not." Perhaps Mary anticipated that Jesus had returned to remain with his followers forever and resume their association. In her anxious desire not to lose him again, she wanted to cling to him to keep him there.

He had to leave again, because he had not yet ascended to his Father. One final event in his great victory—returning to the presence of his Father—remained to be accomplished. As he has promised each of us if we come in faith to him and apply his atoning sacrifice in our lives, he will bring us to be "at one" with the Father again.

Many have asked why Mary Magdalene received this remarkable experience. We could just as easily ask, why not her? We do not need a unique calling, title, or relationship with the Savior different from any other disciple to receive a spiritual witness. We need a broken heart, faith in him, and an opportunity for him to teach us. If for no other reason, she may have received this blessing simply because she lingered in a quiet spot rather than running off to talk with others. Some of our Church leaders have observed that we would have more spiritual experiences if we didn't talk so much about them.[15] Mary Magdalene teaches us to be still and *learn* that he is God (see Psalm 46:10; Doctrine and Covenants 101:16).

Conclusion

In large measure, the women of Galilee remain anonymous, thereby putting the focus and importance where it should be—on Jesus Christ. In a very personal and palpable way, each of those women was a recipient and eyewitness of the Savior's sacrifice not only at the end but *during* his mortal ministry. The Atonement was efficacious in their daily lives in Galilee. The enduring discipleship in each of these women bears witness to the retroactive and infinite power of the Atonement.

The women of Galilee also remind us that God loves all his children and is no respecter of persons. Men and women are alike unto him. They also exemplify that lack of a title or position of authority does not exclude someone from a remarkable spiritual witness. Through the power of the Atonement in experiences that prefigured the Savior's own death and Resurrection, a woman—the widow of Nain—received her only son back to life, and a man—Jairus—witnessed his only daughter die and then live again. And while pondering the meaning of the empty tomb, Mary Magdalene received the visit of the Lord, as did his chosen apostles.

Finally, the women of Galilee prod us to use our agency wisely to come to him, no matter how hopeless our circumstance or how marginalized we may feel in society. Without fanfare or many words, they reinforce the poignant principle that it is by hearing the Lord's teachings and doing them that we join his family, rather than claiming privilege through notable acquaintance or family ties.

During the weeks following the Savior's resurrection, "the women and Mary the mother of Jesus, and his brethren" were numbered among the 120 faithful disciples of Christ (Acts 1:14). When these disciples bore witness "in other tongues" (Acts 2:4) of the "wonderful works of God" (verse 11) on the day of Pentecost, the apostle Peter explained the phenomenon by citing an ancient prophecy: "And it shall come to pass in the last days, saith God, I will pour out of my Spirit upon all flesh: and your sons and your daughters shall prophesy, . . . and on my servants and on my handmaidens I will pour out in those days of my Spirit; and they shall prophecy" (verses 16–18; see also Joel 2:28–29).

In the meridian of time, the church of Jesus Christ commenced after multitudes heard both men and women bear witness of their Redeemer.

Our recognition of the breadth of the Savior's power will likewise increase when we hear and appreciate the testimonies of all those who know the Lord—even those whose perspective may be different from our own. When both men and women fervently testify of the stunning reality of the Atonement in their lives, we are all blessed.

Camille Fronk Olson is a professor emeritus of ancient scripture at Brigham Young University.

Camille Fronk Olson, "They Ministered unto Him of Their Substance: Women and the Savior," in *To Save the Lost*, ed. Richard Neitzel Holzapfel and Kent P. Jackson (Provo, UT: Religious Studies Center, Brigham Young University, 2009), 61–80.

NOTES

1. In Greek, "others" in Luke 8:3 is a feminine plural, clarifying that all those who ministered unto Jesus of their substance were women.
2. Keith J. Wilson, "In Times of Discouragement, Remember the Widow of Nain," *Ensign*, April 2019, 14.
3. Vasiliki Limberis, "Widow of Nain," in *Women in Scripture*, ed. Carol Meyers (Grand Rapids, MI: Eerdmans, 2000), 439–40.
4. Barbara Reid, *Choosing the Better Part? Women in the Gospel of Luke* (Collegeville, MN: Liturgical Press, 1996), 113.
5. Joseph A. Fitzmyer, *The Gospel According to Luke I–IX*, Anchor Bible, vol. 28 (New York: Doubleday, 1981), 689.
6. I. Howard Marshall, *Commentary on Luke*, New International Greek Testament Commentary (Grand Rapids, MI: Eerdmans, 1978), 308–9.
7. Kenneth L. Barker and John R. Kohlengerger III, *The Expositor's Bible Commentary—Abridged Edition: New Testament* (Grand Rapids, MI: Zondervan, 1994), 219–20; Raymond E. Brown, Karl P. Donfried, Joseph A. Fitzmyer, and John Reumann, *Mary in the New Testament* (Philadelphia: Fortress Press, 1978), 154–57; Fitzmyer, *The Gospel According to Luke*, 429–30.
8. Fitzmyer, *The Gospel According to Luke*, 745.
9. Reid, *Choosing the Better Part?*, 139.
10. Reid, *Choosing the Better Part?*, 126.
11. Joseph A. Fitzmyer, *The Gospel According to Luke X–XXIV*, Anchor Bible, vol. 28A (New York: Doubleday, 1985), 1521.
12. F. F. Bruce, *The Gospel of John* (Grand Rapids, MI: Eerdmans, 1983), 379.
13. See Matthew 28:1–6; Mark 16:1–6; Luke 23:55–24:10. In John 20:1, Mary Magdalene alone discovers the empty tomb. In her report to the apostles in the following verse, however, she states, "we" do not know where he is, implying that others accompanied her in making this initial discovery, as the Synoptic Gospels report; see also Raymond E.

Brown, *The Gospel According to John XIII–XXI*, Anchor Bible, vol. 29A (New York: Doubleday, 1970), 977–78, 1001. Rather than suggesting that the women returned to anoint the body with fragrances, the *Gospel of Peter* posits that they came to appropriately "weep and lament" for the loss of a loved one, as "women are wont to do for those beloved of them who die" (verses 50–52, in W. Schneemelcher, ed., Robert McL. Wilson, trans., *New Testament Apocrypha* [Louisville, KY: John Knox, 1991], 1:225).

14. Brown, *The Gospel According to John XIII–XXI*, 992; Bruce, *The Gospel of John*, 389–90.
15. Neal A. Maxwell, quoting Marion G. Romney, in "Called to Serve," *BYU 1993–94 Devotional and Fireside Speeches* (Provo, UT: Brigham Young University, 1994), 137.

Chapter Eight

Jesus Christ and the Feast of Tabernacles

RYAN S. GARDNER

When John alludes to "the Jews' feast of tabernacles" and "that great day of the feast" in John 7:2, 37, he has immediately tapped into a considerable body of cultural, social, and religious images and knowledge in the hearts and minds of an audience from the first century AD who would have been familiar with contemporary Jewish practices.[1] However, youth and young adults in the twenty-first century are less likely to have sufficient understanding of this feast. By making the context of the Feast of Tabernacles explicit, teachers can help students better understand Jesus Christ's declarations in John 7–8 and the miracle he performs in John 9 so they can have greater faith in him and the power of his Atonement.[2]

Overview of the Feast of Tabernacles

Elder Bruce R. McConkie of the Quorum of the Twelve Apostles noted, "It appears to have been our Lord's deliberate design to dramatize the great truths relative to himself by associating them with the religious and social practices then prevailing."[3] Our students will likely miss the deliberate design of the Savior, which John intended to convey in John 7–9,[4] if we do not help them become familiar with the religious and social practices pertaining to the Feast of Tabernacles. Bruce K. Satterfield's research on the Feast of Tabernacles provides a critical foundation for this article, which intends to reinforce key points of his work and suggest further implications between the Feast of Tabernacles and the text in John.[5]

From the direct references to the Feast of Tabernacles in John 7 (see verses 2–3, 8, 10–11, 14, 37), we glean only a few scant details. We know that it was in Jerusalem where the temple was located (see John 7:3). As with all major feasts of the Jews, it was likely crowded—which made it possible for the Savior to arrive and stay "in secret" (John 7:10). The eight-day feast allowed Jesus to teach in the temple "about the midst of the feast" (John 7:14) and again on the "last day" of the feast (John 7:37). We also read that the last day of the feast was called the "great day of the feast" (John 7:37), although the text offers no explanation as to what this means. In other words, allusions to the location, popularity, and duration of the feast require additional explanation in order to optimize the edifying value of the Savior's teachings and healing in John 7–9.

In general, the Jewish feasts were both commemorative and instructive occasions. Activities and rituals during the feasts reminded Israelites of significant historical events and often anticipated future events.[6] The earliest scriptural injunctions concerning the Feast of Tabernacles, also known as the Feast of Booths, indicated to Israel that the feast was to help them remember "when [the Lord] brought them out of the land of Egypt" (Leviticus 23:43). For example, the children of Israel were commanded to construct and dwell in booths throughout the week of the feast to remind them of their years of wandering in the wilderness before the Lord brought them into the promised land. During one of the celebratory processions of the feast, those in the procession carried a lulab (a plume of branches from a tree or bush) in their right hands and a citron (a small citrus fruit) in the left. The lulab represented Israel's traveling through various types of foliage in their journey through the wilderness, and the citron signified the fruit of the land God had promised to his people.[7]

Other aspects of the feast—such as the water-drawing ceremony and the lighting of enormous lampstands in the courts of the temple in conjunction with the reading of messianic passages in Zechariah 14—pointed to the future coming of the Messiah, as will be discussed later in this paper.[8] The timing of the feast, held in the fall around the time of the yearly harvest, or ingathering, pointed both backward to the time when God gathered Israel out of Egypt and forward to the time of "the final harvest when Israel's mission should be completed, and all nations gathered unto the Lord."[9] Thus, Israelites who gathered to the temple in Jerusalem to celebrate the Feast of Tabernacles were inundated with festivities and symbols that inspired thoughts on a variety of themes, such as deliverance (past and future), the coming of the Messiah, and the eventual gathering of all God's children to him.

To help modern students better understand and apply some of the great truths found in John 7–9, teachers can explain four major aspects of the Feast of Tabernacles: (1) dwelling in booths, or *sukkot*; (2) the lighting of the lampstands in the Court of the Women; (3) the additional sacrifices and offerings throughout the week; and (4) the drawing of water from the Pool of Siloam and its pouring on the altar of the temple. Each of these ceremonies was deliberately designed to stir deep religious recollections and feelings in the hearts and minds of the participants.[10]

The Feast of Tabernacles lasted eight days, beginning on a Sabbath and ending on the next Sabbath (see Leviticus 23:39). It was also known as the Feast of Booths, or *sukkot*, because of the temporary booths or shelters participants constructed and lived in during the weeklong festival. Moses instructed the children of Israel throughout their generations to make booths of "the boughs of goodly trees, branches of palm trees, and the boughs of thick trees, and willows of the brook" (Leviticus 23:40). They were to dwell in these booths all week so they would always remember that the Lord "made the children of Israel to dwell in booths, when [he] brought them out of the land of Egypt" (Leviticus 23:43).

Thoughtful dwellers in these temporary booths might have pondered on their continual dependence upon the Lord God of Israel for deliverance (as they contemplated their historic deliverance from Egypt), direction (as they reflected on the Lord leading them through the wilderness), and security (as they gratefully considered the promised land in which they now lived). During the days of Israel's sovereignty, those dwelling in booths during the Feast of Tabernacles may have also thought about the freedom granted to them through the Lord (not entirely different from other holidays celebrating national freedom in many countries).[11] However, in Jesus's day, if celebrants pondered such freedom, their prayers would have been offered as a hope for future deliverance from Roman subjugation.

Following the evening sacrifice on the first day of the Feast of Tabernacles, the gates of the temple were left open so the public could gather in the Court of the Women[12] and participate in the lighting of four giant lampstands, each over seventy feet (twenty-one meters) tall. Each lampstand had four golden bowls filled with oil at their tops. Priests climbed ladders to each bowl and lit the wicks, which were made from the worn-out clothing of the priests collected throughout the year. The light from the lampstands was so bright that it was said to light up every courtyard in Jerusalem. The lighting ceremony was accompanied with music, singing, and dancing that lasted well into the night and even into the early-morning hours. It is unclear whether the ritual was performed anew every day or whether the lamps were simply kept lit throughout the week of the festival.[13]

While most participants in the Feast of Tabernacles would never see the sacred lampstand, or menorah, found in the holy place of the temple where only priests were allowed, this celebration brought a likeness of the same symbol into public view. Just as the golden lampstand in the holy place stood before the most holy place in the temple, these four impressive lampstands may have stirred participants to reflect on the need for inspired enlightenment to prepare them to return to God's presence.[14]

Throughout the Feast of Tabernacles more additional sacrifices were offered than were offered during Passover, the other major sacrificial feast—twice the number of rams and lambs and five times the number of bullocks. In addition, Alfred Edersheim points out that the number of each sacrifice—70 bullocks, 14 rams, 98 lambs, and 336 ephahs of flour for the meat offering—is divisible by seven. The number seven often signifies completion and perfection in Hebraic symbolism.[15] Many Israelites living in Jesus's day seem to have forgotten the true purpose and meaning of these sacrifices, which was to point them toward the Messiah (see 2 Nephi 25:24–25; Jacob 4:5). While sacrifice under the Mosaic law served several purposes, one major reason God instituted these sacrifices was to signify the "great and last sacrifice," which would accomplish the "infinite atonement which will suffice for the sins of the world" (see Alma 34:9–14).

The fourth significant event of the Feast of Tabernacles was "the drawing of water from Siloam and its libation [pouring] on the altar (of this it was said that he who has not seen the joy of the drawing of water at the Feast of Tabernacles does not know what joy is)" (Bible Dictionary, "Feasts"). The parade-like ritual of this ceremony was perhaps the most notable and popular event of the festival:

> During the preparation of the [morning] burnt offering, a procession of priests, with the accompaniment of singing and flute playing, wended their way from the temple down to the Pool of Siloam, where a priest filled a golden flask with water while a choir repeated Isaiah 12:3: "With joy shall ye draw water out of the wells of salvation.". . .
>
> The priests returned to the temple via the Water Gate, a gate on the south side of the wall immediately surrounding the temple within the Court of the Gentiles [where the procession was joined by other pilgrims who had come to the temple for the feast]. When they arrived at the Water Gate, a blast was made on a *shofar,* or ram's horn. . . .
>
> Upon the blasting of the *shofar,* the group moved toward the altar of sacrifice located in the Court of the Priests that immediately surrounded the temple. The priest carrying the golden flask filled with water ascended the altar and prepared to pour the libation on the morning burnt offering. While doing this, the procession [carrying their *lulabs* and citrons] that had followed the priest circled the altar. . . .
>
> The priest who had charge of pouring the water then offered the water libation with a wine libation in two silver bowls on the southwest corner of the altar.[16]

This ceremony was accompanied by great rejoicing and singing from the congregation. It was performed every day of the feast in the same way, "except on the seventh day, when the priests (and perhaps the pilgrims) circled the altar seven times instead of just once."[17]

This ritual performed at the sacrificial altar consists of several aspects that added to its spiritual richness. The Pool of Siloam received its water from the Gihon Spring, a natural water source, making the water in Siloam "living water," or water suitable for ritual purification. The concept of "living water" is critical to understanding the significance of this ceremony. Living water had to come directly from God (via rain or other "pure" or natural sources, such as a spring). It was used for all ordinances and rituals requiring water in the law of Moses. Based on recent archaeological research, the Pool of Siloam was likely a *mikveh*, an ancient ritual bath for purification, and not a reservoir for drinking water.[18] Thus, the water from Siloam symbolized the cleansing and sanctification necessary to prepare one to return to God.

The water from Gihon was channeled into the Pool of Siloam via Hezekiah's Tunnel, which had been dug to preserve the people of Jerusalem during the Assyrian siege in the days of Hezekiah (see 2 Kings 17–18). While the Pool of Siloam in Jesus's day was not likely the same pool as the one from Hezekiah's and Isaiah's day,[19] the site likely still reminded those in Jerusalem of God's power to preserve and deliver them in the face of overwhelming opposition and adversity.

The water-pouring ritual was also accompanied by a prayer of gratitude for the rains that had brought forth the harvest of the previous year and a plea for rain for the coming year to provide another harvest. On the eighth day of the feast, the "great day of the feast," which was also a Sabbath day, the water drawing and pouring ceremony was not performed, but a prayer for rain was still offered with the sacrifices. Thus, reflective participants in this ritual were drawn into a commemorative environment of gratitude and purification that signified their constant dependence on God—all centered on the most significant sacrificial site in all Israel, the altar of the temple.

Messianic Connections with the Feast of Tabernacles

These four aspects of the Feast of Tabernacles were impressive activities and ceremonies for stirring the religious memories and feelings of the people. However, their most significant value in the Savior's day consisted in their power to prepare the people to accept the Messiah and the salvation offered only through him. By the time the Savior arrived in Jerusalem and began teaching in the temple "about the midst of the feast" (John 7:14), the pilgrims there had been living in booths for several days, participated in the stirring ceremonies of the lighting of the lampstands, rejoiced in the pouring of the water on the altar multiple times, and been involved in the additional animal sacrifices. The feast provided an intense physical learning experience that had the potential to prepare the hearts and minds of the people who heard the Savior's teachings to accept him as the Messiah.

This section will explain how four specific passages of scripture in John 7–8 and the miracle found in John 9 become more powerful declarations and demonstrations of the divinity of Jesus Christ and his saving power when understood in context of the Feast of Tabernacles. We will examine them in the order in which they appear in the scriptures.

John 7:37–39

Unfortunately, John did not provide details about what Jesus first began to teach the multitudes in the temple under these circumstances, except that the people "marvelled" at what he taught (John 7:15). He does report the controversy generated by Jesus's presence and his teachings amidst a substantial portion of the Jewish population who had assembled for the feast. This "division among the people" (John 7:43) provided those present with a key opportunity to determine whether or not they believed that Jesus was indeed the Christ (see John 7:15–36, 40–53).

In this environment, Jesus waited until "the last day, that great day of the feast" to stand and cry to all the people within the temple, "If any man thirst, let him come unto me, and drink. He that believeth on me, as the scripture hath said, out of his belly shall flow rivers of living water" (John 7:37–38). The typical position of teachers was to sit while they taught. Jesus emphasized his declaration by standing and speaking in a loud voice.[20] For people who had been so engrossed in expressing gratitude to God and offering supplication to him for water to sustain their physical lives, this declaration brought to their minds the need for spiritual sustenance as well. "The scripture" the Savior referred to is not easily identifiable. He may have been alluding to Isaiah 12:3 and drawing water out of the "wells of salvation," as employed during the water-drawing ceremony. Or he may have been referring to Isaiah 58:11 or Jeremiah 2:13 and Jeremiah 17:13, in which the God of Israel is directly referred to as the "fountain of living waters."[21]

The Savior waited until the "great day of the feast," on which there was no water-pouring ceremony, to publicly declare that he was the source of "living water." In the absence of the celebration involving the waters of Siloam, his words invited the people to come unto him as the only true source for salvation.[22] John clarifies that those who believed in Jesus Christ as the promised Messiah and followed him would receive the Holy Ghost, who would provide consistent spiritual sustenance (see John 7:39).[23] Recipients of this living water would then be able to share their witness of Christ by the power of the Spirit with others, who could then receive the "living water" also.[24]

By referring to himself as the source of "living water," Jesus proclaimed his divinity—he is the "fountain of living waters." Only those who accepted him as the one sent from God to save humankind could be baptized and receive the cleansing through the Holy Ghost necessary for them to return to God (see John 3:5). Elder Joseph B. Wirthlin of the Quorum of the Twelve Apostles explained how faith in Jesus Christ that leads to obedience will bring about the fulfillment of the Savior's promise in John 7:37–38: "By living the gospel of Jesus Christ, we develop within ourselves a living spring that will quench eternally our thirst for happiness, peace, and everlasting life. The Lord explains clearly in the Doctrine and Covenants that only faithful obedience can tap the well of living water that refreshes and enlivens our souls: "But unto him that *keepeth my commandments* I will give the mysteries of my kingdom, and the same shall be in him a well of living water, springing up unto everlasting life" [Doctrine and Covenants]."[25]

Mormon taught that only through a process that begins with "faith unto the fulfilling the commandments" can we receive "the visitation of the Holy Ghost, which . . . filleth with hope and perfect love . . . until the end shall come, when all the saints shall dwell with God" (Moroni 8:25–26). Students who understand more clearly that faith in Jesus Christ is essential to receiving the Holy Ghost may feel inspired to increase their faith in the Savior by being more obedient to his commandments.[26] The abundant joy experienced by those who participated in the water-pouring ceremony pales in comparison with the joy that comes to those who receive the gift of the Holy Ghost, "the greatest gift that can be bestowed upon man" in mortality.[27]

John 8:12; 9:4–5

Although the Feast of Tabernacles was over by the time we come to John 8, it had likely not been over for very long (see John 8:2). Jesus was still teaching in the temple in Jerusalem.[28] Undoubtedly, the recent display of the giant burning lampstands was fresh in the minds of those who heard Jesus proclaim, "I am the light of the world: he that followeth me shall not walk in darkness, but shall have the light of life" (John 8:12). The Pharisees seemed to have missed the main point of his statement in favor of seizing upon a supposed opportunity to catch him in an apparent legalistic argument (see John 8:13–19). We will explore the significance of the Savior's declaration in the context of the Feast of Tabernacles and its implications for our students.

According to ancient sources,[29] Zechariah 14 was read during the lighting ceremony previously described. The four lampstands each had four bowls, a number used frequently in scripture to represent geographic completeness, such as the four corners of the world. As the four bowls on the four lampstands were lit, pilgrims at the feast would have heard the references to light in Zechariah 14:6–7, signifying that the Messiah would ultimately be the Light of the World, and not just for the Jews. Furthermore, the references to "all the nations," "all the families of the earth," and "all nations" in Zechariah 14:16–17, 19 in conjunction with worshipping the Lord in Jerusalem at the time of the Feast of Tabernacles pointed to the eventual gathering together of all God's children through the coming Messiah.[30] By proclaiming himself as the Light of the World and the Light of Life in context of these recently transpired festivities, Jesus declared unequivocally that he was indeed the Messiah of whom the prophets of old had testified. Only through him could the people find the way to salvation and avoid the darkness of sin.[31]

It was said that the light from the great lampstands in the Court of the Women during the Feast of Tabernacles lit up every courtyard in Jerusalem. Likewise, Jesus Christ can be a source of light for each of us during difficult or challenging times. While we often associate darkness with despair and discouragement, light often brings feelings of hope and assurance. Elder Jeffrey R. Holland of the Quorum of the Twelve Apostles taught how Jesus Christ can be a source of light for us personally:

> Every one of us has times when we need to know things will get better. . . . For emotional health and spiritual stamina, everyone needs to be able to look forward to some respite, to something pleasant and renewing and hopeful, whether that blessing be near at hand or still some distance ahead. . . .

> My declaration is that this is precisely what the gospel of Jesus Christ offers us, especially in times of need. There *is* help. There *is* happiness. There really *is* light at the end of the tunnel. It is the Light of the World, the Bright and Morning Star, . . . the very Son of God Himself. . . . To any who may be struggling to see that light and find that hope, I say: Hold on. Keep trying. God loves you. Things will improve. Christ comes to you in His "more excellent ministry" with a future of "better promises."[32]

Students who are taught to look to Jesus Christ as the light of their lives will be taught to look to a source of guidance and hope that will never fail them. Just as those who rejoiced around the giant lamps and sang praises to the God of Israel for his light in their lives, our students can experience joy in their daily lives as they find constant hope and assurance in Jesus Christ, the Light of the World. The Savior's reuse of this metaphor in John 9:4–5 will draw upon this meaning of the Savior as a source for hope amidst darkness.

John 8:31–36

In the Savior's declarations in John 7:37–39 and John 8:12, reference to two key features of the Feast of Tabernacles—the water-pouring ceremony and the lighted lampstands—may be seen as rather overt. In John 8:31–36, the background of the Feast of Tabernacles may be less obvious, but it can still enhance our understanding of the Savior's discourse on spiritual freedom and how he used the occasion of the festival to point to his divinity. For a whole week, the pilgrims who gathered to Jerusalem for the Feast of Tabernacles lived in booths to commemorate their wandering in the wilderness after God delivered them from bondage in Egypt and guided them to freedom in the promised land. As the Savior now addressed those who had at least professed a belief in him,[33] he returned to themes of bondage and deliverance that had just been commemorated during the Feast of Tabernacles.

It may seem that the Savior's audience had forgotten the historical significance of the booths they lived in during the Feast of Tabernacles. How could they say that they were "never in bondage to any man" (John 8:33) when they had just spent a week commemorating their deliverance from Pharaoh and when they were currently subject to the emperor of Rome?

However, when the Savior promised that those who continue in his word would be his disciples and be free (see John 8:31–32), they seem to have followed his transition from physical bondage and deliverance to spiritual bondage. They responded by alluding to their lineage as heirs of Abraham, implying that they had received promises of spiritual liberation and independence regardless of their current political or physical status (see John 8:33).[34] Making this transition from physical bondage to spiritual bondage is important for helping students understand and apply what the Savior teaches next.

Speaking to a group who may have consented to accept Jesus as a prophet or as a potential political Messiah, the Savior draws their attention to his divine spiritual mission by asserting that "whosoever committeth sin is the servant of sin" and that only "if the Son therefore shall make you free, ye shall be free indeed" (John 8:34, 36). Proud of their lineage and stubborn in their traditions, this was something this group of would-be believers would not accept. As one scholar noted, "People do not always, or even usually, realize that they are in bondage. They tend to rest in some fancied position of privilege, national, social, or religious. So these Jews, proud of their religion, did not even know their need to be free."[35] And from what did they need to be free? Elder Bruce R. McConkie answered, "Free from the damning power of false doctrine; free from the bondage of appetite and lust; free from the shackles of sin; free from every evil and corrupt influence and from every restraining and curtailing power; free to go on to the unlimited freedom enjoyed in its fulness only by exalted beings."[36]

Modern audiences may also struggle occasionally with a degree of spiritual complacency and fail to recognize their own spiritual bondage and need for deliverance. However, "all have . . . come short of the glory of God" (Romans 3:23) and need to be freed by the Great Deliverer, Jesus Christ, the Son of God. The Savior drew upon the theme of deliverance during the Feast of Tabernacles to declare his divine power, and modern students who understand this context can gain a greater sense of their need for that power in their own lives.

Students struggling to be free from sin and transgression may also gain greater confidence in the Savior's promise of freedom, as explained by Elder Richard G. Scott of the Quorum of the Twelve Apostles: "I testify that when a bishop or stake president has confirmed that your repentance is sufficient, know that your obedience has allowed the Atonement of Jesus Christ to satisfy the demands of justice for the laws you have broken. Therefore you are now free. Please believe it. To continually suffer the distressing effects of sin after adequate repentance, while not intended, is to deny the efficacy of the Savior's Atonement in your behalf."[37]

When the divine Redeemer of mankind makes us free, we are truly free.

John 8:51–53, 58

While the additional sacrifices were offered during the Feast of Tabernacles, participants sang the Hallel, Psalms 113–18.[38] In these psalms, we can see how the numerous deaths of these animals were accompanied by expressions of great faith and hope for divine help in overcoming the ultimate bondage—death. For example, in Psalm 116, we read,

> The sorrows of death compassed me, and the pains of hell gat hold upon me: I found trouble and sorrow.
>
> Then called I upon the name of the Lord; O Lord, I beseech thee, deliver my soul. . . .
>
> For thou hast delivered my soul from death. . . .
>
> I will walk before the Lord in the land of the living. . . .
>
> What shall I render unto the Lord for all his benefits toward me? . . .
>
> Thou hast loosed my bonds.
>
> I will offer to thee the sacrifice of thanksgiving, and will call upon the name of the Lord. (Psalm 116:3–4, 8–9, 12, 16–17)

We see this hope repeated in the 118th Psalm:

> The Lord is my strength and song, and is become my salvation.
>
> The voice of rejoicing and salvation is in the tabernacles of the righteous. . . .
>
> I shall not die, but live, and declare the works of the Lord. . . .
>
> He hath not given me over unto death. (Psalm 118:14–15, 17–18)

The myriad animal sacrifices during the Feast of Tabernacles combined with these hymns of hope for deliverance from their own eventual demise would have been fresh in the minds of those who heard the Lord declare, "If a man keep my saying, he shall never see death" (John 8:51).

The immediate rejoinder from Jesus's opponents focused on the literalness of the statement "Art thou greater than our father Abraham, which is dead? and the prophets are dead" (John 8:53). However, their objection was not aimed at the eventual triumph of man over death. They had spent the previous week singing about their hope for immortality in the face of animal sacrifices that reminded them of the inevitability of death. Their protest was aimed at the one making the claim. There was no doubt that Jesus was claiming "superhuman power."[39] Therefore, the people asked the real question: "Whom makest thou thyself?" (John 8:53). In one of the most unequivocal declarations of his divinity in the Gospel of John, Jesus of Nazareth answered simply, "Before Abraham was, I am" (John 8:58). He was not claiming to be merely another prophet or messenger from God. Jesus was identifying himself as the Great Jehovah, the God of Israel. Those who rejected his claim as blasphemous took up stones to end his life, but he escaped, for his time had not yet come.

While these well-known statements of the Savior in John 8:51, 58 are inherently powerful, understanding them in the immediate context of the Feast of Tabernacles adds to their poignancy. Observing the deaths of hundreds of animals throughout the festal week may have heightened the pilgrims' sense of their need for deliverance from their own inescapable demise. Their consciousness of the inevitability of death enhanced the power of the Savior's promise to give them everlasting life. As C. S. Lewis noted, "You never know how much you really believe anything until its truth or falsehood becomes a matter of life and death to you. It is easy to say you believe a rope to be strong and sound as long as you are merely using it to cord a box. But suppose you had to hang by that rope over a precipice. Wouldn't you then first discover how much you really trusted it? . . . Only a real risk tests the reality of a belief."[40]

While our students cannot experience the full vicarious nature of the sacrifices at the Feast of Tabernacles, helping them understand and visualize the context can help them better appreciate the Savior's promise to deliver them from death. Perhaps they will also be filled them with the same gratitude repeated in the closing of the Hallel: "His mercy endureth for ever" (Psalm 118:1–4, 29).

John 9:1–7

As Jesus left the temple grounds, he and his disciples "passed by . . . a man which was blind from his birth" (John 9:1). While we never learn the exact age of the man, we understand from his parents' later statement that he is "of age" (John 9:21) and that the man was an adult member of the community who had lived without sight for many years. Here was a man who had spent his entire life in physical darkness. Though he had never known physical light, he could still be brought into the light through Jesus Christ. Regardless of the cause for the man's condition, Jesus affirmed again to his disciples, "'I am the light of the world' [John 9:5], as though to teach: 'Whenever you remember that I opened the blind eyes, physically, remember also that I came to bring light to eyes, spiritually.'"[41]

"In the Old Testament the giving of sight to the blind is associated with God himself (Exodus 4:11; Psalm 146:8). It is also a messianic activity (Isaiah 29:18; 35:5; 42:7), and this may be its significance in the New Testament. It is a divine function, a function for God's own Messiah, that Jesus fulfills when he gives sight to the blind."[42] On at least four previous occasions, Jesus had restored sight to the blind (see Matthew 9:27–31; 12:22–37; 15:29–31; Mark 8:22–26). The miracle was not unique, but the manner in which it was accomplished was. The Savior's deliberate actions were meant to convey yet another proof of his divinity to those who witnessed them.

Closer examination of one piece of the textual context can help us begin to unlock the instructive nature of this miracle for modern students. When Jesus says, "I must work the works of him that *sent* me" (John 9:4; emphasis added), it is the tenth time we have read the word *sent* since the beginning of John 7. The Savior has been emphasizing his role as the one "sent" by the Father for several chapters.[43] This has been prelude for why the Savior now sends the blind man to the Pool of Siloam to be healed. John interprets Siloam to mean simply "Sent" (John 9:7) to correspond with his repeated usage of the term to refer to the divine commission of the Savior.[44] Thus, the Pool of Siloam becomes a symbol for the Savior himself, an especially critical association given the daily processions to the Pool of Siloam during the Feast of Tabernacles.

However, before sending the man to the Pool of Siloam, the Master Healer and Teacher "anointed the eyes of the blind man with the clay" (John 9:6). Similar to Enoch's preparation to receiving spiritual sight in

Moses 6:35, washing the clay from blind eyes may signify cleansing ourselves of the natural, earthly man (see 1 Corinthians 15:47–50). Like the man born blind, the natural man is blind and has no knowledge of the way to salvation—he is enveloped in spiritual darkness. Only by coming to Jesus Christ can we receive spiritual sight and know the way to salvation.

While the Savior could have simply healed the man of blindness, he seems to have had a much broader purpose in this miracle to demonstrate how "the works of God should be made manifest in him" (John 9:3). This miracle is not only about God's compassionate work for one blind man, but about his healing, redemptive power for all mankind. Though there were several pools in Jerusalem where the man may have washed the clay from his eyes, Jesus may have had at least three reasons for sending the man to the Pool of Siloam to have his sight restored.

First, as mentioned earlier, the Pool of Siloam was likely a *mikveh*, used for ceremonial washing and cleansing preparatory to entering the temple and participating in the rituals therein. Thus, the Pool of Siloam provided the blind man with "living water" in which to wash away his symbolic earthly self and receive spiritual, as well as physical, sight.

Second, Siloam was not the closest *mikveh* to where the blind man likely was at the time. According to John 9:1, the Savior and his disciples were not far from the temple when they came upon the man born blind. The closest *mikveh* would have been the Pool of Bethesda, which was only approximately 1,000 feet (300 meters) away, while the Pool of Siloam was approximately 2,100 feet (640 meters) away.[45] The extra distance required the man to exercise faith in the Healer who gave him the instructions, which was the real key to the man's conversion as recorded in John 9:24–38.

Finally, by choosing the Pool of Siloam as the place for the miracle to occur, the Savior was superimposing himself on the most important event of the Feast of Tabernacles. It was as if he was saying, "You come to the Pool of Siloam to 'draw water out of the wells of salvation'—*I am* the well of salvation."

When the blind man goes to the Pool of Siloam to be healed and receive his physical sight, he represents each of us who must come unto the Savior in faith to receive the divine healing and spiritual sight necessary so God can do whatever work is necessary for each of us to receive our immortality and eternal life (see Moses 1:39). And just as the "living water" of Siloam is poured upon the altar of the temple, it is only as we receive the Holy Ghost and the power of Christ's Atonement that this work can be accomplished—"there shall be no other name given nor any other way nor means whereby salvation can come unto the children of men, only in and through the name of Christ, the Lord Omnipotent" (Mosiah 3:17). John continues to emphasize this symbolism of light/sight and dark/blind in Jesus's discussion with the leaders of the synagogue in John 9:39–41, emphasizing to all people that only those who believe in him receive the true light of God.

Conclusion

Understanding the scriptures in context increases faith and inspires action. Chad H Webb reinforced this principle when he taught, "There is power in the principles that are couched within the stories of the scriptures. Part of that power is seeing those principles in context. . . . We teach the principles the Lord intended to preserve in the context and content of scripture. . . . Personal application will come naturally."[46]

Students who learn the Savior's teachings and miracle of healing at the Pool of Siloam in John 7–9 against the backdrop of the Feast of Tabernacles may be more inspired to seek for the gift of the Holy Ghost in their lives through faithful obedience to Jesus Christ. They can have greater spiritual clarity and direction in their lives by focusing on the Light of the World. They can experience increased confidence in the Savior's power to free them from sin through his Atonement, which can increase the likelihood that they will repent and turn to him for deliverance when they feel the bondage of sin. They can find comfort and hope in the Savior's power over death in bringing to pass the resurrection of all mankind. And students who remember the healing at the Pool of Siloam may be more inclined to turn to the Savior for healing and enlightenment, knowing he was "sent" from God for our salvation.

Ryan S. Gardner was a writer for Curriculum Services, Seminaries and Institutes, Salt Lake City Central Office, when this article was first published; he now teaches as part of the Religious Education faculty at Brigham Young University–Idaho.

Ryan S. Gardner, "Jesus Christ and the Feast of Tabernacle," *Religious Educator* 13, no. 3 (2012): 109–27.

Notes

1. Many biblical scholars agree that the Feast of Tabernacles provides important contextual background for John 7–8. See Bruce K. Satterfield, "John and the Feast of Tabernacles," in *The Testimony of John the Beloved: The 27th Annual Sidney B. Sperry Symposium*, ed. Craig J. Ostler, Daniel K Judd, and Richard D. Draper (Salt Lake City: Deseret Book, 1998), 249; Leon Morris, *The Gospel according to John,* rev. ed. (Grand Rapids, MI: Eerdmans, 1995), 371–72; Alfred Edersheim, *The Temple: Its Ministry and Services* (Peabody, MA: Hendrickson, 1994), 222; and F. F. Bruce, *New Testament History* (New York: Doubleday, 1969), 140. This article accepts this conclusion and posits further that the meaning of the healing in John 9 is also enhanced when viewed in context of the Feast of Tabernacles.
2. "In providing context, it is essential to not lose sight of its purpose, which is to contribute to a better understanding of a particular scripture passage. Be careful not to turn context—such as the history, politics, economics, or language of the people in the scriptures—into the main focus of a lesson." *Teaching, No Greater Call: A Resource Guide for Gospel Teaching* (Salt Lake City: The Church of Jesus Christ of Latter-day Saints, 1999), 55.
3. Bruce R. McConkie, *Doctrinal New Testament Commentary* (Salt Lake City: Bookcraft, 1965–73), 1:452.
4. Furthermore, John seems to have constructed his narrative with this in mind: "Passover, the setting of the previous chapter, and Tabernacles (7:2) are some six months apart in the Jewish calendar, leaving a large narrative 'gap' at this point. The symbolism of the Tabernacles setting is probably more important than any attempt to establish a chronology of Jesus' ministry." *Eerdmans Commentary on the Bible*, ed. James D. G. Dunn and John W. Rogerson (Grand Rapids, MI: Eerdmans, 2003), 1180. In other words, John also deliberately chose the teachings of the Savior against the backdrop of the Feast of Tabernacles to emphasize the Savior's divinity and his saving mission.
5. Bruce Satterfield is a faculty member in the Religious Education Department at Brigham Young University–Idaho.
6. See Satterfield, "John and the Feast of Tabernacles," 251; Bible Dictionary, "Feasts."
7. See Morris, *Gospel according to John*, 372; Edersheim, *The Temple*, 217–18; and George Arthur Buttrick, ed., *The Interpreter's Dictionary of the Bible* (Nashville: Abingdon Press, 1962), 1:456.
8. See Satterfield, "John and the Feast of Tabernacles," 256–57.
9. Edersheim, *The Temple*, 213.
10. In Satterfield's research, he proposed that the Mishnah, while redacted around AD 200 to codify much of the oral traditions believed to have been in practice among the Jews from 570–36 BC, still provided an accurate enough description of many of the events and rituals of the Feast of Tabernacles to be useful for a discussion of the feast at the time of Jesus; see especially his footnote 3. Satterfield, "John and the Feast of Tabernacles," 260. Other biblical scholars, such as Edersheim and Morris, have concurred with this assumption. Commentary from other biblical scholars also seems to assume this line

of reasoning, such as Frank E. Gaebelein, ed., *The Expositor's Bible Commentary* (Grand Rapids, MI: Zondervan, 1981), 86, 92; Craig S. Kenner, *The IVP Bible Background Commentary: New Testament* (Downers Grove, IL: InterVarsity Press, 1993), 283, 285; and Richard Nietzel Holzapfel and Thomas A. Wayment, *Making Sense of the New Testament: Timely Insights and Timeless Messages* (Salt Lake City: Deseret Book, 2010), 161.

11. Indeed, according to one commentary, the three major Jewish festivals—Passover, Weeks, and Tabernacles—were critical for marking "the formation of Israel" as a nation. Craig A. Evans and Stanley E. Porter, eds., *Dictionary of New Testament Background* (Downers Grove, IL: InterVarsity Press, 2000), 374.
12. The Court of the Women comprised an area of about two hundred square feet (sixty square meters) between the Court of the Gentiles and Nicanor's gate, which led to the altar of sacrifice. It was likely the most popular place of worship in the temple. See Edersheim, *The Temple*, 225.
13. See Satterfield, "John and the Feast of Tabernacles," 255–56; Edersheim, *The Temple*, 224–25.
14. "The lampstand often symbolically represents God's perfect leadership in showing his people their way. It also represents the Holy Spirit." Lawrence O. Richards, *Zondervan Expository Dictionary of Bible Words* (Grand Rapids, MI: Zondervan, 1991), 388.
15. See Edersheim, *The Temple*, 219; Satterfield, "John and the Feast of Tabernacles," 254–55.
16. Satterfield, "John and the Feast of Tabernacles," 253–54.
17. Satterfield, "John and the Feast of Tabernacles," 254.
18. See Hershel Shanks, "The Siloam Pool: Where Jesus Cured the Blind Man," *Biblical Archaeology Review* 31, no. 5 (September/October 2005): 16–23. Shanks's article reports on the work of Ronny Reich, and the archaeologists' conclusion that the Pool of Siloam was indeed a *mikveh* employs the same line of reasoning that identified the Pool of Bethesda as a *mikveh* in Urban C. Von Wahlde's article, "The Puzzling Pool of Bethesda: Where Jesus Cured the Crippled Man," *Biblical Archaeology Review* 37, no. 5 (September/October 2011): 40–47.
19. See Shanks, "Siloam Pool," 18. The location of this pool has moved around from time to time because of cycles of destruction and reconstruction in Jerusalem. See Nehemiah 3:15, for example.
20. See Morris, *Gospel according to John*, 373–74.
21. Morris suggests that another possible symbolic meaning of the water-pouring ceremony may point to the occasion where God provided water from the rock to satisfy the thirst of the Israelites in the wilderness (see Numbers 20:2–11; Deuteronomy 8:11–18; see also William Barclay, *The Daily Study Bible: The Gospel of John*, volume 1 (Philadelphia: Westminster, 1975), 249. Regardless of the specific allusion, Jesus seems to be using the occasion of the ritual prayer for physical water to point their attention to him as the only one who can satisfy their spiritual thirst. See Morris, *Gospel according to John*, 374.
22. "Just as the Passover setting was appropriate to bread, so the Tabernacles setting, with its celebration of the provision of water in the desert, is appropriate to this part of the discourse." Dunn and Rogerson, *Eerdmans Commentary on the Bible*, 1181.
23. "Most of Judaism did not believe that the Spirit was prophetically active in their own time but expected the full outpouring of the Spirit in the messianic age or the world to come. Water usually symbolized Torah (law) or wisdom in Jewish texts, but John follows Old Testament precedent in using it for the Spirit (Is 44:3; Ezek 36:24–27; Joel 2:28)." Craig S. Keener, *The IVP Bible Background Commentary: New Testament* (Downers Grove, IL: InterVarsity Press, 1993), 283.

24. At least two major functions of the Holy Ghost match the symbolism of the "living water": (1) Those who are "born again" of water and the Spirit receive new spiritual life; and (2) Those who receive the Holy Ghost are cleansed and purified. See 2 Nephi 31:17; 3 Nephi 12:2; Doctrine and Covenants 19:31; 84:33.
25. Joseph B. Wirthlin, "Living Water to Quench Spiritual Thirst," *Ensign*, May 1995, 18. The mysteries of God's kingdom can be known only by the power and gift of the Holy Ghost; see Doctrine and Covenants 76:5–10, 114–18.
26. "Strong faith is developed by obedience to the gospel of Jesus Christ; in other words, faith comes by righteousness" (Bible Dictionary, "Faith," 669).
27. *Teachings of Presidents of the Church: Wilford Woodruff* (Salt Lake City: The Church of Jesus Christ of Latter-day Saints, 2004), 49.
28. In fact, it is likely that Jesus is teaching "in the Court of the Women, the most frequented part of the Temple," where the lamps had been lit throughout the week of the Feast of Tabernacles. See Morris, *Gospel according to John,* 388. "It is most unlikely that Jesus taught in the actual treasure chamber, so the word ['treasury' in John 8:20] probably means that part of the Temple area into which people came to cast their offerings into the chests. This must have been part of the Court of the Women. . . . There were thirteen trumpet-shaped collection boxes there, each with its inscription showing the use to which its contents would be put. In no other writing does the name 'the treasury' appear to be used for a section of the Court of the Women, but it is difficult to give John's words any other meaning. This court was a place to which people resorted and where teaching could take place accordingly." Morris, *Gospel According to John*, 394.
29. See Edersheim, *The Temple*, 213; see also Keener, *IVP Bible Background Commentary: New Testament*, 283.
30. See Satterfield, "John and the Feast of Tabernacles," 257.
31. Modern revelation reiterates and emphasizes Jesus Christ's role as the Light of the World (see Doctrine and Covenants 88:6–13). Modern prophets have also taught specific ways that Jesus Christ can be the light for us in our lives. See Dallin H. Oaks, "The Light and Life of the World," *Ensign*, November 1987, 63–64; Robert D. Hales, "Out of Darkness into His Marvelous Light," *Ensign*, May 2002, 70; and M. Russell Ballard, "You Can Be the Voice," *Ensign*, May 1980, 45.
32. Jeffrey R. Holland, "An High Priest of Good Things to Come," *Ensign*, November 1999, 36.
33. See McConkie, *Doctrinal New Testament Commentary*, 1:456; and Morris, *Gospel according to John,* 404.
34. This line of reasoning seems consistent with a common theme in John: "John presents Jesus as a preexistent messianic figure who comes to rescue his people from this world of darkness, hostility and sin. . . . These images of restoration and exodus suggest that the individual who does not believe in Jesus exists in the realm of darkness, ignorance and death. Since those who do not believe in Jesus are not regarded as 'children of God,' they are in a spiritual sense living in exile because they are alienated from God." Evans and Porter, *Dictionary of New Testament Background*, 351.
35. Morris, *Gospel according to John*, 405.
36. McConkie, *Doctrinal New Testament Commentary*, 1:456–57.
37. Richard G. Scott, "Peace of Conscience and Peace of Mind," *Ensign*, November 2004, 18.
38. See Satterfield, "John and the Feast of Tabernacles," 255.
39. Morris, *Gospel according to John*, 416.
40. C. S. Lewis, *A Grief Observed* (New York: Bantam Books, 1961), 25.

41. McConkie, *Doctrinal New Testament Commentary*, 1:481.
42. Morris, *Gospel according to John*, 422.
43. In fact, the word *sent* occurs in the English King James Version more often in John (59) than in Luke (42), Matthew (35), or Mark (25). It also occurs with greater frequency in John (once per 1.5 pages) than in Mark (once every 0.83 pages), Luke (once every 0.8 pages), or Matthew (once every 0.66 pages). In John 7–9, there are 13 uses of the word *sent*—22 percent of all the occurrences of the word in the Gospel of John. However, if we add the thirteen references found in the critical discourses of John 5–6, where Jesus discourses extensively on his relationship to the Father and his role as Redeemer, we see almost half of the uses of the word *sent* in the Gospel of John clustered in these five chapters. The Savior again refers to himself as the Sent One repeatedly in John 17 (six times) during the great Intercessory Prayer, in which he again stresses his relationship to the Father and his role as Redeemer.
44. The Greek form of Siloam is usually connected with the Hebrew *shiloah* (see Isaiah 8:6). Although this term may be derived from the lexical root *sh-l-h*, "to send," some scholars derive it from a homonym used outside the Bible to designate water channels or canals. This article assumes a connection between Siloam and sh-l-h, "to send," or at the very least a literary play on that meaning, as used by John in John 9:7.
45. Von Wahlde concludes that these two pools were the largest *mikva'ot* in Jerusalem and were likely built for the large crowds that gathered to Jerusalem during the festival seasons, such as the Feast of Tabernacles. See Von Wahlde, "The Puzzling Pool," 47.
46. Chad H Webb, "New-Hire Orientation" (meeting with newly hired teachers of Seminaries and Institutes of Religion, May 19, 2009), 9.

Chapter Nine

Hostility toward Jesus

Prelude to the Passion

JENNIFER C. LANE

By the final Passover of Jesus's life, the plans had been laid for his death. Although he had evaded being captured or being discredited on previous trips to Jerusalem, efforts were now focused to bring closure to what the leaders by this time had convinced themselves was a dangerous threat to the people for whom they had responsibility. At this point, the hostility of the elite had coalesced into a plan for action that was well known among the pilgrims coming to Jerusalem for the Passover festival: "And the Jews' passover was nigh at hand: and many went out of the country up to Jerusalem before the passover, to purify themselves. Then sought they for Jesus, and spake among themselves, as they stood in the temple, What think ye, that he will not come to the feast? Now both the chief priests and the Pharisees had given a commandment, that, if any man knew where he were, he should shew it, that they might take him" (John 11:55–57).

In our reading of the New Testament, we naturally assume this hostility toward Jesus is consistently found throughout all the Gospels. Here I would like to explore some of the background that helps explain why the Pharisees, in particular, had initial concerns about the Savior's actions and then how, over time, those concerns developed into hostility and defensiveness. Seeing how hostility and defensiveness develop in interactions with Jesus recorded in the New Testament can help us better understand the opposition the Savior faced from the leaders of the Jews in the last part of his life.

While we have more records of encounters between the Savior and the Pharisees than between the Savior and any other group in the New Testament, it is important to recognize that it was not the Pharisees who were solely responsible for the efforts to end the Savior's life. The chief priests and the Sadducees had their own religious and political concerns that led them to oppose Christ and develop hostility toward him over time.

The Pharisees were split by different schools of thought, and those who lived in different areas were not directly connected to one another. Thus, interactions in Galilee may not have had an immediate influence on the feelings of those in Jerusalem.[1] In this paper I will, however, focus on the accounts of interactions between the Savior and the Pharisees with hope of clarifying how people seeking to be loyal to the truth may become hardened and hostile when they are challenged to rise to a higher level. In giving an in-depth look into one of the groups that were influential during the life of Jesus, I hope we can see a general pattern of righteous people deciding how to respond to a call to repent and become more holy.

In covenanting with the children of Israel, the Lord commanded, "Ye shall be holy; for I am holy" (Leviticus 11:44). The effort to seek holiness and separate themselves from the world around them was both a challenge and a source of identity for the Israelites throughout their history. This pursuit of holiness continued beyond Old Testament times, into the intertestamental era and the time of the Savior's mortal ministry. During the intertestamental period and the life of Jesus, hellenized culture pressured the Jews to leave the standards of the covenant. Their distinctiveness in diet, circumcision, and Sabbath-day observance were held up to ridicule. One small Jewish group that actively resisted this pressure was the Pharisees. Their efforts focused on ritual purity in food preparation and eating as well as careful observance of the Sabbath. Their strict efforts to live the law of Moses and bring the holiness of the temple into the lives of all the Jews grew out of this defensive position. In their efforts to find holiness, they also criticized others who did not keep their standards.

The New Testament accounts of the Pharisees' critique of the Savior and his followers can be better understood when seen in this historical context.

Their beliefs about the nature of holiness help to explain their initial concerns about the Savior. When Jesus was criticized for his failure to follow the Pharisees' understanding of holiness, he responded to their critique with teachings that pointed to the true nature of holiness. Interestingly, he frequently used the words of Old Testament prophets to make his point, teaching that the divine nature of holiness had already been revealed. As he gave these rebukes to his critics, they were in a position to change their perspective and seek a higher form of holiness. But, as with all inspired chastisement, they were also free to harden their hearts and resist his teaching. As we shall see, for the Pharisees who debated with Jesus the general pattern was that of resisting the call to repentance. When these Pharisees refused to rethink what it meant to be holy, their defensiveness turned into hostility and fueled their active resistance to the Savior and his call to holiness.

The Pharisees' Vision of Holiness

The Pharisees' opposition to Jesus centered on critiques of food practices and Sabbath observance that went against their understanding of true Judaism. At the center of the Pharisees' concern was their confidence in what the Gospels refer to as "the traditions of the elders" (Matthew 15:2; Mark 7:5), also known as "ancestral tradition."[2] A central focus of the law of Moses concerned the sacrifices in the temple and the strict rules governing the ritual purity of the priests while they officiated and ate at the temple. While other Jews of this time believed that these regulations in Leviticus applied only to the priests in the temple, the Pharisees' goal was to bring the holiness of the temple into every home through applying these laws more broadly.

The Pharisees had recently developed a vision of what they believed the law of Moses meant for the holiness of all Jews. The Pharisees' revolutionary claim was that the ritual temple holiness described in the law was God's will for all Jews, not just the priests.[3] All could obtain this holiness by eating "secular food (ordinary, everyday meals) in a state of ritual purity *as if one were a Temple priest*. The Pharisees thus arrogated to themselves—and to all Jews equally—the status of Temple priests."[4]

This desire to bring the purity and holiness of the temple into their homes meant that the Pharisees had to take very seriously a number of things associated with food and eating. It led the Pharisees to focus on the purification of vessels and the washing of hands to make the meals ritually pure. Ritual purity also explains their emphasis on tithes because for them proper tithing of food made the "food ritually acceptable."[5] To keep this level of holiness, it was also essential not to eat with those who did not observe these laws.[6] This combined effort to keep the ritual holiness of the family table is known as table fellowship. As we shall see, much of the Pharisees' initial opposition to Jesus arose over questions of his or his disciples' food practices, particularly as they reflected a breach of table-fellowship regulations. Their critique was that they were not following the standards of holiness.

When we see how the Pharisees sought to live exemplary lives in ordinary circumstances, we can better understand their concerns and see where their Achilles' heel lay. In the Sermon on the Mount, Jesus explained that the Pharisees' righteousness was a high bar that his followers had to surpass: "For I say unto you, That except your righteousness shall exceed the righteousness of the scribes and Pharisees, ye shall in no case enter into the kingdom of heaven" (Matthew 5:20). When we realize that the Pharisees were trying to live a holy life in a world they saw as unclean, we can better identify with their efforts to be righteous, as well as their efforts to justify or defend themselves. Recognizing that their efforts and even their initial opposition grew out of their desire for righteous lives, we more easily "liken them unto ourselves" (1 Nephi 19:23).

Critiques and Responses

Once we understand the Pharisees' vision of holiness, we can see why they would have had concerns about what they saw as lapses in Jesus's and the disciples' behavior, and we can better explain why they opposed it. As we examine the critiques of the Pharisees who are described in the Gospels and the Savior's responses in calling them to a higher level of holiness, we can see the escalation of resistance and hostility that eventually led them to seek his death.

The Pharisees' resistance to the call to rethink holiness helps to explain the source of their hostility to Jesus. It is also helpful to note that the Savior was challenging the Pharisees' role in interpreting the law. His challenge to their vision of ritual holiness surely could have provoked a hostile reaction as it threatened the social status of the Pharisees as the interpreters of the law. But while this context helps to explain pressures and motivations, the response of hostility is not, however, simply a political question. At its core, hostility reflects personal choices and spiritual responses. The hostility we find described in the Gospels was informed by a particular context, but, more importantly, it was a universal spiritual phenomenon—the "universal sin" of pride.

The pattern of questioning turning into hostility because of the Pharisees' defensiveness increasingly characterizes the hostile interactions of the Pharisees and the Savior. We'll look now at two concerns raised against Jesus: that he was eating with sinners and that he was eating with unwashed hands. We can see that these questions grew out of the Pharisees' understanding of the law of Moses. Their religious commitment to ritual purity put them in a position of opposition to what they saw Jesus and his disciples doing. In his responses to their questions, Jesus shows the Pharisees that scripture itself points to a higher form of holiness. In realizing that they are being told that their efforts at spiritual excellence are falling short, they are in a position where—depending on their response—they can be humbled or develop hostility.

Eating with Sinners

New Testament accounts suggest that Jesus was invited to participate in the Pharisees' table fellowship (see Luke 11:37, Luke 14:1), but we also learn that others he ate with were an affront to the Pharisees. Understanding the concept of table fellowship helps us see that by eating with others that were ritually unclean, Jesus would also threaten the purity of his Pharisaic hosts. The tax collectors, or publicans, were specifically excluded from the Pharisees' table fellowship.[7] In the first account of eating with publicans and sinners, we learn that the "scribes and Pharisees murmured against his disciples, saying, Why do ye eat and drink with publicans and sinners?" (Luke 5:30) or "Why eateth your Master with publicans and sinners?" (Matthew 9:11; see also Mark 2:16). For the Pharisees, those who keep the ritual cleanliness of the priests in their homes allow the holiness of the temple to reside in the home. But to keep this level of holiness, it was required that they eat only with others who were equally obedient.

The initial "murmuring" about eating with publicans and sinners is met with Jesus's teachings that the "whole need not a physician, but they that are sick" and "I am not come to call the righteous, but sinners to repentance" (Matthew 9:12–13; see also Mark 2:17; Luke 5:31–32). On its face it might not be clear how these comments would rile the "scribes and Pharisees" because they would naturally concur that the sinners and tax collectors were sick and did need a physician. They could see themselves as righteous and the others as unworthy. One of our greatest challenges as righteous, law-abiding people is to recognize that we all sin. To the extent that our observance of the law becomes our sense of justification before God, then admitting that we are flawed will not be an option. Then, at all costs, we must exactly keep the law and judge others who do not. In Matthew's account, the Savior points out this universal tendency in his accusers with an additional phrase that calls the questioners into question and invites them to a higher level of holiness.

In Matthew 9:13 we read that between the statements about the sick and his mission to call them to repentance, an additional comment is, "But go ye and learn what that meaneth, I will have mercy, and not sacrifice." This is a quotation from the prophet Hosea chastising the unrighteous Israelites: "O Ephraim, what shall I do unto thee? O Judah, what shall I do unto thee? for your goodness is as a morning cloud, and as the early dew it goeth away. For I desired mercy, and not sacrifice; and the knowledge of God more than burnt offerings. But they like men have transgressed the covenant: there have they dealt treacherously against me" (Hosea 6:4, 6–7).

Jesus is challenging the scribes' and Pharisees' interpretation of scripture in telling them, "Go ye and learn what that meaneth." Their understanding of holiness, which required strict adherence to the requirements for priests' ritual purity, had become for them "sacrifice" and "burnt offerings." Jesus is challenging their fundamental conception of holiness and the law by questioning their focus on their own ritual purity while ignoring the spiritually sick among the covenant people.

In using this quote from Hosea, Jesus suggests that his questioners, like the wicked Israelites, were misunderstanding God's will and the nature of God's holiness as they placed their self-justifying obedience over compassion for the less obedient. "For I desired mercy, and not sacrifice; and the knowledge of God more than burnt offerings" (Hosea 6:6). Imbedded in the context of the quote we find a prophetic critique of the ultimate lack of depth and staying power of self-justifying righteousness: "O Judah, what shall I do unto thee? for your goodness is as a morning cloud, and as the early dew it goeth away" (Hosea 6:4). While "by faith was the law of Moses given," Jesus is pointing here to "a more excellent way" (Ether 12:11), a kind of compassionate righteousness that exceeds "the righteousness of the scribes and Pharisees" (Matthew 5:20). He is pointing to a righteousness based on the mercy of God rather than the belief that we can be justified and saved by our own obedience to the law.

Another debate over the nature of holiness is found in the Pharisees' opposition to the Savior's table-fellowship practice and his subsequent questioning of the questioners in Luke 15. Here "the Pharisees and scribes murmured, saying, This man receiveth sinners, and eateth with them" (Luke 15:2). Jesus responds to their critique with the parable of the ninety-nine sheep that are safe and the one sheep that is lost in the wilderness. The imagery of a lost, vulnerable sheep replaces his earlier explanation of the sick needing a physician, but the challenge to the spiritual caretakers is the same. While their concern was based on their desire to maintain the table fellowship that would make their tables as holy as the altar of the temple, Jesus was, however, challenging them to look to an even higher vision of holiness. Just as Hosea had challenged the wicked Israelites to seek "the knowledge of God" rather than merely the temple worship of "burnt offerings" (Hosea 6:6), here Jesus challenges those spiritual leaders that would be holy by describing the nature of divine holiness seen in the imagery of God's care for his covenant people as shepherd (see Ezekiel 34:11–12, 16).

Jesus teaches the Pharisees who disapproved of eating with sinners that as contemporary spiritual leaders the Good Shepherd should be their model. His use of the parable of the ninety and nine suggests that in their focus on their own holiness in table fellowship, they are instead following the example of the ancient "shepherds of Israel" (Ezekiel 34:2) who, concerned with their own advantage, ignored those that were lost. The prophet Ezekiel had been commanded to "prophesy against the shepherds of Israel, prophesy, and say unto them, Thus saith the Lord God unto the shepherds; Woe be to the shepherds of Israel that do feed themselves! should not the shepherds feed the flocks?" (Ezekiel 34:2). In this extended critique against the spiritual leaders of ancient times, the Lord tells them that they have ignored the lost sheep: "And they were scattered, because there is no shepherd: and they became meat to all the beasts of the field, when they were scattered. My sheep wandered through all the mountains, and upon every high hill: yea, my flock was scattered upon all the face of the earth, and none did search or seek after them" (Ezekiel 34:5–6). Those leaders set to represent God cared for themselves and not for those they could have helped. In comparing the lost sheep and the sinners who needed help, Jesus delivers a prophetic rebuke to the Pharisees who sought their own table-fellowship holiness by not eating with sinners.

This neglect of the lost is placed in direct contrast to the care given by Jehovah as the Good Shepherd: "For thus saith the Lord God; Behold, I, even I, will both search my sheep, and seek them out. As a shepherd seeketh out his flock in the day that he is among his sheep that are scattered; so will I seek out my sheep, and will deliver them out of all places where they have been scattered in the cloudy and dark day. . . . I will seek that which was lost, and bring again that which was driven away" (Ezekiel 34:11–12, 16). The holiness and goodness of the Good Shepherd was found in his loving care of those who were scattered and lost. Christ's rebuke against the contemporary "shepherds of Israel" carries with it an invitation to a higher way as he points to the true holiness of forgetting self and reaching out to the lost sinners. But, as with all spiritual correction, this response opens up the possibility of resentment and defensiveness in the hearer.[8]

Not Washing Hands

As the Gospel narratives proceed, an escalation in hostility to Jesus can be seen in the new questions raised by those among the Pharisees. In the earlier issue of eating with sinners, concerns were raised about his and his disciples' practice, but in these exchanges there was no immediate reaction to Jesus's calling the questioners' own holiness into question. When Pharisees begin to question him about not washing hands, we see an escalation of hostility toward Jesus. In Matthew 15 and Mark 7, the question is put to Jesus why his disciples do not also follow "the tradition of the elders" in the washing of hands before eating (Matthew 15:2; Mark 7:3). The earlier comments about eating with publicans and sinners may have implied that these others' ritual uncleanness would diminish the holiness of Jesus and his disciples. In the challenge about not washing hands, they are being accused of not being holy by not living up to the Pharisaic interpretation of how to bring the temple's holiness to every house in Israel.

Christ responds to these accusers' question of holiness by taking on the issue of the authority of the "tradition of the elders" (Matthew 15:2; Mark 7:3). He first illustrates the problems in setting up something beyond the law by discussing how another practice sanctioned under their tradition can be a justification for not keeping the commandments of God (see Matthew 15:3–6; Mark 7:9–13).[9] He also quotes Isaiah's description of a hypocritical people and describes it as a prophecy of his accusers (see Matthew 15:7–9; Mark 7:6–8).

In the prophetic critique found in Isaiah 29:13, the Lord describes a people who appear to want holiness, but their hearts and their understanding are not right with God. The Lord speaks against those who "draw near me with their mouth, and with their lips do honour me, but have removed their heart far from me, and their fear toward me is taught by the precept of men" (Isaiah 29:13). It is not just the lack of correlation between hearts and words, but also "their fear toward me is taught by the precept of men." This fits directly into Jesus's questioning the authority of the "tradition of the elders" and in Mark precedes Jesus's very strong comment that "for laying aside the commandment of God, ye hold the tradition of men, as the washing of pots and cups: and many other such like things ye do. And he said unto them, Full well ye reject the commandment of God, that ye may keep your own tradition" (Mark 7:8–9). In the version of Isaiah that Jesus quotes, the critique on false worship is particularly strong: "But in vain they do worship me, teaching for doctrines the commandments of men" (Matthew 15:9; see also Mark 7:7).

In addition to this strong critique of the Pharisees' vision of holiness, the situation escalates as Jesus calls "the multitude" (Matthew 15:10) to him and publicly teaches that being defiled or impure is not a matter of what we take into ourselves. Instead, our concern should be on what we produce: "Not that which goeth into the mouth defileth a man; but that which cometh out of the mouth, this defileth a man" (Matthew 15:11). In teaching this "more excellent way" (Ether 12:11), Jesus also directly and publicly refutes the authority and interpretation around which the Pharisees' understanding of holiness was built.

It is not surprising, then, that at the end of Jesus's commentary his disciples came "and said unto him, Knowest thou that the Pharisees were offended, after they heard this saying?" (Matthew 15:12). In listening defensively to Jesus's teaching on holiness, these Pharisees had ears to hear the rebuke but not the invitation.

A similar incident is recorded in Luke 11 in which the questioning of Jesus's practice is then turned around and he calls the Pharisees' vision of holiness into question. In this scene it is not the practice of the disciples, but of Jesus himself that is challenged. "A certain Pharisee besought him to dine with him: and he went in, and sat down to meat. And when the Pharisee saw it, he marvelled that he had not first washed before dinner" (Luke 11:37–38). In response to this questioning of his breach of the "tradition of the elders," Jesus begins an extensive critique of the danger of disguising the inner self with outward righteousness. These comments touch on several practices associated with the Pharisees' program of holiness: "[making] clean the outside of the cup and the platter; but your inward part is full of ravening and wickedness" (Luke 11:39), being exacting in tithes, by "[tithing] mint and rue and all manner of herbs, and [passing] over judgment and the love of God" (Luke 11:42). It is, however, significant to note, as in Matthew 23 where similar critiques appear, that these comments are not framed as an attack on the Pharisees' practices, but rather focus on what they yet lack (see Matthew 19:20). Concerning "judgment and the love of God," Jesus says, "These ought ye to have done, and not to leave the other undone" (Luke 11:42). It is the sins of omission that become the barrier to true holiness.

As with the incident of conflict about eating with unwashed hands found in Matthew and Mark, this scene in which the Pharisees are chastised leads to heightened tension. Wanting so much to be holy, the Pharisees who were chastised did not want to hear that their efforts were misguided and were falling short. This would be an indictment of their entire way of life and their confidence of being justified before God through their righteous deeds. We learn that "as he said these things unto them, the scribes and the Pharisees began to urge him vehemently, and to provoke him to speak of many things: laying wait for him, and seeking to catch something out of his mouth, that they might accuse him" (Luke 11:53–54). In this defensive response to the Savior's call to repentance, we can see hostility developing among the Pharisees. The hope of those who spoke with him to "wait for him" and catch him saying something "that they might accuse him" came only "as he said these things unto them."

Resisting the Call to Holiness

What is striking in the New Testament accounts is not that the Pharisees maintained religious or political opposition to Jesus but that some became hostile in that opposition. We have seen here how the Pharisees' initial concerns centered around ritual cleanliness, although the same pattern holds for their emphasis on the Sabbath day.

While the Pharisees' understanding of how to live the law of Moses led to their initial opposition to Jesus, it was not their focus on ritual purity that caused their negative feelings. Their hostility toward Jesus was neither earlier fixed as a part of their program, nor was it a given result of the experiences that they had with him. Their opposition may have been a matter of different beliefs, but the hostility we see reflects the enmity and hardening of heart that grow from pride. This is a pattern that we can see throughout the scriptures and in our own lives.

The Pharisees lived in a time of great challenge for the covenant people. They had a vision of bringing the holiness of the temple into the lives of all the Jews and diligently set about living their lives in harmony with that vision. In this effort they believed that they were living genuinely holy lives. They were trying very hard to keep the highest standards they could. During his ministry the Savior pointed them to a higher level of holiness, portraying sinners not as those who pollute our ritual holiness but as the sick and lost sheep who need the care of those who are well.[10] Hearing this vision of holiness which focused on meeting others' needs rather than merely rejoicing in their own righteousness, they began to recognize changes they could make. The choice was theirs, as it is all of ours, to repent or to harden our hearts. But choosing to resist the call to repent will lead us to increased hostility toward the One calling us to change.

Seeing the escalation of hostility throughout the Savior's ministry, it is not a great surprise when we read that, after the reports of the raising of

Lazarus had reached the Pharisees, "then gathered the chief priests and the Pharisees a council, and said, What do we? for this man doeth many miracles. If we let him thus alone, all men will believe on him: and the Romans shall come and take away both our place and nation" (John 11:47–48). The defensiveness and fear on the part of the leaders of the Jews is palpable in these statements. A pattern of resistance to the Savior's call had eventually developed a sense of Jesus as a threat in the minds of many of the elite.

We can see that the feeling of being threatened became formulated in political terms by the last months of Jesus's ministry. It is not clear from the historical evidence that the Romans did see Jesus as a threat, but it is important to understand the pressures that the elite of the Jews were under. They were an occupied people, ruled by the Romans in Judea and a Roman-supported ruler in Galilee. Although each of the different Jewish groups had found varying strategies of negotiating the political and social pressures of Roman rule and hellenization, it was in nobody's interest to lose what political and religious autonomy they had. This sense of shared threat can help explain why the chief priests and Pharisees were working together to solve what they saw as a shared problem. It may or may not have been an accurate fear, but it was understandable in light of the fragile political situation they faced.

The prophetic statement of the high priest Caiaphas, who unknowingly testified of Christ's Atonement, was also a clear statement of their feeling of justification: "It is expedient for us, that one man should die for the people, and that the whole nation perish not" (John 11:49–50). The subtle escalation of hostility from offense at being challenged and rebuked had grown to the point at which they associated not just their own well-being but also the survival of their nation on eliminating this threat. By the last months of Jesus's life, the defensiveness of the political and religious elite had led them to feel justified in working toward his demise: "Then from that day forth they took counsel together for to put him to death" (John 11:53).

While these leaders have sometimes been portrayed as evil incarnate, their feelings of defensiveness and resistance may be closer to home than we would like. Those who responded defensively sought to protect themselves from the Savior's critique and call to a higher level of holiness. Surely, they thought, we are right and he is wrong. We are living a holy life. We are keeping the commandments. In their hostility we see, as in a mirror, our own response to chastisement as pride rather than humility. Hostility becomes our defense when we resist the call to repentance.

Jennifer C. Lane is a Neal A. Maxwell Research Associate at the Neal A. Maxwell Institute for Religious Scholarship at Brigham Young Universityy.

Jennifer C. Lane, "Hostility toward Jesus: Prelude to the Passion," in *Celebrating Easter: The 2006 BYU Easter Conference*, ed. Thomas A. Wayment and Keith J. Wilson (Provo, UT: Religious Studies Center, Brigham Young University, 2007), 137–55.

NOTES

1. Many of the interactions between Jesus and the Pharisees took place in Galilee, and the Pharisees involved in working for his death were in Jerusalem. While it is not fully clear what relations existed between the different groups interacting with Christ at different times, I believe that the pattern of response we see with the texts we have can give us insights into a broader sense of how hostility developed in those who saw Jesus as their enemy.
2. Martin S. Jaffee, *Early Judaism* (Upper Saddle River, NJ: Prentice-Hall, 1997), 79. Jaffee states, "But what does seem certain—because it is the only thing upon which our otherwise irreconcilable sources agree—is that the Pharisees placed a great premium on something called 'ancestral tradition.'" All sources consistently assent to the Pharisees' focus on "ancestral tradition" that the rabbis would later call the oral law.
3. See Jacob Neusner, *From Politics to Piety: The Emergence of Pharisaic Judaism* (Englewood Cliffs, NJ: Prentice-Hall, 1973), 83. Calvin Roetzel provides a helpful overview to the New Testament era and puts Neusner's insights into conversation with other scholarship on the Pharisees. Calvin J. Roetzel, *The World That Shaped the New Testament*, rev. ed. (Louisville, KY: Westminster John Knox Press, 2002), 38–43.
4. Neusner, *From Politics to Piety*, 83; emphasis in original.
5. Neusner, *From Politics to Piety*, 80.
6. "Pharisees furthermore ate only with other Pharisees, to be sure that the laws were appropriately observed" (Neusner, *From Politics to Piety*, 80).
7. Neusner, *From Politics to Piety*, 73.
8. An important examination of the role of defensiveness and resentment in hardening hearts can be found in Terry Warner, *Bonds That Make Us Free: Healing Our Relationships, Coming to Ourselves* (Salt Lake City: Shadow Mountain, 2001).
9. For background on the practice of corban, see Max Wilcox, "Corban," in *The Anchor Bible Dictionary*, ed. David Noel Freedman (New York: Doubleday, 1992), 1:1134; and "Corban" in *The International Standard Bible Encyclopedia*, ed. Geoffrey Bromily (Grand Rapids, MI: Eerdmans, 1979), 1:772.
10. On this theme, consider Elder Dale G. Renlund's comment, "As the Good Shepherd, Jesus Christ views disease in His sheep as a condition that needs treatment, care, and

compassion. This shepherd, our Good Shepherd, finds joy in seeing His diseased sheep progress toward healing." Dale G. Renlund, "Our Good Shepherd," *Ensign*, May 2017, 30. He notes, "In our lifelong quest to follow Jesus Christ, His example of kindness to those who sin is particularly instructive. We, who are sinners, must, like the Savior, reach out to others with compassion and love. Our role is also to help and bless, lift and edify, and replace fear and despair with hope and joy. The Savior rebuked individuals who recoiled from others they viewed as unclean and who self-righteously judged others as more sinful than they" (31).

Chapter Ten

Jesus Christ

The Savior Who Knows

FRANK F. JUDD JR.

Jesus knows and loves us. This is a powerful and reassuring reality of the restored gospel. The resurrected Savior declared this truth to the Nephites: "I know my sheep, and they are numbered" (3 Nephi 18:31; see also John 10:14, 27). But what does it mean that Jesus knows us? This truth extends beyond the Savior's knowledge of our identity. Elder Richard G. Scott taught, "The Savior knows you; he loves you and is aware of your specific needs."[1] Our Redeemer does not have just a superficial knowledge, but rather he personally understands our true identity, our innermost needs, and our eternal potential. This chapter explores what Jesus Christ knows about each one of us, how he gained that intimate knowledge, and most importantly, why it is imperative that we are aware of this glorious truth. I hope that a clearer understanding of these issues will foster a deeper comprehension of the life, death, and resurrection of our Savior and result in a greater and more joyful appreciation of the Easter celebration.

Different Kinds of Knowledge

Two essential ways of gaining knowledge are by study and by experience.[2] Both means are important. The Lord commanded the Prophet Joseph Smith to learn through his own research: "Study and learn, and become acquainted with all good books, and with languages, tongues, and people" (Doctrine and Covenants 90:15; see also 88:118; 109:7, 14). Joseph Smith was also informed concerning his suffering in Liberty Jail, "All these things shall give thee experience, and shall be for thy good" (Doctrine and Covenants 122:7).

Some languages, such as the Greek of the New Testament, contain different words to distinguish these kinds of knowledge. While they overlap slightly in meaning, the Greek verb *oida* means "to have information about," while the verb *ginōskō* can refer to "familiarity acquired through experience or association with a pers[on] or thing."[3] Unfortunately, however, in the King James Version of the New Testament, these separate and distinct Greek words are both translated into English as the verb "to know." For instance, the Savior taught that we should know the information contained in the scriptures. In the Gospel of Matthew when Jesus rebuked a group of Sadducees, the Greek word for knowledge of facts is used: "Ye do err, not knowing [*oida*] the scriptures" (Matthew 22:29). On the other hand, Jesus also emphasized the need for knowledge by experience. In the Savior's famous Intercessory Prayer, the Gospel of John uses the Greek word for experiential knowledge: "And this is life eternal, that they might know [*ginōskō*] thee the only true God, and Jesus Christ, whom thou hast sent" (John 17:3). This example underscores how deeply we must come to know God the Father and his Son Jesus Christ to gain eternal life.[4]

Modern revelation reinforces the link between gaining knowledge and gaining salvation: "It is impossible for a man to be saved in ignorance" (Doctrine and Covenants 131:6). Certainly, studying the scriptures and other good literature helps us build an essential foundation. But scriptural or literary knowledge is not the ultimate requirement for salvation. The Prophet Joseph Smith said, "Reading the experience of others, or the revelations given to *them*, can never give *us* a comprehensive view of our condition and true relation to God. *Knowledge of these things can only be obtained by experience* through the ordinance of God set forth for that purpose," and added, "Could you gaze into heaven 5 minute[s,] you would know more—than you would by read[ing] all that ever was writ[te]n on the subject."[5] In addition to learning through participation in sacred ordinances and receiving revelation, experiential knowledge can also be gained by internalizing gospel principles. President David O. McKay taught,

> Gaining knowledge is one thing and applying it, quite another. Wisdom is the right application of knowledge; and true education—the education for which the Church stands—is the application of knowledge to the development of a noble and Godlike character. A man may possess a profound knowledge of history and of mathematics; he may be [an] authority in psychology, biology, or astronomy; he may know all the discovered truths pertaining to geology and natural science; but if he has not with his knowledge the nobility of soul which prompts him to deal justly with his fellow men, to practise virtue and holiness in personal life, he is not a truly educated man. Character is the true aim of education.[6]

How does a wise person come to "know the only true God and Jesus Christ" by experience in the way the Savior intended? John the Beloved gave the answer: "And hereby we do know that we know him, *if we keep his commandments*. He that saith, I know him, and keepeth not his commandments, is a liar" (1 John 2:3–4; emphasis added).[7] The most important knowledge is gained by experience—specifically through revelation and obedience to the commandments of God. Thus, the Lord has explained, "Whatever principle of intelligence we attain unto in this life, it will rise with us in the resurrection. And if a person gains more knowledge and intelligence in this life *through his diligence and obedience* than another, he will have so much the advantage in the world to come" (Doctrine and Covenants 130:18–19; emphasis added).[8]

Certain knowledge can be acquired only by those who are obedient. President Gordon B. Hinckley has taught, "Those who live the Word of Wisdom know the truth of the Word of Wisdom. Those who engage in missionary service know the divine wisdom behind that service. Those who are making an effort to strengthen their families in obedience to the call of the Lord know that they reap the blessings of doing so. Those who engage in temple work know the truth of that work, its divine and eternal implications. Those who pay their tithing know the divine promise underlying that great law, the law of finance for the Church. Those who keep the Sabbath know the divine wisdom which provided for the Sabbath day. . . . Simply live the gospel, and everyone who does so will receive in his heart a conviction of the truth of that which he lives."[9] These principles of gaining knowledge through experience and obedience also apply to Jesus Christ.

The Savior's Personal Knowledge

Our Savior is omniscient, all-knowing in both senses of the word *knowledge*—by study and by experience. The prophet Jacob taught, "O the greatness of the mercy of our God, the Holy One of Israel. . . . For he knoweth all things, and there is not anything save he knows it" (2 Nephi 9:19–20).[10] Further, in a modern revelation the Savior declared that He is "the same which knoweth all things, for all things are present before mine eyes" (Doctrine and Covenants 38:2; see also John 16:30).[11]

The Joseph Smith Translation emphasizes the fact that during his lifetime, Jesus did not depend upon earthly teachers to the same degree that others did: "Jesus grew up with his brethren, and waxed strong, and waited upon the Lord for the time of his ministry to come. And he served under his father, and he spake not as other men, neither could he be taught; for he needed not that any man should teach him" (Joseph Smith Translation, Matthew 3:23).[12] Despite his divine sonship, Jesus also gained knowledge as a mortal being, line upon line and precept upon precept. While growing up in Nazareth, "Jesus increased in wisdom and stature, and in favor with God and man" (Luke 2:52).[13]

Jesus gained factual knowledge by study, especially study of the scriptures. He knew the Old Testament scriptures thoroughly and often cited passages during his sermons (see Matthew 5:21–47). While fasting in the wilderness of Judea, the Savior quoted specific scriptures in order to counter Satan's temptations (see Matthew 4:1–11; Luke 4:1–13).[14] At a synagogue in Nazareth, Jesus read from the scriptures and proclaimed himself to be the fulfillment of prophecy (see Luke 4:16–21). On the road to Emmaus, the resurrected Savior walked with some disciples and "beginning at Moses and all the prophets, he expounded unto them in all the scriptures the things concerning himself" (Luke 24:27). As Jehovah, the premortal Savior said, "I am more intelligent than they all" (Abraham 3:19).[15] Concerning this, Elder Neal A. Maxwell explained, "This means that Jesus knows more about astrophysics than all the humans who have ever lived, who live now, and who will yet live. Likewise, the same may be said about any other topic or subject. Moreover, what the Lord knows is, fortunately, *vastly* more—not just *barely* more—than the combination of what all mortals know."[16]

The Savior also gained knowledge by his own experience during his earthly sojourn, encountering the same types of situations that all mortals do. King Benjamin prophesied that Jesus would "suffer temptations, and pain of body, hunger, thirst, and fatigue" (Mosiah 3:7).[17]

During his mortal ministry, Jesus also knew that he was going to suffer and die for the sins of the world (see Matthew 16:21; 17:22–23; 28:18–19). The Savior's own experience through obedience to his Father, however, perfected that knowledge. As Elder Maxwell explained, "Jesus knew cognitively what He must do, but not experientially. He had never personally known the exquisite and exacting process of an atonement before. Thus, when the agony came in its fulness, it was so much, much worse than even He with his unique intellect had ever imagined!"[18]

The Savior's Vicarious Knowledge of Sin

Another dimension of the Savior's knowledge is the fact that he knows what we go through when we sin. As stated above, Jesus understands us because his mortal life, full of temptations, was similar to that of all human beings. A key difference, however, distinguishes the Savior's mortal experience from ours. As the apostle Paul taught concerning us, "All have sinned, and come short of the glory of God" (Romans 3:23). But Jesus Christ "was in all points tempted like as we are, *yet without sin*" (Hebrews 4:15; emphasis added).[19] How can our Savior really understand what it is like to give in to temptation when he never committed a sin? The answer lies in the Savior's experience of the Atonement.[20]

Because of his mortal life, Jesus knows what it is like to be tempted, but because of his experience in the Garden of Gethsemane and on the cross,[21] Jesus vicariously knows our experience with sin. The resurrected Savior declared to the Nephites concerning his experience, "I have drunk out of that bitter cup which the Father hath given me, and have glorified the Father in *taking upon me the sins of the world*, in the which I have suffered the will of the Father in all things from the beginning" (3 Nephi 11:11; emphasis added).[22] While the Savior prayed in the Garden of Gethsemane following the Last Supper, he was in such agony that "his sweat was as it were great drops of blood falling down to the ground" (Luke 22:44).[23] What made Jesus sweat blood from his pores?

It was, of course, the incomprehensible experience of taking upon himself the sins of the world. There is symbolic meaning in the name of the place where these things occurred. Significantly, the Hebrew name *Gethsemane* means "oil press."[24] President Russell M. Nelson explained that in the place where Jesus suffered, "olives had been pressed under the weight of great stone wheels to squeeze precious oil from the olives. So the Christ in the Garden of Gethsemane was literally pressed under the weight of the sins of the world. He sweated great drops of blood—his life's 'oil'—which issued from every pore."[25] But there seems to be a specific element that directly contributed to this horrible physical reaction.

While upon the cross, Jesus cried out, "My God, my God, why hast thou forsaken me?" (Matthew 27:46). It may be hard for some to imagine that God would really forsake, or leave behind, his Only Begotten Son. But that is exactly what happened. President Brigham Young taught, "At the very moment, at the hour when the crisis came for him to offer up his life, *the Father withdrew Himself, withdrew His Spirit*, and cast a vail [*sic*] over him. That is what made him sweat blood. If he had had the power of God upon him, he would not have sweat blood; but all was withdrawn from him, and a veil was cast over him, and he then pled with the Father not to forsake him."[26] It is true that in Gethsemane "there appeared an angel unto him [Christ] from heaven, strengthening him" (Luke 22:43). But this support seems to have been temporary, for, according to the Savior's own allusion to the presses of Gethsemane, he declared, "I have trodden the wine-press alone . . . and none were with me" (Doctrine and Covenants 133:50; see also 76:107; 88:106; Isaiah 63:3).

According to President Young, the withdrawal of the Spirit seems to be the key to understanding why the Savior sweat blood in the Garden of Gethsemane. The Spirit (and a supporting angel) had been providing Jesus with protection from the full extent of his vicarious suffering. The Lord once taught Martin Harris concerning the experience in the garden:

> I, God, have suffered these things for all, that they might not suffer if they would repent;
>
> But if they would not repent they must suffer even as I;
>
> Which suffering caused myself, even God, the greatest of all, to tremble because of pain, and to bleed at every pore. . . .
>
> Wherefore, I command you again to repent, lest I humble you with my almighty power; and that you confess your sins, lest you suffer these punishments of which I have spoken, *of which in the smallest, yea, even in the least degree you have tasted at the time I withdrew my Spirit.* (Doctrine and Covenants 19:16–20; emphasis added)[27]

This revelation reaffirms that unrepented sin and the loss of the Spirit cause terrible suffering. It also confirms that when Martin Harris sinned and lost the Spirit, he experienced the same kind of suffering, though a minuscule portion that the Savior experienced in Gethsemane when he bled from every pore.[28] Conversely, this scripture shows that in the Garden of Gethsemane, Jesus Christ experienced what humans experience when they sin—suffering as a result of the loss of the Spirit of the Lord.[29] Because of the withdrawal of the Spirit, the Savior suffered for the sins of the world *to the fullest degree* and sweat blood from his pores.[30]

Why would God the Father withdraw his Spirit from his Beloved Son in his hour of need? As with Martin Harris, the Holy Ghost withdraws from us when we sin. The Lord has declared in the latter days, "He that repents not, from him shall be taken even the light which he has received; for my Spirit shall not always strive with man" (Doctrine and Covenants 1:33; see also Genesis 6:3; 1 Nephi 7:14; 2 Nephi 26:11; Ether 2:15; Moses 8:17). When Jesus took upon himself the sins of the world, he vicariously—but literally—became guilty in our behalf. The apostle Paul taught, "Christ hath redeemed us from the curse of the law, *being made a curse for us*" (Galatians 3:13; emphasis added).[31] In another epistle, Paul further taught that God "made him [Christ] to be sin for us" (2 Corinthians 5:21).[32] Somehow Jesus took upon himself the sins of humankind in a very real way—becoming "a curse" and "sin" in the process, and as a result the Father withdrew his Spirit from the Savior.[33]

Stephen E. Robinson summarized this principle: "Christ had become guilty of the sins of the world, guilty in our place. . . . In Gethsemane the best among us vicariously became the worst among us and suffered the very depths of hell. And as one who was guilty, the Savior experienced for the first time in his life the loss of the Spirit of God and of communion with his Father."[34] Because Jesus Christ literally took upon himself the sins of the world, vicariously became full of sin, lost the Spirit, and experienced incomprehensible suffering, he not only knows what it is like to be tempted but also intimately knows what we feel like when we disobey. As a result of bearing the heavy burden of guilt and regret caused by sin, the Savior has perfect empathy for the sinful soul.

Additional Knowledge and Suffering

The Savior's knowledge of us, however, includes much more than his comprehension of temptation and sin. How much more? The author of the Epistle to the Hebrews taught concerning Christ, "*In all things* it behoved him to be made like unto his brethren" (Hebrews 2:17; emphasis added).[35] Alma the Younger prophesied that Christ would not only experience his own "pains and afflictions and temptations of every kind" (Alma 7:11) and "take upon him[self] the sins of his people" (verse 13) but also take upon Himself the "pains," "sicknesses," and "infirmities" of humankind (verses 11–12). According to Alma, then, in Gethsemane the Savior gained a complete comprehension not only of sin but also of other negative experiences that we go through. Elder Jeffrey R. Holland concluded that this additional suffering allowed the Savior to "bear every mortal infirmity; feel every personal heartache, sorrow, and loss."[36] Thus, because of Gethsemane, Jesus Christ not only came to fully know what we go through when we sin but also what we go through when we experience grief and sorrow that has nothing to do with sinful behavior.[37]

Why did Jesus undergo additional suffering—in particular, those things that had nothing to do with sin? When Alma prophesied that Jesus would take upon himself the pains, sicknesses, and infirmities of humankind, he also explained that the Savior would do this "that his bowels may be filled with mercy, according to the flesh, that he may know according to the flesh how to succor his people according to their infirmities" (Alma 7:12).[38] Elder Maxwell explained from these passages that Jesus suffered in this additional way "in order that He might be filled with perfect, personal mercy and empathy and thereby know how to succor us in our infirmities. *He thus fully comprehends human suffering*."[39] Jesus Christ really does know what it is like to be each one of us when we experience heartache and sorrow. As a result, he has full compassion for us in our individual situations.

In this way, Jesus has become the ideal judge of our eternal destiny. Only a judge who understands completely the experiences of the defendant can determine the correct verdict beyond question. Otherwise, there would always be the possibility that the judge did not know some important fact that might bring about a different verdict. Concerning this, Elder Glenn L. Pace concluded, "Part of the reason the Savior suffered in Gethsemane was so that he would have an infinite compassion for us as we experience our trials and tribulations. Through his suffering in Gethsemane, the Savior became qualified to be the perfect judge. Not one of us will be able to approach him on the Judgment Day and say, 'You don't know what it was like.' He knows the nature of our trials better than we do, for he 'descended below them all.'"[40]

Additional scriptures shed light on the extent of our Savior's knowledge of us. Christ's knowledge of us is not merely collective; it is individual. While prophesying of the future Messiah, the prophet Isaiah declared, "When thou shalt make his soul an offering for sin, he shall see his seed" (Isaiah 53:10; see also Mosiah 14:10). After the prophet Abinadi quoted this passage to the people of King Noah, he defined those who are the "seed" of Christ: "Whosoever has heard the words of the prophets, yea, all the holy prophets who have prophesied concerning the coming of the Lord—I say unto you, that all those who have hearkened unto their words, and believed that the Lord would redeem his people, and have looked forward to that day for a remission of their sins, I say unto you, that these are his seed" (Mosiah 15:11).[41] Thus, Christ's "seed" are those who have believed the Savior and utilized his Atonement.

What did Isaiah mean that Christ would "see his seed" when he would "make his soul an offering for sin" in Gethsemane?[42] Elder Merrill J. Bateman interpreted this passage in the following way: "In the garden and on the cross, *Jesus saw each of us*," and therefore "the Savior's atonement in the garden and on the cross is intimate as well as infinite. Infinite in that it spans the eternities. Intimate in that *the Savior felt each person's pains, sufferings, and sicknesses*."[43]

As a result of his experience in Gethsemane, not only does our Savior understand what it is like to be tempted and to give in to sin, he also has a personal knowledge of the mortal experience for each person individually. As Elder Maxwell taught, "There is no personal problem through which anyone has passed or will pass but what Jesus understands profoundly, perfectly, and personally."[44] He knows what it is like to be each one of us when we are sick, lonely, depressed, or mistreated.[45] Jesus Christ is in the ideal position to have compassion upon us, precisely because he knows us perfectly and personally, even better than we know ourselves. He therefore has become not only our perfect judge but also our perfect advocate—our perfect friend.

Personal Application

Once we understand that our Savior has a perfect knowledge of us, what should we do about it? The author of the Epistle to the Hebrews declared, "For we have not an high priest which cannot be touched with the feelings of our infirmities; but was in all points tempted like as we are, yet without sin. *Let us therefore come boldly unto the throne of grace, that we may obtain mercy, and find grace to help in time of need*" (Hebrews 4:15–16; emphasis added). The phrase "throne of grace" refers to the "mercy seat" on the top of the ark of the covenant that was placed in the Holy of Holies in the temple at Jerusalem (see Exodus 25:18–22). The mercy seat itself symbolized the presence of God (see Exodus 30:6). Once a year on the Day of Atonement, the high priest would enter the Holy of Holies and sprinkle the mercy seat with blood, "symbolizing the power of the Atonement to cleanse all of repentant Israel from their sins and to render them worthy to be in the presence of the Lord."[46] Coming "boldly unto the throne of grace" symbolizes confidently approaching our Heavenly Father in prayer in the name of his Son, the supernal high priest, that we might take advantage of the mercy and forgiveness available though the Atonement (see Hebrews 3:1, 5:5, 9:11).

We should not timidly seek these blessings, thinking that our Savior will not understand what we have done or what we are going through. He knows! He understands! Elder Maxwell taught, "Jesus knows and takes into account, personally and perfectly, the highly individualized situations of our 'tether and pang,' including the innermost desires and intents of our hearts."[47] Because this is so, we should confidently seek for relief through the Atonement of Jesus Christ, which includes not only forgiveness of sins, but also daily spiritual assistance to live and endure. Elder Gene R. Cook concluded, "What a glorious thought that, in truth, Jesus Christ is capable of bearing the problems and challenges that we each face in our daily lives. He will not only help us to be saved at the Judgment Day, but he and his Father will be involved with us on a regular basis if we will find access to them."[48]

CONCLUSION

During his mortal life, Jesus learned all about temptation. In Gethsemane, Jesus learned what it is like to sin. Because of this, some may think that the Atonement relates only to repentance and forgiveness of sins. But the experience in Gethsemane also gave the Savior intimate knowledge about the mortal experience for each one of us so that he could help us. Elder Holland testified that "the Savior's Atonement lifts from us not only the burden of our sins but also the burden of our disappointments and sorrows, our heartaches and our despair" and that this knowledge gives us "a reason and a way to improve, an incentive to lay down our burdens and take up our salvation."[49]

Elder David A. Bednar taught,

> The Savior has suffered not just for our sins and iniquities—but also for our physical pains and anguish, our weaknesses and shortcomings, our fears and frustrations, our disappointments and discouragement, our regrets and remorse, our despair and desperation, the injustices and inequities we experience, and the emotional distresses that beset us. There is no physical pain, no spiritual wound, no anguish of soul or heartache, no infirmity or weakness you or I ever confront in mortality that the Savior did not experience first. In a moment of weakness we may cry out, "No one knows what it is like. No one understands." But

> the Son of God perfectly knows and understands, for He has felt and borne our individual burdens. And because of His infinite and eternal sacrifice (see Alma 34:14), He has perfect empathy and can extend to us His arm of mercy. He can reach out, touch, succor, heal, and strengthen us to be more than we could ever be and help us to do that which we could never do relying only upon our own power.[50]

Understanding that our Savior has a perfect knowledge of our individual condition and our unique situation, we should join hands with him as we face the road of life ahead. The prophet Nephi declared concerning his mortal condition and relationship with the Savior, "When I desire to rejoice, my heart groaneth because of my sins; nevertheless, I know in whom I have trusted. My God hath been my support; he hath led me through mine afflictions in the wilderness" (2 Nephi 4:19–20). Jesus Christ is truly the Savior who knows. And because he knows, he is uniquely qualified both to save us from sin and to carry us through the unpredictable wilderness of our lives.

Frank F. Judd Jr. is a professor of ancient scripture at Brigham Young University.

Frank F. Judd Jr., "Jesus Christ: The Savior Who Knows," in *Celebrating Easter: The 2006 BYU Easter Conference*, ed. Thomas A. Wayment and Keith J. Wilson (Provo, UT: Religious Studies Center, Brigham Young University, 2007), 113–36.

Notes

1. Richard G. Scott, "The Power to Make a Difference," *Ensign*, November 1983, 70.
2. For a more detailed discussion of the many ways to gain knowledge, see Gerald N. Lund, "An Anti-Christ in the Book of Mormon—The Face May Be Strange, but the Voice Is Familiar," in *Selected Writings of Gerald N. Lund* (Salt Lake City: Deseret Book, 1999), 120–22.
3. See Frederick William Danker, ed., *A Greek-English Lexicon of the New Testament and Other Early Christian Literature*, 3rd ed. (Chicago: University of Chicago Press, 2000), 693, 199.
4. It is interesting to note that this same Greek word for "knowledge by experience" is used in the Greek Old Testament (the Septuagint) to refer to the marital relationship between husband and wife (see Genesis 4:1, 17, 25). Symbolically, our covenant relationship with the Savior is often described in terms of a marriage, with Jesus as the bridegroom and Church members as the bride (see Matthew 9:14–15; 25:1–13; John 3:27–29;

Revelation 19:7–9). See also Stephen E. Robinson, *Believing Christ* (Salt Lake City: Deseret Book, 1992), 24–25.

5. Minutes, 6–9 October 1843, The Joseph Smith Papers; emphasis added. Discourse, 9 October 1843, as Reported by Willard Richards, The Joseph Smith Papers. Note also Elder Jeffrey R. Holland's comments: "Sometimes we seek heaven too obliquely, focusing on programs or history or the experience of others. Those are important but not as important as personal experience, true discipleship, and the strength that comes from experiencing firsthand the majesty of His touch." "Broken Things to Mend," *Ensign*, May 2006, 70.
6. David O. McKay, *Gospel Ideals* (Salt Lake City: Improvement Era, 1953), 440. Concerning this, Elder Neal A. Maxwell taught: "Knowledge—discovery, its preservation, its perpetuation—is very important. Yet, being knowledgeable while leaving undeveloped the virtues of love, mercy, meekness, and patience is not enough for full discipleship. Mere intellectual assent to a truth deprives us of the relevant, personal experiences that come from applying what we profess to believe. There were probably orientation briefings in the premortal world about how this mortal life would unfold for us, but the real experience is another thing! Thus, while knowledge is clearly very important, standing alone it cannot save us." "Becoming a Disciple," *Ensign*, June 1996, 13–14.
7. In this verse, each instance of the English verb "to know" is a translation of the Greek word for knowledge by experience (*ginōskō*).
8. For the connection between obedience and knowledge, see John 7:17; 8:31–32; Mosiah 4:10; Alma 26:22; Doctrine and Covenants 89:18–19.
9. Gordon B. Hinckley, *Teachings of Gordon B. Hinckley* (Salt Lake City: Deseret Book, 1997), 403–4. President Hinckley also taught, "No force on earth can stop the Almighty from pouring down knowledge . . . if we will live in righteousness, obey the principles of the gospel, do what we ought to do as members of The Church of Jesus Christ of Latter-day Saints, and walk in obedience to the commandments of God. *We will then receive enlightenment and knowledge and understanding and faith*, and our lives will be enriched and be made more happy and more fruitful." Quoted in "News of the Church," *Ensign*, October 1995, 75; emphasis added.
10. The Book of Mormon clearly teaches that "the Holy One of Israel" is Jesus Christ (see 2 Nephi 25:29; Omni 1:26).
11. See also Marion G. Romney, "My Testimony of Jesus Christ," *Ensign*, September 1974, 5.
12. See also Thomas A. Wayment, ed., *The Complete Joseph Smith Translation of the New Testament* (Salt Lake City: Deseret Book, 2005), 5.
13. Modern revelation teaches that the Savior "received not of the fulness at the first, but received grace for grace; and he received not of the fulness at first, but continued from grace to grace, until he received a fulness. And thus he was called the Son of God, because he received not of the fulness at first" (Doctrine and Covenants 93:12–13).
14. See also Howard W. Hunter, "The Temptations of Christ," *Ensign*, November 1976, 18.
15. For Jesus's identity as Jehovah, see 3 Nephi 15:4–5 and John 8:58–59.
16. Neal A. Maxwell, *All These Things Shall Give Thee Experience* (Salt Lake City: Deseret Book, 1979), 22.
17. Besides the famous temptations in the wilderness of Judea (see Matthew 4:1–11; Luke 4:1–13), see also Matthew 16:1; 19:3; 22:8, 35. Alma prophesied that Christ would "go forth, suffering pains and afflictions and temptations of every kind" (Alma 7:11).
18. Neal A. Maxwell, "Willing to Submit," *Ensign*, May 1985, 72–73.
19. Paul taught that Christ "knew no sin" (2 Corinthians 5:21).

20. See Robinson, *Believing Christ*, 116–25.
21. Both Elder James E. Talmage and Elder Bruce R. McConkie taught that the terrible type of suffering that the Savior endured in the Garden of Gethsemane "recurred" while he was upon the cross. See James E. Talmage, *Jesus the Christ* (Salt Lake City: The Church of Jesus Christ of Latter-day Saints, 1915), 661; Bruce R. McConkie, *A New Witness for the Articles of Faith* (Salt Lake City: Deseret Book, 1985), xiv, 289; and Bruce R. McConkie, *The Mortal Messiah* (Salt Lake City: Deseret Book, 1979–81), 4:224.
22. See also Alma 34:8: "Christ shall come among the children of men, to take upon him the transgressions of his people, and that he shall atone for the sins of the world."
23. Both the Book of Mormon and the Doctrine and Covenants confirm that the language in this scripture is to be taken literally (see Mosiah 3:7; Doctrine and Covenants 19:18).
24. Ulrich Luz, *Matthew 21–28* (Minneapolis: Fortress Press, 2005), 395.
25. Russell M. Nelson, "Why This Holy Land?" *Ensign*, December 1989, 17–18. See also Robinson, *Believing Christ*, 119–20.
26. Brigham Young, in *Journal of Discourses* (London: Latter-day Saints' Book Depot, 1854–86), 3:206; emphasis added. On this issue, see also Robert L. Millet, "Treading the Winepress Alone," in *The Gospels*, vol. 5 of *Studies in Scripture* (Salt Lake City: Deseret Book, 1986), 434–35. Since the original publication of this chapter in 2007, Elder Jeffrey R. Holland has taught the following: "I testify . . . that a perfect Father did not forsake His Son in that hour. Indeed, it is my personal belief that . . . the Father may never have been closer to His Son than in these agonizing final moments of suffering" (*Ensign*, May 2009). It should be remembered that the English word "forsake" can carry different connotations, including to "permanently abandon" or to "temporarily leave alone." Elder Holland was teaching that the Father did not permanently abandon Christ. But the Father did indeed temporarily leave Christ alone. Elder Holland confirmed that this is the case: "Nevertheless . . . the Father briefly withdrew from Jesus the comfort of His Spirit, the support of his personal presence." To avoid confusion, it should be noted that this temporary experience can also be described by the English word *forsake* and is what Christ was referring to when he cried out "My God, my God, why hast thou forsaken me?" (Matthew 27:46). Elder Holland explained why this temporary leaving alone (or temporary forsaking) was necessary: "It was required, indeed it was central to the significance of the Atonement, that this perfect Son . . . had to know how the rest of humankind—us, all of us—would feel when we did commit such sins. For His Atonement to be infinite and eternal, He had to feel what it was like to die not only physically but spiritually, to sense what it was like to have the divine Spirit withdraw, leaving one feeling totally, abjectly, hopelessly alone." Thus, as Elder Holland explained, the Father did not permanently forsake or abandon Jesus, but he did temporarily forsake or leave Jesus alone as he took upon himself the sins of humankind.
27. At this point in Church history, Martin Harris was having second thoughts about mortgaging part of his farm to pay for the publication of the Book of Mormon. See Stephen E. Robinson and H. Dean Garrett, *A Commentary on the Doctrine and Covenants* (Salt Lake City: Deseret Book, 2000–2005), 1:110–11.
28. Concerning these verses, Robinson and Garrett conclude: "The unrepentant will, however, each suffer *for their own sins* as [Jesus] suffered *for the sins of the world*, suffering exactly the same kind of anguish, but not to the same degree." Robinson and Garrett, *Commentary on the Doctrine and Covenants*, 1:118; emphasis in original.

29. Robert J. Matthews taught, "[Christ] died a physical death on the cross, and he died a 'spiritual death' in the Garden of Gethsemane (as well as on the cross) when he took upon himself the sins of all mankind." *A Bible! A Bible!* (Salt Lake City: Bookcraft, 1990), 260.
30. The Lord has declared in modern revelation that the Savior "descended below" everything that any mortal has experienced. See Doctrine and Covenants 122:8; 88:6. On this issue, see also Millet, "Treading the Winepress Alone," 436–38.
31. Paul was alluding to the reference in the law of Moses, where the Lord declared to ancient Israel: "If a man have committed a sin worthy of death. . . . Thou [shalt] hang him on a tree . . . for he that is hanged is accursed of God" (Deuteronomy 21:22–23).
32. Note the interpretation of C. K. Barrett: "Christ became *sin*; that is, he came to stand in that relation with God which normally is the result of sin, estranged from God and the object of his wrath." *The Second Epistle to the Corinthians* (London: A & C Black, 1973), 180. F. F. Bruce refers to this passage from C. K. Barrett when interpreting Galatians 3:13; see *The Epistle to the Galatians* (Grand Rapids, MI: Eerdmans, 1982), 166. In light of Barrett's interpretation of Paul that Christ became sin and the object of God's wrath, note that modern revelation calls Christ's experience in Gethsemane "the wine-press of the fierceness of the wrath of Almighty God" (Doctrine and Covenants 76:107; see also 88:106).
33. Robert L. Millet interpreted Galatians 3:13 and 2 Corinthians 5:21 to mean the innocent man Jesus vicariously became "the great sinner" in Gethsemane. *The Power of the Word: Saving Doctrines from the Book of Mormon* (Salt Lake City: Deseret Book, 1994), 13, 92, 178.
34. Robinson, *Believing Christ,* 118–19. Recent studies of the experiences of the Savior in Gethsemane can be found in Andrew C. Skinner, *Gethsemane* (Salt Lake City: Deseret Book, 2002) and Terry B. Ball, "Gethsemane," in *The Life and Teachings of Jesus Christ,* vol. 3, *The Savior's Final Hours,* ed. Richard Neitzel Holzapfel and Thomas A. Wayment (Salt Lake City: Deseret Book, 2003), 138–64.
35. The author of the Epistle to the Hebrews also taught that Jesus "was *in all points* tempted like as we are" (Hebrews 4:15; emphasis added).
36. Jeffrey R. Holland, "Special Witnesses of Christ," *Ensign,* April 2001, 14.
37. Elder Neal A. Maxwell explained Alma's prophecy: "Jesus also volunteered to take upon Himself *additional agony* in order that He might experience and thus know certain things 'according to the flesh,' namely *human sicknesses and infirmities and human griefs,* including those *not associated with sin.*" "Becoming a Disciple," *Ensign,* June 1996, 12; emphasis added.
38. The author of the Epistle to the Hebrews similarly taught that the Savior experienced these things "that he might be a merciful and faithful high priest in things pertaining to God, to make reconciliation for the sins of the people. For in that he himself hath suffered being tempted, *he is able to succor them that are tempted*" (Hebrews 2:17–18; emphasis added). It is significant that, following the completion of His experience in Gethsemane and Golgotha, the resurrected Savior declared to the Nephites: "I have compassion upon you; my bowels are filled with mercy" (3 Nephi 17:7).
39. Neal A. Maxwell, "Enduring Well," *Ensign,* April 1997, 7; emphasis added.
40. Glenn L. Pace, "Crying with the Saints," *Ensign,* September 1988, 71. Elder Maxwell also taught, "He [Christ] took upon Himself our sins as well as our pains, sicknesses, and infirmities. (See Alma 7:11–12.) Thus He knew, not in abstraction but in actuality, 'according to the flesh,' the whole of human suffering. He bore our infirmities before we bore them. He knows perfectly well how to succor us. We can tell Him nothing of pain,

temptation, or affliction." *We Will Prove Them Herewith* (Salt Lake City: Deseret Book, 1982), 46–47.

41. See also Mosiah 5:7: "Because of the covenant which ye have made ye shall be called *the children of Christ*, his sons, and his daughters; for behold, this day he hath spiritually begotten you; for ye say that your hearts are changed through faith on his name; therefore, ye are born of him and have become *his sons and his daughters*" (emphasis added).
42. The Hebrew verb "to see" (*ra'ah*) can mean literally "to see" with the eyes, or figuratively "to perceive" with the mind. See Francis Brown, S. R. Driver, and Charles A. Briggs, eds., *A Hebrew and English Lexicon of the Old Testament* (New York: Oxford University Press, 1951), 906–8.
43. Merrill J. Bateman, "The Power to Heal from Within," *Ensign*, May 1995, 14; emphasis added.
44. Neal A. Maxwell, *Plain and Precious Things* (Salt Lake City: Deseret Book, 1983), 43. Note also Elder Maxwell's further teaching: "Jesus knows the sheep of His fold not only for *what they now are* but also for *what they have the power to become.*" *Even As I Am* (Salt Lake City: Deseret Book, 1982), 78.
45. Note Elder Maxwell's plea: "Do we understand—really comprehend—that Jesus knows and understands when we are stressed and perplexed? The complete consecration which effected the Atonement ensured Jesus' perfect empathy; He felt our very pains and afflictions before we did and knows how to succor us." "Swallowed Up in the Will of the Father," *Ensign*, November 1995, 24. See also Neal A. Maxwell, *If Thou Endure It Well* (Salt Lake City: Bookcraft, 1996), 52; Robinson, *Believing Christ*, 122–23.
46. Richard Neitzel Holzapfel and David Rolph Seely, *My Father's House: Temple Worship and Symbolism in the New Testament* (Salt Lake City: Bookcraft, 1994), 60; see also Leviticus 16:14–15; Hebrews 9:7.
47. Neal A. Maxwell, *One More Strain of Praise* (Salt Lake City: Deseret Book, 1999), 40. In a previous book, Elder Maxwell taught, "Jesus knows and cares for each individual; He watches carefully over the seemingly smallest of things." *That Ye May Believe* (Salt Lake City: Bookcraft, 1992), 205.
48. Gene R. Cook, "The Grace of the Lord," *New Era*, December 1988, 4.
49. Jeffrey R. Holland, "Broken Things to Mend," *Ensign*, May 2006, 70–71.
50. David A. Bednar, "Bear Up Their Burdens with Ease," *Ensign*, May 2014, 89–90.

Chapter Eleven

The Loving Christ

JOHN HILTON III

Let me begin with a simple question. How do you think the average member of The Church of Jesus Christ of Latter-day Saints would respond to the following statement: "Although Christ's Atonement was a process, where would you say Jesus *mostly* atoned for our sins? (a) In the Garden of Gethsemane. (b) On the cross at Calvary."

When some colleagues and I surveyed almost a thousand Latter-day Saint adults and asked them this question, 88 percent said, "in the Garden of Gethsemane," and 12 percent said, "on the cross at Calvary." One might think, "That is an unfair question—people were forced to choose between only two options." To remedy this situation, my colleagues and I asked 792 Latter-day Saint adults (who did *not* participate in the first survey) the same question and gave them a third possible response: "equally in Gethsemane and Calvary." But even with this third option, 58 percent—still a strong majority—selected Gethsemane only.[1]

This indicates a tendency among some Latter-day Saint adults to give priority to the atoning significance of Gethsemane over that of Calvary. In this essay, I will show how the scriptures, Joseph Smith, Church leaders collectively, the hymns, and the Savior himself more frequently talk about

Christ's Crucifixion than they do his sufferings in Gethsemane. I will then provide two reasons why studying the Savior's sacrifice on Calvary can help us and share two examples of how focusing on Christ's Crucifixion can strengthen us spiritually. Before I continue, let me be clear that Gethsemane and Golgotha are both vital aspects of Christ's Atonement. They are not in competition with each other. My point is that some Latter-day Saints underemphasize the importance of Christ's Crucifixion. As we more fully embrace scriptural and prophetic teachings about the Savior's death, we will draw closer to him.

When I learned that Latter-day Saints heavily emphasized Gethsemane over Calvary, I was curious. Why was there so much emphasis on Gethsemane? Did it come from the scriptures? Across the standard works, there are two passages of scripture that talk about Jesus Christ suffering for our sins in Gethsemane.[2] In contrast, there are fifty-three passages that talk about Jesus Christ dying for our sins: twenty-one in the New Testament, eighteen in the Book of Mormon, twelve in the Doctrine and Covenants, and two in the Pearl of Great Price.[3] For example, at the beginning of the Book of Mormon, Nephi recounts, "I, Nephi, saw that [Christ] was lifted up upon the cross and slain for the sins of the world" (1 Nephi 11:33).

The emphasis on Calvary also appears in the noncanonized writings and sermons of Joseph Smith, in which he only referred to Gethsemane one time. In this instance, he does not discuss its atoning significance; rather, he uses it as an example of Jesus doing the will of his Father. In contrast, Joseph Smith spoke or wrote about Christ's Crucifixion on thirty-four occasions. Nine of these are explicit statements that Jesus Christ was crucified for the sins of the world.[4] For example, in his 1832 account of the First Vision, Joseph wrote that Jesus said to him, "I am the Lord of glory. *I was crucified for the world,* that all those who believe on my name may have eternal life."[5] On another occasion, Joseph Smith said, "The fundamental principles of our religion are the testimony of the Apostles and Prophets, concerning Jesus Christ, *that He died*, was buried, and rose again the third day, and ascended into heaven; and all other things which pertain to our religion are only appendages to it."[6]

A focus on Calvary also exists when looking at the teachings of Church leaders from 1850 to the present. Collectively, for each one statement from Church leaders about Christ suffering for our sins, there are more than five

The Crucifixion, by Harry Anderson. © Intellectual Reserve, Inc.

about him dying for our sins. If we look only at the words of Church Presidents, the gap widens—for every one statement from a Church President about Christ suffering for our sins in Gethsemane, there are more than twelve about him dying for our sins on the cross.[7]

The hymns likewise share this emphasis. A study of four Latter-day Saint hymnbooks—the three earliest and the current one—shows that less than 1 percent of the hymns refer to Gethsemane, while 16 percent refer to Calvary.[8] For example, a popular sacrament hymn states, "We'll sing all hail to Jesus' name, / And praise and honor give / To him who bled on Calvary's hill / And died that we might live."[9]

To me, what is most significant is the Savior's own emphasis on his gift from Golgotha. In scripture, Christ personally refers to his experience in Gethsemane on one powerful occasion. In contrast, he refers to his death more than twenty times.[10] When Jesus Christ defines his gospel, his Crucifixion is front and center (see 3 Nephi 27:14).

Thus far, I have shown a juxtaposition between what the scriptures, Joseph Smith, later Church leaders, hymns, and the Savior himself have taught and emphasized as far as the atoning significance of Calvary relative to what the average Latter-day Saint adult seems to believe. Before continuing, let me be very clear—the events that took place in Gethsemane are a significant part of the Savior's Atonement; I am certainly *not* recommending we de-emphasize them. Many Latter-day Saints have focused primarily on Christ's sufferings in Gethsemane and not thought as often about his death on the cross. I'm not suggesting we reverse this error by exclusively prioritizing Golgotha and ignoring Gethsemane. Indeed, we should pay more attention to every facet of Christ's life, including his sermons, miracles, and actions.

At the same time, I have found that for many Latter-day Saints, an in-depth study of Christ's Crucifixion is particularly profitable because, in underestimating its significance, some of us have not studied it as carefully as we could. President James E. Faust taught, "Any increase in our understanding of [Christ's] atoning sacrifice draws us closer to Him."[11] Better understanding *any* aspect of Christ's Atonement—including, and perhaps especially his Crucifixion—can deepen our relationship with the Savior.[12]

At this point, many readers are likely wondering, "If there has been such an emphasis on Christ's Crucifixion in the scriptures and elsewhere, why do so many Latter-day Saints seem to prioritize Gethsemane when it comes to the Savior atoning for our sins?" In trying to answer this question, incorrect speculations have been proposed. For example, some have suggested that Christ atoned for our sins and overcame spiritual death only in Gethsemane and then separately conquered physical death on the cross. Elder Gerald N. Lund called this a "doctrinal error" and wrote, "Nowhere in the scriptures do we find indications that the cross alone overcame physical death or that the Garden alone overcame spiritual death."[13]

A related doctrinal error comes if we minimize Christ's experience on the cross by saying, "What Christ experienced on the cross was no different than the suffering experienced by thousands of others who were crucified." That statement is false. The Savior's experience on the cross was completely different from other victims of crucifixion. Jesus did not just die—he "died *for our sins*" (1 Corinthians 15:3); his Crucifixion had atoning efficacy. President Russell M. Nelson taught that the suffering Christ experienced in Gethsemane was "intensified as He was cruelly crucified on Calvary's cross."[14]

Although the space available does not afford a complete answer as to why there is a disconnect between the beliefs of average Church members and collective Church teachings, possible reasons for an emphasis on Gethsemane by Church members include the following: (1) Latter-day Saints have a unique doctrinal understanding of the importance of Gethsemane and so have foregrounded it. (2) A handful of statements from Church leaders from several decades ago prioritized Gethsemane over Calvary. Some of these statements were published in past (but not current) Church curriculum materials, perhaps giving them outsized importance even though they are out of the mainstream of prophetic teachings.[15] (3) Perhaps the most significant reason Church members de-emphasize the atoning significance of Calvary is the lack of Crucifixion artwork and cross iconography in our church buildings.

While not the focus of this essay, the scarcity of Crucifixion imagery merits attention. When Latter-day Saints are asked why their church does not display crosses, they tend to paraphrase words stated by President Gordon B. Hinckley in 1975. In response to a minister's question about the lack of a cross in a temple, President Hinckley responded, "I do not wish to give offense to any of my Christian brethren who use the cross on the steeples of their cathedrals and at the altars of their chapels, who wear it on their vestments, and imprint it on their books and other literature. *But for us, the cross is the symbol of the dying Christ, while our message is a declaration of the living Christ.* . . . The lives of our people must become the only meaningful expression of our faith and, in fact, therefore, the symbol of our worship."[16] It is important to note that in this same talk President Hinckley also referred to "the cross on which [Christ] hung and died," and said, "We cannot forget

that. We must never forget it, for here our Savior, our Redeemer, the Son of God, gave Himself a vicarious sacrifice for each of us."[17] Thus, while de-emphasizing the Church's use of the cross as an institutional symbol, President Hinckley emphasized the atoning significance of Calvary.

Symbols are multifaceted: they permit, even invite, layers of meaning. A cursory look at Church history indicates that the symbol of the cross has been viewed in different ways across the decades. For example, multiple nineteenth-century Latter-day Saints posed for formal photographs while wearing cross jewelry, including a wife and a daughter of Brigham Young. A cross appears on the 1852 European edition of the Doctrine and Covenants, and a floral cross was present at the funeral of John Taylor. In addition, a proposal for a cross to be placed on Ensign Peak was approved by President Joseph F. Smith, and a large cross is on the gravestone of Elder B. H. Roberts of the Seventy.[18] Consider a few quotes

1852 European edition of the Doctrine and Covenants. Photo courtesy of Megan Cutler, used with permission; edition found in L. Tom Perry Special Collections, Harold B. Lee Library, Brigham Young University, Provo, Utah.

The grave of B. H. Roberts. Courtesy of Megan Cutler, used with permission.

Brigham Young's daughter, Nabby Young Clawson (left), and his wife, Amelia Folsom Young, wearing crosses. © Utah State Historical Society.

that illustrate the diversity with which the cross has been viewed by Latter-day Saints:

- Eliza R. Snow referred to "the triumphs of the cross."[19]
- A 1915 editorial published in the *Young Woman's Journal* stated, "The cross . . . has become a symbol of love and salvation."[20]
- A 1933 editorial in the *Relief Society Magazine* said that "Christ changed the cross into a symbol of Glory."[21]
- Elder Edward Dube referred to seeing an image of Christ's Crucifixion as one of the "defining moments" of his life.[22]
- Elder F. Enzio Busche said that looking at a crucifix helped him develop "a tremendous hope" in the redeeming power of Jesus Christ.[23]

Many similar examples could be provided. My point is that throughout the history of Christianity and even within the restored Church, faithful believers have had differing perspectives on how the cross should be used to represent Christ's atoning sacrifice. Regardless of how one views the cross as a symbol, we should focus on the doctrinal reality that Jesus Christ was, in his own words, "crucified for the sins of the world" (Doctrine and Covenants 53:2).

Thus far, I have demonstrated the scriptural emphasis on Christ's Crucifixion and provided a few possible reasons why church members have tended to focus more on Gethsemane. In the remainder of this essay, I will provide two reasons why studying Christ's Crucifixion can be beneficial and then share two examples of how focusing on Christ's Crucifixion can strengthen us spiritually.

Reason 1: Connecting with the Loving Christ

First, studying Christ's Crucifixion can help us connect with the loving Christ. Some Church members focus exclusively on the *living* Christ, and of course it is the living Christ that we worship. At the same time, we also worship a *loving* Christ, and the scriptures repeatedly teach that both Heavenly Father and Jesus Christ manifested their love for us through the Savior's death. For example, Paul declared, "*God commendeth his love toward us,* in that, while we were yet sinners, *Christ died for us*" (Romans 5:8; see also John 10:17; 1 John 3:16; 4:9–10). Jesus Christ himself called the Crucifixion his greatest act of love, saying, "Greater love hath no man than this, that a man lay down his life for his friends" (John 15:13; see also 2 Nephi 26:24; Ether 12:33).

Latter-day Saints throughout the decades have taught this same idea. For example, in 1910 Henry W. Naisbitt wrote, "When I think of the cross, the glorified cross, / On earth as in heaven above, / Resplendent forever undimmed it shall shine, / The eloquent symbol of love!"[24] In 1935 Grace Jacobsen poetically penned, "See the cross and bleeding feet . . . / Hear the message, tender sweet, / Hear him calling, gently calling / All mankind to Him above, / For He gave His life a ransom, / From the depths of perfect love."[25] Marguerite J. Griffin, writing in 1946, taught that Jesus offered his life "on the cross because of his great love for you and me."[26] More recently, Elder Dale G. Renlund stated, "Jesus Christ . . . loves and cares for us. He knows us and laid down His life for His sheep."[27]

Do you and I want to feel more love from Jesus?

Do you and I want to feel more love for Jesus?

Then let us study the Crucifixion—the event Christ personally defined as his greatest act of love. By better understanding the Savior's death, we will feel his love in greater abundance and be increasingly able to share that love with others.

Although we believe in the living Christ, we can also be strengthened by learning more about his sacrifice and death. Jennifer Lane, former dean of the faculty of Religious Education at BYU–Hawaii, wrote, "As we think about the Lamb slain from the foundation of the world, we can also know that he is the life and the light of the world: Christ as the sacrifice and Christ as the living Word. We don't have to pick which one to focus on because we can't have one without the other."[28] Jesus is both the living *and* the loving Christ.

Reason 2: Building Bridges

A second reason to study Christ's Crucifixion is to remember that there are 2.3 billion Christians in the world and that nearly all of them believe Christ died for our sins, providing Latter-day Saints with a perfect opportunity to build on common beliefs. When I was a full-time missionary, if I saw somebody wearing a cross, I probably would have thought, "Oh, they are different." If I were a full-time missionary today, I would be so excited! I would say, "Hi, I can see from your jewelry that you probably believe in Jesus Christ. Could you tell me about your beliefs?" After listening, I might tell them about my beliefs or share a passage from the Book of Mormon that focuses on the importance of the cross, such as 3 Nephi 27:14.

Unfortunately, we don't always take advantage of opportunities to build on common beliefs. A Latter-day Saint woman who lived in the southern United States told me about inviting a neighbor to attend her daughter's baptism. When the neighbor presented the eight-year-old with a cross necklace, both the child and her mother froze, not knowing what to do. Sensing their discomfort, the neighbor took back the cross and said she would get the child a different gift. Regretfully looking back on this experience, the Latter-day Saint said that she wished she had seen this as an opportunity to rejoice with her friend in their shared belief in Jesus Christ rather than let it divide them.

Eric D. Huntsman, professor of ancient scripture at Brigham Young University, recounted the following:

> I remember being surprised once when a . . . Presbyterian friend corrected me when I told her that we preferred to worship a living rather than a dead Christ; she responded that she did too. The cross reminded Protestants that Jesus died for their sins, but it was empty because he was risen and was no longer there on it. I was chastened by her response, realizing that just as we do not appreciate others mischaracterizing our beliefs, neither should we presume to understand or misrepresent the beliefs and practices of others.[29]

Such mischaracterizations happen not only between Latter-day Saints and those of other denominations but also among Latter-day Saints themselves. A young adult told me that she had an institute sticker on her car that allowed her to park in the institute parking lot. She also had a cross hanging from her rearview mirror, which for her signified her belief in the Savior's Atonement. One day she found a note on her car that said, "Why do you have an institute sticker and cross on your car? Pick one!" I'm grateful this individual has remained firm in her commitment to the Church of Jesus Christ but wonder how many visitors or others have left because of unnecessary comments about the cross.

To be clear, I'm not suggesting we all start wearing cross jewelry. I am suggesting that you and I as individuals should let go of any stigma we feel about the cross, and we should certainly never put down somebody who wears or displays one. Let us celebrate those who believe in Jesus Christ and are willing to publicly proclaim their belief in him—however they manifest it. The doctrinal significance of Christ's Crucifixion is much more important than whether one uses a specific symbol. As we embrace and learn more about the Crucifixion of Jesus Christ, we will find that we have something in common with other Christians and a great opportunity to build bridges.

Illustration 1: Understanding Christ's Crucifixion Can Strengthen Us to Carry Our Crosses

I now turn to two illustrations of spiritually strengthening insights we can gain as we study Christ's Crucifixion. First, understanding the Savior's death can help us press forward despite extreme difficulties. The book of Hebrews teaches, "Jesus . . . for the joy that was set before him endured the cross, despising the shame, and is set down at the right hand of the throne of God" (Hebrews 12:2). Similarly, the Book of Mormon prophet Jacob spoke of those "who have endured the crosses of the world, and despised the shame of it, they shall inherit the kingdom of God, which was prepared for them from the foundation of the world, and their joy shall be full forever" (2 Nephi 9:18). Note that in both passages, there is a connection between enduring a cross, despising the shame of the cross, and finding joy.

As we follow the path of Christian discipleship, we will bear crosses and perhaps be shamed by others for our belief in Christ and his teachings. But Jesus endured his cross and received great joy; he says to each of us, "If any want to become my followers, let them deny themselves and take up their cross daily and follow me" (Luke 9:23 NRSV).[30] Note that we are instructed to take up our crosses *daily* and do so while *following* Jesus.

Today when we hear the phrase "take up the cross," we perhaps think metaphorically about carrying our different burdens. How would Christ's disciples have thought about this phrase? The Greek word translated as "cross" in Luke 9:23 is the same word used to describe Jesus on the physical cross where he was crucified (see Luke 23:26). The disciples had likely seen others literally take up their crosses on the way to execution. Is it possible that to Jesus's disciples the phrase "take up your cross" had a more graphic feel than it does to us today? Evangelical scholar Dr. D. A. Carson writes,

> In the first century it was as culturally unthinkable to make jokes about crucifixion as it would be today to make jokes about Auschwitz. To carry your cross does not mean to move forward with courage despite the fact you lost your job or your spouse. It means you are under sentence of death; you are taking up the horizontal cross-member on your way to the place of crucifixion. You have abandoned all hope of life in this world. And then, Jesus says, and only then, are we ready to follow him.[31]

Contemplating the realities of Roman crucifixion can deepen our understanding of Christ's call to deny ourselves, take up our crosses daily, and follow him. If we consider this invitation in a first-century context, as suggested by Dr. Carson, the vivid connection between Christ's taking up his cross and our taking up our own can move us to greater courage when we face challenging circumstances. The Savior did not flinch from the cross he faced; rather, as Paul wrote, Jesus "emptied himself . . . and became obedient to the point of death—even death on a cross" (Philippians 2:7–8 NRSV; see also 2 Nephi 9:18). Pondering Christ on his cross can strengthen us to deny ourselves, despise the shame of the world, carry our crosses *daily*, and follow Jesus—even when we feel like giving up.

Illustration 2: Crucifying the Sin Within

A second illustration of a spiritually enriching insight related to Calvary is how Christ's Crucifixion can help us overcome sin. The apostle Paul writes, "Those who belong to Christ Jesus have crucified the flesh with its passions and desires" (Galatians 5:24 NRSV). Thus, Paul uses crucifixion language to motivate us to destroy any remnants of evil lying within us. In effect, Paul encourages us to nail our sins to the cross of Jesus Christ and leave them with him on Calvary.[32]

In this same epistle, Paul writes, "I am crucified with Christ" (Galatians 2:20). This visceral image suggests that to follow Christ, we must follow him to the cross and spiritually crucify the natural man or woman in each of us. In fact, at the conclusion of Galatians, Paul writes, "In the cross of our Lord Jesus Christ, . . . the world is crucified unto me" (Galatians 6:14). Think about those words: *the world is crucified unto me*. Paul seems to suggest that because of Christ's Crucifixion, sin can become less appealing, eventually becoming dead to us. While such a state may not come immediately, it will come as we increasingly draw closer to Jesus and understand his atoning sacrifice (see Alma 13:12).

How can we crucify our lustful flesh and thus decrease our desire to sin? At least one approach is to accept the Savior's personal invitation to fix our eyes on his crucifixion wounds. The living Christ has said, "Behold [meaning "fix your eyes upon"[33]] the wounds which pierced my side, and also the prints of the nails in my hands and feet" (Doctrine and Covenants 6:37). The more we remember what he did for us, the more we will do what he asks of us. Perhaps this is why the Book of Mormon prophet Jacob wanted all to "view [Christ's] death" (Jacob 1:8), and Mormon encouraged his son to let the death of Christ rest in his mind forever (see Moroni 9:25). Accepting the scriptural invitations to "behold [Christ's] wounds," "view his death," and let Christ's death "rest in [our] mind[s] forever" can strengthen us to, in Paul's words, crucify "the flesh with its passions and desires" (Galatians 5:24 NRSV).

Conclusion

Although Latter-day Saints tend to give atoning priority to Gethsemane, the scriptures, Joseph Smith, Church leaders, the hymns, and Jesus Christ himself all more heavily emphasize Calvary. Throughout the history of The Church of Jesus Christ of Latter-day Saints, there has been a diversity of opinions about the meaning of the cross as a symbol. Many Latter-day Saints have viewed it as a symbol of love, glory, and triumph, perhaps suggesting that some of us today could reevaluate our current feelings toward the cross as a symbol.

We will fortify our relationship with the Savior as we focus on an event he often uses to identify himself. Our feelings for Jesus will grow as we recognize him as both the living and the loving Christ. We will feel a greater abundance of the Spirit as we rejoice with other Christians in our common belief that Christ died for our sins. A deeper understanding of Christ's Crucifixion will strengthen us in our trials and help us to nail our sins to his cross—and leave them there. These and many other powerful principles will distill in our souls as we, in the words of the apostle Paul, "glory . . . in the cross" (Galatians 6:14). Studying Christ's death can change our lives.

Of course, the Savior's Crucifixion should not be the sole focus of our studies. His life and his parables, his resurrection and his miracles also merit a lifetime of careful examination. President Russell M. Nelson has promised, "The more we know about the Savior's ministry and mission—the more we understand His doctrine and what He did for us—the more we know that He can provide the power that we need for our lives."[34]

In Doctrine and Covenants 46, the Lord lists several spiritual gifts. The *very first gift listed* is to know through the Holy Ghost "that Jesus Christ is the Son of God, and that *he was crucified for the sins of the world*" (Doctrine and Covenants 46:13, emphasis added). This testimony is a spiritual gift each of us can receive and develop at increasingly deeper levels. President M. Russell Ballard taught that every member of the Church is entitled to and can "develop an apostolic-like relationship with the Lord."[35] Learning more about every aspect of Christ's life and atoning sacrifice will help us gain this witness.

My heart is filled with gratitude for the Savior. He is "Christ crucified," "the Lamb slain from the foundation of the world" (1 Corinthians 1:23;

Revelation 13:8). He is the one who "liveth, and was dead; and . . . [is] alive for evermore" (Revelation 1:18). He is "our peace," "our passover," "our life," and "our Lord Jesus Christ" (Ephesians 2:14; 1 Corinthians 5:7; Colossians 3:3; Philippians 4:23). May we each strive to learn all we can about him—including the sacrifice he made on Calvary.

John Hilton III is a professor of ancient scripture at Brigham Young University.

John Hilton III, "The Loving Christ," in *The Power of Christ's Deliverance*, ed. Jan J. Martin and Alonzo L. Gaskill (Provo, UT: Religious Studies Center, Brigham Young University; Salt Lake City: Deseret Book, 2022), 67–90. Significant portions of this chapter are drawn from John Hilton III, *Considering the Cross: How Calvary Connects Us with Christ* (Salt Lake City: Deseret Book, 2021), used with permission.

NOTES

1. John Hilton III, Anthony Sweat, and Joshua Stratford, "Latter-day Saints and Images of Christ's Crucifixion," *BYU Studies Quarterly 60*, no. 2 (2021): 49–70, available at http://johnhiltoniii.com/crucifixion.
2. See Mosiah 3:7; Doctrine and Covenants 19:16–19. Other verses, such as Isaiah 53:4 and Alma 7:11–13, may connect to the Garden of Gethsemane, but the verses themselves do not directly reference Christ's sufferings there. Luke 22:44 speaks of Christ's sweat being like great drops of blood; however, it does not attach atoning significance to this event.
3. See John 3:14–15; 12:32; Romans 5:6, 8, 10; 1 Corinthians 5:7; 15:3; 2 Corinthians 5:15; Galatians 3:13; Ephesians 2:16; Colossians 1:20, 21–22; 2:14; 1 Thessalonians 5:10; Hebrews 9:15, 26; 10:10, 12; 1 Peter 2:24; 3:18; Revelation 5:8–9, 1 Nephi 11:33; 2 Nephi 2:7–8; 9:5; 26:24; Mosiah 14:12; 15:7–9, 12; 18:2; Alma 21:9; 22:14; 30:26; 33:22; 34:15; Helaman 14:15–16; 3 Nephi 9:21–22; 11:14; 27:14; Ether 12:33; Doctrine and Covenants 18:11; 20:23–25; 21:9; 35:2; 45:2–5; 46:13; 53:2; 54:1; 76:41; 138:2, 35, 57; Moses 7:45–47, 55. For a discussion of these passages, see John Hilton III, "Teaching the Scriptural Emphasis on the Crucifixion," *Religious Educator* 20, no. 3 (2019): 132–53, available at http://johnhiltoniii.com/crucifixion.
4. For a comprehensive discussion of Joseph Smith's teachings regarding these topics, see John Hilton III, "The Teachings of Joseph Smith on Gethsemane and Jesus Christ's Crucifixion," in *How and What You Worship: Christology and Praxis in the Revelations of Joseph Smith*, ed. Rachel Cope, Carter Charles, and Jordan Watkins (Provo, UT: Religious Studies Center, Brigham Young University; Salt Lake City: Deseret Book, 2020), 303–29.
5. "Circa Summer 1832 History," [1], The Joseph Smith Papers.
6. "*Elders' Journal*, July 1838," [44], The Joseph Smith Papers.
7. For an analysis of these references, see John Hilton III, Emily K. Hyde, and McKenna Grace Trussel, "The Teachings of Church Leaders Regarding the Crucifixion of Jesus

Christ, 1852–2018," *BYU Studies Quarterly* 59, no. 1 (2020): 49–80, available at http://johnhiltoniii.com/crucifixion.

8. John Hilton III, Emily K. Hyde, and Megan Cutler, "An Atoning Priority in the Hymns of Calvary and Gethsemane," *Journal of Mormon History*, in press.
9. Richard Alldridge, "We'll Sing All Hail to Jesus' Name," *Hymns* (Salt Lake City: The Church of Jesus Christ of Latter-day Saints, 1985), no. 182.
10. In mortality, Christ referred to his death at least ten times: Matthew 16:21; 17:22; 20:18; 26:2; John 3:14; 8:28; 10:15, 17; 12:32; 15:13 (this list does not include references in Mark and Luke that parallel those given by Matthew). In addition, after his Crucifixion, he referred to his death at least eleven times: 3 Nephi 9:21–22; 11:14; 27:14; 28:6; Doctrine and Covenants 6:37; 27:2; 35:2; 45:4–5; 52; 53:2; 110:4.
11. James E. Faust, "The Atonement: Our Greatest Hope," *Ensign,* November 2001, 18.
12. A careful study of the Savior's Atonement is vital; as Elder Joseph B. Wirthlin explained, "No other doctrine will bring greater results in improving behavior and strengthening character than the doctrine of the Atonement of Jesus Christ." "You'll Grow into It," *New Era*, November 2000, 40. For a short but powerful exposition of the atoning significance of Christ's Crucifixion, see Gaye Strathearn, "The Crucifixion," in *New Testament History, Culture, and Society: A Background to the Texts of the New Testament*, ed. Lincoln Blumell (Provo, UT: Religious Studies Center, Brigham Young University; Salt Lake City: Deseret Book, 2019), 353–71.
13. Gerald N. Lund, "The Fall of Man and His Redemption," in *The Book of Mormon: Second Nephi, The Doctrinal Structure*, ed. Monte S. Nyman and Charles D. Tate Jr. (Provo, UT: Religious Studies Center, Brigham Young University, 1989), 94.
14. Russell M. Nelson, "The Correct Name of the Church," *Ensign*, November 2018, 88.
15. Here I am referring to statements that specifically put down Calvary relative to Gethsemane. See John Hilton III and Joshua P. Barringer, "The Use of Gethsemane by Church Leaders, 1859–2018," *BYU Studies Quarterly* 58, no. 4 (2019): 49–76, and John Hilton III, *Considering the Cross: How Calvary Connects Us with Christ* (Salt Lake City: Deseret Book, 2021), 96–100.
16. Gordon B. Hinckley, "The Symbol of Christ," *Ensign*, May 1975, 92, emphasis added. This talk was slightly modified to become a First Presidency message in the April 2005 *Ensign* and also appears in the March 1989, April 1990, and April 1994 editions of the *Liahona*. This phrase has been quoted more than twenty times in Church magazines, manuals, and other writings of Church leaders.
17. Hinckley, "Symbol of Christ," 93.
18. For an in-depth discussion of these and other indications that the cross was favorably viewed by some early Latter-day Saints, see Michael G. Reed, *Banishing the Cross: The Emergence of a Mormon Taboo* (Independence, MO: John Whitmer Books, 2012).
19. Eliza R. Snow, cited in "Lucy Mack Smith, History, 1845," 334, The Joseph Smith Papers.
20. "The Drawing Power of the Risen Redeemer," *Young Woman's Journal*, April 1915, 260.
21. "The Light of the World," *Relief Society Magazine*, April 1933, 235.
22. Edward Dube, "Gaining My Faith One Step at a Time," *New Era*, April 2020, 31.
23. F. Enzio Busche and Tracie A. Lamb, *Yearning for the Living God: Reflections from the Life of F. Enzio Busche* (Salt Lake City: Deseret Book, 2004), 52.
24. Henry W. Naisbitt, "'Twas Calvary's Cross," *Young Woman's Journal*, March 1910, 137.
25. Grace C. Jacobsen, "Gently Calling," *Relief Society Magazine*, August 1935, 528.
26. Marguerite J. Griffin, "Echoes of Hope," *Relief Society Magazine*, April 1946, 226.

27. Dale G. Renlund, "Our Good Shepherd," *Ensign*, May 2017, 32.
28. Jennifer C. Lane, *Finding Christ in the Covenant Path: Ancient Insights for Modern Life* (Provo, UT: Religious Studies Center, Brigham Young University; Salt Lake City: Deseret Book, 2020), 148.
29. Eric D. Huntsman, "Preaching Jesus, and Him Crucified," in *His Majesty and Mission*, ed. Nicholas J. Frederick and Keith J. Wilson (Provo, UT: Religious Studies Center, Brigham Young University; Salt Lake City: Deseret Book, 2017), 73.
30. Christ invites his followers to take up their cross in Matthew 10:38; 16:24; Mark 8:34; 10:21; Luke 9:23; 14:27; 3 Nephi 12:30; Doctrine and Covenants 23:6; 56:2; 112:14. In this chapter I occasionally use the NRSV because of its gender-inclusive and simpler language.
31. D. A. Carson, *Scandalous: The Cross and Resurrection of Jesus* (Wheaton, IL: Crossway, 2010), 25. At the same time, Joel Marcus argues that those who instigated or wrote about crucifixion at times did so with "grisly humor." "Crucifixion as Parodic Exaltation," *Journal of Biblical Literature* 125, no. 1: 73–87.
32. Elder D. Todd Christofferson taught, "If we are among the penitent, with His Atonement our sins are nailed to His cross, and 'with his stripes we are healed.'" "The Love of God," *Liahona*, November 2021.
33. Noah Webster, *An American Dictionary of the English Language* (New York: S. Converse, 1828), s.v. "behold."
34. Russell M. Nelson, "Drawing the Power of Jesus Christ into Our Lives," *Ensign*, May 2017, 39.
35. M. Russell Ballard, cited in "We Are Witnesses," *Ensign*, July 2019, 17.

Chapter Twelve

Mourning with Hope

HANK R. SMITH

On the spring morning of Sunday, March 20, 1842, Joseph Smith stood in a grove of trees near the construction site of the Nauvoo Temple. He was speaking to a group of Saints who had gathered to hear him preach on baptism. However, because of the recent death of a young child, a two-year-old girl named Marian S. Lyon, the Prophet had altered his remarks to include thoughts on death and resurrection. At one point in his sermon, the Prophet said, "[We] mourn the loss but we do not mourn as those without hope."[1]

Joseph's statement may be taken to mean that in The Church of Jesus Christ of Latter-day Saints we do mourn the deaths of our beloved friends and family members, but we mourn differently than others. One might say we mourn with hope. Where does the hope that Joseph spoke of stem from? The answer to this question is significant. Death is both universal and personal—perhaps more than any other experience of mortal life. All of God's children must deal with deep loss throughout mortal life, and all must eventually contemplate their own assured death.

THE STING OF DEATH

Each individual has experienced or will experience the aching and sometimes overwhelming grief that comes with the passing of a cherished individual. Our Heavenly Father has given each of us a remarkable mind. With concentration, we can recall in our minds the voices and the laughter of those we love who have died. The human mind's ability to draw on memories from even decades ago is astounding. In our mind's eye, many can still recall a smile of a loved one now passed on or a familiar phrase they would often repeat. Despite the time that has gone by, in a still moment we may hear the voice of a cherished family member or friend echoing across our memories, often with incredible clarity—a voice of a person whom we long to see again, to talk to again, to laugh with again. In such moments we feel both sweet happiness and piercing heartache. These experiences bring to mind the scriptural phrase "the sting of death"[2]—the deep and inescapable pain of missing terribly a beloved mother or father, grandmother or grandfather, sister or brother, aunt or uncle, a close friend, or perhaps most painful of all, a child.

Jacob, the fifth son of Lehi, described death and hell as a monster.[3] With this unique description, Jacob may teach us, at least in part, why human beings are naturally afraid of death. The word "monster" might take us back to our childhood bedrooms. How is death like the monsters of a dark closet or the dreaded monsters we were sure were lurking under our bed? What is it that children actually fear? Perhaps our fear of a monster was actually a fear of the unknown. Without knowing what the monster actually looked like, our young imagination was free to create the most hideous and fearsome creature it could devise. We knew the monster was both powerful and merciless. We knew that no matter how we struggled to fight or how sincerely we cried out for sympathy, the monster could not be stopped and would not choose to stop until we were destroyed.

Perhaps Jacob used this description because death may seem both unknown and merciless. The fear of death is natural to our human experience and it, amid other reasons, keeps us striving to stay alive as long as possible. Like children, we feel vulnerable in the face of the unknown, the powerful, and the merciless. The ancient Greek philosopher Epicurus wrote, "Against all other hazards it is possible for us to gain security for ourselves but so far as death is concerned all of us human beings inhabit a city without walls."[4] In other words, death brings a sense of vulnerability unmatched by any other fact of life. We stand in its path, completely exposed and without any form of defense.

When we experience the passing of a loved one, we may, in the grip of inescapable grief, even cry out in anguish or anger against the monster of death and hell. Said Ralph Waldo Emerson, "Sorrow makes us all children again—destroys all differences of intellect. The wisest know nothing."[5] The monster seems to steal our cherished loved ones without remorse. The following comments found on an online forum for those mourning a death may give us a glimpse of the experience:

> There are no words and not enough tears to reflect the immensity of our loss. Everything is changed. A [thief] has robbed me of my future. The space she inhabited in our lives has become a void where her laughter and light no longer lives, where questions remain unanswered.[6]

> The first few days were a surreal nightmare—I actually asked people to wake me up. Then I just started putting one foot in front of the other and walking through all the logistics of a death and learning to be alone. . . . I live in a wide awake coma. I'm here walking, talking, writing but not really here at all. All the meaning of life was drained from me in that one horrible moment.[7]

> It has been over a decade for me now. . . . She is fixed in time, she never grew older the way I have. She remains the vital woman she was before the cancer in my memory. But even now, something will make me think of something about her and first I smile and get happy and then I get really sad. You remember the blessings and then you remember the loss. It still hurts.[8]

> I cannot describe how the loss affects you physically, emotionally, spiritually—every way possible. I only know that it did—and my whole body ached with sorrow. I didn't think it was possible to cry that much, but I did. I didn't think it was possible to be so sad and miss someone so much, but I did.[9]

> My husband of almost 20 years died suddenly 2 1/2 years ago. I was numb at first, but the devastation set in very quickly. Half of me disappeared. I felt empty, lost, disoriented, and totally depressed. I only need the simplest reminder of Sam and I start tearing up. He was my best friend first, then my love.[10]

Dealing with Death

Cultures and individuals across the globe seek to cope with this knowledge and mitigate the pain in unique ways. The "sting of death" is no respecter of persons. Said the Roman poet Horace, "Death with impartial step knocks at the huts of the poor and at the palace of kings."[11] All humanity will experience death—as an observer and as a participant. Sorrow, fear, and despair are the common response, especially to those without the knowledge of the plan of salvation. Modern philosopher and Cambridge professor Stephen Cave has said, "We have to live in the knowledge that the worst thing that can possibly happen one day surely will, the end of all our projects, our hopes, our dreams, of our individual world. We each live in the shadow of a personal apocalypse. And that's frightening. It's terrifying."[12] British novelist Howard Jacobson wrote, "How do you go on knowing that you will never again—not ever, ever—see the person you have loved? How do you survive a single hour, a single minute, a single second of that knowledge? How do you hold yourself together?"[13] Ancient Greek playwright Euripides wrote to a loved one who had passed away, "Come back! Even as a shadow, / even as a dream."[14]

There are some who seek to avoid death entirely. They hope to sidestep the sting and search for a way to escape the grasp of the monster. Corporate executive Larry Ellison is on record declaring his desire to live forever and has donated more than 430 million dollars to antiaging research. "Death has never made any sense to me," he told his biographer, Mike Wilson. "How can a person be there and then just vanish, just not be there?" Larry Page, another corporate executive, has made the biggest bet on longevity yet, founding California Life Company, an antiaging research center, with an investment of up to 750 million dollars. Despite the fortunes that have been poured into the fight against death, none have proven to be very effective.[15]

This reality caused author Susan Jacoby to write, "Acceptance of the point at which intelligence and its inventions can no longer battle the ultimate natural master, death, is a true affirmation of what it means to be human."[16]

Some take a lighthearted approach. Billy Standley of Mechanicsburg, Ohio, purchased three burial plots so he could be buried in a large casket, allowing his body to sit atop his 1967 Harley Davidson.[17] George Swanson of Hempfield County, Pennsylvania, purchased twelve burial plots so he could be buried in the driver's seat of his white 1984 Corvette (which had only 27,000 miles on the odometer).[18] The family of Pittsburgh Steelers fan James Smith transformed the funeral home with a small stage and furniture from Smith's living room. The deceased was placed in his favorite recliner, remote control in hand, so he could comfortably watch a loop of Steelers football on TV.[19] When Judy Sunday passed away in 2013, her family and friends held a memorial at her favorite bowling alley, where they spelled "RIP Judy" in pins and then knocked them down with the dolly-mounted casket.[20]

Humor can be a coping mechanism for those dealing with death. Actor Woody Allen is said to have remarked, "I'm not afraid to die, I just don't want to be there when it happens." Eighty-eight-year-old prankster Chet Finch of Oregon had his barber mail handwritten cards to friends two months after Chet's death with heaven as the return address.[21] British prime minister Winston Churchill is said to have remarked, "I am prepared to meet my Maker. Whether my Maker is prepared for the great ordeal of meeting me is another matter."[22] Legend holds that on his deathbed, Oscar Wilde said, "Either that wallpaper goes or I do." Some believe that he actually said, "This wallpaper and I are fighting a duel to the death. Either it goes or I do."[23] Bertrand Russell once quipped, "We are all like the turkey who wakes up [Thanksgiving] morning expecting lunch as usual. Things can go wrong at any time."[24]

Different cultures have passed down ancient death traditions for thousands of years. Famadihana is a funerary tradition of the Malagasy people in Madagascar. The Malagasy, in what is termed "the turning of the bones," bring forth the bodies of their ancestors from the family tombs and rewrap them in fresh cloth, then dance with the corpses around the tomb to live music. This tradition, akin to Memorial Day in the US, is a time for the Malagasy people to remember their dead relatives and loved ones.

For Torajans on the Indonesian island of Sulawesi, the death of the family member isn't an abrupt, final, severing event like it is in the West. Instead, death is just one step in a long, gradually unfolding process. The bodies of deceased loved ones are tended to in the home; they are dressed, offered food, and are even part of family pictures for weeks, months, or even years after death.

Most human beings deal with death in a much more traditional way. Many turn to mourning in private. These can be the darkest and most difficult times of life. After returning to her home the night of the funeral for her husband, who was killed in an accident in the streets of Paris, the famed scientist Madame Marie Curie wrote this entry in her diary: "They filled the grave and put sheaves of flowers on it. Everything is over. Pierre is sleeping his last sleep beneath the earth; it is the end of everything, everything, everything."[25]

Latter-day Saints are not immune to the tragedy of death. The faithful are not exempt from grief. Try to imagine the heartache of Stillman Pond, who, with his wife Maria, joined the Church in 1841. The Ponds had been among the first group to flee Nauvoo in February of 1846. Later that year, in Winter Quarters, Nebraska, the Saints were ravaged by malaria, cholera, and consumption. It was there where Stillman Pond buried nine of his eleven children and his sweet wife. Historian Richard E. Bennett estimated that a minimum of 723 Latter-day Saint pioneers died between June 1846 and May 1847 in settlements on both sides of the Missouri River and back along the Iowa trail. Nearly half the deaths were infants two years old and younger.[26] (Comparatively, approximately 250–70 handcart pioneers died in the Willie and Martin companies in 1856.)[27] Words cannot express the heartbreak Stillman Pond and those like him experienced. In *Macbeth* Shakespeare wrote, "Give sorrow words. The grief that does not speak whispers the o'erfraught heart and bids it break."[28]

The painful reality of mourning is also not foreign to prophets and apostles. All men and women, including the Lord's anointed servants, must wrestle with the pain of death. Job asked, "If a man die, shall he live again?"[29] The Lord has said, "Thou shalt weep for the loss of them that die" (Doctrine and Covenants 42:45). President Gordon B. Hinckley, who lost his beloved wife, Marjorie, after sixty-seven years of marriage, said the following:

> When the last of life's breath is drawn, there is a finality comparable to no other finality. When a father and mother lay the remains of a beloved child in the cold of the grave, there is grief almost inconsolable. When a husband buries the companion of his life, there is a loneliness that is poignant and unrelieved. When a wife closes the casket on the remains of her beloved husband, there are wounds that seem never to heal. When children are bereft of parents who loved and nurtured them, there is an abject destitution comparable to none other. Life is sacred, and death is somber. Life is buoyant and hopeful. Death is solemn and dark. It is awesome in its silence and certainty.[30]

A testimony does not exempt anyone from the deep sense of loss that accompanies death.

Speaking of the loss of one of his wives, Sarah, whose death was followed shortly by one of his daughters, Zina, President Joseph F. Smith said, "I cannot yet dwell on the scenes of the recent past. Our hearts have been tried to the core. Not that the end of mortal life has come to two of the dearest souls on earth to me, so much as at the sufferings of our loved ones, which we were utterly powerless to relieve. Oh! How helpless is mortal man in the face of sickness unto death!"[31] In his first general conference address following Marjorie's death, President Hinckley remarked, "Before I married her, she had been the girl of my dreams, to use the words of a song then popular. She was my dear companion for more than two-thirds of a century, my equal before the Lord, really my superior. And now in my old age, she has again become the girl of my dreams."[32]

Recent apostles such as Richard G. Scott, L. Tom Perry, Dallin H. Oaks, and Russell M. Nelson have buried spouses during their lives. Speaking of the passing of his wife, Dantzel, President Nelson recounted the following experience:

> While I was at home on a rare Saturday with no assignment, we had worked together. She had washed our clothing. I had helped to carry it, fold it, and put it in place. Then while we were sitting on the sofa, holding hands, enjoying a program on television, my precious Dantzel slipped peacefully into eternity. Her passing came suddenly and unexpectedly. Just four days earlier, our doctor's report at a routine checkup indicated that her laboratory tests were good. After my efforts to revive

> her proved fruitless, feelings of shock and sorrow overwhelmed me. My closest friend, angel mother of our 10 children, grandmother of our 56 grandchildren, had been taken.[33]

Stories like these tug on our heartstrings because we all will experience (or we are conscious of the reality that we someday will experience) scenes like them.

Without hope, death's finality is crushing. This monster's power is devastating. Its sting is piercing and agonizing. The light and energy of life are gone, and a heavy and complete darkness closes in until the bereaved is entirely overcome, engulfed in impenetrable grief.

LIGHT, LIFE, AND HOPE

When the people of the Book of Mormon were encompassed in the overwhelming darkness described in 3 Nephi 8, the record states that they were "mourning and howling and weeping" (3 Nephi 8:21). Sometime toward the end of the three days of complete darkness, they heard a voice. Amid the message given to them they heard, "I am Jesus Christ the Son of God. . . . I am the light and the life of the world."[34] Not long after the voice had spoken, "the darkness dispersed from off the face of the land . . . and the mourning, and the weeping, and the wailing. . . . did cease; and their mourning was turned into joy, and their lamentations into the praise and thanksgiving unto the Lord Jesus Christ, their Redeemer."[35]

Not long after, the resurrected Lord appeared to the Nephite people. Their confusion about what was happening slowly turned into comprehension. As they processed the reality of his presence, and all that it meant, they fell to the earth in worship. This was not a dream. This was not a hallucination. It was Jesus Christ. He was right there in front of them to see, hear, and touch. It was overwhelming in every sense. Among many other things, his presence was an irrefutable witness of life after death—his life after death and the life after death of so many loved ones. Annihilation quickly became a myth of yesterday. After this day, all about yesterday would seem like a completely different life. It is no wonder why Elder Jeffrey R. Holland referred to it as "the day of days!"[36]

The Lord Jesus Christ, our Savior and Redeemer, our brother and friend, turns darkness into light and mourning into joy. His entire existence witnesses the reality that death is not the end. Like the first glimmer of dawn turns into a glorious morning sun after the darkest and coldest of nights, he has gloriously risen as the supreme embodiment of light and life. Weeping did endure for a night, but joy has come with the rising Son.

Without the slightest equivocation, Latter-day Saints declare the reality of historical Christianity. We declare, "Christ actually lived, died, and was resurrected and that the glad tidings of His Resurrection spawned a movement and a doctrine that continue to change lives. If there is one recurring theological constancy of the Book of Mormon, it is that Christ was born, that He lived and died in Jerusalem, that He was literally resurrected, and that His atoning sacrifice for sin happened in time and place."[37] G. Stanley Hall, an American psychologist, wrote in 1915, "The most essential claim of Christianity is to have removed the fear of death and made the king of terrors into a good friend and boon companion."[38]

The Resurrection of Jesus Christ is the very core of who we are as a Church and who we are as disciples of Christ. Joseph Smith declared, "The fundamental principles of our religion are the testimony of the Apostles and Prophets, concerning Jesus Christ, that He died, was buried, and rose again the third day, and ascended into heaven; and all other things which pertain to our religion are only appendages to it."[39] Latter-day Saints boldly believe in literal everlasting life. We do not fear an unending consciousness. Said President Dieter F. Uchtdorf, "In light of what we know about our eternal destiny, is it any wonder that whenever we face the bitter endings of life, they seem unacceptable to us? There seems to be something inside of us that resists endings. Why is this? Because we are made of the stuff of eternity. We are eternal beings, children of the Almighty God, whose name is Endless and who promises eternal blessings without number. Endings are not our destiny."[40]

In the Bible Dictionary we read, "Christianity is founded on the greatest of all miracles, the Resurrection of our Lord. If that be admitted, other miracles cease to be improbable."[41] In other words, if Jesus Christ was really resurrected, if he really does now live forever as a glorified being, what else can he do? What else will he do? Certainly, having a young man translate the Book of Mormon and restore his (Christ's) Church does not fall outside the expertise of one who has power over life and death. Such an orchestration would seem simple for such a being. In fact, using *unlikely* scenarios may be the preferred method to a being whose Resurrection was an achievement which had never been accomplished before in the history of the world. Wrote scientist Henry Eyring, "The Creator of the universe almost certainly knows enough about how things work to control and manipulate event to meet his purposes. . . . Revelations and miracles seem like the natural consequences of having a compassionate and just Creator of the universe interested in human events."[42]

The reality of the Resurrection of Jesus Christ has been and continues to be witnessed by many. Among the first to see the resurrected Lord was the chief apostle Peter, who wrote, "We have not followed cunningly devised fables . . . but were eyewitnesses of his majesty."[43] Elder James E. Talmage referred to Christ's Resurrection as "the greatest miracle and the most glorious fact of history . . . and is attested by evidence more conclusive than that which rests our acceptance of historical events in general."[44] Mary Magdalene, Cleophas, Peter, James, John, Thomas, Paul, Joseph Smith, Lorenzo Snow, and many others, both ancient and modern, have witnessed that they have seen him and have heard his voice.

The text of the New Testament reveals Jesus's followers gaining, not losing, confidence following his death. This is explained best by a powerful belief in his Resurrection. In promoting the gospel message, the ancient Apostles appealed, even when encountering their most ruthless opponents, to seemingly common knowledge concerning the reality of the Resurrection. Peter and John and the others of Christ's followers did not leave the area to declare that Christ was raised from the dead. Rather, they went right back to the city of Jerusalem, where, if what they were teaching was false, the deceptiveness would be most blatantly evident. The Pharisee Gamaliel suggested that what Peter and John preached may "be of God."[45] Why would he do such a thing if he had any compelling evidence that their message was spurious? Concerning the value of the testimonies of Matthew, Mark, Luke, and John, F. F. Bruce, Rylands Professor of Biblical Criticism at the University of Manchester, says, "Had there been any tendency to depart from the facts in any material respect, the possible presence of hostile witnesses in the audience would have served as a further corrective."[46]

There are those who say the record of the New Testament cannot be trusted. Archaeological discoveries have bolstered the veracity of the New Testament manuscripts. Because of its unlikely claims, the Bible is held to a higher standard than other records. Said Christian scholar F. F. Bruce, "If the New Testament were a collection of secular writings, their authenticity would generally be regarded as beyond all doubt."[47]

Of course, there will be those who insist that Jesus Christ's Resurrection is simply foolish in the enlightened world. They disregard the idea of such a miracle and the notion that miracles exist at all. Renowned intellectual E. F. Schumacher wrote, "The modern world seems to be skeptical about everything that makes demands on man's higher faculties. But it is not at all skeptical about skepticism, which demands hardly anything."[48] Instead, these enlightened skeptics sometimes seek to replace the Christian God with godless science. In writing about what he called the belief "that living beings suddenly made their appearance by pure chance," Schumacher wrote sarcastically, "One can just see it, can't one: organic compounds getting together and surrounding themselves by membranes—nothing could be simpler for these clever compounds—and lo! there is the cell, and once the cell has been born there is nothing to stop the emergence of Shakespeare, although it will obviously take a bit of time. There is therefore no need to speak of miracles."[49]

Now, that isn't to say that we as a church do not appreciate scientific discovery, particularly the theory of evolution. Our gospel is a search for truth, no matter where it is found. However, most Latter-day Saints would probably agree with Dr. Henry Eyring when he wrote, "The [theory] has to include the notion that the dice have been loaded from the beginning in favor of more complex life forms. That is, without intelligent design of the natural laws in such a way as to favor evolution from lower forms to higher forms of life, I don't think the theory holds water."[50] Within a broader perspective produced by acknowledging the omniscience of God, our significant scientific discoveries can be put in their proper place and can be incredibly useful. Elder Russell M. Nelson modeled this when he taught, "Yes, compounds derived from dust—elements of the earth—are combined to make each living cell in our bodies. The miracle of the Resurrection, wondrous as it will be, is marvelously matched by the miracle of our creation in the first place."[51] The methods of science can teach us many things, but they should not be misused to tear down faith—they were never designed to do so.

Despite what critics may say, the fact remains that with his Resurrection, Jesus Christ has driven back and conquered the monster of death. Christ has healed the sting of death and has allowed courage and strength to fill the human heart. Followers of Christ witness as the prophet Abinadi testified when he faced his own impending death. After being falsely accused and condemned to death, Abinadi turned to his captors and affirmed, "There is a resurrection, therefore the grave hath no victory, and the sting of death is swallowed up in Christ. He is the light and the life of the world; yea, a light that is endless, that can never be darkened; yea, and also a life that is endless, that there can be no more death."[52] When one is focused on the Savior and his Resurrection, confidence replaces darkness; hope replaces fear.

In 1842, Eliza R. Snow penned the following poem in which she addressed death itself:

> The darkness that encompass'd thee, is gone;
> There is no frightfulness about thee now…
> Since the glorious light
> Of revelation shone upon thy path
> Thou seem'st no more a hideous monster, arm'd
> With as thou art, by inspiration's light,
> Thou hast no look the righteous need to fear.[53]

EASTER

Each spring, the Lord teaches us that life and warmth follow the fall and the winter. The "fortunate fall"[54] of man brought about spiritual and physical death. These deaths, crucial to the Lord's plan of salvation, were meant to be overcome. With the budding of the trees and flowers, God teaches us each year that life overpowers death, warmth replaces cold, and light banishes darkness. Martin Luther is credited with saying, "Our Lord has written the promise of the resurrection, not in books alone, but in every leaf in spring-time."[55]

If grading by the significance of what is being celebrated, Easter could be (perhaps should be) thought of as the most important of all the modern holidays. The Resurrection is the "greatest of all events in the history of mankind." President Dieter F. Uchtdorf wrote, "On Easter Sunday we celebrate the most long-awaited and glorious event in the history of the world. It is the day that changed everything. On that day, my life changed. Your life changed. The destiny of all God's children changed. When I think of what the Savior did for us . . . that first Easter Sunday, I want to lift up my voice and shout praises to the Most High God and His Son, Jesus Christ! The gates of heaven are unlocked! The windows of heaven are opened!"[56] For believers, the Easter holiday is a personal recognition of devotion to a literally resurrected Lord.

The scriptures are rife in the reassurance not only that Christ rose from the dead but that all humankind will follow him through their individual resurrection. Wrote Phillips Brooks, "Let every man and woman count himself immortal. Let him catch the revelation of Jesus in his resurrection. Let him say not merely, 'Christ is risen,' but 'I shall rise.'"[57] The promise is sure. Without any doubt, without any uncertainty, Christ's followers declare each individual will see, hear, talk with, laugh with, and embrace their cherished loved ones again. Their kind mother, their gentle father, their grandparents, their siblings, their best of friends—all will live again. Is there any more important message in all the world?

While we do not know what difficulty the Savior had to endure to ensure resurrection for all mankind, we can assume it was not done with ease. Each time the sting of death is used in the Book of Mormon, it is followed by the word "swallowed."[58] Mormon states simply that the "sting of death" is "swallowed up." Abinadi comments that the "sting of death is swallowed up in Christ." Aaron teaches King Lamoni's father that the "sting of death should be swallowed up in the hopes of his glory." The word "swallow" is often thought of encompassing, covering, or completely surrounding something. In that regard, the knowledge of Christ's Resurrection does swallow up and balm the sting of death. However, the Savior has also repeatedly told us that He has drunk out of "the bitter cup." With such a picture in mind, the sting of death being swallowed up in Christ takes on a different meaning. It was in Christ's partaking of the bitter cup that death was swallowed up and overcome.

MERCIFUL HOPE

The certainty of the Resurrection is the only force able to mitigate the shock and bereavement of losing a beloved family member or friend to death. No matter where we "search for peace," every other source will "cease to make [us] whole."[59] While the deep pain of loss and trauma of a changed daily life is not taken away, the surety of the Resurrection of Jesus Christ can calm the stormy seas of the heart. We are bereaved, but such grief is, mercifully, only temporary. Because of Jesus Christ, "even the darkest night will end and the sun will rise."[60] Our knowledge of the plan of salvation, the Fall of man, the role of death, and the Atonement of Jesus Christ enable us to mourn with hope.

In the April 2009 general conference, President Thomas S. Monson related the story of a member of the Church who was saved, both physically and spiritually, by her knowledge of a certain Resurrection. She and her family lived in East Prussia, but her husband was killed in World War II. She was left alone to care for their four children, the oldest being only seven. While fleeing Prussia for West Germany, a journey of over one thousand miles, she and her children were forced to gather food from fields and forests along the way. As they continued, the weather turned freezing. Without the necessary supplies, she and the children had little protection. One by one, this faithful sister lost each of her children to death—at times digging their graves with a spoon. Her grief was overwhelming and she contemplated ending her own life. President Monson continued:

> And then, as these thoughts assailed her, something within her said, "Get down on your knees and pray." She ignored the prompting until she could resist it no longer. She knelt and prayed more fervently than she had in her entire life: "Dear Heavenly Father, I do not know how I can go on. I have nothing left—except my faith in Thee. I feel, Father, amidst the desolation of my soul, an overwhelming gratitude for the atoning sacrifice of Thy Son, Jesus Christ. I cannot express adequately my love for Him. I know that because He suffered and died, I shall live again with my family; that because He broke the chains of death, I shall see my children again and will have the joy of raising them. Though I do not at this moment wish to live, I will do so, that we may be reunited as a family and return—together—to Thee."

The woman eventually reached Germany, starving and emaciated. Shortly thereafter, she bore testimony in a Church meeting. She stated "that of all the ailing people in her saddened land, she was one of the happiest because she knew that God lived, that Jesus is the Christ, and that He died and was resurrected so that we might live again. She testified that she knew if she continued faithful and true to the end, she would be reunited with those she had lost and would be saved in the celestial kingdom of God."[61]

Among other hopeful doctrines, the woman must have been bolstered by the knowledge that her children and husband we together in the spirit world. They were now in the company of many family members, ancestors who had passed on before them. President Nelson once remarked, "Our limited perspective would be enlarged if we could witness the reunion on the other side of the veil, when doors of death open to those returning home."[62]

At the funeral of his friend King Follett, Joseph Smith taught that these thoughts can even bring cheerfulness in times of sorrow. He said, "[Our] relatives and friends are only separated from their bodies for a short season: their spirits which existed with God have left the tabernacle of clay only for a little moment, as it were; and they now exist in a place where they converse together the same as we do on the earth. . . . The expectation of seeing my friends in the morning of the Resurrection cheers my soul and makes me bear up against the evils of life."[63] John Taylor bore a second witness to this knowledge when he said, "While we are mourning the loss of our friends, others are rejoicing to meet them behind the veil."[64]

President Henry B. Eyring shared similar sentiments when he told of what happened the day his mother died:

> The afternoon my mother died, we went to the family home from the hospital. We sat quietly in the darkened living room for a while. Dad excused himself and went to his bedroom. He was gone for a few minutes. When he walked back into the living room, there was a smile on his face. He said that he'd been concerned for Mother. During the time he had gathered her things from her hospital room and thanked the staff for being so kind to her, he thought of her going into the spirit world just minutes after her death. He was afraid she would be lonely if there was no one to meet her.

> He had gone to his bedroom to ask his Heavenly Father to have someone greet Mildred, his wife and my mother. He said that he had been told in answer to his prayer that his mother had met his sweetheart. I smiled at that too. Grandma Eyring was not very tall. I had a clear picture of her rushing through the crowd, her short legs moving rapidly on her mission to meet my mother. When I saw in my mind my grandmother rushing to my mother, I felt joy for them and a longing to bring my sweetheart and our children to such a reunion.[65]

Mourning with Hope: A Personal Account

Almost twenty years ago, I met the girl who would eventually, through great persuasion on my part, become my wife. I have been forever changed because of her. I have also been blessed to have known and learn from her incredible parents, Rod and Marlene Savage. This is their story:

Rod Savage describes his early years, growing up in Richfield, Utah, as incredibly happy. He has always been, according to his friends and family, "naturally cheerful." It was during this blissful childhood, around age seven, that a significant event occurred that would stay in his memory forever.

Throughout each week Rod would often find himself inside Richfield's local dairy, either there on errands from his parents or to pick up a treat for himself—and often, both. It was during one of these routine visits, that the bell hanging above the entrance rang and Rod turned to see who had come in. To his surprise, it was a girl, about his own age, that he had never truly noticed before. Like Rod, she had lived in Richfield all her life, and they attended the same school, but seeing her today was different. He was, in his words, "struck" by her. He was completely "fascinated." He watched her intently as she perused the penny candy and soda fountain flavors.

His goggling must have been noticeable because his mother asked him why he was "studying that girl." He promptly replied that he was doing no such thing and was ready to leave when she was. He quickly left with his mother, but the impression made by that little girl never left him.

As the years passed, Rod filled his life with his natural loves, hunting and fishing. However, he kept his eye on the little girl year after year, but he rarely spoke to her. He discovered her name was Marlene Baker. As they entered Richfield High School, Rod preferred the fun crowd while Marlene preferred friends who took school more seriously. Rod said, "My friends and I thought school was fun, but all those classes and all that homework kept getting in the way."

In a casual conversation with his school counselor one day late in Rod's junior year, he was asked, "Rod, who are you taking to prom?" "Nobody," Rod said quickly. "I'll probably go hunting." "That's too bad," the counselor replied, "I think every girl deserves to go to prom." That sentiment had never crossed Rod's mind before. "Maybe I should ask someone to prom," he thought. "But who?" It was then he thought of Marlene. He worked up the courage and asked her to prom that evening.

Almost fifty years later, when speaking of their date, Rod said, "That date was so wonderful. She laughed harder than she'd ever laughed in her life, and she got me to think more about the importance of school than I ever had in my life. We never went on a date with a different person after that night." Rod and Marlene Savage were sealed in the St. George Temple the summer after they graduated from high school.

Though they tempered each other, Rod and Marlene kept the traits of their youth. She was reserved and careful; he was spontaneous and playful. They were loyal to each other. They were the best of friends. Eventually, they decided their little family needed to grow.

The day they brought their newborn son, Justin, home from the hospital, Rod had an idea. The baby (who was a just a few days old), he said, needed a tour of the home. He took the baby, with Marlene in tow, through a tour of the entire home: the living room (where he told Justin they would have family home evening), the family room (where he told Justin they would watch countless hours of John Wayne movies), the kitchen (where he promised Justin the cookie jar would always be full), and each bedroom, each picture, each faucet, and any other detail Rod could find. Needless to say, it was a long and extensive tour.

"The tour" became a tradition. When Rod and Marlene brought a new baby home (they brought home six in total), the entire family would take the baby on a tour of the home. Even new nieces and nephews went on the tour. As the years passed, grandchild after grandchild were taken, with an ever increasing entourage, through the home. While each tour started with everyone present in the home, most would trickle back to other activities and each tour would usually end with Grandpa Rod, Grandma Marlene, and the new baby.

Then, as it always does in this mortal classroom, tragedy struck their home. It had been a visitor before, but perhaps never in such a catastrophic way. Marlene was diagnosed with advanced liver cancer. They fought with faith. They prayed and begged the Lord for an outcome different than those predicted by their doctors. Less than a year later, however, the cancer grew too powerful, and Marlene was placed on hospice care, where she could pass away in the home she loved and surrounded by the family she adored.

This is where I learned personally what it means to mourn with hope. They both remained optimistic and sometimes even cheerful throughout the entire ordeal. They discussed at length, with and without their children present, their plans for the next life. Though heartbroken, Marlene expressed certainty of her soon seeing her mother and father, brother, and other family members. They laughed and cried together as they reminisced and mourned this unwanted change of plan. They faced the last months, then weeks, and then days with grace, humility, and unshakable faith.

As Marlene approached what the hospice nurses recognized as her last hours, it was decided that Rod should place her in bed for the last time. He stood up and took his place behind her wheelchair and began to slowly make his way to the bedroom with their adult children and some grandchildren following. In the hallway, however, he stopped. He quietly asked the nurse something, and she nodded affirmatively. Rod slowly turned the wheelchair around and softly said to his children and grandchildren with an attempt of quiet cheerfulness, "Let's take Mom on one last tour."

The group made their way toward the living room, where Rod knelt down in front of Marlene and said through visible tears, "Marlene, we are in the family room. . . . Forty-seven years of family home evening. . . . How did you put up with all of us? . . . Thank you."

The group moved on to the kitchen and the closest bedrooms, while Rod complimented, thanked, and kissed his bride of almost five decades. The children and grandchildren then held back and allowed Rod and Marlene time alone. After a few minutes, they all made their way into the bedroom, where they all watched this spiritual giant lift his equally spiritual wife and place her in bed, where he would stay with her until she peacefully passed away a few hours later.

As Rod knelt next to the bed where Marlene lay, he thought of his children. This was a significant moment for the entire family. He decided it would be an appropriate time to tell them once again about the day he first saw their mother. He began, "One day, when I was just seven years old, I was in the Richfield Dairy . . ."

Mourning with hope means celebrating the time spent in mortality with those we love. It means we look forward with anticipation to joyful reunions, both in the spirit world and in the Resurrection. Mourning with hope means placing all your hope in the power of the Lord Jesus Christ to return you and those you love to your heavenly home. It means acting in faith upon his commandments until you regain the presence and behold the face of your Heavenly Father.

When I leave this frail existence,
When I lay this mortal by,
Father, Mother, may I meet you
In your royal courts on high?
Then at length, when I've completed
All you sent me forth to do,
With your mutual approbation
Let me come and dwell with you.[66]

Hank R. Smith is an assistant teaching professor of ancient scripture at Brigham Young University.

Hank R. Smith, "Mourning with Hope," in *His Majesty and Mission*, ed. Nicholas J. Frederick and Keith J. Wilson (Provo, UT: Religious Studies Center, Brigham Young University; Salt Lake City: Deseret Book, 2017), 121–54.

NOTES

1. Andrew F. Ehat and Lyndon W. Cook, *The Words of Joseph Smith: The Contemporary Accounts of the Nauvoo Discourses of the Prophet Joseph* (Salt Lake City: Bookcraft, 1980), 20 March 1842. See also Wilford Woodruff, "Sabbath Scene in Nauvoo," *Times and Seasons*, April 15, 1842, 751.
2. 1 Corinthians 15:56; Mosiah 16:8; Alma 22:14; Mormon 7:5.
3. 2 Nephi 9:10.

4. Norman Wentworth DeWitt, *Epicurus and His Philosophy* (Minneapolis: University of Minnesota Press, 1964), 182.
5. William H. Gilman and Ralph H. Orth, eds., *The Journals and Miscellaneous Notebooks of Ralph Waldo Emerson*, 16 vols. (Cambridge: Belknap, 1960–82), 8:165.
6. Simon Smith, comment on Betsy Megas, "What Does It Feel Like to Have Your Spouse Die?," Quora.com/What-does-it-feel-like-to-have-your-spouse-die.
7. Anonymous, comment on Megas, "What Does It Feel Like to Have Your Spouse Die?"
8. Paul Kukuca, comment on Megas, "What Does It Feel Like to Have Your Spouse Die?"
9. Anonymous, comment on Megas, "What Does It Feel Like to Have Your Spouse Die?"
10. Lorna W., https://answers.yahoo.com/question/index?qid=20090506165547AASRWHg.
11. Steele Commager, *The Odes of Horace: A Critical Study* (New Haven: Yale University Press, 1962), 267.
12. Stephen Cave, "The 4 Stories We Tell Ourselves about Death," TED Talks, http://www.ted.com/talks/stephen_cave_the_4_stories_we_tell_ourselves_about_death/transcript?language=en.
13. Howard Jacobson, *The Finkler Question* (London: Bloomsbury, 2010), 14.
14. Anne Carson, *Grief Lessons: Four Plays by Euripides* (New York: New York Review Books, 2006), 38.
15. Ariana Eunjung Cha, "Tech Titans' Latest Project: Defy Death," *Washington Post*, April 4, 2015, A1.
16. Susan Jacoby, *Never Say Die: The Myth and Marketing of the New Old Age* (New York: Pantheon Books, 2011), 224.
17. Nina Golgowski, "Ohio Man Buried Riding His 1967 Harley-Davidson Motorcycle in Extra-Large Grave," *New York Daily News*, 31 January 2014.
18. "Pennsylvania Man Buried with his Beloved Corvette," History Channel, History.com.
19. Associated Press, "Family Has Unique Viewing at Funeral Home," ESPN News, July 6, 2005, http://www.espn.com/nfl/news/story?id=2101713.
20. Evan Bleier, "Family Holds Funeral at Bowling Alley," UPI, December 2, 2013, http://www.upi.com/Odd_News/2013/12/02/Family-holds-funeral-at-bowling-alley/5471386003239/.
21. Associated Press, "Dead Man Sends Cards from 'Heaven,'" *NBC News*, December 25, 2007, http://www.nbcnews.com/id/22394223/ns/us_news-weird_news/t/dead-man-sends-cards-heaven/#.WBPR3S0rJaQ.
22. Antony Jay, *Lend Me Your Ears: Oxford Dictionary of Political Quotations* (New York: Oxford University Press, 2010), 70.
23. "Oscar Wilde Wallpaper," *Los Angeles Times*, 2016, http://www.latimes.com/books/jacketcopy/la-et-jc-13-lastminute-gift-ideas-for-readers--008-photo.html.
24. *The Oxford Companion to Philosophy,* ed. Ted Honderich (Oxford: Oxford University Press, 1995), 610.
25. Françoise Giroud, *Marie Curie: A Life* (New York: Holmes & Meier, 1986), 141.
26. Richard E. Bennett, "Winter Quarters: Church Headquarters, 1846–1848," *Ensign*, September 1997, 49.
27. LaRene Porter Gaunt and Linda Dekker, "Go and Bring Them In," *Ensign*, December 2006, 43.
28. William Shakespeare, *Macbeth*, act 4, scene 3.
29. Job 14:14.
30. Gordon B. Hinckley, "The Empty Tomb Bore Testimony," *Ensign*, May 1988, 65.
31. Joseph F. Smith to Hyrum Smith, 3 November 1915, Joseph F. Smith Papers, Church History Library.

32. Gordon B. Hinckley, "The Women of our Lives," *Ensign*, November 2004, 82.
33. Russell M. Nelson, "Now Is the Time to Prepare," *Ensign*, May 2005, 16.
34. 3 Nephi 9:15–18.
35. 3 Nephi 10:9–10.
36. Jeffrey R. Holland, *Christ and the New Covenant: The Messianic Message of the Book of Mormon* (Salt Lake City: Bookcraft, 1997), 251.
37. Richard E. Bennett, "From Calvary to Cumorah: What Mormon History Means to Me," *Religious Educator* 8, no. 3 (2007): 101–12.
38. G. Stanley Hall, "Thanatophobia and Immortality," *American Journal of Psychology* 26, no. 4 (October 1915): 561.
39. *Teachings of Presidents of the Church: Joseph Smith* (Salt Lake City: The Church of Jesus Christ of Latter-day Saints, 2011), 49.
40. Dieter F. Uchtdorf, "Grateful in Any Circumstances," *Ensign*, May 2014, 76–77.
41. Latter-day Saint Bible Dictionary, "Miracles."
42. Henry Eyring, *Reflections of a Scientist*, ed. Harden R. Eyring (Salt Lake City: Deseret Book, 1983), 93.
43. 2 Peter 1:16.
44. James E. Talmage, *Jesus the Christ* (Salt Lake City: Deseret Book, 1979), 649, 699.
45. Acts 5:39.
46. F. F. Bruce, *The New Testament Documents: Are They Reliable?* (Grand Rapids, MI: Eerdmans, 1960), 45–46.
47. Bruce, *New Testament Documents*, 10.
48. E. F. Schumacher, *A Guide for the Perplexed* (New York: Harper & Row, 1977), 61.
49. Schumacher, *A Guide for the Perplexed*, 131.
50. Eyring, *Reflections of a Scientist*, 61.
51. Russell M. Nelson, "Life after Life," *Ensign*, May 1987, 10.
52. Mosiah 16:8–9.
53. Eliza R. Snow, "Apostrophe to Death," *Times and Seasons*, December 15, 1842, 48.
54. Daniel K Judd, *The Fortunate Fall: Understanding the Blessings and Burdens of Adversity* (Salt Lake City: Deseret Book, 2011).
55. *Watchwords for the Warfare of Life from Dr. Martin Luther* (New York: M. W. Dodd, 1869), 317.
56. Dieter F. Uchtdorf, "The Gift of Grace," *Ensign*, May 2015, 107–11.
57. Phillips Brooks, *The Spiritual Man and Other Sermons* (London: R. D. Dickinson, 1895), 151–52.
58. Mosiah 16:8; Alma 22:14; Mormon 7:5.
59. Emma Lou Thayne, "Where Can I Turn for Peace?," *Hymns* (Salt Lake City: The Church of Jesus Christ of Latter-day Saints, 1985), no. 129.
60. Edward Behr and Claude-Michel Schönberg, *The Complete Book of Les Misérables* (New York: Arcade, 1989), 28.
61. Thomas S. Monson, "Be of Good Cheer," *Ensign*, May 2009, 92.
62. Russell M. Nelson, "Doors of Death," *Ensign*, May 1992, 72–74.
63. *Teachings of Presidents of the Church: Joseph Smith* (Salt Lake City: The Church of Jesus Christ of Latter-day Saints, 2011), 171–81.
64. John Taylor, in *Journal of Discourses* (London: Latter-day Saints' Book Depot, 1854–86), 21:177.
65. Henry B. Eyring, "Write upon My Heart," *Ensign*, November 2000, 87.
66. Eliza R. Snow, "O My Father," *Hymns*, no. 292.

Part Three

ACTS TO REVELATION

Chapter Thirteen

The Church in the First Century

GAYE STRATHEARN AND JOSHUA M. SEARS

> "And God hath set some in the church, first apostles, secondarily prophets, thirdly teachers, after that miracles, then gifts of healings, helps, governments, diversities of tongues."
>
> 1 Corinthians 12:28

In the well-known 1842 Wentworth Letter, Joseph Smith included thirteen statements about the beliefs of The Church of Jesus Christ of Latter-day Saints, known today as the Articles of Faith. The sixth statement says, "We believe in the same organization that existed in the Primitive Church, namely, apostles, prophets, pastors, teachers, evangelists, and so forth" (Articles of Faith 1:6). Later, Elder James E. Talmage wrote, "In the dispensation of the Savior's ministry, Christ established His Church upon the earth, appointing therein the officers necessary for the carrying out of the Father's purposes. . . . Every person so appointed was divinely commissioned with authority to officiate in the ordinances of his calling; and, after Christ's ascension, the same organization was continued, those who had received authority ordaining others to the various offices in the priesthood. In this way were given unto the Church, apostles, prophets, evangelists, pastors, high priests, seventies, elders, bishops, priests, teachers, and deacons."[1]

Both the ancient and modern Church grew from a rather small number of believers to a much larger community of believers, developing offices and structures to deal with its growth.[2] For example, the restored Church in 1830 was led by the first and second elders with apostolic keys. Additionally, several men were ordained to various offices, including deacon, teacher, and priest. Later, additional offices were added, including bishop (1831), high priest (1831), patriarch (1833), and seventy (1835). By 1835 the First Presidency, Quorum of the Twelve, and the Quorum of the Seventy had been organized to help administer an expanding Church membership.[3] A similar development had occurred in the first century. The early Church, moved by inspiration, revelations, and needs, expanded its organizational structure as membership increased and new situations called for change.

As we examine the development of the early Christian Church organization and government within the first century, two important questions emerge: "Did Jesus organize a church during his mortal ministry?" and "How did the Church function after Jesus's ascension?" To help answer this latter question, we will specifically examine the function of apostles and other titles and offices in the early Church, the administrative impact of a growing church, and Jesus's designation in Matthew 16:18 of the Church as "my church."

Did Jesus Organize a Church during His Mortal Ministry?

Is there evidence of a formal church existing during the mortal ministry of Jesus? The answer is difficult to determine and is dependent to some extent on how we define the word *church.* The Greek word for "church" used throughout the New Testament is *ekklēsia.* In its basic sense, it refers to a legislative body or assembly, but it can also refer to a casual gathering of people or a community of people with shared beliefs.[4] It is the last of these meanings that most closely reflects the New Testament concept of church, but we must remember that a community of people with shared beliefs can exist without a formal organization that includes initiatory rituals, priesthood, scripture, and so forth. Without doubt, the word eventually takes on all these meanings, but the question is, when? One of the difficulties comes because the word *church* appears only three times in the four Gospels, and all those occurrences are in just two verses in Matthew (Matthew 16:18; 18:17). By the time we reach Acts, however, we find a very different scenario. In Acts through Revelation, the word occurs more than one hundred times. Thus, the distinct existence of an individually functioning Christian Church is much more significant or well-known *after* Jesus's mortal ministry.

Nevertheless, some indicators suggest that a basic organization did exist during Jesus's mortal ministry, at least a community with priesthood. First, there is one cryptic comment in John that indicates Jesus's disciples performed baptisms that seem to be independent of those performed by John the Baptist: "When therefore the Lord knew how the Pharisees had heard that Jesus made and baptized more disciples than John, (Though Jesus himself baptized not, but his disciples)" (John 4:1–2). The Joseph Smith Translation amends the parenthetical portion to read, "Now the Lord knew this, though he himself baptized not so many as his disciples; for he suffered them for an example, preferring one another" (JST, John 4:3–4). Unfortunately, neither the Johannine passage nor the Joseph Smith Translation tells us about the purpose of this baptism. Was it like John the Baptist's—for the remission of sins—or was it an initiation into a formal church? The texts simply give no answer. The fact that they were baptizing, however, implies that they had at least the Aaronic Priesthood.

Second, some of the followers of Jesus were part of an inner circle, showing that there was at least some basic level of hierarchy within the community. All three Synoptic Gospels record that Jesus called apostles (Matthew 10:1–5; Mark 6:7–13; Luke 6:13–16).[5] The Greek word for *apostle* is *apostolos* and comes from the verb meaning to "send forth." When used in conjunction with people, *apostolos* indicates that they were sent forth with a specific purpose.[6] This definition fits well with the accounts in Matthew and Mark, but there is no indication at this point that the term *apostle* refers to a specific priesthood office, although, as we will suggest, it does at a later time in Jesus's ministry. Rather, according to Matthew, the apostles are directed to heal (Matthew 10:8) and to "preach saying the kingdom of heaven is at hand" (Matthew 10:7). In the New Testament, there is little evidence that the apostles engaged in either of these activities until after Jesus's ascension in Acts 1. Prior to this time, the Gospels portray them as accompanying Jesus as he healed and preached.[7] Even within this inner circle of apostles, there is a further division with Peter, James, and John being privy to some events, such as the raising of Jairus's daughter, the events on the Mount of Transfiguration, and the invitation to come further into the Garden of Gethsemane than the other eight apostles.

That the apostles (in a general sense) eventually became Apostles (in the sense of a priesthood office) during Jesus's mortal ministry is implied, rather than explicitly stated. At Caesarea Philippi, Peter receives the promise from Jesus, "I will build my church" (Matthew 16:18). Here the promise of a church is in the future tense. Immediately after this first promise, Jesus says, again in the future tense, "I will give unto thee [singular] the keys of the kingdom of heaven: and whatsoever thou [singular] shalt bind on earth shall be bound in heaven: and whatsoever thou shalt loose on earth shall be loosed in heaven" (Matthew 16:19). The promise of a church with priesthood keys given specifically to Peter strongly suggests a shift to an official church, rather than simply a collection of like-minded people.[8] It must be remembered, however, that in this passage it is a promise, not a statement of fact—yet. Latter-day Saints understand that Jesus, Moses, and Elijah gave these promised keys to Peter, James, and John on the Mount of Transfiguration about a week after the events at Caesarea Philippi (Matthew 17:1–13; compare Doctrine and Covenants 110:11, 13–16).[9]

It is therefore probably not happenstance that in Matthew 18, the chapter that immediately follows the events on the Mount of Transfiguration, Jesus delivers the Church Discourse. Here, the word *church* is found twice in verse 17, in a context of establishing boundaries for participation in the Church and the use of the sealing power. Jesus teaches the process that should be followed if "thy brother shall trespass against thee." First, the injured party should go and discuss it with the offender. If that doesn't work, he or she should bring in witnesses. Finally, if reconciliation is still not achieved, "tell it unto the church: but if he neglect to hear the church, let him be unto thee as an heathen man and a publican" (i.e., he should be put out or excommunicated from the Church). "Verily I say unto you, Whatsoever ye [plural] shall bind on earth shall be bound in heaven: and whatsoever ye [plural] shall loose on earth shall be loosed in heaven" (Matthew 18:15–18). Here the Church is spoken of as a present reality, rather than as a future promise. In addition, the power to bind is now available, not just to Peter but to the disciples—presumably the Twelve.

In addition to the Twelve, Luke also mentions the calling of seventy.[10] Luke tells us that Jesus "sent them two and two before his face into every city and place, whither he himself would come" (Luke 10:1). Jesus instructed them, "Carry neither purse, nor scrip, nor shoes" (Luke 10:4). In Luke's sequence of events, these seventy were called after the events on the Mount of Transfiguration and the bestowal of the priesthood keys. Their responsibility is similar to that given to the Twelve in Luke 9:1–6. The specific mention that they go in pairs may reflect the rejection and hostility that Jesus experienced in Samaria (Luke 9:52–53).[11] Unfortunately, we know very little about this group. Luke gives no account of their mission; he simply records that when they returned, they rejoiced because "even the devils are subject unto us through thy name" (Luke 10:17). After Luke 10:20 they are never mentioned again.[12] Luke probably includes them because the number seventy represents the whole world—in the Table of Nations in Genesis 10, the world after the flood is divided into seventy nations—and even though this group seems to teach only among the Jews, they foreshadow the time when the gospel will be taught "in Jerusalem, and in all Judaea, and in Samaria, and unto the uttermost part of the earth" (Acts 1:8).

How Did the Church Function after Jesus's Ascension?

The limited information we have about Jesus's forty-day ministry tells us little about the Church and its organization. Robert J. Matthews suggests, "It is probable that it was during this period that the church was organized with quorums and various officers."[13] If this is indeed the case, then it helps us understand why in Acts, much more clearly than in the Gospels, we see the apostles using the priesthood in the workings and organization of a church.

Ephesians includes two passages on Church organization that are particularly important for Latter-day Saints: "Now therefore ye are no more strangers and foreigners, but fellowcitizens with the saints, and of the household of God; and are built upon the foundation of the apostles and prophets,

Jesus Christ himself being the chief corner stone" (Ephesians 2:19–20); "And he gave some, apostles; and some, prophets; and some, evangelists; and some, pastors and teachers; for the perfecting of the saints, for the work of the ministry, for the edifying of the body of Christ: till we all come in the unity of the faith, and of the knowledge of the Son of God, unto a perfect man, unto the measure of the stature of the fulness of Christ: that we henceforth be no more children, tossed to and fro, and carried about with every wind of doctrine, by the sleight of men, and cunning craftiness, whereby they lie in wait to deceive" (Ephesians 4:11–14).

The emphasis on Christ is the bedrock of all teaching from the very beginning of Christian missionary work, but the list of offices included in Ephesians is neither exhaustive nor uniform in the New Testament. Ephesians does not mention, for example, the seven (Acts 6:3), elders (Acts 15:4), bishops (1 Timothy 3:1), or deacons (1 Timothy 3:10). While mention of the importance of apostles is very early and extensive, the New Testament descriptions of prophets, evangelists, pastors, and teachers are fragmentary.

The Apostles

Luke records the process of calling a new member of the Twelve in some detail, outlining a pattern which may be assumed later in his account when other apostles are mentioned. The prerequisite for considering someone to become a member of the Twelve was that they "have companied with us all the time that the Lord Jesus went in and out among us, beginning from the baptism of John, unto that same day that he was taken up from us, must one be ordained to be a witness with us of his resurrection" (Acts 1:21–22). The language of the KJV in this passage is a little misleading. There is no Greek word in the sentence that can be translated as "ordained." Instead, the Greek literally reads "one of these must *become* a witness (Greek *martyra*) with us of his resurrection" (authors' translation). The language of this verse, then, does not require a priesthood ordination. Nevertheless, it is significant that the first thing Peter does after the Ascension is to fill the vacancy in the Twelve. This action indicates that, in Peter's mind, having a group of eleven was *not* the same as having a group of twelve and that the latter was important for the Church to move forward.

Luke records the Twelve doing the two things Jesus had assigned them to do in Matthew 10: perform miracles and teach the gospel. Peter and John now heal "in the name of Jesus Christ" (Acts 3:6). As a representative example of their healings, Luke recounts Peter's healing of a man "lame from his mother's womb" (Acts 3:1–11), but he also notes "by the hands of the apostles were many signs and wonders wrought among the people" (Acts 5:12; compare 2 Corinthians 12:12). The apostles also teach the gospel, initially at and around the temple and later in Samaria and the rest of the known world. In addition, when Peter and John are in Samaria, Luke records that they laid "their hands on [the new converts], and they received the Holy Ghost" (Acts 8:17), giving evidence that they had the authority of the Melchizedek Priesthood.

We also see that the Twelve had administrative responsibility, both in Jerusalem and also in regional centers of the Church. Initially, when the members of the Church brought the money from the sale of their lands and possessions, they "laid them down at the apostles' feet: and distribution was made unto every man according as he had need" (Acts 4:35). When there was a problem with the Grecian widows being neglected, the issue was brought to the Twelve (Acts 6:1–4). When Paul and Barnabas and "certain men which came down from Judaea" disputed over whether Gentile converts needed to be circumcised, they agreed to take the question to "the apostles and elders" in Jerusalem (Acts 15:1–2).[14]

What is not evident is whether all the apostles in the early Church were members of the Twelve. Our earliest Christian text that mentions the apostles, 1 Corinthians (written ca. AD 55), seems to make a distinction between the Twelve and the apostles. When discussing the Resurrection appearances, Paul mentions Jesus's appearance to the Twelve and then noted that afterward he appeared to all the apostles: "He was seen of Cephas, then of the twelve. . . . After that, he was seen of James; *then of all the apostles*" (1 Corinthians 15:5, 7; emphasis added).

This situation seems to be corroborated in other New Testament sources. We know that Herod Agrippa I killed James, the brother of John, at an early date (Acts 12:1–2). Unlike Acts 1, Luke does not give any details of the Twelve meeting to find a replacement for James. In chapter 14, when Paul and Barnabas are on their first missionary journey, Luke begins to identify them as apostles (verses 4, 14), which could mean that there were at least thirteen members of the Twelve. In addition, at the conclusion of Paul's letter to the Romans, he mentions Andronicus and Junia (a female name) as apostles (Romans 16:7). In 2 Corinthians, Paul mentions the "messengers [Greek *apostoloi*] of the churches" (8:23) and, more specifically, in Philippians he refers to Epaphroditus as "my brother, and companion in labour, and fellowsoldier, but your messenger [Greek *apostolos*], and he that ministered to my wants" (2:25). Here Epaphroditus is not an apostle for the entire church but only an apostle for the Philippians—an envoy or representative for the Philippian branch of the Church. In these instances, we should probably understand *apostle* in a general sense, rather than as an office of the Melchizedek Priesthood.

In antiquity, there was some debate in the Church over Paul's status as an apostle. Paul did not fit the requirements for being a member of the Twelve, as outlined in Acts 1; although he was witness of the Resurrection, he was not a disciple "beginning from the baptism of John, unto that same day that he was taken up from us" (Acts 1:22). This may be the reason that some in Corinth questioned his apostolic status, especially in relation to Cephas (Peter) and the other apostles (1 Corinthians 9:1–5). Paul declares, "If I be not an apostle unto others, yet doubtless I am to you: for the seal of mine apostleship are ye in the Lord" (1 Corinthians 9:2). Is he suggesting that he was only an apostle for the Corinthians? Although Luke identifies him as an apostle during his first missionary journey (Acts 14:4, 14), Paul does not seem to be one of the apostles at the Jerusalem Council (Acts 15), and he does not call himself an apostle in his earliest epistles to the Thessalonians written during his second missionary journey.[15]

In latter epistles, however, Paul begins each epistle with a reference to his being an apostle. In Romans 1:1 and 1 Corinthians 1:1, he specifically says that he was "called to be an apostle." It is worth noting that there are three particular epistles where Paul has to justify his authority: Romans, 1 Corinthians, and Galatians. In Galatians, he calls himself an apostle but does not say that he was "called to be an apostle," as he does in Romans 1:1 and 1 Corinthians 1:1. This suggests that when Paul wrote Galatians, his apostolic status may have been as a missionary, not yet called as a member of the Twelve (as was the case by the time he wrote Romans and 1 Corinthians).[16] Although Paul calls himself the "least of the apostles" (1 Corinthians 15:9), it is clear that he fights to be recognized along with the other apostles.

Prophets

In addition to mention of the apostles, we also find frequent reference to prophets. During the apostolic ministry, a number of unnamed and named individuals are called prophets: a group of prophets traveling from Jerusalem to Antioch (Acts 11:27); Agabus (Acts 11:28; 21:10); Barnabas, Simeon, Lucius, Manaen, and Saul (Acts 13:1); and Judas and Silas (Acts 15:32). Prophecy as a spiritual gift within the early Church is mentioned on numerous occasions and is also featured prominently in John's Revelation.[17] With the exception of the apostles, we have on record only the prophecies of Agabus, who first prophesied of a coming famine (Acts 11:27–28) and later of Paul's Roman incarceration (Acts 21:10–11).

What was the role of a prophet? Within the Israelite context from which Christianity grew, being a prophet (Hebrew, *nābî'*) was not a description of an office but of an endowment of the gift of prophecy. When Eldad and Medad prophesied in the Israelite camp, Joshua was concerned by what he perceived to be a challenge to Moses's leadership. Moses, however, responded that he wished "that *all* the Lord's people were prophets, and that the Lord would put his spirit upon them!" (Numbers 11:29; emphasis added). To Moses, such prophesying did not in itself give one hierarchical authority and thus was not a challenge to his position. This understanding prevailed throughout the Old Testament and continued into the New Testament world.[18] Although prophets are frequently mentioned in the New Testament, we never read of them being ordained in any sense. Thus, to be a prophet meant that one possessed the gift of prophecy but did not necessarily mean one held an ecclesiastical office.

What was the relationship between apostles and prophets? With the exception of Jesus's statement in Luke 11:49, Paul is the only writer ever to mention apostles and prophets together, and whenever he does, apostles are always listed first (1 Corinthians 12:28; Ephesians 2:20; 3:5; 4:11). The ordering in the sentences was most likely deliberate and perhaps suggests Paul's recognition that though the gift of prophecy was valuable, it was subject to those formally authorized to administer.[19] Paul himself demonstrates this when, writing to the Saints at Corinth in his capacity as an apostle (1 Corinthians 1:1), he gives instructions to help regulate the speaking and interpreting of prophecies among them (see 1 Corinthians

14:26–40). Within this same passage, he also counsels them to "covet to prophesy" (verse 39), instruction that would certainly have created chaos had prophecy been thought of in itself as giving a right to leadership.

Prophets, then, were an important feature of the early Christian Church. The presence of prophets was evidence that "the manifestation of the Spirit [was being] given to every man to profit withal. For to one is given by the Spirit the word of wisdom; to another the word of knowledge by the same Spirit; to another faith by the same Spirit; to another the gifts of healing by the same Spirit; to another the working of miracles; to another prophecy" (1 Corinthians 12:7–10). Being a prophet was not an office or position; rather, all Saints were encouraged to seek "the testimony of Jesus [which] is the spirit of prophecy" (Revelation 19:10).[20]

Evangelists

A rather enigmatic office is that of evangelist (Greek *euangelistēs*). In addition to the Ephesians passage, the term is found only two other times in the New Testament to describe Philip (Acts 21:8) and Timothy (2 Timothy 4:5), but these passages give no indication of the meaning of the term. Linguistically the word refers to someone who declares the "good news," or gospel (Greek *euangellos*). Although it is clear that apostles were evangelists in the sense that they declared, not all evangelists were apostles. Neither Philip nor Timothy were ever considered to be apostles. Outside the New Testament, *euangelistēs* is found in an inscription from Rhodes, describing "one who proclaims oracular sayings."[21] This definition fits well with the Prophet Joseph Smith's explanation that "an Evangelist is a Patriarch."[22]

Pastors

The term "pastor" (Greek *poimenas*) refers to someone who looks after sheep, and so is used to refer to shepherds or leaders. Christ identified himself as the Good Shepherd (John 10:14), and he instructed Peter three times to "feed my lambs/sheep" (John 21:15–17). Ephesians 4 is the only place in the New Testament where the word *pastor* is used in a technical sense of a

Church office, but variations of the Greek stem are often found in conjunction with other Church offices such as elder and bishop (1 Peter 5:1–2; Acts 20:17–35) and may indicate "their initial synonymous use as designations for Christian leaders."[23]

Teachers

In the New Testament, *teacher* seems to be a descriptive term, rather than a priesthood office. Twice Paul identifies himself as an Apostle and "a teacher of the Gentiles" (1 Timothy 2:7; 2 Timothy 1:11). Likewise, Luke identifies prophets and teachers in the Church at Antioch such as Barnabas and Saul (Paul), whom we know about from other places, but others we do not: Simeon, Lucius of Cyrene, and Manaen (Acts 13:1). Paul also encourages women to be "teachers of good things" (Titus 2:3). But the New Testament also warns against those who desire to be teachers but who understand "neither what they say, nor whereof they affirm" (1 Timothy 1:7) and "false teachers among you, who privily shall bring in damnable heresies, even denying the Lord that bought them, and bring upon themselves swift destruction" (2 Peter 2:1).

Elders

In both the Greek Old and New Testaments, the term *elder* (Greek *presbyteros*) is often used to refer to older men who were respected for their experience and wisdom.[24] In this context it appears frequently to denote the elders of the Jews, a group often in opposition to Jesus and his ministry. However, in a Christian context the term seems to refer to a specific office, received by appointment (Acts 14:23, Greek *cheirotoneō*; Titus 1:5, Greek *kathistēmi*). In Acts, elders work in close association with the apostles (Acts 15:2, 4, 6, 22–23; 16:4). Peter even identifies himself as a "co-elder"[25] (see 1 Peter 5:1; Greek *sympresbyteros*). Luke records that Paul and Barnabas, on their first missionary journey, "ordained [or appointed; Greek *cheirotoneō*] them elders in every church" (Acts 14:23). Paul similarly instructs Titus to "ordain [or appoint] elders in *every* city, as I had appointed thee" (Titus 1:5; emphasis added).

The responsibilities of these elders were many and varied: they received and distributed welfare goods (Acts 11:29–30); helped settle doctrinal disputes (Acts 15:2, 4, 6, 22–23; 16:4); oversaw and fed the flocks of God (Acts 20:28; 1 Peter 5:1–3); received reports of missionary efforts (Acts 21:17–20); sought to correct misunderstandings among Church members (Acts 21:18–25); ordained others to the ministry (1 Timothy 4:14); ruled (1 Timothy 5:17); labored in "the word and doctrine" (1 Timothy 5:17); anointed and blessed the sick (James 5:14–15); and served as examples for the rest of God's flock (1 Peter 5:3).

Elders appear to have held a priesthood office on the local level and led the Saints in the absence of traveling apostolic authorities like Paul. At the end of Paul's third mission, he went to Miletus and sent for the elders of the Church from Ephesus to come to him. Knowing that he would not return to the area (Acts 20:25), he directed them, "Take heed therefore unto yourselves, and to all the flock, over the which the Holy Ghost hath made you overseers [Greek *episkopoi*], to feed the church of God" (Acts 20:28).

Bishops

The Greek word for bishops is *episkopoi* and refers to "overseers." The KJV is not always consistent in its translation of *episkopoi.* Sometimes it will translate it literally as "overseers" (Acts 20:28) and sometimes technically as bishops (Philippians 1:1; 1 Timothy 3:2; Titus 1:7). The only time we find the term *bishop* (Greek *episkopos*) in the New Testament in a singular form is when Peter uses it to describe Christ (1 Peter 2:25). Again we are reminded of the fluid boundaries in the early Church between elders and bishops; both are described as overseers who shepherd their flocks. According to Paul's letters to Timothy and Titus, bishops were responsible to teach (1 Timothy 3:2); take care of the Church (1 Timothy 3:5); serve as stewards of God (Titus 1:7); and exhort and convince gainsayers (Titus 1:9). It is not until the early second century that we find concrete evidence, in the writings of Ignatius, bishop of Antioch, of a clear distinction between elders and bishops, with elders yielding to the bishop who is *the* representative of

Christ and the leader of the congregation (*To the Ephesians*, 1:3; 4:1; *To the Magnesians*, 2:1; 3:1; *To the Trallians*, 1:1). In Ignatius's letters, the bishop is now the only one who is described as a shepherd or pastor (*To the Philadelphians*, 1–2; compare *To the Romans*, 9:1–2).[26]

Deacons

Paul writes to the Philippians, "Paul and Timotheus, the servants of Jesus Christ, to all the saints in Christ Jesus which are at Philippi, with the bishops [Greek *episkopoi*] and deacons [Greek *diakonoi*]" (1:1). Not only were bishops associated with elders, they were also associated with deacons. The difficulty again in understanding the many passages that use *diakonoi* is determining whether it is being used in the general sense of one who ministers, or in the technical sense of the office of deacon.[27] For example, Paul describes himself and Apollos as "ministers [Greek *diakonoi*] by whom ye believed" (1 Corinthians 3:5), yet at the beginning of the epistle he identifies himself as an apostle (1:1). Is he, therefore, identifying himself as an apostle who ministers to the Saints at Corinth, or is he indicating that he is a deacon in the Church? In another epistle, Paul commends to the Roman church a woman by the name of Phebe, whom he describes as "our sister, which is a servant [Greek *diakonon*] of the church which is at Cenchrea" (Romans 16:1). In most cases in the New Testament the context suggests that *diakonoi* should be translated as "ministers," rather than "deacons." One exception to this may be 1 Timothy 3:8–13, which describes the qualifications for being a *diakonos*. The passage says nothing about the duties of a *diakonos* but indicates that he must be serious, not double-tongued, not addicted to wine or money, and must hold to the mystery of the faith with a clear conscience. Then Paul instructs Timothy that an individual must be tested and, if he is found blameless, let him serve as deacon (Greek *diakoneitōsan*). In this context, it does not appear to be a general reference to ministering, because people who are not blameless can still effectively minister to others.

We have noted that on two occasions deacons are mentioned in conjunction with bishops. We see the same kind of pairing in *1 Clement*, 42:4, and the *Didache*, 15:1, Christian texts which date to around the turn of the first century. Ignatius encourages the Trallians: "Let everyone respect the deacons as Jesus Christ, just as they should respect the bishop" (3.1). However, it is clear that Ignatius does not consider deacons to enjoy equal status with bishops; rather they are subject to the bishop and the elders (*To the Magnesians*, 2). He specifically describes "Philo, the deacon from Cilicia, a man with a good reputation, who even now assists me [Ignatius, who was a bishop] in the word of God" (*To the Philadelphians*, 11:1). Deacons, he writes to the Trallians, "are not merely 'deacons' of food and drink, but ministers of God's church. Therefore they must avoid criticism as though it were fire" (2:3). Thus, it appears that the role of deacons was to aid the bishop by helping with the temporal welfare of the Church and by teaching the word, which, as we will see, corresponds remarkably with the seven who are called to minister in Acts 6.

The Administrative Effects of a Growing Church

Having examined the various groups in the early Church, we are now in a position to examine the ways it may have functioned. According to Acts, the Church began with very few members; only one hundred and twenty people were gathered with the apostles and women when the vacancy in the Twelve was filled (Acts 1:15). But events that followed led to an exponential increase in Church membership. After Peter's teaching at Pentecost, "about three thousand souls" joined the Church (Acts 2:41). After Peter and John's teaching at the temple, "many of them which heard the word believed; and the number of the men was about five thousand" (Acts 4:4), although the number could have been much greater if it included women and children. As a result of the "many signs and wonders wrought among the people" by the apostles, "believers were the more added to the Lord, multitudes both of men and women" (Acts 5:12, 14).

The rapid growth of the Church inevitably led to some administrative difficulties. Acts 6 records that "when the number of the disciples was multiplied, there arose a murmuring of the Grecians [Greek-speaking Jews] against the Hebrews [Aramaic-speaking Jews], because their widows were neglected in the daily ministration" (verse 1). During this time the Church members were consecrating their wealth (Acts 4:37; contrast 5:1–11),[28] but due to the administrative difficulty of keeping up with the Church's growth, some of the members—specifically the widows—were being neglected. This was a problem because they had given all to the Church and were relying on the Church for support.

When made aware of the situation, Peter realized that the apostles did not have the time to take care of these matters. He declared, "It is not reason that we should leave the word of God, and serve tables. Wherefore, brethren, look ye out among you seven men of honest report, full of the Holy Ghost and wisdom, whom we may appoint over this business. But we will give ourselves continually to prayer, and to the ministry of the word" (Acts 6:2–4). As a result, we have the first administrative expansion of the Church leadership. Acts does not tell us much about these seven men, though Peter does say that the Twelve would "appoint" them. The Greek word is *kathistēmi*, which means to "put in charge."[29] Elsewhere in the KJV it is translated as "ordain" (Titus 1:5; Hebrews 5:1; 8:3), perhaps suggesting a formal priesthood role. The only information that we have about any of them, specifically Stephen and Philip, describes them out preaching the gospel (Acts 6:8–7:60; 8:5–40). At least in the case of Philip, they seem to be operating under the authority of the Aaronic Priesthood, rather than the Melchizedek, because while Philip baptized, it was Peter and John who came to Samaria and "prayed for them, that they might receive the Holy Ghost. . . . Then laid they their hands on them, and they received the Holy Ghost" (Acts 8:15, 17).

Beyond what specific duties the seven performed, the most important feature of this account is its demonstration of how the organizational structure of the Church was able to grow and adapt to meet new needs. Christ did not establish his Church, initially, in all its organizational potential. Initially there was simply no need for an extensive structure including bishops, welfare administrators, deacons, councils of elders, and so forth. Rather, he revealed the offices and organization of his Church gradually, line upon line, as the Church had need. Although the New Testament does not provide a record of how most Church offices developed, the calling of the seven serves as a potential model. First, there was a practical need for adaptation. Second, the apostles considered the situation and—no doubt under inspiration—came to a solution. Third, they implemented an organizational change, and as a result, "the word of God increased" (Acts 6:7), and the Lord blessed the Church.

The rapid growth of the Church must have also caused difficulties for the Church members in finding places to worship. While they "continu[ed] daily with one accord in the temple" (Acts 2:46) and continued to attend the synagogue (Acts 13:4; 19:8; 26:11), they also needed places where they could meet together as followers of Christ. Houses seem to have been the gathering places of choice for members of the Church. Acts 1:13 says that the Church members met in an upper room of someone's home, possibly the same one where Jesus instituted the sacrament (see also Mark 14:15). Luke says, "Breaking bread from house to house, [they] did eat their meat with gladness and singleness of heart" (Acts 2:46). When Peter was delivered out of jail, "he came to the house of Mary the mother of John, whose surname was Mark; where many were gathered together praying" (Acts 12:12). Archaeologists have uncovered in Capernaum a house that seems to have been used as a Christian "place of meeting or worship as early as the end of the first century."[30]

This practice of meeting in houses continued as missionary work expanded among the Gentiles and seems to have become the basic unit of the Church. Paul rarely speaks of the "whole church" (Romans 16:23; 1 Corinthians 14:23). Instead, he usually speaks of the Church in somebody's house (Greek *hē kat' oikon ekklēsia*). Thus, Priscilla and Aquila, Paul's companions in Corinth and Ephesus, hosted a branch of the Church in their house (1 Corinthians 16:19; Romans 16:3–5). Likewise, Philemon hosted a branch in Colossae (Philemon 1:2), and Nymphas hosted a branch in Laodicea (Colossians 4:15). These house-churches "enabled the followers of Jesus to have a distinctively Christian worship and fellowship from the very first days of the apostolic age."[31] It is probable that in larger cities more than one house-church existed. This state may be reflected in the groupings of salutations Paul sends in Romans 16:14–15.[32] The patrons of these house-churches, some of which may have been women (e.g., Lydia and Chloe), were probably not only responsible for providing the space for the Christian gathering, they probably also provided the meal that was a part of the sacramental celebration.[33]

House-churches were a natural outgrowth of the societal emphasis on the extended family in the first century.[34] Cornelius was "a devout man, and one that feared God *with all his house*" (Acts 10:2; emphasis added). While he waited for Peter to come, he "called together his kinsmen and near friends" to listen to Peter (Acts 10:24). This household and friends were the first gentile converts. Likewise, when Paul taught in Philippi, he baptized Lydia "and her household" (Acts 16:15), and in Corinth he "baptized also the household of Stephanas" (1 Corinthians 1:16). A household could consist of parents, children, grandparents, and other extended family members as well as servants and slaves. Not all members of the household, however, automatically joined the Church, as seen in the case of Onesimus who, as a slave, did not convert with his owner, Philemon (Philemon 1:1–2, 10).[35] It is possible that the early missionaries sought to baptize households that could become the nucleus of the Church in a new city.

While the Church was small, the house was a viable meeting place, where all the membership could gather together, but the exponential growth must have eventually made it impossible to gather everyone into one place (see Acts 12:17). Therefore, in any one city there was probably more than one house-church. Given the huge distances between cities and the difficulty of communication in the first century, a centralized Church government was difficult to administer and maintain with house-churches, which probably existed with a fair amount of autonomy, except for the infrequent visits from the apostles and the letters that they sent. It appears that the contention in Corinth may have resulted from conflicts between different house-churches that were established by different Christian missionaries (1 Corinthians 1:10–16). Likewise, 3 John may be describing a rogue leader of a house-church in its description of Diotrephes (3 John 1:9–10). Only in one instance is there a suggestion that one of these house-churches, the house of Stephanas, may have been viewed in a leadership capacity for other members of the Church (1 Corinthians 16:15–16).

"My Church"

When Jesus promised Peter at Caesarea Philippi that he would build a church, he specifically called it "my church" (Matthew 16:18). In 3 Nephi 27:8, Jesus identifies two qualifications for a church to belong to him: "And how be it my church save it be called in my name? For if a church be called in Moses' name then it be Moses' church; or if it be called in the name of a man then it be the church of a man; but if it be called in my name then it is my church, if it so be that they are built upon my gospel." Jesus then gives a definition of *gospel.* He encloses it within two bookends, so to speak. He begins this definition with "Behold I have given unto you my gospel, and this is the gospel which I have given unto you," and he closes with "Verily, verily, I say unto you, this is my gospel" (3 Nephi 27:13, 21). Within these two statements, he teaches that the gospel, or good news, is that he came to do the will of the Father and to be lifted up on the cross that he might draw all men unto him so that they can "stand before me, to be judged of their works, whether they be good or whether they be evil" (verse 14). But the good news is not just what *Jesus* has done; it also includes what *we* must do: repent, be baptized, remain faithful to the end, wash our garments in Christ's blood, and "be sanctified by the reception of the Holy Ghost" (verse 20). All these principles and ordinances were taught and practiced in the New Testament. According to Jesus's definition, therefore, the New Testament contains a fullness of the gospel and the New Testament Church qualifies to be called "my church."

The New Testament, however, does not give us many indications of how the early Church members were identified, though in Acts we learn of two. In Acts 9:2, Paul seems to be calling them the "way." Before going to Damascus, he went to the high priest, desiring letters to the synagogues in Damascus so that "if he found any of this way [Greek *tēs hodou*], whether they were men or women, he might bring them bound unto Jerusalem" (Acts 9:2). Scholars have argued that the word *way* may be a term used to identify members of the Church.[36] And the Revised Standard Version contains the phrase "so that if he found any belonging to the Way." Similar language is also found in Acts 19:23; 22:4; 24:14, 22. "The Way" may thus have been the earliest means to identify Church members who were still considered to be Jews but who were traveling a different path. Later, when Paul was arrested in Jerusalem, another name for the members of the Church was used when he was accused of being "a ringleader of the sect of the Nazarenes" (Acts 24:5).

But how did the earliest members of the Church identify themselves? The most frequent self-designation in the New Testament is "saints," from the Greek word *hagioi*, "dedicated to God" or "holy." This designation is used sixty times from Acts to Revelation, but only once in the four Gospels (Matthew 27:52). In Antioch, Ananias worries about "how much evil [Paul] hath done to thy saints at Jerusalem" (Acts 9:13). Twice Paul teaches about those who are "called to be saints" (1 Corinthians 1:2; Romans 1:7). Both these references follow Paul's declaration that he was "called to be an apostle" (1 Corinthians 1:1; Romans 1:1), perhaps indicating that he saw membership in the Church as something more than an individual's decision to join. One of the principal reasons for a Church organization is for the "perfecting of the saints" (Ephesians 4:12).

But there is also another possible self-designation. Like the people who inhabited Qumran (4QpPs37 3.10; "the community of the poor"), they simply identified themselves as the poor. As we have noted, Acts makes it clear that the members of the Church donated their wealth to the Church, similar to the lifestyle practiced by those at Qumran. Twice Paul identifies the members of the Church in Jerusalem as *ho ptōchoi* ("the poor"). In Galatians, Paul describes James, Cephas, and John's directions that as he and Barnabas preach to the Gentiles, "they would that we should remember the poor" (Galatians 2:10). Paul writes, "For it hath pleased them of Macedonia and Achaia to make a certain contribution for the poor saints which are at Jerusalem" (Romans 15:26). Both these instances have reference to the collection Paul is making to take to the Jerusalem church and, on one level, may refer to their economic state after the famine prophesied by Agabus (Acts 11:27–28), but it may also refer to a life of consecration.[37]

The term *Christian* seems to have come later. In two of the three occasions in the New Testament, it is outsiders who use the term *Christian*. Acts 11:26 describes the period when Barnabas and Paul are teaching in the Church at Antioch: "And it came to pass, that a whole year they assembled themselves with the church, and taught much people." Then it records, "The disciples were called Christians first in Antioch." The passive voice in this verse suggests that outsiders, rather than insiders, coined this name.[38] In the second instance King Agrippa tells Paul, "Almost thou persuadest me to be a Christian" (Acts 26:28). Thus, it seems that the term *Christian*, like the term *Mormon*, was originally coined by outsiders, although it eventually became a self-designation, as we see in 1 Peter 4:16: "Yet if any man suffer as a Christian, let him not be ashamed; but let him glorify God on this behalf." By the beginning of the second century, Ignatius frequently uses it as a self-designation (see his letters *To the Ephesians*, 11:2; *To the Magnesians*, 4; *To the Romans*, 3:2; and *Polycarp*, 7:3).

There is no doubt that the Church of the first century qualifies to be called Jesus's church on the basis of its teaching of judgment, atonement, repentance, baptism, enduring to the end, and sanctification. The case for its qualifying as his church because it was called in Jesus's name is more difficult to make in our present New Testament, although *Christian* did eventually become a self-designation.

Conclusion

From the information we have in the New Testament and early Christian literature, we see that the organization of Christ's Church on earth developed over a period of time, in a way similar to the organization of the Church in this dispensation.[39] This development came as the fledgling Church grew and expanded both in numbers and geography. As we read the New Testament, it is important for us to understand that it gives us only the equivalent of snapshots of what the Church looked like at any one time. But the nature of the text, as it stands today, often does not join all the pictures together into a movie of the Church in the first century. Oftentimes we have more questions than we have answers. What is true, however, is that the early Church was grounded on the teachings and Atonement of Jesus Christ, just as it is today; that it operated under the power and authority of the priesthood, just as it does today; and that the offices of the Church developed as the needs of the members and the administration dictated.

Joseph Smith did not simply study the New Testament as did other Christian Primitivists (Restorationists) in the nineteenth century who attempted to pattern their organizations after the church outlined in the book of Acts. The Church of Jesus Christ was organized as revealed to the Prophet by the Lord Jesus Christ. In this sense, "We believe in the same organization that existed in the Primitive Church" (Articles of Faith 1:6), that is, a church led by revelation and inspiration that adapts to the current needs of the times and to the growing membership of the Church spread across the earth.

Gaye Strathearn is a professor of ancient scripture at Brigham Young University.
Joshua M. Sears is an assistant professor of ancient scripture at Brigham Young University.

Gaye Strathearn and Joshua M. Sears, "The Church in the First Century," in *The Life and Teachings of the New Testament Apostles: From the Day of Pentecost to the Apocalypse*, ed. Richard Neitzel Holzapfel and Thomas A. Wayment (Salt Lake City: Deseret Book, 2010), 35–62.

NOTES

1. James E. Talmage, *The Articles of Faith: A Series of Lectures on the Principal Doctrines of The Church of Jesus Christ of Latter-day Saints* (Salt Lake City: Deseret News, 1899), 201.
2. Jared W. Ludlow, "The Book of Acts: A Pattern for Modern Church Growth," in *Shedding Light on the New Testament: Acts–Revelation*, ed. Ray L. Huntington, Frank F. Judd Jr., and David M. Whitchurch (Provo, UT: Religious Studies Center, Brigham Young University, 2009), 1–29.
3. See "Adjustments to Priesthood Organization," Church History Topics, https://www.churchofjesuschrist.org/study/history/topics/adjustments-to-priesthood-organization.
4. "ἐκκλησία; *ekklēsia*," in Walter Bauer, William F. Arndt, and F. Wilbur Gingrich, *A Greek-English Lexicon of the New Testament and Other Early Christian Literature*, 3rd ed., ed. Frederick W. Danker (Chicago: University of Chicago Press, 2000), 303–4 (hereafter abbreviated as *GEL*).
5. John P. Meier, "The Circle of the Twelve: Did It Exist during Jesus' Public Ministry?," *Journal of Biblical Literature* 116, no. 4 (1997): 637. The Gospel of John does not contain any specific reference to the calling of the apostles, and it uses the word *apostolos* only once (John 13:16) but in a very general sense. John does, however, refer to the Twelve (John 6:67–70; 20:24). The synoptic Gospels also refer to the Twelve, but only twice do we find the phrase "twelve apostles" (Matthew 10:2; Luke 22:14).
6. "*Apostolos,*" in Bauer, Arndt and Gingrich, *GEL*, 122. See also Eric D. Huntsman, "Galilee and the Call of the Twelve Apostles," in Richard Neitzel Holzapfel and Thomas A. Wayment, eds., *From Bethlehem through the Sermon on the Mount,* vol. 1 of *The Life and Teachings of Jesus Christ* (Salt Lake City: Deseret Book, 2005), 228–38.
7. The one exception *may* be when the disciples failed to heal a boy who was possessed of a spirit. The text never calls them apostles but the context, most clearly in Matthew, suggests they may have been the nine apostles who did not go up into the mountain. The question is whether the disciples attempted to heal the boy through the power of the priesthood or simply through the power of faith. Jesus's response to the disciples' question, "Why could not we cast him out?" suggests that it may have been the latter. He says that they could not heal the boy "because of your unbelief" (Matthew 17:19–20).
8. S. Kent Brown, "Peter's Keys," in *The Ministry of Peter, the Chief Apostle*, ed. Frank F. Judd Jr., Eric D. Huntsman, and Shon D. Hopkin (Provo, UT: Religious Studies Center, Brigham Young University; Salt Lake City: Deseret Book, 2014), 91–102.
9. History, 1838–1856, Volume C-1 [2 November 1838–31 July 1842], p. 11, The Joseph Smith Papers.

10. A number of manuscripts say that Jesus called seventy-two, not seventy (e.g., Sinaiticus, a; Alexandrinus, A; Ephraemi, C; Bezae, D; and Freer, W).
11. Joel B. Green, *The Gospel of Luke,* The New International Commentary on the New Testament (Grand Rapids, MI: Eerdmans, 1997), 412–13.
12. The fourth-century Church historian Eusebius claims that Matthias, who was called to fill the vacancy left in the Twelve by the death of Judas, had served among the Seventy, as had Barnabas and an otherwise unknown figure named Thaddaeus. He recounts that "after [Christ's] resurrection from the dead and ascent into heaven, Thomas, one of the twelve Apostles, was divinely moved to send Thaddaeus to Edessa, himself listed among the number of the Seventy disciples of Christ, as a herald and evangelist of the teaching about Christ." *Ecclesiastical History*, 1:13. He also cites Clement of Alexandria, who wrote that after the resurrection the apostles passed divine instruction on to the Seventy. *Ecclesiastical History*, 2:1. If these records have a historical basis, it would indicate that the Seventy continued as an organized body in the Christian Church beyond the Resurrection under apostolic direction.
13. Robert J. Matthews, *Unto All Nations: A Guide to the Book of Acts and the Writings of Paul* (Salt Lake City: Deseret Book, 1975), 1. Robert L. Millet suggests that the phrase "speaking of the things pertaining to the kingdom of God" (Acts 1:3) could indicate that it was at this time that Jesus "provided the more complex church organization" to the apostles. "The Saga of the Early Christian Church," in Robert L. Millet, ed., *Acts to Revelation*, vol. 6 of *Studies in Scripture* (Salt Lake City: Deseret Book, 1987), 2. After surveying various interpretations of the forty-day ministry, Hugh Nibley concludes that Jesus's desire to better prepare the Twelve was "the argument most confidently put forth today." "Evangelium Quadraginta Dierum: The Forty-day Mission of Christ—The Forgotten Heritage," in *Mormonism and Early Christianity,* vol. 4 of *The Collected Works of Hugh Nibley* (Salt Lake City: Deseret Book and FARMS, 1987), 12.
14. For a detailed discussion of the Jerusalem Council, see Richard Neitzel Holzapfel and Thomas A. Wayment, "Unto the Uttermost Part of the Earth," in *The Life and Teachings of the New Testament Apostles: From the Day of Pentecost through the Apocalypse*, ed. Richard Neitzel Holzapfel and Thomas A. Wayment (Salt Lake City: Deseret Book, 2010), 63–79.
15. Nor does Paul identify himself as an apostle in Philippians 1:1; Titus 1:1; or Philemon 1:1. In these instances it may be because there is no question about his apostolic status.
16. Thomas A. Wayment, *From Persecutor to Apostle: A Biography of Paul* (Salt Lake City: Deseret Book, 2006), 153.
17. Acts 2:16–18; 19:6; 21:9; Romans 12:6; 1 Corinthians 11:4–5; 12:10; 13:2, 8–9; 14:1–6, 22–26, 31–32, 37, 39; 1 Thessalonians 5:20; 1 Timothy 1:18; 4:14; 2 Peter 1:19; Revelation 1:3; 10:11; 16:6; 18:20, 24; 19:10; 22:6–7, 9–10, 18–19.
18. This explains why such women as Miriam (Exodus 15:20), Deborah (Judges 4:4), Huldah (2 Kings 22:14; 2 Chronicles 34:22), and Anna (Luke 2:36) could be considered prophetesses despite a gender-based priesthood restriction. See also Acts 2:16–17; 1 Corinthians 11:5.
19. The Dead Sea Scrolls demonstrate that other Jews who were near-contemporaries with Paul similarly regulated that people speaking prophetically were subject to the leadership and correction of those with priestly authority. See Joshua M. Sears, "False Prophets as a Construction of Authority at Qumran," in *The Prophetic Voice at Qumran: The Leonardo Museum Conference on the Dead Sea Scrolls, 11–12 April 2014*, ed. Donald W. Parry,

Stephen D. Ricks, and Andrew C. Skinner, Studies on the Texts of the Desert of Judah 120 (Leiden: Brill, 2017), 115–27.

20. Andrew T. Lincoln, *Ephesians,* Word Biblical Commentary 40 (Dallas: Word, 1990), 153.
21. "εὐαγγελιστής; *euangelistēs,*" in Gerhard Kittel and Gerhard Friedrich, eds., *Theological Dictionary of the New Testament,* 10 vols., trans. Geoffrey W. Bromiley (Grand Rapids, MI: Eerdmans, 1964–76), 2:736.
22. History, 1838–1856, Volume C-1 [2 November 1838–31 July 1842], 9, The Joseph Smith Papers. John W. Welch has noted, "Today we cannot be certain of the origins of the new testament term *euangelistēs.* But of all the meanings attributed to the word *evangelist* over the years, the Prophet Joseph Smith's identification of this office as that of a patriarch who gives spiritual and prophetic blessings to individuals still comes closest to the meaning of this term in its earliest known occurrence." "Word Studies from the New Testament," *Ensign,* January 1995, 29.
23. John H. Elliott, "Elders as Leaders in 1 Peter and the Early Church," *Harvard Theological Studies* 64, no. 2 (2008): 687.
24. In fact, "throughout the ancient world, both in Greco-Roman and Israelite circles, heads of households respected for their age and prestige were known as 'elders' (*zekanim, presbyteroi, gerontes, seniors*) and exercised the role of local leadership." Elliott, "Elders as Leaders," 686.
25. Elliott, "Elders as Leaders," 685.
26. Elliott, "Elders as Leaders," 688.
27. Other places where *diakonos* is translated as the generic "minister" include Matthew 20:26; 22:13; Mark 9:35; 10:43; John 2:5, 9; 12:26; Romans 13:4; 15:8; 16:1; 1 Corinthians 3:5; 2 Corinthians 3:6; 6:4; 11:15, 23; Galatians 2:17; Ephesians 3:7; 6:21; Philippians 1:1; Colossians 1:7, 23, 25; 4:7; 1 Thessalonians 3:2; 1 Timothy 3:8, 12; 4:6. This is clearly the predominant sense of the word.
28. There is no evidence that this practice was entered into by Church members outside Jerusalem.
29. "καθίστημι; *kathistēmi*" in Bauer, Arndt and Gingrich, *GEL,* 492.
30. John J. Rousseau and Rami Arav, *Jesus and His World: An Archaeological and Cultural Dictionary* (Minneapolis: Fortress, 1995), 40.
31. Floyd V. Filson, "The Significance of the Early House Churches," *Journal of Biblical Literature* 58 (1939): 109.
32. Wayne A. Meeks, *The First Urban Christians: The Social World of the Apostle Paul* (New Haven: Yale University Press, 1983), 75.
33. For more on early Christian worship, see Erik Odin Yingling, "Worship and Ritual Practices in the New Testament," in *New Testament History, Culture, and Society: A Background to the Texts of the New Testament,* ed. Lincoln H. Blumell (Provo, UT: Religious Studies Center, Brigham Young University; Salt Lake City: Deseret Book, 2019), 586–602.
34. See Ken M. Campbell, ed., *Marriage and Family in the Biblical World* (Downers Grove, IL: InterVarsity Press, 2003).
35. Meeks, *First Urban Christians,* 76.
36. S. Vernon McCasland, "The Way," *Journal of Biblical Literature* (1958): 222–30.
37. The early Church Fathers knew of an early group of Christians, whom they regarded as heretical, who lived the law of Moses (cf. Acts 21:20) and were called the Ebionites, from the Hebrew word for poor, *ebyônîm.* See Irenaeus, *Against Heresies,* 1.26.2; 3.11.7, 21.1; 4.33.4.

38. For examples of outsiders using the term, see Josephus, *AJ,* 8.3.3, Pliny, *Letters,* 10.96, and Suetonius, *Claudius,* 25.13–15, where the word *Chrestus* is used. "'Christus' was often confused with 'Chrestus' by non-Christians, and sometimes even by Christians. This confusion arose from two sources, of meaning and sound. The Greek 'Christos' and its Latin equivalent 'Christus' would have suggested a strange meaning to most ancients, especially those unfamiliar with its Jewish background. Its primary Greek meaning in everyday life suggests the medical term 'anointer' or the construction term 'plasterer.' These meanings would not have the religious content that 'Christ' would have to someone on the inside of Christianity. These unusual meanings could have prompted this shift to a more recognizable, meaningful name. Due to a widespread phonetic feature of Greek, 'Christus' and 'Chrestus' were even closer in pronunciation than they appear to be today." Robert E. Van Voorst, *Jesus outside the New Testament: An Introduction to the Ancient Evidence* (Grand Rapids, MI: Eerdmans, 2000), 34.
39. Change and development are a feature, not a bug, of a "living Church" (Doctrine and Covenants 1:30). In response to changes being made to the organization of the Seventy in the late nineteenth century, the Lord gave a revelation to the First Presidency on April 14, 1883 and explained, "Let not your hearts be troubled, neither be ye concerned about the management and organization of my Church and Priesthood and the accomplishment of my work. Fear me and observe my laws and I will reveal unto you, *from time to time*, through the channels that I have appointed, everything that shall be necessary for the future development and *perfection* of my Church, for the adjustment and rolling forth of my kingdom, and for the building up and the establishment of my Zion." As cited in Earl C. Tingey, "The Saga of Revelation: The Unfolding Role of the Seventy," *Ensign*, September 2009, 56; emphasis in original.

Chapter Fourteen

Peter, Cornelius, and Cultural Boundaries

THOMAS A. WAYMENT

In the second half of the New Testament, the letters of Paul and the book of Acts are particularly and carefully focused on the issue of the church's early missionary efforts among Greek-speaking gentile communities in Asia Minor, Macedonia, Rome, and Greece.[1] In fact, the interest in and focus on the gentile mission might be considered a unifying theme in Paul's letters and in Acts. For example, discussions on important doctrinal topics such as grace and foreordination were necessary in light of the increasing numbers of gentiles joining the church. Some important questions arose in the early church as a result of the gentile mission: Would God accept gentiles into heaven, and if he did so, would *they* need grace to enter, unlike Jews, who were guaranteed a place in heaven through birthright? Were God's people forever chosen despite the fact that Jews were only infrequently accepting baptism and joining the fledgling Christian church? These questions shaped Paul's letters and forced him to address these topics on multiple occasions. They also direct us to some of the interesting points of discussion that arise out of the letters and histories from the first three decades of the church's existence (AD 30–60).[2]

One particularly perplexing and thematic issue is the resistance that some early Jewish members of the church felt toward teaching the gospel to gentiles. Additionally, it is possible that some early church leaders may have been culturally conditioned to feel a need to place restraints on the teaching of the gospel to gentiles. A study of this length cannot consider all of the attitudes that early church members expressed towards gentiles or whether or not there were even different opinions expressed towards different ethnic groups within the church: Macedonians, Greeks, Romans, Egyptians, or Samaritans. Some would have been more culturally different—Egyptians—while the Samaritans shared many of the same beliefs and practices as ethnic Jews. Despite the limitations of a study such as this, it will be possible to consider briefly how Peter treated gentiles within the church and how his actions shaped early church policy and practice. Peter is at least emblematic of the wide spectrum of attitudes that existed in early Christianity, and his attitudes and actions are woven into the fabric of an ethnically diverse, multilingual, geographically distant, early Christian church. The modern reader will find in this discussion an important study of how cultural boundaries shaped the growth of the early church and how the Lord guided early church leaders to navigate an ethnically diverse organization.

Ultimately, this paper will seek to establish the thesis that Peter, the church's leader and most recognizable member, was both part of the hesitance in initially limiting the mission to the gentiles and a significant part of the solution in initiating the mission to the gentiles after his vision in Joppa. Moreover, this paper will attempt to establish the fact that Peter's actions were representative of the attitudes and opinions of Jewish Christians regarding the evangelization of gentiles and regarding the early hesitance to permit gentiles into full fellowship without first requiring them to be circumcised and live the kosher laws (i.e., the *kashrut*). This study will not consider the successes or the failures of the early gentile mission, nor will it address the doctrinal question of whether a gentile mission was even permissible. Instead, this paper will focus closely on whether Luke's portrayal of events, particularly those involving Peter, intentionally suggests that Peter had reservations in taking the gospel to the gentiles.

A Brief Survey of Previous Studies

A number of careful and contemplative studies on the subject of Acts and the gentile mission have been carried out by Latter-day Saint scholars, all of which appear to be genetically linked to Bruce R. McConkie's seminal series on the books of the New Testament.[3] Each of the subsequent major studies on Acts builds on the position advanced in Elder McConkie's work and argues with minor alterations that Peter was hesitant to accept gentiles into the church in full fellowship but that he eventually, through revelation, accepted them, thus paving the way for a full-blown gentile mission.[4] There has been little discussion about the ramifications of Peter's act of hesitation, and almost no discussion of where Peter's attitudes came from and whether they represented those of other members of the early church or whether the Galilean Peter was predisposed to exclude gentiles. These questions have major ramifications for the development of Christianity because they provide us with an awareness of the outlook of the early disciples and whether or not they had considered taking the gospel beyond Judea and Galilee.

Outside of Latter-day Saint circles of scholarship, the question of attitudes toward gentiles within early Christianity has been closely considered with emphasis on the chronological development of the question and the social impact of those attitudes.[5] As a general rule, these studies typically assume that early Christian leaders held attitudes that were very similar to or even identical to other first-century Jews who did not convert to Christianity.[6] This is, of course, certainly possible, but upon careful scrutiny of the evidence it is not necessarily certain that early Christians felt the same way about gentiles that their Jewish counterparts did. In addition to that concern is the question of whether the early disciples shared the common cultural bias that their Jewish counterparts exhibited.

Some of Jesus's teachings in the Gospels clearly point in the direction of an eventual gentile mission. Following Luke's overall interest in the mission to the gentiles, he was careful to narrate Simeon's blessing of the infant Jesus: "A light to lighten the Gentiles, and the glory of thy people Israel" (Luke 2:32). Although the disciples would not have heard Simeon speak the prophecy, Luke's recording of the story shows that it was foundational for understanding Jesus and the purpose of his ministry. An additional saying in Matthew 12:21 records a saying of Jesus that points clearly in the direction of the gentiles coming to accept the gospel: "And in his name shall the Gentiles trust." The quotation itself is derived from Isaiah 42:1–4, but Jesus changed the wording: "He shall bring forth judgment unto truth. He shall not fail nor be discouraged, till he have set judgment in the earth: and the isles shall wait for his law" (Isaiah 42:3–4). By changing Isaiah's "isles" to gentiles, Jesus unequivocally changed the meaning and helped his disciples see that a gentile mission was possible.

It is certainly time to relook at the issue of the gentile mission and to reappraise the evidence. That evidence will help us determine whether Peter was caused to accept gentiles through visionary prompting after expressing early reluctance to do so or whether Peter and other early Christians were simply anti-gentile in their attitudes because they had been culturally conditioned via Judaism to be that way.[7]

A Mission to the Gentiles? The Purpose of Acts

It is important for this study to note that writing and recording history in the first century was fundamentally different than writing history today. For the purposes of this study, it is worthwhile to consider what it might mean to us if Luke wrote with a particular agenda and how he treated his ancient eyewitness sources. Oral history was preferred over written history.[8] The oft-quoted saying of Papias is helpful here and is worth including in full:

> I shall not hesitate also to put into properly ordered form for you everything I learned carefully in the past from the elders and noted down well, for the truth of which I vouch. For unlike most people I did not enjoy those who have a great deal to say, but those who teach the truth. Nor did I enjoy those who recall someone else's commandments, but those who remember the commandments given by the Lord to the faith and proceeding from the truth itself. And if by chance anyone who had been in attendance on the elders should come my way, I inquired about the words of the elders—[that is,] what [according to the elders] Andrew or Peter said, or Philip, or Thomas or James, or

> John or Matthew or any other of the Lord's disciples, and whatever Aristion and the elder John, the Lord's disciples, were saying. *For I did not think that information from books would profit me as much as information from a living and surviving voice.* (Eusebius, *Historia Ecclesiastica* 3.39.3–4)[9]

This cautionary type of attitude, if representative of the attitudes held by others towards book reading in the early church, should not cause us to question the accuracy of books per se, but to evaluate books that claim to present firsthand experiences differently than we might evaluate an ancient book that was not written by eyewitnesses. That is to say, books that advocate that their information was derived from eyewitnesses were superior, according to Papias, to books where the author has collected written sources and evaluated them. A modern scholarly book would not fare well in ancient Christianity. But additionally it should be pointed out that a book that promotes eyewitness accounts may also be taking advantage of the skepticism of writing history via reading books and promoting its own account as superior to other books on the subject. Two canonical Gospels intentionally promote eyewitnesses as the source of their writing: Luke and John.[10]

Although we cannot take up the discussion of John as an eyewitness, we do have space to consider Luke's eyewitness sources.[11] He, more than any other New Testament writer, established his credentials in writing at the outset of his account: "Forasmuch as many have taken in hand to set forth in order a declaration of those things which are most surely believed among us, *Even as they delivered them unto us, which from the beginning were eyewitnesses*,[12] and ministers of the word; it seemed good to me also, having had perfect understanding of all things from the very first, to write unto thee in order" (Luke 1:1–3; emphasis added).[13] What is useful to this study are two features from this discussion: first, Luke may have intentionally wanted his readers to recognize his *written* Gospel as more authoritative than the oral reports circulating in his day, and second, his confidence that his report was based on a "perfect understanding." For the present study, this evidence points in the direction of an author who had something definitive and authoritative to say and that there may also be undertones of a corrective interest. It would appear safe to say that Acts, also written by Luke, bears a similar interest in setting forth the story that was based on eyewitness accounts and was reliant upon a "perfect understanding."[14]

A parallel situation occurs in Joseph Smith's 1838 journal history, where he also records history with an overt purpose, "Owing to the many reports which have been put in circulation by evil-disposed and designing persons, in relation to the rise and progress of The Church of Jesus Christ of Latter-day Saints, all of which have been designed by the authors thereof to militate against its character as a Church and its progress in the world—I have been induced to write this history, to disabuse the public mind, and put all inquirers after truth in possession of the facts, as they have transpired, in relation both to myself and the Church, so far as I have such facts in my possession" (Joseph Smith—History 1:1).

Discovering Luke's Agenda

Building upon the proposition that Luke wrote with a particular agenda in mind and that he intentionally wanted to advertise his account as one that was built upon better eyewitness sources, it should be possible to at least describe the contours of that agenda.[15] Several features of Luke's account reasonably represent at least a portion of his agenda.[16] First, Paul is formally introduced into the story in Acts 9:1 and takes over the narrative almost completely by Acts 13:1. Even though Luke began by retelling the history of Christianity and the early experiences of the apostles, he no longer does so in a significant way after narrating Paul's first mission. Second, the stories that are told after Paul's introduction are almost exclusively focused on the question of the gentile mission: Cornelius, Peter's vision at Joppa, the church expanding into Antioch (a gentile city), and the death of an old nemesis from the Herodian family.[17] Although Luke certainly had additional intentions in writing his Gospel and history, such as the role of women in the church and the plight of the poor, we can be fairly confident that one of the items of central importance was his interest in describing the gentile mission.

The gentile mission was arguably the foremost interest driving Luke's narrative: he was searching for causes and solutions.[18] And he may have taken his narrative structure in part from Paul's letter to the Romans, "For

I am not ashamed of the gospel of Christ: for it is the power of God unto salvation to every one that believeth; *to the Jew first, and also to the Greek*" (Romans 1:16, emphasis added; see also 2:10).[19] The taking of the gospel to the "Jew first, and also to the Greek" accurately describes Luke's account where he abbreviates the story of taking the gospel to the Jews (Acts 1–8) and then expands the discussion of the gospel to the Gentiles (Acts 9–21).[20] Luke also foreshadowed his greater interest in the gentile mission when he reported a cautionary statement by a leading Jewish leader of the day that has prophetic hints at the success of the gentile mission, "Refrain from these men, and let them alone: for if this counsel or this work be of men, it will come to nought: but if it be of God, ye cannot overthrow it; lest haply ye be found even to fight against God" (Acts 5:38–39). Luke went on to demonstrate that the growth of Christianity among the gentiles was something that could not be overthrown. Having discussed both Luke's agenda in writing as well as his interest in establishing his history as authoritative, we can now look at how Luke's portrayal of Peter fits into this developing narrative.

Peter's Role in the Gentile Mission

Returning directly to the original focus of this paper, it is necessary to consider Peter's part in the unfolding story of the gentile mission. In the Gospel of Luke, Peter is mentioned by name in eighteen verses, with twelve of those references coming from two stories: the Mount of Transfiguration and Peter's denial (see Luke 5:8; 6:14; 8:51, 45; 9:20, 28, 32–33; 12:41; 18:28; 22:8, 34, 54–55, 58, 60–62). Peter is mentioned fifty-six times in Acts, with fifty-five of those references coming in Acts 1–12 (see also Acts 15:7). Of necessity, Peter is portrayed differently in the two sources: in the Gospel of Luke he is the impetuous disciple who faithfully seeks to testify and demonstrate his faith, whereas in the book of Acts he is the relentless leader of the church who is carefully guided through revelation (see Acts 10) to lead the church in a new age. The two viewpoints are congruous, and in the Gospel of Luke, Peter can be described as learning to be a disciple, and in Acts he demonstrates that he has learned and is capable of leading.

Some of the features that are characteristic of Peter in the Gospel of Luke are that he is frequently portrayed as asking questions and giving answers (see Luke 8:45; 9:20). He is also the voice for the other disciples and frequently uses the first person plural when speaking, "Then Peter said, Lo, we have left all, and followed thee" (Luke 18:28). In Acts this portrayal of Peter subtly shifts when he asks the disciples, "Men and brethren, what shall we do?" (Acts 2:37). This question is characteristic of Peter as portrayed in the Gospel, but after Pentecost it appears that Peter only asks questions to which he already knows the answer. To be precise, after Acts 2:37 he asks questions on two different occasions: In Acts 5:3, 8, and 9, Peter asks questions of Ananias and Sapphira where he already knew through inspiration what they had done, and in Acts 10:21 he asks Cornelius, "Behold, I am he whom ye seek: what is the cause wherefore ye are come?" Effectively, Peter has become the leading disciple in Acts that is on some level omniscient of the answers he will receive, a contrast that Luke highlights by making the final verse in his Gospel that specifically mentions Peter to say, "And Peter went out, and wept bitterly" (Luke 22:62). In the Gospel he is also human and subtly weak, but the weakness also serves to heighten the contrast of the new Peter in Acts.

In a diachronic retelling of the history of Christianity and the story of Peter and the early gentile mission, Luke was faced with several challenges of how to incorporate some of the difficulties that arose when ethnic Jews were faced with the possibility of dining with gentiles in their Christian house-churches where nonkosher foods were offered and where the gentile members were uncircumcised. The trauma of such an event is recognizable in Paul's description of one such encounter in Antioch, "But when Peter was come to Antioch, I withstood him to the face, because he was to be blamed. For before that certain came from James, he did eat with the Gentiles: but when they were come, he withdrew and separated himself, fearing them which were of the circumcision" (Galatians 2:11–12).[21] In structuring the story, Paul may have supposed that Peter ceased eating with gentiles because he was afraid of what ethnic Jews might think of him for eating with gentiles.[22] Luke does not report the story in the way that Paul does, and he omits the story of conflict, perhaps because he was more sensitive to Peter's actual motives. What Peter's concerns were is a subject to which we will return.

Part of Luke's narrative in Acts may initially appear to depict Peter as part of the obstacle in taking the gospel to the gentiles, an important part of the discussion considered in this study. The key verses treating this theme read, "And there came a voice to him, Rise, Peter; kill, and eat. But Peter said, *Not so, Lord; for I have never eaten any thing that is common or unclean*" (Acts 10:13–14; emphasis added) and later in the chapter, "Ye know how that it is an unlawful thing for a man that is a Jew to keep company, or come unto one of another nation; but God hath shewed me that I should not call any man common or unclean" (Acts 10:28). Both of these passages convey the idea that Peter was in part an obstacle to a gentile mission because he had never considered the unclean (the gentiles) and because even after the vision of the sheet and the unclean animals, Peter still maintained that he was a "Jew" (and not a Christian) and that it was "unlawful" for him to come into the home of a gentile. Both of these obstacles should naturally have been resolved in the Resurrection and the command to take the gospel to all nations, but Luke is here subtly reminding the reader that there were still cultural obstacles to overcome and Peter was pivotal in resolving those obstacles (see Matthew 28:19–20). Assuming that Luke was intentionally retelling this story to help demonstrate to the reader that he was aware of the implications of Peter calling himself a Jew after the Resurrection of Christ, then this story has great meaning in understanding some of the cultural boundaries that existed between Jewish Christians and gentile Christians.

Simplifying the story in this way, however, misses the opportunity to ask whether or not Luke may have shaped the story in a way to express to his audience the validity—the revelatory foundation—of the gentile mission. In other words, when Peter expressed his hesitancy to the angel, "I have never eaten any thing that is common or unclean," he may have revealed his deep-seated concerns about a mission to the unclean gentiles, but Luke may have recorded that particular part of the story because it so adequately described the sentiments of Judean/Jewish Christians. In analyzing the story further, it becomes apparent that Peter may have been savvier to the meaning of the vision than we might have initially assumed. Luke reports, "Peter went up upon the housetop to pray about the sixth hour: and he became very hungry, and would have eaten: but while they made ready, he fell into a trance, and saw heaven opened, and a certain vessel descending unto him, as it had been a great sheet knit at the four corners, and let down to the earth: wherein were all manner of fourfooted beasts of the earth, and wild beasts, and creeping things, and fowls of the air. And there came a voice to him, Rise, Peter; kill, and eat" (Acts 10:9–13). By drawing attention to Peter's concluding statement we overlook two important features: (1) there were clean beasts on the sheet and (2) Peter knew he was being asked to eat the unclean beasts, which is surprising given that observant Jews would certainly assume they were only to eat the clean animals.[23] For an observant Jew, the command to eat from the sheet would typically be understood as a request to avoid the unclean and to eat only the clean: Peter saw it differently.

It can be stated with some confidence, that on a simple reading of Acts 10, Peter is part of the hesitance in expanding the mission to the gentiles, but that upon closer inspection, Peter knew the way forward and saw how the Lord was directing him to take the gospel beyond Judea and Galilee. Luke spends more time on this part of the discussion between Peter and Cornelius than he does on any other aspect.[24] He reports Peter's words, "Then Peter opened his mouth, and said, Of a truth I perceive that God is no respecter of persons: But in every nation he that feareth him, and worketh righteousness, is accepted with him" (Acts 10:34–35). Luke is careful to note that Peter's declaration caused some concern for ethnic Jews when they heard his report, "While Peter yet spake these words, the Holy Ghost fell on all them which heard the word. And they of the circumcision which believed were astonished, as many as came with Peter, because that on the Gentiles also was poured out the gift of the Holy Ghost" (Acts 10:44–45). By retelling the story in this way, Luke has helped the reader see that the common attitude that gentiles could not receive the Holy Ghost had been unequivocally answered through Peter and through revelation.

Peter at the Jerusalem Conference (AD 49)

To fully appreciate the importance of Acts 15 and its account of the Jerusalem Conference that was convened to settle the matter concerning the gentile needs to be circumcised and to maintain the kosher standards of Judaism, we must first take a closer look at Peter's vision of the sheet and its aftermath. This will be important to the discussion because it will help demonstrate how the early church resolved the issue of the cultural divide between its members.

The most important verse in this discussion will be "When they heard these things, they held their peace, and glorified God, saying, Then hath God also to the Gentiles granted repentance unto life" (Acts 11:18). Because the verse reads as a declaration of the early church's position on gentile conversion and because of its pivotal nature in this discussion, it will be helpful to scrutinize the translation. In Greek, the passage reads, "ἀκούσαντες δὲ ταῦτα ἡσύχασαν καὶ ἐδόξασαν τὸν θεὸν λέγοντες, Ἄρα καὶ τοῖς ἔθνεσιν ὁ θεὸς τὴν μετάνοιαν εἰς ζωὴν ἔδωκεν," which translated in a very literal way reads, "Having heard this thing, they were silent and were glorifying God, saying, 'Then God has given to the Gentiles the repentance that leads to life.'"

An important feature of this verse is the statement that they were "silent" and "glorifying," the latter of which is not a particularly silent gesture, which indicates that they were probably silent in their resistance to the gentile mission but vocal in their praise of God. The "thing" that caused them to rejoice openly was the unequivocal statement "Forasmuch then as God gave them the like gift as he did unto us, who believed on the Lord Jesus Christ; what was I, that I could withstand God?" (Acts 11:17). In other words, they could no longer withstand the will of God. But perhaps most important is the verb translated as "has given" (ἔδωκεν), which conveys a past tense action or an action that had occurred prior to the speech being reported. God "has given" the gentiles an opportunity to enter the fold and who can "withstand God?"

In looking closer at Peter's experience, another interesting facet of the story catches our attention. By reporting Peter's declaration that being commanded to eat unclean foods helped Peter see that *people* should not be declared unclean (Acts 10:15, 28), Luke has subtly made the connection that people are equal to the unclean food in the vision. Through this connection, Luke is able to draw out the idea that the center of the divide between gentiles and Jews in early Christianity was an issue of food.[25] At the very heart of the debate was the real-life concern that in giving up the kosher laws of the Old Testament, ethnic Jews were turning their back on their religious identity and uniqueness. And one of the fundamental reasons gentiles were considered unclean is because they partook of unclean foods. Now Jewish Christians would be unclean in the eyes of their non-Christian countrymen.[26]

This brings us to what appears to be Luke's clearest expression of frustration that the issue continued to divide ethnic gentiles like Luke and ethnic Jews like Peter. In reporting the Jerusalem Conference, Peter states with authority,

> And when there had been much disputing, Peter rose up, and said unto them, Men and brethren, ye know how that a good while ago God made choice among us, that the Gentiles by my mouth should hear the word of the gospel, and believe.
>
> And God, which knoweth the hearts, bare them witness, giving them the Holy Ghost, even as he did unto us;
>
> And put no difference between us and them, purifying their hearts by faith.
>
> Now therefore why tempt ye God, to put a yoke upon the neck of the disciples, which neither our fathers nor we were able to bear?
>
> But we believe that through the grace of the Lord Jesus Christ we shall be saved, even as they. (Acts 15:7–11)

Peter's redeclaration of God's will in Acts 15 was the second announcement of church policy, and the fact that God had already declared his will on the matter in Acts 11:18 as ἔδωκεν ("hath given") was already sufficiently clear.

Peter, following the direction God had given him, announced the decision on two separate occasions, which is why Acts 15:20 represents a step backwards in the narrative: "But that we write unto them, that they abstain from pollutions of idols, and from fornication, and from things strangled, and from blood." These strictures all relate to the *kashrut*, the kosher requirements of the law of Moses, and they were given despite Peter's clear declaration on the matter. Phrases such as "put no difference between us and them" are in open conflict with "But that we write unto them."

It is to be expected that Luke, Paul's traveling companion, would hold an opinion similar to Paul's regarding the Jerusalem conference (for Paul's view, see Galatians 2:12–13)—that is, that he saw the resolution of the conflict of cultural boundaries as foundational to the success of the gentile mission. When Paul denounced Peter in Antioch, he perhaps failed to apprehend that though he was commissioned to take the gospel to the gentiles, Peter was commissioned to take the same message to the Jews so that their hearts could be softened to accept the gentiles that Paul would convert. Paul appears to have interpreted the situation through its effects on his mission in Antioch and not in light of the larger issue of harmony within the church between Jewish and gentile Christians. Luke, however, shows some sensitivity in not taking either side in the conflict, but in focusing on the resolution.

Why Joppa?

Finally, it is helpful to see that there may be a larger symbolic undertone to why Peter was at Joppa when he received the revelation that Cornelius was awaiting him. According to the story in Acts, Cornelius was at Caesarea Maritima when he had the vision telling him to send for Peter, while Peter was a short distance away in the coastal city of Joppa (see Acts 10:1).[27] Acts reports simply, "And now send men to Joppa, and call for one Simon, whose surname is Peter" (Acts 10:5). The significance of Joppa is easily overlooked in the story, but it may have a connection to an earlier prophet who was similarly called to teach the gospel to gentiles. In the book of the prophet Jonah, when the Lord commanded Jonah to go to Nineveh, Jonah fled in the opposite direction, "But Jonah rose up to flee unto Tarshish from the presence of the Lord, and went down to Joppa; and he found a ship going to Tarshish: so he paid the fare thereof, and went down into it, to go with them unto Tarshish from the presence of the Lord" (Jonah 1:3). Jonah's starting point for taking the gospel to the Assyrians was the same city where Peter was later praying on his roof.

The symbolic significance is overt: Jonah fled the command to take the gospel to the gentiles, while Peter in the same city accepted the call of the Lord to take the gospel to the gentiles. Interestingly, Jonah was originally called upon to deliver a message of doom, "Arise, go to Nineveh, that great city, and cry against it; for their wickedness is come up before me" (Jonah 1:2). Peter was given the command to take a message of peace and of good news.[28] Although the actual occurrence of the vision in Joppa is probably little more than happenstance, given Luke's careful documentation of the gentile mission, it is possible that he recorded the location with the intent that the reader would see the connection to the mission of Jonah and see the parallel that is mentioned here.

Conclusion

Looking carefully at the New Testament texts and their accounts of the early gentile mission may raise concerns in the minds of some readers: concern that there was discord in the early church, concern that James and Paul may have handled the issue of kosher requirements very differently, and concern that Peter's revelation was only gradually adopted.[29] But those concerns are really only minor when we compare the issues in the early church with any other day and age where the faithful have wrestled to accept all of God's words: We have seen that there is at times discord in the way we understand revelation; we have teachings that appear to offer differing opinions; and ultimately we have a prophet who reveals the mind of the Lord that we are obligated to accept. The history of the early church is the history of God's people. Luke's honesty is refreshing and insightful.

Reconstructing what Luke appears to intend, we can conjecture that Peter was initially resistant to accepting gentiles into the church without the gentiles previously having committed themselves to live the full law of Moses as he had done. With revelatory prompting, Peter came to see a way forward through grace wherein the gentiles could enter the church in full fellowship. Some early missionaries, notably not referred to as apostles in Acts, disagreed on how Peter's revelation should be implemented. And perhaps the most resounding message comes from Peter, who understood fully the impact of what the Lord had revealed to him. The gentiles were and are the future of the church, and Peter opened the door through which they entered. Elder Hales noted the pivotal nature of Jesus's words to Peter when he said, "Brothers and sisters, do we really understand the teachings of the Savior, 'When thou art converted, strengthen thy brethren'? (Luke 22:32). Feed my lambs. Feed my sheep. Feeding the lambs could well be missionary labors working with newly baptized members, who must be nurtured and given caring warmth and fellowship in the family of Saints. Feeding the sheep could well refer to the mature members of the Church, some active and some less active, who need to be cared for and brought back to the flock."[30]

It is the conclusion of this paper that seeing Peter as the resistant disciple is perhaps too simplistic and that the development of the gentile mission was in fact much more complicated. In the end, there simply is not enough evidence to distinguish Peter's personal views about gentiles from those of his Judean peers, although I expect that they were different. Ultimately, the church was slow to take the gospel to the gentiles. A multitude of reasons exist to explain this occurrence, but the most likely reason is that cultural attitudes were the root cause. Luke, a fellow traveling companion of Paul's, saw the need to document the gentile mission and sought to help the reader see it as part of the larger historical portrait of Christianity.

Thomas A. Wayment is a professor of classics at Brigham Young University.

Thomas A. Wayment, "Peter, Cornelius, and Cultural Boundaries," in *The Ministry of Peter, the Chief Apostle*, ed. Frank F. Judd Jr., Eric D. Huntsman, and Shon D. Hopkin (Provo, UT: Religious Studies Center; Salt Lake City: Deseret Book, 2014), 211–26.

NOTES

1. The New Testament term denoting "Gentile" is ἔθνος (ethnos), which functionally indicates a group of people unified by family or culture. Typically the term is modified by a genitive description of the people, i.e., "the people of the Samaritans" or "the people of the Greeks." Often it is used in the sense of those who have another faith, regardless of their ethnicity (see Matthew 10:18).
2. For example, Paul's teaching that the law of Moses acted like a schoolmaster to bring Israel to Christ in Galatians 3–4 may be understood as a conversation arising out of the Gentile mission. See also Romans 1–3.
3. Bruce R. McConkie, *Doctrinal New Testament Commentary*, 3 vols. (Salt Lake City: Bookcraft, 1965–73). The series is now published by Deseret Book in both electronic and print editions.
4. See Robert J. Matthews, "Unto All Nations," in *Acts to Revelation*, vol. 6 of *Studies in Scripture*, ed. Robert L. Millet (Salt Lake City: Deseret Book, 1987), 34–36; Gaye Strathearn, "The Jewish and Gentile Missions: Paul's Role in the Transition," in *The Apostle Paul: His Life and His Testimony* (Salt Lake City: Deseret Book, 1994), 194–96; Gaye Strathearn, "Law and Liberty in Galatians 5–6," in *Go Ye into All the World* (Salt Lake City: Deseret Book, 2002), 62–63; Jared W. Ludlow, "The Book of Acts: A Pattern for Modern Church Growth," in *Shedding Light on the New Testament: Acts–Revelation*, ed. Ray L. Huntington, Frank F. Judd Jr., and David M. Whitchurch (Provo, UT: Religious Studies Center, 2009), 1–29; Eric D. Huntsman, "The Impact of Gentile Conversions in the Greco-Roman World," in *The Life and Teachings of the New Testament Apostles: From the Day of Pentecost through the Apocalypse*, ed. Richard Neitzel Holzapfel and Thomas A. Wayment (Salt Lake City: Deseret Book, 2010), 80–96.

5. An excellent recent study on the question is a collection of essays edited by David C. Sim and James S. McLaren, *Attitudes to Gentiles in Ancient Judaism and Early Christianity* (London and New York: T&T Clark, 2013). A particularly helpful article in the collection is Elizabeth V. Dowling, "'To the Ends of the Earth': Attitudes to Gentiles in Luke–Acts," 191–208. See also James Carleton-Paget, *Jews, Christians and Jewish Christians in Antiquity* (Tübingen: Mohr Siebeck, 2010).
6. D. C. Sim, "Gentiles, God-Fearers and Proselytes," in *Attitudes to Gentiles in Ancient Judaism and Early Christianity*, ed. David C. Sim and James S. McLaren (London and New York: T&T Clark, 2013), 4–8.
7. I recognize that this is a somewhat simplistic dichotomy and is not likely to express all of the nuances in the excellent studies already in print. The dichotomy is admittedly a characterization of the two different sides of the discussion. What is not at issue is the simple fact that both sides accept a certain anti-Gentile attitude in earliest Christianity.
8. See Thomas A. Wayment, "From Jesus to the Written Gospels: The Oral Origins of the Gospel," in Holzapfel and Wayment, *Life and Teachings of the New Testament Apostles*, 11–34.
9. I have taken the translation of this passage from Richard Bauckham's excellent study on the topic, *Jesus and the Eyewitnesses: The Gospels as Eyewitness Testimony* (Grand Rapids, MI: Eerdmans, 2006) 15–16: his translation of the passage is the most nuanced and careful of which I am aware.
10. Some will note that Matthew (9:9) was also an eyewitness to the events told in his account, but Matthew as a personal witness to events is not a developed theme in the first Gospel.
11. For John as an eyewitness, see John 1:35–40 and 19:26.
12. The phrase "Even as they delivered them unto us, which from the beginning were eyewitnesses" could be read to imply that Luke was including himself as an eyewitness. In Greek, however, the phrase is not ambiguous and it unquestionably refers to the eyewitnesses, i.e., Luke was stating that the unnamed eyewitnesses passed on things to "us," a group that included Luke.
13. For a discussion of this passage, see Richard Neitzel Holzapfel and Thomas A. Wayment, "Introduction: The World of the New Testament," in *From Bethlehem through the Sermon on the Mount*, vol. 1 of *The Life and Teachings of Jesus Christ*, ed. Richard Neitzel Holzapfel and Thomas A. Wayment (Salt Lake City: Deseret Book, 2005), xxii–xxix.
14. Acts 16:10 begins a series of first-person plural passages, the so-called "we" passages, that point to Luke being physically present for the events he is narrating.
15. This approach has often been viewed with skepticism because scholars who seek to determine Luke's method of writing history often use terms such as *myth*, which has been offensive to many Latter-day Saint scholars. In telling a story with an overt agenda, however, the author is not obligated to create a mythical account or an account built upon fabricated sources. Even the act of selecting which stories to tell is an act of writing with an agenda. For a recent discussion of Luke's agenda, see Mikeal C. Parsons, *Luke: Storyteller, Interpreter, Evangelist* (Peabody, MA: Hendrickson, 2007).
16. Adele Berlin, *Poetics and Interpretation of Biblical Narrative*, Bible and Literature 9 (Sheffield: Almond, 1983), 46, details the difficulties in identifying an author's agenda in writing. See also David L. Cowles, "Formalism," in *The Critical Experience: Literary Reading, Writing, and Criticism*, ed. David L. Cowles, 2nd ed. (Dubuque, IA: Kendall/Hunt Publishing, 1994), 11–12.

17. Acts 10:45 preserves an allusion to what I will argue is Luke's agenda, "And they of the circumcision which believed were astonished, as many as came with Peter, because that on the Gentiles also was poured out the gift of the Holy Ghost."
18. Luke also expresses a clear interest in the Samaritan mission in the early part of Acts. See Elizabeth V. Dowling, "'To the Ends of the Earth': Attitudes to Gentiles in Luke–Acts," in *Attitudes to Gentiles in Ancient Judaism and Early Christianity*, 191–208.
19. Somewhat surprisingly, two passages from Mark that emphasize gentile involvement are not retold in Luke (Mark 7:24–30; 8:1–10).
20. This emphasis has been noted by numerous other scholars. See, for example, Jeffrey S. Siker, "'First to the Gentiles': A Literary Analysis of Luke 4:16–30," *Journal of Biblical Literature* 111 (1992): 73–90.
21. James D. G. Dunn, "The Incident at Antioch (Gal 2:11–18)," *Journal for the Study of the New Testament* 18 (1983): 3–57; John G. Gager, "Jews, Gentiles, and Synagogues in the Book of Acts," in *Christians among Jews and Gentiles: Essays in Honor of Krister Stendahl on His Sixty-Fifth Birthday*, ed. George W. E. Nickelsburg and George W. MacRae (Philadelphia: Fortress, 1986), 93, thinks Gentiles were welcome in the synagogues. Most scholars today seem to refute Gager's findings, but it remains a possibility that in diaspora communities Gentiles were frequently in attendance.
22. The participle *foboumenos* (φοβούμενος) in Galatians 2:12 conceptually conveys genuine fear and apprehensiveness. See H. Balz, "φοβέω," in *Theological Dictionary of the New Testament*, ed. Gerhard Kittel and Gerhard Friedrich, trans. G. W. Bromily, 9 vols. (Grand Rapids, MI: Eerdmans, 1978), 208–19.
23. It may be that the instruction to eat the unclean was implied in the injunction. "Rise, Peter; kill, and eat." The inference was that Peter was to eat everything on the sheet, clean and unclean. Clinton Wahlen, "Peter's Vision and Conflicting Definitions of Purity," *New Testament Studies* 51 (2005): 515 notes that the impure (κοινόν) and unclean (ἀκάθαρτον) animals symbolized impure (κοινόν) and unclean (ἀκάθαρτον) people, a possible reference to two types of Gentiles: God-fearers and idolaters, respectively.
24. R. W. Wall, "Peter, 'Son' of Jonah: The Conversion of Cornelius in the Context of the Canon," in R. W. Wall and E. Lemcio, eds., *The New Testament as Canon: A Reader in Canonical Criticism*, JSNTSS 76 (Sheffield: JSOT Press, 1992), 129–40 argues that the Cornelius episode has historical foundations in a conversion story of a gentile household.
25. See Dunn, "The Incident at Antioch (Galatians 2:11–18)," 3–57, who comes to similar conclusions through looking at the incident in Galatians.
26. C. K. Barrett, *Acts: Volume I, I–XIV*, 2 vols. (Edinburgh: T&T Clark, 1998), 494.
27. For an excellent discussion of how Luke wrote with intent, see Walter T. Wilson, "Urban Legends: Acts 10:1–11:18 and the Strategies of Greco-Roman Foundation Narratives," *Journal of Biblical Literature* 120 (2001): 77–99.
28. For a discussion of the mythology associated with Joppa, see Paul B. Harvey, "The Death of Mythology: The Case of Joppa," *Journal of Early Christian Studies* 2 (1994): 1–14.
29. A similar idea is touched upon in Doctrine and Covenants 64:8: "My disciples, in days of old, sought occasion against one another and forgave not one another in their hearts; and for this evil they were afflicted and sorely chastened."
30. Robert D. Hales, "When Thou Art Converted, Strengthen Thy Brethren," *Ensign*, May 1997, 82–83.

Chapter Fifteen

Women and the World of the New Testament

CATHERINE GINES TAYLOR

The New Testament is a rich resource for learning about the women who walked beside Jesus during his ministry, who served as patrons and key actors within the early church, and who spread the good news of salvation after Christ's death and resurrection. Thinking critically about women's roles in the Roman world of the New Testament is a task taken up by multiple academic disciplines and within the complexities of Christianity.[1] Thoughtful, faithful, analytical readers look to female exemplars in scripture and material culture to help both women *and* men utilize the narratives of women in their own devotional practices. New Testament women are presented in distinct scriptural accounts that underscore profoundly symbolic and archetypal meanings. Our understanding of these meanings is enhanced through the practice of careful reading, scriptural exegesis, and hermeneutics. These rigorous practices expand the way we see and understand women in ever-growing and capacious ways.

Women in scripture are presented to us by their writers through a variety of lenses. We read their stories and narratives and often wish that our limited view of them was more informed or that we could see further than the distance offered by the text. Paying attention to the language and imagery of archetypes is important in studying scripture precisely because they speak directly to our understanding in both individual and communal ways.[2] This chapter focuses on a few specific archetypes of New Testament women that represent signify their position and power, while also considering the *realia* of lived religious experience for women. It is also important to examine the models for women who were not in traditional positions of power or who were marginalized. This kind of close reading and thinking requires a courageous and self-critical willingness to revisit the texts that we know so well. We must imagine, consider, and investigate these narratives so that they may open our hearts and minds.

While much has been written about the many women, both named and unnamed, who appear in pages of the New Testament, this study will uniquely contribute by underscoring their roles, their voices, and their archetypal examples. From patronizing familial networks to the propertied women of Paul's letters, women played pivotal roles in scripture and the successes of earliest Christianity. One of the best ways to understand the scriptural context of New Testament women is through the material culture that belongs to the age. This chapter will combine text and, at times, images from the earliest Christian sources.

This chapter is divided into three sections. The first section presents two case studies where the narratives of two women in the New Testament, Mary (the mother of Jesus) and Tabitha, are presented within the context of early Christian art. The purpose of this section is to demonstrate how well-known and lesser-known scriptural stories were received by early Christians in ways that may surprise our modern reading of those same stories. The second section gives an illustrative sampling of named but lesser-known women in the New Testament whose stories present compelling questions and spark interest in further investigation. Finally, the third section focuses on unnamed women in the New Testament, whose archetypal symbolism help the reader understand them in sophisticated ways beyond their narratives. While this chapter can in no way provide a comprehensive look at all New Testament women, it will explore some ways in which gender is ordered, represented, and patterned within the scriptural and historical narrative.

Contextual Case Studies

As a primary case study, we should begin by illuminating the account of Mary as she is introduced to us in the moment of Annunciation.[3] Canonical sources for the Annunciation are found in Luke and Matthew. The account in Luke details the angel Gabriel's assignment by God to appear to Mary in the city of Nazareth in Galilee to proclaim her as favored and blessed, and to deliver a message. After his initial salutation, Gabriel presents a succinct and powerful message: "Behold, thou shalt conceive in thy womb, and bring forth a son, and shalt call his name Jesus. He shall be great, and shall be called the Son of the Highest; and the Lord God shall give unto him the throne of his father David; and he shall reign over the house of Jacob for ever; and of his kingdom there shall be no end" (Luke 1:31–33). Gabriel answers Mary's concerns and generally describes the holy event that will occur. He gives her a witness sign in the pregnancy of her cousin Elizabeth, who was called barren. Mary's incredulity and fears are allayed in the infinite possibilities of God, and she submits to the will of the Lord. This glorious dialogue is secondary to the nucleus of the message: Christ is the Son of God, who will be born in the flesh to his mother, Mary, through the royal bloodlines of Judah, and who is the King of kings, reigning over the household of celestial and terrestrial inheritance forever and without end. The message of Gabriel has been celebrated and analyzed over centuries; however, the iconography of the Annunciation has not been considered in association with the reception of the most important part of the announcement, that the household of kings, royal and divine, would receive its heir apparent on earth through Mary's flesh and would be favored within the household construct of the *materfamilias* ("mother of the family").

As early as the second century, there was both curiosity and confusion regarding the role of Mary. We have good reason to suspect that the apocryphal texts that detail the extracanonical details of Mary's life were formulated as popular tales in the early church and became well known enough to be written down by the second century (see chapter 19).[4] The degree to which the stories and tales that became Christian apocrypha are evidence of the earliest Marian cult cannot be overemphasized. The iconography of the Virgin Annunciate spinning naturally developed out of ancient iconographies that already celebrated motherhood and the pious Matron.

Apocryphal writings on the annunciation "display great literary and theological imagination, . . . and, of course, it was these stories that not only reproduced the folk traditions about Mary and developing Mariology, but in themselves also fueled that theology."[5] The infancy narrative found in the Protevangelium of James, originally composed in the second century, is the only known surviving textual source available to readers of the fifth century that incorporates spinning as a dominant symbol in the Annunciation story. A fifth-century sarcophagus named for the Pignatta family, today in Ravenna, Italy, features the Virgin Mary in the guise of the spinning Roman matron. She is seated on a low stool, drawing woolen roves vertically to her distaff from a large woven basket (fig. 1).[6] Her pose is characteristically classical as she sits in profile facing the angel Gabriel.[7] The Virgin wears a simple stola with her palla wrapped around her shoulders and draped over her head, demonstrating her traditional piety and modesty. Mary's gaze is directed simultaneously toward her handiwork and Gabriel.[8]

The Protevangelium of James provides the noncanonical sequence of events that surrounds the birth of Mary to Joachim and Anna as well as the early life of the Virgin. In these earliest Annunciation motifs, text and image intersect in both formal and intimate ways, informing and legitimizing each other. These narratives become typical examples of divine intervention; but, amid the seemingly impossible miracles that surround the Virgin as she is prepared for her role, it is also possible to find suggestions of the common and ordinary. For example, it is Mary's lot to spin the purple and the scarlet for the temple veil, combining the mundane act of spinning with sacred material. Mary's task does not fall to her by accident. She is the sole legal heir to her father's inheritance, he being a rich man and a direct descendent of the royal line of David. She is specifically taken before the chief priests at her birth and receives "a supreme blessing which cannot be superseded,"[9] the undefiled daughters of the Hebrews serve her, and at the age of three her parents take her to the temple for the priest to bless her, saying, "The Lord has magnified your name among all generations."[10] Her genealogy was known, and the whole house of Israel revered her; she was to the second-century Christians of the Roman world the archetypal materfamilias, the mother as a rightful sovereign and legally powerful figure within the household.

Figure 1

Mary as the spinning Annunciate was the Christian archetype of exemplary womanhood, marriageability, motherhood, and fertility well before she was given the exclusive title Theotokos, or "God-bearer," by the church in AD 431 at Ephesus and later described as "Mother of God" (*mētēr theou*) in ecclesiastical texts.[11] Averil Cameron has pointed out that Christology was the center point around which the figure of Mary developed, attracted interest, popular devotion, and early images.[12] Though references to Mary in Gospel accounts were limited to events like the Annunciation, Visitation, Nativity, Adoration of the Magi, and the Flight into Egypt, other ideas about Mary and her role grew out of nonexplicit and apocryphal traditions, many of which were developing before the fifth century.[13]

As a second case study in scriptural reception, we can also look to the less familiar account of Tabitha from Acts 9, who was raised from the dead by Peter in similitude of Christ's raising the daughter of Jairus.[14] The story of Peter in Tabitha's house has traditionally been used to highlight the widow's experience in the early church or to illustrate charitable love within early Christian communities. Tabitha gives us insight into the archetypal complexity of the philanthropic rescuer in her own community, and the capacity of widows who also acted as mothers and providers to those in need. Again, little attention has been given to the reception of early Christian images that address the iconography of Peter and the household of Tabitha. Peter's interaction with Tabitha is found at an interdisciplinary crossroads, where Acts 9 meets the earliest visual representations of Peter in Tabitha's house.

Luke introduces us to the woman called Tabitha, whose Aramaic name translated into Greek is "Dorcas," with both names meaning "gazelle." Tabitha's character has been associated with the gazelle as a symbol of a nurturer or life giver. It is easy to see how Peter's attentions to Tabitha accentuated her acts as symbols of love, compassion, service and graciousness, and as a type of proselyte for the new community of Christians. This narrative was useful in expanding Christianity's borders beyond Jewish believers to gentile converts. It is important for us to examine how the image of Peter raising Tabitha was depicted in the earliest years of the church and its specific historicity for the fourth century.

A fourth-century Roman style sarcophagus gives us an excellent example today at the Basilique Saint-Marie-Madeleine in Saint-Maximin-la-Sainte-Baume, France (fig. 2). On the left end, we find the scene with Peter raising Tabitha in a well-appointed room complete with draperies, a luxurious bed, an architectural column, and a pipe organ. Figures of the poor are diminutively small and kneel or sit near the side of the bed. Two women, widows, are standing behind Tabitha with their gaze and gestures directed toward her. Tabitha is proportionately large and fills the picture plane. Her dress is a simple stola and her head remains uncovered, though her hair is neatly coiffed and prepared for burial. Tabitha is depicted here as a type of crossroads figure as demonstrated in the varied figures she is shown helping. Besides the two widows standing behind Tabitha's bed, we find three smaller figures representing the poor in the foreground next to

Figure 2

Tabitha's bed. Indeed, they are small, according to the standards of hierarchy of scale, precisely because they are poor and are of a distinctively different social class in comparison to Tabitha and the stately, matronly widows. Tabitha's left hand rests on the head of the small female figure at her left who supports a seated, naked figure with her hands and right knee. The third kneeling figure is set apart from these and reaches out to touch the hem of Peter's garment, an act in similitude of the woman with an issue of blood touching Christ's garment. This third figure wears a peculiar head covering, akin to the Phrygian cap of foreign magi, often shown wearing similar hats in artistic representations of the Adoration of the Magi. The widows and the woman with the naked boy are easy to situate into the Levitical laws regarding the care of the widows and the fatherless. However, the inclusion of the Phrygian capped figure indicates that Tabitha's generosity was considered, within the fourth century, to include the foreign poor as well, a notion that coincides with the nature of diverse port cities like Joppa and the conversion of gentiles.

While we typically focus on Peter's raising Tabitha from the dead as a miracle with the convenient effect of conversion, we have long hesitated in defining the role Tabitha occupied in performing acts of charity, specifically by bestowing goods and clothing on the widows and less fortunate of Joppa. There is some discussion that Tabitha was likely a widow herself, but one who had means to maintain her household and expand her philanthropic reach to her community. That Peter goes to Tabitha's house to raise her is not just to demonstrate her ability as a non-Jewish proselyte to expand the cause of Christianity but to also normalize a new type of patron within the early church, that of the *Matrona*.

Choosing Christ Jesus: Named Women in the New Testament

When we talk about women in scripture, we often think first of named women who offer significant examples or embodiments of traits and characteristics, some of which resonate with us. In many ways, women in scripture provide personified archetypes or depictions of our own reality that, in addition to what we learn by historical and theological analysis, can be read as valuable and insightful to our own practice and devotion. We rarely talk about what it means to view women in the New Testament through the lens of archetypal models or how that perspective might shape our own practical and devotional lives. As Latter-day Saints, it is imperative that we increase our grasp of iconographic types for women in scripture so that we can recognize the competence and influence of women within the full scope of their power, holiness, and humanity. Particularly for Latter-day Saint women, how we understand scriptural accounts involving women impacts the way we reflect the text into our own personal narrative. If we are serious in our consideration of these women, if they matter to us, we must do the work it takes to know them.

Named women within the New Testament embody multifaceted roles including that of matron, businesswoman, head of household, wise woman, prophetess, and philanthropist. These positions are often ignored in favor of the traditional roles of virginal maid, wife, and mother. If we confine ourselves to archetypes that only embrace the roles or symbolism that we find comfortable, or which have been promoted as culturally normative, we will find ourselves not only limited but also incomplete.

There are a number of named women in the New Testament who are not well known or who fall too easily into the shadow of more illustrious actors. However, there is a synergistic familiarity that comes with careful attention to women like Anna, Joanna, Lydia, Phoebe, Prisca, and Rhoda alongside women who are more often discussed like the Marys, Martha, and Elizabeth. Even someone as well-known as Mary, the mother of Jesus, may find herself featured in significant accounts like the wedding at Cana that are often unremembered in favor of her role in the Nativity. Without attempting to provide an encyclopedic accounting, commentary, and biography for all of the named women in the New Testament, I will consider only an illustrative sample of women who are not often highlighted or studied with much care.

Anna

Many of us can clearly imagine the prophetess Anna as a matronly, exemplary, wise woman abiding in God's temple. The Gospel of Luke pays careful attention to widows and women generally, perhaps revealing his benevolent concern for the poor and oppressed.[15] As a widow, Anna may have been part of an order of consecrated elderly women who enjoyed social respectability within the Jewish world,[16] even if they were also very poor and reliant on the welfare of those who made offerings in the temple or gave alms. As a prophetess, she reflects the "tradition of Miriam, Deborah, and Huldah, and she foreshadows the honorable Christian calling held by, among others, the daughters of Philip (Acts 21:9)."[17] Anna's experience in Luke 2:36–38 closely parallels that of Simeon's from Luke 2:25–35. Simeon recognizes Jesus as the Christ and praises God. Simeon's words are included in the story, but even though Anna is recognized as a prophetess, devoted to temple worship and prayer, her voice is only mentioned, her words are absent. Luke pairs Anna with Simeon in a way typical to his practice of using both male and female characters, like Zechariah and Elizabeth, in his narrative.[18] Simeon speaks words of praise and consolation to Mary and Joseph, but Anna's audience is different; her audience is *all* who seek the Savior. She, like Elizabeth, initiates a new messianic pronouncement as she "began to praise God and to speak about the child to all who were looking for the redemption of Jerusalem."[19]

Joanna

As an attestation for active, female disciples of Jesus, Luke 8:3 is remarkable. The verse names three women, who by presumably independent will and means, joined Jesus, and presumably used their resources to provide for the community of believers. We are introduced to Joanna by reference to her husband, Chuza, whose title *epitropos* may indicate that he managed property for Herod.[20] Joanna's husband is mentioned without indicating if he is a believer, thereby giving us pause to consider that perhaps Chuza is very lenient about his wife's movements and beliefs or, like other "rebel" women from noncanonical Acts of Apostles, Joanna has taken her dowry or her independent means and left her home to follow Jesus.[21] Joanna takes on the archetype of a rather unorthodox truth seeker. Her consecrated piety, which perhaps lay outside traditional social structures, demonstrated Joanna's humility and her utter devotion to act in favor of spiritual discipleship.

Joanna is also second in the list of women in Luke 24:10 who witness the empty tomb. Whereas Mark 16:1–8 indicates an angelic commission for the women witnesses to tell the apostles, Luke 24 adds subtlety to the story by placing the initiative with the women themselves to go and tell.[22] Matthew 28:9 nuances the account even further when Jesus suddenly meets the women on their way. The women take hold of Jesus's feet and worship him before also receiving the commission to go and tell. In all cases, Joanna, along with Mary Magdalene, Mary the mother of James, Salome, and "other women" are given the role of first messengers, envoys, even *apostoloi* or apostles,[23] commissioned to tell the good news.

Lydia

Lydia is a woman living in Philippi, a Roman province in Macedonia, whom Paul meets and baptizes near the beginning of his ministry, along with her entire *oikos*, during his first journey. The late antique Roman household, the Latin *domus* or the Greek *oikos*, extended beyond the nuclear family and often included "several generations, a large number of slaves, other dependents and even unrelated clients."[24] The household was the essential locus for the spread of early Christianity, and the first churches were associated with the organized house church and the assembly of the Christian community. One of the most powerful examples of this phenomenon in the apostolic period is found within the household of Lydia, mentioned in Acts 16.

Lydia is first encountered among other women who gathered at "a place of prayer," a location in which it was proper and appropriate for women to hear Paul preach.[25]

Lydia's name has caused some scholars to question her historicity. The region of Lydia in Asia Minor was where the city called Thyatira, Lydia's hometown, was located. This connection caused some to think that she was a fictitious figure with her name adopted by Luke as a personification of this place.[26] However, it is at Philippi where Paul and Lydia meet. Philippi is home to the Dionysian cult and polytheistic goddess worship. Many women gather there for worship purposes. Placing Lydia and her conversion at Philippi makes a theological statement,[27] especially when that statement is directed toward converting women who are possibly participating in these mystery cults. Shelly Matthews has further studied the historicity of women like Lydia—identifying real women and finding them in scripture between the lines of narrative. Rather than conceding that Lydia's narrative is fictional, she points to Paul's letters that reveal women as primary hosts for house churches.[28] Matthews finds the pattern of fiscally independent women who support Paul to be an attestation of Lydia's reality. Furthermore, what she finds most suspect in the narrative is that such a woman as Lydia is presented only as a "convert accommodating Paul and his mission, and not as a missionary/leader in her own right."[29] Archetypally, Lydia demonstrates how religious piety *and* independent work were not mutually exclusive.

Phoebe

At the end of Paul's epistle to the Romans (16:1–2), we are introduced to a woman called Phoebe. She is commended by Paul as a *diakonos*, or deacon, from a regional church at Cenchreae, to the hospitality of the saints in Rome.[30] Phoebe's title, deacon, is sometimes translated as "servant" (KJV, NIV), but Paul clearly uses the term in Greek, without gendered distinctions, to also refer to his own ministry of preaching and teaching within the church.[31] Paul asks that the Roman believers welcome and aid Phoebe in part because he is under obligation to her as his patron or benefactor. Phoebe was probably the person who carried the letter, which would arguably become one of the most important books in the New Testament.[32] As a patron, Phoebe provides funds for the church and may also publicly represent believers within the church. Significantly, Phoebe is also described as *prostatis*, the feminine form of a noun that means "one who stands before" and can be interpreted as leader. In this context, it likely emphasizes her role as patron.[33] Both designations are evidenced in association with women during late antiquity. For example, a stele from Jerusalem with an epigraph dating to the second half of the fourth century reads, "Sophia, a deacon, a second Phoebe."[34]

Paul clearly identifies women like Phoebe as part of his circle of coworkers. She has work to do in Rome and is independent enough to accomplish it of her own accord. Some scholars have suggested that she may have been traveling "to or through Rome as a missionary or Church worker."[35] Paul acknowledges Phoebe's role as a patron and as a teacher, but he also describes her as an archetypal networker, someone who enhances the unity of the church by sharing information. She is a mentor and advocate with Paul and carries words and wisdom to the nascent church.

Prisca

Among Paul's coworkers in Christ Jesus, Priscilla (the diminutive form of Prisca) is mentioned six times in the New Testament (Acts 18:2–3, 18–19, 24–26; Romans 16:3–5; 1 Corinthians 16:19; 2 Timothy 4:19). Acts contextualizes the circumstances of Paul's meeting with Prisca and her husband Aquila as they, and other Jews, have left Rome under the orders of Claudius.[36] Paul finds both work and hospitality in the household of Prisca and Aquila as they also dealt in the textile trade. After a considerable time, Paul, accompanied by Prisca and Aquila travel to Ephesus, where they part ways but are not forgotten by Paul. He further addresses their efforts and the church that met in their house. We come to know Prisca as she traveled with her husband, spreading the gospel to Rome, Ephesus, and Corinth. One encounter that demonstrates Prisca's perceptive and authoritative wisdom is found in connection with the preaching of another believer, Apollos the Alexandrian.[37] After moving on from their ministry in Corinth, Prisca and Aquila seem to be functioning like Barnabas, Timothy, Silas, and other Pauline missionaries.[38] Their teaching roles naturally take them to the synagogue at Ephesus, where they cross paths with Apollos, a well-educated and effective orator. He had "been instructed in the way of the Lord and spoke as one stirred up by the Spirit."[39] Prisca and Aquila hear him and bring him into their circle of friends, and Prisca takes the authoritative initiative to instruct him privately and "more accurately" in God's way.[40]

Questions had arisen in Ephesus and Corinth among believers concerning baptism, ways of staying in the path, and gifts of the Spirit.[41] Prisca, as an educated businesswoman, uses her benevolent influence, wisdom, and authority to protect and teach others. She is loyal in her relationships and faithful in her pioneering enterprises that sustain the spread of the good news to many people. Although the account of Prisca and Aquila in Acts has been approached with some caution because some scholars believe it may include highly idealized narratives,[42] further attestations in Romans, 1 Corinthians, and 2 Timothy underscore the fact that Prisca's name and her work were known and respected, even highly esteemed, by communities of Christian believers. For Prisca and Aquila to be able to perform as itinerant preachers and welcome congregants into their house church may speak to the success of their business enterprises as well as their capacity to sustain a prominent and well-funded missionary effort.

Prisca is a missionary, but she is also a wife. Naming Prisca first in the pair is significant and may point to her status as a propertied *materfamilias* and to the status of her family according to Roman social constructs.[43] The vision of household dynamics glimpsed in these few verses reflects a sense that, at least in some early Christian communities, egalitarian attitudes toward women existed within marriage.[44] These structures also held up under the scrutiny of Roman law, whereby women of property or important families were designated as the *materfamilias* and head of household.[45] Prisca's devotion and dedication to her vocational work are matched by external supports in many facets of her life. Her husband partners with her in devotion, she enjoys the friendship and contemplative notice of the apostle Paul, and she finds herself as an organizational and economic life force in relationship with her community.

Without diminishing their contribution as a secondary force, we must also acknowledge the wave of named women who were also known as "workers in Christ Jesus." Prisca and her husband Aquila join a number of named New Testament women who are faithful evangelists, workers in the Lord, and devotees: the many Marys—not including Mary the mother of Jesus and Mary Magdalene ([Mary 1] John 11:1–33; 12:1–8; [Mary 2] John 19:25; 20:1–18; [Mary 3] Matthew 27:56; [Mary 4] John 19:25; [Mary 5]

Acts 12:12; [Mary 6] Romans 16:6)—Tryphaena and Tryphosa (Romans 16:12), Lois (2 Timothy 1:5), Eunice (2 Timothy 1:15), Persis (Romans 16:12), and Junia (Romans 16:7). Paul also admonishes two other women called Euodia and Syntyche in Philippians 4:2–3, to be of "the same mind in the Lord" as they have also "struggled beside me in the work of the gospel." This critical mass of named women takes up a significant role in the building up of the church. They are visionary seekers, they challenge social systems in favor of spiritual communion, they are empathetic with their fellow believers, and they displayed an uncanny openness to the powerful life force of the Spirit. Examining the textual and historical context for these women helps us to reconstruct the stories of those who have been consistently overlooked in our study of the Bible and the earliest Christian church.

Sustained in Christ Jesus: Unnamed Women of the New Testament

Unnamed women in the New Testament are easily recognizable within archetypal constructs, partially because they are explicitly known according to their symbolic modalities. Unnamed women fall into patterned categories that describe their familial relationships, their social position, their sexual status, their bodily state of being, and their actions or behaviors. Nearly all unnamed women are categorized according to their physicality, their essential bodies, and the external manifestations of their internal selves. Rarely are we privy to their thoughts or words. Unnamed men in the New Testament may also fall into these same categories, but they often have the capacity to act with social independence. For example, the rich man from Mark 10:25, the good Samaritan from Luke 10:36, or even the crippled beggar at the temple gate in Acts 3:1–10 act or speak in ways independent of customary gendered restrictions. Unnamed men also speak for themselves or others when they interact with Jesus like the centurion and his servant from Matthew 8:5, 9 or the father of the boy with a spirit from Mark 9:14–29. As unnamed women speak less often than men, it is imperative that we examine and enumerate the ways that they are archetypally present in the New Testament and then consider the ways their stories illuminate and complicate the way we understand them. We must never lose sight of the fact that their narratives were connected to communities and that the way we read them can reflect our own receptive biases.

Unnamed Women and Familial Relationships

Unnamed women are often described in relation to men as mother, daughter, wife, widows, mother-in-law, daughter-in-law, and so forth. Although many women are only noted by their familial affiliations, they still exerted influence without words. One example that leads us to consider these connections is the mother-in-law of Simon Peter, whom Jesus heals from a fever in Mark 1:30. She, as proof of her cure, immediately begins serving the men gathered in the tradition of hospitality. We must also acknowledge the woman absent from the narrative, Peter's wife, who is caring for her mother within her marital household, most likely because she is widowed.[46] Widows, virgins, and celibates are often noted for their extraordinary circumstances within the early church. Widows, wise women, and virgins are sometimes archetypally associated with visionaries and prophetesses, like Philip's four daughters, who in Acts 21:9 reflect the prophecy in Joel 3. Even in their silence, Philip's daughters are still noted for their devotional relationship to the believers.[47] Unfortunately, these women and other women in Acts, even those with considerable familial affiliations, for the most part, do not speak.[48] Even if his exclusion is not deliberate, Luke has left us without a record of their prophetic words. We must concede that, without language, women may lack public credibility. Even in the case of the household slave, Rhoda, who speaks the truth and brings news of Peter's liberation from prison, she is not believed.[49] Beverly Roberts Gaventa has underscored the fact that mothers, daughters, wives, and widows in the Acts of the Apostles may not have words or may be absent altogether, but some do, especially in the case of virgins and widows, manage to act independently and in alignment with God's relentless fulfillment of his promises.[50]

Marital status and familial relationships define women in the ancient Greco-Roman world. The lived constructs of marriage in the first-century Mediterranean world are surprisingly diverse because they depend on the social and religious laws and customs held by many different groups of people. Marriage under Augustan Roman law reforms applies to Roman citizens.[51] These laws formalize the rights of women, based on their fertility, to maintain their own property independent of their husbands, allowing women under certain circumstances to divorce.[52] Gender parity is an issue that Paul addresses, particularly for unmarried women in 1 Corinthians 7:32–33, who are anxiously concerned with the Lord's work in contrast to married women who necessarily have other kinds of material responsibilities.[53]

Unnamed Women Defined by Their Sexual Status

Some unnamed women are defined by their sexual status in the New Testament. They include the woman who is looked at lustfully (Matthew 5:28), the adulterous woman (John 8:3-11), divorced women (Matthew 5:31–32, 19:3–9; Mark 10:2–12; Luke 16:18), prostitutes (Matthew 21:31–32; Luke 15:30; 1 Corinthians 6:15–16), those who had been married multiple times (Matthew 22:23–30; Mark 12:18–25; Luke 20:27–36), bridesmaids (Matthew 25:1–13), unmarried women (1 Corinthians 7), those who take part in unnatural intercourse (Romans 1:26), and virgins (Luke 1–2; 1 Corinthians 7). Sexualized language, image, and metaphor are used largely and almost exclusively in connection with women, their bodies, and their behaviors. One example, adulteresses, as discussed in John 8:3–11 and generally in James 4:1–13, are read as actors who operate within the larger christological condemnation of disloyal, unchaste behavior.[54] Social constructs surrounding female sexuality had very real-life effects when it came to marriage expectations, pregnancy, sexual behaviors, coercion, and even rape. We would do well to read these sexual archetypal descriptions with some compassion, some mercy, and the clear realization that the male partner is often absent from the narrative. Often, women privileged their material, spiritual, social, and physical security over their own power, will, and ability to act, and were prone to both the social stigma and physical consequences of the behavior of themselves and others.

Whereas issues of purity laws are the focus of sexual behaviors, especially as we take our cue from unnamed women, we must recognize and deliberately consider the way we read narratives that harm or exclude women for merely being female. The anonymity of unnamed women, in its most frustrating guise, perpetuates the objectification of women designated by their sexual actions by proclaiming a judgment akin to damnation. Even if the sinning female from these narratives is forgiven, the hermeneutics of imagination may perpetuate her as an exile within the biblical context, and perhaps, beyond.

We must further complicate our thinking toward unnamed women in the New Testament who are reduced to their sexual identity. It is to our advantage to ask questions like the following: How does women's sexuality determine control over their bodies by others or demonstrate control over their own bodies and possessions? What burdens and advantages does reality place upon the lives of married, single, divorced, and ascetic women? What issues arise around health and cleanliness laws specific to women? Does pointing out special cases of healing for women unduly highlight their vulnerable positioning for shame? These questions can be particularly helpful because they help us recognize the complex nature of these women who are otherwise relatively passive in the restorative accounts of their bodies.

On the other hand, desexualizing women can be detrimental. By denying their specifically female sexual power in creation, we find that women are transmuted into anonymity or rhetorically into the male domain where all of mankind becomes men and sons. The devaluation of marriage, motherhood, and other creative capacities for sexually engaged women within the familial dynamic can also remove women's power from the long-held mother archetype of the *creatrix*.

Unnamed Women and Social Relationships

Unnamed women are also categorized in the New Testament as social outsiders and insiders. Outsiders like the Canaanite woman (Matthew 15:21–28) and the Samaritan woman at the well (John 4:1–42) were faced with initial social resistance in their narratives but were also instrumental in drawing former outsiders into the larger covenant community.[55] The responsibility to hold faith in divine promise is also relevant for unnamed Greek women, "outsiders" who were also believers, as well as the unnamed "insider" companions to male disciples and apostles. Unnamed women were often described according to their social status. At one end of the spectrum were women of elect status, leading women, and at the other end, slaves. Unnamed women within the community of believers also acted in roles concerning civic action and well-being. For example, the woman, a widow, in Luke 18:20 who pleads or acts as an advocate for herself against an unjust judge, is recognized for her strength and persistence as she is successful in her case. Others within the community tended to the physical needs of others, especially the most vulnerable, generally in the role of a nurse (Matthew 24:19; Mark 13:17; Luke 21:23; 1 Thessalonians 2:7).

To find women participating in socially and theologically instructive ways, it is sometimes useful to incorporate imaginative and inquisitive ways of reading the scriptural narrative. For example, Elaine Wainwright asks important questions regarding Jesus's interaction with the Syro-Phoenician woman. She demands of us as readers to consider the anonymity of her possessed daughter, whose ailment is at the center of the narrative.[56] The interpersonal conversation takes place in the border region between Israel and Tyre/Sidon, a place of marginalization.[57] Jesus initially ignores the woman's plea to heal her daughter, citing her ethnic designation as a Canaanite in order to argue that "it is not fair to take the children's food and throw it to the dogs" (Matthew 15:26 NRSV). From her position of vulnerability, she still bravely replies as an advocate for her ill, foreign daughter, "Yes, Lord, yet even the dogs eat the crumbs that fall from their masters' table" (Matthew 15:27 NRSV), and is ultimately blessed with a healing miracle.

The sociality of unnamed women was also intricately connected to their bodily state of being. For example, the woman who hemorrhages, the bent woman, and various iterations of pregnant, laboring, and nursing women provide very clear images of women whose social narrative is specifically bound to their bodies. Many of these accounts are acutely essentialist, meaning that the narrative is wholly dependent upon their female bodies. Their physical circumstances are framed in ways connected with shame, issues of gendered cleanliness, and the commodification of their sexuality. These women have endured over time, not because they merely tolerated their circumstances or survived them but because they were extraordinary actors in spite of their bodies, who autonomously reached beyond their physical circumstances. Their stories are not necessarily different from many other women around them who could have also been exemplars, but they are prioritized into the New Testament text in ways that call our attention to their bodies in specific ways, often as a contrast point for Christ's healing touch.

Women's social actions were also connected bodily to gendered expectations regarding hospitality, work, patronage, and household chores. New Testament women were socially connected to acts of hospitality. They were the actors who fed others, washed others, prepared meals, and leavened the bread of life and their communities. Parables often feature domestic tasks accomplished by women who sweep, provide sustenance, and even offer coins. Women's affiliation with hospitality is deeply connected to their role as patrons to the disciples. Without question, women were at hand within the household, acting as and staying with the disciples of Jesus in shared fellowship.

Unnamed Women and Holy or Devotional Acts

The largest group of unnamed women is those identified by their actions. Holy and devotional acts are underscored in the New Testament by the accounts of women who anoint, praise, teach, lament, pray, and prophesy. Women take action as true believers; they are baptized, persecuted, and devoted (at places of prayer). They are witnesses to Jesus's resurrection and are called deacons, profess reverence, and are moved on by the Holy Spirit.

We sometimes understand women's devotional practices in the early church through the reaction of men toward them rather than from an explicit record of the acts themselves. For example, in 1 Corinthians 11:5 it is clear from Paul's letter that women in the Corinthian church prayed and prophesied publicly, a tradition that "may perhaps go back to the example of Prisca"[58] as a founding missionary in Corinth. Paul argues in behalf of these women and stresses that a woman should have *exousia*, or authority over her own head, and "appeals to the new church order marked by mutual interdependence of men and women."[59] In the same chapter,[60] Paul also adds ambiguity to his former statements by expressing the persistence of nature and custom in the acceptable quality of women's devotions, the subordination of which is traditionally emphasized over other interpretations.[61] This has led many scholars to argue for one of these two perspectives, rather than seeing the productive tension inherent in Paul's own arguments.[62]

Apart from arguing for the official capacities of women in devotional settings, there are also customary circumstances in which women were primary actors. Anointing women, female messengers, and women participating in rites of death and burial come immediately into view as we examine the events surrounding Christ's passion, crucifixion, death, burial, and resurrection. Women in the New Testament perform holy acts that indicate a high level of perception, foreknowledge, or intuitive understanding of coming events.

The realms of hospitality and death are simultaneously the domains of women. The act of the anointing woman, recorded anonymously in the Synoptic Gospels and named as Mary the sister of Martha and Lazarus in the Gospel of John, is not outside of her office, even if its enactment is somewhat unconventional. Dennis McDonald will prioritize female participation and its significance by underscoring the anointing act as one that moves beyond hospitality into the realm of prophetic seership.[63] The woman acts from recognition of Jesus's forthcoming passion, and she does so without the need of an exterior revelatory sign. MacDonald compares the varied story of the woman anointing Jesus with ointments, oils, and tears to the account of the nurse Eurycleia, who recognizes Odysseus's feet as she washes them on his return to Ithaca.[64] This trope of recognition is presented as a specifically female act of wisdom and is enacted in moments of birth, death, and rebirth—all realms where women stand at the gates, attend, participate, and witness.

Unnamed women are dominantly present at the cross as well as in the burial and resurrection accounts. Their presence was credible to the audience of the New Testament, which illuminates the acceptability of women within rituals and practices of mourning, watching, waiting, and lamenting the dead. Carolyn Osiek has highlighted the incongruities of the New Testament world, where apotheosis accounts and Messianic rhetoric were crucial to the communal memory of first-century believers, and yet when that message was delivered first by women, they were not believed.[65]

Unnamed Women and Unholy or Profane Actions

In addition to unnamed women being associated with holy acts, there are also those who are anonymously associated with tale-tellers, silly women, and even the false female prophetess Jezebel, who is typified and vilified in Revelation 2:20. The term Jezebel is, of course, associated with the Israelite queen from 1 Kings 16 who encourages her husband, King Ahab, to abandon the worship of Jehovah in favor of the deities Baal and Asherah. Women who speak falsely are first presented in the example of Sapphira, the first female speaker in Acts, whose words are lies and is struck dead (Acts 5:1–11). Women as tale-tellers are a problem because their words are seen in conflict with the true faith. The Pastoral Epistles of 1 and 2 Timothy and Titus include warnings relevant to the last days. Part of their rhetoric warns against "false teachings," adhering to extreme behaviors like asceticism or celibacy, and believing legends or old wives' tales rather than gospel teachings.[66] The practice of describing women as tellers of tales was dually problematic for the early church, which collectively set its hope in the living God. First, by associating these practices specifically with women, the writer(s) immediately connects women with irrational and emotional superstitions in opposition to men's spiritual or rational mind. Secondly, the common refrain from 1 Timothy 5:13, describing women as "gossips and busybodies" aligns women's idle nonsense against sayings that are "sure and worthy of full acceptance" within the gospel framework from 1 Timothy 4:9. By associating women with the foolish woman as an archetype, we can naturally focus on her naïveté, but we would be wise to also consider that those who ultimately find a path of mature thinking, even the path of Woman Wisdom, begin with questioning, simple discourse, and new experience.

By gendering authoritative voices, there is a clear bias against women's "silly" narratives. Even though there were legitimate concerns over correct teachings perpetuated amongst the faithful, this diminutive name-calling is rhetorically dismissive. As mentioned in 2 Timothy 3:6 within the context of the apocalyptic discussion of the last days, silly women are those who are most vulnerable to false teachers. They are swayed by their desires and never arrive "at a knowledge of the truth" (3:6).[67] The struggle for authentic instruction, especially within the nascent church at Ephesus, indicates both the growing nature of the congregation and the fact that the church was conceptually faced with the prospect of apocalyptic finality. Time is perceived as essentially short, and women who professed proper and correct reverence for God are put in high contrast with women, personified or real, who are traditionally denigrated for their silly ways.

Conclusions

In thinking through the experiences of New Testament women, there is a need to focus attention on the fact that they were holy, nurturing, humble, and submissive as well as decisive, revelatory, intuitive, resilient, powerful, and fallible human beings. It is not the intention of this study to use gender as a tool of categorization, especially if it limits and marginalizes women as other or differentiates or separates them from the powerful discourses within scripture. Each of the women discussed here contributes to a larger, more holistic way of comprehending women in the world of the New Testament.

Suggesting specific archetypal meanings for New Testament women is not meant to be the definitive or final word on the matter. This kind of examination attempts instead to be helpful in highlighting patterns and characteristics in the text. The entirety of each scriptural account and all iterations of commentary for each woman would be impossible to convey here. However, when we encounter their pericopes, it is useful to consider these New Testament women, if not from all perspectives, at least from broader vantage points. What we are offered, as faithful and conscientious readers, is an intimately deep, and often surprising, engagement with the expansive lives of women whose devotion, in many ways, reflects that of modern women.

Catherine Gines Taylor is the Hugh W. Nibley Postdoctoral Fellow at the Neal A. Maxwell Institute for Religious Scholarship at Brigham Young University.

Catherine Gines Taylor, "Women and the World of the New Testament," in *New Testament History, Culture, and Society: A Background to the Texts of the New Testament*, ed. Lincoln H. Blumell (Provo, UT: Religious Studies Center, Brigham Young University; Salt Lake City: Deseret Book, 2019), 514–31.

NOTES

1. Volumes of commentaries, dictionaries, and academic studies are available. See, for example, Richard Bauckham, *Gospel Women: Studies of the Named Women in the Gospels* (Grand Rapids, MI: Eerdmans, 2002); Christine E. Joynes and Christopher C. Rowland, eds., *From the Margins 2: Women of the New Testament and their Afterlives* (Sheffield: Sheffield Phoenix Press, 2009); Elizabeth A. McCabe, ed. *Women in the Biblical World* (Lanham, MD: University Press of America, 2009); Carol Meyers, Toni Craven, and Ross S. Kraemer, eds., *Women in Scripture* (Grand Rapids, MI: Eerdmans, 2000); Camille Fronk Olson, *Women of the New Testament* (Salt Lake City: Deseret Book, 2014).
2. Archetypes are patterns or models from which copies, examples, or imitations can be derived. The origin of archetypes is ancient and dates back to the forms within Platonic thought. Archetypal criticism is used in the assessment of literature and art and is

expansive and useful when considering symbolic language in scripture. See, for example, Carl Jung, *Man and His Symbols* (Garden City, NY: Doubleday, 1964).

3. Compare Catherine C. Taylor, "The *Pignatta Sarcophagus*: Late Antique Iconography and the Memorial Culture of Salvation," *Biblical Reception* 3 (2014): 30–56.
4. David R. Cartlidge, *Art and Christian Apocrypha* (London; New York: Routledge, 2001), 1–20.
5. J. K. Elliott, *A Synopsis of the Apocryphal Nativity and Infancy Narratives* (Leiden and Boston: Brill, 2006), ix.
6. The combination of images on this sarcophagus, including the annunciation scene, may indicate that this imagery was specifically chosen by or for a particular client rather than being part of the typical decorative repertoire readily available in the workshop.
7. This pose is commonly seen in numismatic evidence as female members of the imperial household take on this seated profile or three-quarter pose demonstrating *pudicitia*, or modest virtue.
8. All facial features have been weathered or worn away, yet her face remains in profile without indication of any sideward or forward glance.
9. *Protoevangelium of James*, 6:2, in J. K. Elliott, *The Apocryphal New Testament* (Oxford: Oxford University Press, 2005), 59.
10. *Protoevangelium of James* 7:2 in Elliott, *Apocryphal New Testament*, 60.
11. Ioli Kalavrezou, "Images of the Mother: When the Virgin Mary Became *Meter Theou*," *Dumbarton Oaks Papers* 44 (1990): 165–72.
12. Averil Cameron, "The Early Cult of the Virgin," in *Mother of God: Representations of the Virgin in Byzantine Art*, ed. Maria Vasilake (Milan, New York: Skira, 2000), 3.
13. J. K. Elliott, *The Apocryphal New Testament* (Oxford: Oxford University Press, 1993), 48–51.
14. Compare Catherine C. Taylor, "Peter in the House of Tabitha: Late Antique Sarcophagi and Christian Philanthropy," in *The Ministry of Peter, the Chief Apostle*, ed. Frank F. Judd Jr., Eric D. Huntsman, and Shon D. Hopkin (Provo, UT: Religious Studies Center, Brigham Young University; Salt Lake City: Deseret Book, 2014), 191–210.
15. Bonnie Bowman Thurston, *The Widows: A Women's Ministry in the Early Church* (Minneapolis: Fortress Press, 1989), 23.
16. Thurston, *The Widows*, 24.
17. Thurston, *The Widows*, 25.
18. Thurston, *The Widows*, 23.
19. Luke 2:38 NRSV.
20. Richard I. Pervo, "Joanna," in *Women in Scripture: A Dictionary of Named and Unnamed Women in the Hebrew Bible, The Apocryphal/Deuterocanonical Books, and the New Testament*, ed. Carl Meyers, Toni Craven, and Ross S. Kraemer (Grand Rapids, MI: Eerdmans, 2000), 102–3.
21. Pervo, "Joanna," 103.
22. Pervo, "Joanna," 103.
23. Richard Bauckham, *Gospel Women: Studies of the Named Women in the Gospels* (Grand Rapids, MI: Eerdmans, 2002), 109–202.
24. Eric D. Huntsman, *Jesus Christ and the World of the New Testament* (Salt Lake City: Deseret Book, 2006), 161.
25. Acts 16:13–15 NRSV.
26. Valerie Abrahamsen, "Lydia," in Meyers, Craven, and Kramer, *Women in Scripture*, 111.
27. Abrahamsen, "Lydia," 111.

28. Shelly Matthews, "Elite Women, Public Religion, and Christian Propaganda," in *A Feminist Companion to the Acts of the Apostles*, ed. Amy-Jill Levine (London, New York: T&T Clark International, 2004), 130–33.
29. Matthews, "Elite Women," 132.
30. Elizabeth McCabe, "A Reevaluation of Phoebe in Romans 16:1–2 as a *Diakonos* and *Prostatis*: Exposing the Inaccuracies of English Translations," in *Women in the Biblical World*, ed. Elizabeth A. McCabe (Lanham, MD: University Press of America, 2009), 99.
31. McCabe, "A Reevaluation of Phoebe," 99–101.
32. Brian Dodd, *Problem with Paul* (Downer's Grove, IL: InterVarsity, 1996), 23.
33. Richard B. Hays, "Paul on the Relation between Men and Women," in *A Feminist Companion to Paul*, ed. Amy-Jill Levine (London, New York: T&T Clark International, 2004), 144.
34. Elizabeth McCabe, "A Reevaluation of Phoebe," 100.
35. Jouette M. Bassler, "Phoebe," in Meyers, Craven, and Kramer, *Women in Scripture*, 135.
36. Jouette M. Bassler, "Prisca," in Meyers, Craven, and Kramer, *Women in Scripture*, 136.
37. Ross Shepard Kraemer, *Her Share of the Blessings* (Oxford: Oxford University Press, 1992), 144.
38. F. Scott Spencer, "Women 'of the Cloth' in Acts: Sewing the Word," in *A Feminist Companion to the Acts of the Apostles*, ed. Amy-Jill Levine (London, New York: T&T Clark International, 2004), 152.
39. Acts 18:25 CEB.
40. Acts 18:26 NRSV.
41. Acts 19:1–10 NRSV.
42. Dennis MacDonald, "Lydia and Her Sisters as Lukan Fictions," in Levine, *A Feminist Companion to the Acts of the Apostles*, 105–10.
43. Bassler, "Prisca," 137.
44. T. J. Wray, *Good Girls, Bad Girls of the New Testament: Their Enduring Lessons* (Lanham, MD: Rowman & Littlefield, 2016), 193.
45. Kate Cooper, "Household and Empire: The Materfamilias as *Miles Christi* in the Anonymous *Handbook for Gregoria*," in *Household, Women, and Christianities, in Late Antiquity and the Middle Ages*, ed. Anneke B. Mulder-Bakker and Jocelyn Wogan-Browne (Turnhout: Brepols, 2006), 91–108.
46. Ross Kraemer, "Mother-in-Law of Simon (Peter)," in Meyers, Craven, and Kramer, *Women in Scripture*, 422.
47. Beverly Roberts Gaventa, "What Ever Happened to Those Prophesying Daughters?," in Levine, *A Feminist Companion to the Acts of the Apostles*, 60.
48. Gaventa, "What Ever Happened," 58–60.
49. Acts 12:12–15 NRSV.
50. Gaventa, "What Ever Happened," 60.
51. Susan Treggiari, *Roman Marriage:* Iusti Coniuges *from the Time of Cicero to the Time of Ulpian* (Oxford: Clarendon Press, 2002), 3–37.
52. Treggiari, *Roman Marriage*, 435–83.
53. Sheila Briggs, "Married Women (and Men), Unmarried Women (and Men), and Women (and Men) Married to Unbelievers," in Meyers, Craven, and Kramer, *Women in Scripture*, 471–74.
54. Adele Reinhartz, "Adulterous Woman," in Meyers, Craven, and Kramer, *Women in Scripture: A Dictionary of Named and Unnamed Women in the Hebrew Bible, The Apocryphal / Deuterocanonical Books, and the New Testament*, 454–55.

55. See, for example, Gale R. O'Day, "Surprised by Faith: Jesus and the Canaanite Woman," in *A Feminist Companion to Matthew*, ed. Amy-Jill Levine (Sheffield: Sheffield Academic Press, 2001), 114–25; Elaine Wainwright, "Not without My Daughter: Gender and Demon Possession in Matthew 15:21–28," in Levine, *A Feminist Companion to Matthew*, 126–37.
56. Wainwright, "Not without My Daughter," 132–34.
57. Wainwright, "Not without My Daughter," 132.
58. Margaret M. Mitchell, "Women Praying and Prophesying," in Meyers, Craven, and Kramer, *Women in Scripture*, 476.
59. Mitchell, "Women Praying and Prophesying," 476.
60. 1 Corinthians 11:14–16 NRSV.
61. Mitchell, "Women Praying and Prophesying," 477.
62. Mitchell, "Women Praying and Prophesying," 477.
63. Dennis MacDonald, "Renowned Far and Wide," in *A Feminist Companion to Mark*, ed. Amy-Jill Levine (Sheffield: Sheffield Phoenix Press, 2001), 135.
64. MacDonald, "Renowned Far and Wide," 128–31.
65. Carolyn Osiek, "The Women at the Tomb: What Are They Doing There?" in Levine, *A Feminist Companion to Matthew*, 214–20.
66. Lucinda A. Brown, "Women Tale Tellers," in Meyers, Craven, and Kramer, *Women in Scripture*, 491.
67. Lucinda A. Brown, "'Silly' or Little Women," in Meyers, Craven, and Kramer, *Women in Scripture*, 494.

Chapter Sixteen

The Life of the Apostle Paul

An Overview

NICHOLAS J. FREDERICK

> "Few figures in Western history have been the subject of greater controversy than Saint Paul. Few have caused more dissension and hatred. None has suffered more misunderstanding at the hands of both friends and enemies. None has produced more animosity between Jews and Christians."[1]

These words, taken from a recent study of Paul by emeritus Princeton University professor John G. Gager, speak to the impact Paul has had in the two thousand years since the emergence of the Christian faith. Paul continues to be the topic of much debate in the modern era, with books describing Paul as everything from the "real founder of Christianity"[2] to a "Jewish cultural critic."[3] While it may be close to impossible to retrieve the historical Paul from the pages of the New Testament, this essay will attempt to construct a brief biographical overview of Paul and his life, synthesizing information from the book of Acts and from Paul's own letters while also remaining cognizant that there are several places where the New Testament sources are reticent or in disagreement.

The Early Life of Paul

The majority of Paul's life prior to his shift toward Christianity remains shrouded in mystery and must be reconstructed from the small glimpses given us through Paul's letters and Luke's history. One of the most revealing statements comes from Paul's letter to the Philippians, where he writes,

> Circumcised the eighth day, of the stock of Israel, of the tribe of Benjamin, an Hebrew of the Hebrews; as touching the law, a Pharisee; Concerning zeal, persecuting the church; touching the righteousness which is in the law, blameless. (Philippians 3:5–6)

While these may seem like small details, they are actually quite revealing. Paul's statement to the Philippians reveals that religiously and ethnically he saw himself as a Jew. His descent through the tribe of Benjamin likely explains the origin of his actual name, Saul. While it is often thought that "Saul" was Paul's name prior to becoming a Christian and that he took the name "Paul" after he became Christian, this is incorrect. "Saul" is a Hebrew name, and "Paul" a Roman name. The most notable member of the tribe of Benjamin was King Saul, the ruler who preceded David. While Saul is remembered somewhat negatively today, mainly due to his improper offering of sacrifice and his acrimony toward David, he remained an important figure in Israelite history, and it is not surprising that Paul's Jewish parents would pass on that name to him. On the other hand, "Paul" means "short" or "small" in Latin and is a name likely connected with his family. Rather than being two names connected with two periods of his life, the names rather represent two cultural spheres. When Paul interacted with those of a Jewish background, he went by "Saul"; when his travels took him into gentile areas, he went by "Paul."

Paul's statement that he was "circumcised the eighth day" tells us that his parents were observant Jews, a reflection that finds support in Acts 23, where Paul announces that "I am a Pharisee, the son of a Pharisee" (Acts 23:6). This suggests that Paul would have been raised in a devout Jewish home. Beginning at about age six, Paul would likely have begun studying the Law and the Prophets, probably committing several passages to memory. Quotations from the Hebrew Bible are strewn throughout Paul's letters, perhaps as a direct result of his early education. He probably used the Greek translation of the Hebrew Bible, the Septuagint, as his primary text, but his education likely included the study of Hebrew and Aramaic as well.[4]

This Jewish education would have come in addition to the regular education he would have received growing up in the Hellenistic atmosphere of the city of Tarsus, where Luke tells us Paul was born (see Acts 21:39). Tarsus, located in the northeastern Mediterranean area of what is now south-central Turkey, was a prosperous city, full of both economic and intellectual opportunities for Jewish families seeking to establish themselves in the diaspora. Receiving an education in Tarsus would very likely have brought Paul into contact with not only the Greek alphabet and language but also the writings of those whose works were considered the pinnacle of Greek literary achievement, such as the epics of Homer and the tragedies of Sophocles and Euripides. This exposure to Greek literature may explain why Paul, when speaking at Athens on Mars Hill, summons quotes from not one but two Greek poets, Epimenides and Aratus (see Acts 17:28).

In addition to his Jewish religious background and his Greek cultural background, Paul also appears to have been raised as a Roman citizen. While Paul himself never mentions his citizenship in his letters, Luke mentions it on multiple occasions (see Acts 16:37–38; 22:25–28; 25:11). This citizenship was highly prized and would have entitled Paul to many important benefits, such as the three-part Roman name (*tria nomina*), exemption from ill-treatment at the hands of Jewish and Roman authorities, and the right to have a capital legal case brought before the Roman emperor himself. There were several ways one could obtain Roman citizenship. If one's father was a Roman citizen, then so were his children. One could be granted citizenship for military service or other favors to Rome. Likewise, one could also purchase it, although the price would be high and the practice prohibited (at least officially). Finally, slaves were given Roman citizenship at the time of their manumission from a Roman household. In Acts 22:28, Paul tells the Roman military tribune Claudius Lysias that he was born with his citizenship, meaning that his father would have been a Roman citizen as well. The two most likely scenarios are that either Paul's father (or perhaps grandfather) were manumitted slaves, or that someone in Paul's genealogical line had been granted citizenship based upon service rendered to Rome. The origins of Paul's Roman citizenship may also help explain the roots of the name *Paulus.* If Paul's progenitors were manumitted slaves, they may have adopted the name of the person who granted them their freedom as a family name or nickname. Or perhaps, as others have suggested, "Paul" was selected simply because it was the closest sounding gentile name to "Saul."[5]

At some point early in his education, Paul appears to have moved to Jerusalem. According to Acts, Paul was "yet brought up in this city at the feet of Gamaliel, and taught according to the perfect manner of the law of the fathers, and was zealous toward God, as ye all are this day" (Acts 22:3; compare 26:4). Depending on how the Greek participle *anatethrammenos* ("brought up") is understood, Paul could be seen as moving to Jerusalem with his family early in his life and thus receiving the majority of his education in Jerusalem, or he could be seen as receiving his primary education in Tarsus and then being sent to Jerusalem for more specialized education. Scholars remain divided as to when Paul made this move. Acts does contain the tantalizing detail that a nephew of Paul's, his "sister's son" (Acts 23:16), resided in Jerusalem during the time of his trial before the Sanhedrin, which may give weight to the idea that his family had moved to Jerusalem together. However, Acts also relays that Paul returned to Tarsus following his vision of the Savior, which could suggest existent family ties in Tarsus (see Acts 9:30; 11:25). Perhaps the safest conclusion is that Paul "came to and settled in Jerusalem as a young adolescent and received his principal education there."[6] Keeping in mind the arbitrary nature of dating the events of Paul's life, especially the early events, this move likely occurred sometime between AD 15 and AD 25.

Acts further informs us that Paul received some of his education from Gamaliel (see Acts 22:3). Gamaliel appears only once in the New Testament as a leading Pharisee who offers a somewhat sympathetic take on the early Christian movement (see Acts 5:34–40). Traditionally, there were two primary schools among the Pharisees, the school of Shammai and the school of Hillel. The school of Shammai tended to be a more conservative approach to the Judaism of the Pharisees, with Hillel being more liberal. Several of Jesus's teachings, such as his stance on divorce as recorded in Matthew 19:3, can be seen as negotiating these two positions. Gamaliel later became the leader of the school of Hillel (he may even have been Hillel's son or grandson) and is described by Luke as a *nomodidaskalos*, or "doctor of the Law" (Acts 5:34).[7] According to later Jewish tradition recorded in the *Mishnah*, "Since Rabban Gamaliel the elder died there has been no more reverence for the law; and purity and abstinence died out at the same time" (*m. Soṭah* 9:15). Gamaliel's emphasis upon "reverence for the law" and "purity" may help us understand where Paul developed the zealousness for Judaism and its preservation that defines so much of his early career as a Christian antagonist.

There is also a fair amount of debate as to whether or not Paul was married. The only statement Paul himself ever makes regarding his marital situation comes in his discussion on marriage in 1 Corinthians 7. Paul writes, "I say therefore to the unmarried and widows, It is good for them if they abide even as I" (1 Corinthians 7:8). The implication is that Paul is currently not in a marital relationship. The question is whether he has always been single, or whether he was once married but was single at the time he wrote 1 Corinthians. Several ancient Jewish sources indicate that it was unusual for men who were dedicated to study of the Torah to be unmarried, although there are exceptions.[8] One later piece of folklore claims that Paul was involved with the daughter of the high priest, and that her rejection of Paul led to his animosity toward Judaism:

> Paul was a man of Tarsus and indeed a Greek, the son of a Greek mother and a Greek father. Having gone up to Jerusalem and having remained there a long time, he desired to marry a daughter of the (high?) priest and on that account submitted himself as a proselyte for circumcision. When nevertheless he did not obtain the girl, he became furious and began to write against circumcision, the Sabbath and the Law.[9]

This story contains a clear anti-Pauline bias, and it is unlikely to contain anything historical. However, in a provocative move, some of Paul's biographers have tentatively suggested that not only was Paul married, but that he lost his wife and possibly children at some point prior to becoming a Christian;[10] it was this loss of family that angered Paul and sparked his persecution of Christianity. One scholar, Jerome Murphy-O'Connor, speculates:

> Jerusalem is sited in an earthquake zone, and it cannot have been immune to the domestic tragedies of fire and building collapse, which were so frequent at Rome. Had Paul's wife and children died in such an accident, or in a plague epidemic, one part of his theology would

> lead him logically to ascribe blame to God, but this was forbidden by another part of his religious perspective, which prescribed complete submission to God's will. If his pain and anger could not be directed against God, it had to find another target. An outlet for his pent-up desire for vengeance had to be rationalized.[11]

Paul's frustration at a perceived injustice in the loss of his family, combined with the importance placed upon purity by Gamaliel and his school, may have kindled a fiery zeal within Paul that led him to pursue the path that first brought him directly into the pages of the New Testament—namely, as an antagonist and persecutor of Christians. However, this scenario is entirely unsubstantiated and pure speculation.

Paul the Persecutor (ca. AD 33)[12]

Paul's role as persecutor of the nascent Christian movement is supported by both the accounts related in Acts and Paul's own epistles. In the years following his vision of Jesus, Paul would write that "I persecuted the church of God" (1 Corinthians 15:9), "beyond measure I persecuted the church of God, and wasted it" (Galatians 1:13), and "concerning zeal, persecuting the church" (Philippians 3:6). It is difficult to know exactly what form these persecutory activities took and to what extent Paul went in punishing perceived violations. Paul is first introduced in Acts as being present and complicit in the execution of Stephen. While seemingly a minor character in the Stephen account, Luke's mention that the witnesses "laid down their clothes at a young man's feet, whose name was Saul" (Acts 7:58) suggests that Paul had already gained a stature or reputation as a punisher of Christians.[13] Following Stephen's stoning, Paul took the initiative and sought out permission from the high priest (see Acts 9:2), or chief priests (see Acts 26:12), to pursue, punish, and if necessary extradite Christians back to Jerusalem. One crucial point to understand here is that Paul appeared to have had no legal or judicial authority granted by Rome that would have allowed him to make arrests. Additionally, whatever legal or judicial authority the Jewish high priest and the Sanhedrin held likely did not extend outside of Jerusalem. What Paul likely sought from the high priest and took to Damascus were letters condemning Christianity and strongly recommending that any supporters be identified and strongly encouraged to deny any connections between Jesus and the Messiah. Paul relates in 2 Corinthians that "of the Jews five times received I forty stripes save one" (2 Corinthians 11:24), referring to judicial floggings in the synagogues (compare Deuteronomy 25:1–3). Paul and his supporters may have cowed synagogue leaders into inflicting a similar punishment if members of their synagogues chose not to retract their stance on Jesus's messianic role. To resist this punishment would have left the Christians open to the far more damaging punishment of excommunication from the synagogue. Paul may have even relied upon the threat of a potential charge of blasphemy, which carried with it a punishment of death by stoning. How successful these threats were is unclear. While Paul may have been exaggerating when he wrote to the Galatians that he persecuted the Christians "beyond measure," it is difficult not to see his activities having real consequences. Arrests, beatings, violent assaults, home invasions—all are very real means through which Paul would have attempted to suppress the "heretical" Christians. In the words of one author, "Paul did real damage over a period of time impossible to estimate."[14]

Paul's Encounter with Jesus (ca. AD 34)

It was this charge to suppress Christianity that led Paul onto the road to Damascus. Separated from Jerusalem by about 135 miles, Damascus had a relatively large Jewish population and apparently had become a location for Christians to gather as well, as evidenced by Ananias's presence there. Paul set out with his letters and was apparently near the city when he encountered the resurrected Jesus. Luke records three versions of this visionary experience in Acts, and all three of them differ in certain respects (see Acts 9:3–9; 22:6–14; 26:12–18). The two consistent elements throughout all three accounts are the bright light Paul saw and the loud voice he heard. While Paul does not explicitly say that he actually saw Jesus Christ in Acts, Paul's letters imply it.[15] The message relayed by Jesus was clear: the God Paul had been following and the leader of those he had been persecuting were one and the same. Jesus's statement to Paul, "It is hard for thee to kick against the pricks" (Acts 26:14), is perhaps better rendered "It is hard to kick a cactus (especially when wearing open-toed sandals)."[16] The kingdom spoken of by Jesus was going to move forward, and for Paul to try to stop its growth would be as fruitless and senseless as trying to "kick a cactus."

It is common to speak of this visionary encounter as Paul's "conversion" to Christianity. However, it is unclear whether or not Paul would have seen himself being converted in the same sense in which we use the term today. He may have processed this experience as something closer to a commission or call. Prior to his vision, Paul was a zealous defender of the God of Israel and the covenant relationship that had been implemented between God and Israel (i.e., the law of Moses). Following his vision, Paul remained a zealous defender of the God of Israel and his covenant. What changed was his understanding of how Jesus fit into this schema. Paul essentially went from one form of Second Temple Judaism (Pharisaism) to another (Jesus-centered messianism). Jesus never tells Paul to get baptized or to join his church. He simply asks him why Paul has been persecuting him. However, it is notable that Paul is baptized shortly after regaining his sight (see Acts 9:18).

Damascus, Arabia, and the "Missing Years" (ca. AD 34–47)

Being left blind as a result of his vision, Paul was led by his companions the rest of the way to Damascus, where he met Ananias, who subsequently healed Paul and may have performed his baptism (see Acts 9:18). At this point, Paul's movements and whereabouts for the next decade of his life become very difficult to pin down with any kind of surety. Luke tells us that Paul was "certain days with the disciples which were at Damascus. And straightway he preached Christ in the synagogues" (9:19–20), suggesting that Paul remained in Damascus and preached. Luke also suggests that Paul went straight from Damascus to Jerusalem, where he tried to join up with some of the other Christian disciples (see 9:26). However, Paul's own letters suggest a different series of events. In his letter to the Galatians, Paul writes that "I went into Arabia, and returned again unto Damascus. Then after three years I went up to Jerusalem to see Peter, and abode with him fifteen days" (Galatians 1:17–18). Luke's account of Paul's activities following his vision are clearly not all-inclusive, perhaps because Paul rarely spoke about them, or perhaps Paul's activities outside Jerusalem and its surrounding areas were not germane to Luke's focus on the Holy Land as the site of Christianity's founding and early growth.

Paul's reference to time spent in Arabia likely refers to the kingdom of the Nabataeans, an area stretching from Damascus down into the Hijaz (modern Saudi Arabia). The king of the Nabataeans at this time, Aretas IV (9 BC–AD 40; see 2 Corinthians 11:32), was embroiled in a dispute with Herod Antipas, the tetrarch of Galilee due to the latter's divorcing of Aretas's daughter in order to marry Herodias.[17] Paul does not tell us why he first turned to Arabia.[18] Perhaps he needed time to think and consider what he had learned on the road to Damascus. Jesus's words were no doubt life changing for Paul, and required a period of reorientation. Perhaps, like Moses and Jesus, he needed to pass through the wilderness, removed from his regular environment, to commune with God. Or perhaps he, demonstrating the zeal for truth that had defined his previous career as a persecutor, selected an area that had not been heavily proselytized by Christians and turned his efforts toward an area populated by non-Jews of Semitic origins. Whatever Paul's motivations for going to Arabia, he apparently did enough to rouse the ire of King Aretas IV. Paul writes in 2 Corinthians that "in Damascus the governor under Aretas the king kept the city of the Damascenes with a garrison, desirous to apprehend me: And through a window in a basket was I let down by the wall, and escaped his hands" (2 Corinthians 11:32–33). The implication is that Paul had done something to upset King Aretas (who was already frustrated with Jews because of the scandal of his daughter's divorce), and had then left Arabia and returned to Damascus. However, the governor of Damascus, likely acting under Aretas's orders, attempted to arrest Paul. Paul was then forced to flee Damascus in a humiliating fashion, by being lowered out of the city in a basket (see Acts 9:25). It is only at this point that Paul returned to Jerusalem.

These small details preserved in Galatians and 2 Corinthians are significant for three specific reasons. First, it establishes, for the first time, a historical date for an event in Paul's life. It is unlikely that Aretas would have been able to exercise influence over Damascus until near or after the death of the Emperor Tiberius in AD 37 and the subsequent ascension of Gaius.[19] Taking into consideration the "three years" mentioned by Paul in Galatians, this would put Paul's experience on the road to Damascus around AD 34.

While we have no direct information on when Paul was born, his vision of Jesus on the road to Damascus could have occurred when he was around thirty years old, putting his birth somewhere between AD 1 and 10.

The second and third reasons are what these experiences tell us about Paul's own self-perception and understanding of his mission and role within the nascent Christian movement—namely, that he considered his primary responsibility to proselytize to the gentiles and that he would pursue this responsibility somewhat independent of the Jerusalem leadership. Paul mentions specifically that one of the things Jesus revealed to him was that "I might preach him among the heathen [*ethnos*]" (Galatians 1:16). He later remarks that a division of responsibilities between Jewish and gentile spheres was officially made between himself and Peter (see Galatians 2:9). Paul's subsequent travels to cities such as Ephesus, Corinth, and Rome demonstrate that he took this responsibility seriously. Yet while Paul certainly viewed his missionary efforts as complementing what Peter and others were doing, he goes to great lengths to establish his own independence. He states that he preached for three years before he even met Peter, and emphasizes that his understanding of the gospel came straight from Jesus Christ, for after his vision "I conferred not with flesh and blood" (Galatians 1:16). Paul's sentiment is clear; he owes none of what he teaches to the influence of anyone other than Jesus.[20] Later on, in his letter to the church at Rome, Paul made a point to say that "so have I strived to preach the gospel, not where Christ was named, lest I should build upon another man's foundation" (Romans 15:20). Paul's normal method was to establish and build up churches in areas that had not already been evangelized by other Christians, and likewise he expected other Christians to not impose their ideas or directions upon his converts.[21]

This attitude, of course, raises a question about what exactly Paul means when he refers to himself as an apostle. While Latter-day Saints have a very definite idea of what it means to be an apostle, it is important to remember that the word literally means "one who is sent forth," and Paul's understanding of the title seems to come from that broad definition. Certainly Paul would include Peter and the eleven at Jerusalem as apostles, but he also includes himself, James (see Acts 9:19), and those to whom the Lord appeared as well: "After that, he was seen of James; then of all the apostles" (1 Corinthians 15:7). In Romans, Paul also includes two otherwise unknown individuals, Junia and Andronicus, as being "among the apostles" (Romans 16:7). Paul's understanding of what qualified someone to be considered an apostle was whether or not they had personally encountered Jesus Christ: "Am I not an apostle? am I not free? have I not seen Jesus Christ our Lord? are not ye my work in the Lord?" (1 Corinthians 9:1; compare Acts 1:21–22). This does not mean that Paul could not have become part of the official quorum of the twelve apostles, only that his self-identification as an apostle should not be taken to mean that he was.[22] Additionally complicating the matter is the fact that outside of the selection of Matthias in Acts 1:21–26, the New Testament records no instances where the body of the twelve apostles is reconstituted following the death of one of its members, making it difficult to draw firm parallels between this ancient organization and the modern quorum of today.

It is with this understanding of Paul that we should approach Paul's long-awaited return to Jerusalem following his escape from Damascus. Paul tells us that the purpose of this trip was to finally meet and become acquainted with Peter (see Galatians 1:18). Acts adds the detail that Barnabas brought Paul to Peter and provided a recommendation of Paul's character and experiences since his vision. This introduction was likely necessitated because of Paul's prior reputation as a persecutor, which apparently had not dwindled in the three years he was away (see Acts 9:26). Paul states that he spent fifteen days with Peter (see Galatians 1:18). This time would not have been devoted to Paul seeking a greater understanding of the gospel, as Paul already felt like he understood all he needed to. Probably Paul approached Peter in order to get what he needed most—namely, information from Peter on the life and ministry of the Savior from one who had witnessed it with his own eyes. During his time in Jerusalem, Paul also engaged in conversation and debate with some Hellenized Jews, the result being that "they went about to slay him" (Acts 9:29). In a striking turn, Paul the persecutor had become Paul the persecuted. Clearly it was dangerous for Paul to remain in Jerusalem, so friends sent Paul to a place he likely hadn't seen in several years, his home of Tarsus (see Acts 9:30). At this point the events of Paul's life become nearly impossible to trace. All Paul says is that "I came into the regions of Syria and Cilicia" (Galatians 1:21), and it is likely that some of the events Paul describes in 2 Corinthians 11:23–29 happened during this time in Tarsus. This may also be the time during which Paul developed the craft and skill of a tentmaker or leatherworker, a trade that would be a great asset once he began his extensive missionary travels (see Acts 18:3). What else Paul may have done during these missing years is impossible to know, and a lengthy period of time may have passed (ca. AD 37–46) before the details of Paul's life are picked up again.

ANTIOCH (CA. AD 47)

Two significant events led to Paul's reemergence in the affairs of the Christian movement. First, Peter's groundbreaking vision recorded in Acts 10 gave divine sanction to the idea that circumcision was no longer a requirement for covenant membership. Prior to Acts 10, those who wished to become Christians essentially had to become Jews if they were not already, meaning that they had to agree to follow the law of Moses and be circumcised. After Peter's vision, however, this barrier to membership was removed, meaning that one could become a Christian without having to become a Jew first. It is hard to overstate just how controversial this decision was, and it is likely that the gradual realization of this new policy, especially after its affirmation in Acts 15, would have caused many to part ways with Christianity. Second, Stephen's harsh condemnation of the Jewish people in Acts 7 had earlier led to an increased persecution of the Christians (see Acts 8:1; 11:19). Those fleeing persecution found a haven in the city of Antioch, the capital of the Roman province of Syria and at the time the third-largest city in the Roman Empire.[23] Antioch quickly became a center for Christian growth, particularly among the gentiles, and it is here that Christians were first called "Christians" (Acts 11:26). Previously, those who adhered to the messianic movement surrounding Jesus had been called simply followers of "[the] way" (Acts 9:2), an enigmatic title that perhaps refers to the "way of Jesus" (see John 14:6) or perhaps connotes the "other way" of being a Jew.

It was to Antioch that Barnabas, a Christian who hailed from Cyprus, traveled in about AD 47 at the behest of the Jerusalem leadership, likely to strengthen and support what was quickly becoming a significant group of followers. Perhaps realizing that the task at hand was more than one person could adequately handle, Barnabas took a detour to Tarsus with the express purpose of finding Paul. Together, they travelled to Antioch and spent "a whole year" teaching the new converts and likely evangelizing others (Acts 11:26). During Barnabas and Paul's tenure in Antioch, a prophet named Agabus arrived from Jerusalem and prophesied that a famine was imminent (see Acts 11:28). Recognizing the dangers that the lack of food presented and mindful of the Christians in Jerusalem, the disciples at Antioch gathered relief (likely financial) and sent it to Jerusalem with Barnabas and Paul, the second time Paul had been to Jerusalem since his vision. While in Jerusalem, Paul reports that he met privately with some of the church leaders, including Peter, James, and John, and that they extended to him and Barnabas "the right hand of fellowship" (Galatians 2:9). It was also at this meeting that it was formally decided that Paul and Barnabas would spearhead the mission to the gentiles, while Peter would oversee the evangelizing of the Jews (see Galatians 2:9). Finally, Peter reminded Paul and Barnabas to "remember the poor," likely a reference to the famine and the relief Barnabas and Paul had brought from Antioch.[24]

Paul's First Mission (ca. AD 48–49)

Following their brief stay in Jerusalem, Barnabas and Paul returned to Antioch, taking with them a young man named John Mark, the nephew of Barnabas and future author of the Gospel of Mark (see Acts 12:25). At some point after their return, the leaders of the church in Antioch, acting upon the inspiration of the Holy Ghost, selected Barnabas and Paul to begin moving the gospel out into the gentile world. They first traveled to the island of Cyprus, about sixty miles from Antioch, likely because Cyprus was Barnabas's home. After a short time spent preaching in Salamis, the missionaries arrived in Paphos, the imperial capital of Cyprus. Barnabas and Paul must have been making strides in their evangelizing efforts, because they were summoned to meet with Sergius Paulus, the Roman proconsul governing Cyprus. In the first of what would become several encounters between Paul's Christianity and the larger supernatural world, Paul was challenged by Sergius Paulus's deputy, a "sorcerer" and false prophet named Elymus (Acts 13:7–8). Elymus is described as a "*magos*," a wise man or magician and may have filled the role of court astrologer. Elymus appears to have resented Sergius Paulus's interest in Barnabas and Paul and tried to turn him against the missionaries. But Paul, "filled with the Holy Ghost," blinded Elymus and denounced him as a "child of the devil" (Acts 13:9–11). The result of this encounter was that Sergius Paulus "believed, being astonished at the doctrine of the Lord" (Acts 13:12).

Following their time preaching in Cyprus, Barnabas and Paul decided to travel to the mainland of Asia Minor and continue their work. Traveling to Asia Minor may have been part of their plan all along, or perhaps their success with Sergius Paulus encouraged them to continue preaching. After landing in Perga, Barnabas and Paul headed for Pisidian Antioch, a city north of the Taurus Mountains. At this point, John Mark returned to Jerusalem, perhaps feeling that traveling through Asia Minor was more than he wanted to do (see Acts 13:13). That Paul bore some resentment at John Mark's early departure becomes clear in events that follow the Council of Jerusalem the following year (see Acts 15:37–40). In Pisidian Antioch, Barnabas and Paul entered a synagogue on the Sabbath and Paul proceeded to give a lengthy speech, his earliest recorded oration. Themes that become focal points in Paul's letters can be observed in this speech: God's role in directing history, the extension of the Abrahamic covenant to all believers, and the justification of the sinner that comes through faith in the Messiah's sacrifice. Not surprisingly, the gentiles in Pisidian Antioch responded favorably to Paul's message, while the Jews raised up opposition to the missionaries by stirring up resentment among the city's elite, which forced the missionaries to leave the city.

The two missionaries headed next for Iconium, a prosperous city that lay about eighty miles from Pisidian Antioch. Again Barnabas and Paul preached in the synagogue, and this time they found success among both Jews and gentiles. However, resistance was again stirred up against them, and again they were forced out of the city to avoid being stoned. From Iconium they travel to Lystra, about twenty-five miles to the south. In Lystra, Paul healed a man who had been a cripple since birth. This miracle did not escape the notice of the Lystrans, who concluded that Barnabas and Paul must be gods in disguise, specifically Zeus and Hermes.[25] The priest of Jupiter brought oxen and garlands to begin officiating in sacrifices to Barnabas and Paul, but they stopped him by speaking about the "living God" who created the "heaven, and earth, and the sea, and all things that are therein" (Acts 14:15). Unfortunately, this scene is quickly followed by the arrival of Jews from

Pisidian Antioch and Iconium, who had traveled a considerable distance (about one hundred miles in the case of those from Pisidian Antioch) simply to track down Barnabas and Paul. After convincing several of the Lystrans to join their efforts, the Jews stoned Paul and dragged him out of Lystra, where they dumped his body, presuming him to be dead. In a fascinating scene, the Lystrans who were sympathetic to Paul formed a circle around him, and Paul was healed to the point where he was able to stand up and even depart from Lystra the following day (see Acts 14:19–20). Following a brief trip to Derbe, Barnabas and Paul turned around and retraced their steps, visiting Lystra, Iconium, and Pisidian Antioch before finally sailing back home to Antioch, bringing their first mission to a close.

Paul's first mission included several key elements that would become part of the evangelizing process in Paul's subsequent missionary endeavors. First, Paul began his work in each city he visited by preaching in the local synagogues. He seemed to feel that, even though his primary responsibility was to take the gospel to the gentiles, he must first present it to the Jews (see Acts 13:46–48). Second, Paul found success among the gentiles but alienated the Jews, and the Jews remained Paul's frequent opponents throughout his ministry. As is typical, Paul obtained a sympathetic reaction from the Roman leaders he encountered. Generally when problems arose in the cities Paul visited, it was at Jewish instigation rather than from Roman interference. Third, Paul presented a message centered on God's role in initiating a new age through the death and resurrection of his Son. This age, Paul argued, is the time history hinges upon, a turning point where the covenant is extended and the world prepares to enter into a new messianic period. Fourth, Paul's life as a missionary was not simply difficult; it was also dangerous. The stoning at Lystra is just one of several such threats Paul encountered over the next fifteen or so years until his eventual death in Rome.

Trouble in Antioch and the Council of Jerusalem (ca. AD 49)

Barnabas and Paul returned to Antioch only to find that trouble awaited them in the form of the "Judaizers," conservative Jewish-Christians who insisted that gentile converts to Christianity must be circumcised according to the law of Moses or "[they could not] be saved" (Acts 15:1). Peter's vision combined with Barnabas and Paul's evangelization efforts had clearly raised tensions in Jerusalem. Paul recorded an encounter in Galatians that may well have resulted from this tension or perhaps even exacerbated it.[26] Paul tells us that while he and Barnabas were in Antioch, it was customary to enjoy table fellowship with gentiles. When Peter came to Antioch to visit, he also shared table fellowship with gentiles. This all changed, however, when "certain [men] came from James" (Galatians 2:12). These men represented the conservative, orthodox faction of the Jerusalem church, and upon their arrival both Peter and surprisingly Barnabas separated themselves from the gentiles, "fearing them which were of the circumcision" (Galatians 2:12). The reactions of Peter and Barnabas are difficult to understand, especially after the events of Acts 10 and Acts 13–14. Perhaps they were concerned that table fellowship might be seen as scandalous to those in the Jerusalem church and make an already tense situation worse. Or perhaps the concern was what those Jews outside the church would think if they heard that seemingly orthodox Jews like Peter and Barnabas were behaving in a contradictory manner, leading the Jews to begin persecuting converts and severely hampering evangelization. Paul, however, felt no such concerns: "But when I saw that they walked not uprightly according to the truth of the gospel, I said unto Peter before them all, If thou, being a Jew, livest after the manner of Gentiles, and not as do the Jews, why compellest thou the Gentiles to live as do the Jews?" (Galatians 2:14). For Paul, the issue of gentile circumcision had already been decided, and to suggest anything else, for whatever reason, was extremely problematic. Unfortunately, we don't have Peter's side of this debate, and Paul gave us no further information on how Peter and Barnabas took his public criticism.

It was perhaps this incident, or else others like it, that led to a gathering of important church leaders in Jerusalem around AD 49. The immediate issue was to finally resolve the vexing question of gentile circumcision, a matter that was causing "no small dissension and disputation" (Acts 15:2). Barnabas, Paul, and "certain other of them" traveled to Jerusalem from Antioch with Peter, James (the brother of Jesus), and "the apostles and elders" also in attendance (Acts 15:2). Peter spoke first, presenting a theological argument that the grace of the covenant that had been extended by God to the Jews for centuries had now been extended to the gentiles. The gentiles had received the Holy Spirit; they were also purified through faith. This was God's will, and the church would do well to embrace this shift in covenant understanding rather than resist it. Barnabas and Paul spoke next. Although Luke did not give a recounting of anything specific that they said, he did mention that they declared "what miracles and wonders God had wrought among the Gentiles" (Acts 15:12). Barnabas and Paul would have provided a valuable witness of the reality that God was now working among the gentiles, a substantiation of Peter's theological position. Finally, James spoke and added an additional witness to Peter's words through the use of Amos 9:11–12. James argued that Amos's prophecy about the raising up of David's fallen tent had been fulfilled in the birth, death, and resurrection of Jesus Christ—he is David's heir, the Messiah. One of his primary reasons for coming when he did, James argued, was so that "the residue of men might seek after the Lord, and all the Gentiles" (Acts 15:17). James then delivered the final decision of the leadership: "Wherefore my sentence is, that we trouble not them, which from among the Gentiles are turned to God" (Acts 15:19).

Paul was no doubt thrilled at the decision reached at the Jerusalem conference.[27] The acceptance of gentiles into the Christian church regardless of circumcision and other Jewish observances had been his position for some time. Armed with a letter from "the apostles and elders and brethren" that summarized the decision of the conference, Barnabas and Paul and a few associates traveled back to Antioch. After the letter had been read, the Christians "rejoiced for the consolation" (Acts 15:31). Likely encouraged by the results of both the conference and the reception in Antioch, Barnabas and Paul decided to undertake another mission to spread news of this milestone "in every city where we have preached the word of the Lord" (Acts 15:36). Barnabas agreed, but wanted John Mark to accompany them. Paul, apparently still resentful after John Mark's departure during their first mission, "thought [it] not good to take him with them" (Acts 15:38). Sadly, the argument became heated enough that Barnabas and Paul split up, with Barnabas taking John Mark as a companion and Paul taking with him Silas, one of those who had accompanied Paul to Antioch to deliver the decision of the conference. Fortunately, Paul's letters hint at a future reconciliation with both Barnabas and John Mark (see 1 Corinthians 9:6; Colossians 4:10).

Accompanied by Silas, Paul first traveled "through Syria and Cilicia" (Acts 15:41) and later Derbe and Lystra, apparently revisiting the cities he and Barnabas had evangelized a few years earlier. There are likely two reasons why Paul decided to retrace his earlier steps rather than set out for new territory. First, Paul wanted to spread the news from town to town regarding the decision reached in the Jerusalem conference. It is quite likely that questions about circumcision and Jewish observance had arisen during his first mission, and now Paul had good news that brought his converts no small relief. Notably, it is during his time in Lystra that Paul met Timothy, a young man who would be invaluable to Paul's ministry in the coming years. Paul wanted Timothy to travel with him and Silas and even offered to circumcise Timothy. While this may seem strange based upon the decision of the conference and Paul's own stance on circumcision, the decision was likely a practical one. As the uncircumcised son of a mixed marriage, Timothy would be regarded with suspicion by Jews and might then be a hindrance to further missionary efforts, especially since it was Paul's custom (at least according to Luke) to begin his evangelization in the synagogues upon reaching a new city. Paul's circumcision of Timothy should be seen as practical rather than theological.

A second reason why Paul may have chosen to retrace his earlier steps was the continued persistence of the Judaizers. As discussed earlier, "Judaizers" is the name given to the conservative faction of the Christian church, those who insisted upon full conversion to Judaism for those wishing to worship as Christians. It was likely that this group (or one like them) was responsible for Peter's actions in Antioch, and it was likely the actions of this group that provided the impetus for the conference at Jerusalem. Acts 15:1 relates that "certain men which came down from Judea taught the brethren, and said, Except ye be circumcised after the manner of Moses, ye cannot be saved." It is quite possible that these "certain men" did not stop in Antioch, but actually continued traveling to other places where the Christian message had been preached, including the congregations founded by Barnabas and Paul during their first mission. The Judaizers were apparently quite convincing, because Paul soon received word that his converts had either been circumcised or at least were under the assumption that they needed to be. It is this situation that provides the occasion for Paul to write his epistle to the Galatians, a fiery invective against the Judaizers and all those who would listen to them. While the exact dating of this epistle remains the topic of much debate, the circumstances immediately preceding the Jerusalem conference seem to indicate that this is the most likely time period.[28] It is also possible that the Judaizers, finding themselves rebuffed in Jerusalem, began to more aggressively spread their message, which could also have taken them to Galatia. This would mean that Galatians was written shortly after the Jerusalem conference, perhaps while Paul and Barnabas were still in Antioch. Perhaps Paul's visit to his converts in Iconium and Lystra was to see how they had responded to his letter: Had they been convinced by his argument, or were the Judaizers still posing a threat? If either of these scenarios is correct, then Galatians would be Paul's earliest extant epistle, with a date of AD 49–50.

Paul's Second Mission (ca. AD 50–52)

After consolidating the concerns of the church in the cities of Galatia, Paul began what is generally referred to as his second mission. Whereas his first mission had been largely local and constrained to the cities in Galatia, this second mission took Paul through Asia Minor and into what we call Europe. Whether or not he initially planned to travel as far as he did is unknown, but two key spiritual experiences provided a sense of direction and scope for Paul as he ventured farther out into the gentile world. First, Luke tells us that Paul and Silas initially attempted to continue their travels north into Bithynia, but "the Spirit suffered them not" (Acts 16:7). Instead, Paul and Silas turned westward, toward Troas. Second, while in Troas, Paul experienced a dream or vision of a man in Macedonia who pled with Paul to "come over into Macedonia, and help us" (Acts 16:9). Paul immediately departed for Macedonia, convinced "that the Lord had called us for to preach the gospel unto them" (Acts 16:10). The inclusion of the first "we" passage in Acts 16:11 suggests that Luke joined Paul, Silas, and Timothy at this point.

From Troas, Paul and his party landed in Neapolis and traveled ten miles to Philippi, one of the most prosperous and important Roman colonies in Macedonia. In Philippi, Paul met and baptized Lydia and her household. Lydia's occupation as a "seller of purple" meant that she sold cloth or wool that had been dyed with rare and precious purple dye, which was difficult to obtain (purple dye was typically extracted from shellfish). This profession would have granted her a fair amount of financial success and prosperity, and thus it is no surprise that she offered herself as a hostess for Paul and his party. This success with Lydia was quickly tempered by an encounter between Paul and a young slave girl who served as a fortune-teller. Unlike Lydia, who appeared to be quite successful and financially independent, this girl was a slave who was completely dependent upon her masters. Even her body was not her own, as she was possessed to some degree by a spirit. However, the girl obviously recognized something special in Paul and his party and spent many days following them around and shouting, "These men are the servants of the most high God" (Acts 16:17). Paul, seemingly annoyed by this behavior, exorcised the spirit from the girl, freeing the girl but angering her masters, who were now faced with losing the financial benefits the girl had provided them.

What happened next is curious. The girl's masters complained to the Philippian authorities that Paul and Silas "do exceedingly trouble our city" (Acts 16:20). The response from the authorities was to take Paul and Silas, strip off their clothes, beat them with rods (a standard Roman punishment against those threating civil order), and finally cast them into prison. Additionally, their feet were held "fast in the stocks" (Acts 16:24), a measure that would greatly have increased their discomfort (compare 1 Thessalonians 2:2). Paul and Silas remained in prison throughout the night, patiently singing praises to God, until miraculously the doors of the prison opened up because of an earthquake. The reason this story is so curious is that Paul and Silas were both Roman citizens and therefore should have been exempt from this type of harsh punishment.[29] So why did Paul and Silas only identify themselves as Roman citizens *after* they had spent the night in prison? When the magistrates heard that Paul and Silas were citizens, they were justly fearful, for they could lose their positions as a result of this violation, and their attempt to quietly usher Paul and Silas out of Philippi is certainly understandable. Perhaps Paul felt that his suffering and persecution were part of the discipleship process—just as Jesus suffered, so should those who follow him suffer. Or perhaps Paul hoped that the magistrates would be more sympathetic toward his recent converts (now that he had an advantage over the magistrates), should any future trouble arise. Regardless, Paul and Silas departed from Philippi soon after. Based upon Paul's later letter to the

Philippians, this congregation was one he felt very close to, and it is clear he valued their friendship throughout his life.

From Philippi (where Paul apparently left Luke), Paul and his companions traveled west to Thessalonica, where again Paul ran afoul of the locals. As was his custom, Paul began by preaching in the synagogue of the Jews, where he preached three times. However, a group of Jews became annoyed at Paul's success, and in order to rid themselves of Paul's presence they attempted to bring Paul to the city magistrates. Not finding Paul, they instead attacked a man named Jason, possibly because he was providing the house in which Paul was staying. Jason and his associates were forced to pay a bond or fine and were then released. Paul and his associates were quickly ushered out of the city and continued on their way toward Athens.

In Athens, the intellectual capital of the world, Paul continued his teaching and debates. Curious about what "new doctrine" (Acts 17:19) Paul was presenting, Paul was brought before the court of the Areopagus, a venerable body located on the Hill of Ares, immediately southwest of the Acropolis. Here Paul was given the chance to explain Christian theology to an intellectual audience that included Stoics and Epicureans, an audience that would appreciate its novelty even if they rejected the message (see Acts 17:18–32). Paul's subsequent speech is a masterstroke, one contrasting supposed Athenian piety with the truth about humanity, their origins, and their relationship to the true God. Without a knowledge and an understanding of God, Paul argued, even the intellectual elite, such as the Athenians, fall short. The Athenians, Paul argued, had created a God in their own image, rather than seeking to change themselves to match the image of God. While God may have acted with patience in the past, divine judgment is a reality for those who do not repent. However, when Paul brought up the topic of the Resurrection, his Greek audience lost interest and sent him on his way.

From Athens, Paul continued about forty miles west to Corinth, a port city that was the capital of the Roman province of Achaia. Unlike previous cities where Paul spent a short time and then moved on, Paul remained in Corinth for at least eighteen months and possibly even longer. While in Corinth, Paul continued his custom of preaching in the synagogue on the Sabbath and also plied his trade of working with leather. Paul lived for a time with two Jews who had come to Corinth from Rome, a husband and wife named Aquila and Priscilla, who practiced a similar trade (see

Acts 18:3). It is possible that Paul converted Aquila and Priscilla, although they may have been Christians prior to their expulsion from Rome because of the edict of the Emperor Claudius.[30] It is likely during his time spent in Corinth that Paul wrote 1 and 2 Thessalonians, helping his Thessalonian congregation navigate the problems of persecution and Jesus's return. Paul apparently had a fair amount of success in Corinth, including the baptism of Crispus, the chief ruler of the synagogue, and his family. However, Paul once again incurred the resentment of the Jews living in Corinth, who brought Paul to Gallio, the proconsul of Achaia, on a trumped-up charge of being a lawbreaker.[31] Gallio saw through the charade and responded to the Jews that they should "look ye to it; for I will be no judge of such matters" (Acts 18:15). In a curious turn of events, Sosthenes, the leader of the synagogue, was taken and beaten in full view of Gallio, who "cared for none of those things" (Acts 18:17). Paul then left Corinth with Aquila and Priscilla, leaving Silas and Timothy behind to continue ministering to the Corinthians. After a brief stay in Ephesus, where Paul left Aquila and Priscilla, he returned to Jerusalem and then Antioch, concluding this second mission.

Paul's Third Mission (ca. AD 53–56)

Little time appears to have passed between Paul's return from his second mission and the beginning of his third mission (see Acts 18:22–23). After his visit to Jerusalem, Paul again commenced his evangelization, similarly beginning in Antioch and moving to Galatia before finally arriving in Ephesus. Unlike Luke's account of Paul's second mission, which showed Paul traveling extensively throughout the Aegean, Paul's third mission was largely spent in Ephesus, a city Paul had briefly visited at the end of his second mission. In all, Paul spent approximately three years in Ephesus, by far his lengthiest stay in any one city during his missions (see Acts 20:31). The abnormal period of time Paul spent in Ephesus could be attributed to the importance the city held in the ancient world. Ephesus was one of the largest cities in the Roman Empire, with a population approaching a quarter million. Nearly all communication throughout western Asia went through Ephesus, and Ephesus was also a commercial and cultural center. Of paramount importance was the worship of Diana, whose temple constructed outside the city walls was considered one of the seven wonders of the ancient world. If Paul was searching for a locale where he could spread his religious message far and wide, Ephesus provided the perfect environment.

Luke provides glimpses of what Paul did during those years in Ephesus. In addition to following his regular pattern of preaching in the Jewish synagogues, Paul also spent time in the "school of one Tyrannus," where presumably he gathered disciples and those interested in the Christian message and held various discussions (Acts 19:9). The result was that "all they which dwelt in Asia heard the word of the Lord Jesus, both Jews and Greeks" (19:10). Luke goes to great lengths to portray Paul's ministry as charismatic and inspired during this time. Handkerchiefs and aprons that touched Paul's body were used to heal various diseases and even to cast out devils. In a rather humorous aside, Luke tells of the seven sons of Sceva who also tried their hand at casting out devils but failed miserably when the evil spirit they are attempting to cast out "leaped on them, and overcame them, and prevailed against them, so that they fled out of that house naked and wounded" (19:16). This encounter resulted in many more embracing the message of Jesus Christ and bringing their magical texts together and burning them (see 19:19). Apparently, Paul became so successful at turning people away from their former religious beliefs that resentment began to build among those whose livelihood revolved around the selling of silver statues of Diana. These silversmiths rioted in protest and were only subdued when the Ephesian town clerk warned the rioters that their actions lacked legal foundation. While Luke portrays Paul's time in Ephesus as largely successful and without incident, it is possible that Paul was imprisoned for some time during his stay at Ephesus, as he mentions to the Corinthians that he "fought with beasts at Ephesus" (1 Corinthians 15:32).[32]

Perhaps concern for affairs in Corinth caused Paul to leave Ephesus. Paul had earlier sent Timothy and Erastus to Macedonia, and Timothy's return to Ephesus likely alerted Paul to the apostasy that had crept into the Corinthian branch. Paul had probably already written two letters to Corinth from Ephesus, one that did not survive (mentioned in 1 Corinthians 5:9–10) and one that did (1 Corinthians). However, Timothy's report made Paul realize that the situation required his actual presence. Luke reports that Paul traveled back to Greece, with stops in Troas and Macedonia. Once Paul arrived in Corinth, where he stayed for three months (see Acts 20:3;

likely the winter season), Paul realized just how far things had deteriorated. Mocked for his timid appearance and whiny voice, Paul left Corinth undermined and frustrated. He then likely wrote a letter he described as written "with many tears" (2 Corinthians 2:4), which is now lost. Paul sent this letter with Titus and likely continued traveling back through Macedonia and Troas; it was likely during that stay in Macedonia that Paul wrote part of 2 Corinthians (2 Corinthians 2:13). Fortunately, Titus appears to have been favorably received by the Corinthians, and he was even able to raise money for the collection while at Corinth (see 2 Corinthians 7:15). Happy to be reconciled, Paul wrote that he planned to visit Corinth a third time (see 2 Corinthians 12:14), although it is unknown whether or not Paul ever made a return visit to Corinth.

One of the reasons Paul may not have returned to Corinth was his eagerness to return to Jerusalem for Pentecost. Paul apparently avoided returning to Ephesus while traveling back from Greece because he worried that a stop in Ephesus would delay him from reaching Jerusalem in time. Pentecost may not have been Paul's only concern. He may have wanted to deliver the collection in conjunction with the festival, or he may have become excited about undertaking a possible voyage to Rome, a trip that had apparently been on his mind since his time in Ephesus (see Acts 19:21). It is likely that Paul began composing his epistle to the Romans during this time as a sort of introductory letter (see Romans 15:25–26) to what he appears to have fully expected to be part of a fourth mission. Paul did allow himself one brief stop at Miletus, a coastal town located about thirty miles from Ephesus. There, Paul gathered the elders of the church and delivered a warning that in the near future "grievous wolves enter in among you, not sparing the flock. Also of your own selves shall men arise, speaking perverse things, to draw away disciples after them" (Acts 20:29–30). Then, in Caesarea, despite a warning given him by the prophet Agabus that he would be bound and handed over to the Gentiles while in Jerusalem (see Acts 21:11), Paul insisted on continuing his journey to Jerusalem.

Jerusalem and Imprisonment (ca. AD 57)

Paul arrived in a Jerusalem full of anxiety and unrest. Felix, the Roman procurator of Judea (ca. AD 52–60), was no friend of the Jews and had on several occasions shown little hesitation in killing those Jews who would not quietly submit to his rule.[33] Nationalistic attitudes ran high among the Jews, and Jewish resentment for Roman rule manifested itself in a general anti-gentile sentiment. The celebration of Pentecost would have done nothing to diminish these views. About this time Luke records that accusations had been brought against Paul himself—namely, that he was teaching Jews living in the diaspora to disregard the law of Moses and to refrain from circumcising their sons (see Acts 21:20–21). When Paul met with James (the brother of Jesus), James asked Paul to prove his devotion to Judaism by accompanying a few Jews who were in the process of completing their Nazarite vows: according to the law, Paul would have needed to go through his own period of purification due to his time spent in gentile territory (see Numbers 19:11–13). James must have felt that this act would assuage any concerns about Paul's respect and devotion for Jewish law and tradition while away in the diaspora. To agree to such a proposal was not a guarantee of safety since Paul would have had to make his presence in the temple public and thus alert his enemies to his whereabouts. Paul nonetheless agreed, perhaps realizing that his reputation had put him in a precarious position or perhaps because he feared that the collection he and his colleagues had worked so hard to gather would be rejected if it came from someone who was viewed as anti-Jewish (see Romans 15:30–31).

Unfortunately, James's plan did not work out. Luke relates that "the Jews which were of Asia" (Acts 21:27) stirred up the crowd by accusing Paul (falsely) of bringing gentiles into the temple, a capital offense that would desecrate the temple. Paul was seized by an angry mob, dragged out of the temple, and nearly killed, an appropriate punishment (under the law) if Paul had in fact done what the mob accused him of. Fortunately, the Roman tribune Claudius Lysias, likely already on high alert due to the festival, intervened and rescued Paul with soldiers garrisoned in the nearby Antonia Fortress. Claudius Lysias was apparently under the impression that Paul was a revolutionary zealot, an Egyptian pseudo-Messiah who had led four thousand *sicarii* into the wilderness, and was thus surprised to learn not only that Paul could speak Greek but that he was also a citizen of Tarsus.[34] Paul requested to speak to the crowd and told them of his background, his vision, and his mission. Unsatisfied, the Jewish mob pushed for Paul's execution, and Claudius Lysias ordered Paul to be brutally scourged in order to extract more specific information about Paul's identity and presence in Jerusalem. Recognizing that Roman law forbade the use of scourging, or *verberatio*, on a Roman citizen, Paul asked the centurion in charge of scourging him, "Is it lawful for you to scourge a man that is a Roman, and uncondemned?" (Acts 22:25). Alarmed at this revelation, Claudius Lysias ordered a cessation to Paul's punishment, although he continued to keep Paul in his custody.

Claudius Lysias thereupon ordered Paul to stand before the Sanhedrin. This move should not be understood as an attempt by Claudius Lysias to ignore his responsibilities and allow Jewish law to settle the dispute. Rather, it is more likely that Claudius Lysias needed further insight into why Paul and his Jewish opponents were engaged in such a heated religious dispute. Before the Sanhedrin, Paul maintained his innocence and successfully won over the Pharisees to his side by highlighting his pharisaic pedigree, although not before insulting Ananias, the high priest (see Acts 23:1–9). Worried that the conflict between the Sadducees and the Pharisees over Paul's testimony might become violent, Claudius Lysias was forced once again to take Paul back into custody. Later that night the Lord appeared to Paul, comforting him: "Be of good cheer, Paul: for as thou hast testified of me in Jerusalem, so must thou bear witness also at Rome" (Acts 23:11). The following morning, likely frustrated at their inability to see Paul executed, a band of about forty Jews swore an oath that they would not eat or drink until they had killed Paul (see Acts 12–13). They attempted to enlist the help of the chief priests and elders in contacting Claudius Lysias and asking him to return Paul for another hearing before the Sanhedrin, with the intent of killing Paul before he arrived. Alerted to this plot by a nephew of Paul's, Claudius Lysias realized that Paul would not be safe in Jerusalem and ordered him to be extradited to Caesarea Maritima to be interrogated by Antonius Felix, the Roman procurator (AD 52–60). The number of men sent to escort Paul, 470 (see Acts 23:23), is extraordinary, but it may indicate the dedication Claudius Lysias had to ensure Paul's safe travel.

Before Felix and Festus (ca. AD 58–60)

Paul's trial before Felix took the form of a debate. Tertullus, a skilled prosecutor hired by the Jews, attempted to portray Paul as a seditious person intent on stirring up trouble for both the Jews and Rome. Paul responded by refuting Tertullus's accusations and reemphasizing his own beliefs in the God of Judaism and the law. When the debate was over, Felix declined to declare a verdict, instead stating that he would wait for Claudius Lysias to arrive. Paul was ordered to remain in custody but to have some liberties, such as the companionship of friends. However, Felix continued to delay his decision, ostensibly because he wanted to discuss Christianity and its beliefs with Paul, but Luke includes the more likely cause of the delay—namely, that "he hoped also that money should have been given him of Paul" (Acts 24:26). Felix's holding out for a bribe is not surprising, given what is otherwise known about his character, although the act of taking bribes from prisoners was strictly prohibited according to the Roman *Lex Julia de pecuniis repetundis.* Rather than obtaining the quick release from prison he may have been expecting, Paul instead spent two years in captivity in Caesarea under the watch of Felix.

Likely due to questionable administrative practices, Felix was removed from office in AD 60 and replaced by Porcius Festus (AD 60–62).[35] By all accounts a decent administrator, Festus initially acted impartially but likely underestimated the hatred Paul's Jewish opponents had for Paul. Festus rejected the Jewish appeal to transfer Paul to Jerusalem (where he would have been ambushed and killed along the way; see Acts 25:3) but invited Paul's opponents to travel to Caesarea and accuse Paul in person. However, once everyone gathered in Caesarea and both sides again pled their case, Festus sided with the Jews and asked Paul if he would be willing to travel to Jerusalem and be judged there. Festus likely had no knowledge of the Jewish plot to ambush Paul; rather he was trying to please his constituency and thus was "willing to do the Jews a pleasure" (Acts 25:9). Well aware that certain death awaited him if he traveled to Jerusalem and sensing that Festus was more sympathetic to the Jews than to him, Paul again relied on his Roman citizenship. According to the Roman *Lex Julia de vi publica seu privata*, a Roman citizen could at any time appeal (*provoco*) to the emperor to have his case heard, and that is what Paul did here: "I stand at Caesar's judgment seat, where I ought to be judged: to the Jews have I done no wrong, as thou very well knowest. For if I be an offender, or have committed any thing worthy of death, I refuse not to die: but if there be none of these things whereof these accuse me, no man may deliver me unto them. I appeal unto Caesar" (Acts 25:10–11).

Festus did not immediately send him to Rome. Rather, it was his responsibility to write up a report outlining the charges brought against Paul. Festus, being procurator only a short time, likely struggled with how to describe Paul's circumstances in a way that looked to be worth the emperor's time, rather than a silly cultural dispute that (at least in the emperor's eyes) any competent administrator should have been able to resolve. Thus, it is likely with a certain amount of relief that Festus welcomed Herod Agrippa II and his sister Bernice, who had arrived in Caesarea to welcome the new procurator. The last of the Hasmonean rulers over Judea, Herod Agrippa II would have been able to help Festus understand the complexities of Paul's circumstances. Paul again related his vision and offered a brief summary of his travels, including his capture in the temple. Festus was unimpressed with Paul's presentation and declared Paul to be mad. Herod Agrippa II was more sympathetic, and his famous response, "Almost thou persuadest me to be a Christian" (Acts 26:28) is ambiguous and could be read either respectfully or ironically. The important outcome of the encounter is that Herod Agrippa II declared that Paul "doeth nothing worthy of death or of bonds" and lamented that "this man might have been set at liberty, if he had not appealed unto Caesar" (Acts 26:31–32).

Paul's Imprisonment in Rome (ca. AD 60–62) and Execution (ca. AD 64)

Following his hearing with Herod Agrippa II, Festus agreed to send Paul to Rome to have his appeal heard. After a series of near-disastrous events that included a shipwreck and a viper's bite, Paul arrived in Rome. Luke records that he spent two years in Rome under some kind of confinement. Paul's case was likely not considered a serious offence by the Romans, and he was granted a lightened form of custody. Paul was allowed to dwell in a small, modest residence that he (or more likely his supporters) paid for (see Acts 28:16), although he remained in the custody of a Roman soldier (see Acts 28:16), perhaps even bound to the soldier by a chain (see Acts 28:20). Unfortunately, Luke's account ends with Paul under arrest in Rome, leaving many questions unanswered. The likeliest scenario for what happened next is that Paul's case was dismissed, probably due to the absence of his accusers. First Clement (5:5–7) mentions that Paul reached "the limits of the west," possibly suggesting that Paul achieved his goal of traveling to Spain (see Romans 15:24, 28). However, on the way home from the west Paul found himself once again in a difficult situation, one that he would not escape from. Eusebius wrote that after being released from his initial Roman imprisonment and undertaking an additional ministry, Paul came "a second time to the same city [and] suffered martyrdom under Nero."[36] Eusebius additionally relays the detail that Paul suffered death by beheading, the proper means of execution for a Roman citizen.[37] If this scenario is accurate, while Paul's death could have taken place as early as AD 62 it may have extended as late as AD 68 (the year of Nero's death).[38] Of course, it is also possible that Paul was executed during his first stay at Rome, and Luke simply chose not to include that detail, which would likely place Paul's execution sometime between AD 62 and 64.

It is probable that 2 Timothy (if genuinely Pauline) preserves some of the last thoughts Paul ever recorded. In this revealing epistle, Paul laments that some of his colleagues, such as Demas, have left him, save Luke (see 2 Timothy 4:10–11). His request that Timothy bring him the "cloak that I left at Troas with Carpus" (2 Timothy 4:13) may reveal conditions indicative of a harsher imprisonment than his previous one (see 2 Timothy 4:16). Yet Paul's ever-present optimism does not wane. Using a series of athletic metaphors, Paul confidently declares, "I have fought a good fight, I have finished my course, I have kept the faith" (2 Timothy 4:7). In other words, Paul has wrestled a good match, he has run a good race, and he has maintained, through it all, his loyalty to and confidence in Jesus Christ.

With these words, Paul leaves his modern-day readers with a valuable archetype of discipleship. Over two (possibly three) decades of missionary work, Paul made no shortage of enemies, parted ways with friends and colleagues, wrote epistles fiery (Galatians) and contemplative (Philippians), and yet through it all he endured because of his faith. Paul's experiences tell us that the life of a disciple is not an easy one; it requires sacrifice and patience centered on the conviction that faith in Jesus Christ has not been misplaced or found wanting. As Paul (rather explicitly) writes to the Philippians, "I have suffered the loss of all things, and do count them but dung, that I may win Christ" (Philippians 3:8). Paul's legacy comes through to help his readers understand that life is hard and takes its toll, that true commitment can lead to a shortage of earthly satisfaction, and that obtaining a "crown of righteousness" (2 Timothy 4:8) is not about perfection, but about perseverance.

Nicholas J. Frederick is an associate professor of ancient scripture at Brigham Young University.

Nicholas J. Frederick, "The Life of the Apostle Paul: An Overview," in *New Testament History, Culture, and Society: A Background to the Texts of the New Testament*, ed. Lincoln H. Blumell (Provo, UT: Religious Studies Center, Brigham Young University; Salt Lake City: Deseret Book, 2019), 393–418.

Notes

1. John G. Gager, *Who Made Early Christianity? The Jewish Lives of the Apostle Paul* (New York: Princeton University Press, 2015), 17.
2. This has been the approach of some biographies of Paul aimed at popular audiences, such as A. N. Wilson, *Paul: The Mind of the Apostle* (New York: W. W. Norton, 1997); and Hyam Maccoby, *The Mythmaker: Paul and the Invention of Christianity* (New York: Harper and Row, 1986); however the origin of the idea goes back to F. C. Baur, in particular, *Paul: The Apostle of Jesus Christ: His Life and Works, His Epistles and Teachings* (London: Williams and Norgate, 1845).
3. Daniel Boyarin, *A Radical Jew: Paul and the Politics of Identity* (Berkeley: University of California Press, 1994).
4. For Paul's early education, see Jerome Murphy-O'Connor, *Paul: A Critical Life* (Oxford: Clarendon Press, 1996), 46–51.
5. For a discussion of the arguments for and against Paul being a Roman citizen, see Udo Schnelle, *Apostle Paul: His Life and Theology*, trans. M. Eugene Boring (Grand Rapids, MI: Baker Academic Press, 2003), 60–62. A classic study of Roman law and the New Testament is A. N. Sherwin-White, *Roman Society and Roman Law in the New Testament* (Oxford: Oxford University Press, 1963).
6. James D. G. Dunn, *Christianity in the Making, vol 2: Beginning from Jerusalem* (Grand Rapids, MI: Eerdmans, 2009), 335.
7. See Jacob Neusner, *The Rabbinic Tradition about the Pharisees before 70*, vols. 1–3 (Leiden: Brill, 1971), 1:341–76.

8. See *m. Yebamot* 6:6; *b. Yebamot* 62b–63b, *b. Qiddušin* 29b; *b. Sanhedrin* 36b. For a discussion of exceptions to this understanding, see John P. Meier, *A Marginal Jew: Rethinking the Historical Jesus*, vol. 1, *The Roots of the Problem and the Person*, The Anchor Bible Reference Library (New York: Doubleday, 1991), 336–41.
9. Epiph. *Pan.* 30.16.9.
10. "It is much more probable, however, that Paul cheerfully bowed to the expectation that young men should marry in their early twenties." Murphy-O'Connor, *Paul: A Critical Life*, 63.
11. Murphy-O'Connor, *Paul: A Critical Life*, 64–65.
12. Dating events in the life of Paul is a difficult task, and there are as many chronological time lines for the life of Paul as there are biographies. The dates presented here in this essay represent my best estimation. For a discussion of the issues involved and other Pauline time lines, see Dunn, *Beginning from Jerusalem*, 497–512.
13. "The fact that the witnesses laid their clothes at Saul's feet suggests that he was already the acknowledged leader in the opposition to the early church." David G. Peterson, *The Acts of the Apostles* (Grand Rapids, MI: Eerdmans, 2009), 268. Compare Acts 4:35, 37; 5:2.
14. Murphy-O'Connor, *Paul: A Critical Life*, 67.
15. See Galatians 1:16; 1 Corinthians 9:1.
16. See Thomas A. Wayment, *From Persecutor to Apostle: A Biography of Paul* (Salt Lake City: Deseret Book, 2006), 41.
17. Josephus, *Antiquities* 18.109–15. It is the denouncement of this marriage by John the Baptist that provides the setting for his execution. Compare Matthew 14: 3–12.
18. One possible link between Paul and Arabia is his comment in Galatians that Hagar represents "mount Sinai in Arabia" (Galatians 4:25). This opens up the intriguing possibility that Paul went to Arabia to visit Mount Sinai and find answers to his questions in a similar fashion as Moses did.
19. See Murphy-O'Connor, *Paul: A Critical Life*, 5–7.
20. "The only point Paul chose to make is that his time in Arabia further underlined his independence from the Jerusalem leadership; in Arabia there was no one whom he could have consulted." Dunn, *Beginning from Jerusalem*, 265.
21. Compare 1 Corinthians 3:10; 2 Corinthians 10:13–16.
22. For those who want to argue that Paul was a member of the Quorum of the Twelve Apostles, the best textual evidence is Acts 14:4, 14, and Galatians 2:9.
23. Josephus, *Jewish War* 3.29.
24. It is important to note that at this juncture two possible sequences of events are introduced by Luke in Acts and Paul in Galatians. The first one, which I follow, is that the famine relief mentioned in Acts 11 is the same event discussed by Paul in Galatians 2:1–10. In support of this position is F. F. Bruce, who writes, "The view taken here is that it is to be identified with the visit of Acts 11:30, in the fourteenth year of Paul's conversion." F. F. Bruce, *The Epistle to the Galatians* (Grand Rapids, MI: Eerdmans, 1982), 108–9; see also Ben Witherington III, *The Acts of the Apostles* (Grand Rapids, MI: Eerdmans, 1998), 439–43. The other position is that Galatians 2:1–10 refers to the events mentioned in Acts 15. There are good arguments supporting both views. For an even-handed treatment of both positions, see Dunn, *Beginning from Jerusalem*, 446–70.
25. As recorded by Ovid in his charming collection of tales, *Metamorphoses*, Zeus and Hermes often would travel to Earth in the guise of men as a test of hospitality. After several rejections, Zeus and Hermes found an acceptance in the house of the elderly couple Baucis and Philemon, who are rewarded for their hospitality by becoming priests

in the temple of Zeus; see *Metamorphoses*, 8:611–724. This story apparently occurred nearby the city of Lystra, and it is likely that the inhabitants' reaction to Barnabas and Paul stems from their knowledge of this story.

26. Again, we experience questions in regard to the sequence of Paul's life as described in Galatians 2:11–14. Some scholars, such as F. F. Bruce, argue that the encounter between Peter and Paul in Antioch occurred between the first mission and the Council of Jerusalem, which issued the decree granting full membership to uncircumcised Gentiles. See Bruce, *Galatians*, 128–30; see also See Ben Witherington III, *Grace in Galatia* (Grand Rapids, MI: Eerdmans, 1998), 149–52. Others, such as Joseph A. Fitzmyer, argue that the encounter between Peter and Paul happened after the Council of Jerusalem (and presumably the decree); see Joseph A. Fitzmyer, *The Acts of the Apostles* (New Haven: Yale University Press, 1998), 541. Again, for a full discussion, see Dunn, *Beginning from Jerusalem*, 446–70. See also the work of David G. Peterson, who writes, "We cannot be certain when the next incident mentioned by Paul in Galatians 2:11–14 took place, though it is most likely to have been before the resolutions of the Jerusalem Council brought public agreement between Peter, James, Paul, and Barnabas on such matters." Peterson, *The Acts of the Apostles*, 420.
27. For more on the Jerusalem conference, including the events that led up to it and the outcomes that followed, see Robert J. Matthews, "The Jerusalem Conference," in *The Apostle Paul: His Life and Testimony*, ed. Paul Y. Hoskisson (Salt Lake City: Deseret Book, 1994), 96–109.
28. For a useful discussion of the issues surrounding the epistle to the Galatians, including its dating, occasion, and audience, see Bruce, *Galatians*, 1–56. Bruce himself argues for an early date for Galatians, believing that a date sometime near the events of the Council of Jerusalem "would yield the most satisfactory correlation of the data of Galatians and Acts and the most satisfactory dating of Galatians" (55).
29. The *Lex Porcia de provocatione* specifically forbade the flogging of one who was a *civis romanus*, or a "Roman Citizen" (compare Livy, *Ab. Urb. Cond*, 10.9.5). "In a Roman colony it appears that arrest, beating, and imprisonment were normal for aliens, but that it was potentially dangerous to give citizens the same treatment." Peter Garnsey, *Social Status and Legal Privilege in the Roman Empire* (Oxford: Oxford University Press, 1970), 268.
30. Suetonius records that Claudius expelled Jews from Rome because of uprisings resulting from "impulsore Chresto," which could mean that either divisions over belief in Jesus Christ had led to these uprisings or it could simply refer to someone named Chrestus who had no connection with Christianity (see Suet. *Claud.* 25.4). Either way, Jews were likely banned from Rome somewhere around AD 49 and likely did not return until after the death of Claudius in AD 54.
31. Gallio's tenure as proconsul of Achaia can be firmly dated from spring AD 51 to spring AD 52. The majority of attempts at establishing a Pauline chronology use Gallio's proconsulship as a primary foundation.
32. For more on the argument for an Ephesian imprisonment, see Dunn, *Beginning from Jerusalem*, 777–80.
33. See Josephus, *Jewish War* 2.12.2; 2.13.4,7. Compare Tacitus, *Hist.* 5.9; *Ann.* 12.54.
34. See Josephus *Jewish War* 2.13.5. Felix had been working on quelling the Egyptian's revolt and had largely been successful, although the Egyptian remained at large. Claudius Lysias appears to believe that the man he has apprehended, who had caused such a disturbance in the temple, was this Egyptian.
35. See Josephus, *Jewish Antiquities* 20.182.

36. Eusebius, *Hist. Eccl.* 2.22.2; compare 2 Timothy 4:16.
37. Eusebius, *Hist. Eccl.* 2.25.5; compare 1 Clem. 5.7; Tert. *De. Praescriptione Haer.* 36.
38. For a fuller discussion of these issues, see H. W. Tajra, *The Martyrdom of St. Paul: Historical and Judicial Context, Traditions, and Legends* (Tübingen: Mohr [Paul Siebeck], 1994).

Time Line for the Life of Paul

(Note: Because these dates are based upon limited historical evidence and the text of the New Testament, this time line should be seen as a *speculative* reconstruction of Paul's life).

AD 1–10 (+/-5)	Paul's birth
30	Crucifixion of Jesus
31–33	Paul persecutes the Hellenists
34	Paul's "conversion"
34–37	Damascus and Arabia (the "missing years")
37	First visit to Jerusalem
37–46	Years spent in Syria and Cilicia
47	Paul and Barnabas preach in Antioch
48–49	Paul's first mission: Galatia
49	Council of Jerusalem (Incident at Antioch either closely preceding or closely following the council)
50	Paul returns to Galatia (*Galatians*)
50–52	Paul's second mission: Corinth (*1 and 2 Thessalonians*)
53–56	Paul's third mission: Ephesus (*1 and 2 Corinthians, Romans*)
57	Return to Jerusalem and arrest
58–60	Imprisonment in Caesarea (*Philippians, Ephesians, Colossians*, and *Philemon*)
60–64	Imprisonment in Rome and execution (*Pastorals*)

Further Reading

Latter-day Saint

Anderson, Richard Lloyd. *Understanding Paul.* Salt Lake City: Deseret Book, 1983.
A work that was written more recently than Sidney Sperry's. It is more useful for engaging Paul's theology and the context of the epistles than as a study of Paul's life, but it is still a valuable resource for Latter-day Saints.

Hoskisson, Paul Y., ed. *The Apostle Paul, His Life and His Testimony: The 23rd Annual Sidney B. Sperry Symposium.* Salt Lake City: Deseret Book, 1994.
A collection of essays, some scholarly, others devotional, devoted to the life of Paul and the issues that arise surrounding him in Acts and his letters.

Sperry, Sidney B. *Paul's Life and Letters.* Salt Lake City: Bookcraft, 1955.
A classic Latter-day Saint treatment of Paul. It is heavily Protestant and somewhat outdated, but it is still useful, especially in its treatment of Paul's letters.

Wayment, Thomas A. *From Persecutor to Apostle: A Biography of Paul.* Salt Lake City: Deseret Book, 2006.

A highly readable biography of Paul written by a Latter-day Saint and New Testament scholar. It is the best place to start for readers looking for a one-volume treatment of Paul's life.

Other

Dunn, James D. G. *Christianity in the Making*, vol 2: *Beginning from Jerusalem*. Grand Rapids, MI: Eerdmans, 2009.

All three volumes in Dunn's *Christianity in the Making* series are must-reads, but this second volume masterfully navigates the primary and secondary literature on Paul to provide a cogent picture of Paul's role in the early Christian church.

Murphy-O'Connor, Jerome. *Paul: A Critical Life*. Oxford: Clarendon Press, 1996.

An engaging and provocative biography of Paul by an outstanding New Testament scholar. Readers looking for an academic treatment of Paul's life from a non–Latter-day Saint perspective should begin here.

Schnelle, Udo. *Apostle Paul: His Life and Theology*, trans. M. Eugene Boring. Grand Rapids, MI: Baker Academic Press, 2003.

A thorough treatment of Paul's life and thought for those who want something similar to Richard Lloyd Anderson's *Understanding Paul* but from a non–Latter-day Saint perspective.

Witherington III, Ben. *The Paul Quest: The Renewed Search for the Jew of Tarsus.* Downer's Grove, IL: InterVarsity Press, 1998.

Witherington brings together all the arguments and issues involved in the search for the "historical Paul." A useful resource for those wanting to know more about what can and cannot be said about Paul himself.

Chapter Seventeen

Peter and Paul in Antioch

GAYE STRATHEARN

"When Peter was come to Antioch, I withstood him to the face, because he was to be blamed. For before that certain came from James, he did eat with the Gentiles: but when they were come, he withdrew and separated himself, fearing them which were of the circumcision" (Galatians 2:11–12). So wrote the apostle Paul to the Galatian Saints. This passage is a difficult one. Just as ancient Saints were not comfortable with the public tension between Christianity's most prominent leaders, neither are modern Saints today.

Peter's importance comes from his close association with Jesus during his mortal ministry and his prominence among the Twelve as the chief apostle. In the Synoptic Gospels "he is always spokesperson for and representative of the disciples as a group,"[1] and as Acts opens, after Christ's Ascension, it is clear that Peter is the one leading out and shepherding the church. In contrast, Paul comes on the scene only after the Ascension. Not only does he play no role in Jesus's mortal ministry, but when he does first appear in Acts he is making "havoc of the church, entering into every house, and haling men and women committed them to prison" (Acts 8:3). Luke's decision in Acts to shift focus from Peter's ministry to that of Paul's has undoubtedly impacted the course of early Christian history. Paul's importance comes from the sheer weight of his writings that were collected into the canon and because he is arguably the one who most shapes the Christian message in a way that is both acceptable and enticing to the Gentile world.

Given the importance of both leaders, it can be difficult to understand what would cause Paul to publicly confront and question Peter's actions. Latter-day Saint commentators on this passage acknowledge the tension. In trying to explain it, sometimes Paul's actions are criticized,[2] but sometimes he is vindicated.[3] Generally, if addressed at all in Latter-day Saint writings, the passage is used to simply explain that leaders in the church can disagree,[4] but rarely is the passage analyzed in its Galatian context.

Frankly, there is no simple explanation for Galatians 2:11–12 because the incident is complicated by many issues, three of which we will try to address in this paper. First, Jesus's command to the apostles on the Mount of Olives to "be witnesses unto me both in Jerusalem, and in all Judea, and in Samaria, and unto the uttermost part of the earth" (Acts 1:8) exposed deep-seated tensions between Jews and gentiles, especially with respect to Israel's status as God's covenant people and the place of the law of Moses in the church as it began to expand its missionary work among the gentiles. The early church struggled to envision a church that proselyted both Jews and gentiles: how would the law of Moses function in such a church, and how would it impact Israel's calling as God's chosen people?

Second, the issue in Galatians 2:11–12 is further complicated because we only have access to one side of the story. The New Testament does not include Peter's perspective, only Paul's. It might be helpful, for example, if we had more information about questions such as the following: Why had Peter come to Antioch? What was the nature of the gathering? What was Peter thinking as "he withdrew and separated himself"? If we had Peter's side of the story, we might be able to gain a more balanced perspective of the event. Without his perspective we can only postulate possibilities.

Third, the issue is also compounded by the fact that Paul is clearly upset as he writes to the Galatian Saints because both his authority as an apostle and the gospel that he taught were under attack. This leaves modern readers trying to recreate the events and motives from an account that has a decided agenda, with rhetorical language that is sometimes used to heighten, rather than downplay, the tension.

The purpose of this paper, therefore, is to provide some context for Galatians 2 that may help modern readers better understand the relationship between Peter and Paul and why the issues were so important to them. In doing so we will first briefly overview the historical interaction between Jews and gentiles to understand the early church's reluctance to widen the scope of its missionary activities. Then we will discuss the Antioch incident in its larger Galatian context, which includes two other meetings between the two apostles: Paul's first visit to Jerusalem after his conversion (see Galatians 1:16–19) and the Jerusalem Council (see Galatians 2:1–10; Acts 15:1–11). While it is impossible, without further information, to come to a definitive and comfortable answer to explain the tension in Antioch, I will argue that the incident took place sometime after the Jerusalem Council but before the apostolic decree described in Acts 15:12–21. Therefore, while the issue of circumcision for gentiles had been decided by the Jerusalem Council, the issue of table fellowship, which is at the heart of the Antioch incident, had not been settled by the church. Therefore, I will argue that what we see in Galatians 2:11–14 is evidence of a theological debate between Peter and Paul that had not yet been decided by the church leadership.

Teaching All Nations

The tension in Galatians 2 is broader than the one incident between Peter and Paul; it is between two fundamentally different ways of interpreting Jesus's command on the Mount of Olives to expand their missionary activities beyond the house of Israel (see Matthew 28:19; Acts 1:8). This Olivet command must have raised some questions for the early church leaders and members; especially since Jesus, on calling the Twelve, had directly instructed them, "Go not into the way of the Gentiles, and into any city of the Samaritans enter ye not: but go rather to the lost sheep of the house of Israel" (Matthew 10:5–6). Historically and theologically, Abraham and his descendants, the house of Israel, had been called to enter into a covenant with God that *they* would be his covenant people. As part of that covenant, Abraham and his seed were promised two blessings that sometimes stood in tension with each other: that they would become "a great nation"

(Abraham 2:9) and that through them "all the families of the earth [would] be blessed" (Abraham 2:11; Genesis 12:3).

On the one hand, to make Israel into a great nation God required that Israel distance themselves from other nations in order to establish its geographical, political, and religious boundaries. At Mount Sinai, God reiterated that *they* would "be a peculiar treasure [i.e., a treasured possession; Hebrew *sĕgullāh*] unto me above all people, . . . a kingdom of priests, and an holy nation" (Exodus 19:5–6; 1 Peter 2:9). They were to be "the people of the Lord" (2 Samuel 1:12; Ezekiel 36:20), distinct from the other nations of the world. As they entered the promised land, God knew that the nations of Canaan would be a constant threat to the covenantal integrity of his chosen people (see Deuteronomy 12:1–3, 29–32). Therefore, they were directed not to marry outside of the covenant: "For they will turn away thy son from following me, that they may serve other gods" (Deuteronomy 7:4) and they were directed to "make no league with the inhabitants of this land" (Judges 2:2). Nevertheless, Israel always struggled with these commands and so the prophets routinely called them to repentance on this account.

Two watershed events heightened Israel's sense of isolation from the other nations: the Exile (ca. 597–538 BC) and the Maccabean Revolt (ca. 167–160 BC). Prior to the exile, "the identity of the people had been shaped and supported by a number of complementary factors—common territory, political loyalty, ethnic continuity, common language, religious observance, and tradition."[5] But during the exile, the people had to find ways to maintain their identity in a Gentile environment. Thus, their "religious tradition and observance assumed an ever greater role in maintaining distinctive identity."[6] They had to learn to "sing the Lord's song in a strange land" (Psalm 137:4). When they returned to Judea, Ezra and Nehemiah focused on establishing the social, religious, and political boundaries that separated the returnees from outsiders in an effort to reestablish a holy people (see Ezra 3–4, 9–10; Nehemiah 3–4; 8:1–8).

The second watershed event was the Maccabean Revolt. Alexander the Great had invaded Palestine militarily and culturally, and one of his successors attempted to unify the Seleucid kingdom under the banner of the worship of Zeus. This highlighted the tension between the desire to be a peculiar people and the yearning for acceptance among the other nations. The Maccabean Revolt championed religious independence, but it did not advocate cultural independence.[7] It did, however, force the Jews to identify what the core elements were that gave them their cultural and religious identity and enabled them to be a peculiar nation: worship at the temple, circumcision as the sign of the covenant, keeping the Sabbath day holy, and table fellowship.[8] The last of these, table fellowship, included not only the dietary restrictions outlined in Leviticus 11, but by the intertestamental period they were expanded to include elements of ritual purity.[9] As we will see, two of these elements, circumcision and table fellowship, will be issues central to the interactions between Peter and Paul. Table fellowship, in particular, created a wall of isolation for some Jews from gentiles, particularly those living in the diaspora. In a blessing reportedly given by Abraham to Jacob recorded in the *Book of Jubilees*, we read, "Separate yourself from the gentiles, and do not eat with them, and do not perform deeds like theirs. And do not become associates of theirs. Because their deeds are defiled, and all of their ways are contaminated, and despicable, and abominable" (22.16). Similarly, in the *Letter of Aristeas*, we read that Moses "surrounded us with unbroken palisades and iron walls to prevent our mixing with any of the other peoples in any matter. . . . So, to prevent our being perverted by contact with others or by mixing with bad influences, he hedged us in on all sides with strict observances connected with meat and drink and touch and hearing and sight, after the manner of the Law" (139, 142). Thus it is not surprising that Cicero, as an outsider, notes that in Rome the Jews stick together as a large, close-knit group (*Flaccus* 28.66).

In the Roman Empire, Jews were generally afforded freedom to practice their religion (Josephus, *Antiquities of the Jews* 19.288–90). But that did not mean that they were exempt from episodes of persecution. The emperors Tiberius and Claudius both ordered expulsions of Jews from Rome (*Antiquities of the Jews* 18.83–84; Acts 18:2).[10] Philo describes riots that took place in Alexandria in AD 38 because of the destruction of Jewish synagogues (*Flaccus* 41–54; *On the Embassy to Gaius* 132–37).[11] Undoubtedly these attacks from without only served to fuel their sense of religious isolationism, especially when living in the midst of gentile communities.

But we must not let these issues overshadow the very real efforts that Jews made to bless "all the families of the earth" (Abraham 2:11; Genesis 12:3; 28:14). Although God covenanted with Israel that they would be a peculiar people, the covenant was never intended to be an exclusive affair.[12]

Abraham left Haran with "the souls that they had gotten in Haran" (Genesis 12:5), and when Israel left Egypt "a mixed multitude went up also with them" (Exodus 12:38). Ruth, a Moabite, converted to the Abrahamic covenant through Naomi (see Ruth 1:16); Jonah was called to cry repentance to the inhabitants of Nineveh (see Jonah 1–4); and Isaiah prophetically declared that Israel would be "a light to the Gentiles" (49:6), that "the Gentiles shall come to thy light" (60:3), and that "the Gentiles shall see thy righteousness" (62:2).

During the intertestamental period there appears to be a heightened awareness of, and attraction to, Judaism by gentiles.[13] The antiquity of the religion and the ethical guidelines of the law of Moses were two characteristics that appealed to some gentiles.[14] Two Jewish writers, Josephus and Philo, make significant comments about Jewish proselytes. Josephus records that the Jews welcomed those who wished to adopt their laws (*Against Apion* 2.28) and that "the masses have long since shown a keen desire to adopt our religious observances" (*Against Apion* 2.39). Philo says that those who have chosen to follow a single creator must be looked upon "as our friends and kinsmen" (*On the Virtues* 33.179).[15] In part, this is because "those men . . . have left their country, and their friends, and their relations for the sake of virtue and holiness (Greek *hosiotēs*)" (*The Special Laws* 1.9.52). What is their motivation for conversion? According to Philo, it was because of their search for "the certainty and clearness of truth, and of the worship of the one true and living God" (*On the Virtues* 20.102).[16] In the New Testament, Jesus confirms that Jews actively proselyted converts. He declares that scribes and Pharisees "compass sea and land to make one proselyte" (Matthew 23:15).[17] Josephus also records the conversion of the royal house of Adiabene in the first century AD (*Antiquities of the Jews* 20.2.3–4).

In addition to proselytes to Judaism, we also find evidence for people who were attracted to Judaism, but who did not convert. Philo mentions proselytes who have not undergone circumcision and insists that they are not true converts (*Questions and Answers on Exodus* 2.2). Josephus, in describing those who sent contributions to the temple, makes a distinction between the "Jews throughout the habitable world" and "those who worshipped God" (Greek *sebomenōn ton theon*; *Antiquities of the Jews* 14.7.2). The same Greek phrase is also found in the New Testament to describe Lydia (see Acts 16:14) and Justus (see Acts 18:7). Another parallel New Testament phrase that seems to also describe gentiles who participate in Judaism to a limited degree is those who "fear God" (*phoboumenoi ton theon*; see Acts 10:2, 22, 35; 13:16, 26, 43, 50; 17:4, 17). Scholars sometimes identify this group of Jewish sympathizers with the technical term of "God-fearers,"[18] which may help us understand why two gentiles, the centurion and the Canaanite woman, could appeal to Jesus with such extraordinary faith (see Matthew 8:5–10; 15:21–28). Both the proselytes and the God-fearers seem to have been a fruitful source for early Christian missionary activity.

In summary, the Abrahamic covenant was designed to accomplish two tasks: to create a peculiar and holy people who would become a great nation and to bless all the nations of the earth. This brief sketch of Israelite and Jewish history highlights that there was sometimes a pulsating tension between these two goals. At times an emphasis on the first goal overshadowed the importance of the second, but in the intertestamental period we see the planting of seeds that would mature to harvest in the New Testament. Although there is no evidence for an organized, large-scale Jewish program of proselyting, there is evidence to suggest that missionary work did exist on some level (see Matthew 23:15).[19]

When the resurrected Jesus stood on the Mount of Olives and gave his command to take the gospel to all the world, he initiated a major shift in direction for the early church. Given the evidence in Acts, it is fair to say that the church and its leaders struggled to comprehend and act upon the new direction. The Twelve, as represented by Peter and John, did not immediately respond. Rather they continued to concentrate their missionary work among the Jews, particularly those that they found in and around the temple precinct (see Acts 2; 3:11–26; 4:1–22; 5:12–16, 19–21, 27–42).

Two events seemed to shift the momentum. The first event was Saul's persecution of Christians after the death of Stephen. This persecution forced Christians to be "scattered abroad" and, as a result, they "went every where preaching the word" (Acts 8:4). In particular, Acts represents this expansion with the work of Philip among the Samaritans and with the Ethiopian eunuch (see Acts 8:5–40). The second event was Peter's vision of the unclean animals that he reluctantly received in Joppa and that led to him teaching the Roman centurion Cornelius and his household (see Acts 10:9–48). What is significant about the results of both of these events is that the missionary work only expanded to those who already had a relationship with

Israel: the Samaritans who had a connection with Israelite religion and lived the law of Moses (although not the oral law), a eunuch who was probably a proselyte because he was returning home after worshipping in Jerusalem (Acts 8:27–28), and the God-fearer Cornelius, "a devout man, and one that feared God [*phoboumenoi ton theon*] with all his house, which gave much alms to the people, and prayed to God alway" (Acts 10:2). The reaction of the Jerusalem church to these missionary endeavors was mixed. Apparently they approved of Philip's work among the Samaritans, because Peter and John came down and conferred the Holy Ghost upon the converts (see Acts 8:14–17).

Unfortunately, Acts is silent on the reaction of the Jerusalem church to the conversion of the eunuch. However, they react heatedly to the news of Peter's dealings with Cornelius: "And when Peter was come up to Jerusalem, they that were of the circumcision contended with him, saying, thou wentest in to men uncircumcised, and didst eat with them" (Acts 11:2–3). This reaction of the Jerusalem church focuses on two of the four elements that, as we have seen, were identified as the key essentials in Jewish cultural and religious identity. Circumcision and table fellowship are also the two issues that are at the very heart of the tension between Peter and Paul in Antioch and evoked important questions for the early church. For example, not only did the early leaders and members struggle to envision a church that included both Jews and gentiles, they also struggled with the questions of the doctrinal and practical implications of gentiles becoming part of the seed of Abraham. The command on the Mount of Olives and Peter's vision to include gentiles in the missionary work, however, did not give specific instructions for how it was to be carried out. Paul's missionary work "to bear [Christ's] name before the Gentiles" (Acts 9:15) brought the issue to a head, and Antioch became the test case for two competing approaches.

Peter and Paul in the Epistle to the Galatians

Paul wrote to the Galatians in response to charges against him by Christian missionaries who had come to Galatia with a very different approach to the gentile mission. Although he never specifically mentions their charges, we can get a pretty good sense of them because of the issues Paul chose to address in his response. The three overarching concerns in the epistle seem to center on the issues of Paul's authority and the gospel, how gentiles *become* a part of the seed of Abraham, and how they then *live* within the covenant.

Scholars generally identify Paul's opponents in Galatia as a group of Jewish Christians, known as Judaizers, who insisted that gentiles enter the church through the law of Moses. As we have seen in Acts, the Judaizers' approach probably represents the church's earliest interpretation of the Olivet command. From their perspective they were continuing the established method of proselyting gentiles who were already attracted to Judaism. Paul's earliest missionary endeavors seem to be situated within this same paradigm: when he entered into a new city at the beginning of his first missionary journey he went and taught in the synagogue. There he was able to address both Jews and those who "fear God" (*phoboumenoi ton theon*; Acts 13:16, 26). But by Acts 13:46–47, Paul shifted his missionary focus to the gentiles. Acts does not provide us with the specific details of how that shift in focus impacted his preaching. At the end of that first mission, however, Christian missionaries from Jerusalem (probably Judaizers) came to Antioch criticizing him for not requiring the Gentile converts to be circumcised (see 15:1). The result was "no small dissension and disputation with them" (15:2), meaning that there was major contention over the issue.

Similar conflict over Paul's missionary work with the gentiles is again a prominent concern underlying his epistle to the Galatians. That there is an added criticism of his apostolic authority seems certain given Paul's opening declaration: "Paul, an apostle, (not of men, neither by man, but by Jesus Christ, and God the Father, who raised him from the dead)" (Galatians 1:1).[20] In no other epistle does Paul immediately begin with a justification for his apostolic authority. Generally he simply acknowledges that he was "called to be an apostle" (Romans 1:1), sometimes adding the statement "through the will of God" (1 Corinthians 1:1; 2 Corinthians 1:1; Ephesians 1:1; Colossians 1:1; 2 Timothy 1:1). The criticism by Paul's opponents in Galatia, however, is not just about his apostleship. The question of authority is directly tied to the gospel that he taught. With language that is closely tied to the opening verse, Paul also defends the veracity of his gospel message:

"But I certify you, brethren, that the gospel which was preached of me is not after man. For I neither received it of man, neither was I taught it, but by the revelation of Jesus Christ" (Galatians 1:11–12).

Paul's feelings about the attack on his authority and the gospel are reflected in his pejorative choice of words to describe the situation in Galatia. He argued that "false brethren" (Galatians 2:4) had "bewitched" (Galatians 3:1) the Galatian churches, and he fears that he has become their enemy (Galatians 4:16). It is therefore not surprising that immediately after his opening salutation he forgoes his usual thanksgiving and immediately writes:

> I marvel that ye are so soon removed from him that called you into the grace of Christ unto another gospel:
>
> Which is not another; but there be some that trouble you, and would pervert the gospel of Christ.
>
> But though we, or an angel from heaven, preach any other gospel unto you than that which we have preached unto you, let him be accursed.
>
> As we said before, so say I now again, If any man preach any other gospel unto you than that ye have received, let him be accursed.
>
> For do I now persuade men, or God? or do I seek to please men? for if I yet pleased men, I should not be the servant of Christ. (Galatians 1:6–10)

The more specific issues from the law of Moses that the Judaizers seem to be pushing in both Galatia and Antioch, and that Paul is opposing, is that the church, and all who join it, should continue the practices of circumcision and table fellowship. Remember that these practices were two of the four core elements that enabled Jews to live in a gentile world while still maintaining their religious covenantal identity. From the Judaizers' perspective, Paul's missionary efforts, if unchecked, placed their very identity in jeopardy.

In responding to these accusations, Paul makes reference to three meetings that he had with Peter: two in Jerusalem and one in Antioch. Even though all of these meetings occur outside of Galatia, it is clear that Paul believes that they have a bearing on the argument that he will make to the Galatians. In appealing to these three meetings, it is also clear that there is an underlying tension in the rhetoric of Paul's description of them. On the one hand, he specifically meets with Peter (and James) when he travels to Jerusalem some three years after his conversion (see Galatians 1:17–19); he also acknowledges the importance of Peter, James and John as pillars of the church (see 2:9); and he seeks their approval for his missionary activities among the gentiles (see 2:9). Yet, on the other hand, he is quick to remind his opponents that "they [Peter, James, and John] . . . added nothing to me" (2:6), and, in fact as we have noted, in Antioch he "withstood [Peter] to the face, because he was to be blamed" (Galatians 2:11).

In recounting Paul's first visit with Peter (Galatians 1:15–19), he seems to be trying to correct "possible misperceptions . . . as to where [he] got his Gospel and how much contact he may have had with the Jerusalem authorities."[21] Paul writes that "it pleased God, who separated me from my mother's womb, and called me by his grace, to reveal his Son in me, that I might preach him among the [Gentiles]" (Greek *ethnoi*; Galatians 1:15–16). Paul addresses the concern about his authority in two ways. First, he uses language that hearkens back to Jeremiah 1:4–5. In doing so, Paul implies that he, like Jeremiah, was foreordained to his call. Second, by referring to his revelatory experience on the road to Damascus, he reminds his audience that his call to preach came directly from the resurrected Jesus.

Paul then insists that "immediately I conferred not with flesh and blood: Neither went I up to Jerusalem to them which were apostles before me; but I went into Arabia, and returned again unto Damascus" (Galatians 1:16–17). His point is that just because his contact with the Jerusalem authorities was limited, it did not weaken his authority to teach the gentiles because his authority did not come from humans, but from God. In making this claim it is important to note that here Paul is not attacking Peter and the other apostles. Rather, he acknowledges that there were people in Jerusalem who had been apostles before him, and as one scholar has noted, "He does not call them so-called or pseudo-apostles (contrast 2 Cor. 11:13), there is no pejorative tone to this mention of these persons. . . . [Rather,] this is a tacit admission of the legitimacy of these persons, and that they had a certain pre-eminence over Paul as authorities having been commissioned before Paul."[22]

In some important ways, however, Paul was not like Peter and the other apostles; he did not come through the same ranks, so to speak.[23] For example, Paul did not meet all of the requirements that were established in Acts 1:21–22 for a person to fill the vacancy in the Twelve: He had not "companied with [the other disciples] all the time that the Lord Jesus went in and out among us, Beginning from the baptism of John, unto that same day that [Jesus] was taken up from us." His experience on the road to Damascus, however, did qualify him for the second requirement: "one of these must become a witness with us to his resurrection" (Acts 1:22 NRSV).

Since Paul often uses the language of his opponents' rhetoric,[24] perhaps one of their issues that they had against him was that he didn't qualify as an apostle because he had not been associated with Jesus's ministry from the beginning, and therefore, his brand of missionary work among the gentiles was invalid. Paul's response is that he received his authority directly from God, not from any human, not even from Peter. When eventually he did go to Jerusalem, not until three years after his conversion, he went to get the "history" (Greek *historeō*) from Peter. The Greek word *historeō* can mean that he went to meet Peter, probably because Paul recognized his status as a pillar in the early church, but the fact that he stayed with him for fifteen days suggests that he also went to get information from him. Perhaps that information included, among other things, Peter's reminiscences of Jesus's ministry. While in Jerusalem, Paul also met with James, the Lord's brother. This visit suggests that Paul also recognized James's importance in the Jerusalem church. But he is quick to note, "But other of the apostles saw I none" (Galatians 1:19). In other words, Paul acknowledges the importance of Peter and James, but his point is that his authority did not come from them; it came because of the revelation that he had experienced on the road to Damascus.

Whereas chapter 1 focuses on Paul's personal credibility, chapter 2 describes his second visit to Jerusalem (Galatians 2:1–10), but this time the focus is on the credibility of his gospel message to the gentiles.[25] Unfortunately, the nature and timing of this visit is the subject of considerable scholarly debate. Paul writes, "Then fourteen years after I went up again to Jerusalem with Barnabas, and took Titus with me also" (2:1). The text is unclear as to whether this date was fourteen years after his conversion or after his first visit to Jerusalem. In addition, there is considerable debate over whether this account refers to the Jerusalem Council that Luke describes in Acts 15.[26] There are some significant parallels. Both the Jerusalem Council and the meeting described in Galatians 2 are the result of people criticizing Paul's missionary activities among the gentiles; in both, the issue centers on Paul not requiring gentiles to be circumcised; both accounts include the same major players: Paul, Barnabas, Peter, James, and the Judaizers; both deal with issues of how gentiles join the church; both conclude that circumcision is not required for gentiles to become members of the church; and both agree that this issue involved participation in the Christian church and had nothing to do with "the relationship between non-Christian Jews and Christians"[27] (see Galatians 2:1–10; Acts 15:1–11).

Certainly, there are also some differences in the two accounts,[28] something that we would expect given that Luke and Paul have very different agendas for recording their accounts. Since Galatians 2 reflects a firsthand account of the events, its details should be given priority, when necessary, over Luke's secondhand account. Some of the unique material that Paul includes in Galatians 2, but is missing in Acts 15, is that he and Barnabas took Titus with them to Jerusalem (Galatians 2:1). Titus becomes an important living witness that a gentile could be an acceptable member of the church without being circumcised.[29] The passive voice in Galatians 2:3 opens the possibility to infer from this verse that neither Paul nor the Jerusalem authorities required that he be circumcised. In addition, Paul indicates that he went up to Jerusalem by revelation, which again reminds readers that his call in Galatians 1:16 continues to be the undergirding moving force of his missionary work.[30] Such a statement does not need to be, as some have argued, a conflict with the account in Acts that they went because of the dispute with those who "came down from Judea" (15:1).[31]

Paul notes two outcomes of this meeting. First, the conference decided that the church would have two parallel missions: "the gospel of the uncircumcision" over which Paul and Barnabas would have stewardship, and "the gospel of the circumcision" over which Peter was given stewardship (Galatians 2:7). There is nothing in this verse to indicate that Paul considered "the gospel of the circumcision" to be "another gospel" which "would pervert the gospel of Christ" (1:6–7) that he strongly objects to in chapter 1. Rather, Galatians 2:7 indicates that Peter, Paul, and Barnabas were united in their missionary efforts, although they recognized that their approaches would have different emphases according to their audience. In addition, we should note that this verse does not necessarily mean that their responsibilities were exclusive to the mission over which they had stewardship. Paul's commission by the Savior was that he was "a chosen vessel unto me, to bear my name before the Gentiles, and kings, and the children of Israel" (Acts 9:15), and in his letter to the Romans he notes, "Brethren, my heart's desire and prayer to God for Israel is, that they might be saved" (Romans 10:1). Likewise, it appears that Peter was active in gentile locations such as Antioch, where he was eating with gentile members and also gained some missionary converts in Corinth (1 Corinthians 1:12).

Second, Paul notes that "James, Cephas [Peter], and John,"[32] who he acknowledges are recognized (Greek *dokeō*) as "pillars, perceived the grace that was given unto me, they gave to me and Barnabas the right hands of fellowship; that we should go unto the Gentiles [Greek *ethnoi*], and they unto the circumcision" (Galatians 2:9). Paul's point in verse 6 that the Jerusalem leadership "added nothing to me," in the context of verse 9, indicates that, unlike the "false brethren" of verse 4, they did not want to change Paul's methods or insist that gentiles had to do any more than Paul and Barnabas required of them. The only exception was that the gentiles should remember the poor,[33] which Paul says he was eager to do (Greek *ho kai espoudasa auto touto poiēsai*) (1:10). Instead, James, Peter, and John gave them the "right hands of fellowship" (2:9). Thus Paul's second visit with Peter, like the first, was amicable. Paul recognized the status of Peter as one of the leading apostles in Jerusalem and came seeking his seal of approval on Paul's missionary work.

The question then remains, if on the Mount of Olives Jesus gave the command to teach the gospel to all the world, why did it take around fifteen years for the church in Jerusalem to come to a decision on how gentiles were to join the church? The simple answer is that the issue would have had a higher priority for the church in Antioch than it would have for the church in Jerusalem. The evidence in the New Testament suggests that the church in Jerusalem consisted predominantly of Jewish Christians, people who were already living the law of Moses, and who continued to live it even after their conversion to Christianity (see Acts 21:20). Christian Jews continued to worship at the temple (see 21:23–26) and at the synagogue (see 9:20; 13:5, 14–15; 14:1; 17:1–17; 18:4, 7, 19; 19:8), to participate in the Jewish festivals of Passover (see 18:21) and Pentecost (see Acts 2:1; 20:16; 1 Corinthians 16:8), and to make Jewish vows (see Acts 18:18).

For all intents and purposes, Christianity was initially viewed as just another one of the varieties of Judaism.[34] That's certainly how Saul viewed it as he embarked on his persecutions. In Antioch, however, the situation would have quickly become very different. Although the Christian congregation there began within the synagogue, the city was predominantly gentile, and the converts to the church eventually were attracted from outside the sphere of the synagogue and the gentile proselytes and God-fearers. But it wasn't until Judaizers came from Jerusalem the first time that the status quo was upset. The Jerusalem Council settled the issue of how gentiles should *enter* the church: gentiles did not need to be circumcised, but it did not address the question of how gentiles should live *in* the church. That issue came to a head when the Judaizers came to Antioch a second time.

Paul now moves to address his third meeting with Peter, this time in Antioch. He claims that the reason that he "withstood [Peter] to the face" was because "before that certain came from James, he did eat with the gentiles: but when they were come, he withdrew and separated himself, fearing them which were of the circumcision." Even more problematical in Paul's eyes was that "the other Jews [played the hypocrite (Greek *sunupekrithēsan*)] likewise with him; insomuch that Barnabas also was carried away with their [hypocrisy (Greek *hypokrisei*)]" (Galatians 2:11–13). Therefore, Paul confronted Peter, "But when I saw that they walked not uprightly according to the truth of the gospel, I said unto Peter before them all, If thou, being a Jew, livest after the manner of Gentiles, and not as do the Jews, why compellest thou the Gentiles to live as do the Jews?" (Galatians 2:14).

At the heart of the tension between Peter and Paul on this occasion was the issue of table fellowship. It seems clear that initially Peter had no reservations about eating with gentiles, and the imperfect tense of the verb "did eat" (Greek *sunēsthien*) suggests that his actions were not a once-off event but had taken place over a period of time. Such an understanding corresponds with Peter's experience with Cornelius in Acts 10 and the general statement that he gave at the Jerusalem Council, "Now therefore why tempt ye God, to put a yoke [i.e., the law of Moses] upon the neck of the disciples, which neither our fathers nor we were able to bear? But we believe that through the grace of the Lord Jesus Christ we shall be saved, even as they" (Acts 15:10–11). Paul does not tell us what the men from James said or did that caused Peter to withdraw, but it seems certain that they disapproved of his eating with gentiles, just as the Jerusalem church had when they heard that he had done likewise with Cornelius and his household (see Galatians 2:12; Acts 11:1–3).

Again, we reiterate that any understanding of this incident is limited because we do not have access to Peter's side of the story. Nevertheless, we can say a few things. First, it seems likely that the men from James came to Antioch insisting on a strict separation of "the gospel of the circumcision" and "the gospel of the uncircumcision" that had been established at the Jerusalem Council. Thus, they would have argued that Peter should continue to live the law of Moses, as did the Christians in Jerusalem.[35] Peter may have felt that his actions to withdraw from the meal would alleviate the tension, at least on the part of the Judaizers. Perhaps he felt that he needed to do what Paul claimed for himself: "And unto the Jews I became as a Jew, that I might gain the Jews; to them that are under the law, as under the law, that I might gain them that are under the law" (1 Corinthians 9:20).[36] After all, at one point Paul seemed to have done likewise when he had Timothy circumcised "because of the Jews" (Acts 16:1–3).

Second, the imperfect tense of the verbs "withdrew" (Greek *hypestellen*) and "separated himself" (Greek *apōrizen*) indicates that Peter's withdrawal and separation was done over a period of time. Perhaps this indicates that Peter came to the realization that to maintain the unity of the church the separation of the two missions should indeed be maintained and that he should focus on his particular stewardship.

Third, it seems to me that the best way of understanding the account of the Jerusalem Council in both Galatians 2 and Acts 15 is to recognize that the Lukan account conflates two different meetings: the first of which, where Peter presided, dealt with the issue of circumcision of gentiles, and that the second, where James seems to be in charge, dealt with the issue of table fellowship.[37] This reading helps a number of issues. For example, it explains why Peter seems to be in charge in Acts 15:6–11 but then falls into the background when James delivers the apostolic decree in Acts 15:13–19. It also helps us understand why Paul makes no reference to the apostolic decree when he confronts Peter in Galatians 2:11–14. Lastly, it also helps us understand James' comment in Acts 15:24, "Forasmuch as we have heard, that certain which went out from us have troubled you with words, subverting your souls, saying, Ye must be circumcised, and keep the law: to whom we gave no such commandment." Acts 15 indicates that Paul's opponents "came down from Judea" (Acts 15:1). There is no mention of their relationship with James; that is found only in Galatians 2. If this reading is correct, then the crisis in Antioch precipitated a return to Jerusalem where the matter would be sorted out by James, since the Judaizers were claiming their authority through him. Therefore Peter's actions in Antioch, Paul's response notwithstanding, would *not* have been a betrayal of guidelines already established by the church. Rather they would simply be evidence of the ongoing development of the church to understand, line upon line, the practical implications of Jesus's direction to take the gospel to all the world.

So why was Paul so angered over this incident in Antioch, especially since his two previous meetings with Peter had been both cordial and amicable, with Paul implicitly acknowledging Peter's position? Again, there are a number of factors that we should consider. First, we must recognize the tone of Paul's letter to the Galatians. The lack of any kind of thanksgiving section, which he normally includes after his salutation, suggests that Paul is upset as he pens this epistle.[38] Second, the reason for Paul writing this epistle is that members in the Galatian churches are in a situation where they are returning to a law-observant understanding of the Christian message. Thus Paul implores them, "Stand fast therefore in the liberty wherewith Christ hath made us free, and be not entangled again with the yoke of bondage," which he understands to be the law of Moses (Galatians 5:1). I have argued elsewhere that this situation is best understood if the Galatian churches consist predominantly of gentile God-fearers who, prior to being taught the gospel by Paul, were already attracted to the law of Moses.[39] These were Paul's converts. He had taught them that the Christian message is founded on Christ's grace, which is now incompatible with the law of Moses. True, the law was indeed a "schoolmaster to bring us unto Christ," but only so that they could be made righteous or justified by faith (3:24). Paul himself had been "more exceedingly zealous of the traditions of my fathers" than "my equals in mine own nation" (1:14). He had lived the law as well as it was possible for a human to do so, but it was God's grace, not the law, that led to his revelation on the road to Damascus and his conversion. In Paul's mind, Peter's actions at Antioch were a type of what the Saints in Galatia were doing: having received the gospel that comes through Christ's grace, they were trying to turn back to their old ways of understanding God, ways that were not consistent with "the truth of the gospel" (2:5). It is possible that Paul's language in describing this incident is so strong because his opponents were using Peter's actions as evidence that the Galatians should also return to a law-observant understanding of the Christian message. The whole message of Galatians is that all people, both Jew and gentile, are made righteous through the faith of Jesus Christ and not, as the Judaizers argued, through the law of Moses (see 2:16). According to Paul, the Christian approach to inviting gentiles into the kingdom of God was meant to be very different from the Jewish approach. Clearly, Paul had strong feelings on this topic, and it may well be that, in an effort to convince his readers that they were headed in the wrong direction, he intentionally employed rhetoric that heightened the tension of the Antioch incident.

Conclusion

Paul's account of the incident at Antioch is part of a larger rhetorical effort to crush the inroads that Judaizers were making in the churches in Galatia. His description has troubled readers who are uncomfortable with such tension between the early church's most influential leaders. While not explicitly referring to the incident at Antioch, the Petrine epistles make a significant effort to emphasize the unity between Peter and Paul. The epilogue of 1 Peter (5:12–13) includes the names of two individuals who are known to be missionary companions of Paul: Silvanus (see 2 Corinthians 1:19; 1 Thessalonians 1:1; 2 Thessalonians 1:1) and Marcus (see Acts 13:13; 15:37; Colossians 4:10). The inclusion of these two individuals emphasizes the ties (rather than any rift) between the Pauline and Petrine missionary efforts. In 2 Peter 3:15–16, Paul is described as "our beloved brother," and his epistles, although they are described as having "some things [which are] hard to be understood," are judged to be equivalent to scripture.

The incident in Antioch is a reminder that history, even religious or sacred history, is rarely neat and straightforward. Even though the resurrected Jesus directed his apostles to expand the missionary work to take the gospel to all the world, the early church clearly struggled to grasp and comprehend all of the implications of such a command. Paul's account in Galatians 2 reminds us that leaders of the church, even after receiving revelation, must still wrestle with complex doctrinal issues. As Elder Bruce R. McConkie taught, even though Peter received a revelation and opened the door for missionary work among the gentiles, "there would yet be difficult doctrinal, administrative, and procedural problems to be solved."[40]

Gaye Strathearn is a professor of ancient scripture at Brigham Young University.

Gaye Strathearn, "Peter and Paul in Antioch," in *The Ministry of Peter, the Chief Apostle*, ed. Frank F. Judd Jr., Eric D. Huntsman, and Shon D. Hopkin (Provo, UT: Religious Studies Center; Salt Lake City: Deseret Book, 2014), 227–46.

NOTES

1. Pheme Perkins, *Peter: Apostle for the Whole Church* (Minneapolis: Fortress Press, 2000), 20.
2. For example, in 1853 Jedediah M. Grant wrote, "But if you pass on in their history to seek for uniformity and beauty, you will find some grand flare-ups among them. Look, for instance, at Paul and Peter, disputing and quarrelling with each other [2 Peter 3:15–16; Galatians 2:11]; and Paul and Barnabas contending, and parting asunder with angry feelings [Acts 15:36–41]. 'When Peter came to Antioch,' says Paul, 'I withstood him to the face, because he was to be blamed,' [Galatians 2:11] &c. Paul does not gain much credit with the Mormons for taking this course. We know he had no right to rebuke Peter; but some man said he was like Almon Babbit, *he wanted to boast of rebuking Peter*. He thought it was a feather in his cap because he coped with Peter and rebuked him. Had that affair come before a 'Mormon' tribunal, they would have decided in favor of Peter and against Paul. We believe when Paul rebuked Peter, he had in him a spirit of rebellion, and was decidedly wrong in rebelling against the man who held the keys of the kingdom of God on the earth." In *Journal of Discourses*, 26 vols. (London: Latter-day Saints' Book Depot, 1854–86), 1:346.
3. Bruce R. McConkie, *Doctrinal New Testament Commentary*, 3 vols. (Salt Lake City: Bookcraft, 1971), 2:463–64.
4. D. Kelly Ogden and Andrew C. Skinner, *New Testament: Apostles Testify of Christ: A Guide for Acts through Revelation* (Salt Lake City: Deseret Book, 1998), 161.
5. John J. Collins, *Between Athens and Jerusalem: Jewish Identity in the Hellenistic Diaspora*, 2nd ed. (Grand Rapids, MI: Eerdmans, 2000), 1.
6. Collins, *Between Athens and Jerusalem*, 1.
7. The Maccabean rulers appropriated many Greek cultural traits. They adopted Greek names, their burial monuments and graves "reflect a significant appropriation of Hellenistic forms," their coins begin to have both Greek and Hebrew inscriptions and symbols, and the literature of the time, even if the text berates Hellenism, often reflects strong Greek stylistic influence (e.g., 1 & 2 Maccabees). For a further discussion, see L. Levine,

"Hasmonean Jerusalem: A Jewish City in a Hellenistic Orbit," *Judaism* 46, no. 2 (1997): 143–46.

8. See the account in 2 Maccabees 6, where Jews revolt against the edict of Antiochus outlawing the practice of Judaism by openly displaying their loyalty to these four aspects of Judaism. In the decree of Sardis, Jewish citizens are afforded the right to meet together to offer prayers and sacrifices to their God, and market officials are directed to have "suitable food for them brought in." *Antiquities of the Jews* 14.259–61. Josephus also records Caesar Augustus's decree that Jewish monies sent to the temple are inviolable and that they are exempt from appearing in court on the Sabbath or Sabbath eve. *Antiquities of the Jews* 16.6.1–8. Cicero says that each year Jews from Italy sent gold to the temple in Jerusalem. *Pro Flacco* 28.66–69; see also Tacitus, *Histories* 5.5. In addition, as we will see, the New Testament shows that for Judaizers, the main areas for concern about letting gentiles join the Church center around circumcision (see Acts 15:1; Galatians 5:1–13) and eating with gentiles (see Acts 11:3; Galatians 2:11–13). Worship on the Sabbath does not appear to be an issue because the early Christians continued to participate in the synagogue on the Sabbath and then added their service on Sunday. In addition, the early Christians continued to worship at the temple (Acts 21:23–26). For a discussion on pagan attacks on Jewish circumcision, Sabbath observance, and dietary laws, see Louis H. Feldman, *Jew and Gentile in the Ancient World: Attitudes and Interactions from Alexander to Justininian* (Princeton, NJ: Princeton University Press, 1993), 153–70.
9. See James D. G. Dunn, "The Incident at Antioch (Gal. 2:11–18)," *Journal for the Study of the New Testament* 5, no. 3 (1983): 12–25.
10. The reference in Acts 18 aligns well with the account of a Roman writer, Suetonius: "Since the Jews constantly made disturbances at the instigation of Chrestus [probably a misspelling for Christos], he expelled them from Rome." *Claudius* 25.4.
11. Dunn, "Incident at Antioch," 7–11.
12. For a discussion of early Jewish proselytism, see Feldman, *Jew and Gentile*, 288–341.
13. Tacitus records that proselytes "increase their [i.e., the Jews'] numbers." *Histories* 5.5.
14. Emile Schürer, *The History of the Jewish People in the Age of Jesus Christ*, 3 vols., rev. & ed. Geza Vermes, Fergus Millar, and Martin Goodman (Edinburgh: T&T Clark, 1986), 3.1:150–76.
15. Unless noted otherwise, all Philo quotations are from *The Works of Philo: Complete and Unabridged; New Updated Version*, trans. C. D. Yonge (Peabody, MA: Hendrickson Publishers, 1993).
16. We find the most detailed description of a conversion to Judaism in a late apocryphal work entitled *Joseph and Aseneth* (third–fourth centuries AD). The impetus for Aseneth's conversion is meeting Joseph and realizing that he is not interested in marrying anyone who does not share his religious beliefs. The account, however, goes to great length to show that Aseneth's conversion is spiritual in nature.
17. The only specific extracanonical evidence for "an organized Jewish proselytizing campaign is found in the policies of the Hasmoneans toward the Idumeans and Itureans in the late second century B.C.E." Collins, *Between Athens and Jerusalem*, 262.
18. There is some debate whether the term *God-fearers* is a technical term for a well-defined class of gentiles that were connected with the synagogue. The evidence suggests that there were many levels of attachment. For careful discussions on issues, see Feldman, *Jew and Gentile*, 342–82, and Collins, *Between Athens and Jerusalem*, 264–72.
19. An opposing view is found in Dieter Georgi, *Opponents of Paul in Second Corinthians* (Philadelphia: Fortress Press, 1986), 84, 175n1.

20. To the Corinthians, Paul declared, "for in nothing am I behind the very chiefest apostles, though I be nothing" (2 Corinthians 12:11). The question of Paul's apostolic authority is complex. On the one hand, the Biblical text does not give any specific information of when he was called to be an apostle. In Acts, Luke first calls him an apostle when he was at Lystra during his first missionary journey (Acts 14:14). On the other hand, the New Testament uses the word apostle (Greek *apostolos*) in different ways. The basic meaning of *apostolos* is "messenger," and the New Testament uses it in this sense, particularly when talking about messengers who are sent out representing various branches of the church (e.g., Philippians 2:25). Sometimes the New Testament uses it in the sense of a priesthood office that is synonymous with the Twelve (Acts 1:21–26), but sometimes the Twelve and the apostles seem to be two different groups (1 Corinthians 15:5–7). On one occasion Paul refers to a woman, Junia, who is "of note among the apostles" (Romans 16:7). It seems certain that Paul's opponents in Galatia did not recognize Paul as an apostle on the same level as Peter and the other apostles. Paul's point here is that his apostolic authority came directly from Christ himself.
21. Ben Witherington, *Grace in Galatia: A Commentary on Paul's Letter to the Galatians* (Grand Rapids, MI: Eerdmans, 1998), 96.
22. Witherington, *Grace in Galatia*, 116.
23. This is a fact that Paul readily admits in his epistle to the Corinthians. He describes himself as "the least of the apostles, that am not meet to be called an apostle, because I persecuted the church of God" (1 Corinthians 15:9).
24. Paul writes his letters in response to specific events that are taking place in the respective church communities. Scholars have long noted that in Paul's Corinthian epistles he uses slogans from his opponents' rhetoric. For an example, see Denny Burk, "Discerning Corinthian Slogans through Paul's Use of the Diatribe in 1 Corinthians 6:12–20," *Bulletin for Biblical Research* 18, no. 1 (2008): 99–121. It is therefore not unreasonable to assume that he may also have included the stories of his interactions with Peter to correct misinformation that his opponents are disseminating about Paul's relationship with Peter.
25. B. R. Gaventa, "Galatians 1 and 2: Autobiography as Paradigm," *Novum Testamentum* 28, no. 4 (1986): 316–17.
26. For examples of those who argue for two different events, see Witherington, *Grace in Galatia*, 15. See also the discussions in F. F. Bruce, *The Epistle to the Galatians*, The New International Greek Testament Commentary (Grand Rapids, MI: Eerdmans, 1982), 106–27; Joe Morgado Jr., "Paul in Jerusalem: A Comparison of His Visits in Acts and Galatians," *Journal of the Evangelical Theological Society* (March 1994): 55–68. See also Richard Neitzel Holzapfel, Eric D. Huntsman, and Thomas A. Wayment, *Jesus Christ and the World of the New Testament: An Illustrated Reference for Latter-day Saints* (Salt Lake City: Deseret Book, 2006), 216–17.
27. Witherington, *Grace in Galatia*, 14; Richard Lloyd Anderson, *Understanding Paul* (Salt Lake City: Deseret Book, 1983), 156.
28. Witherington, *Grace in Galatia*, 15. See also the discussions in Bruce, *The Epistle to the Galatians*, 106–27; Morgado, "Paul in Jerusalem," 55–68.
29. Hans Dieter Betz, *Galatians*, Hermeneia (Philadelphia: Fortress Press, 1979), 88–89.
30. Gaventa, *Galatians 1 and 2*, 316.
31. For examples of those who see Paul's statement in verse 2 as a reason to separate the two accounts, see Witherington, *Grace in Galatia*, 15; Morgado, "Paul in Jerusalem," 61–62.

32. Bart Ehrman argues that the Cephas in Galatians 2:9 refers to someone other than Peter. "Cephas and Peter," *Journal of Biblical Literature* 109, no. 3 (1990): 463–74. For a response to his arguments, see Dale C. Allison Jr., "Peter and Cephas: One and the Same," *Journal of Biblical Literature* 111, no. 3 (1992): 489–95.
33. This verse is the genesis for the collection that Paul encourages the Gentile converts to contribute to in order to help the poor saints in Jerusalem (1 Corinthians 16:1–3; 2 Corinthians 8:1–11; 9:1–12; Romans 15:25–27).
34. James D. G. Dunn, *Unity and Diversity in the New Testament: An Inquiry into the Character of Earliest Christianity*, 3rd ed. (London: SCM, 2006), 255–57; Lawrence H. Schiffman, "At the Crossroads: Tannaitic Perspectives on the Jewish-Christian Schism," in *Jewish and Christian Self-Definition*, vol. 2, *Aspects of Judaism in the Graeco-Roman Period*, ed. E. P. Sanders (London: SCM, 1981), 115–56.
35. Betz, *Galatians*, 108.
36. Tertullian, *Against Marcion*, 1.20, in *Tertullian, Adversus Marcionem*, ed. Ernest Evans (London: Oxford, 1972), 51–53.
37. Dunn, "The Incident at Antioch," 38. Latter-day Saint descriptions of the Jerusalem Conference generally assume that Acts 15:6–35 refers to a single event. For examples, see Robert J. Matthews, "The Jerusalem Council," in *The Apostle Paul: His Life and His Testimony* (Salt Lake City: Deseret Book, 1994), 96–109; Wayment, *From Persecutor to Apostle*, 93–104; Jared Ludlow, "The Book of Acts: A Pattern for Modern Church Growth," in *Shedding Light on the New Testament: Acts–Revelation*, ed. Ray L. Huntington, Frank F. Judd Jr., and David M. Whitchurch (Provo, UT: Religious Studies Center, 2009), 22–24; Richard Neitzel Holzapfel and Thomas A. Wayment, "Unto the Uttermost Part of the Earth," in *The Life and Teachings of the New Testament Apostles: From the Day of Pentecost through the Apocalypse*, ed. Richard Neitzel Holzapfel and Thomas A. Wayment (Salt Lake City: Deseret Book, 2010), 76–78; Frank F. Judd Jr., "The Jerusalem Conference: The First Council of the Christian Church" *Religious Educator* 12, no. 1 (2011): 55–71.
38. For examples of Paul's thanksgiving sections in other epistles, see Romans 1:8; 1 Corinthians 1:4; Philippians 1:3; Colossians 1:3; 1 Thessalonians 1:2; 2 Thessalonians 1:3; 2 Timothy 1:3; Philemon 1:4.
39. See Gaye Strathearn, "Law and Liberty in Galatians 5–6," in *Go Ye into All the World: Messages of the New Testament Apostles* (Salt Lake City: Deseret Book, 2002), 59–62.
40. Bruce R. McConkie, *Doctrinal New Testament Commentary*, 3 vols. (Salt Lake City: Bookcraft, 1979), 2:101.

Chapter Eighteen

The Occasional Nature, Composition, and Structure of Paul's Letters

ERIC D. HUNTSMAN

> "Even as our beloved brother Paul also according to the wisdom given unto him hath written unto you; as also in all his epistles, speaking in them of these things; in which are some things hard to be understood, which they that are unlearned and unstable wrest, as they do also the other scriptures, unto their own destruction."
>
> 2 Peter 3:15–16

The heart of much Catholic and especially Reformation theology, the Pauline epistles frequently prove to be unfamiliar and difficult territory for many Latter-day Saints.[1] Some of Paul's teaching, taken in isolation and out of context, can seem confusing or even to be in contradiction with gospel principles explicated elsewhere in the scriptures generally or even in the rest of the Pauline corpus itself.[2] This is partly because the letters of Paul, by and large, are not treatises of systematic theology, a fact that undercuts the efforts of some to establish extensive theological positions based largely upon the apostle's writings alone.[3] Instead, the letters were written to congregations or individuals in response to specific circumstances or problems and therefore emphasize or apply specific aspects of gospel principles in response to the original situation.

Paul was a prolific and lengthy writer. Whereas the average ancient letter was 87 words long, the literary letters of the Roman authors Cicero and Seneca averaged 295 and 995 words respectively. The average letter of Paul, however, was 2,495 words long![4] Often covering a variety of subjects and addressing each with complex argumentation, his letters can be difficult to follow, especially in translation. However, by considering the original context of the letters and Paul's original reasons for writing them, the types of writing that these letters represent, and how he actually composed and formatted them, the modern student of the Pauline epistles can better interpret the letters and understand both their original and current applications, thereby avoiding "wresting" them improperly.

Occasional Nature

Although an occasion, or reason for writing, can be identified for all of the letters of the Pauline corpus, the occasional nature is particularly apparent in some of the earliest of the apostle's letters, each of which is a response to specific situations in the early branches of the Church.[5] While the principles that these letters teach are abiding and applicable in our age, understanding the original occasion of each letter is especially important for understanding and interpreting it,[6] as can be seen particularly in some of the early letters of Paul such as those written to the Saints in Thessalonica, Galatia, Corinth, and Rome.

Paul, Silvanus (Silas), and Timothy had come to Thessalonica early in the Second Missionary Journey, about AD 50, and had spent only a few weeks in the city where they had established a largely gentile congregation. Dated to AD 50 or 51, Paul's two letters to the Thessalonians are generally considered to be the earliest of his preserved writings, and the formal occasion for Paul's writing is his concern for the further instruction of these new Saints.[7] Lacking Paul's later focus on righteousness by faith rather than by the works of the law, much of these letters consist of ethical exhortations as Paul endeavors to teach these new Christians how to live as Saints (see 1 Thessalonians 4:1–12; 5:12–22; 2 Thessalonians 3:6–15).

Nevertheless, considerable portions of both letters to the Thessalonians are devoted to treating the specific topic of the Parousia, or glorious return of Jesus Christ (see 1 Thessalonians 4:13–5:11; 2 Thessalonians 2:1–12), which included the promise that those who were Jesus's at his coming would live with him forever.[8] While this part of Paul's teaching is best preserved in 1 Thessalonians 4:13–18, this same passage also makes clear that it caused some confusion among the Thessalonians that Paul's letter sought to resolve: because the Thessalonians, and possibly Paul himself, expected the Lord to return soon, they were concerned when the Parousia did not happen immediately and, furthermore, when members of the congregation began to die before Jesus's return. Accordingly, Paul explained in his first letter that "the dead in Christ shall rise first" to be followed by those who were alive at his coming who would be "caught up together with them in the clouds, to meet the Lord in the air" (1 Thessalonians 4:16–17). This preoccupation with Jesus's return, however, seems to have been at the heart of Paul's second letter, where he needed to moderate the enthusiasm of the Thessalonians, noting some of the significant signs that would precede the Parousia (see 2 Thessalonians 2:1–12) and encouraging the Saints with admonitions to work that seem to have been occasioned by the "disorderly walk" (*ataktos peripatountos*) or idle behavior of Saints whose indolence seems to have been the result of an unrealistic expectation of an imminent Second Coming (see 2 Thessalonians 3:6–15).

The letter to the Galatians, conventionally dated AD 54–55 but perhaps composed as early as AD 48 if it were written before the Council of Jerusalem in AD 49, was written in response to a very specific and real problem in the churches spread throughout the southern or northern parts of the Roman province of Galatia. These congregations also consisted largely of gentile converts, but in Paul's absence a subsequent group of missionaries had disturbed the new converts by teaching them "a different gospel" (see Galatians 1:6–10). Paul's succeeding arguments, especially in Galatians 5:2–12, have suggested that these false teachers had convinced some of the Galatians of the necessity of adopting certain aspects of the Mosaic law—notably circumcision—leading many modern scholars to refer to them as "Judaizers."[9] This context and Paul's efforts to counter this false teaching are necessary to understand properly one of his central points in the letter: "Knowing that a man is *not* justified *by the works of the law,* but by the faith of Jesus Christ, even we have believed in Jesus Christ, that we might be justified by the faith of Christ, and *not by the works of the law: for by the works of the law shall no flesh be justified*" (2:16; emphasis added). On the other hand, Paul may have had a second group of opponents, because his letter later seeks to counter the efforts of those who think that the grace of Christ had made all obedience and law unnecessary. In reaction to the false teaching of these "libertines," a second emphasis is found in a strong ethical section of the letter, where Paul enjoins the Galatians to reject the works of the flesh in favor of the fruits of the Spirit (see 5:16–26).

Paul's first letter to the Corinthians, one of a series of letters of which only two are preserved, was written as a result of problems within one of the largest congregations that he had established. A mixed congregation of converted Jews and Gentiles in the cosmopolitan Roman capital of the province of Achaia (Greece), this branch had been established during Paul's second missionary journey, AD 50–52, when he had stayed there for eighteen months (see Acts 18:7–11). The beneficiaries of thorough gospel instruction, upon Paul's departure the Corinthian Saints developed internal divisions arising from factionalism, pride over special knowledge and gifts, and moral misbehavior arising from doctrinal speculation.[10] Accordingly, Paul devoted considerable portions of his letter to dealing with problems in Corinth such as factions (see 1 Corinthians 1:10–4:21); moral misbehavior, including problems of sex and property (see 5:1–6:20); problems regarding marriage and celibacy (see 7:1–40); Christian freedom and its abuse (see 8:1–11:1); correct and incorrect Christian worship, including the veiling of women (see 11:2–16); abuses of the Lord's Supper (see 11:17–34); misunderstanding and misusing spiritual gifts (see 12:1–14:40); and doctrinal correction regarding the nature of the Resurrection and its application to Christians (see 15:1–58).

Paul's important letter to the Romans is significant both because Paul wrote it to a congregation with which he was not yet familiar and also because of the particular history of the congregation there. He seems to have written it from Corinth in the winter of AD 57–58, when Paul began making plans to visit Rome on his way to Spain and the west after first delivering a collection of money to the poor Saints in Jerusalem (see Romans 15:14–33). Since he knew individual Saints from Rome but had not yet been there himself, the letter was partially intended as a letter of introduction in which he hoped to familiarize the Roman congregation with "his" gospel, perhaps recognizing that his views had been incorrectly represented to the Roman Saints by others (see Romans 3:8).[11] Furthermore, Paul wrote this letter with over a decade of preaching and writing behind him, including the letters to the Thessalonians, Galatians, Corinthians, and perhaps to the Philippians and to Philemon. As a result, in this letter Paul provides a masterful survey of many of the issues he treated in earlier letters to other congregations, producing in the process what is perhaps his most systematic treatment of the issue of justification by faith (see Romans 1:16–8:39).[12]

The background of the Roman church itself influenced both how Paul approached the issue of justification and why he also introduced another topic, God's promises to Israel. Christianity had been brought to Rome by others, presumably Jewish Christians, perhaps as early as the AD 40s or even earlier since Jews from Rome had been among those in Jerusalem at the time of Pentecost (see Acts 2:10). The introduction of Christianity in the capital had apparently led to conflict within the large Jewish community in the city, leading the emperor Claudius to expel all Jews from the city in AD 49.[13] Consequently, in Romans, Paul addresses many of the same issues as he did in Galatians, but here the situation is reversed. In Galatians, Paul addressed a congregation that he had founded but which had subsequently been infiltrated by Judaizers bringing with them old practices of the Mosaic law. In Romans he was addressing a church founded by others and one in which Jewish Christians had been significant but were no longer dominant. As a result, he is less strident and more diplomatic about some of the same principles.

After the death of Claudius in AD 54, Jews and Jewish Christians were allowed to return to Rome, but in the meantime the Church had continued to grow among gentiles, perhaps resulting in some tension between them and the returning Jewish Christians. The failure of the majority of ethnic Israel to accept Christ and the confusion about what role Jewish Christians should play in the Church led to questions such as whether the gentiles had superseded the Jews or whether the promises of Israel had passed to the Church, subjects that Paul addresses in his treatise on God's promises to Israel (see Romans 9:1–11:36). Largely misunderstood by sectarian Christianity, Paul's arguments here regarding such issues as God's election of Israel (see 9:1–29), Israel's unbelief (see 9:30–10:5), the availability of salvation to all (see 10:6–21), the fact that Israel's rejection is not final (see 11:1–10), Paul's allegory of the ingrafted branches and the salvation of the gentiles (see 11:11–24), and the promise that all righteous Israel will be saved *as a group* (see 11:25–32) have a particular importance in the context of the restored gospel.[14]

The Genres of Paul's Letters

When a specific occasion influenced Paul to write regarding certain topics, he employed the basic letter form common in the Mediterranean world at that time. However, as noted above, Paul's letters were unusually long, and he adapted the standard letter format to meet each occasion. Although the differences in the types of writing found in the Gospels, the book of Acts, the book of Revelation, and the various "epistles" or letters in the New Testament are fairly obvious, distinctions in genre also exist among the various letters themselves. Part of this is a result of the fact that New Testament letters vary according to intended audience and how widely the authors expected them to be circulated beyond their original audiences. Paul's letter to Philemon and his family, for instance, reads very much like a personal letter about a particular subject of concern to the sender and recipient—namely how Philemon should treat his slave, Onesimus, who is also Paul's convert. Accordingly, Philemon is termed a "real letter," as opposed to a literary or philosophical exercise intended for wider publication. Paul's other early letters—such as 1–2 Thessalonians, Galatians, Philippians,[15] 1–2 Corinthians, and Romans—were written to individuals or congregations, but, like Greek philosophical letters, they were considerably longer than an average ancient letter and were meant to teach and exhort. Nevertheless, these are still considered "real letters" because they were written to specific individuals or communities and addressed practical and theological issues relevant to their recipients.

In Ephesians and Colossians, however, there are indications that Paul expected the letters to be circulated among a broader audience. (See Colossians 4:16. Some early manuscripts of Ephesians 1:1 lack "at Ephesus," opening the possibility that the letter was meant for more than just the branch at Ephesus.)[16] This concept of an encyclical, or circular letter, is further developed in 1 Peter and in the other "general epistles." Some scholars, in fact, have tried to reserve the term "epistle" for letters of this type, comparing them to the literary letters of classical authors such as Cicero and Pliny, who, even when they were writing "real letters" to specific individuals, expected their letters to be more widely published and so often wrote with a broader audience in mind.[17] While being familiar with the circumstances that faced Christianity in the first century is still important for understanding the general epistles, as a whole these letters tend to address more than one congregation or were even directed to the entire Church, much like a First Presidency message or letter is today. Ephesians and Colossians, midway between real and circular letters, follow the same general structure of most of Paul's other letters, whereas the general epistles of other authors, although they open and close as letters, are generally shorter and have a less complex structure than a Pauline letter.[18]

The remainder of Paul's letters either fall into different generic categories or combine different types of writing. First Timothy and Titus, commonly called "pastoral epistles," are in effect priesthood handbooks or collections of instructions for the practical organization and regulation of branches of the church. In them Timothy and Titus are given instructions for the selection and appointment of church officials, warnings against false teachings, and practical advice on community behavior and belief. While 2 Timothy also addresses some of these issues, it also takes the form of a "testament" or final expression of belief before Paul met his death. Hebrews, which has been closely associated with Paul in both ancient tradition and Restoration teaching despite being significantly different in style and theme from the secure Pauline letters, has been identified as a work that "begins like a treatise, proceeds like a sermon, and closes like an epistle."[19] Nevertheless, it is not simply a theological treatise but rather has an apologetic purpose, defending the superiority of Christ and preventing the readers from lapsing back to the Mosaic system. Furthermore, it is more of a homily, which is an explication closely connected to scriptural text, rather than a sermon, which is generally more topical. Only at Hebrews 13:1–25 does it read like a letter or epistle.

The Mechanics of Writing an Ancient Letter

While the occasion helped determine *what* Paul wrote and to some extent the *form* the letter took, the realities of ancient letter writing affected *how* he wrote. Contrary to modern notions of letter writing, Paul did not sit alone at a desk quietly composing his epistles. Instead, the composition process was a more lengthy procedure that involved others at every step.[20] Paul probably stayed with other Christians in his travels and would have enjoyed little privacy.[21] But more significantly, his letters frequently included in their opening formula references to coauthors, who are different from others, such as scribes, who, if mentioned by name, are usually noted in the conclusion.

Examples of coauthors include Silvanus and Timothy in 1–2 Thessalonians; Timothy in 2 Corinthians, Philippians, Colossians, and Philemon; Sosthenes in 1 Corinthians; and "all the brethren" with Paul in Galatians. These individuals can be viewed as collaborators in the composition process and may have contributed substantively to much of the initial material that the scribe, under Paul's direction, later wove into the final draft.[22] The involvement of Silvanus and Timothy in the Thessalonian correspondence makes particular sense because they had been involved with Paul in the initial evangelizing of Thessalonica, and Timothy was often Paul's messenger to the congregation there, as he was in the case of other letters where he is listed as coauthor. The nature of their participation in the formulation of the material used in the letter is best described by Richards, who notes that Paul worked as leader of a missionary team, the members of which would have discussed and prayed with him about problems facing the congregations to which they were writing.[23] The case of Sosthenes—who may well be the same individual mentioned in Acts 18:17 as the former ruler of the synagogue, as well as an opponent of Paul, in Corinth—is intriguing. Familiar with both Jewish customs and scripture on the one hand and Greek philosophy and lifestyle in Corinth on the other, he may have been particularly sensitive to the problems facing the congregation there.[24]

The involvement of a secretary or scribe in the actual writing of an ancient letter is more important than modern readers might suspect. Professional writers were used for virtually every letter written in antiquity. For those who were themselves illiterate and needed someone to write for them, a scribe usually took down notes regarding the subjects that concerned the sender and then employed a standard format and used conventional expressions to write the letter. For those who were themselves able to read and perhaps write, scribes were still often used to take down literal dictation—although the skill involved often made this prohibitively expensive—or to take notes from which they wrote a first draft, which the "author" then reviewed, altered, and approved. Two New Testament scribes are identified by name: Tertius in Romans 16:22 and Silvanus in 1 Peter 5:12. In both cases, they seem to have been fellow Christians who were competent in letter writing. In the case of Paul's scribe Tertius, he may have been a professional secretary who was able to take dictation in ancient shorthand and had volunteered his services since Romans has many oratorical features that seem to reflect spoken composition.[25]

Most of Paul's letters, however, were probably not the result of such transcription, which would have taken hours of continuous dictation: by some estimates 1 Thessalonians and Philippians could have been dictated in about two and a half hours, but 1 Corinthians would have required over ten hours, and Romans itself over eleven if an expensive professional not using shorthand were transcribing it.[26] While scribes are not named in any Pauline epistle other than Romans, they can be presumed in the other letters, where their involvement in the actual composition of the letter and the degree to which they were involved in wording of the final draft could vary greatly. Nevertheless, their involvement in the composition process may, in fact, help to explain the differences of style and diction between the different letters of Paul.27

Because parchment and especially finer quality papyrus were expensive, scribes may have first taken notes and even written initial drafts on tablets of wood or ivory coated with wax. The scribe then composed, or in the case of a dictated letter, revised the letter and set it down in a neat, professional hand on a good paper, usually papyrus. Letters often went through several drafts before the author reviewed it and then either applied his seal or "signed it" with a postscript at the end. While a postscript could in fact be additional information added after the close of a letter, as is often the case today, in antiquity an "author" more generally used a postscript to guarantee that the contents written by a scribe reflected his thinking. In such a postscript, the author might summarize the contents and then sign his name or affirm the contents in some other fashion.[28] Such postscripts that are actual parts of the preserved text differ from the postbiblical subscriptions that copyists began to add in the fourth century to note assumed facts about a letter but which are often wrong.[29]

Noted examples of postscripts in the Pauline corpus include 1 Corinthians 16:21–24, Galatians 6:11–18, Colossians 4:18, 2 Thessalonians 3:17–18, and Philemon 1:19, where Paul uses his own name and mentions that he is writing this "with mine own hand." Other possible, but unsigned, postscripts include 1 Thessalonians 5:27–28 and Romans 16:21–23.[30] Therefore, regardless of the role of a coauthor or scribe in the composition of a letter, the final product was reviewed and accepted by Paul, who thereby attributed to it apostolic authority. Second Thessalonians 3:17, "The salutation of Paul with mine own hand, which is the token in every epistle: so I write," is a clear example of an authoritative postscript, and it is particularly interesting since the authenticating postscript seems also to have been a device used to prevent forgery by a letter purporting to be from Paul. Apparently this had occurred, because 2 Thessalonians 2:2 suggests that the eschatological fervor that Paul was trying to counter in that letter had been inflamed by such a forgery: "That ye be not soon shaken in mind, or be troubled, neither by spirit, nor by word, *nor by letter as from us,* as that the day of Christ is at hand."[31]

After the postscript was added, the letter was either folded or rolled and then sealed. The entire process of composition, dictation, writing, revision, review, and approval was not only time-consuming but also expensive. The cost of the finished letter included both the cost of the papyrus and secretarial labor and could be quite high. According to some calculations, Romans (979 manuscript lines) would have cost $2,275 in 2004 US dollars, and even short Philemon (44 lines) would have cost $101![32] The letter was then dispatched, sometimes being carried by a friend or associate traveling to the recipient's destination but sometimes just sent with some traveler who was found going to the intended destination. The imperial post carried only official government correspondence, so it was not available to Paul and other New Testament letter writers.

The Structure and Format of Paul's Letters

In antiquity, even personal letters were read aloud.[33] Letters to groups, such as Paul's letters to various congregations, were often read to a majority of the recipients (the probable meaning of Colossians 4:16), so most individuals never actually read the letters themselves. As a result, care was given to the way the letter was written, both in its language and its structure, so that it could best be understood, remembered, and repeated to others. Most ancient letters followed a standardized format, one that can often be discerned in other letters of the New Testament, but the length of Paul's letters and the fact they would generally be heard rather then read required additional organization. Briefly analyzing this format and the rhetorical structure of Paul's letters allows a reader to see how Paul used, and in many instances changed, the conventional letter format in order to emphasize certain points.

Ancient letters began with an *opening formula*, identifying the sender (which we saw above could include coauthors) and the recipient (which could be a local congregation, specific members of a branch, or an individual).[34] For example, "Paul, and Silvanus, and Timotheus, unto the church of the Thessalonians which is in God the Father and in the Lord Jesus Christ: Grace be unto you, and peace, from God our Father, and the Lord Jesus Christ" (1 Thessalonians 1:1). While ancient Greek letters consistently included the salutation *chaire*—"be well" or "rejoice"—in the opening formula, here Paul seems to have changed the conventional greeting by substituting *charis*, or "grace," a typically Pauline usage that immediately called to mind the saving work of Jesus Christ. Then, rather than refer to his earthly family or household as a typical letter writer would have done (e.g., "Paul, son of X, of Tarsus . . ."), he identified himself with a new, spiritual household and identified his position to emphasize his authority (e.g., "Paul, a servant or apostle of Jesus Christ" as in 1–2 Corinthians, Galatians, Ephesians, Colossians, 1–2 Timothy, and Titus).[35]

The introductory formula of an ancient letter was routinely followed by either a prayer for health or a *thanksgiving* to the gods. This section of the letter is often considerably extended in Christian letters, particularly the letters of Paul, where it includes expressions of gratitude to the one true God, doxologies or expressions of praise, and even extended prayers.[36] A short example from what is perhaps Paul's earliest extant letter illustrates the thanksgiving section of one of his letters: "We give thanks to God always for you all, making mention of you in our prayers; remembering without ceasing your work of faith, and labour of love, and patience of hope in our Lord Jesus Christ, in the sight of God and our Father; knowing, brethren beloved, your election of God" (1 Thessalonians 1:2–4). These thanksgivings were so standard in Pauline letters that their absence is obvious, as in the letter to the Galatians, where Paul's anger is apparent.[37]

The *body* of a longer letter was frequently structured according to the principles of classical rhetoric, varying the style depending upon the purpose of the letter, while a shorter letter could be written quite simply. The body of a longer letter of Paul also often contained some of the elements found in the literary letter of a classical philosopher, such as containing a section of instruction or teaching followed by a section of exhortation. Hence the body of a letter is often divided then into distinct parts, sometimes referred to as "Pauline Indicative" for the section of instructions and "Pauline Imperative" for the section containing admonitions,[38] as can be seen in the body of 1 Thessalonians, in which Paul begins with an indicative section reviewing his relationship to the Thessalonians (2:1–3:13) and follows with an imperative section of exhortations and instructions (4:1–5:22), which includes not only a subdivision of ethical admonitions (4:1–12) but also a further subsection that gives the Saints directions on how they should live given their expectation of the Parousia (4:13–5:11).

This frequent twofold division into indicative and imperative sections is important because many commentators focus on Paul's doctrinal teaching without sufficiently noting that almost every letter also discussed how the reality of the message of Christ should affect how Saints should *live* as Christians. For instance, the weighty doctrinal section of Romans (1:16–11:36) is followed by a shorter but still significant imperative or hortatory section (12:1–15:13) that includes important discussions of Christian ethics (12:1–13:14) and relations between the strong and the weak (14:1–15:13). Even when indicative and imperative sections alternate or are otherwise spread throughout the body of a letter, the modern reader must always keep in mind that Paul's letters not only teach *doctrine* but also call to *action* and insist that Christians must live according to the highest ethical and moral standards, that their "whole spirit and soul and body be preserved blameless unto the coming of our Lord Jesus Christ" (1 Thessalonians 5:23).[39]

While formal divisions into indicative and imperative sections may have helped a listening audience follow one of Paul's letters, what was even more significant to an ancient audience was his use of rhetorical styles. Dubbed "the art of persuasion," classical rhetoric involved both the pleasing use of language—which was meant to help it be both understood and remembered—and appropriate use of argumentation. The three modes of argumentation were forensic or judicial, often meant to defend a position; deliberative or hortatory, intended to persuade an audience to make practical decisions; and demonstrative or "epideictic," which sought to inspire, praise, affirm common beliefs, and gain support. According to these divisions, Galatians, meant to defend both Paul's teaching of the gospel and his own authority, is an example of judicial oratory; 1 Corinthians, intended to correct behavior, is an example of deliberative writing; and Romans, which sought to introduce Paul, affirm his doctrine, and gain the support of the Saints in Rome, serves as an example of demonstrative rhetoric.[40] The rhetorical intent of a letter could, in fact, dictate the way Paul organized the body of the letter. For instance, the indicative section of Galatians (1:6–5:1) takes the form of a courtroom speech in which the introduction of Paul's argument that there is no other gospel (see 1:6–10) is followed by a formal *apologia* or "defense" (see 1:11–21) and a series of six proofs demonstrating that one is indeed saved by the faith of Jesus Christ and not by the works of the law (see 3:1–5:1).[41]

The simple *concluding formula* of a Greek or Roman letter is considerably developed in New Testament letters. In place of a simple expression of affection and the occasional wish for strength and health for the recipient, the letters of Paul, for instance, frequently include a final blessing, greetings to various individuals in the community receiving the letter, sometimes the instructions "to greet with a holy kiss," and a final peace wish.[42] Most letters then concluded with a postscript like those discussed above, written and often signed by Paul.

Paul's Letters, Then and Now

The frequent personal greetings often appended to the end of Paul's letters—such as the list of twenty-six individuals and five groups in Romans

16:3–16—remind us that these were actual letters written to real people in the first century AD. One must try to understand the circumstances in which these individuals and groups found themselves in order to understand what and how Paul was trying to teach them. Nevertheless, Paul's final doxology, or expression of praise, at the end of his letter to the Romans reminds us that his fervent testimony is as vital and true today as it was then: "Now to him that is of power to stablish you according to my gospel, and the preaching of Jesus Christ, according to the revelation of the mystery, which was kept secret since the world began, but now is made manifest, and by the scriptures of the prophets, according to the commandment of the everlasting God, made known to all nations for the obedience of faith: to God only wise, be glory through Jesus Christ for ever. Amen" (Romans 16:25–27).

Eric D. Huntsman is a professor of ancient scripture at Brigham Young University.

Eric D. Huntsman, "The Occasional Nature, Composition, and Structure of Paul's Letters," in *How the New Testament Came to Be: The Thirty-fifth Annual Sidney B. Sperry Symposium*, ed. Kent P. Jackson and Frank F. Judd Jr. (Provo, UT: Religious Studies Center, Brigham Young University; Salt Lake City: Deseret Book, 2006), 190–207.

NOTES

1. See the representative excerpts of Augustine's AD 427 treatise *On Grace and Free Will,* and Martin Luther's 1531 "Lectures on Galatians," in *The Writings of St. Paul*, ed.Wayne A. Meeks (New York: Norton, 1972), 220–50.
2. See Richard L. Anderson, *Understanding Paul* (Salt Lake City: Deseret Book, 1983), 177–83.
3. Morna D. Hooker, *A Preface to Paul* (New York: Oxford University Press, 1980), 8–9, 16–18.
4. E. Randolph Richards, *Paul and First-Century Letter-Writing: Secretaries, Composition, and Collection* (Downers Grove, IL: InterVarsity, 2004), 163–64.
5. Hooker, *Preface to Paul*, 9.
6. Hooker, *Preface to Paul*, 9–11.
7. In this note and subsequent notes, I have given a representative chronological sampling of scholarship from both academic and Latter-day Saint commentators who consider the occasion of each of the letters briefly discussed here. For 1–2 Thessalonians, see Sidney B. Sperry, *Paul's Life and Letters* (Salt Lake City: Bookcraft, 1955), 94–98; Anderson, *Understanding Paul,* 72–90; Jo Ann H. Seely, "Hope for the 'Children of Light' as the

Darkness Descends (1, 2 Thessalonians)," in *Acts to Revelation*, vol. 6 of *Studies in Scripture*, ed. Robert L. Millet (Salt Lake City: Deseret Book, 1987), 146–50; Charles A. Wanamaker, *The Epistles to the Thessalonians*, New International Greek Testament Commentary (hereafter NIGTC) (Grand Rapids, MI: Eerdmans, 1990), 53–63, 164–90; E. P. Sanders, *Paul* (New York: Oxford University Press, 1991), 26–33; Raymond E. Brown, *Introduction to the New Testament* (New York: Doubleday, 1997), 459–62.

8. Sanders, *Paul,* 21–22.
9. Sperry, *Paul's Life and Letters,* 158–71; F. F. Bruce, *The Epistle to the Galatians,* NIGTC (Grand Rapids, MI: Eerdmans, 1982), 19–32; Anderson, *Understanding Paul,* 152–58; George A. Horton Jr., "Concern, Correction, and Counsel for Converts (Galatians)," in Millet, *Acts to Revelation*, 83–88; Sanders, *Paul*, 44–64; Brown, *Introduction to the New Testament*, 468–77.
10. Sperry, *Paul's Life and Letters*, 118–37; Anderson, *Understanding Paul*, 95–129; David R. Seely, "'Is Christ Divided?' Unity of the Saints through Charity (1, 2 Corinthians)," in Millet, *Acts to Revelation*, 57–66; Brown, *Introduction to the New Testament*, 511–35; Anthony C. Thiselton, *The First Epistle to the Corinthians,* NIGTC (Grand Rapids, MI: Eerdmans, 1982), 29–40.
11. Sperry, *Paul's Life and Letters*, 179–200; Anderson, *Understanding Paul*, 172–95; Robert L. Millet, "The Just Shall Live by Faith (Romans)," in Millet, *Acts to Revelation*, 46; Sanders, *Paul*, 65–76; Joseph A. Fitzmyer, *Romans* (New York: Doubleday, 1993), 25–36; Brown, *Introduction to the New Testament*, 559–75.
12. Brown, *Introduction to the New Testament*, 563, notes that "Romans was in a way a summary of Paul's thought, phrased with an air of finality as he pulled together his ideas before going to Jerusalem where he would have to defend them."
13. See Suetonius, *Claudius*, 25.3, which attributes the expulsion order to riots over one *Chrestus*, the Latin form of a common Greek slave name meaning "useful" or "serviceable" (*Chrestos*), which apparently he had confused with the name *Christos.* Priscilla and Aquila, whom Paul met in Corinth, were Jewish Christian refugees from Rome (see Acts 18:1–3; Romans 16:3–4). Paul himself had relatives who later returned to the city (Andronicus and Junia; see Romans 16:7).
14. Early in the postapostolic period and in the centuries since, many Christians have seen the necessity of accepting Jesus Christ and the failure of Israel to do so as a sign that the Christian Church, as New Israel, had superseded, or taken the place, of ethnic Israel. This view of supersession, sometimes called "replacement theology," saw the Mosaic law and the old covenant of God with his people as being replaced by the new covenant ushered in by Jesus's sacrificial death. In addition to early patristic authors such as Justin Martyr, Tertullian, and Origen, later reformers such as Martin Luther and John Wesley subscribed to some degree of supersessionism. In contrast, for a Latter-day Saint understanding of Romans 9–11, see Millet, "The Just Shall Live by Faith," 53–54.
15. Although Philippians, as one of the "imprisonment epistles," has been traditionally associated with Paul's (first) Roman imprisonment, circa AD 61–63, this is based largely upon the text's later subscription (see below) as well as to references to "the palace" (Greek *praitorion*, Philippians 1:13) and Saints "of Caesar's household" (Greek *hoi ek te-s kaisaros oikias*, 4:22), both of which terms were not, in fact, limited to Rome itself. Consequently, alternative suggestions include a postulated Ephesian imprisonment, circa AD 54–55, or Paul's detention in Caesarea, circa AD 58–60, both of which would allow for an earlier letter to the Philippians, proposals that are attractive because of Philippians' similarity in style, content, and situation to Galatians and 1 Corinthians. See Brown, *Introduction to*

the New Testament, 493–96, and Peter T. O'Brien, *The Epistle to the Philippians*, NIGTC (Grand Rapids, MI: Eerdmans, 1991), 19–26. See Brown, *Introduction to the New Testament*, 507–9, for similar arguments that have been made about the dating of Philemon.

16. Brown, *Introduction to the New Testament*, 600–601, 626–27, 631–33.
17. First proposed by Adolph Deissmann, *Bible Studies* (Edinburgh: Clark, 1901), 3–59, the strict distinction between an actual *letter* and a literary *epistle* has largely been abandoned by New Testament scholarship. Nevertheless, "real letters" and "apparent letters" continue as basic categories, especially if the latter are considered to include circular letters, treatises, homilies, and other kinds of writing that only contain superficial epistolary features. See Jerome Murphy-O'Connor, *Paul the Letter-Writer: His World, His Options, His Skills* (Collegeville, MN: Liturgical Press, 1995), 42–45.
18. 1–2 Peter, 2–3 John, and Jude do not divide the body of the letter into the two usual sections of instruction and admonition. Paul's letters often do. James, although it begins as a letter, continues as a homily based on scriptural references and the teachings of Jesus, employing the diatribe style. Shaped in letter format in its opening and focusing on practical religion, it is somewhat in the tradition of Old Testament wisdom literature. First John does not read like a letter at all but is probably best seen as a theological treatise or a doctrinal homily rather than a letter, although it was sent to a "general" audience and is usually termed an epistle.
19. H. E. Dana, *Jewish Christianity: An Expository Survey of Acts I to XII, James, I and II Peter, Jude and Hebrews* (New Orleans: Bible Institute Memorial, 1937), 201.
20. See Richards, *Paul and First-Century Letter Writing*, 19–31.
21. Richards, *Paul and First-Century Letter Writing*, 36–44.
22. Murphy-O'Connor, *Paul the Letter-Writer*, 16–19; Richards, *Paul and First-Century Letter Writing*, 33–36.
23. Richards, *Paul and First-Century Letter Writing*, 32–33.
24. Murphy-O'Connor, *Paul the Letter-Writer*, 20–24, reviews carefully both 1 Corinthians and considerable commentary on said letter to try to discern what contributions Sosthenes indeed made to the letter. He suggests that the more theologically involved passages, such as 1:18–31 and 2:6–16, may possibly represent Sosthenes' presumably exegetical and philosophical bent, whereas Paul insisted on pragmatic counsel. How the involvement of Sosthenes and his concerns for Corinthian customs might have affected some of the more controversial sections of 1 Corinthians (e.g., the role of women) is unrecoverable.
25. Richards, *Paul and First-Century Letter Writing*, 92.
26. Richards, *Paul and First-Century Letter Writing*, 92.
27. Murphy-O'Connor, *Paul the Letter-Writer*, 8–16, 34–35; Richards, *Paul and First-Century Letter Writing*, 59–93.
28. Murphy-O'Connor, *Paul the Letter-Writer*, 110–13; Brown, *Introduction to the New Testament*, 419; Richards, *Paul and First-Century Letter Writing*, 171–75.
29. For instance, the subscription to 1 Thessalonians reads: "The first epistle unto the Thessalonians was written from Athens." First Thessalonians 3:1–6, taken together with Acts 18:1–5, make it clear that Paul wrote the letter from Corinth, after he had left Athens and when Timothy had come to Corinth with news about the Church in Thessalonica. See Anderson, *Understanding Paul*, 72.
30. Murphy-O'Connor, *Paul the Letter-Writer*, 112–13, and Richards, *Paul and First-Century Letter Writing*, 174–75, differ in their assessments of 2 Corinthians—Murphy-O'Connor seeing 2 Corinthians 1–9 and 10–13 as two different letters (and all of 2 Corinthians 9

as the postscript of the first letter), whereas Richards sees 10–13 as an after-the-fact postscript or addition to the original letter.

31. Sperry, *Paul's Life and Letters*, 102, 104–5, notes, "A careful reading of [2 Thessalonians 2:2] . . . gives the impression that some person might have forged a letter purporting to come from Paul, which gave faulty information to the Thessalonians and caused them to be shaken in mind and considerably troubled. . . . These reports from Macedonia together with accounts of continued persecution, convinced the great missionary that he ought to write the Thessalonian Saints another letter. . . . In this one and some others he writes a greeting toward the end in his own distinctive handwriting, to give a warm personal touch and also to prevent forgery."
32. Richards, *Paul and First-Century Letter Writing*, 169.
33. Richards, *Paul and First-Century Letter Writing*, 202.
34. Murphy-O'Connor, *Paul the Letter-Writer*, 45–55; Brown, *Introduction to the New Testament*, 413–15.
35. Murphy-O'Connor, *Paul the Letter-Writer*, 45–53; Richards, *Paul and First-Century Letter Writing*, 128–29.
36. Murphy-O'Connor, *Paul the Letter-Writer*, 55–59; Richards, *Paul and First-Century Letter Writing*, 129–30.
37. Murphy-O'Connor, *Paul the Letter-Writer*, 60–61.
38. See Brown, *Introduction to the New Testament*, 416n16.
39. Sanders, *Paul*, 22.
40. The classical point of discussion begins with Aristotle, *Ars rhetorica*, 1.3 (§1358b) and includes Quintillian, *Institutio oratorio*, 3.4.12–15. See Brown, *Introduction to the New Testament*, 411–12, for a brief review and this particular application to Paul's letters, as well as the more detailed discussion of Murphy-O'Connor, *Paul the Letter-Writer*, 65–95.
41. Brown, *Introduction to the New Testament*, 412.
42. Murphy-O'Connor, *Paul the Letter-Writer*, 98–110; Brown, *Introduction to the New Testament*, 418–19.

Chapter Nineteen

Agency and Self-Deception in the Writings of James and 1 John

TERRANCE D. OLSON

> "Therefore, to him that knoweth to do good, and doeth it not . . . "
>
> James 4:17

Think of the last time you felt it was right to do something and you refused to do it. Perhaps it was a little thing like reading a book to your five-year-old at bedtime or visiting your brother in the hospital. It could have been an act that demanded more in time, such as driving to your niece's wedding in a neighboring state or giving a Saturday of service cleaning up girls' camp. No matter what the example, each consists of something you sense is right to do. But you are a moral agent—capable of living true or false to your sense of what is right. If you act favorably and willingly on your feeling regarding what is right, you proceed to read the book, make the visit, drive to the wedding, or help with girls' camp. You do these things without a second thought and probably without moral fanfare. As examples or stories of moral or ethical conduct, there is little to tell about these incidents except to recall the memories.

However, if we do not do these things or we do them resentfully, there is a story to tell. Suddenly, an otherwise straightforward and perhaps even mundane event becomes significant. Now the story is a moral tale, for the heart of the story is in our refusal to do as we believe. Had we been true to our sense of what was right, it would not occur to us to explain ourselves. But when we are false to our beliefs, there is much to explain.

When my response to my five-year-old is to go against what I believe is right, I might say to myself, *I am really tired tonight*, or, *He wasn't very well-behaved at dinner*, or, *I have a big report due tomorrow*. When these kinds of comments are delivered by someone who "knoweth to do good, and doeth it not" (James 4:17), they become rationalizations of wrong-doing. They become attempts to make the wrong we are doing appear to be right—or at least not wrong.[1] They are symptoms of a problem being experienced by someone who is no longer living the truth in relationships with others. These symptoms are evidence of more than mere ignorance and more than being blinded by the demands or pressures of life. They are signs of self-deception.

In everyday life and in our attempts to explain ourselves to each other, it seems we have neglected the idea and implications of being self-deceived. Yet the scriptures indicate that when responsible agents engage in self-deception, they engage in sinful activity. Evidently, self-deception is more than an abstract term that describes someone who does not see the truth. It is a concept that accounts for how it is possible to be blind to the truth. By definition, to be self-deceived is to participate in an act that produces a false view of one's circumstances. To be self-deceived is to be blind to the truth of a situation. This blindness includes at least two features: (1) seeing the truth falsely—as untruth—and (2) being blind to the fact that one's own act has produced the false view.

Given this kind of blindness, it seems that if I am self-deceived, I cannot access the knowledge that would set me free, so I cannot escape. Also, since I do not know I am deceived and do not know I have produced the deception, I will even reject the attempts of observers to enlighten me. I will see such efforts as evidence that they are meddlers, prejudiced, or irrational. Clearly, to take the idea of self-deception seriously might seem impossible to the self-deceived.

The epistles of James and John address the problem of self-deception more than any other place in the scriptures, and both of them ground the problem as a symptom of wrongdoing.

James on Double-Mindedness

James understood the link between knowing the truth and living the truth, and described the instability in life that comes when we are "double minded" (James 1:8) and willfully refuse to live that which we know:

> Be ye doers of the word, and not hearers only, deceiving your own selves.
>
> For if any be a hearer of the word, and not a doer, he is like unto a man beholding his natural face in a glass;
>
> For he beholdeth himself, and goeth his way, and straightway forgetteth what manner of man he was. (James 1:22–24)

The complete rendition of James 4:17 is "Therefore to him that knoweth to do good, and doeth it not, to him it is sin." Thus, sin and self-deception are inextricably linked.

Sin is not a popular explanation of what our culture has come to see as mere imperfection or inescapable human failings. To deny sin as a source of some mortal troubles can itself be a symptom of being self-deceived. After all, if I can attribute my sins to things I can't help—imperfections—I have nothing to repent of, and the best I can do, even with those failings, is cope. Besides, if James is going to lay blame at my feet for something that is just human nature, then it creates guilt. I certainly do not need guilt as an additional stumbling block! But perhaps there is a better answer. Perhaps we can actually be free of certain recurring attitudes and feelings that seem inescapable. Perhaps James takes seriously an idea our culture too readily dismisses. Perhaps dismissing James's testimony is already an act of self-deception, and that dismissal leaves us blind and trapped in a self-deceived world.

John on Self-Deception

John sustains James's witness regarding wrongdoing and blindness. The book of 1 John is a testimony of Jesus Christ and a call to obedience. In almost every chapter, the author contrasts the condition of the obedient with that of the disobedient. In testifying of the fellowship the Saints can experience with the Father and the Son, John unequivocally declares,

> This then is the message which we have heard of him, and declare unto you, that God is light, and in him is no darkness at all.
>
> If we say that we have fellowship with him, and walk in darkness, we lie, and do not the truth:
>
> But if we walk in the light as he is in the light, we have fellowship one with another, and the blood of Jesus Christ his Son cleanseth us from all sin.
>
> If we say that we have no sin, we deceive ourselves, and the truth is not in us. (1 John 1:5–8)

So a contrast is established immediately between walking in light and walking in darkness. Walking in darkness is characterized by our *doing not the truth;* by the truth not being *in us.* This is significant commentary, because it suggests that those who are self-deceived no longer see, experience, or understand the truth. This blindness to the truth is not due to ignorance but to a refusal to walk in the light. But that refusal is something we are *doing* ("and do not the truth"), and that kind of doing makes the truth inaccessible to us ("the truth is not in us").

In 1 John chapter 2, the author continues the theme:

> He that saith, I know him, and keepeth not his commandments, is a liar, and the truth is not in him. . . .
>
> He that loveth his brother abideth in the light, and there is none occasion of stumbling in him.
>
> But he that hateth his brother is in darkness, and walketh in darkness, and knoweth not whither he goeth, because that darkness hath blinded his eyes. (verses 4, 10–11)

And in a final example from chapter 4:

> There is no fear in love; but perfect love casteth out fear: because fear hath torment. He that feareth is not made perfect in love. . . .
>
> If a man say, I love God, and hateth his brother, he is a liar: for he that loveth not his brother whom he hath seen, how can he love God whom he hath not seen. (verses 18, 20)

Perhaps the reason obedience is the first law of heaven is that without obedience, we do not see clearly the possibility or reality of heaven. We do not see that the Savior is the light of the world. We are in darkness, we stumble, we "forget" what manner of person we are. But we cannot attribute these problems to sources outside ourselves. We are blind because of our own refusal to see. As Jacob, the son of Lehi, noted, "Wo unto the blind that *will not see*; for they shall perish" (2 Nephi 9:32; emphasis added). It is likely that the first casualty of refusing to see is a loss of an understanding of the truth, because "that darkness hath blinded his eyes" (1 John 2:11).

It is evident, then, that it is in our *response* to the gospel—how we act upon it, and not how it acts upon us—that reveals who and what we see; who and what we are, in any given moment. Our disobedience changes our world—what we see and what we understand, and how we relate to others. Being blind to the truth is the condition of those who refuse to live by the truth they have been offered.

Since our blindness is produced by walking in darkness and since we are "free" to walk in darkness, our blindness to the truth is self-inflicted. Or, regarding the stumbling metaphor used by James, we do not stumble at all spiritually when the hallmark of our life is love for our brother. It is our refusal to love that creates our spiritual problems, and those problems cause us to stumble.

The Blindness of Self-Deception

Thus far we know that self-deception is produced by disobedience, which is, by definition, sin. So what? Either this is a conclusion so obvious that it need not take up too much of our time or we have failed to see its significance in our everyday lives—especially for those who generally seek to take the gospel seriously. Seemingly, the counsel to those self-deceived is to repent—end of story. But since to be self-deceived is to be blind to the truth, including the truths that others might tell us about our being in sin, how does a person who is self-deceived respond to the truth telling of others? If self-deception is produced by a refusal to walk in the light, self-deceived persons will resist light offered them about their sin.

This act of refusal is evidence of humans as moral agents, for if the act of refusal were not voluntary—freely chosen—the individual could not be held accountable for the act. As affirmed by Samuel the Lamanite in the Book of Mormon,

> And now remember, remember, my brethren, that whosoever perisheth, perisheth unto himself; and whosoever doeth iniquity, doeth it unto himself; for behold, ye are free; ye are permitted to act for yourselves; for behold, God hath given unto you a knowledge and he hath made you free.
>
> He hath given unto you that ye might know good from evil, and he hath given unto you that ye might choose life or death; and ye can do good and be restored unto that which is good, or have that which is good restored unto you; or ye can do evil, and have that which is evil restored unto you. (Helaman 14:30–31)

When we have a sense of what is right to do and we do not do it, we create a false way of seeing—and a false way of being—to which we are blind. We are as blind to the solutions to these types of problems as we are to our role in creating them in the first place. My own experience affirms this possibility.

When I was irritated about how one of the neighbor's children had stomped through my newly planted garden, I confess that there was no room in my heart, during my irritation, for forgiveness. Nor, if you had asked me at the time why I was troubled, would I have thought I had any need for repentance. Yet, at that moment, I was neither forgiving nor repentant. Rather, I was consumed with how my gardening efforts had been ruined by a thoughtless child. And make no mistake, in my irritation, that child had become my enemy. No other way of seeing the situation made sense to me.

On another occasion, I found myself delayed at an intersection where I was waiting with my signal flashing to turn left. I had to wait because of one—only one—oncoming and amazingly slow-moving car. It seemed that I had been waiting for an eternity for this creeping mass of metal to get by me. Then as the car entered the intersection, it turned left without warning. Had I known earlier of the driver's intention, my path would have been clear. Because the driver hadn't exercised the same courtesy I had—using the left turn signal as automakers and the state driving manual had intended—I had waited unnecessarily. That wait must have cost me at least twenty seconds—all because some other driver was so frivolous and discourteous as to not use a simple turn signal. My car's tires squealed as I made my long-awaited left turn. I'm sure I muttered something about what kind of people they let drive these days. I don't recall the phrase "Do unto others" or "Love thy neighbor" coming into my mind as I drove the final few blocks to my house. Such ideas would have seemed so unrealistic in that situation anyway.

I also remember once speaking in a public meeting where I was being critical of the practices of one of my child's teachers. I didn't name the teacher, but my wife was pulling on my sleeve. I successfully ignored her until I realized the teacher about whom I was complaining was in the audience. It was not enough that the audience didn't know who I was speaking of. The teacher knew. I knew. I felt, fleetingly, that it was a shame someone's incompetence had to be publicly displayed like that. Unfortunately, the idea of conducting myself with meekness and lowliness of heart was foreign to me in that meeting.

These are everyday incidents, I know. Some would even claim that they are merely mundane evidences that we are imperfect or that we lose control, or that all of us are trying to learn to cope better with the challenges of life. Those who see the garden or turn-signal incident as trivial might even say that there are so many much-greater things to worry about in life, that we should bite our collective tongues over the little things and worry about coping with the big things.

I believe that these so-called everyday incidents—these so-called "little things"—have much to do with the quality of our lives, and are the foundation of the quality of our marriage, family, business, and Church relationships, not only in the present moment, but in the kingdoms we look forward to inheriting after this life. In each of these incidents, the person telling the stories—me—is self-deceived. That means in the moment I am living these stories, I am more than merely ignorant. It means I am doing more than denying the truth of the situation. The truth of the situation is that I don't even see the truth. If, during my irritation with the child, or during my impatience with the driver, or during my public criticism of the teacher, someone had told me I was hard-hearted, unforgiving, or unrepentant, I would have met the charge with what I would have considered to be justified disbelief. I would have been blind to the need for my compassion for the child (I would have seen such a notion as mere indulgence), for the driver of the other car (who didn't deserve to be rewarded for being inconsiderate), or for the teacher. In fact, instead of considering *my* attitude, *my* actions, as being a problem in these situations, I would have considered myself as being victimized by the other people. *They* are causing the problem. *They* are responsible for disrupting my world. *They* are the source of my difficulties. Preach to *them*, I might say to anyone challenging my responses. Moreover, I would have seen even those challenging my responses as stumbling blocks.

These responses are more than human failings that we can't help doing, or mere denials of the truth. They are expressions of having refused to see and live by the truth. Such refusals are symptoms of disobedience, of a refusal to walk in the light, if you will. As James and John testify, such disobedience means we begin to deceive ourselves about the truth. I know this because these are my stories. I know now what I didn't know during those incidents: that while I was being uncompassionate, hard-hearted and so on, I was absolutely blind to the truth. Only when I later quit refusing to live the truth did I see the truth I had been refusing to live. I began living obediently to all that I knew about how I am to treat my neighbors (and let's see—who is my neighbor?). The truth was now a blessing to me, whereas in my refusal, I found the truth unrealistic and a burden. It may be that only moral agents can become self-deceived.

Once I gave up my sin, John's testimony made perfect sense to me, and his phrases began echoing in my soul. I was saying I had no sin. I was deceiving myself. The truth was not in me (see 1 John 1:8). John's description of the reality of self-deception and of the cause—my refusal to admit to sin when I was, in fact, sinful—was either lost on me or an irritant. But once I repented and returned to the light, the idea of self-deception made perfect sense and became a relatively important feature of my understanding the human condition. After all, if through disobedience, I become blind to the truth—the truth is not in me—how am I to understand the truth of myself and my condition at all? In such a condition, all my explanations of my actions will also be self-deceived.

It is not the truth that the reason I did not read the book to my child was because he or I was tired or that he had misbehaved or that I had a report looming. Those explanations only occurred to me *after* I had become self-deceived. I became self-deceived when I became disobedient. In my disobedience, my "explanations" became justifications or rationalizations for wrongdoing, rather than straightforward descriptions of an honest, moral choice. Similarly, I was walking in darkness in my attitude toward the oncoming car, and my irritation over their lack of use of a turn signal was just self-righteousness. My complaints against the teacher in a public meeting were not "honest criticism" but dishonest resentment. All those meanings eventually changed for me, not because any of those people changed, but because I did. I have wondered how my change came about.

Other Symptoms of Self-Deception

James and John identify additional symptoms of how we are when self-deceived. They see the consequences fully. James links many specific acts of disobedience to rationalizations born of blindness. One example is, "Let no man say when he is tempted, I am tempted of God; . . . neither tempteth [God] any man" (James 1:13). Do we see ourselves as victims of God when in temptation? This is a deceived view compared to the truth: "But every man is tempted, when he is drawn away of his own lust, and enticed" (James 1:14). This is an example of being a hearer of the word and not a doer, and thus "deceiving your own selves" (James 1:22). Also, "If any man among you seem to be religious, and bridleth not his tongue, but deceiveth his own heart, this man's religion is vain" (James 1:26). To *seem* to be religious stands in contrast to being religious, and is an expression of being self-deceived. Think for a moment. The last time your tongue was unbridled, did you feel justified? What was your rationalization?

Similarly, John notes that to be self-deceived is to be a liar. Yet, in sin, we not only lie about the truth, but believe the lie that we tell. Terry Warner calls this more than telling a lie—it is living a lie.[2] A simple example is that one who uses tobacco while ignorant of the spiritual law against it may suffer health problems but does not perish spiritually over it unless he refuses to obey the law once it is received by him. In other words, the prices we pay for our ignorance do not include the cost to us of knowing to do good and doing it not. Self-deception is resistance to light and truth, while ignorance is lack of knowledge of light and truth.[3] As described by John, "the truth is not in him" (1 John 2:4); or, "If a man say, I love God, and hateth his brother, he is a liar: for he that loveth not his brother whom he hath seen, how can he love God whom he hath not seen?" (1 John 4:20). The idea of simultaneously loving God and hating a brother is conceptually and practically impossible. But those immersed in hate, those who are self-deceived by their own sin of a refusal to love, are blind to the truth of that statement.

The common threads of how self-deceived persons see themselves and their circumstances include, not surprisingly, a sense of being helpless in the face of what others are doing to them, and a defensiveness that looks absolutely necessary to them. This view swallows up any sense of personal responsibility for creating or perpetuating the problem and obliterates the possibility that they are participating in any way in a willful refusal to walk in the light. Nor would it occur to the self-deceived that they are engaging in a freely chosen walk in darkness. But these are the fruits of self-deception consistent with how self-deception is described in James and 1 John. When we're in that darkness, born of our refusal to do the good that we know, we do not see our way out. After all, we now don't see how we played any role in getting ourselves in (to self-deception). Moreover, no sense of being personally responsible for the helplessness is experienced either. If so, the individual would not be deceived about their role in producing the problem. This illustrates the reality of "the truth is not in us" (1 John 1:8).

At a more general level, being self-deceived is to find the gospel to be a burden. This is not because the Lord's commandments are burdensome, but because, when we fail to respond to them in humility and meekness, we deceive ourselves about their meaning. Seeing the commandments as a burden is a perfect way to rationalize and justify our refusal to respond to them in humility. When we "do not the truth," we are "doing" a lie. That lie includes the self-deceived view that our refusal to give our best and call upon the atonement is someone else's fault—perhaps even God's fault. The self-deceived see their own imperfections, the gospel, and often life itself, as a burden instead of a blessing.

The Avenue of Escape

Escaping self-deception begins with a willingness to admit that we are, after all, moral agents. The crucial point about being moral agents is not in the mere matter of choice, but in our free, unrestricted opportunity and obligation to choose the right. Lehi's witness about moral agency matches the position of Samuel the Lamanite, cited earlier. Lehi affirms that when we do not choose the right, we choose consequences that we cannot escape: "men are free according to the flesh, . . . free to choose liberty and eternal life, through the great Mediator of all men, or to choose captivity and death" (2 Nephi 2:27).

Remember, John, in his discourse on living the truth, identified the problem of self-deception and also declared the avenue of escape: "if we walk in the light, as he is in the light, we have fellowship one with another, and the blood of Jesus Christ his Son cleanseth us from all sin" (1 John 1:7).

Giving up a self-deceived view of others reveals that we have not only become free of our resentments toward them, but often, that they had never sinned against us in the first place. When we *do* not the truth, the truth of the motives, attitudes, and actions of others is unavailable to us, and our fellowship with one another can range from being shallow to hypocritical.

In a way, the difference between doing the truth and doing self-deception is the difference described by King Benjamin of the mighty change of heart: "because of the Spirit of the Lord Omnipotent, which has wrought a mighty change in us, or in our hearts, that we have no more disposition to do evil, but to do good continually" (Mosiah 5:2). Essentially, we have awakened from the evil, resistant, alternative way of living described elsewhere as being in a deep sleep as to the things of God (see Alma 5:7).

The attitudes and even emotions of the two worlds (doing self-deception versus doing the truth) are incompatible. A disposition to do evil, or walking in darkness, cannot simultaneously be an expression of having lost that disposition, and be walking in the light. So the world of sin and self-deception are absolutely distinguishable from the alternative world of obedience. Once a person is living (or doing) qualities associated with obedience, the alternative disobedient qualities are not "in us." Examples of these incompatibilities from James and John include

1. Be swift to hear rather than slow (James 1:19),
2. Be slow to wrath rather than quick-tempered (James 1:19),
3. Be doers of the word, not hearers only (James 1:22),
4. Bridleth his tongue, versus unbridled—and thus "deceiveth his own heart" (James 1:26),

5. Visit the fatherless and widows, versus neglecting them (James 1:27),
6. Faith without works, versus faith "by my works" (JST James 2:15), and
7. Knoweth to do good, versus doeth it not (James 4:17).

None of the categories of being obedient can coexist with the categories of a refusal to be obedient. And in that refusal comes our self-deceived understanding of what we have done.

Consider this—if self-deception is produced by a free act, then escaping it must be a free act also. If being self-deceived is a refusal to live the truth, then giving up that refusal is the heart of being restored to an understanding—even a vision—of the truth. Thus, the problem is not a matter of ignorance or lack of skill or even lack of practice in some behavior. Being free of self-deception begins in willingness, not ability. If being free of self-deception requires a change of heart, then only a moral agent willing to be true to the light can experience the fellowship with Christ promised those who walk in the light. The change necessary to be free of self-deception is a matter of obedience. Yet all of us have sinned and fallen short of the glory of God (see Romans 3:23), so all of us are imperfect; thus, all of us have participated in self-deception.

A harsh term for our condition is hypocrisy, and many Christians whose failings are all too visible have been subjected to such an accusation. Also, other hearers of the word who fail to be doers sometimes report they feel guilty—so guilty that they are burdened by the commandments, ever fearful that since they can never be perfect, they are doomed to guilty despair. This presents a curious situation. The gospel is a gospel of hope, not despair, and James and John are issuing a call to obedience meant to nourish the idea that "If we confess our sins, he is faithful and just to forgive us our sins, and to cleanse us from all unrighteousness" (1 John 1:9).

An honest rendition of gospel principles reveals there is no need for would-be Saints to experience burdensome, paralyzing guilt when they read passages such as James 4:17: "Therefore to him that knoweth to do good, and doeth it not, to him it is sin." Rather, they are free to see it as merely "guilt unto repentance" and an invitation to give up their burdened world of experience. At the least, we can propose that those whose response to the call of the gospel is to despair, are somehow deceived about the spirit and meaning of the call in the first place. And, according to James and John, seeing the truth falsely is evidence of *self*-deception. The truth is "not in" those who are offended by the truth or burdened by the light, precisely because they are "do[ing] not the truth" (1 John 1:6).

Specifically, we can offer hope for people like me who, although disobedient (hard-hearted) in past moments, can, in the present moment, give it all up and be left with compassion for neighbor children, fellow drivers, and imperfect teachers. I neither need to indulge others when they are engaged in wrongdoing by excusing them or by pretending they have not sinned, nor will I feel to condemn others harshly as a way of justifying my own hostility. I will tell the truth in love and sorrow. If I must testify to an officer regarding how a car weaving in traffic startled a girl whose car then rolled three times, I will do so in sorrow, not in arrogance or in a self-promoting way. In brief, I will love others, pray for them in humility, sorrow when they sin, and nourish them in their concern for others. Only by walking in the light myself, and repenting of the times I do not, will I likely be able to invite others to live a life of love and sacrifice and commitment and humility. Others will either take offense (Terry Warner's term for becoming hard-hearted or in sin) at my self-deceptive way of being—or even at my humility—or they will see me honestly. If, in their honesty, they see I am being hard-hearted, they will sorrow. If they see a person of compassion and humility, we will resonate. Their response to me reveals whether they have joined me in my world of self-deception or have remained true to the faith, being an example to me to repent. Either way, it is always possible for us to continue to offer responses in the light, even if others begin or continue to walk in darkness.

The world others live in may include rejecting our honest offerings, but we need not join them in darkness. To consider ourselves above or below them are examples of dark responses. We must continue in love and humility and boldness as our concern for them and the Spirit prompts us. To give up self-deception is to be realistic, honest, full of hope and to experience all the "symptoms" of walking in the light.

Self-deception, then, is an inescapable consequence of wrongdoing. Giving up self-deception is only possible in the act of obedience, that act that comes from within. It is that act moral agents are capable of. It is an affirmation of our love of God to love our brother. The Savior's call to us who labor and are heavy laden to come unto him is absolutely realistic and absolutely the source of hope and healing.

Terrance D. Olson is a professor emeritus in the School of Family Life at Brigham Young University.

Terrance D. Olson, "Agency and Self-Deception in the Writings of James and 1 John," in *Go Ye into All the World: Messages of the New Testament Apostles* (Salt Lake City: Deseret Book, 2002), 290–304.

NOTES

1. C. Terry Warner and Terrance D. Olson, "Another View of Family Conflict and Family Wholeness," *Family Relations* 39 (October 1981): 493–503.
2. C. Terry Warner, *Bonds That Make Us Free: Healing Our Relationships, Coming to Ourselves* (Salt Lake City: Shadow Mountain, 2001).
3. To be ignorant of a law, including the law of the gospel, may mean we suffer the practical, temporal consequences of our ignorance. But we can not be accountable for that law to which we have not been exposed. This is important, for the solution to our ignorance of spiritual things is in being introduced to or confronted by them. If we have not been given the law, then as Jacob, from the Book of Mormon, reminds us, "Wherefore, he has given a law; and where there is no law given there is no punishment; and where there is no punishment there is no condemnation; and where there is no condemnation the mercies of the Holy One of Israel have claim upon them, because of the atonement; for they are delivered by the power of him. But wo unto him that has the law given, yea, that has all the commandments of God, like unto us, and that transgresseth them" (2 Nephi 9:25, 27).

Chapter Twenty

New Testament Prophecies of Apostasy

KENT P. JACKSON

The Church of Jesus Christ of Latter-day Saints has proclaimed to the world consistently since its beginning that there was an apostasy of the church founded by Jesus during his earthly ministry and led by his apostles following his ascension.[1] This is a fundamental belief; in fact, the apostasy of early Christianity provides much of the very justification for the existence of the Latter-day Saint faith. If there had not been an apostasy, there would have been no need for a restoration.[2] Latter-day Saint theology asserts that the church of Jesus and his apostles came to an end within a century of its formation; the doctrines which its inspired leaders taught were corrupted and changed by others not of similar inspiration, the authority to act in God's name was taken from the earth, and the Christian systems that then remained did not enjoy divine endorsement. It was precisely the question of divine endorsement—in Joseph Smith's words, "which of all the sects was right" (Joseph Smith–History 1:17)—that led to the glorious event that ushered in the Restoration of the gospel, the appearance of the Father and the Son to the young Prophet. In response to Joseph Smith's search for a true church, he was told to join none of them, "for they were all wrong," and all their creeds were "an abomination" in the sight of God (Joseph Smith–History 1:19).

The message of the Latter-day Saints is that following seventeen centuries since the days of the apostles, the heavens were again opened, divinely authored doctrines were revealed anew, the authority to speak and act in God's name was brought back to earth, and the Church of Jesus Christ was established by divine command.

Prophecies about Apostasy

The best single witness of the apostasy of New Testament Christianity is the New Testament itself. In it there are several statements made by Jesus and his apostles about the future of their work. Though they labored with great zeal to bring souls to the Lord and establish the church throughout the world, still their prophetic utterances concerning the end result of their efforts foretold tragedy. In short, they knew that the church would fall into apostasy shortly after their time, and they bore candid testimony of that fact. In this study we will examine selected prophetic passages in which Jesus and his apostles foretold the falling of the church or events associated with it. In the church's earlier years, those prophecies pointed to the future. In the later years, the anticipated future had arrived. In these somber prophecies, words like "latter times," "last time," "last hour," and "last days" refer not to our own time but to the last days of the early Christian church. For some passages, we will draw from responsible modern translations when they express the intended meaning better than does the King James translation.[3]

Matthew 24:5, 9–11

One of the most significant sermons of the Savior is that which is recorded in Matthew 24–25, the Olivet Discourse. In response to questions of the Twelve regarding the destruction of the temple and the destruction of the world, Jesus prophesied of events that would transpire in the near and distant future. Matthew 24:9–11 records a prophecy of great importance concerning the future of the church:

> Then shall they deliver you up to be afflicted, and shall kill you: and ye shall be hated of all nations for my name's sake.

> And then shall many be offended, and shall betray one another, and shall hate one another.
>
> And many false prophets shall rise, and shall deceive many.

The rendering of this passage in the Joseph Smith Translation places it clearly in the context of the last days of the early church (Joseph Smith—Matthew 1:4–21).

A number of important statements are contained in these verses. Verse 9 foretells the fate of the apostles themselves: affliction, hatred, and death for Christ's sake. The only scripturally attested fulfillment of the martyrdom prophecy is the death of James at the hands of Herod Agrippa I (Acts 12:1–2), but early Christian tradition tells of similar fates for other apostles.[4] Yet the killing of the apostles was not the cause of the apostasy. Other references clearly teach that true Christianity died from an internal wound, the rejection of true doctrine by the members of the church. Still, the death of those who alone held the authority to lead the church could only mean the death of the church itself.

Verse 10 provides an important prophecy of the rejection of truth by the saints. Unfortunately, the King James translation obscures its intended meaning with the phrase "Then shall many be offended." "Offended" translates from the Greek verb *skandalízō,* the core meaning of which is to "trip." In a religious context such as this, the passive voice here (a third-person plural, future tense) means to "give up one's faith." This is expressed in some recent translations: "Many will turn away from the faith" (TNIV), or "Many will fall from their faith" (REB). *Many*, the Savior foretells, will leave the faith in that day.

Verse 11 records an additional prophecy—namely, that many false prophets would arise and would "deceive many." In that day, when the apostles would be afflicted, hated, and killed, taking their places would be "many false prophets." The related passage in verse 5, which Joseph Smith—Matthew places in the early Christian period (Joseph Smith—Matthew 1:6), is also significant: "For many shall come in my name, saying, I am Christ; and shall deceive many." Notice that there would be *many* false Christs, and, like the *many* false prophets, they would deceive *many*. One can only lament the fact that the available sources, scriptural and nonscriptural, do not give us a complete history of the fulfillment of these words.

Acts 20:29–31

On his way from Greece to Jerusalem at the end of his third missionary journey, the apostle Paul stopped at the city of Miletus and called for the elders of nearby Ephesus (see Acts 20:18–35). On their arrival he gave an important address of which Luke records only excerpts. The prophecy relevant to the future of the church, Acts 20:29–31, reads as follows:

> For I know this, that after my departing shall grievous wolves enter in among you, not sparing the flock.
>
> Also of your own selves shall men arise, speaking perverse things, to draw away disciples after them.
>
> Therefore watch, and remember, that by the space of three years I ceased not to warn every one night and day with tears.

Paul warned the elders of the province of Asia that following his departure, forces would damage the church. "Grievous wolves" would enter in and would not spare the flock. At this point in Paul's career, he had experienced years of trouble with Judaizers trying to thwart his work of taking the gospel to Gentiles. Perhaps it was similar infiltration of apostate forces that Paul foresaw. The Judaizers, who had already had great success opposing Paul (see, for example, Galatians 1:6), were members of the church. In spite of the wolf metaphor, what Paul alluded to here was undoubtedly not physical attack or external persecution. Instead, he was describing the ascension of opposing forces within the church and their gaining power over the Saints. This is borne out as he continued by speaking about people who were part of the church in that area—and who were perhaps in Paul's audience at that very moment—who would come forward "speaking twisted things, to draw away the disciples after them" (Acts 20:30, ESV).

Paul ended his tragic prophecy by testifying that for three years he had warned the Saints there constantly, "with tears" (Acts 20:31). Similarly, in his prophecy of apostasy in 2 Thessalonians, which we will examine next, he also bore witness to the saints that he had warned them well in advance of the coming rebellion (see 2 Thessalonians 2:5).

2 Thessalonians 2:1–12

In Paul's second letter to the Thessalonians, he had to respond to the belief among the Thessalonian Saints that the "day of Christ" was "at hand" (2 Thessalonians 2:2). We do not know the details of the problem in Thessalonica, nor do we know its origin. The Greek verbal conjugation *enéstēken*, translated in the King James Bible as "is at hand," has been rendered in a variety of ways in other translations. The basic meaning of the word is "is present," so perhaps readings such as "has come" (ESV) and "is already here" (NRSV), as found in the majority of the versions, are more accurate than the ambiguous "at hand."[5] Whatever the exact misunderstanding of the Thessalonians may have been, Paul responded clearly that the day of Christ's coming would not happen until the "falling away" had taken place (verses 3–4):

> Let no man deceive you by any means: for that day shall not come, except there come a falling away first, and that man of sin be revealed, the son of perdition;
>
> Who opposeth and exalteth himself above all that is called God, or that is worshipped; so that he as God sitteth in the temple of God, shewing himself that he is God.

The King James words "falling away" are translated from the Greek noun *apostasía*, from which we have our word *apostasy*. Whereas the words "falling away" may give the incorrect impression of a process of drifting or gradually losing ground, the original term means something much more dramatic. Some modern translations use terms like "the rebellion" (ESV, NRSV, TNIV) and "the Great Revolt" (NJB). The two Greek elements combined in *apostasía* are the verb *hístēmi*, "to stand," and *apó*, "away from." The basic meaning of the word is "revolt" or "rebellion," and ancient sources use the term to describe political rebellion and revolution.[6] *Apostasía* is not an invasion from without but an uprising from within. What Paul was describing in the future of Christianity was a mutiny against God and his position in the church—a mutiny by members of the church. The meaning of the word, and the evidence from the New Testament and from history, show us that the *apostasía* would be an inside job. And, as Paul wrote in the following verses, the rebellion would succeed.

The chief feature of this time of rebellion would be the triumph of the "man of sin." The metaphor is striking: the "man of sin" would supplant God in God's temple. Latter-day Saint commentators generally equate the "man of sin" mentioned in these verses with Satan, and that is clearly what Paul had in mind.[7] But the message of the passage is a general one about the replacement of a true church with a counterfeit one not acknowledged by God. As part of the *apostasía*, as Paul noted, Satan would be made manifest as he would exalt himself over all that is called divine. Paul used the words "temple of God" here to refer to the church, as he also did in some other places.[8] Of historical and theological significance is the fact that in this prophecy, a form of the church would survive, but as God would not be at its head, it would no longer be the church of God.

Paul's words correspond well with evidence that we have from other scriptures. When the Lord appeared to Joseph Smith in the spring of 1820, he told the young Prophet that all the Christian churches of his day were "wrong" (Joseph Smith—History 1:19). The Book of Mormon prophet Nephi envisioned in the latter days following the restoration only two churches: "the church of the Lamb of God" and "the church of the devil" (1 Nephi 14:10). The virtuous and godly would belong to "the church of the Lamb of God," and all wickedness would be classified as "the church of the devil." Paul told us the same thing as he foretold the "man of sin" supplanting God as a result of the rebellion.

No one should conclude that Paul's metaphor of the "man of sin" sitting in God's temple means that Christianity after the time of the apostles would be satanic. The apostasy was the early process by which church members rejected the teachings and authority of the apostles, so it is not accurate to blame the later victims of that process—medieval and modern Christians. Nor is it accurate to call the later centuries "the apostasy." Latter-day Saints should rejoice—as the heavens undoubtedly do—at the great works of righteousness and faith, and the leavening influence on the world, of those whose lives are touched in any way by Jesus Christ.

The Lord called The Church of Jesus Christ of Latter-day Saints "the only true and living church upon the face of the whole earth" (Doctrine and Covenants 1:30). It possesses "the power of God unto salvation" (Romans 1:16). The restoration of the fullness of the gospel, with its priesthood and other blessings, took place because it is only in its light that salvation in its truest sense is possible to humankind. In times and places where those blessings are absent, Satan succeeds by hindering God's children from returning to their Father's glory. The latter-day restoration of the gospel brought back Christ's ancient church, with God again at its head.

In Paul's next verse (2 Thessalonians 2:5), he punctuated his prophecy by reminding the saints that he had taught them of the apostasy when he had been with them personally: "Remember ye not, that, when I was yet with you, I told you these things?" But his message did not stop there. Even at that time, said Paul, the man of sin was being restrained until he would be "revealed in his time" (verse 6, ESV). "For the mystery of lawlessness [KJV, 'mystery of iniquity'] is already at work. Only he who now restrains it will do so until he is out of the way. And then the lawless one will be revealed" (verses 7–8, ESV). In these verses, Paul stated that the overt manifestation of Satan in the church was still in the future. Yet even then the "mystery of iniquity" was operating, waiting in the wings, as it were, for its chance to come to the fore. Paul wrote of some force which restrained the man of sin from making his appearance before his time, perhaps the Lord, the collective power of the apostleship, or something or someone else as the obstacle to the day of the man of sin. In any case, the message comes through clearly that Satan and his works were at that time already operational but were being held back until the divine power that restrained them would "be taken out of the way. And then shall that wicked one be revealed" (verses 7–8, Joseph Smith Translation).[9]

In verses 9–12, Paul told of Satan's deceptive power with his church and false priesthood. They would come with "power and signs and lying wonders, and with all deceivableness of unrighteousness." Those who would follow them are they who "received not the love of the truth," who "believe a lie," and who "believed not the truth, but had pleasure in unrighteousness." In short, Satan's work, accompanied by signs and miracles meant to counterfeit those of the Lord's true servants, would prosper because the Saints would reject the truth and believe falsehood.

1 Timothy 4:1–3

In Paul's first letter to Timothy, he prophesied concerning the departure of some of the Saints from the faith (1 Timothy 4:1–3):

> Now the Spirit speaketh expressly, that in the latter times some shall depart from the faith, giving heed to seducing spirits, and doctrines of devils;
>
> Speaking lies in hypocrisy; having their conscience seared with a hot iron;
>
> Forbidding to marry, and commanding to abstain from meats, which God hath created to be received with thanksgiving of them which believe and know the truth.

This prophecy has a number of features that make it of considerable interest. First, Paul specifically stated that his belief in the future defection was the result of revelation. In fact, not only did the Spirit speak these words to Paul, but it did so "expressly." The chronological note is also important. Paul used the term "latter times" (*hústeroi kairoí*) to denote the period in which the developments that he foretold would take place. Paul was not speaking of our day but of the "latter times" of the early church. The message is consistent in the New Testament. A few decades later, Jude announced to his readers that they were then in "the last time" (*éschatos chrónos*; Jude 1:18). Similarly, John expressed to the readers of his first letter the certainty of the fact that they themselves were living in "the last hour" (*eschátē hṓra*; 1 John 2:18). They knew that they were in the final days of the Christian church, the period of time concerning which the Spirit spoke expressly to Paul. Paul's term "the last days" in 2 Timothy 3:1 (*eschátai hēmérai*) should be understood in the same light.

As we have seen in other prophecies examined so far, the departure from the faith would be a defection from true principles of doctrine. Paul wrote that those who would depart would give heed to what he called "seducing spirits" and "doctrines of devils." What Paul saw was not an abandonment of religion but a shifting of loyalties, from "the faith" to a false faith. Accompanying this defection would be the manifestation of the negative behaviors cited in verse 2 (see also 2 Timothy 3:2–4).

Verse 3 is interesting because it mentions two examples of the false ideas that the counterfeit religious system would foster: a prohibition against marriage and a prohibition against certain foods. Beyond that, the apostle gave no further details.

In his prophecy in 1 Timothy, Paul did not express any of the feelings of doom or urgency that are so obvious in the letters of his fellow apostle John, written about thirty-five years later. Yet for Paul, the present danger was real enough that he admonished Timothy personally to reject strange ideas (verse 7) and to remind "the brethren" of his warnings (verse 6).

2 Timothy 3:1–5, 13

In the prophecy in 2 Timothy 3, which parallels that of 1 Timothy 4, Paul told his beloved coworker that "perilous times" would come in the last days (verse 1). In this passage, he emphasized the spiritual depravity that would be characteristic of the world in that era (verses 1–4):

> This know also, that in the last days perilous times shall come.
>
> For men shall be lovers of their own selves, covetous, boasters, proud, blasphemers, disobedient to parents, unthankful, unholy,
>
> Without natural affection, trucebreakers, false accusers, incontinent, fierce, despisers of those that are good,
>
> Traitors, heady, highminded, lovers of pleasures more than lovers of God.

Paul continued his sentence as follows: "having a form of godliness; but denying the power thereof" (verse 5). Latter-day Saints recognize these words as being among those spoken by the Lord to the Prophet Joseph Smith (Joseph Smith—History 1:19). Paul's point within the context of this prophecy of apostasy is that despite the inward corruption, the outward trappings of sanctity would remain, yet the power of God would not be found there.

As Paul continued his warning to Timothy of "perilous times" ahead, he spoke with increasing concern. In verse 13 we read, "But evil men and seducers shall wax worse and worse, deceiving, and being deceived." The fact that Paul knew that those "perilous times" were not far in the future is demonstrated by his personal plea to Timothy in verse 14: "But continue thou in the things which thou hast learned and hast been assured of, knowing of whom thou hast learned them." Paul was confident of Timothy's unceasing faithfulness if he would but continue in the things that the apostle had taught him and also in the words of the scriptures (verse 15). For others of Timothy's generation, there was more cause for concern.

2 Timothy 4:3–4

Paul's final prophecy of the abandonment of true religion is found in the last chapter of 2 Timothy. From the English Standard Version we read (2 Timothy 4:3–4):

> For the time is coming when people will not endure sound teaching, but having itching ears they will accumulate for themselves teachers to suit their own passions,
>
> And will turn away from listening to the truth and wander off into myths.

This passage paints a picture of rejection of the truth that is consistent with the other prophecies examined so far. In the verses that precede it, Paul charged Timothy strongly to "preach," "reprove, rebuke, and exhort" (ESV). Verse 3 reveals that the reason for his urgency is the fact that he knew that a time was coming in which the Saints would no longer accept the truth.

Paul's desire in this, his last preserved letter, was to hold off the onslaught of the inevitable rebellion. What he foresaw was not an abandonment of religion but a willful rejection of true doctrine and its replacement by doctrines which were untrue but more to the liking of the hearers. Notice that the people involved, although unwilling to put up with correct teachings, desired teachings nonetheless. Having "itching ears," that is, a desire to hear religion, they would acquire teachers whose doctrines were acceptable to them. The final outcome of their actions would be the abandonment of truth and the acceptance of "myths."

2 Peter 2:1–3

Paul was not alone among the apostles in prophesying doom for early Christianity. In 2 Peter, the chief apostle foretold the introduction of false teachers into the church (2 Peter 2:1–2):

> But there were false prophets also among the people, even as there shall be false teachers among you, who privily shall bring in damnable heresies, even denying the Lord that bought them, and bring upon themselves swift destruction.
>
> And many shall follow their pernicious ways; by reason of whom the way of truth shall be evil spoken of.

These false teachers, according to Peter, would secretly bring in "damnable heresies." So successful would they be that as a result of their efforts, "the way of truth" would be blasphemed (future passive from *blasphēméō*).[10] Verse 3 tells us more: "In their greed they will exploit you with false words" (ESV). This tells us something concerning their purpose: to exploit the members of the church (KJV, "make merchandise of you"), and their method of doing so: by making up doctrine.

1 John 2:18; Jude 1:4, 17–18

There are a few passages in the New Testament that give evidence indirectly that an apostasy had been foretold. Of these, the most informative are found in 1 John 2:18 and Jude 1:4, 17–18. These verses actually speak of apostasy already present in the church, and while doing so they make mention of the fact that the saints knew that it would come and had been warned appropriately. John wrote: "Little children, it is the last time: and as ye have heard that antichrist shall come, even now are there many antichrists; whereby we know that it is the last time" (1 John 2:18). What is important at this point is the fact that John reminded the Saints to whom he wrote that they had heard earlier that a time would come—called the "last time" (*eschátē hṓrā*)—in which "antichrist" would come among the church. The foretold time had now arrived.

Similarly, Jude wrote: "For certain people have crept in unnoticed who long ago were designated for this condemnation, ungodly people, who pervert the grace of our God into sensuality and deny our only Master and Lord, Jesus Christ" (Jude 1:4 ESV). This passage tells that the readers had received warning in the past of the coming of "ungodly people" who would pervert the gospel and reject the Lord. After writing more about those predicted apostates and likening them to some of more ancient times, Jude continued (Jude 1:17–19 ESV):

> But you must remember, beloved, the predictions of the apostles of our Lord Jesus Christ.
>
> They said to you, 'In the last time there will be scoffers, following their own ungodly passions.'
>
> It is these who cause divisions, worldly people, devoid of the Spirit.

According to Jude, the apostles had foretold the coming in the "last time" (*éschatos chrónos*) of those who would scoff at the true faith. The "last time" had arrived, and those scoffers had come.

Revelation 13:1–9

The final prophecy to be examined is found in Revelation 13. Here we read John's vision of the victory of the forces of Satan over the saints of the Lord. In chapter 12, John characterized the continual conflict between Satan and the works of God as the efforts of a dragon, Satan, to destroy a woman and her children. In Revelation 12:17 we read, "And the dragon was wroth with the woman, and went to make war with the remnant of her seed, which keep the commandments of God, and have the testimony of Jesus Christ." This is part of an ongoing conflict that has existed since before humankind was placed on the earth, and it will continue until Satan suffers final defeat following the Millennium (see Revelation 20:10).

The episode from that conflict that is recorded in chapter 13 is directly relevant to the end of the early Christian church. As the vision continued, John saw the appearance of a beast, "having seven heads and ten horns, and upon his horns ten crowns, and upon his heads the name of blasphemy" (Revelation 13:1). This beast was the agent of the dragon, Satan, from whom he had received "his power and his throne and great authority" (Revelation 13:2 ESV). In John's narrative, we find the beast blaspheming God, God's name, his dwelling place, and those who live in heaven (compare *blasphēméō* in 2 Peter 2:2). John continued: "And it was given unto him to make war with the saints, and to overcome them: and power was given him over all kindreds, and tongues, and nations" (Revelation 13:7).

The information provided seems sufficient for us to draw two confident conclusions about the beast metaphor, its identity, and its work. First, it is a deputy of Satan; it derives its power from him and does his work (see Revelation 13:2, 4). As God's work is "to bring to pass the immortality and eternal life of man" (Moses 1:39), Satan's and that of his beast is to do the opposite. The Joseph Smith Translation notes that the beast was "in the likeness of the kingdoms of the earth" (Revelation 13:1). "Kingdom" in a scriptural context can mean any kind of institution, movement, force, or power—religious, political, or otherwise. The second statement that we can make concerning the beast is that it accomplished what it was sent to do. Verse 7 records the tragic fact that it succeeded: it overcame the Saints.

In viewing John's beast in the light of its context in Revelation 13 and other prophetic statements concerning the fall of the church, we can identify it as the institutions or forces of Satan that prevailed over early Christianity following the time of the apostles. As for the nature of those forces, it should be remembered that the scriptures we have examined so far present in clear focus the prophetic vision of the apostles: the cause of the apostasy would be the rejection of the truth by the members of the church. In this light, the beast seen by John that overcame the saints might be interpreted best as being Christianity itself—not the Christianity of Jesus, Peter, John, and Paul, but the Christianity that overcame the Saints and apostles and transformed the church.

The Great and Abominable Church

There is more to the story than what we have seen in these verses. Other New Testament passages show the process by which errant behaviors and false doctrines made their way into the early church, issues that the apostles had to deal with in their visits and letters. The New Testament epistles are almost all corrective, dealing with problems that had come to the apostles' attention that needed inspired responses. By examining the epistles in chronological order, we see the apostasy taking place as it happened, progressing in severity as time went on.[11] Letters written in the mid-first century deal with issues that may not seem overly serious to us today, but within a few decades the apostles were dealing with trends that were serious dangers to the church's existence. Descriptions in Revelation 2–3 show widespread problems in the church, and the New Testament's latest document, 3 John, tells of a local church leader who rejected the authority of the last remaining apostle in the church (see 3 John 1:9–10). These circumstances were likely representative of what was happening elsewhere as well.

Nephi wrote about the time of the early apostles and prophesied of a "great and abominable church." Its founder would be the devil, and it would remove things "which are plain and most precious" both from the scriptures and from the teachings of the church. The Bible would not go forth to the nations until it had been corrupted "through the hands of the great and abominable church," leaving it less pure and reliable than it had been when it was first written (1 Nephi 13:4–6, 20–29). When reading these passages, some Latter-day Saints have identified the medieval Christian church as the abominable church of which Nephi wrote. This cannot be, because Nephi wrote that the corruption of the biblical text and the removal of plain and precious things from the gospel would take place *before* the Bible would go to the world (1 Nephi 13:29), and the spread of the Bible to the world was under way early in the second century AD.[12] Medieval Christianity was no more responsible for the apostasy than are today's Christian churches. All Christians after the first century inherited the effects of the apostasy; they did not bring the apostasy about. By about the end of the first century, the church of the apostles was gone, the keys of the kingdom were no longer on earth, and the prophesied doctrinal evolution was already in progress.[13]

So what was the great and abominable church? It was the early church itself as it went through the process of rejecting the teachings and authority of the apostles and as it charted a path that was more pleasing to the philosophies of the world. In the New Testament passages that we have examined, Jesus and his apostles foretold, and then they later witnessed, the time when church members would look beyond the simple doctrines of the gospel and bring new ideas into the Christian faith. It was *apostasía* that brought about the end of the church, willful rebellion against God and his chosen servants. Church members, no longer content with "sound doctrine" but having "itching ears" (2 Timothy 4:3–4), sought out teachers whose words they found to be more "pleasing unto the carnal mind" (Alma 30:53). The early church died from internal, self-inflicted wounds. The structure survived for a time, but what was left of the institution was no longer acknowledged of Jesus as his own.

Jesus and his apostles knew that the church that they headed would come to an end shortly after their generation. They bore a somber witness to that knowledge in the record that they left behind for later readers—the New Testament. All Christians who take seriously the apostolic testimony must reckon with the prophetic word of the inspired witnesses that the forces of false religion would prevail over those of the truth and that the church which was guided by the power of the apostleship in the first century would no longer exist in the second. We thank God for the latter-day restoration of what was lost.

Kent P. Jackson is a professor emeritus of ancient scripture at Brigham Young University.

Kent P. Jackson, "New Testament Prophecies of Apostasy," in *Sperry Symposium Classics: The New Testament*, ed. Frank F. Judd Jr. and Gaye Strathearn (Provo, UT: Religious Studies Center, Brigham Young University; Salt Lake City: Deseret Book, 2006), 394–406.

NOTES

1. See, for example, James E. Talmage, *The Great Apostasy* (Salt Lake City: Deseret Book, 1909); James E. Talmage, *Articles of Faith* (Salt Lake City: The Church of Jesus Christ of Latter-day Saints, 1913), 198–216.
2. After the original publication of this article in 1983, I expanded on the theme in "Watch and Remember: The New Testament and the Great Apostasy," in *By Study and Also by Faith: Essays in Honor of Hugh W. Nibley on the Occasion of His Eightieth Birthday*, vol. 1, ed. John M. Lundquist and Stephen D. Ricks (Salt Lake City: Deseret Book and FARMS, 1990), 81–117. A brief article I wrote on the same topic appeared earlier as "Early Signs of the Apostasy," *Ensign*, December 1984, 8–16. My book *From Apostasy to Restoration* (Salt Lake City: Deseret Book, 1996), 8–18, summarizes the same thoughts and puts the apostasy in the broader context of early Christian history and the Restoration. This article is revised and expanded from the original publication.
3. All biblical quotations are from the King James Version unless indicated otherwise by the following acronyms: ESV—English Standard Version; NJB—New Jerusalem Bible; NRSV—New Revised Standard Version; REB—Revised English Bible; TNIV—Today's New International Version.
4. John Foxe, *Book of Martyrs* (London: Seeley and Burnside, 1837), 1:27–32.
5. Albrecht Oepke, "*Enistemi*," *Theological Dictionary of the New Testament*, ed. G. Kittel, 10 vols. (Grand Rapids, MI: Eerdmans, 1964), 2:543–44.
6. Heinrich Schlier, "*Apostasia*," *Theological Dictionary of the New Testament*, 1:513–14; F. F. Bruce, *1 and 2 Thessalonians*, vol. 45 of Word Biblical Commentary (Waco, TX: Word Books, 1982), 166.
7. See, for example, Bruce R. McConkie, *Doctrinal New Testament Commentary*, 3 vols. (Salt Lake City: Bookcraft, 1973), 3:63; Sidney B. Sperry, *Paul's Life and Letters* (Salt Lake City: Bookcraft, 1955), 103.
8. See 1 Corinthians 3:16; Ephesians 2:21.
9. See also Bruce, *1 and 2 Thessalonians*, 170–71.
10. Hermann W. Beyer, "*Blasphemeo*," *Theological Dictionary of the New Testament*, 1:621–25.
11. See "Watch and Remember," 95–112; "Early Signs of the Apostasy," 10–16; *From Apostasy to Restoration*, 12–18. Relevant passages (in chronological order) include 1 Thessalonians 4:13–17; 2 Thessalonians 2:1–15; James 2:14–26; much of 1 Corinthians;

2 Corinthians 11–12; Galatians 1:6–12; 3:1–5; 4:9–11; 5:2–4; Colossians 1:12–23; 2:6–18; 1 Timothy 1:3–4; 6:3–5, 20–21; Titus 1:10–14; 3:8–9; 2 Timothy 1:15; 2:16–18, 23–26; 3:5; Jude 1:3–8, 17–19; Revelation 2–3; 1 John 2:18–26; 4:1–6; 2 John 1:7–11; 3 John 1:9–10.

12. This is evident in the fact that New Testament passages are quoted or cited often in the earliest Christian writings of that period. See Richard D. Draper, "The Earliest 'New Testament,'" in *How the New Testament Came to Be: The Thirty-fifth Annual Sidney B. Sperry Symposium*, ed. Kent P. Jackson and Frank F. Judd Jr. (Provo, UT: Religious Studies Center, Brigham Young University, 2006), 260–91.
13. See Jackson, *From Apostasy to Restoration*, 19–30.

Chapter Twenty-One

"By His Own Blood He Entered in Once into the Holy Place"

Jesus in Hebrews 9

RICHARD D. DRAPER

With penetrating and inspired insight, the author of Hebrews bore a powerful witness of the nature and work of Jesus Christ. Unfortunately, history has not preserved who that inspired author was. Though from the second century onward, many attributed the work to the apostle Paul, the epistle itself gives no clear indication as to who wrote it. Due to both the epistle's strikingly different style and treatment of subject matter from that found in Paul's writings, the authorship of Hebrews has been much debated, both anciently and today.[1] Nevertheless, this work, and chapter 9 in particular, presents a commanding christological argument that underscores the work's inspiration and status as scripture. This paper, by taking an in-depth and careful look at Hebrews chapter 9, explores the witness of this author concerning the effect, power, and result of the self-sacrifice of Jesus for the believer.

THE AUTHOR'S PURPOSE IN WRITING

Hebrews 9 reveals that the author's purpose in writing was twofold. The first was to fully expose the insufficient nature of the sacrifices of the old covenant to make a change in the worshippers' "conscience" (*syneidēsis*). The Greek noun denotes a sense of moral awareness, but in a broader sense, the word carries the nuance of the pain people sense when they knowingly break a moral law.[2] The author played on this nuance. He insisted that, through participation in the observances of the Mosaic law, each person could be ritually cleansed, *but* a cleansing of the conscience did not take place. An inward uncleanliness remained that caused discomfort among the participants and acted as a barrier between the worshipper and God.[3]

The author's second purpose was to stress that by his obedient sacrifice, Jesus Christ made the all-sufficient atonement through which the believer's conscience could be fully cleansed. To have a cleansed conscience meant being freed from the pain of guilt. The author expanded on this idea and in doing so gave the idea of a cleansed "conscience" an even stronger thrust: the sanctification of the soul. In this way, the cleansing of the conscience provided the way for the disciple to gain access to the transforming power of grace. By that means, the believer was prepared to enter into God's glory. In sum, "Christ's obedience empowers the faithful to live in obedience and in fellowship with God (see [Hebrews] 10:5–10). [Each disciple comes] through him to God's 'throne' in order to find grace for living this life of faithfulness" (4:14–16; 10:19–25).[4]

A HIGH PRIEST OF GOOD THINGS TO COME

It would appear that the specific audience to which the author directed his epistle were Jewish Christians who, because of the difficulty of belonging to the faith, were tempted to leave the gospel and return to Judaism. The author thus appealed to them on the basis of Old Testament practices and teachings, but he gave these a decidedly Christian spin.[5]

The epistle states that the Levitical high priest ministered in a holy but earthly tabernacle, "but Christ being come an high priest [ministered in] a more perfect tabernacle, not made with hands" (Hebrews 9:11). The author's use of the phrase "but Christ" presents a sharp contrast between his focus in verses 1–10 that looked at the work of the mortal high priest with his focus in verses 11–14 that looked at the work of the eternal High Priest. The author of Hebrews has shown that the earthly holy place provided no access to heaven, "but Christ" has now opened the way. The emphasis in the first set of verses is on the tabernacle itself,[6] while that of the latter is on the full sufficiency of the Lord's sacrifice that provides complete access to God. In 9:12–14, the author provides his most thorough analysis of Christ's fulfillment of the typological sacrificial rites established by the Mosaic covenant. Throughout the verses the author emphasizes "blood," "self-sacrifice," and "cleansing." He makes it clear in these verses that the reason the Lord was able to enter the heavenly realm and make way for others to do so was because he did what the old covenant failed to do; he purged sins and cleansed the conscience of the worshipper. The author is careful to help his readers see that the whole of the Levitical system was restricted exclusively to external purification. The best it could do was but point to that internal purification so necessary to enter the presence of God.[7]

From an Old Testament perspective, it was a victim's blood that contained a vital force capable of opposing and subduing evil and quashing spiritual death. In instituting the Mosaic rites, Jehovah explained that "the life of the flesh is in the blood, and I have given it to you on the altar to make atonement for your souls; for its blood shall makes atonement for the soul" (Leviticus 17:11;[8] compare Deuteronomy 12:23). "But in the sacrifice of Christ, the relationship was reversed: whereas in the Old Testament, it was the blood that gave value to the sacrifices, in the case of Christ, it is his sacrifice that gave value to his blood."[9]

Evidencing the fully sufficient work of Christ is the epistle's note in Hebrews 9:12 that Jesus entered heaven "once for all" (*ephapax*), "a term that excludes both the necessity and the possibility of repetition."[10] The Lord's redeeming work was full, complete, and final—requiring nothing more, forever.[11]

In Hebrews 9:14 the work clearly states the benefits of Christ's atonement. The author first describes what it cleanses: "our conscience" (*syneidēsis*). When God established his covenant with Israel, he also gave them his law. In doing so, he laid down the standard he expected his people to follow. At the same time, he created a condition in which the individual conscience had a standard external to itself. That meant that a person did not decide what was right and what was wrong—the law did. The person, however, could choose to conform to the law or not. The result of choosing not to conform is a transgression (*parabasis*).[12] The word denotes a heavy sin because the person knows the law and the consequences of breaking it and yet chooses to do so. Even so, the Atonement of the Lord is so strong that it can reach even those who have broken the law in this manner and redeem them if they will but repent and follow him. This option places the consequences of a person's choice squarely on her or his shoulders.

The effect of the Lord's self-sacrifice was directed not at an outward cleansing as was the old covenant. Instead, it focused on the inward cleansing of "the conscience." The Atonement also had the deeper effect of *purifying* it. Both cleansing and purifying "refer to the same reality." Cleansing emphasizes "the removal of sinful pollutions" while purifying refers to "the readiness of the cleansed heart to approach God."[13] Taken together they denote the "moral transformation of the worshipper."[14]

The term *conscience*, as used by the author, carries much of the same scriptural nuance as does the term *heart* (*kardia*). Both refer to the center of a person's religious life that "embraces the whole person in relationship to God" and where each individual confronts God's holiness.[15] It is on the basis of the conscience and the heart that people decide for themselves if they want to remain with the Father and Son in the heavenly realm (see 2 Nephi 9:46; see also Alma 5:15–25; 34:33–34).

The author next states that the conscience is cleansed from "dead works" (*nekrōn ergon*). His reference is likely not to the works of the Mosaic law that, though not fully effective, were able to point the faith-filled follower to Christ. Rather, it refers to the inner state of impurity that the old covenant could not remove—that of an "evil, unbelieving heart" (Hebrews 3:12), which acted as the seat for faithlessness, disobedience, and, all too often, outright rebellion (see 3:7–4:11), and became an effective barrier between the sinful soul and God. The fault of the Levitical performances was that, though they prepared the worshipper outwardly for temple service, they did not transform the heart such that it became the pure receptacle of faith resulting in obedience. As a result, the worshipper was not freed from propensities that led to misdeeds and the threat of spiritual death.

The author of Hebrews emphasizes that this condition stands opposite the atonement's positive result, namely the worshippers' ability to "serve the living God." With the sinful pollutions removed from the conscience, the soul is cleansed and the barrier between it and God is removed. This cleansing not only delivers the soul from the wrath of God but also enables it to enter the most holy place, God's true sanctuary.[16] But it does more—it acts in mortality to empower the worshipper to follow God's ways and have fellowship with him. Thus, having realized the promise of the Atonement, the saints are not only prepared but also anxious to serve him in his way.

Mediator of a New Covenant

In 9:15, Hebrews clearly states how those who transgressed under the old covenant "might receive the promise of eternal life," and in doing so the work intimates that the same is true for those under the new. It was because of the role Christ played. He was the *mesitēs*, which the King James Version translates as "mediator"; however, that translation falls far short of the nuance of the Greek noun. A more accurate understanding would be that of one who stands as a guarantee that promises will be realized. How so? Though the idea of a go-between is an ever-present aspect of the Greek word, the requirements for the salvation of humankind "necessitated that the Mediator should Himself possess the nature and attributes of Him towards whom He acts, and should likewise participate in the nature of those for whom He acts (sin apart); only by being possessed of both deity and humanity could He comprehend the claims of the one and the needs of the other; further, the claims and the needs could be met only by One who, Himself being proved sinless, would offer Himself in expiatory sacrifice on behalf of men."[17] In that way, he became the guarantee of salvation to the faithful. He did so by securing the salvation that could otherwise not be obtained. Thus, as the author states, Jesus is the "surety" (*engous*) of the "better covenant" (*kreittonos diathēkēs*, see Hebrews 7:22; 8:6; 9:15; 12:24) by guaranteeing that the terms of the new covenant would be fully met for his people.

Hebrews 9:15 points out how Christ became the guarantor of the blessings of the new covenant for those who failed in the old—it was because his blameless life made his self-offering acceptable to God. As a result, Jesus was able to redeem those who transgressed because of the weakness inherent in the first covenant. His sacrifice brought to an end all Mosaic sacrifices that could only cleanse "the flesh" (9:10). "Thus, by establishing an effective way of approaching God, [Christ] terminated the Old Covenant as a way of salvation and inaugurated the New that it typified."[18] His sacrifice was, then, one of covenant inauguration. Of its new promise, he became not just the mediator but the guarantor.

Hebrews 9:15 then stresses the result of Jesus becoming the guarantor of the new covenant for those who failed under the old one. The author focuses on "former transgressions" committed under the Mosaic law because the Israelites' redemption from those sins laid the foundation that made the new covenant possible. Their forgiveness made way for the new law to be written on their hearts because they were justified and could, thereby, receive the influence and power of the Holy Ghost (see Hebrews 8:10; 10:16; see also Jeremiah 31:33).[19]

Remarkably, the Lord's sacrifice was retroactive—reaching back to all people of all ages. The author of Hebrews makes a point in line with that of the angel who declared to King Benjamin that Christ's "blood atoneth for the sins of those who have fallen by the transgression of Adam." The angel went on to teach Benjamin that those who lived before the coming of the Lord who believed "that Christ should come, the same might receive remission of their sins, and rejoice with exceedingly great joy, even as though he had already come among them" (Mosiah 3:11–13).

Hebrews refers to those whose conscience has been cleansed as "those who have been called" (*hoi keklēmenoi*). This group is composed not only of those whose lives are directed by faith and the resultant obedience but also of those who continually persevere in the service of the Master.[20] The author's words do not exclude those who rebelled during the Mosaic era.[21] There is a subtle hint here of vicarious work for the dead through which even those rebellious souls can become "the called" and, with the living, receive the promise of an eternal inheritance (see 1 Peter 3:18–20; 4:6; compare Doctrine and Covenants 76:73).

The author's words reveal both the length and width of the Lord's atonement. Its length is vast, covering all those who come to him throughout the entire history of the world. Its width is very narrow, for it excludes all those who do not come to him. The Lord himself made it abundantly clear that all must enter "at the strait gate: for wide is the gate, and broad is the way, that leadeth to destruction, and many there be which go in thereat: Because strait is the gate, and narrow is the way, which leadeth unto life, and few there be that find it" (Matthew 7:13–14; see also 2 Nephi 31:18; 33:9; 3 Nephi 27:33; Doctrine and Covenants 132:22).

The epistle makes clear that redemption comes to all only by the means of the Lord's death (Hebrews 9:15). As we look at the substitutionary or ransom model of the atonement used by the author of Hebrews, the question naturally arises: Why would God demand the suffering and death of Jesus as the means of removing the consequences of sin from the Father's other children? Was there no other way the Father could free them except through such a brutal and torturous means? Neither in Hebrews nor in the New Testament as a whole—nor specifically in the recorded words of Jesus—is this question ever addressed. The Lord made it clear that "the Son of Man came not to be served but to serve, and to give his life as a ransom for many" (Mark 10:45). These words are revealing because they show the voluntary nature of the self-sacrifice affected by the Lord. To stress the point, Christ's words emphasize that his atonement was a deliberate, willful act of obedience to God that allowed for a substitution in which one life could be given for others. That life paid the ransom that freed, potentially, all others from the consequences of sin and spiritual death. Hebrews 9:14 clarifies that the ransom is paid to God, allowing him to free others from the demands of justice and, if they will, to come under the power of his mercy (see also 2 Nephi 9:26; Alma 42:13–28).

The author of Hebrews takes this idea for granted. It was "fitting" (*prepō*), he insists, that Christ should suffer and die to redeem his people and make them "perfect [*teleioō*] in respect to conscience" (9:9). Thus, the author never questions why it was necessary for the Father to treat the Son in such a manner. He is satisfied to understand that it was simply necessary for the Lord Jesus to bow to the will of God by giving himself as the ransom. The author's writing, therefore, leaves unexplored the reason behind the divine will.

The same is true regarding the other New Testament writers (compare Matthew 11:25–26; Mark 13:32; 14:35–36; 15:34). We can say that the

> complete subjection to God's will is an integral part of the service which Jesus renders to God. For Jesus, God does not owe anyone, not even the Son, a manifestation of His reasons, let alone a justification of

> His acts and demands. What God wills and does, He does for reasons which are holy, just and wise. But this does not mean that He will disclose the reasons. There is a purpose behind God's will; it is not caprice. But man can know this purpose only if and in so far as God reveals it to him. What is here revealed to man is that the death of Jesus is service to God, and that it is a vicarious death for many in virtue of which they find freedom from sin.[22]

Whatever else the case, Jesus serves as the model for devotion to God; therefore, what he requires of the rest of us is no more than what he has given. His obedience is the essence, ground, and revelation of the law of sacrifice we as Christians are asked to follow. *And no one knows the cost more than does he.*

In Hebrews 9:18 the author makes his point: as with most covenants, the Mosaic law was inaugurated and ratified by the death of the sacrificial victim and the administration of its blood. Having validated his position by the use of scripture, the author makes this point: blood, and only blood, brings forgiveness. His appeal is to Jehovah's statement in Leviticus 17:11 that he has given to Israel the blood "on the altar to make atonement for your souls; for [the sacrifice's] blood shall make atonement for the soul."[23] The Hebrew verb translated "to atone" (*kpr*) carries the basic meaning to "cover over" with the extended sense of "atone, make amends."[24] The purpose of such covering is to put a barrier between a wrongful deed and its ill effects. When such a deed broke the relationship between persons, the purpose of the *kaphar* was to expiate the wrongdoing and propitiate or placate the offended party. It was by this means that the offense was covered over and a good relationship restored.

The purpose of the Mosaic sacrifices was to atone for sin and thus bring about a reconciliation between the offender and Jehovah.[25] According to the view of sin during the Mosaic period, committing a transgression could not simply be forgotten and walked away from. The only way sin could be forgiven was by one of the expiatory rituals defined in the law. Jehovah allowed for the transgression to be passed onto a sacrificial animal and, with its death, the guilt to be removed from the person (see Leviticus 16:20–22; compare 17:11). The act emphasizes that it is God alone who can forgive sins but that this requires an act of atonement.

Hebrews emphasizes that, on the basis of the Mosaic law, no forgiveness could be achieved without the shedding of blood. This fact becomes the ground on which the author will next make his case for the necessity of the Lord's sacrifice. He has carefully shown that both purification and redemption were associated with the new covenant's inauguration. Both old and new covenants required the death of the sacrificial victim. In Hebrews 9:23–28 the author stresses the finality of the Lord's "once for all" cleansing (*ephapax*, Hebrews 10:10) at the time when he inaugurated and put in force the new covenant (9:12). To stress that finality, he contrasts it with both the initiation of the old covenant and the ritual of the Day of Atonement. On the basis of his model, he insists that since everything associated with the first covenant had to be cleansed by sacrificial means so, too, did all corresponding heavenly things.

A Pattern of Things in Heaven

Having made that point, the author of Hebrews presents his definitive evidence for the full effectiveness of the Lord's sacrifice. He boldly affirms that Christ, the High Priest, has entered into the holy place, that is, heaven itself, and proclaims that the all-sufficient sacrifice of the Lord has procured for the disciple an entrance into heaven (see Hebrews 9:23–24).

Extrapolating based on tabernacle typology, in Hebrews 9:23 the author uses both the necessity and the method of purification of the tabernacle to explain why there had to be an atonement. As the earthly tabernacle with its furnishings had to be purified and dedicated through the administration of blood, so too did the heavenly tabernacle. He stresses, however, that heavenly purification requires far more than the mere fleshly sacrifices that worked for the temporal order (see 9:23).

The author's comments that "heavenly things themselves" needed to be cleansed and that what Christ offered were "better sacrifices" brings two questions to mind. First, how is it that "heavenly things" must be cleansed and second, why does the author denote the Lord's offering as "sacrifices"? To answer, it is best to address the second question first, for it lays down the basis for understanding the first.

Hebrews uses the plural term *sacrifices* to equate what the Savior did with that of the continual offerings the high priest had to administer annually on the Day of Atonement. The author states clearly that the very necessary purification rites associated with the earthly tabernacle typify the need for the same to be done to the true heavenly things themselves. His point is that, by analogy, the way the sacrificial offering cleansed "the pattern" (*typos*; that is, the Mosaic tabernacle and all its furnishing), so Christ cleanses the heavenly. Furthermore, since cleansing the tabernacle was a prerequisite to a priest's entrance into it, the cleansing of the "true" was necessary for entering it. This the Savior accomplished by his one-time sacrifice (9:12) that allowed him, as the eternal High Priest, to enter the heavenly holy place.[26]

So far as the first question is concerned, what polluted the earthly tabernacle was not its location but the sins of the people (see Exodus 30:10; see also Leviticus 16:16, 19). "Their sins formed a barrier that prevented them from coming into God's presence and exposed them to his wrath. If sin erected a barrier forbidding entrance into the earthly sanctuary, how much more did it bar the way into the 'true' Sanctuary in which God dwells."[27] Thus, such defilement was an objective impediment to entrance into God's presence and had to be cleansed.[28]

In sum, it seems likely that Hebrews uses the imagery of the need for a cleansing of the heavenly holy place as a metaphor for the need to cleanse the people in preparation for their entrance into heaven. It is human intransigence that produces an impregnable barrier that threatens the soul with eternal recompense. The cleansing represents Christ's removal of that barrier so that the repentant can enter into the presence of God. In doing what he did, the Lord made it possible for genuine fellowship with the Father to occur.[29] Furthermore, we must stress, a rite of the purification does not necessarily imply the object was previously impure any more than a rededication of a holy site means the first dedication did not work.[30] Even so, there is no doubt that Christ's act was one of both consecration and inauguration.

Hebrews points out clearly that Jesus did what he did in behalf of the saints (see 9:24). On the basis of the author's temple imagery, entrance into the "true" holy place involves not only the consecration of the place but also the purification of those who would enter. In this way, the work expresses both the subjective and objective significance of the Lord's sacrificial act.

The subjects are the individuals within the Christian community and the object is to bring them eternal life by preparing the way.

In Hebrews 9:25 the author points out the vast difference between what the Levitical high priest did and the work that Christ did. In doing so, he sets the stage to showcase the grandeur of the sacrifice the Lord had to effect in order to cleanse heavenly things. He shows that there were three differences: First, the Lord presented himself as the sacrifice, while the high priest presented an animal; second, Christ did not have to perform the sacrifice over and over as did the high priest; and third, he used his own blood, not that of some sacrificial animal like the high priest used.

In 9:26, Hebrews shows that through his sacrifice, Jesus did more than merely weaken or restrain the effects of sin; he brought about their abolishment (*athetēsis*) once for all. He took the entire weight of the consequences of sin—not just the believers' deserved punishment—and bore it away.[31] Doing so enabled him to deliver people from its demands. In other words, the Lord did more than deliver his people from the consequences of sin. He also delivered them from its pollution and domination and thus made way for their total liberation from its demands.[32] Through his self-sacrifice, he annulled the effects of sin, reducing them to nothingness. As a result, sin will never be able to regain its destructive power. In short, Christ vanquished sin with all its consequences "once for all" (Hebrews 10:10). Through that act, he inaugurated the purification of the cosmos (see Hebrews 8:10–12). Thus, his atonement, inaugurated in Gethsemane, implemented on Golgotha, and climaxed at the tomb on Sunday, dominates all history from the beginning to the end of time.[33]

Through his work, Jesus provided for humankind the perfect antidote for what has been called the universal human predicament. All face impending death, and, whether they know it or not, they will also face judgment. The latter will become appallingly clear to the ignorant, the denier, and the wicked upon the moment of death. If death has its sting, so much more will be the fear of judgment (see Jacob 6:13; see also Alma 40:11–14; Moses 7:1). Since judgment was a well-known principle among the readers of Hebrews (see 6:2; compare Alma 12:27), the author's words would have rung abundantly clear.

Jesus was the Father's offering "to bear the sins of many," the author states in Hebrews 9:28. Christ's return will confirm the Father's faith in that offering. The focus of the Son's first coming was on the atonement with the objective of obliterating sin. And it worked for all those who had and would have faith in him. Because of his successful efforts, sin no longer had force and therefore could not determine the final state of its once victims. That work having been accomplished, the Lord has now moved to the work of his second coming. To those who look for him to appear, he shall come to their vindication and bequeath their reward (see Revelation 6:9–11; 21:1–4).

Richard D. Draper is a professor emeritus of ancient scripture at Brigham Young University.

Richard D. Draper, "'By His Own Blood He Entered in Once into the Holy Place': Jesus in Hebrews 9," in *Thou Art the Christ, the Son of the Living God: The Person and Work of Jesus in the New Testament*, ed. Eric D. Huntsman, Lincoln H. Blumell, and Tyler J. Griffin (Provo, UT: Religious Studies Center; Salt Lake City: Deseret Book, 2018), 244–59.

NOTES

1. For a discussion of this issue from a Latter-day Saint perspective, see Richard Neitzel Holzapfel, Eric D. Huntsman, and Thomas A. Wayment, *Jesus and the World of the New Testament* (Salt Lake City: Deseret Book, 2006), 254–56. Latter-day Saint scholars are not in agreement on this issue. For two examples of those who favor Pauline authorship, see Richard Lloyd Anderson, *Understanding Paul* (Salt Lake City: Deseret Book, 1983), 197; and Terrence L. Szink, "Authorship of the Epistle to the Hebrews," in *How the New Testament Came to Be: The 35th Annual Sidney B. Sperry Symposium*, ed. Kent P. Jackson and Frank F. Judd Jr. (Salt Lake City: Deseret Book, 2006), 243–59. For an example of those who do not favor Pauline authorship, see Richard Neitzel Holzapfel and Thomas A. Wayment, *Making Sense of the New Testament: Timely Insights and Timeless Messages* (Salt Lake City: Deseret Book, 2010), 446–47.
2. Frederick William Danker, ed., *A Greek-English Lexicon of the New Testament and Other Early Christian Literature,* 3rd ed. (Chicago: University of Chicago Press, 2000), 967–68 (hereafter cited as BDAG). On the moral aspect, see Moisés Silva, ed., *New International Dictionary of New Testament Theology and Exegeses*, 5 vols. (Grand Rapids, MI: Zondervan, 2014), 4:405 (hereafter cited as *NID*).
3. *NID*, 4:402–6.
4. Gareth Lee Cockerill, *The Epistle to the Hebrews*, The New International Commentary on the New Testament (Grand Rapids, MI: Eerdmans, 2012), 386.
5. The greater audience of Hebrews likely included proselytes and God-fearers (Gentiles attracted to Judaism) who also came into the Christian fold. See Holzapfel, Huntsman, and Wayment, *World of the New Testament*, 258. The epistle's view that much of the Mosaic law witnessed the work and ministry of the Lord through types and shadows

follows the same trajectory as the Book of Mormon (see Mosiah 13:31; 16:14; Alma 25:15–16).

6. Albeit in Hebrews 9:9b–10, the epistle does note that the insufficiency of the sacrifices of the old covenant were the reason access to God could not be obtained.
7. Cockerill, *Epistle*, 397.
8. My translation throughout.
9. Albert Vanhoye, *Letter to the Hebrews: A New Commentary*, trans. Leo Arnold (New York: Paulist Press, 2015), 148.
10. William L. Lane, *Hebrews 9–13*, Word Biblical Commentary 47b (Dallas: Word Books, 1991), 239.
11. Gustav Stählin, *Theological Dictionary of the New Testament*, ed. Gerhard Kittel, trans. Geoffrey W. Bromiley (Grand Rapids, MI: Eerdmans, 1967), 1:383–84 (hereafter cited as *TDNT*).
12. or a study, see Johannes Schneider, *TDNT*, 5:739–40.
13. Cockerill, *Epistle*, 401.
14. Luke Timothy Johnson, *Hebrews: A Commentary* (Louisville, KY: Westminster John Knox, 2006), 238.
15. Lane, *Hebrews 9–13*, 240–41.
16. The main object of the Day of Atonement ritual was to accomplish such a purification. See Johnson, *Hebrews*, 71.
17. "The New Strong's Expanded Dictionary of the Words in the Greek New Testament," in James Strong, *The New Strong's Expanded, Exhaustive Concordance of the Bible* (Nashville: Thomas Nelson, 2001), 161. For additional studies, see Albrecht Oepke, *TDNT*, 4:598–624; *NID*, 3:284–88.
18. Cockerill, *Epistle*, 402.
19. Vanhoye, *Letter*, 151–52.
20. Cockerill, *Epistle*, 403. Those who composed this group may have roots that go back to the premortal existence. See Orson F. Whitney, *Saturday Night Thoughts* (Salt Lake City: Deseret Book, 1921), 129–30, http://gospelink.com/library/contents/620. This applies to those who are called to priesthood authority. As the author of Hebrews states, people do not take this honor upon themselves, but they must be called of God (Hebrews 5:4). Some of those to whom he wrote were members of this group (see Hebrews 3:1). In modern history, the Lord has noted that "many are called" but due to unfaithfulness do not remain part of this group (Doctrine and Covenants 121:40, compare Matthew 24:14).
21. By this means, the author shows that "the called" could include even those who rebelled under Moses if they repented. Johnson, *Hebrews*, 240.
22. Friedrich Büschel, *TDNT*, 4:344.
23. In the LXX, the verb translated as "atonement" is *exilaskomai* and means "to appease" (see BDAG, 350). In its religious but broader context, it portrays the idea that sin causes the gods to become angry and this can bring upon the offending party divine wrath. To appease them, a gift had to be given or some action completed. When such was offered and accepted, then the gods were appeased and good relations restored.
24. Frances Brown, S. R. Driver, and Charles A. Briggs, *A Hebrew and English Lexicon of the Old Testament* (Oxford: Clarendon Press, reprint 1987), 497–98 (hereafter cited as BDB).
25. BDB, 497–98.
26. Cockerill, *Epistle*, 416.

27. Cockerill, *Epistle*, 416.
28. Lane, *Hebrews 9–13*, 247.
29. Cockerill, *Epistle*, 416–17.
30. Paul Ellingworth, *The Epistle to the Hebrews*, The New International Commentary on the New Testament (Grand Rapids, MI: Eerdmans, 2015), 477.
31. The singular here stands in contrast to the plural "sins" used in 1:3; 2:17; 9:28; 10:1 and thereby connotes, with emphasis, "sin" as *the* principle and force that stands between the individual and God. Cockerill, *Epistle*, 422–43, 427.
32. F. F. Bruce, *The Epistle to the Hebrews*, The New International Commentary on the New Testament, rev. ed. (Grand Rapids, MI: Eerdmans, 1990), 232.
33. Cockerill, *Epistle*, 423n22. For the cosmic nature of the Lord's atonement, see Doctrine and Covenants 76:23–24.

Chapter Twenty-Two

Make Your Calling and Election Sure

ROBERT L. MILLET

Joseph Smith the Prophet declared that "Peter penned the most sublime language of any of the apostles."[1] While it is in the first chapter of Peter's second epistle that we encounter the invitation for us to become "partakers of the divine nature" (2 Peter 1:4), both epistles point us powerfully toward that supernal ideal.

Let me first speak of the procedure we will follow in discussing this sacred and sensitive matter. It might be appropriate in a traditional academic conference to spend a significant portion of time reviewing the literature of scholars of other faiths on the writings of 2 Peter, debating the authorship and dating of the epistle, or detailing the various interpretive avenues that New Testament experts from the past have pursued. To be sure, we can learn much from scholars and church leaders from other faiths regarding the history, language, or culture behind a scriptural text. What follows, however, is a faith-based, Restoration-centered, doctrinal investigation of the subject. We do not turn to Roman Catholic scholars to teach us how to build temples or to Protestant theologians to receive insights into the proper place of covenants and ordinances. When it comes to doctrinal interpretation, our principal and primary source must be the scriptures of the Restoration and the writings and sermons of latter-day apostles and prophets. This is a topic that can only be engaged seriously by a people well acquainted with premortal existence, temples, priesthood keys, sealing powers, and kingdoms of glory hereafter.

To avoid or ignore the distinctive insights provided by modern revelation is foolish at best and spiritually perilous at worst. In a revelation given in March of 1831, the Savior declared, "I have sent *mine everlasting covenant* into the world, *to be a light to the world, and to be a standard for my people*, . . . and to be a messenger before my face to prepare the way before me" (Doctrine and Covenants 45:9; emphasis added). In September of that same year, the Lord offered similar counsel: "Behold, I, the Lord, have made my church in these last days like unto a judge sitting on a hill, or in a high place, to judge the nations. For it shall come to pass that *the inhabitants of Zion shall judge all things pertaining to Zion*" (Doctrine and Covenants 64:37–38; emphasis added).

Latter-day Saint writers, including general church leaders, have not written or spoken of the doctrine of calling and election very often, not because it is a forbidden subject, but rather a sensitive one. Furthermore, because the Brethren have said very little about it publicly, that is not an announcement that we should avoid it like a plague, that the teaching has somehow fallen on hard times, that it has been officially relegated to the category of folklore or pop theology, that it is out of date, or that it is no longer held to be the doctrine of the church. For heaven's sake, this precious truth is found in the standard works, within the New Testament, the Doctrine and Covenants, and the sermons of the Prophet Joseph Smith. And when it comes to relevance or timeliness in the twenty-first century, what could be more everlastingly pertinent than the quest for eternal life and the sweet assurance that one's salvation is secure?

The Sanctification of the Soul

Peter begins with a description of the people of the church of Jesus Christ as the "elect according to the foreknowledge of God," those who have, through the sanctifying blood of the Redeemer, been begotten into what Peter calls a "lively hope," that is, a living hope—a sweet expectation, a sturdy anticipation, a dynamic assurance—of a glorious resurrection. These have placed themselves in a condition to enjoy "an inheritance incorruptible, and undefiled, and that fadeth not away, reserved in heaven for you," those who "are kept by the power of God through faith unto salvation" (1 Peter 1:1–5).

In the second chapter of the first epistle, Peter reminds us that our Lord was guileless, that he never sinned. Thus a significant step toward becoming a partaker of the divine nature is being engaged in the imitation of Christ, the emulation of the sinless Son of Man, following in the steps of the Prototype or standard for all saved beings (1 Peter 2:21–22).[2] C. S. Lewis observed, "Whatever may have been the powers of unfallen man, it appears that those of redeemed man will be *almost* unlimited. Christ is bringing up human nature with Him. Where He goes, it goes too. It will be made 'like Him.'" Lewis pointed out that divine miracles "anticipate powers which all men will have when they also are 'sons' of God and enter into that 'glorious liberty.'" Christ becomes not a prodigy, but "a pioneer. He is the first of His kind; He will not be the last."[3]

In the fourth chapter, Peter challenges the Saints to gain "the same mind" as Christ (compare 1 Corinthians 2:16). "For you who have suffered in the flesh should cease from sin, that you no longer the rest of your time in the flesh, should live to the lusts of men, but to the will of God" (Joseph Smith Translation, 1 Peter 4:1–2). Peter also reminds the members that because they are living at the end of the age, the final days of the meridian dispensation, they should be sober and watchful. "And above all things have fervent charity among yourselves: for charity preventeth a multitude of sins" (Joseph Smith Translation, 1 Peter 4:8).

In the fifth and final chapter of the first epistle, a passage of profound significance, the members are counseled tenderly: "Humble yourselves therefore under the mighty hand of God, that he may exalt you in due time: casting all your care upon him; for he careth for you" (1 Peter 5:6–7). The New Jerusalem Bible renders this as follows: "Bow down, then, before the power of God now, so that he may raise you up in due time; unload all your burden on to him, since he is concerned about you." Or, as paraphrased in Eugene Peterson's *The Message*: "So be content with who you are, and don't put on airs. God's strong hand is on you; he'll promote you at the right time. Live carefree before God; he is most careful with you."[4]

In the tenth verse of this final chapter, Peter provides a summation of the means by which weak and fallen men and women are made right with God, are made whole, and are established and grounded in the faith: "But the God of all grace, who hath called us unto his eternal glory by Christ Jesus, after that ye have suffered a while, make you perfect, stablish, strengthen, settle you" (1 Peter 5:10).

Like Precious Faith

As we turn our attention to Second Peter, it is fascinating that the senior apostle begins his letter by addressing himself to "*them that have obtained like precious faith with us* through the righteousness of God and our Savior Jesus Christ" (2 Peter 1:1; emphasis added). *Like precious faith.* Those who have come out of the world by covenant, who have been baptized and become members of the household of faith, these have acquired the same kind of faith as the apostles. There is not one gospel for prophets and another for the rank and file of the church. No, theirs is a like precious faith, the faith that is centered in the Lord Jesus Christ, the faith that trusts totally in, has complete confidence in, and relies wholly upon the Savior. This is the faith that enables one to move steadily through the vicissitudes of life, to make decisions based on gospel priorities, the faith that empowers one to overcome every temptation of the devil (see Alma 37:33), the faith that leads to life and salvation. Such faith brings an actual knowledge that the course one is pursuing in life is according to the divine will,[5] which knowledge is accompanied by "exceeding great and precious promises." By receiving these promises, the peace in this world that is a forerunner of the ultimate peace associated with eternal life in the world to come (Doctrine and Covenants 59:23), the faithful begin to become partakers of the divine nature.

Peter then reports that the fruits that flow from such faith are endowments of the Spirit that represent the Christlike character, the character of one who has begun to enjoy what Paul described as the "fruit of the Spirit" (Galatians 5:22–25). Peter mentions virtue, knowledge, temperance, patience, godliness, brotherly kindness, and charity. A modern revelation teaches that such qualities ought to be found in the hearts and lives of those who aspire to teach the gospel and bring people into the faith (Doctrine and Covenants 4:5–6). Respected New Testament scholar N. T. Wright translated this passage: "So, because of this, *you should strain every nerve to supplement your faith with virtue*, and your virtue with knowledge," and so on (The Kingdom New Testament; emphasis added). Perhaps a word or two about each of these qualities or attributes would be helpful.

Virtue is a condition of uprightness, moral excellence, goodness, and a life that demonstrates consistency with truth or with the way things really are (see Jacob 4:13; see also Doctrine and Covenants 93:24).

Knowledge is vital because one cannot be saved in ignorance (see Doctrine and Covenants 131:6) and because a saving conviction is always predicated upon propositions of truth. We cannot live consistent with that which we do not know, nor can we endure faithfully to the end when we do not understand that which requires our lifetime loyalty.

Temperance is self-control. It was Jesus himself who taught, "Blessed are the meek: for they shall inherit the earth" (Matthew 5:5). It is the meek person who is restrained, not alone by social prohibitions but, more importantly, through *temperance*, or self-control.

Patience is that virtue, that Godlike quality that demonstrates one's trust in God's program, trust in the Lord's purposes, and acquiescence to the divine timetable. To have patience is to have hope, to be willing to wait upon the Lord.

Godliness is a quality of a man or woman who has yielded his or her heart unto God (see Helaman 3:35), a believer whose genuine piety is reflected in his or her willing conformity to divine law.

Brotherly kindness is more than nice and attractive; it is a fundamental and vital feature of the outworking of the Spirit of Jesus Christ in our lives. One of the ways we assess our growth unto godliness is the extent to which we have begun to value the children of God, to love our brothers and sisters. Christianity is only partially about individual transformation and personal salvation; it is also concerned with community and corporate growth, how and in what manner we have come to treasure and respect humanity.

Charity, the pure love of Christ, is of course the highest of all spiritual gifts, the grandest of all heavenly endowments, and that "more excellent way" (1 Corinthians 12:31; Ether 12:11). It was Mormon who taught us that true followers of Christ are those who have become by spiritual regeneration the sons and daughters of God, persons who have been lifted, purified, and transformed by this sacred love into the image of Christ. These will see the returning King for who he is, for they will be like him (Moroni 7:47–48).

Truly, as Peter states, a man or woman who possesses these qualities and gifts is neither "barren nor unfruitful in the knowledge of our Lord Jesus Christ," while the person who lacks them is "blind, and cannot see afar off, and hath forgotten that he was purged from his old sins" (2 Peter 1:8–9). That is, the Saint who manifests such attributes is not idle, is not unprofitable; rather, he or she is alive, spiritually productive, contributing regularly and meaningfully to the life of the Church of God and the betterment of God's world. On the other hand, one who lacks such qualities is living as though there had been no redemption made (see Moroni 7:38); he or she has a warped perspective on life, views things through the lenses of the natural man, is self-absorbed, is spiritually myopic, and has little sensitivity to sacred things. Such persons cannot see the distant scene.

Note that Peter observes that a member of the church who enjoys this character is fruitful "in the knowledge of our Lord Jesus Christ" (2 Peter 1:8). Such a person is enjoying both the cleansing and enabling powers of the Lord's Atonement and is experiencing the enlivening companionship of the Holy Spirit, which is the midwife of such spiritual traits. It is by the blood that we are sanctified from sin and by the medium of the Lord's Spirit that we grow in spiritual graces and in our relationship with God and man. In writing of one who has undergone this mighty change of heart, Elder Parley P. Pratt explained,

> His mind is quickened, his intellectual faculties are aroused to intense activity. He is, as it were, illuminated. He learns more of divine truth in a few days than he could have learned in a lifetime in the best merely human institutions in the world. His affections are also purified, exalted, and increased in proportion. He loves his Heavenly Father and Jesus Christ with a perfect love. He also loves the members of the Church, or the body of Christ, as he loves his own soul; while his bosom swells with the tenderest sympathies and emotions of good will and benevolence for all mankind. He would make any sacrifice that might be expedient to do good. He would lay down his life most cheerfully, without one moment's hesitation or regret, if required of him by the cause of truth.[6]

It was Paul, Peter's apostolic colleague, who wrote so eloquently of the transformation of his own soul following his conversion to Christ and Christianity: "But what things were gain to me [before conversion], those I counted loss for Christ. Yea doubtless, and *I count all things but loss for the excellency of the knowledge of Christ Jesus my Lord*: for whom I have suffered the loss of all things, and do count them but dung, that I may win Christ, and be found in him, not having mine own righteousness, which is of the law, but that which is through the faith of Christ, the righteousness which is of God by faith: *that I may know him*, and the power of his resurrection, and the fellowship of his sufferings, being made conformable unto his death" (Philippians 3:7–10; emphasis added). Indeed, the knowledge that matters, the knowledge that settles and sanctifies the human heart, and the knowledge that prompts purity and motivates one to selfless service, is the knowledge that Jesus Christ is the Son of God and the Savior of all humankind; that through him and him alone, we are able to be delivered from sin and death and hell and endless torment; that there is no weakness he cannot turn to strength, no emptiness he cannot fill, no sickness that the great Physician cannot heal. Again quoting Paul, "thanks be to God, [who gives] us the victory through our Lord Jesus Christ" (1 Corinthians 15:57).

Called and Elected

Having spoken of the need to become partakers of the divine nature, the need to acquire the fruit of the Spirit that produces Christlike character, Peter then counsels us, "Wherefore the rather, brethren, give diligence to make your calling and election sure: for if ye do these things ye shall never fall: for so an entrance shall be ministered unto you abundantly into the everlasting kingdom of our Lord and Savior Jesus Christ" (2 Peter 1:10–11). The first part of this verse is difficult to understand, particularly as it has been rendered in the King James Version. Alternate translations of "Wherefore the rather, brethren" include "All the more reason, brethren" (Revised English Bible) or "Be all the more eager to confirm your call and election" (New Revised Standard Version) or "Be all the more eager to make your calling and election sure" (New International Version). That is to say, "Don't be shortsighted or spiritually vacuous, but instead do all within your power to make your calling and election sure."

The words *calling* and *election* are often used interchangeably. In scripture they tend to refer to a duty or an assignment, a responsibility within God's kingdom. Elder Bruce R. McConkie explained,

> To be called is to be a member of the Church and kingdom of God on earth; it is to be numbered with the saints; it is to accept the gospel and receive the everlasting covenant. . . . It is to be born again; to be a son or a daughter of the Lord Jesus Christ . . . it is to have a conditional promise of eternal life; it is to be an inheritor of all of the blessings of the gospel, provided there is continued obedience to the laws and ordinances thereof.
>
> The Lord's calls are the result of foreordination and grow out of faithfulness in the [premortal existence]. . . . That is, the saints were foreordained in the councils of eternity to believe the truth, to be sanctified, and to save their souls; and then in this life they are called to that gospel whereby these eternal promises can be fulfilled. . . . And if by a long course of trial and obedience, while yet in this life, a man proves to the Lord that he has and will abide in the truth, the Lord accepts the exhibited devotion and issues his decree that the promised blessings shall be received. The calling, which up to that time was provisional, is then made sure. The receipt of the promised blessings is no longer conditional; they are guaranteed. Announcement is made that every gospel blessing shall be inherited. . . .
>
> To have one's calling and election made sure is to be sealed up unto eternal life; it is to have the unconditional guarantee of exaltation in the highest heaven of the celestial world; it is to receive the assurance of godhood; it is, in effect, to have the day of judgment advanced.[7]

In other words, the apostle Peter pointed the minds of the former-day Saints toward their eternal possibilities. He encouraged them, knowing of trying times which lay ahead as they moved toward the end of the age, the end of the dispensation. In the words of Paul, the Saints were to "press toward the mark for the prize of the high calling of God in Christ Jesus" (Philippians 3:14). Would they make mistakes after receiving the assurance of salvation? Of course they would. Would they sin? Yes, for no person, except the Lord Jesus, has walked this earth and remained free from sin. While the inclination to commit serious sin will generally have been banished from the soul of such a righteous man or woman (see Mosiah 5:2; Alma 13:12; 19:33), yet the pull of the flesh will remain as long as we reside on a telestial earth.

President Brigham Young asked,

> *Will sin be perfectly destroyed? No, it will not, for it is not so designed in the economy of heaven. . . . Do not suppose that we shall ever in the flesh be free from temptations to sin.* Some suppose that they can in the flesh be sanctified body and spirit and become so pure that they will never again feel the effects of the power of the adversary of truth. Were it possible for a person to attain to this degree of perfection in the flesh, he could not die neither remain in a world where sin predominates. . . . I think we shall more or less feel the effects of sin so long as we live, and finally have to pass the ordeals of death.[8]

Consequently, persons who have made their calling and election sure to eternal life are required to be vigilant, humble, and dependent upon the Lord for spiritual protection, and to strive to be true to their covenants until they pass through the veil and are safely dead! When they fall, they "shall rise again" (Doctrine and Covenants 117:13). As President Young said on another occasion: "It requires all the atonement of Christ, the mercy of the Father, the pity of angels and the grace of the Lord Jesus Christ to be with us always, and then to do the very best we possibly can, to get rid of this sin within us, so that we may escape from this world into the celestial kingdom."[9]

In a revelation given at the time of the organization of the restored church, we learn, "And we know that justification through the grace of our Lord and Savior Jesus Christ is just and true; and we know also, that sanctification through the grace of our Lord and Savior Jesus Christ is just and true, to all those who love and serve God with all their mights, minds, and strength." Now note this warning: "But *there is a possibility that man may fall from grace* and depart from the living God; therefore *let the church take heed and pray always,* lest they fall into temptation; yea, and even *let those who are sanctified take heed also*" (Doctrine and Covenants 20:30–34; emphasis added).

The Presbyterians in Joseph Smith's day taught that one could not fall from grace and that once salvation was received, it could not be lost. The Methodists taught, on the other hand, that one could in fact fall from grace and be renewed and restored. Joseph taught that the fulness of truth took a road between them both—that in general while people could fall from grace and repent, there was a sin, known as the unpardonable sin or sin against the Holy Ghost, against which even the supernal power of Elijah could not seal an individual.[10] The message is clear: every living soul, no matter the spiritual heights to which he or she may have ascended, must endure in faith until the end. Those who have passed the tests of mortality are forgiven of their sins through genuine repentance, just like all of God's children. While much is required of those who have gained the supernal assurance of exaltation (see Doctrine and Covenants 82:3), all of humankind are saved by obedience to the laws and ordinances of the gospel (see Articles of Faith 1:3; see also Doctrine and Covenants 82:3).[11]

In this context Peter adds that "an entrance shall be ministered unto you abundantly into the everlasting kingdom of our Lord and Saviour Jesus Christ" (2 Peter 1:11). To say this another way, "For if you practice these qualities you will never fall. For in this way there will be richly provided for you an entrance into the eternal kingdom" (English Standard Version). Or, "For in this way, entry into the eternal kingdom of our Lord and Savior Jesus Christ will be richly provided for you" (New Revised Standard Version). Or, "you will receive a rich welcome into the eternal kingdom" (New International Version).

In summary, we are speaking here of what Paul called the "hope of eternal life, which God, that cannot lie, promised before the world began" (Titus 1:2), being made sure, made solid, made secure. We are reminded of the marvelous words of the Prophet Joseph when he taught: "After a person hath faith in Christ, repents of his sins, and is baptized for the remission of his sins and receives the Holy Ghost (by the laying on of hands), . . . then let him continue to humble himself before God, hungering and thirsting after righteousness, and living by every word of God, and the Lord will soon say unto him, Son, thou shalt be exalted. When the Lord has thoro[ugh]ly proved him, and finds that the man is determined to serve him at all hazards, then the man will find his calling and Election made sure."[12]

THE MORE SURE WORD

The senior apostle then turns himself to testimony. He alludes to the fact that he knows he will soon "put off this my tabernacle, even as our Lord Jesus Christ hath shewed me" (2 Peter 1:14). He then bears witness of the message of the gospel, that Jesus of Nazareth is all that the prophets said he would be, and that he is indeed the Lord of glory: "For we have not followed cunningly devised fables, when we made known unto you the power and coming of our Lord Jesus Christ, but were eyewitnesses of his majesty" (2 Peter 1:16). That is, "We are not making all of this up. This is not some devious and fictitious sham." We "were not following cleverly devised myths. Rather, we were eyewitnesses of his grandeur" (Kingdom New Testament). Peter then makes reference to the transcendent experience he and James and John had enjoyed with the Savior on the Mount of Transfiguration some six months before the Crucifixion: "For [Christ] received from God the Father honour and glory, when there came such a voice to him from the excellent glory, This is my beloved Son, in whom I am well pleased. And this voice which came from heaven we heard, when we were with him in the holy mount" (2 Peter 1:17–18).

Christians have generally viewed the Transfiguration as a display of "a new and greater Moses," a reminder of the baptism of Jesus where that same voice was heard, and a foreshadowing of the glory their Master would receive in the Resurrection.[13] Christian pastor and theologian John MacArthur has written,

> The Jesus who had been living for over thirty years in ordinary human form was now partially seen in the blazing effulgence of God (compare Hebrews 1:1–3). From within himself, in a way that defies full description, much less full explanation, Jesus's divine glory was manifested before Peter, James, and John. Here is the greatest confirmation of his deity yet in the life of Jesus. Here, more than on any other occasion, Jesus revealed Himself as He truly is, the Son of God. . . . As with the Shekinah [holy cloud] manifestations of the Old Testament, God here portrayed Himself to human eyes in a form of light so dazzling and overwhelming that it could barely be withstood.

MacArthur added, "That awesome experience was but a foretaste of the day in which 'the Son of man shall come in the glory of his Father with his angels (Matthew 16:27).'"[14]

Latter-day Saints have received additional insights pertaining to what took place on the mount. We know from modern revelation and prophetic teaching that Peter, James, and John—the meridian First Presidency—were granted a most unusual vision of the future. The Savior declared in August 1831, "Nevertheless, he that endureth in faith and doeth my will, the same shall overcome, and shall receive an inheritance upon the earth when the day of transfiguration shall come"—at the Second Coming, when the earth will be changed, lifted to a terrestrial condition—"when the earth shall be transfigured, even according to the pattern which was shown unto mine apostles upon the mount; of which account the fulness ye have not yet received" (Doctrine and Covenants 63:20–21).

Joseph Smith explained, "The Savior, Moses, and Elias gave the keys to Peter, James, and John, on the mount, when they were transfigured before him"—that is, when the three apostles were also transfigured with their Lord.[15] We would presume that these keys were the same as those conferred upon Joseph Smith and Oliver Cowdery in the Kirtland Temple on April 3, 1836 (Doctrine and Covenants 110:11–16). Further, President Joseph Fielding Smith has suggested that it was on the mount that the chief apostles received what we would know today as the temple endowment.[16]

Finally, James Burgess reported that the Prophet Joseph made the following comments in a sermon in Nauvoo on August 27, 1843: "Men will set up stakes and say thus far will we go and no farther. Did Abraham when [he was] called upon to offer his son? And did the Savior? No. View [the Savior] fulfilling all righteousness again on the banks of Jordan. Also, *on the Mount transfigured before Peter and John, there receiving the fulness of priesthood* or the law of God, setting up no stake but coming right up to the mark in all things."[17] According to Wilford Woodruff's journal, the Prophet said, "If a man gets a fullness of the priesthood of God he has to get it in the same way that Jesus obtained it, and that was by keeping all the commandments and obeying all the ordinances of the house of the Lord."[18]

Peter testified, "We have also a more sure word of prophecy; whereunto ye do well that ye take heed, as unto a light that shineth in a dark place, until the day dawn, and the day star arise in your hearts" (2 Peter 1:19). When the

Prophet Joseph Smith was engaged in his inspired translation of the King James Bible, he altered this verse as follows: "We have therefore *a more sure knowledge of the word of prophecy*, to which word of prophecy ye do well that ye take heed" (emphasis added). Now there is no question that Peter and his apostolic colleagues understood, through supernal and ineffable experience with the Master, "the word of prophecy," what we call the spirit of revelation, and that those within the faith who were less seasoned in utilizing or comprehending the gifts of the Spirit, and particularly the gift of prophecy, were well advised to look to those acknowledged prophets, seers, and revelators as both mentors and interpreters. It seems clear that the Prophet Joseph did not, at this early stage of his spiritual development (between 1832 and 1833),[19] understand the doctrine of calling and election and the more sure word of prophecy. Like all the Saints of God, the choice seer grew in understanding and experience line upon line, precept upon precept.[20]

In May 1843, a decade after his inspired translation of 2 Peter, Brother Joseph declared, "The more sure word of prophecy means a man's knowing that he is sealed up unto eternal life, by revelation and the spirit of prophecy, through the power of the Holy Priesthood. It is impossible for a man to be saved in ignorance" (Doctrine and Covenants 131:5–6). Also,

> Notwithstanding the Apostle Exhorts them to Add to their faith virtue knowledge temperan[c]e, &c., yet he Exhorts them to make their calling & election shure & though they had he[a]rd the audible voice from heaven bearing testinoy [testimony] that Jesus was the son of God yet he says we have a more sure word of Prophecy, whare unto ye do well that ye take heed as unto a light shining in a dark place. Now wharein could they have a more sure word of prophecy than to hear the voice of God saying this is my Beloved son &c Now for the secret & grand [*drawing of a key*] key. though they might hear the voice of God & know that Jesus was the son of God this would be no evidence that their election & calling was made shure that they had part with Christ & was a Joint heir with him, they then would want that more sure word of prophecy that they were sealed in the heavens & had the promise of eternal life in the kingdom of God— then having this promise sealed unto them it was an anchor to the soul sure & steadfast.[21]

Joseph then added that "this hope & knowledge would support the soul in evry hour of trial trouble & tribulation." [22] The Prophet then made a statement that clarifies and expands upon Peter's words—that having acquired faith, virtue, knowledge, temperance, patience, godliness, brotherly love, and charity, we become fruitful "in the knowledge of our Lord Jesus Christ" (2 Peter 1:8): "Then knowledge through our Lord and Savior Jesus Christ is the grand key that unlocks the glories and mysteries of the kingdom of heaven."[23] Knowledge of anything that is "virtuous, lovely, or of good report or praiseworthy" (Articles of Faith 1:13) is worthwhile and commendable, but the knowledge about which Peter and Joseph Smith are speaking is the knowledge that saves, the knowledge that one's course in life is pleasing to God and that one will go on to eternal life and exaltation. The Prophet beckons to us: "Then I would exhort you to go on and continue to call upon God until you make your calling and election sure for yourselves, by obtaining this more sure word of prophecy, and wait patiently for the promise until you obtain it."[24]

CONCLUSION

In reflecting on this glorious doctrine, we might ask, "Is this something we should desire or seek for?" In response, who among us, living in a fallen world filled with disappointment, distress, and hopelessness, does not long to know that our lives are acceptable to God, that we are on course and will one day inherit a better world? As Elder McConkie has written, "Among those who have received the gospel, and who are seeking diligently to live its laws and gain eternal life, there is an instinctive and determined desire to make their calling and election sure. Because they have tasted the good things of God and sipped from the fountain of eternal truth, they now seek the divine presence, where they shall know all things, have all power, all might, and all dominion, and in fact be like Him who is the great Prototype of all saved beings—God our Heavenly and Eternal Father (see Doctrine and Covenants 132:20). This is the end objective, the chief goal of all the faithful, and there is nothing greater in all eternity, 'for there is no gift greater than the gift of salvation'" (Doctrine and Covenants 6:13).[25]

King Benjamin offered this timeless counsel: "Therefore, I would that ye should be *steadfast and immovable*, always abounding in good works, *that Christ, the Lord God Omnipotent, may seal you his, that you may be brought to heaven, that ye may have everlasting salvation and eternal life*, through the wisdom, and power, and justice, and mercy of him who created all things, in heaven and in earth, who is God above all" (Mosiah 5:15; emphasis added). Steadfast and immovable—those are the key words, for they are the scriptural description of balance and spiritual stability.

It was while wrestling with his assignment as a new and inexperienced priesthood leader and struggling to know how best to assist those who were in transgression, that Alma the Elder, a very good man who "feared that he should do wrong in the sight of God," poured out his heart in prayer to God. Alma was commended for choosing to respond affirmatively to the power and invitation of Abinadi's words, for being willing to repent of his sins, and be a part of the Church of Jesus Christ. "Thou art my servant," the Lord stated, "and I covenant with thee that thou shalt have eternal life" (Mosiah 26:13–20). We note that Alma was not seeking to be truer than true when this glorious assurance came to him. He was not on a calling and election crusade. Rather, he was busily engaged in doing his duty, striving with all his heart to bless, lift, and strengthen his brothers and sisters. There's a message there for us.

We must be willing to come to that point of personal commitment where whatever the Lord calls upon us to do, we will do. Such unconditional surrender of self is always prerequisite to gaining the ultimate victory. The Prophet and the early brethren taught that only by being willing to sacrifice all things, including our own life if necessary, can we gain the actual knowledge that our course in life is in harmony with the heavens. Thus "a religion that does not require the sacrifice of all things never has power sufficient to produce the faith necessary unto life and salvation. . . . It was through this sacrifice, and this only, that God has ordained that men should enjoy eternal life; and it is through the medium of the sacrifice of all earthly things that men do actually know that they are doing the things that are well pleasing in the sight of God."[26] In short, the Lord essentially asks us, "Do you want me to give you all that I have?" We of course respond positively. And then the Savior answers, "Then be willing to give me all that you have."

It is worthwhile to read how and why Joseph Smith himself received the assurance of eternal life. The Lord addressed his modern seer: "For I am the Lord thy God, and will be with thee even unto the end of the world, and through all eternity; for verily *I seal upon you your exaltation*, and prepare a throne for you in the kingdom of my Father, with Abraham your father. Behold, *I have seen your sacrifices*, and will forgive all your sins; I have seen your sacrifices in obedience to that which I have told you" (Doctrine and Covenants 132:49–50, emphasis added; compare 97:8).

Surely there are few things more important in this life than striving to live in such a manner as to always enjoy companionship with the Holy Ghost. The clearer are our views, the more we will strive to avoid anything that would cost us the influence of that Holy Spirit. It is that Spirit that testifies, that confirms, that informs and inspires, and that sanctifies. And it is that Spirit that brings peace (see Doctrine and Covenants 6:23). In August 1831 the Lord counseled the early Saints to "learn that he who doeth the works of righteousness shall receive his reward, even peace in this world, and eternal life in the world to come" (Doctrine and Covenants 59:23). In this light, President Marion G. Romney explained, "The fulness of eternal life is not attainable in mortality, but *the peace which is its harbinger and which comes as a result of making one's calling and election sure is attainable in this life*."[27]

Latter-day Saints who have received the ordinances of salvation—including the blessings of the temple—may press forward in the work of the Lord and with quiet dignity and patient maturity seek to be worthy of gaining the certain assurance of salvation before the end of their mortal lives. But should one not formally receive the more sure word of prophecy in this life, he or she has the scriptural promise that faithfully enduring to the end—keeping the covenants and commandments from baptism to the end of their lives (see Mosiah 18:8–9)—leads one to the promise of eternal life, whether that promise be received here or hereafter (see Doctrine and Covenants 14:7; 53:7; 2 Nephi 31:20; Mosiah 5:15). "But blessed are they who are faithful and endure, whether in life or in death, for they shall inherit eternal life" (Doctrine and Covenants 50:5). God grant that such will be our sweet privilege and our supernal blessing.

Robert L. Millet is a professor emeritus of ancient scripture at Brigham Young University.

Robert L. Millet, "Make Your Calling and Election Sure," in *The Ministry of Peter, the Chief Apostle*, ed. Frank F. Judd Jr., Eric D. Huntsman, and Shon D. Hopkin (Provo, UT: Religious Studies Center; Salt Lake City: Deseret Book, 2014), 267–82.

NOTES

1. Discourse, 17 May 1843–A, as Reported by William Clayton, p. 16, The Joseph Smith Papers.
2. See *Lectures on Faith* (Salt Lake City: Deseret Book, 1985), 75–76, 7:9.
3. C. S. Lewis, *Miracles* (New York: Touchstone, 1996), 178; emphasis added.
4. Eugene H. Peterson, *The Message: The Bible in Contemporary Language* (Colorado Springs, CO: NavPress, 2002), 2216.
5. See *Lectures on Faith*, 67–69, 6:2–7.
6. Parley P. Pratt, *Key to the Science of Theology* (Salt Lake City: Deseret Book, 1985), 59–60.
7. Bruce R. McConkie, *Doctrinal New Testament Commentary*, 3 vols. (Salt Lake City: Bookcraft, 1965–73), 3:326, 327–28, 330–31.
8. Brigham Young, in *Journal of Discourses*, 26 vols. (London: Latter-day Saints' Book Depot, 1854–86), 10:173; emphasis added.
9. Young, in *Journal of Discourses*, 11:301.
10. Wilford Woodruff Journal, 10 March 1844, The Joseph Smith Papers.
11. Citing the apostle Paul (see Hebrews 10:26) and the Prophet Joseph Smith, Elder McConkie points out that those who have made their calling and election sure who then become guilty of serious sin "must then pay the penalty of their own sins, for the blood of Christ will not cleanse them." More specifically, those who commit adultery or murder break the seal and go to the telestial kingdom, while those who commit the unpardonable sin break the seal and become sons of perdition. *Doctrinal New Testament Commentary* 3:343; *A New Witness for the Articles of Faith* (Salt Lake City: Deseret Book, 1985), 232; Wilford Woodruff Journal, March 10, 1844, 2:363.
12. History, 1838–1856, volume C-1 (2 November 1838–31 July 1842), The Joseph Smith Papers.
13. See W. D. Davies and Dale C. Allison, *A Critical and Exegetical Commentary on the Gospel According to Saint Matthew*, 3 vols. (Edinburgh: T & T Clark, 1988–97), 2:687.
14. John MacArthur, *The MacArthur New Testament Commentary—Matthew*, 3 vols. (Chicago: Moody Press, 1985–89), 3:63–64.
15. Discourse between 26 June and ca August 1839-A, The Joseph Smith Papers.
16. Joseph Fielding Smith, *Doctrines of Salvation*, 3 vols., comp. Bruce R. McConkie (Salt Lake City: Bookcraft, 1954–56), 2:165, 170; see also Bruce R. McConkie, *Doctrinal New Testament Commentary* 1:400.
17. Ehat and Cook, *Words of Joseph Smith* 246; punctuation supplied.
18. *Words of Joseph Smith*, 307.
19. See Robert J. Matthews, *A Plainer Translation: Joseph Smith's Translation of the Bible—a History and Commentary* (Provo, UT: Brigham Young University Press, 1975), 96.

20. Other examples of alterations in the King James text indicate that Joseph did not grasp, at the time of the translation, what he would understand and teach in later years, including the JST of Hebrews 11:40 and the JST of Revelation 1:5–6.
21. Discourse, 14 May 1843, as Reported by Wilford Woodruff, 31–32, The Joseph Smith Papers.
22. Discourse, 14 May 1843, as Reported by Wilford Woodruff, 32.
23. History, 1838–1856, volume D-1 [1 August 1842–1 July 1843], p. 1549, The Joseph Smith Papers.
24. Wilford Woodruff Journal, 14 May 1843, The Joseph Smith Papers.
25. McConkie, *Doctrinal New Testament Commentary*, 3:325.
26. *Lectures on Faith*, 69, 6:7.
27. Marion G. Romney, in Conference Report, October 1965; in *Look to God and Live* (Salt Lake City: Deseret Book, 1971), 125–26; emphasis added.

Chapter Twenty-Three

The Paradoxical Lamb and the Christology of John's Apocalypse

NICHOLAS J. FREDERICK

With the exception of a few chapters, the book of Revelation is the written record of a magnificent vision beheld by a man identified only as "his servant John" (Revelation 1:1). Over the course of this vision, John is taken to the throne room of God, witnesses a series of bizarre events as the earth descends into chaos, and finally sees the creation of a "new heaven and a new earth." Central to the book of Revelation's theological project is the introduction and development of its central protagonist, Jesus Christ. While Jesus appears briefly in the very first chapter, over the course of John's lengthy vision Jesus is most often symbolized by a *lamb*, a figure that appears twenty-eight times before the conclusion of the vision. This lamb, in the words of one scholar, is "the leading Christological expression of the book, central for understanding John's rhetorical argument and theology."[1] But this is no ordinary lamb. John's lamb is both victim and leader, one who conquers through his own death and overcomes evil through his own suffering. Achieving victory through vulnerability, the lamb is simultaneously *conquered* and *conqueror.*

The lamb, then, is a paradoxical image brimming with tension, a tension that is not easily resolved but itself leads to a series of questions: What Christological understanding is John (and his audience) expected to glean from this lamb imagery? How does John's vision speak to the fundamental nature of Jesus Christ and his mission? What elements of the lamb must we as his disciples develop if we are truly to become his sons and daughters?

It's important to remember that "the book of Revelation is notoriously difficult to interpret, and it is an impossible book to interpret completely."[2] All that readers of the book of Revelation can successfully do is study and analyze John's vision with an eye toward *possible* answers, since the book of Revelation seems almost intended to provoke questions rather than provide answers. With this in mind, exploring the paradox of John's lamb Christology and attempting to alleviate some of its tensions through a close examination of the lamb imagery makes clear the remarkable portrait of Jesus in John's vision. The focus of the paper will be on the sections of Revelation that present the heaviest Christological emphasis—namely, chapters 5, 7, 12, 19, and 21.

At this point, it may be useful to further explore how the figure of a lamb was used in Jewish and Christian literature prior to John's writing. The Greek word John uses that is translated in the King James Bible as "lamb" is the Greek term *arnion*, a diminutive of *arēn*.[3] While Jesus is called a "lamb" by other New Testament authors, John the Revelator is the only one to use *arnion*. In 1 Corinthians 5:7, Paul refers to Jesus as "our passover lamb" (Greek *to pascha hēmōn*), while John the Baptist twice calls Jesus "the Lamb of God" (*ho amnos tou theou*; John 1:29, 36). Notably, the only other place where the Greek term *arnion* appears outside the book of Revelation is in reference to those who believe in Jesus, as in John 21:15 when Jesus tells Peter to feed "my lambs" (*ta arnia mou*). If we look earlier into the Hebrew Bible (the Old Testament), the Hebrew word *keḇeś* appears 130 times, making it the most common Hebrew word referring to lamb.[4] The majority of these references to lamb are in a sacrificial context, specifically the lamb as a burnt offering. In the Septuagint, the Greek translation of the Hebrew Bible, *keḇeś* is normally rendered as *amnos*. When *arnion* (or *arēn*) does appear in the Septuagint, it is primarily in a symbolic or metaphorical context.[5] While semantic discussions are usually hazy and difficult to derive conclusions from, it can safely be said that the book of Revelation is applying to Jesus a Christological title unique from other New Testament authors and one that is often applied in symbolic or metaphorical discussions.

JESUS AS THE "CONQUERING" LAMB

With this background in mind, let us now turn our attention to the text of John's vision. Revelation 5 finds John the Revelator in the throne room of God, observing a scene that unfolds, as much of the book of Revelation does, rather curiously. God holds in his hand a scroll and seeks one that is worthy to take the scroll and open it.[6] John begins to weep because the book is sealed with seven seals, and "no man in heaven, nor in earth, neither under the earth, was able to open the book, neither to look thereon" (Revelation 5:3).[7] Fortunately, John is assured that someone—a figure described as "the Lion of the tribe of Juda" and "the Root of David" (5:5)—has successfully opened the scroll.

The titles of "Lion of the tribe of Juda" and "Root of David" are familiar from the Hebrew Bible and are titles charged with Jewish messianic expectation. Jacob had likened Judah to a lion ("Judah is a lion's whelp; from the prey, my son, you have gone up. He crouches down, he stretches out like a lion, like a lioness—who dares rouse him up?") and had declared that the "scepter shall not depart from Judah" (Genesis 49:9–10). The latter proved to be true, as the Davidic kings came through Judah's line, as did Jesus. The description of the lion as "the Root of David" alludes to Isaiah 11, where Isaiah prophesies that "a shoot shall come out from the stump of Jesse, and a branch shall grow out of his roots" (Isaiah 11:1). Isaiah's language further links the tribe of Judah with Davidic kingship and points to a future messianic figure.[8] The choice of the word *conquer* (*enikēsen*) to describe the lion's actions serves to prepare John and his readers for a regal, military figure.

However, what John then sees is something strikingly different. When John looks around for this lion, he sees only a lamb,[9] and not just any lamb, but a lamb that has been slaughtered as a sacrifice (*esphagmenon*).[10] This juxtaposition is potent and forces readers to ask the critical question: Did the elder err in describing the lamb as a lion, or did we as readers err in expecting that Judah's most powerful representative would be anything other than a conquered, bloody, and apparently (previously) dead lamb? As mentioned earlier, in the Hebrew Bible the image of a lamb was often used metaphorically to connote vulnerability.[11] For example, Jeremiah states that "I was like a gentle lamb led to the slaughter" (Jeremiah 11:19) and prophesies that at the arrival of Babylon "the little ones of the flock shall be dragged away" (Jeremiah 50:45). In a passage that may lay behind the application of the lamb imagery to Jesus, Isaiah speaks of the suffering servant as "a lamb that is led to the slaughter." A further possible origin for the usage of lamb imagery in Revelation 5 is that it is meant to evoke the Passover lamb, an image Paul utilizes in 1 Corinthians 5:7.[12] Whether John has in mind Jeremiah's imagery, Isaiah's suffering servant, or the Passover lamb, by promising a lion and then introducing a lamb the throne-room scene in Revelation 5 suggests a critical reversal in Jewish messianic expectations. Rather than a militaristic, warrior messiah (a lion) who will restore the glory of Israel through a physical conquest,[13] the true redemption of Israel will be obtained only through the blood of the lamb, an ultimate victory won through a temporary defeat.[14] It is at this point, then, that readers are introduced to John's "paradoxical lamb," a figure that is at once both dead and alive, victim and victor, one who finds the ultimate expression of life only in death. As one scholar has noted, John employs the image of the lamb in order to "emphasize that it was in an ironic manner that Jesus began to fulfill the OT prophecies of the Messiah's kingdom. Wherever the OT predicts the Messiah's final victory and reign, John's readers are to realize that these goals can begin to be achieved only by the suffering of the cross."[15]

The irony of this scene is further developed through the attribution of "seven horns" and "seven eyes" to the lamb. In Hebrew Bible passages such as Deuteronomy 2:3; Daniel 7:20–21; 1 Samuel 2:1; and Psalm 89:17, "horn" tended to symbolize power and strength.[16] The image appears throughout the Psalms, in passages such as this: "The Lord is my rock, and my fortress, and my deliverer; My God, my strength, in whom I will trust; My buckler, and *the horn of my salvation*, and my high tower" (Psalm 18:2; emphasis added; compare Psalms 75:10; 89:17, 24; 92:10; 112:9).[17] Physically, a horn is typically associated with a ram rather than a sheep, adding an additional level to John's already complex paradox.[18] The description of the lamb having "seven eyes" is likely an allusion to the lamps of the temple menorah in Zechariah 4:10 (compare Revelation 4:6), while eyes themselves can be viewed as symbolic of knowledge or wisdom.[19] Combined with the presence of the number seven, an indicator of "fullness" elsewhere in the book of Revelation and in biblical literature,[20] John's lamb emerges as a figure who is both *omnipotent* and *omniscient*, qualities one would expect from the Davidic Messiah, the lion from the tribe of Judah. The attribution of these two divine traits to a "slaughtered lamb" only serves to heighten the paradoxical imagery of John's throne-room scene.

The paradoxical juxtaposition of the "messianic lamb" is accentuated through the scene of praise that follows the appearance of the lamb. After the lamb approaches the throne of God and takes the book sealed with seven seals from God's right hand, the four beasts and the twenty-four elders who had been gathered around the throne fall down and begin to praise the lamb. Significantly, the focus of their praise is not the power or knowledge of the lamb, but the fact that the lamb had been slaughtered: "Thou art worthy to take the book, and to open the seals thereof: *for thou wast slain*, and hast redeemed us to God *by thy blood* out of every kindred, and tongue, and people, and nation" (Revelation 5:9; emphasis added). The literal meaning of "redeemed" as "to buy back" appears to be intended here, with the lamb's blood being the "currency" used in the "purchase."[21] The result of this divine transaction is that the lamb "hast made us unto our God kings and priests: and we shall reign on the earth" (5:10).[22] While the "power" and "sight" of the lamb are certainly impressive and noteworthy, John emphasizes that the lamb's worthiness and redemption come through its *vulnerability* and *sacrifice.* Significantly, no mention is made of the lamb *conquering death*—the Resurrection is not mentioned as part of the lamb's worthiness. Rather, the focus is upon the lamb's conquering *through* death, an important distinction for John to make.

Jesus as the "Redemptive" Lamb

The blood that flows from the conquering lamb becomes a critical theme in Revelation 7, where John describes what might be termed the "redemptive" lamb. In Revelation 5:9, John had introduced the idea that the blood of the slaughtered lamb acts as a redemptive element for those who follow the lamb. In Revelation 7:14, John further develops the redemptive nature of the lamb's blood through an additional paradoxical image. Here, in Revelation 7, John witnesses the sealing of the 144,000 (12,000 from each tribe). Following the sealing, John notices "a great multitude" standing before God's throne, each "clothed with white robes, and palms in their hands" (Revelation 7:9). When asked by one of the elders for the identity of this party, John responds that he does not know. The elder answers, "These are they which came out of great tribulation, and have washed their robes, and made them white in the blood of the Lamb" (7:14). The idea that "blood" can wash an article of clothing and render it white presents a striking paradox and an additional ironic image for John's readers to grapple with. In the ancient world, one washed one's clothes to remove the dirt, after which a fuller would often bleach the clothing white to remove stains, such as blood. However, the elder's answer is paradoxical, for, as Craig Koester has noted, "even though blood normally stains, here it cleanses."[23] John's imagery of cleansing through blood again highlights Jesus's power. As we sin and thus accumulate spiritual "dirt" or "stain," Jesus offers his cleansing power to those who will receive it.[24] Significantly, we cannot perform this act of cleansing by ourselves—it is his blood, and only he can offer it to us. Understood in this sense, cleansing through blood becomes an act of grace, offered freely to those who have made and kept their covenants and thus "[stand] before the throne" (7:9).[25] Notably, John will return to this imagery later in Revelation, as readers are informed that the devil is overcome "by the blood of the Lamb" (12:11), and the climactic encounter between Jesus Christ and the beasts finds Jesus clothed "with a vesture dipped in blood" (19:13).

The challenge presented by the image of the lamb, particularly throughout the book of Revelation, is how to interpret it. What does the New Testament want us to understand about Jesus and his sacrifice? Front and center is the idea of Jesus Christ as the high priest who offers himself willingly as the true Passover lamb, whose sacrifice will "take away the sin of the world." This conquest of death comes about through slaughtering of the lamb on the cross, as victory over death comes only through submission to it. It is through the violently shed blood of the slaughtered lamb that "sin" is taken away and the "clothing" of those who have faith in his name is made "white."[26] All this leads readers of the New Testament to encounter what one author has termed "the great Christian paradox"—namely, that in order for there to be life, the Son of God must die.[27]

Jesus and the "Parodied" Lamb

At this point in John's vision, the lamb moves to the periphery of events as the focus shifts to other dramatic events and enigmatic characters: the opening of the seventh seal (Revelation 8–9), John's eating of a book (Revelation 10), the slain witnesses (Revelation 11), and the introduction of an unholy trinity, a dragon and two beasts (one from the sea and one from the wilderness). The dragon is identified as the "Devil and Satan, the deceiver of the whole world" (Revelation 12:9), and may also be representative for the chaos that arises as the vision builds toward the creation of a new heaven and earth.[28] The second beast, the one from the land, is described as a prophet who speaks for the beast and promotes worship of the beast (compare Revelation 19:20).[29] It is the first beast, the beast from the sea, that interests us here. Here is how John describes it:

> And I stood upon the sand of the sea, and saw a beast rise up out of the sea, having seven heads and ten horns, and upon his horns ten crowns, and upon his heads the name of blasphemy. And the beast which I saw was like unto a leopard, and his feet were as the feet of a bear, and his mouth as the mouth of a lion: and the dragon gave him his power, and his seat, and great authority. And I saw one of his heads as it were wounded to death; and his deadly wound was healed: and all the world wondered after the beast. And they worshipped the dragon which gave power unto the beast: and they worshipped the beast, saying, Who is like unto the beast? who is able to make war with him? (Revelation 13:1–4)

Like the lamb, the beast receives power and authority from a higher source (God and the dragon). Like the lamb, this beast was wounded in a manner that should have resulted in death, yet miraculously the beast is healed. Like the lamb, the beast receives worship from those who witness it. This beast from the sea, then, represents a *parody* of the true lamb: "Where God's Messiah is Jesus, the slain and living lamb (Rev 5:6), the dragon's . . . vicegerent is the slain and living beast (13:3). Where the death and resurrection of the lamb convey the redemptive power of sacrifice, the purported death and healing of the beast disclose the resilient power of evil. The question for readers is which form of power and authority will claim their loyalty."[30] In this fashion, the book of Revelation sets up its final denouement as being between the potency of the paradoxical lamb and the dragon with his parodied lamb.

Jesus as the "Providing" Lamb

The actual encounter between the lamb and the dragon finally occurs in Revelation 19, but not before John narrates a wedding feast celebrating the union of the lamb and the church. This union introduces a further dimension to the paradoxical lamb—namely, the lamb as "caretaker" or "provider." Typically, sheep require a shepherd to feed and manage the flock. In return, the sheep obey the shepherd and hearken to his voice. Yet in Revelation 19 the lamb is described as a bridegroom ready to wed his bride. In the Hebrew Bible, Hosea speaks of the "marriage" between God and Israel in a very poignant manner: "And I will betroth thee unto me for ever; yea, I will betroth thee unto me in righteousness, and in judgment, and in lovingkindness, and in mercies. I will even betroth thee unto me in faithfulness: and thou shalt know the Lord" (Hosea 2:19–20).[31] In this sense, it is God (Jehovah) who provides for and loves Israel. The realization of this wedding feast, then, provides a beautiful complexity to the book of Revelation's Christology. Jesus functions as the lamb because he followed the will of his own Shepherd, his Father. But as the lamb takes his place as the Bridegroom, ready to join his bride, who is "arrayed in fine linen, clean and white" (Revelation 19:8), the lamb now becomes the Shepherd, and he will protect and care for those who respond to his name and follow him as if they were his own bride.

The Revelation of the Lamb

It is, finally, at this point that the lamb appears in his true form. The book of Revelation had begun with the promise that what would be revealed was "Jesus Christ" (Revelation 1:1). Until this point, this "unveiling" of Jesus has largely been through paradoxical symbols, but here, finally, readers encounter the revealed Jesus Christ. In a visually impressive description, John states,

> And I saw heaven opened, and behold a white horse; and he that sat upon him was called Faithful and True, and in righteousness he doth judge and make war. His eyes were as a flame of fire, and on his head were many crowns; and he had a name written, that no man knew, but he himself. And he was clothed with a vesture dipped in blood: and his name is called The Word of God. And the armies which were in heaven followed him upon white horses, clothed in fine linen, white and clean. And out of his mouth goeth a sharp sword, that with it he should smite the nations: and he shall rule them with a rod of iron: and he treadeth the winepress of the fierceness and wrath of Almighty God. And he hath on his vesture and on his thigh a name written, King of kings, and Lord of lords. (Revelation 19:11–16)

One of the striking characteristics of this description is that John mentions three titles or names for Jesus: "Faithful and True," the "Word of God," and "King of kings, and Lord of lords."

The first, "faithful and true," could refer to Jesus's role as the fulfillment of Jewish messianic expectations.[32] Throughout the Hebrew Bible, prophets such as Isaiah promised that the Lord of Hosts would descend from Mount Zion and defeat and judge Israel's enemies.[33] In the descent of Jesus from heaven, this promise has been fulfilled; Jesus has been "faithful and true" to his promise.

The title the "Word of God" may suggest to readers a connection with the Gospel of John, which also speaks of Jesus being "the word" (John 1:1). For this reason, this title could be a reference to Jesus's close association with the Father. Jesus is the *logos* because he is the Father's agent; the Father expresses his will that an action be brought to pass, and the *logos* is the one who fulfills the Father's "words." However, based upon the context, this title is likely describing Jesus's role as judge, since "the rider will judge by means of God's word."[34] The association of the title the Word of God with judgment is supported by the weapon that Jesus carries. According to Revelation 19:21, Jesus slays his enemies with a sword, specifically a sword that "proceeded out of his mouth." In other words, Jesus's foes are defeated by the weapon of his words—that is, the judgment that he brings upon the wicked.[35]

The final title, "King of kings, and Lord of lords,"[36] is written in a very visible location, on Jesus's "vesture and on his thigh."[37] In verse 12, John had said that Jesus's name was one "that no man knew," but here, in a movement "from concealment to disclosure,"[38] Jesus chooses to reveal his name to everyone.[39]

In addition to the three names, Jesus is also described as having eyes that were "as a flame of fire," a head with "many crowns," and a robe "dipped in blood." The presence of fire speaks directly to Jesus's mission; just as fire both destroys and cleanses, Jesus has arrived to destroy the wicked and cleanse the earth (compare Revelation 1:14; 2:18). The image of a crown carries with it a sense of rule or authority. While kings and monarchs currently upon the earth may have an individual crown, Jesus has "many crowns," suggesting that his authority trumps theirs. Additionally, the dragon and the beast wear a specified number of crowns, but the number of Jesus's crowns remains unspecified. He has authority over not only the human rulers of the earth, but the forces of evil as well.[40] The implication of Revelation 19:12 is that Jesus's name may have been written on the crowns. This would serve as a parallel to both the blasphemous names written on the beast's crowns but also the appearance of the name of the Lord on the Jewish high priest's forehead. Finally, while the robe "dipped in blood" could refer to the blood of Jesus's vanquished enemies,[41] the fact that the robe is dipped in blood prior to the commencement of the battle indicates that the robe was bloody prior to Jesus's arrival. In that case, the presence of blood on his robe would likely be due to his redemptive actions during his mortal ministry—namely, the atonement and crucifixion.[42] Just as those who follow Jesus have their robes "washed white" though his blood (Alma 5:21), Jesus's own robe remains bloodstained.

All these images prepare readers for an additional element of the book of Revelation's Christology—namely, Jesus's function as warrior. The forces of the dragon—namely, the two beasts and the rulers of the earthly kingdoms who have been swayed by the promises of the dragon—have been gathering since chapter 16 in preparation for the battle of Armageddon, which finally takes place in chapter 19. The battle itself, however, unfolds differently than some readers might think. In actuality, there is little that could be termed a battle. Rather, Jesus arrives on the scene and promptly casts the two beasts into "a lake of fire burning with brimstone" (Revelation 19:20). Those who foolishly aligned themselves with the dragon are subsequently slain with the sword of Jesus, a sword that "proceeded out of his mouth" and thus likely refers to an act of preaching and spreading the message of Jesus Christ rather than a literal slaying. While the dragon had boasted of his power and might, all that remains of his forces is a feast for the crows, who "were filled with their flesh" (19:21).

A New Paradox—Jesus as "God"

The remaining chapters, those describing the millennial reign of Jesus and the eventual establishment of a celestial earth, provide the final piece of the book of Revelation's Christology. While Jesus's power and abilities have been alluded to in previous chapters, such as the lamb with seven horns and the seven eyes or the rider upon the white horse, it is in this climactic section that Jesus's association with the Father comes through most vividly. Consider the following passages:

> And I saw no temple therein: for the Lord God Almighty and the Lamb are the temple of it. (Revelation 21:22)
>
> And the city had no need of the sun, neither of the moon, to shine in it: for the glory of God did lighten it, and the Lamb *is* the light thereof. (Revelation 21:23)
>
> And he shewed me a pure river of water of life, clear as crystal, proceeding out of the throne of God and of the Lamb. (Revelation 22:1)
>
> And there shall be no more curse: but the throne of God and of the Lamb shall be in it; and his servants shall serve him: And they shall see his face; and his name *shall be* in their foreheads. (Revelation 22:3–4)

These statements imply a relationship where the Father and the Son exist as *one* being. Together the Lord God Almighty and the lamb form *one* temple. Both God and the lamb are the "light" of the city. Both God and the lamb share *one* throne. Significantly, those who serve "God and the Lamb" serve "him." Referring specifically to Revelation 22:3, G. K. Beale writes, "That 'they will serve *him*' likely does not refer only to God or only to the Lamb.

The two are conceived so much as a unity that the singular pronoun can refer to both. . . . That both are sitting on only one throne and together form one temple (21:22) enhances their perceived unity."[43] This is not to say that Jesus hadn't shared divinity with the Father prior to the creation of the "new heaven and the new earth" or that his divinity was a result of his conquest in Revelation 19, only that this divinity is made explicit through the enthronement scene narrated in Revelation 22. Curiously, the paradoxical Christology of Revelation that appeared to have been resolved in chapter 19 has now returned. How can two beings be one? How can two deities share one throne? These questions have troubled Christian thinkers for two thousand years, and ascertaining exactly what John has in mind in using this language remains a challenge for readers of his text. Perhaps the simplest way to understand these closing chapters is not to try to resolve the paradox but to embrace it, remembering that, ultimately, John leaves little doubt as to who Jesus is—he is God himself.

In summary, what can be said about the Christology of the book of Revelation? Many of the Christological elements we would expect as Latter-day Saints are present. First and foremost, Jesus Christ is God; he is *one* with the Father. He is described as having seven horns and seven eyes, images that suggest a high degree of *power* and *knowledge*. Further, he is a *warrior*. It is he who rides down from heaven and with his sword dispenses justice to the unrepentant. He is also the rightful *ruler* of the earth, the only one who bears the name "King of kings and Lord of lords."

However, one of the most significant messages of the book of Revelation is that Jesus is one with the Father not simply because Jesus is, by nature, divine (although he may be). Rather, the book of Revelation suggests that Jesus's eventual status should be attributed to the personal qualities he demonstrated in the previous chapters. The twenty-four elders do not bow down to the lamb because he is God, but because he is *worthy.* This worth comes through Jesus's *submissiveness* in accepting the book offered by the Father, even though the result was that he became the slaughtered lamb. He suffered and bled and was ultimately crucified. In this action, Jesus also demonstrated a degree of *loyalty*; what the Father asked, he would do, no matter how much anguish he was forced to endure. The result of these experiences was that Jesus became our *Redeemer*; it is his blood that washes our garments white, our sins and pains that leave his garment red. This union between sinner and savior is characterized through the wedding supper of the lamb, where Jesus, as *caretaker*, unites with his bride.

It is this confluence of qualities that perhaps accounts for John's paradoxical Christology. Jesus may now sit enthroned as God, but only because he submitted himself to mortality. Jesus can boast of conquest, but the true sign of his victory was his own vulnerability. As the author of Hebrews poignantly observed, "For we have not an high priest which cannot be touched with the feeling of our infirmities; but was in all points tempted like as *we are, yet* without sin. Let us therefore come boldly unto the throne of grace, that we may obtain mercy, and find grace to help in time of need" (Hebrews 4:15–16; compare Alma 7:11–12). Jesus is the "great high priest" of Hebrews precisely because of the experiences highlighted in the book of Revelation.[44] As Latter-day Saint readers of the book of Revelation, it is critical that we don't forget or ignore this fundamental element of John's vision—namely, that he has endured our pains and our sufferings *for us*, so that in him we can find the peace, the redemption, and ultimately the salvation that so gracefully he offers us.

Nicholas J. Frederick is an associate professor of ancient scripture at Brigham Young University.

Nicholas J. Frederick, "The Paradoxical Lamb and the Christology of John's Apocalypse," in *Thou Art the Christ, the Son of the Living God: The Person and Work of Jesus in the New Testament*, ed. Eric D. Huntsman, Lincoln H. Blumell, and Tyler J. Griffin (Provo, UT: Religious Studies Center; Salt Lake City: Deseret Book, 2018), 260–80.

NOTES

1. Laszlo Gallusz, *The Throne Motif in the Book of Revelation* (New York: Bloomsbury T&T Clark, 2014), 142.
2. Richard Neitzel Holzaphel and David Rolph Seely, *My Father's House: Temple Worship and Symbolism in the New Testament* (Salt Lake City: Bookcraft, 1994), 209.
3. ἀρνίον is technically the diminutive form of ἀρήν, though it is unlikely that such detail would have been recognizable enough to carry theological weight by the first century CE. See discussion in *The New International Dictionary of New Testament Theology*, ed. Colin Brown (Grand Rapids, MI: Zondervan, 1976), s.v. "Lamb."

4. According to one scholar, the word *sheep* appears a total of 742 times in the Old Testament. Roy Pinney, *The Animals of the Bible: The Identity and Natural History of All the Animals Mentioned in the Bible* (Philadelphia: Chilton Books: Philadelphia, 1964), 108. See also the lengthy discussion in *Theological Dictionary of the Old Testament*, ed. G. Johannes Botterweck (Grand Rapids, MI: Eerdmans, 1995), 7:43–52.
5. See discussion in Loren L. Johns, *The Lamb Christology of the Apocalypse of John* (Tübingen: Mohr Siebeck, 2003), 28–32.
6. According to Doctrine and Covenants 77:6, the scroll contains "the revealed will, mysteries, and the works of God; the hidden things of his economy concerning this earth during the seven thousand years of its continuance, or its temporal existence."
7. According to Doctrine and Covenants 77:7, the seven seals represent temporal periods of the earth's history: "We are to understand that the first seal contains the things of the first thousand years, and the second also of the second thousand years, and so on until the seventh."
8. "The emphases on the tribe of Judah and on Davidic descent together underline one of the crucial qualifications of the Jewish royal Messiah: he must be a descendant of the royal house of David (*Psalms of Solomon* 17:21; Mark 12:35–37; John 7:42), sometimes conceived as David *redivivus* (Jer 23:5; 30:9)." David E. Aune, *Revelation 1–5* (Dallas: Word Books, 1998), 350.
9. It should be noted that the lamb "stood" (ἑστηκὸς). In other words, it did not lie down or limp, as one would expect an animal to do that was wounded. The lamb clearly bears the marks of its wounds but not the effects.
10. "The perfect participle ἐσφαγμένον ("having been slain") expresses an abiding condition as a result of the past act of being slain," with the result that not only does the lamb stand before the throne, he "continues to exist as a *slaughtered* lamb." G. K. Beale, *The Book of Revelation: A Commentary on the Greek Text* (Grand Rapids, MI: Eerdmans, 1999), 352.
11. This vulnerability should not, however, be interpreted as weakness. As Ekkehardt Mueller points out, "The servant of God does not defend himself. No evil is found in him. In him truth resides. He is righteous and yet lives for others and is willing to bear their sin and guilt. *However, the Lamb is not a symbol of weakness. It is a symbol of strength in suffering.* In spite of its vulnerability it is victorious." Ekkehardt Mueller, "Christological Concepts in the Book of Revelation—Part 3: The Lamb Christology," *Journal of the Adventist Theological Society* 22, no. 2 (2011): 45; emphasis added.
12. "There are two different proposals for the background of the 'slain Lamb.' Some prefer to see it as a reference to the OT Passover lamb, while others favor Isa. 53:7: 'he was led as a sheep to the slaughter' (cf. Isa. 53:8ff). However, neither should be excluded, since both have in common with the metaphorical picture in Rev. 5:6 the central function and significance of the sacrifice of a lamb, which accomplishes redemption and victory for God's people. The Isaiah 53 background especially highlights the atoning aspect of the lamb's sacrificial death, as well as applying the metaphors of both 'root' (ῥίζα; cf. Isa. 52:2 and Rev. 5:5) and 'lamb' (ἀμνός, LXX) to the sacrificial victim. In fact, 'root' occurs also in Isa. 11:1, 10, alluded to in Rev. 5:5, which may have inspired attraction to the same metaphor in 53:2. The Passover/Isaiah 53 backgrounds are also suggested by the use of ἀρνίον ("lamb"), behind which could lie Aramaic *ṭalia'*, which means not only 'lamb,' but also 'servant' and 'boy.' If that is the case, then ἀρνίον would be a most suitable word to combine the Passover lamb with the servant lamb of Isaiah 53." Beale, *Book of Revelation*, 351.

13. This is not to suggest that all Jewish Messianic expectation centered upon a militant figure. See John J. Collins, *The Scepter and the Star: The Messiahs of the Dead Sea Scrolls and Other Ancient Literature* (New York: Doubleday, 1995).
14. "This scene lies at the theological heart of the Apocalypse. It is specifically designed to communicate the shock, irony, and ethical import of his message that the *Conquering One conquers by being a slain lamb*, not a devouring lion" (Johns, *Lamb Christology*, 159). Of the expectation of seeing a lion and the actual realization of seeing a lamb, David L. Barr writes, "A more complete reversal of value would be hard to imagine." David L. Barr, "Apocalypse as a Symbolic Transformation of the World: A Literary Analysis," *Interpretation* 38 (January 1984): 41.
15. Beale, *Book of Revelation*, 353–54.
16. "The horn was a symbol of power and honor (Pss 89:17, 24; 92:10; 112:9; 1 Sam 2:1; 1QM I, 4) and the ability to save (Ps 18:2; 2 Sam 22:3)." Craig Koester, *Revelation: A New Translation with Introduction and Commentary* (New Haven: Yale University Press, 2014), 377.
17. The attribution of horns to a messianic figure does appear in literature from outside the Hebrew Bible, such as the Dead Sea Scrolls (1Q28b Col. V:26) and the Pseudepigrapha (*1 Enoch* 90:37). What impact passages such as these may have had upon John's lamb is unknown. Craig Koester writes, "The imagery in Revelation both affirms and transforms earlier connotations. The seven horns affirm Jesus' messianic identity, yet as the Lamb, he saves through his own self-sacrifice." Koester, *Revelation*, 377. The key difference, however, is that "the Messiah is never symbolized as a lamb in Judaism, and the special attributes of seven horns and seven eyes together suggest that this composite image is the creation of the author, though the elements are drawn from traditional imagery." Aune, *Revelation 1–5*, 353–54.
18. "But this lamb had horns, and so we have a fusion of sacrificial lamb and ram features, conveying a deliberate paradox." Ben Witherington III, *Revelation* (Cambridge: Cambridge University Press, 2003), 121.
19. "God was understood to see all things, so no one was exempt from his scrutiny." Koester, *Revelation*, 377. Witherington calls the eyes "symbols of omniscience." Witherington, *Revelation*, 120. Compare Revelation 4:5–6, where the four beasts were themselves "full of eyes."
20. "Seven is a symbolic number, denoting wholeness and completeness." Jay A. Parry and Donald W. Parry, *Understanding the Book of Revelation* (Salt Lake City: Deseret Book, 1998), 14.
21. "The verb 'purchase' (*agorazein*) has connotations of the marketplace (Rev 13:17; 18:11), where some people purchased others to be their slaves. *Vita Aesopi* 15; 20. In the divine economy, however, Jesus purchases people for God, which is a redemptive action." Koester, *Revelation*, 379–80. Compare 1 Corinthians 6:20; 7:23, where the same verb is used in a similar sense.
22. Technically, "kings and priests" (βασιλείαν καὶ ἱερεῖς) should be translated "a kingdom and priests," likely an allusion to Exodus 19:6.
23. Koester, *Revelation*, 422. Additionally, the book of Revelation may be drawing upon the Old Testament imagery of sacrifice with this imagery. Psalm 51:7 contains the injunction "Wash me, and I shall be whiter than snow." Isaiah, in a similar fashion, promises that "though your sins be as scarlet, they shall be as white as snow" (Isaiah 1:18).
24. John may have in mind Isaiah 1:18 or Exodus 19:10–14 here.

25. When John describes the group standing before God's throne who receive "white robes" (Revelation 7:9), he may well have the Abrahamic covenant specifically in mind. As G. K. Beale observes, the phrase "a great multitude, which no man could number," possibly "evokes the promise to Abraham and Jacob that God would multiply their descendants. . . . Therefore, the multitudes in Rev. 7:9 are the consummate fulfillment of the Abrahamic promise and appear to be another of the manifold ways in which John refers to Christians as Israel." Beale, *Revelation*, 427.
26. Other New Testament passages add to this imagery. John declares in 1 John 1:7 that "the blood of Jesus Christ his Son cleanseth us from all sin." In two places Paul alludes to this, in Romans 3:25, where he speaks of Jesus's "sacrifice of atonement by his blood" (NRSV), and in Ephesians 1:7, where Paul declares that through his grace we have "redemption through his blood." Finally, the author of Hebrews asserts "without the shedding of blood there is no forgiveness of sins" (Hebrews 9:22 NRSV).
27. Grant R. Osbourne, *Revelation* (Grand Rapids, MI: Baker Academic, 2002), 254.
28. As Koester notes, "In Revelation the dragon has the qualities of a mythic monster. The LXX calls sea monsters (Hebrew, *taninim*) and Leviathan 'dragons' (Ps 74:13–14 [73:13–14 LXX]). Such dragons represented the chaotic forces that needed divine control (Job 7:12; 26:13; 41:1; Ezek 32:2 LXX)." Koester, *Revelation*, 544.
29. This second beast also hints at the chaos that precedes the new creation through its allusion to Behemoth, another monster described in the Hebrew Bible (compare Job 40:15–24; Revelation 13:11).
30. Koester, *Revelation*, 581. Beale adds, "The expression of Satanic incomparability is an ironic use of OT phraseology applied to Yahweh (cf. esp. Exod. 8:10; 15:11; Deut. 3:24; Isa. 40:18, 25; 44:7; 46:5; Pss. 35:10; 71:19; 86:8; 89:8; 113:5; Mic. 7:18). This is a further attempt at Satanic imitation of God. In all these OT texts Yahweh's incomparability is contrasted polemically with false gods and idols." Beale, *Revelation*, 694.
31. In the Hebrew Bible, it was common to speak of the covenant as a marriage between God and Israel (compare Ezekiel 16:8; Jeremiah 31:32; Isaiah 54:5). However, the relationship between the Messiah and the church was rarely, if ever, described in this fashion. In Christian texts, such as Matthew 19:15; John 3:29; and Ephesians 5:28–32, the application of the marriage imagery to the Messiah and the Church became the norm, as reflected here in Revelation 19.
32. "This dual name occurs in Greek only in *3 Macc.* 2:11 (πιστὸς εἶ καὶ ἀληθινός), where it refers to a hope in God's faithfulness, namely that in answering Israel's prayer God will defend the honor of his name by judging Israel's persecutor (cf. *3 Macc.* 2:9–14). The verbal identity and similarity of contextual theme indicate that John is probably alluding to *3 Maccabees* here, and this strengthens the contextual theme of Christ as a divine figure and as the one who executes a just and vindicating judgment." Beale, *Revelation*, 950.
33. Compare Isaiah 24:21–23; 31:4–5; 34:12.
34. Beale, *Revelation*, 957. Compare Wisdom of Solomon 18:15–16.
35. "To be slain by the sword that projected from the mouth of the warrior on the white steed certainly invites metaphorical interpretation; i.e., the "sword" must be the words spoken by the warrior." David E. Aune, *Revelation 17–22* (Dallas: Word Books, 1998), 1067.
36. "These titles were ordinarily reserved for God but here are given to Christ, who acts on God's behalf." Koester, *Revelation*, 766.
37. It is more likely that the name is only written once, on the cloak, with the reference to "his thigh" being appositional or epexegetical, introduced by "and." Understood in

this way, the name would have appeared on the cloak but on the part of the cloak that covers the thigh, in other words where a soldier would carry his sword. See discussion in Koester, *Revelation*, 758. Additionally, in the Old Testament one typically made an oath by placing one's hand underneath the thigh (compare Genesis 24:2; 47:29), an idea that may allude back to the "faithful and true" title in verse 11.

38. Koester, *Revelation*, 754.
39. Concealed names play an important role in the book of Revelation. Believers are given a white stone with a name written on it that remains secret to all but the believer (Revelation 2:17), while the whore in Revelation 17 has a name written that is supposed to remain a mystery, but John reveals it anyway (Revelation 17:5).
40. Coincidentally or not, earlier in the book of Revelation Christians are promised that they will obtain a "crown of life" as a reward for their endurance, while the twenty-four elders who surround the throne of God are also described as wearing "golden crowns." Compare Revelation 2:10; 4:4.
41. This seems to be the implication of Isaiah 63:2–3: "Wherefore art thou red in thine apparel, and thy garments like him that treadeth in the winefat? I have trodden the winepress alone; and of the people there was none with me: For I will tread them in mine anger, and trample them in my fury; and their blood shall be sprinkled upon my garments, and I will stain all my raiment."
42. As Koester notes, "There are two principal interpretations concerning the source of the blood. The most probable is that this is Christ's own blood." Koester, *Revelation*, 755.
43. Beale, *Revelation*, 1113. Aune adds, "By sharing the throne of God, the Lamb also shares the sovereignty of God." Aune, *Revelation 17–22*, 1177.
44. Jesus does appear in language reminiscent of the Jewish high priest in Revelation 1:11–20. Here Jesus is described as being "in the midst of the seven candlesticks," likely implying that he has entered the holy place of the temple.

Appendix

"Seek Ye Out of the Best Books"

Scholarly Books on the New Testament

THOMAS A. WAYMENT

As a scholar of the New Testament, I am often asked which books on the New Testament are the best ones. The question sometimes baffles me because to answer such a question I must first narrow the selection to a specific area of interest, understand the audience who will be reading the book, and know the purpose for which the book is being read. Reading for enjoyment, for example, is not the same as reading to understand a subject. Moreover, when a person asks about the best books, does the adjective *best* imply the most important, the most influential, the most enjoyable, or the best of some other category?

Another important facet of this discussion is a general feeling of skepticism that pervades Latter-day Saint impressions of modern biblical scholarship and scholars generally. The modern academy operates under the assumption that belief and faith often predetermine academic outcomes.[1] The scholarly ideal is one who recognizes and acknowledges bias (although this can never fully be achieved) in his or her conclusions and can present findings without appeal to emotion, predetermined positions, or working toward a favorable outcome. This approach has attracted backlash from believers who seek to defend their beliefs against what they feel are encroachments from secular idealism.

Interestingly, the two approaches—sometimes popularly referred to as faith-based versus academic—which seem to be at odds with one another, are fairly compatible. With both approaches, the scholar or the believer, approaches the text with an acknowledged validity of the text under discussion. For one, the quest may lead to a search for absolute truth and for the other, the quest may lead to understanding is origins, compositional history, theological impact, or a host of other questions that assume a certain level of validity of the text. Scholars who seek for answers must remain open to all hypotheses regardless of the scholars' religious attitudes. With their biases put aside, scholars must painstakingly explore all possible answers, whether popular or not. If they allow their religious beliefs to influence their findings, their findings become subjective, tainted, and unusable by the larger scholarly and believing communities. This is not an argument for the postmodern scholarly ideal of absolute unbiased historicism; rather, it describes the direction and intent of the academic mindset. The academy invites those who believe and those who do not: the university, as the word implies, is inherently the joining of unity and diversity under one roof.

Some critics may feel that this approach encourages secularism, and it does look at the text differently than what would be achieved if the goal were apologetic. The results of any singular-minded or single-vantage-point approach would be a self-perpetuating system that dominates discussions of religion and that could not tolerate diversity of opinion, such as advocated for in our own unique understanding of history and faith. If our own tradition guided the scholarly enterprise, then perhaps we would feel more at ease, but this would admittedly be a selfish endeavor. If the discussion is to be applicable to the widest possible audience, it must remain detached, unbiased, and guided by an acceptance that the religious texts under consideration are valid for a religious community or communities and are also robust enough to stand up to academic inquiry.

As a scholar trained in academic thinking and as one who exists within a community that professes faith in text as scripture with a living prophetic voice, the challenges of navigating both worlds are obvious. When working within a believing community there are two differing approaches: those who accept a body of religious texts as scripture and who view academic discussions through the lens of inherited and prophetic faith, and those who while accepting a body of scriptural texts and prophetic speech allow their academic training to inform their beliefs while remaining open to scholarly conversations about the text. There tends to be a significant amount of friction between the two camps, as one side defines itself as more firmly rooted in prophetic tradition while the other side sees itself as accepting the prophetic tradition but also accepting a certain level of responsibility to accept historical findings.

A pitfall of the faith-first approach may be that it engages in the practice of distilling scholarly materials into Latter-day Saint discussions or using academia as a smorgasbord of facts, choosing only those things in the buffet that appear satisfying. For scholars who attempt to see themselves simultaneously as good scholars and good believers, they wrestle with the right degree of balance and not criticizing others or allowing one of their two polarities to speak louder in the presentation of their findings.

There are other challenges for the two types of scholars, regardless of their approach. Scholarship functions on the rigid application of methodology and discipline specific academic approaches, neither of which were developed for the sole purpose of obtaining answers about truth or even for assessing the truth claims of a text. Therefore, the scholar who relies on the distillation of current scholarship builds upon a shifting foundation that will require each subsequent generation to reconsider the position of the academy and then redefine current positions through new distillations of scholarship. Each new generation of scholars acknowledges a body of both responsible and careful scholarship and scholars from whose work the new generation can freely draw.

The academic approach to understanding a religious text will never achieve something that might be termed the final answer or even an absolute statement of fact. The scholarly enterprise is not designed to debate questions such as "Was Jesus the Savior of the world?" Instead, it accepts the position that some thought that he was, and then it moves to consider what was meant by that belief and how were people treated who did not hold that belief. It might also ask what the origin of such a belief was and whether that origin was with Jesus or an earlier source.

Interestingly, the Restoration has been characterized by an emphasis on eternal truths while leaving many historical matters alone. For example,

President Russell M. Nelson recently stated that the Book of Mormon "is not a textbook of history, although some history is found within its pages."[2] That is not to say that the book is ahistorical, but that the book is something other than a history. A scholar working on the text would then seek to categorize it by genre: If not history, then what? When no prophetic or church counsel has been offered on a subject, Latter-day Saint scholars are left to navigate the field for themselves. If the tools of scholarship had never been fully cultivated, this endeavor would have led to less-than-desirable results.

In this spirit, I present what I feel are some of the most influential works on the New Testament today—publications that continue to have the greatest impact in our scholarly lives. These works have shaped the way we ask questions of the New Testament. Only by working with the same sources will we be able to enter the arena of their discussions as well as acquire valuable and enduring information from those discussions.

The Quest of the "Historical Jesus"

In the twentieth century, following the English translation of Albert Schweitzer's *The Quest of the Historical Jesus*, a group of scholars began thinking about Jesus and his life in important new ways.[3] They recognized that public understanding of Jesus had been filtered through the larger institution of the church and that to appreciate who Jesus was, they would have to peel away the layers of tradition to discover the "historical Jesus." *The church* was initially loosely defined as any institution that altered or shaped the way the story of Jesus was presented, whether it be a first-century or a nineteenth-century institution. When these successive layers of tradition were peeled back, a more perfect picture of Jesus would thus emerge, defined by a more precise understanding of what he said, did, and experienced. The first so-called quest of the historical Jesus concluded that he was an apocalyptic prophet who promised the dawning of a new millennial age.

The first quest was followed by a second quest, which of course has been followed by other tangential quests.[4] Recognizing certain deficiencies in the first quest, such as a limited interpretation of the way historical context informed New Testament narratives, inspired the efforts of the second-generation scholars. They felt that Jesus could not be understood or defined simply as the sum of his experiences and sayings (that is, by his historical setting alone); rather, he should be understood dynamically as a composite of his experiences and sayings and by how his peers—the church and early institutional leaders—defined him. Interestingly, the new quest has been bogged down for some time as scholars have attempted to clarify the progression of leadership from Jesus's death to the apostles and to the late first-century bishops and elders. The new quest also attempts to develop a clearer understanding of the relationship of first-century sources to the life of Jesus.

A number of vitally important works have emerged from this quest. No single work has yet emerged as the defining monograph, but the majority of books about Jesus trace their ancestry to this quest in some way; in other words, modern studies of Jesus's life are part of the dialogue of this quest. For the Latter-day Saint tradition, James E. Talmage's *Jesus the Christ* is an early response to the first quest. Remaining uninformed about how the quest has shaped the modern discussion can, in fact, lead us to interpret findings and then draw certain conclusions without seeing the larger implications. In essence, it is somewhat like purchasing a new house because we like the front door.

My own experience has led me to esteem the following books as the best books on the quest. Albert Schweitzer's *The Quest of the Historical Jesus* is still essential reading in the field as well as James M. Robinson's *A New Quest of the Historical Jesus*. Still timely, but not as comprehensive as Schweitzer or Robinson, is Bart D. Ehrman's *Jesus: Apocalyptic Prophet of a New Millennium.*[5] Ehrman's work signals a call to return to the findings of Schweitzer and, in essence, is an attempt to reign in the more tangential quests. His work, however, demonstrates that scholars still consider Jesus an apocalyptic prophet who prophesied of a new age and asserts that titles such as *Savior* and *Redeemer* were later descriptions applied to Jesus by his second- and third-generation followers.

- Albert Schweitzer, *The Quest of the Historical Jesus* (Mineola, NY: Dover, 2005)
- James Robinson, *A New Quest of the Historical Jesus* (London: SCM Press, 2012)

- Bart Ehrman, *Jesus: Apocalyptic Prophet of a New Millennium* (Oxford: Oxford University Press, 2001)
- Gerd Theissen and Annette Merz, *The Historical Jesus: A Comprehensive Guide* (Philadelphia: Fortress Press, 1998)
- John Meier, *A Marginal Jew: Rethinking the Historical Jesus*, 5 vols. (New York: Doubleday, 1991–2009)
- Richard Bauckham, *Jesus and the Eyewitnesses: The Gospels as Eyewitness Testimony*, 2nd ed. (Grand Rapids, MI: Eerdmans, 2017)

Kyrios Christos, or Lord Jesus

Perhaps more properly considered a subset of the quest for the "historical Jesus" is one of the most important and long-lasting works ever written in the field: Wilhelm Bousset's *Kyrios Christos: A History of the Belief in Christ from the Beginnings of Christianity to Irenaeus*[6] traced the development of changing perceptions about Jesus, which the first quest had posited would exist, through the first Christian century. This enormously successful monograph has defined the way many scholars present the life of Jesus and brought incredible scholarly acumen and breadth to New Testament studies.

In 1992, a group of scholars met at Princeton under the direction of the influential James H. Charlesworth to work out some of the categories emanating from Bousset's work. Although not instigated directly as a response to Bousset, the seminar participants felt that the recent publications of a wealth of primary materials—the Dead Sea Scrolls, the Nag Hammadi Codices, the Cologne Mani Codex, and other works—warranted a reinvestigation. The resulting publication of their discussions, *The Messiah: Developments in Earliest Judaism and Christianity*,[7] continues to be a must-read for students of the New Testament and early Christianity.

Even more recently, Larry Hurtado's *Lord Jesus Christ: Devotion to Jesus in Earliest Christianity*[8] has challenged the towering presence of Bousset in the field, presenting one of the most careful and thoughtful scholarly monographs to date. Hurtado's work, which rightly challenges the fundamentals and categories of the quest for the "historical Jesus," attempts to reconfigure the way we think about the transition between the living Jesus and the way early Christians interpreted his life. These studies could prove vitally important for the dynamics of late first-century Christianity and the developing ecclesiastical structure that arose out of this period.

- Dale Allison, *Constructing Jesus: Memory, Imagination, and History* (Ada, Michigan: Baker, 2010)
- Chris Keith and Anthony Le Donne, eds., *Jesus, Criteria, and the Demise of Authenticity* (London: T&T Clark, 2012)
- James D. G. Dunn, *Christianity in the Making, Volume 1: Jesus Remembered* (Grand Rapids, MI: Eerdmans, 2003)
- Larry Hurtado, *Lord Jesus Christ: Devotion to Jesus in Earliest Chrsitianity* (Grand Rapids, MI: Eerdmans, 2005)
- Wilhelm Bousset, *Kyrios Christos: A History of the Belief in Christ from the Beginnings of Christianity to Irenaeus* (Waco: Baylor University Press, 2013)

New Testament Textual Criticism

The growing discipline of New Testament textual criticism, once a subset of New Testament studies but now a burgeoning field in itself, has developed under careful scholarly scrutiny and is now on the verge of making some major breakthroughs, the equivalent of which has not been seen for nearly a hundred years.[9] The pioneers of the field, Karl Lachmann, Constantin von Tischendorf, Brooke Foss Westcott, Fenton John Anthony Hort, Eberhard Nestle, Irwin Nestle, Hermann Freiherr von Soden, and others, developed methodological approaches and categories that are still in place today.

More recently, however, a trend has developed that has caused scholars to rethink some of the older approaches in the field and reconfigure the way we discuss the text of the New Testament and how we reconstruct its text. Primary among the new approaches are two books that advocate more eclectic or reasoned approaches to recovering the original text of the New Testament as well as maintaining certain methodologies advanced by earlier New Testament textual critics. Kurt and Barbara Aland's *The Text of the New Testament* is foremost in this regard, with a particular emphasis on rewriting the categories of New Testament textual families.[10] The fourth edition of Metzger's influential *Text of the New Testament*, revised and expanded by Bart D. Ehrman, is also exemplary.[11]

- Kurt and Barbara Aland's *The Text of the New Testament* (Leiden: Brill, 1987)
- Bart D. Ehrman, Michael W. Holmes, and Bruce M. Metzger, eds., *The Text of the New Testament in Contemporary Research. Essays on the Status Quaestionis*, 2nd ed. (Grand Rapids, MI: Eerdmans, 2012)
- David C. Parker, *An Introduction to the New Testament Manuscripts and Their Texts* (Cambridge: Cambridge University Press, 2008)
- Metzger, Bruce M. and Bart D. Ehrman, *The Text of the New Testament: Its Transmission, Corruption, and Restoration*, 4th ed. (New York and Oxford: Oxford University Press, 2005)
- Patrick J. Hartin, H. J. Petzer, and Bruce Manning, *Text and Interpretation: New Approaches in the Criticism of the New Testament* (Leiden: Brill, 1991)

PAUL: THE AUTHOR OF CHRISTIANITY?

Perhaps no other figure in the New Testament besides Jesus has garnered such attention and created such diversity of opinion as Paul the apostle. In my opinion, the area of Pauline studies is the most difficult to navigate today, so the following ideas can only sweepingly describe the present state of the field and what books might be best.

In pre–World War II Germany, with the rise of the *Religionsgeschichtliche Schule* (History of Religions School), which sought to describe Christianity as a social phenomenon of the Greco-Roman world, Paul came to be seen as a product of Jewish apocalyptic anxiety and Christian liberalism. In other words, Jewish expectations of the coming of the Messiah and the associated frustration that the coming of the Messiah appeared to be delayed caused many Jews to feel disappointment and lack of confidence in God. Those same Jews, like Paul, purportedly began to look for other expressions of God's grace. According to the theory, Christianity opened new possibilities for these frustrated Jews.

With Paul at the helm of this reenvisioning of Judaism, which came to be called Christianity, the early Christian church developed according to

Paul's personal outlook and perspective.[12] Early interactions among church leaders, therefore, began to be interpreted as competing forms of Christianity, seeking to imply their own forms of orthodoxy on the others. Of course, this less-than-flattering view of early Christianity places great emphasis on Paul's role in shaping the church. In these studies, the typical findings are that Paul is the most important figure in Christianity besides Jesus or that Paul, rather than Jesus, is responsible for making Christianity what it is today.

Thousands of books have been written on the life of Paul. But before anyone reads one of them, he or she would be wise to connect the particular study into the family tree of Pauline scholarship. Certain important questions should be asked. Is the book in question a reaction to the Religionsgeschichteschule, or does it advance their ideas? Further questions should follow—does Paul appear as a Jew trying to change Christianity, or is he a Christian trying to make sense of his Jewish heritage?

Some excellent works on Paul's life are Alan F. Segal's *Paul the Convert: The Apostolate and Apostasy of Saul the Pharisee*, and Jerome Murphy-O'Connor's *Paul: A Critical Life*.[13] These two works are both carefully researched and provide the reader with cautiously constructed views of how Paul fits into the overall picture of developing Christianity. Segal sees Paul as a radical convert to Christianity whose divergent beliefs encouraged his conversion from Judaism to Christianity, whereas Murphy-O'Connor sees Paul as a humble convert of dynamic personality and boundless energy.

Another invaluable study of Paul can be found in Wayne A. Meeks's *The First Urban Christians: The Social World of the Apostle Paul*.[14] This work provides the reader with the necessary Greco-Roman background for understanding Paul's life. Its major shortfall is that it omits Paul's early period prior to his conversion. For that period, *Paul's Early Period* by Rainer Riesner is essential reading.[15]

- Alan F. Segal, *Paul the Convert: The Apostolate and Apostasy of Saul the Pharisee* (New Haven, CT: Yale University Press, 1992)
- Jerome Murphy-O'Connor, *Paul: A Critical Life* (Oxford: Oxford University Press, 1996)
- Wayne A. Meeks, *The First Urban Christians: The Social World of the Apostle Paul* (New Haven, CT: Yale University Press, 2003)

- Rainer Riesner, *Paul's Early Period: Chronology, Mission Strategy, Theology* (Grand Rapids, MI: Eerdmans, 1997)
- Michael Bird, ed., *Four Views on the Apostle Paul* (Grand Rapids, MI: Zondervan, 2012)
- N. T. Wright, *The Paul Debate: Critical Questions for Understanding the Apostle* (Waco, TX: Baylor University Press, 2015)

Dictionaries

New Testament dictionaries are abundant today and approach the New Testament from a variety of different vantage points. Unfortunately, no single dictionary satisfies every need of the New Testament scholar. Although it unfortunately comes in a six-volume set, the *Anchor Bible Dictionary*, edited by David Noel Freedman, is perhaps the most comprehensive dictionary of the Bible today.[16] Some of its entries are now outdated, and some important subjects receive only minor treatment when readers might expect otherwise. It is, however, an excellent starting point for biblical study. The *Eerdmans Dictionary of the Bible* is also a handy reference companion.[17] Its brevity notwithstanding, the entries are mostly up to date and reflect the recent scholarship in the field today.

For the more serious student of the New Testament, Gerhard Kittel and Gerhard Friederich's *Theological Dictionary of the New Testament*, translated by Geoffrey W. Bromily, is a standard in the field.[18] Unfortunately, it is probably used to the exclusion of the equally important three-volume work by Celsas Spicq, *Theological Lexicon of the New Testament*, edited by James D. Ernest.[19] These two works combined are an essential part of any New Testament library, particularly when readers are studying the meaning of New Testament terms in Greek and the implications of certain words in their larger Greco-Roman context.[20]

- David Noel Freedman, ed., *Anchor Bible Dictionary*, 6 vols. (New York: Doubleday, 1992)
- Celsas Spicq, *Theological Lexicon of the New Testament*, 3 vols., ed. James D. Ernest (Cambridge: Tyndale House, 1995)
- David Noel Freedman, ed., *Eerdmans Dictionary of the Bible* (Grand Rapids, MI: Eerdmans, 2000)

- Gerhard Kittel, Gerhard Friederich, and Geoffrey W. Bromily, *Theological Dictionary of the New Testament*, 10 vols., trans. Geoffrey W. Bromily (Grand Rapids, MI: Eerdmans, 1976)

New Testament History: Greco-Roman or Jewish

In the academy today, two schools of thought prevail regarding the sociological background and historical development of Christianity in the first few centuries. Certainly, this is a simplification to some degree, but the vast majority of studies in this area can be classified in one of two ways—either Christianity was a social phenomenon growing out of the larger Greco-Roman world or it was a small Jewish reformist movement that eventually broke from its Jewish moorings.

The essential question facing students of the New Testament is whether studying Classics or studying Judaism will be more helpful to understanding the New Testament world; in other words, is Greek or Hebrew more beneficial for New Testament study? The question is not easily resolved, and Latter-day Saint scholars have typically adopted both approaches. The obvious answer seems to be that both approaches have their merits; unfortunately, very few schools today approach the question from both viewpoints. It is essentially an either-or proposal.

For the student of the New Testament, the following works are still important and largely influential. Emil Schürer's *The History of the Jewish People in the Age of Jesus Christ (175 B.C.–A.D. 135)*, revised and edited by Geza Vermes and Fergus Millar, explores the theory that Christianity grew largely from Jewish origins.[21] Although only available in German, Hermann Strack and Paul Billerbeck's six-volume *Kommentar zum Neuen Testament aus Talmud und Midrasch* is the best source to reference primary sources on the intersections between Judaism and Christianity.[22] Joachim Jeremias's *Jerusalem in the Time of Jesus: An Investigation into Economic and Social Condition during the New Testament Period* is also helpful and still contains insights that are pertinent today, even though the work is now dated.[23]

On the Greco-Roman world, the revised edition of *The New Testament Background*, edited by Charles Kingsley Barrett, is careful and cautious in providing source materials for understanding the world of the New Testament.[24] F. F. Bruce's *New Testament History*, although dated, is still a favorite among Latter-day Saint scholars.[25] Bruce's work is not generally highly regarded among scholars today because its presentation is no longer on the cutting edge, but it is still a competent introduction to the subject. I personally like Luke Timothy Johnson's *The Writings of the New Testament*, although at times his religious views lead him to dismiss scholarly discussions unnecessarily.[26]

- Emil Schürer, *The History of the Jewish People in the Age of Jesus Christ (175 B.C.–A.D. 135)*, 4 vols., rev. and ed. Geza Vermes and Fergus Millar (London: T&T Clark, 2000)
- Hermann Strack and Paul Billerbeck, *Kommentar zum Neuen Testament aus Talmud und Midrasch*, 6 vols. (München: C. H. Beck'sche, 1974)
- Joachim Jeremias, *Jerusalem in the Time of Jesus: An Investigation into Economic and Social Condition during the New Testament Period* (Philadelphia: Fortress Press, 1969)
- F. F. Bruce, *New Testament History* (New York: Doubleday, 1980)
- Luke Timothy Johnson, *The Writings of the New Testament*, 3rd ed. (Philadelphia: Fortress Press, 2010)
- Charles Kingsley Barrett, *The New Testament Background* (London: S.P.C.K., 1956)

COMMENTARIES

The value of New Testament commentaries is that they provide a reference point for interpretation of selected passages. Today, various commentaries are aimed at teachers, preachers, academics, and lay students. Therefore, no single commentary can satisfy every need or answer every question. One important reason for readers to purchase New Testament commentaries is obvious because they typically provide the most up-to-date bibliographic information for a given book of scripture; moreover, they also often represent a summary of the various scholarly approaches to a specific book, which can help the reader understand simple facts such as why scholars often quote references to the Gospel of Mark first even when the same story is also found in Matthew and Luke.

One commentary series stands out as exemplary for beginning students of the New Testament: *Black's New Testament Commentaries*.[27] For the really serious student of the New Testament, the conservative *Anchor Bible Commentary* series, the liberal *Hermeneia* series, and the *New International Greek Testament Commentaries* are helpful and informative resources.[28]

- *Black's New Testament Commentaries* (Bloomsbury)
- *Anchor Bible Commentary* series (Yale University Press)
- *Hermeneia* series (Philadelphia)
- New International Greek Testament Commentaries (Bloomsbury/ T&T Clark)
- *Baker Exegetical Commentaries* (Baker)
- *Word Biblical Commentaries* (Baker)

Development of the Canon

Although the history of the New Testament canon is a specialized subset of New Testament studies, it is an essential part of understanding how to use and interpret the text of the New Testament. Often, I am asked what the "original Greek" says in this or that passage. This question, however, cannot be answered today because we do not have the original and because we do not know for certain the relationship of the earliest surviving written texts (all of them in Greek) and their earlier Aramaic sources (the language of Jesus and the language of the first oral accounts).

Another important reason for our studying the history of the New Testament canon is to avoid the reliance upon emotive arguments intended to demonstrate the superiority of one translation over another. Certainly, some translations are better than others, but no single translation in English today is superior to the words of Jesus as he spoke them. Every translation, including the Greek, Latin, Syriac, English, Spanish, or any other language, can only approximate what Jesus said and what he meant. These translations will always remain secondary sources that report to the best of their ability what Jesus said. As far as we can tell today, we have only very few words in the New Testament that actually represent the words as Jesus spoke them, while everything else is preserved in translation. Those words are "Amen," "talitha cumi," "abba," "mammon," "Cephas," "eloi eloi lama sabachthani," and "raca." Because the translations of his words are the only way we can access his words, it is important to understand the history of those translations. Bruce M. Metzger's *The Canon of the New Testament: Its Origin, Development, and Significance* is still the standard in the field and is very accessible for the beginning student.[29]

- Bruce M. Metzger's *The Canon of the New Testament: Its Origin, Development, and Significance* (Oxford: Clarendon Press, 1997)
- F. F. Bruce, *The Canon of Scripture* (Downers Grove, IL: IVP, 1988)
- David Trobisch, *The First Edition of the New Testament* (Oxford: Oxford University Press, 2000)
- Harry Gamble, *The New Testament Canon: Its Making and Meaning* (Philadelphia: Fortress, 1985)
- Lee Martin McDonald, J. A. Sanders, *The Canon Debate* (Peabody, MA: Hendrickson, 2002)

Conclusion

No single list of books on the New Testament can feasibly represent all the best books available today. Differences of opinion will always arise about which ones are best, and Latter-day Saint scholars may have significant differences of opinion. On the other hand, a fairly wide consensus exists on which books should be considered best in the sense that they have been the most influential and should be required reading for anyone who wishes to pursue further study of the New Testament and early Christianity.

This article is an attempt to give a beginning point for someone who wishes to pursue a more detailed study of the New Testament, but who has not had formal academic training in New Testament studies. The list would be significantly different if I were creating one for an introductory class at Brigham Young University or if I were teaching a graduate level seminar. I hope that these suggestions will give the reader a clear beginning point in the conversation, although I openly acknowledge that the field of New Testament studies has moved in different directions in many cases, and so in a sense this list of best books is not up to date, but it is represents an entrypoint into a lively discussion about the meaning of the New Testament, its people, and places.

Thomas A. Wayment is a professor of classics at Brigham Young University.

Expanded from an article in the *Religious Educator* 8, no. 2 (2007): 87–99. This article discusses biblical scholarship from an academic perspective and surveys only these types of resources rather than specifically Latter-day Saint biblical scholarship. For Latter-day Saint views on the New Testament, consider Lincoln H. Blumell, *New Testament History, Culture, and Society: A Background to the Texts of the New Testament* (Provo, UT: Religious Studies Center, Brigham Young University; Salt Lake City: Deseret Book, 2019).

NOTES

1. Michael V. Fox, "Bible Scholarship and Faith-Based Study: My View," SBL Forum, http://www.sbl-site.org/Article.aspx?ArticleId=490.
2. Russell M. Nelson, "2016 Seminar for New Mission Presidents," *Church News*, June 30, 2016.
3. Albert Schweitzer, *The Quest of the Historical Jesus*, trans. John Bowden (Minneapolis: Fortress, 2001; originally published in 1906).
4. James M. Robinson, *A New Quest of the Historical Jesus and Other Essays* (Minneapolis: Fortress, 1983; first published SCM Press, London, 1959).
5. Bart D. Ehrman, *Jesus: Apocalyptic Prophet of the New Millennium* (Oxford: Oxford University Press, 1999).
6. Wilhelm Bousset, *Kyrios Christos: A History of the Belief in Christ from the Beginnings of Christianity to Irenaeus*, trans. John E. Steely (Nashville: Abingdon, 1970).
7. James H. Charlesworth, ed., *The Messiah: Developments in Earliest Judaism and Christianity: The First Princeton Symposium on Judaism and Christian Origins* (Minneapolis: Fortress, 1992).
8. Larry W. Hurtado, *Lord Jesus Christ: Devotion to Jesus in Earliest Christianity* (Grand Rapids, MI: Eerdmans, 2003).
9. The series *Textus Criticus Maior* promises to be the most comprehensive collection of textual variants of the New Testament ever assembled.
10. First published as *Der Text des Neuen Testaments* (Stuttgart: Deutsche Biblegesellschaft, 1981); English translation by Erroll F. Rhodes (Grand Rapids, MI: Eerdmans, 1987).
11. Bruce M. Metzger and Bart D. Ehrman, *The Text of the New Testament: Its Transmission, Corruption, and Restoration*, 4th ed. (Oxford: Oxford University Press, 2005).
12. My own study of Paul's life seeks to place him within the context of the larger ecclesiastical or church structure and to show how his personality developed according to the Spirit of God rather than how his personality shaped Christianity: see Thomas A. Wayment, *From Persecutor to Apostle: A Biography of Paul* (Salt Lake City: Deseret Book, 2006).

13. Alan F. Segal, *Paul the Convert: The Apostolate and Apostasy of Saul the Pharisee* (New Haven, CT: Yale University Press, 1990); Jerome Murphy-O'Connor, *Paul: A Critical Life* (Oxford: Oxford University Press, 1996).
14. Wayne Meeks, *The First Urban Christians: The Social World of the Apostle Paul*, 2nd ed. (New Haven, CT: Yale University Press, 2003).
15. Rainer Riesner, *Paul's Early Period: Chronology, Mission Strategy, Theology* (Grand Rapids, MI: Eerdmans, 1998).
16. David Noel Freedman, ed., *Anchor Bible Dictionary*, 6 vols. (New York: Doubleday, 1992).
17. David Noel Freedman, Allen C. Myers, Astrid B. Beck, eds., *Eerdmans Dictionary of the Bible* (Grand Rapids: Eerdmans, 2000).
18. Gerhard Kittel and Gerhard Frieric, *Theological Dictionary of the New Testament*, trans. Geoffrey W. Bromily (Grand Rapids, MI: Eerdmans, 1985).
19. Celsas Spiqc, *Theological Lexicon of the New Testament*, ed. James D. Ernest, 3 vols. (Peabody, MA: Hendrickson, 1994).
20. It is important to note that this does not imply that the Greco-Roman worldview approach is preferable but rather that the language of translation (Greek) is significantly informed by Greco-Roman usage of those same terms.
21. Emil Schürer, *The History of the Jewish People in the Age of Jesus Christ (175 B.C.–A.D. 135)* 3 vols., rev. and ed. by Geza Vermes and Fergus Millar (Edinburgh: T & T Clark, 1973).
22. Hermann Strack and Paul Billerbeck, *Kommentar zum Neuen Testament aus Talmud und Midrasch*, 6 vols. (München: C. H. Beck, 1922–56).
23. Joachim Jeremias, *Jerusalem in the Time of Jesus: An Investigation into Economic and Social Condition during the New Testament Period* (Philadelphia: Fortress, 1975).
24. Charles Kingsley Barrett, ed., *The New Testament Background*, rev. ed. (San Francisco: Harper & Row, 1987).
25. F. F. Bruce, *New Testament History* (Garden City, NY: Doubleday, 1980).
26. Luke Timothy Johnson, *The Writings of the New Testament*, rev. ed. (Minneapolis: Fortress, 1999).
27. Black's New Testament Commentaries (Peabody, MA: Hendrickson).
28. *Anchor Bible Commentary* (New York: Doubleday); *Hermeneia* (Philadelphia: Fortress); *New International Greek Testament Commentaries* (Grand Rapids, MI: Eerdmans).
29. Bruce M. Metzger, *The Canon of the New Testament: Its Origin, Development, and Significance* (Oxford: Clarendon, 1987).

Index

M

S

About the Editors

JOHN HILTON III is a professor of ancient scripture at Brigham Young University. Previously, he worked with the Seminaries and Institutes program for eleven years in a variety of capacities. He has a master's degree from Harvard and a PhD from BYU, both in education. His research focuses on issues relating to both religious topics and Open Educational Resources (OER). His most recent book is *Considering the Cross: How Calvary Connects Us with Christ.*

NICHOLAS J. FREDERICK is an associate professor of ancient scripture at Brigham Young University. He has a PhD in the history of Christianity with an emphasis in Mormon studies. His research focuses primarily on the intertextual relationship between the text of the Bible and Latter-day Saint scripture, specifically the Book of Mormon. He enjoys teaching courses on the Book of Mormon and the New Testament, particularly the writings of Paul and the book of Revelation.